NORTH AMERICAN
MUSHROOMS

A Field Guide to
Edible and Inedible Fungi

DR. ORSON K. MILLER JR.
AND HOPE H. MILLER

FALCONGUIDE®

GUILFORD, CONNECTICUT
HELENA, MONTANA
AN IMPRINT OF THE GLOBE PEQUOT PRESS

Text design: Sue Cary
All photos are by the authors.
Top front cover image: Russula flavida by Orson Miller
Three insets on front and back cover, from left to right: Mycena haematopus, Lactarius indigo, and Hygrophorus speciosus, all by Orson Miller

Library of Congress Cataloging-in-Publication Data is available.

Manufactured in China
First Edition/Second Printing

To buy books in quantity for corporate use
or incentives, call **(800) 962–0973, ext. 4551,**
or e-mail **premiums@GlobePequot.com.**

We dedicate this book with our love to our three daughters: Andrea, Annelise, and Ginny. They spent their summers following us all over the country, and in the process made many contributions to our efforts.

Amanita excelsa

Laetiporus cincinnatus

CONTENTS

ACKNOWLEDGMENTS

Coprinopsis lagopus

We wish to thank our reviewers, Dr. Cathy Cripps and Dr. Walter Sundberg, for a very professional and thorough job of reviewing the manuscript. We also greatly appreciate the review of the ecological material by Dr. Steve Stephenson, as well as Marilyn Shaw's review of the fungal toxin section. The excellent artwork done for the visual key was by artist Paulette Gaudry. Pictures of the fungi were mostly taken by the senior author. However, images were contributed by the Emily Johnson Slide Collection at the University of Arkansas, through the courtesy of Dr. Steve Stephenson. In addition, the following mycologists contributed images: Blain Askew, Dr. Howard Bigelow, Dr. Gerald Bills, Dr. Dennis Desjardin, Robert Farnsworth, Hal Horowitz, Dr. Steve Miller, Paul Noel, Don Simons, Paul Stamets, Dr. James Trappe, and the North American Truffling Society.

We also want to thank our graduate students, and the amateur and professional mycologists, and our friends from the North American Mycological Association (NAMA) with whom we have spent many delightful trips in the field, at home and abroad. We also greatly appreciate the support over the years by the Virginia Tech Department of Biology, the University of Montana Biological Station, at Flathead Lake, Montana, and the members of the Mycological Society of America (MSA).

We would especially like to acknowledge the guidance and assistance of Erin Turner, Executive Editor, and the layout and design work of Sue Cary. Their help was invaluable.

Polyporus squammosus

INTRODUCTION

Our objective is to produce a guide that can be used in North America by the casual observer of mushrooms, the amateur mycologist, students of mycology, professional mycologists, and biologists. We have presented a general visual and written key to identify and place a fungus into one of the major groups, such as agarics, chanterelles, boletes, polypores, fungi with spines, coral fungi, bird's nest fungi, earth stars, puffballs, stinkhorns, jelly fungi, true morels, false morels, cup fungi, earth tongues, truffles, false truffles, and others. Following this is a key to the families of mushrooms with lamellae (Agarics) divided into groups by spore print colors. This key will aid the reader in deciding which family to check first to get into the right genus. Keys, descriptions of the species, and color illustrations are provided. An illustrated glossary, as well as a regular glossary, is also included. Monographs and detailed professional papers are cited for those who wish to study further.

Fungi are considered one of the six Kingdoms, which are Fungi, Plantae, Animalia, Straminopila (oömycetes, diatoms, and kelp), Protista (slime molds, and cellular slime molds), and Prokaryots (bacteria, blue-green algae, and archaea). This book covers that part of the Fungi referred to as the higher or larger fungi. These produce very visible fruiting bodies such as the mushrooms, boletes, puffballs, stinkhorns, morels, and cup fungi. There are many very small fungi, which are not included here, that produce a vast array of fruiting bodies on leaves, branches, and a host of plant and animal parts. Mycology textbooks and technical monographs describe these small fungi, which are usually identified using both the dissecting and compound microscope, and are beyond the objective of this guide.

It is imperative that a spore print be taken. To do this, remove the pileus from the specimen and place it lamellae side down on a piece of white bond paper. This paper should be kept as clean as possible, so we cut pieces about 1½ inches by 4 inches and keep them in a small Ziploc bag so they will not be contaminated by spores that might be in the air. You may wrap the pileus in waxed paper or cover it with a bowl to keep the humidity up. If it is very hot, put the packaged spore print in cool place. Spores will not be cast if it is too hot. The spores may take a few hours up to overnight to leave a print on the paper. It is necessary to record the color.

If one takes the time to follow the keys while looking at the fungus in hand, the determination should be much easier. For example, if the fungus in hand has a stipe, pileus, and lamellae beneath the pileus (Fig. 35, page 544), start by checking the agarics. This group will be found in the Key to the Families of Fungi with Lamellae, and the spore print color is important. The key to the families will lead to a given family and the genera within that family. This method is meant to create an ability to diagnosis the family and hence the genus. It has the strong advantage of placing together all of the species in a given genus, such as *Amanita,* so one can obtain a concept of the genus.

It is highly recommended that a part of your field gear be hand lens, which enables one to see minute pores on a polypore or fine hairs on the pileus, for example. A ruler in both meters and inches provides the size conversions between the two measuring standards. We prefer centimeters and millimeters. Very small measurements are more easily handled by using 2–4 mm instead of $\frac{1}{3}$–$\frac{1}{8}$ of an inch, for example. Spot reagents are used to further identify specific genera and/or species. These include KOH, Melzer's solution, $FeSO_4$ (see glossary). Lastly, the color plates were selected with care to illustrate key traits of a species as one might see it in the field. Study the picture carefully and read the description along with it. Staining reactions of *Leccinum,* the red pores of *Boletus satanus,* and the yellow stains of *Agaricus xanthoderma* at the stipe base, for example, can be easily observed. These field characters make the identification process much easier.

Geographic Coverage & Plant Biomes

The area covered here includes Canada, Alaska and Continental United States. No doubt many of the fungi described herein may be found in Mexico, but no attempt has been made to delve into areas south of the southern border of the United States. Alpine and Arctic tundra are not covered in any detail. Space limitations and the enormous number of fungi in the rest of the area of coverage simply limited the inclusion of tundra. Collectively, the following regions provide a setting in which a combination of plant floras of great complexity yields a staggering array of associated higher fungi.

The taiga and boreal forest region extends over much of northern North America, including Alaska, Canada and a small portion of the northern tier of the United States. Conifers such as spruce, fir, larch, and jack pine are the usual dominants, but some communities also contain aspen and birch.

The temperate deciduous forest region occurs in the eastern United States and adjacent regions of southern Canada and the southern portion of the Maritime Provinces. This region is characterized by communities containing beech, birch, maple, ash, oak, pine, hemlock and (prior to the introduction of the chestnut blight fungus into the United States) American chestnut.

The temperate mixed forest region covers southeastern United States, extending from Maryland south to Georgia. Various species of oak and hickory, along with the southern hard pines, are the dominant tree species throughout most of the region.

 The subtropical mixed forest region occurs from northern Florida, along the Gulf Coast, on west to the Big Thicket country of Texas. Among the more important trees are the southern pines, deciduous oaks, and live oaks.

The western mountain forest region encompasses the major ranges of the Rocky Mountains, which extend well beyond the United States into Canada and Mexico. Typical forest communities contain spruce, fir, Douglas fir, hemlock, larch, pine, and aspen. However, in the more southern portion of the region, these are found only at higher elevations.

The desert and semi-desert region of southwestern United States contains a wide range of different plant communities. Prominent and widespread examples include pinyon pine-juniper and mountain mahogany-scrub oak woodlands on less arid sites, at generally higher elevations, and communities dominated by sagebrush, saltbush, and greasewood on somewhat more arid sites. At the very lowest elevations in the region, various cacti become important elements of the flora.

The coastal forest region of the western United States is a mixed forest made up of both conifers and broad-leafed trees, including several species of pine, Sitka spruce, coastal redwood and various live oaks.

The Pacific Northwest region of the United States is characterized by a temperate rain forest consisting almost exclusively of conifers, including coastal redwood, Sitka spruce, western hemlock and western red cedar.

The grassland region occupies the central portion of North America and covered about a third of the area of the entire United States at one time. As the very name of the region suggests, various grasses are the most abundant plants present, but riparian communities containing cottonwood, elm, hackberry, alder and willow occur along the stream courses.

General Groups of Fungi

The Basidiomycetes are a diverse group of fungi composed of agarics, boletes, fungi with spines, chanterelles, coral fungi, polypores, aphyloporales, and jelly fungi. Although the majority of the Basidiomycetes forcibly discharge their spores, the Gasteromycetes do not. These include puffballs, earth stars, stinkhorns, earth balls, false truffles, bird's nest fungi, and sequestrate fungi. The Ascomycetes, include the cup fungi, true morels, false morels, ear fungi, and true truffles. They also forcibly discharge their spores, with the exception of the truffles. The truffle fruiting body develops below ground. Their spores become thick-walled and the asci are oval and merely split when mature. The volatile odors emanating from the mature truffle attract rodents, deer, and insects who dig them up and eat them, thus distributing the spores in the process.

An estimated 6,000 common higher fungi in North America means that there are fungi that will not be able to be included in this guide. The criteria for selection of the species to be included here are based on their wide and common distribution or high local distribution in a region. Other criteria are their unique structures or the particular habitats where they occur.

Fortunately, there are a growing list of local field guides that can be accessed for additional information about a particular area. These have been referred to and are listed in the literature cited.

Mycological Organizations

Mycological Society of America (MSA): The professional society of mycologists. The members include mycologists from many parts of the world. *Mycologia* is the journal of this society and is published bimonthly.

North American Mycological Association (NAMA): The amateur society made up of local mushroom clubs in the United States and Canada. It has an annual meeting somewhere in the United States or Canada each year. It also publishes a newsletter, *The Mycophile,* and a journal, *McIlvania.*

Edibility and Nutrition

It is important to know your mushrooms when collecting in the wild. Just because you have collected and eaten something in the East or in Europe or Asia, this does not mean it is the same species in another area of this country or the world. Make sure you have accurate, local information. Joining a club or contacting a professional in the area where you can learn what is good and what is not is most important. Remember, **when in doubt, throw it out!**

Many people have said for years that there is no nutritional value in mushrooms. That is not correct. Mushrooms contain the following: Vitamins A, C, D, and all the B complex (thiamin, riboflavin, niacin, pyridoxine, pantothenic acid, and biotin), calcium, phosphorus, iron, copper, manganese, and potassium. Recently scientists have identified folic acid and selenium as well.

We do know that there are very few calories in mushrooms, no fat, little sodium and no cholesterol. We add these things along with calories by adding such things as sour cream, butter, and other fattening ingredients when we cook them.

It is important to take proper care of mushrooms you plan to eat. This is the same for those that come from the grocery store or the forest. Keep them cool until you can put them in the refrigerator. Take the plastic off the containers and put them in a brown paper bag and place in the cool place. Don't leave them in the hot sun in your car or on the kitchen counter. If you are collecting in the forest do not use plastic bags since this may create a warm, moist chamber that encourages bacteria to grow. Also keep different ones apart, in separate packets. We use aluminum foil, waxed paper, or small containers so that you don't make the mistake of putting a good one with a bad one. Mushrooms may be dried over a food dehydrator or in the microwave (following the instructions for drying vegetables for your microwave). The oven will just cook them rather than drying them. Once completely dried, they may be stored in a cool, dry place in clean, glass jars or Ziploc bags for up to 2 years.

Toxins Produced by Mushrooms

There are no simple guidelines that can be used to distinguish edible from poisonous mushrooms. The only safe way to eat wild mushrooms is to learn to identify the edible species as well as the poisonous species. Field guides should be consulted whenever one is in doubt. We advise that if one is still in doubt throw it out! In general the vast majority of mushrooms just do not taste good and are neither poisonous nor edible. However, there are eight types of toxins known and their action and symptoms are described below. The toxins are distributed among a number of different families of mushrooms. Most families that contain toxic species also contain edible species. It is very important to consult good, recent field guides or seek the help of trained mycologists.

Most toxic species are not fatal to man. They usually produce only nausea, act as a laxative, or induce mild to strong hallucinations. Unfortunately, a small number of mushrooms have toxins that are fatally poisonous while others affect the central nervous system and are very debilitating. Those toxins with **longer onset of symptoms,** including **Type 1** Amatoxins, **Type 5** Monomethylhydrazine, and **Type 7** Orellanine, indicate one of the more destructive and possible fatal toxins. The types of toxins are discussed below, commencing with the most deadly. However, it should, however, be remembered that many mushrooms have never been tested and therefore their potential toxins are unknown. Also each person may have a personal allergy to some fungi so, therefore, eat only one new species at a time. This way if a problem occurs you will be able to identify the culprit.

Type 1 toxins, Amatoxins: These are the toxins that result in the majority of fatalities in adult humans. The toxin, complex cyclic heptapeptide molecules, consists primarily of proteins composed of amino acids. When the toxin is first ingested, the taste of the fungus is pleasant and there is no indication of the consequences. The **delayed onset of symptoms** is usually 5 to 7 hours after ingestion. In the intervening time the toxin enters the bloodstream and amanitin inhibits protein synthesis in liver cells. Initial symptoms include extreme pain, profuse vomiting, lethargy, diarrhea, and distorted vision. However, a period of remission follows and during the interim the victim may even feel somewhat better. In 3 to 4 days symptoms of damage to the liver and kidneys begin to appear (Spoerke & Rumack, Ch. 9, 1994). The onset of severe pain then continues from 3 to 6 days when kidney failure usually culminates in death. Even when death does not result, the illness lasts several weeks and may do permanent damage to the liver. Spoerke & Rumack, Ch. 10, (1994) provide information on treatment, which may avoid death and or limit subsequent liver damage.

Known members of this type include *Amanita verna, A. virosa, A. phalloides, A. ochreata, A. bisporigera, Conocybe filaris = Pholiotina filaris, Galerina marginata, G. autumnalis,* and *G. venenata.* In addition, *Lepiota helveola, L. castanea* and *L. subincarnata* also contain amatoxins.

Type 2 toxins, Muscarine: The symptoms of toxicity include heavy perspiration, salivation, and lacrimation or the PSL syndrome. Additional symptoms are pin-point pupils, blurred vision, diarrhea, urgent urination, bronchial asthma, lowered blood pressure and reduced heart rate (Spoerke & Rumack, Ch. 14, 1994). The symptoms occur in ½ to 2 hours and vomiting, induced or spontaneous, is often treated by giving atropine in severe cases. Atropine has long been used to counteract the effect of muscarine. However, some fungi such as *Amanita muscaria* have more than one toxin, and atropine as an antidote may not be warranted, see **Type 3** Ibotinic Acid and Muscimol for additional information. Symptoms may last up to 24 hours. High concentrations of muscarine are present in many species of *Inocybe* and *Clitocybe.*

Known members of this type include *Inocybe patouillardii, I. rimosa (=I. fastigiata), I.*

lanuginosa, I. geophylla, and also the white species of *Clitocybe,* including *C. dealbata, C. rivulosa,* and *C. candicans.* However, no member of the genus *Inocybe* nor any of the white or light colored species of *Clitocybe* should be eaten.

Type 3 toxins Ibotenic acid and Muscimol: The symptoms include delirium, loss of coordination, drowsiness, dilated pupils, muscle spasms, stomach upset and vomiting, often accompanied with a hangover for at least the next day. The onset of symptoms occurs about an hour after ingestion. The toxins affect the central nervous system and the level of response is dose dependent. Sometimes deep comatose sleep occurs from which it is difficult or impossible to arouse the patient. Some species, such as *Amanita pantherina,* contain populations which have high levels of muscimol and the toxicity is more acute than in other species. The ibotinic acids and not muscarine, which is also present in small amounts, comprise the chief toxins in *Amanita muscaria.* When a large amount of *A. muscaria* containing these toxins is ingested, it often results in severe illness, but victims usually recover.

Known members of this group include *Amanita muscaria, A. pantherina, A. solitaria, A. porphyria, A. gemmata, A. cauthurnata,* and *A. citrina.*

Type 4 toxins Psilocybin and psilocin: These toxins effect the central nervous system and the result is moderate to strong hallucinogenic reactions. Symptoms include sensory distortion, visual distortion, brilliant colors, with both impaired ability to concentrate and objects appearing longer or bigger than they really are. In some cases subjects experience depression, anxiety, or fear. These symptoms are often felt in a very short time, 15 minutes to an hour. In some cases nausea and vomiting occur. The compounds involved are in the LSD (lysergic acid) family of hallucinogenic compounds. The period of toxicity usually lasts 6 to 12 hours but this is very much dose dependent. Children may experience seizures. If a large number of mushrooms are consumed, the severity of the toxicity will be much greater (Spoerke & Rumack, 1994). Stamets (1996) provides details on the identification of the hallucinogenic species and information on their potency.

Known members of this group covered in this guide include *Psilocybe cubensis, P. semilanceata, P. cyanescens, P. pelliculosa, P. stuntzii, Conocybe cyanopus, Gymnopilus spectabilis,* and *G. aeruginosus.* Suspected or very weak in toxins are *Panaeolus foenisecii* and *P. castaneifolius.*

Type 5 toxins Monomethylhydrazine (MMH) and Gyromitrins: The delayed onset of symptoms occur in 5 to 12 hours but maybe longer. Symptoms include nausea, a bloated feeling, diarrhea, vomiting, muscle spasms, cramps, and a loss of muscle coordination. Severe headaches and pains may linger for some time. The tolerance of individuals, the amount of MMH present in the fungus, and the method of cooking may combine to cause widely varying toxic reactions. There have been a number of fatalities in Europe from ingestion of false morels. Monomethylhydrazine is water soluble and volatile when the mushroom is cooked or boiled. However, the steam can be breathed in by the cook and have a toxic effect. Severe toxicity can cause the death of red blood cells, liver damage, and a carcinogenic effect shown in laboratory animals. It is absolutely essential to thoroughly cook false morels in a well ventilated area (Spoerke & Rumack, Ch. 13, 1994).

Known members of this group include *Gyromitra esculenta, G. montana = G. gigas, G. fastigiata, G. californica, G. infula,* and, in all probability, other closely related species of *Gyromitra.*

Type 6 toxins Coprine (disulfiram-like toxins): Symptoms such as nausea, vomiting, confusion, and a flushed appearance following ingestion of *Coprinus atramentarius,* coupled within 5 days of an alcoholic drink, are well known. It is reported that the symptoms may occur if alcohol is consumed even a number of hours after the ingestion of the mushroom. The effects may linger longer but the toxicity is usually of short duration and is similar to the disulfiram-like reaction used as a deterrent to alcoholism.

Known species include: *Coprinus atramentaria*

Type 7 toxins Orellanine: The **delayed onset of symptoms** occurs 2 to 17 days following ingestion of the mushroom and involves nausea, vomiting, chills, shivering, sweating, and often extreme thirst. Symptoms may follow for days leading to renal failure and, in some cases fatalities result. Recovery may be dependent upon prolonged dialysis or a kidney transplant (Spoerke & Rumack, Ch. 11, 1994).

Known species include *Cortinarius gentilis, C. rainierensis,* and *C. speciosissimus,* which are rarely encountered and found in the northern boreal forests and in western North America. (Thorn & Malloch, 1993).

Type 8 toxins Gastrointestinal Irritants: Symptoms result from a number of unknown toxins, are rarely fatal, but cause nausea, diarrhea, vomiting, or intestinal cramps. Recovery is usually total after 3 to 5 days. However, young children could be more acutely affected when ingesting the same amounts of the mushroom as adults. This group comprises the largest aggregation of species and requires much additional study. The toxic effects of these and other species are further discussed under the individual species. See Spoerke and Rumack (1994) for an additional list and more information.

A partial list of known members of this group includes *Agaricus xanthoderma, A. placomyces, Boletus luridus, B. satanus, B. sensibilus, B. subvelutipes, B. calopus, Leccinum* species, *Clitocybe dealbata, Gymnopus dryophilus = Collybia dryophila, Entoloma lividum, E. strictius, Hebeloma crustuliniforme* and other *Hebeloma* species, the genus *Inocybe, Lactarius piperatus, L. rufus, L. torminosus, L. uvidus, L. chrysorrheus, Chlorophyllum molybdites, Omphalotus illudens* and other *Omphalotus* species, *Paxillus involutus, Gomphus floccosus, G. bonari, Ramaria formosa, Russula nigricans, R. compactae, R. albonigra, R. emetica, R. fragilis, R. densifolia,* and *Tricholoma pardinum.*

Role of Fungi in Nature

Saprophytes of plant and animal remains

Perhaps the largest numbers of mushrooms and their allies are decomposers of plant parts referred to as saprophytes. These fungi recycle leaves, needles, wood of various kinds, as well as dying mosses, lichens, and the husks of various nuts. Some saprophytes are called white rots and produce enzymes which can degrade lignin essential to decomposing wood. Other saprophytes are called brown rots and can degrade cellulose and hemicellulose, as well as the sugars in plant parts. Each mushroom has a specific role in the decomposition process. *Marasmius oreades,* for example, grows in fairy rings in grass decomposing the dead grass. *Laetiporus sulphureus* grows on stumps and logs and decomposes the wood. *Stropharia hornemanni* grows on conifer needles and decomposes them. These are just a few examples of the specific substrates where each of the mushrooms will be found. Knowing these relationships enables the mushroom collector to seek out a given fungus with specific knowledge of where it grows and where to find it.

Parasites of plants and insects

Parasites invade and kill plants by attacking the roots or, in some cases, the living cells called cambium in the stem or branches of a tree or shrub. Very few of the mushrooms and their allies covered in the field guide are parasites of plants and animals. However, *Heterobasidion annosum* is a root parasite of both conifers and hardwoods, causing infection centers in forests. *Cryptoporus volvatus* is a weak stem parasite, often following beetle infestations, on conifer trunks. These forest parasites can have a long-term effect on the composition of forest stands or in damaging valuable trees in parks or private yards. Being aware of them allows one to take action before multiple infections occur. It is important to remove infected trees to avoid additional infections in healthy trees. *Cordyceps militaris* is a parasite of beetles. It infects the larval stage and kills the beetle. There are many different species of *Cordyceps* that are specific to particular insects.

Mycorrhizal symbionts of higher plants

Before the turn of the 20th century, it was discovered that some mushrooms and their allies were in a beneficial association with the roots of trees and some shrubs. Since the associations were with the rootlets of trees, the term mycorrhizae, greek for fungus/root, was used to describe the association. The fungus mycelium grows through the soil, contacting the tiny rootlets of a receptive or host tree. The fungus establishes a sheath surrounding the tree rootlet and the hyphae, or individual fungal cells, surround the outer cells of the rootlet, forming a glovelike sheath called a Hartig net. Here the fungus supplies the tree with hard-to-get nitrogen and phosphorus, while the tree, which makes carbon through photosynthesis, supplies the fungus with carbon. It is this mutual association that benefits both the fungus and the host tree. When a mushroom participates in this association and a Hartig net is formed, it is called an ectomycorrhizae. Mycorrhizal experts have learned that only certain plants, mostly trees, and certain mushrooms participate in this association. In the North American Northern Hemisphere, which is covered in this field guide, certain trees are ectomycorrhizal. Among the trees only one family of Conifers, the Pinaceae, is involved with ectomycorrhizae. These include pine, spruce, fir, Douglas fir, hemlock, and larch. Among hardwoods, certain families, including the Fagaceae (oak, beech, hickory etc.), Betulaceae (birch and alder), and Salicaceae (willow, poplar, and aspen), fulfill this role. In many cases only certain mushrooms are specifically associated with only one species of tree. For example, *Suillus americanus* and *S. pictus* are only found associated with eastern White Pine *(Pinus strobus)*, while *S. grevillei* and *S. cavipes* are only associated with larch (tamarack). These associations are pointed out under comments for a given species. In addition, specific families of mushrooms such as the Amanitaceae and Gomphidiaceae are all ectomycorrhizal with tree species. It would not be possible to find an *Amanita* or a *Gomphidius,* for example, fruiting in a grasslands, devoid of the tree hosts. An additional fact learned in more recent times is that as a given tree, a pine for example, grows over its lifespan, which may be 200 or 300 years, it associates with different mushrooms, some only colonizing the roots of young trees and others not until the tree is much older. Old growth trees may have a mushroom associated with the roots that is never found in young forests. As we gain additional knowledge of these ecological associations, we become more aware of where and when to hunt for and find certain species of mushrooms.

Anatomy of Fungi

Macroscopic anatomy

The understanding of the anatomy, and terms used to describe it, is essential to rapidly diagnosing and identifying a given mushroom. Each description uses the appropriate terms to characterize each major group of fungi. A glossary, in part visual, is included to help you quickly read and understand the descriptions of each species. The reference to figures in the text will illustrate and explain a given term. In some cases it is desirable to find, for example, a membranous flaring partial veil, which will illustrate the term better than an illustrated glossary. For example, look up *Stropharia hornemannii* to see this type of partial veil.

Microscopic morphology

Technical descriptions are usually long and deal with precise anatomical details. This type of description is not used in this or most field guides. It would make the guide too long and unwieldy. In addition everyone would need to own a microscope and this would severely limit both the number of successful users and the number of species that could be included because of the space needed. However, the most important microscopic character is the anatomy and size of the spores, as well as the type and kind of ornamentation when present. Also of great importance is the amyloid reaction of some spores in Melzer's solution, which colors some spores blue. The reason is because certain families, genera, subgenera, and species can be identified for certain only by observing this character. However, a solid knowledge of the macroscopic characters replaces the need to use the microscope in the majority of the cases. In addition, in some genera, the sterile cells on the surface of the lamellae called cystidia are included after the description of the spores. This is for the people who do use a microscope and it serves to alert them to the need to not only look for the cystidia, but also to consult more detailed works given in the literature cited. Occasionally, mycelium (the vegetative minute threads of the fungus vegetative plant) and hyphae (individual cells in the mycelium) are mentioned as part of the description. The mycelium is usually seen surrounding the base of the fruiting body and the plant from which the fruiting body initiates and fruits. In addition rhizomorphs (stringlike cords of fungal hyphae) are mentioned when they are present and sometimes is the key to the identification of a given species. These are also seen surrounding the base or emanating from the base of the fruiting body in soil or wood debris. For additional study with a microscope, it is suggested that Largent, et al. (1980) and Miller & Miller (1988) be consulted for explanations of the microscopic features of the higher fungi.

How the Fungus Operates

The hymenium (spore-bearing surface or area) contains the reproductive cells that give rise to the spores that reproduce a given species of fungus. The hymenium is either oriented on a surface of the fruiting body (a lamella in an agaric or inside a tube in the boletes, for example), and the spores are forcibly discharged into the air. The spores may develop deep within the fruiting body (the gleba of a puffball) and they are not forcibly discharged. In the Basidiomycetes, the sexual cell is called a basidium (Fig. 16, page 542). The spores are borne on small "pegs" called sterigma (Fig. 17, page 542). There are usually 4 per basidium, and the spores, when mature, are discharged into the air from the basidium. The Basidiomycete hymenium may also contain cystidia among the basidia, or sometimes they form a totally sterile area on the edge of the lamellae. These cells serve to separate the basidia and orient them for discharge. They also may serve to collect and discharge waste from the fruiting body. Sometimes they serve as a center for pigment formation giving the characteristic color to the lamellae.

However, in the Ascomycetes the spores are formed inside a long narrow to oval cell called an ascus (or sac) (Fig. 18, page 542). At maturity forcible discharge occurs from the tips of the ascus into the air. There are also sterile cells in the hymenium, which are called paraphyses. They are often numerous and serve the same functions that are described above for the cystidia of the Basidiomycetes. See the scarlet surface of *Sarcocypha coccinea,* where the pigment is contained in the thousands of paraphyses.

KEY TO THE MAJOR GROUPS OF FUNGI

1. Fleshy mushrooms, stipe present or absent, with lamellae (A = **Agarics**); stipe present, hymenium with ridges, intervenose, to smooth (B = **Chanterelles**); central stipe present, hymenium comprised of tubes with pores (C = **Boletes**)

1. Fruiting bodies tough to woody, rarely fleshy --- 2

    2. Tough, woody, or fleshy with pores, on wood (D = **Polypores**); stipe present or absent, fleshy, tough, or woody fruiting bodies with spines (or teeth) (E = **Fungi with spines**); or coral-like, erect, fleshy to tough (F = **Coral Fungi**)

    2. Fruiting bodies not as above -- 3

3. Spores develop in a sac, with or without a sterile base or stalk (G = **Puffballs**); or star-like with spore sac in the center (G = **Earthstars**)

3. Not as above -- 4

    4. Fruiting bodies small, nestlike or urnlike with oval or lens-shaped "eggs" inside (G = **Bird's Nest Fungi**)

    4. Fruiting bodies not as above -- 5

5. Fruiting bodies usually stalked, often with a volva, with an olive-brown to green, slimy top; and a disagreeable odor (H = **Stinkhorns**)

5. Fruiting bodies not as above -- 6

    6. Fruiting bodies above ground or on wood-- 7

    6. Fruiting bodies underground or partially buried in the soil ---------------------------- 8

7. Fruiting bodies jelly-like, gelatinous, pliant; on wood or on the ground (I = **Jelly Fungi**)

7. Fruiting bodies fleshy, pine cone-shaped, with ridges and pits or wrinkled spore bearing surface; on the ground (J = **True Morels** and **False Morels**); cuplike (J = **Cup Fungi**); or small, with stalks and flattened or small wrinkled heads (K = **Earth Tongues**)

    8. Fruiting bodies, in cross-section, appearing marbled without locules (minute cavities) --- (L = **True Truffles**)

    8. Fruiting bodies, in cross-section, with locules (L = **False Truffles**)

Plate A

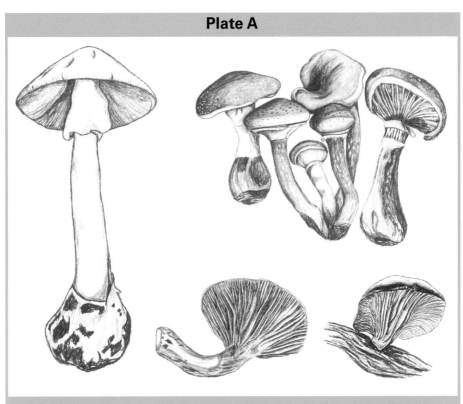

Fleshy mushrooms with lamellae; stipe central, lateral or absent AGARICS

Plate B

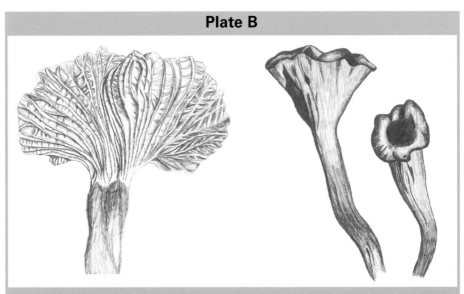

Fleshy with blunt, often interconnected ridges, or nearly smooth and slightly wrinkled; always on the ground CHANTERELLES

Plate C

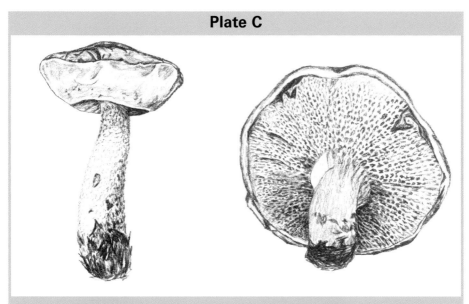

Fleshy with pores; central stipe; always on the ground under trees BOLETES

Plate D

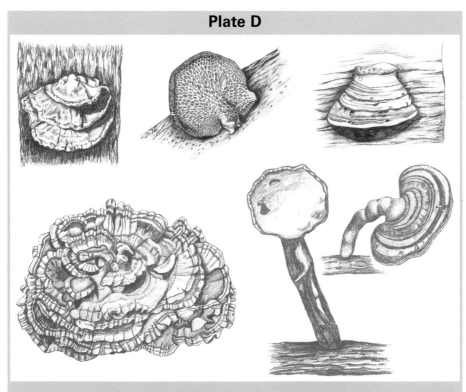

Tough, woody, or fleshy with pores; stipe central, lateral or absent POLYPORES

Plate E

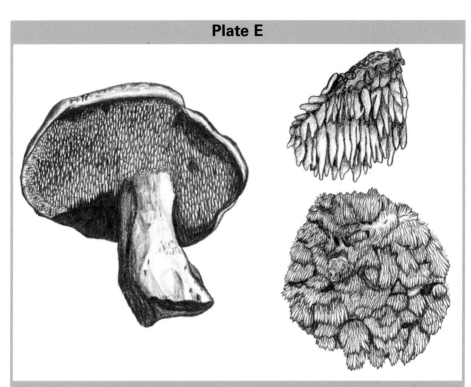

Fleshy to tough; with teeth; central stipe or stipe absent; on ground, wood, pine cones or plant debris; annual FUNGI WITH SPINES

Plate F

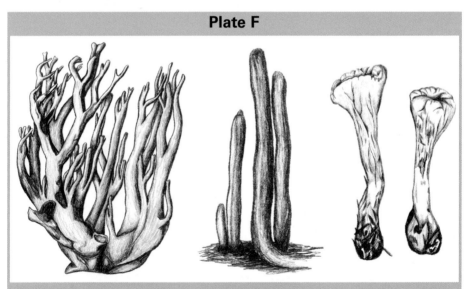

Fleshy to tough; with upraised fingers like coral, single fingers to large fruiting bodies with complicated branching; on ground or occasionally on twigs and decayed wood CORAL FUNGI

Plate G

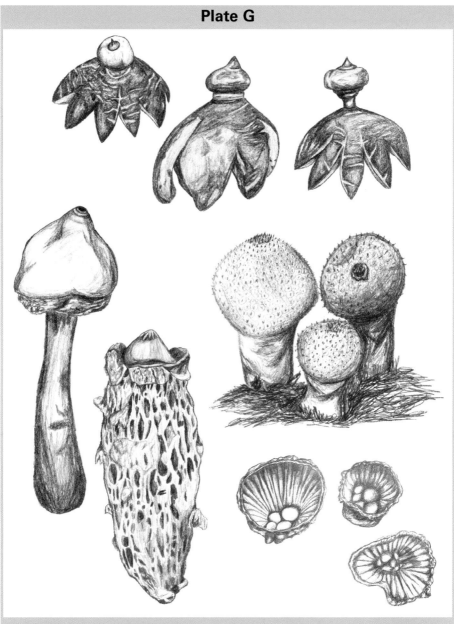

Star-shaped; with a central spore sac and ostiole ("mouth") for spore discharge; on ground or in litter EARTH STARS

Round to oval spore sacs; with or without a stalk or sterile base, on ground or well decayed wood or mulch STALKED PUFFBALLS, PUFFBALLS

Small urnlike or nestlike fruiting bodies with round peridioles ("eggs") inside; on mulch or litter BIRD'S NEST FUNGI

Plate H

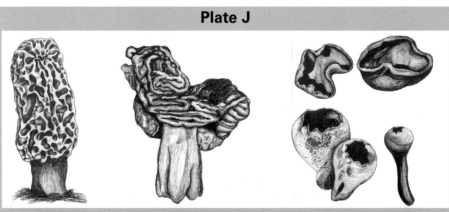

Fleshy and fragile; with a volva or cup surrounding the base; green slime over the top or on the arms; attracts flies; have a very disagreeable odor; on ground in humus STINKHORNS

Plate I

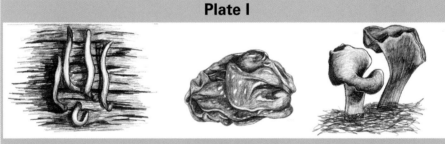

Jellylike to tough jellylike; brightly colored, white, yellow, orange; on wood, humus or litter JELLY FUNGI

Plate J

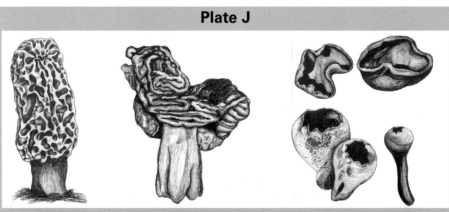

Fleshy; on ground; head with ridges and pits (pine conelike) TRUE MORELS

Fleshy; on ground; head with wrinkles and skirt or saddle-like FALSE MORELS

Fleshy; on ground; cuplike with spores inside CUP FUNGI

Plate K

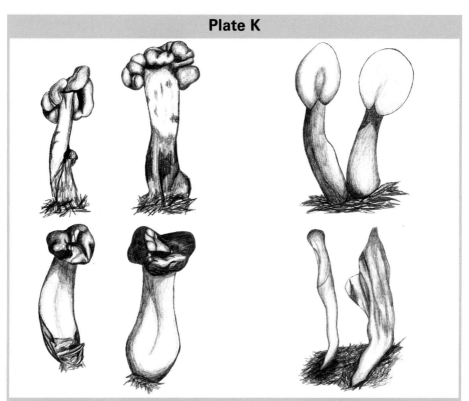

Fleshy to tough, small; on ground; stipe with head, variously shaped **EARTH TONGUES**

Plate L

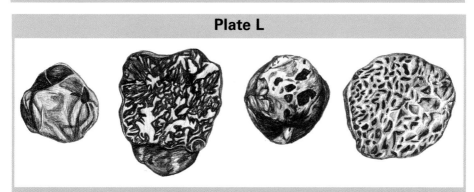

Fruiting bodies, in cross-section, appearing marbled; without locales **TRUE TRUFFLES**

Fruiting bodies, in cross-section, with locules **FALSE TRUFFLES**

BASIDIOMYCETES

Amanita flavoconia

The Basidiomycetes are a large group of fungi that include the agarics, chanterelles, coral fungi, boletes, fungi with spines, polypores, Aphyllophorales, puffballs, earth balls, stalked puffballs, bird's nest fungi, false truffles, sequestrate fungi, and jelly fungi. The sexual cells, called basidia, are clavate cells with four prongs called sterigmata on which the basidiospores develop. These cells form the spore-bearing surface called a hymenium, which covers the lamellae of the agarics, inside the tubes of the boletes or polypores, and develops within the spore mass called the gleba in the puffballs. The spores are forcibly discharged from the basidium at maturity, except in the Gasteromycetes, in order to distribute the spores and reproduce the fungus. However, this fact allows us to place the pileus of a fruiting body on a white sheet and obtain a spore print. The spore print color is often an essential part, in the agarics for example, of determining the family to which the mushroom belongs. Basidiospores are either smooth or ornamented, variously shaped, entire or with an apical pore, amyloid or nonamyloid. The physical structure of the fruiting body and its appearance allows us to recognize major groups of Basidiomycetes. The visual key provides examples of the major groups listed above and allows the user to go directly to that group to identify a given species.

KEY TO THE FAMILIES OF MUSHROOMS WITH LAMELLAE (AGARICS)

Spore print white, cream color, buff to ochre

1. Lamellae free from the stipe -- 2
1. Lamellae attached to the stipe --- 3
    2. Lamellae free; universal veil (volva) present as a "cup" surrounding the stipe base or as patches, warts or granules loose on the surface of the pileus; partial veil may leave an annulus on the stipe or absent ----------------------------------- Amanitaceae
    2. Lamellae free; universal veil absent, small scales or fibrils on the pileus are part of the pileipellis; partial veil often present as a loose ring or as a fibrillose zone on the stipe --- Lepiotaceae
3. Lamellae often thick, white or brightly colored, fleshy, waxy when rubbed, well separated; pileus often brightly colored; always on the ground; partial veil if present viscid or weekly fibrillose; stipe always present and central -------------------- Hygrophoraceae
3. Lamellae thick, thin, white or colored, not waxy or with a latex; on ground, wood, humus, litter, dung or other fungi --- 4
    4. On ground; usually in woods under or near trees; partial veil absent; flesh usually brittle; latex present or absent; spores globose to subglobose with amyloid (blue) warts or reticulations in Melzer's solution ------------------------------------- Russulales
    4. On ground, wood, leaves, needles, litter, dung, other fungi or from wounds on living trees; flesh soft to tough; stipe central, laterally attached to absent; spores, if amyloid not globose or not with warts or reticulations in Melzer's solution -- Tricholomataceae

Spore print salmon, pinkish brown to pink

1. Lamellae free from the stipe; usually on wood, or wounds on living trees, occasionally on humus or litter; universal veil (volva) present or absent; spores smooth, subglobose to elliptic; cystidia often as thick-walled metuloids ----------------------------- Pluteaceae
1. Lamellae attached and not free from the stipe; usually on the ground, if on wood stipe absent or very short and lateral; universal veil (volva) absent; spores angular to longitudinally striate; cystidia if present, thin-walled, hyaline -------------------- Entolomataceae

Spore print black, black-brown to smoky gray

1. Lamellae decurrent, thick, never turning to "ink" (deliquescent); always on the ground under or near conifers (pine, fir, spruce, larch or hemlock); pileus tissue amyloid (blue)

or not in Melzer's solution; spores subfusiform thick-walled, without an apical pore; cystidia long, thin- or thick-walled protruding above the basidia; pileus dry, viscid to slimy glutinous -- Gomphidiaceae

1. Lamellae usually free, never decurrent, often becoming inky (deliquescent); on horse or cow dung, manured grass, decayed wood, wood in service in many habitats; pileus tissue never amyloid; spores elliptic thick-walled with an apical pore; cystidia not long usually ovoid, pear-shaped or ten-pin shaped ---------------------------------- Coprinaceae

Spore print purple-brown, yellow-brown to chocolate-brown

1. Spores purple-brown to orange-brown; spores subglobose to elliptic, thick-walled with an apical pore or not; lamellae adnate, white to tan when young; on wood, litter, grass, dung or occasionally from buried wood; context or surface not bruising yellow, orange or red but some bruise blue --- Strophariaceae

1. Spores chocolate-brown, subglobose to elliptic, thick-walled, apical pore present or absent; lamellae free, pink, grayish pink to gray when young; in grass, humus, manured pasture but never on wood; context or surface yellow, orange, red or not   Agaricaceae

Spore print bright yellow-brown, rusty-brown, cinnamon-brown, earth-brown to clay-brown

1. Spores clay-brown to light yellow-brown; pileus convex to fan-shaped; stipe absent or very reduced and lateral; on logs, stumps, limbs or wood debris; spores globose to elliptic, smooth or spiny; fresh tissue never green in ferric sulphate ---- Crepidotaceae

1. Not with the above combination of characteristics -- 2

    2. Spores clay color, smooth, subfusiform without an apical pore; lamellae decurrent; stipe present or absent; on ground, wood or wood debris; flesh always green in ferric sulphate --- Paxillaceae

    2. Not with the above combination of characteristics ------------------------------------- 3

3. Spores bright yellow-brown, clay-brown to earth-brown smooth with an apical pore; lamellae often free, never inky (deliquescent); on dung, humus, manured grass, wood mulch; partial veil absent or if present membranous ---------------------------- Bolbitiaceae

3. Spores rusty-brown, cinnamon-brown to dark earth brown, smooth, nodulose, rugose without an apical pore; lamellae attached never inky (deliquescent); on the ground, wood or on moss; partial veil cortinous (cobweblike), membranous or absent -- Cortinariaceae

MUSHROOMS WITH LAMELLAE (AGARICS)

AMANITACEAE

There is an estimated total of more than 130 species of *Amanita* in North America. Some of the common species will be presented and others referred to under comments rather than fully described. The fruiting body in *Amanita* develops from a round or oval button that is surrounded by a protective tissue layer known as the universal veil. The young button contains the immature pileus, lamellae, stipe. At this stage they have sometimes been mistaken for puffballs and eaten with disastrous results. One should cut the button in half lengthwise, it will reveal a typical young mushroom inside. If something other than a tissue which looks similar to a block of cream cheese is observed, it could be an *Amanita*. When the stipe of the *Amanita* button starts to elongate, very soft universal veil fragments of some species are carried up on the expanding pileus as a series of warts (Fig. 35) or patches of tissue. If it is a tough, outer membrane, it will be split by the expanding pileus and stipe and nothing of the universal veil left on the pileus. Instead, a well-formed volva (Fig. 35) surrounds the base of the stipe. In the genus *Limacella,* the universal veil is a thick, slimy, gelatinous tissue, but the development is the same as in *Amanita*. *Volvariella* is the third genus in the lamellate fungi in which one encounters an obvious volva. However, all species of *Volvariella* (Pluteaceae) have pink spores, while *Amanita* and *Limacella* have white spores. A third important character possessed by *Amanita* and *Limacella* is free lamellae, so called because they do not touch the stipe. Therefore, a fungus in the Amanitaceae must have white spores, free lamellae, and a universal veil, which leaves either veil fragments on the pileus or a volva surrounding the stipe. If the volva is cottony or membranous, it is an *Amanita*. A gelatinous universal veil and volva signify a *Limacella*. One must be careful to dig down under the stipe and lift the entire fungus out of the ground to be able to see the volva. The fragmented remains of the universal veil can often be seen in the surrounding soil. Two additional characters can be verified with a microscope. All the spores of the Amanitaceae produce a white spore print. They are entire, smooth, and thin-walled (Figs. 1–4), and a significant number of species have amyloid spores (see glossary). Figures 6–10, illustrate non *Amanita* spores, which, by contrast, are thick-walled, ornamented, or are not entire and possess an apical pore. Lastly, if one cuts down through the lamellae of a young fruiting body, the tissue in the center of the lamella is divergent, that is, it grows outward from a central strand (Fig. 28). This character must also be viewed microscopically, but occurs in all species in the Amanitaceae.

Edibility: There are, indeed, both edible and very poisonous species of *Amanita* in North America. However, several of the species have been eaten in Europe for centuries. We have many more species of *Amanita* in North America, many in which the toxins are inadequately known, and we have several poisonous species that closely resemble the edible ones. We would therefore not recommend eating any Amanitas. The toxins possessed by Amanitas are described under Mushroom Toxins and include deadly cyclopeptide toxins in Type 1, muscarine in Type 2, and ibotinic acid toxins in Type 3. There is little doubt that these large, attractive, showy mushrooms have caused the majority of fatalities attributable to mushrooms and more than all other mushrooms combined.

KEY TO AMANITA

1. Volva a saclike cup surrounding the stipe base --- 2
1. Volva in fragments over the pileus as warts and/or appressed to the stipe or in the soil surrounding the stipe --- 7
    2. Partial veil forming a superior annulus or skirtlike annulus---------------------------- 3
    2. Partial veil absent, only a saccate volva present --- 6
3. Pileus white, smooth; stipe with a saclike cup surrounding the base; white, superior, hanging partial veil; globose, amyloid spores --- *A. virosa*
3. Pileus green, brownish green, orange-red, pink to ochraceous ----------------------------- 4
    4. Pileus green to brownish green; stipe, partial veil and volva white------ *A. phalloides*
    4. Pileus pink, ochraceus to orange red--- 5
5. Pileus orange-red striate; partial veil yellow; volva white ---------------------- *A. caesarea*
5. Pileus light orange-yellow; partial veil yellow; volva white ------------------ *A. arkansana*
                          (See comments under *A. caesarea*)
    6. Pileus gray-brown to yellow-brown; white saccate volva; widely distributed -- *A. vaginata* complex
    6. Pileus pink to ochraceus; white saccate volva; known from California ---- *A. velosa*
7. Pileus red, orange, olivaceous brown to brown or gray-brown, with scattered patches of tissue, but not floccose and powdery; usually odorless ------------------------------- 8
7. Pileus white, with white or colored warts or powdery remains of the universal veil, rest of fruiting body white; often floccose patches on the bulb or stipe base, sometimes rooting; often with an unpleasant odor -- 19
    8. Pileus red, orange to straw-yellow, viscid; universal and partial veil white; stipe with an enlarged base with 2 or 3 concentric rings of tissue ------------ *A. muscaria*
    8. Pileus variable in color; stipe base lacking 2–3 concentric rings of tissue ---------- 9
9. Pileus bright orange to yellow--- 10
9. Pileus not as above--- 11
    10. Pileus bright orange to yellow-orange; veil whitish; flesh and/or cuticle of stipe near base white --- *A. flavoconia*
    10. Pileus deep yellow, even; veil yellow; flesh and /or cuticle of stipe tinted red --- *A. flavorubescens*
11. Pileus dark brown with white patches; bulb cleft or split longitudinally; spores globose, amyloid--- *A. brunnescens*
11. Bulb not split; with other combinations of characters ------------------------------------- 12

12. Pileus citrine green, yellowish tinted green, with lavender or white patches of universal veil remains; white fragile annulus; globose amyloid spores -------- *A. citrina*

12. Pileus another color; universal veil white or colored ---------------------------------- 13

13. Pileus dull yellowish, yellow-gray, orange-brown to dark brown;
universal veil white --- 14

13. Pileus reddish brown to brownish gray; universal veil colored --------------------------- 16

14. Pileus dull yellow with a pinkish cast;
basal bulb with a narrow collar -- *A. gemmata*

14. Pileus orange-brown to dark brown; white superior annulus ------------------------ 15

15. Pileus dark brown to pale brown; margin lighter, with white warts over the surface;
partial veil often ragged superior skirtlike; nonamyloid spores -------------- *A. pantherina*

15. Pileus orange-brown with yellowish brown margin, numerous white warts; annulus
white, flaring and persistent; spores elliptical, thin-walled, amyloid -------- *A. francheti*

16. Pileus red-brown with pinkish warts; stipe base flushed red; volva with reddish
patches -- *A. rubescens*

16. Pileus dark brown to red-brown, warts not pinkish; no red stains;
volva a different color --- 17

17. Partial absent; pileus with a striate margin; universal veil of gray warts ---- *A. ceciliae*

17. Partial veil present, ash gray-- 18

18. Pileus dark brown with many small gray warts; gray fibrillose material over the
stipe base; spores subglobose to elliptic, thin-walled, amyloid ------------ *A. excelsa*

18. Pileus deep dark brown with large gray to pinkish gray patches of universal veil
remains; stipe evenly gray with round to flattened bulb at the base ---- *A. porphyria*

19. Pileus with a dense gray to brownish gray, granulose to powdery surface, margin
striate; spores nonamyloid -- *A. farinosa*

19. Pileus without a gray powdery to granulose surface, margin not striate;
spores amyloid --- 20

20. Pileus 8–20 cm broad chalk white, with white powdery universal veil remains;
base bulbous but not rooting; strong unpleasant odor;
spores 9.0–13.5 x 5.5–9.0 µm amyloid ---------------------------------- *A. polypyramis*
(Note: *A. chlorinosma* is a rare, smaller species with smaller spores, see comments)

20. Pileus white or colored with colored universal veil material; stipe rooting or not;
spores amyloid--- 21

21. Pileus 5–10 cm broad, white with pointed white warts; stipe with abrupt round bulb;
odorless; amyloid spores 7–9 x 5.5–8.5 µm --------------------------------------- *A. abrupta*

21. Not with the above combination of characters --- 22

    22. Pileus 6–25 cm broad, white with powdery to granulose reddish to pinkish brown universal veil material also on the large rooting bulb; odor of old ham bones or soap -- *A. daucipes*

    22. Smaller species or the universal veil differently colored; unpleasant odor or odorless --- 23

23. Pileus 6–21.5 cm broad, yellowish white to gray, covered with small reddish brown to gray-brown warts; rounded basal bulb covered with rings of reddish brown scales; amyloid spores 9.0–12.5 x 5.5–8.0 µm ------------------------------------ *A. atkinsoniana*

23. Not with the above combination of characters --- 24

    24. Pileus 5–10 cm broad, covered with flattened gray to brownish gray warts; club-shaped bulb with rooting base and erect, recurved, gray scales; odor mild--- *A. onusta*

    24. Pileus larger, more robust, white with brownish orange universal veil; bulb ovoid and without erect gray scales; odor present or not ------------------------------------ 25

25. Pileus large 8–17 cm broad, white, with concentric rows of brownish orange scales, stocky and robust with a large white rooting basal bulb; odor of "chloride of lime"--- *A. ravenelii*

25. Pileus medium 6–15 cm broad, white with brownish orange pyramidal warts which grade into sticky fibrils over the margin; stipe tall and thin with a round bulb at base with scales arranged in several rows; odorless ------------------------------------ *A. cokeri*

Amanita virosa (Fr.) Quél.
DEADLY POISONOUS

Pileus 3.0–9.5 cm broad, conic to ovoid, convex to plane, pure white, smooth, viscid when wet to sticky, margin smooth, not striate or only obscurely so, no volval warts. Flesh firm, white. Lamellae free, close to subdistant in age, narrow, white. Stipe 14–24 cm long, 1.0–2.3 cm wide, enlarging gradually to a club-shaped base, dry, white, finely fibrous above ring, hairy below. Volva white, membranous, persistent, saclike, and free from the stipe, often 3–4 cm high. Partial veil membranous, white, smooth, faintly striate on upper surface, leaving a tattered or skirtlike, superior ring, which on occasion is almost missing. Odorless or slightly unpleasant. Do not taste this fungus.

Spores 8–10 (-12) x 6.5–9.5 µm globose to short elliptic, smooth, entire, thin-walled, amyloid. Spore print white.

Habit and distribution: Solitary but usually several together under oaks and hardwood forests or in mixed woods. Widely distributed in eastern North America. Fruiting in the summer and fall.

Comments: Amanita virosa is known around the world as the "Destroying Angel" or the "Death Angel." On the Pacific Coast A. ocreata Peck is very similar and is also a species with subglobose to elliptic, amyloid spores. It is found under live oak (especially Quercus agrifolia) in California, Oregon, and Washington and fruits from January to March. The two-spored A. bisporigera G. F. Atk. is distributed in the eastern and northern U.S. and Canada, and usually fruits in the spring or early summer. Amanita volvata (Peck) Martin is another white species with a thick, saccate volva (Fig. 30) and amyloid, elliptic spores (Jenkins, 1986). It is found in the southeastern United States. They all should be treated as deadly poisonous and the characters described above apply equally well to all of the species. None of these species has an odor. If an odor of old ham bones or old tennis shoes is present see A. polypyramis or A. ravenelii.

This group of species is one of the most deadly of the mushrooms. The Type 1 toxins, cyclopeptides, kill liver cells that, without a liver transplant, often cause fatalities. Note the button stage in the picture. It can be confused with a small puffball or assumed to be an edible button of A. caesarea or Volvariella volvacea, both of which are edible mushrooms. All pure white species of Amanita especially those with a saccate volva should be avoided.

Amanita phalloides Fr.
DEADLY POISONOUS

Pileus 7–15 cm broad, convex, viscid, smooth, pale yellow-green, brownish green to green, with flattened radiating hairs, margin not striate, universal veil patches on surface. Flesh firm, white to light green just below pileus cuticle. Lamellae free, close, broad, white. Stipe 8–14 cm long, 1–2 cm wide enlarging somewhat toward the base, white, smooth. Volva membranous, persistent, saclike, white. Partial veil membranous, remains as superior ring hanging skirtlike on stipe. Odor slightly disagreeable. Do not taste!

Spores 8–11 x 7–9 μm subglobose to globose, smooth, entire, thin-walled, amyloid. Spore print white.

Habit and distribution: Several to numerous, on ground, under or near European trees such as Norway spruce or in plantations established in America. Known from New Jersey, Virginia, Minnesota, and California, but likely established elsewhere. Fruiting in the summer and early fall.

Comments: This species is frequently referred to as the "Green Death Cap." In addition, the subglobose to globose spores are amyloid. This species was introduced into the United States in the early part of the century on European root stock and is now widespread, even mycorrhizal, with native trees. It is as deadly as *A. virosa* and *A. ochreata* and has the Type 1 toxins, cyclopeptides, typical of this complex. Young buttons can easily be mistaken for *Volvariella volvacea* (Bull.:Fr.) Singer, the "Paddy straw mushroom," and Asian immigrants to the United States living on the West Coast should be especially careful to correctly identify their finds. *Volvariella volvacea* has a volva; no partial veil; and pink lamellae at maturity with a pink spore print. Prior to the introduction of *A. phalloides, A. brunnescens,* an edible species, was often mistaken for *A. phalloides* (Coker, 1917).

Amanita caesarea (Fr.) Schwein.
NONPOISONOUS

Pileus 5–15 (-30) cm broad, conical at first, convex, sometimes with a low umbo, viscid, smooth with long striations toward the margin, margin bright yellow shading to orange or dark orange-red toward the center, no warts. Flesh firm, white, yellowish just under pileus cuticle. Lamellae free, close, broad, yellow. Stipe 9–23 cm long, 0.7–2.0 cm wide, nearly equal, hollow, yellow, dry, smooth, glabrous or floccose. Volva membranous, persistent, saccate, white cup enclosing the base at maturity. Partial veil membranous, soft, yellow to orange, as a persistent, skirtlike ring on upper stipe. Odorless. We do not recommend tasting any Amanitas.

Spores 7.5–14.5 x 5–8.5 μm oval, smooth, entire, thin-walled, nonamyloid. Spore print white.

Habit and distribution: Scattered in groups, sometimes in fairy rings, under hardwood forests in eastern North America, across the South to New Mexico (Jarmie & Rogers, 1993). Frequent. Fruiting in summer and fall.

Comments: This species is known around the world as "Caesar's Mushroom. *Amanita flavoconia* G. F. Atk. looks similar but the volva breaks up into yellow pieces and the lamellae are white with a nearly white to buff stipe. *Amanita parcivolvata* (Peck) Gilb., which fruited in our neighborhood in Virginia, has a bright red pileus and yellow stipe, but lacks a partial veil and it has a saccate, white volva. A third species, *A. arkansana* Rosen. has an orange-yellow pileus; a yellow partial veil; pale yellow lamellae; and a white, saccate volva. In Asia we have collected and photographed *A. hemibapha* (Berk. & Broome) Sacc. and it appears identical to our material of *A. caesarea*. In Europe we have seen variation in the presence of orange scales on the stipe as well as those that have very reduced scales and marginal striations on the pileus that are not as pronounced as our taxon in the North America. Only additional study, especially with sequence data, will determine if the minor differences in populations are enough to recognize several species. Often recorded as edible but there are too many similar Amanitas in North America for us to recommend it for the table.

Amanita vaginata (Fr.) Vittad.
NONPOISONOUS

Pileus 5–9 cm broad, nearly conic, plane in age often with a small umbo, viscid, brown, gray-brown to yellow-brown, without hairs, with a conspicuously striate margin, warts absent. Flesh soft, thin, white. Lamellae free, close, narrow, fairly well separated in age, white. Stipe 10–20 cm long, 1.0–1.5 cm wide, white, enlarging to an oval or club-shaped, basal bulb, smooth or with some flattened hairs over the center. Volva white, membranous, saclike (Fig. 30), persistent, unattached to stipe. Partial veil absent. Odorless. Do not taste.

Spores 7–14 x 7–13 µm globose, smooth, entire, thin-walled, nonamyloid. Spore print white.

Habit and distribution: Single to numerous under both hardwood and conifers. Widely distributed. Fruiting spring through fall.

Comments: This species is commonly called the "Grisette." Several varieties (for example, var *alba* and var *livida*) have also been described, using pileus color as the criterion. *Amanita sinicoflava* Tuloss has a "olive-tan to brownish olive" pileus (Tuloss, 1988) and a "graying volva" well illustrated by Roody (2003) and known from Virginia to Maine. It is similar to the widely distributed *A . fulva* (Schaeff.) Pers., which is based on the orange pileus variant of this species and *A. pachycolea* D. E. Stuntz, which is a large dark brown species found on the West Coast. Some people eat this species but we would not recommend that anyone eat Amanitas.

Amanita velosa (Peck) Lloyd
NONPOISONOUS

Pileus 4–15 cm broad, convex to plane in age, viscid, glabrous, pink to ochraceous, margin striate, typically with a large patch or patches of white universal veil remains over the center. Flesh soft, thin, and white. Lamellae free, subdistant, white often tinted pinkish. Stipe 8–15 cm long, 0.6–1.7 cm wide, equal, white, dry, floccose, no partial veil, base with a thick, saccate, white volva. Odorless. Do not taste.

Spores 8.5–13.0 x 6–10 µm broadly elliptic, smooth, entire, thin-walled, nonamyloid. Spore print white.

Habit and distribution: Single or several under live oak or in mixed oak forests. Found in California and Oregon. Fruiting in winter, February to March.

Comments: *Amanita calyptrata* Peck (= *A. calyptroderma* G. F. Atk.) is very similar but the pileus is brown to orange-brown and it is most often found associated with Madrone in a narrow range in California and adjacent Oregon. Both species are nonpoisonous. However, we strongly favor not eating any species of *Amanita*.

Amanita muscaria (Fr.) Gray
POISONOUS (INTOXICATING)

Pileus 8–24 cm broad, convex to plane in age, viscid, usually straw-yellow, orange to bright blood-red, usually darkest at the center, but can be all white, adorned with whitish, warts or small patches and, at first, hanging marginal veil remains, white. Flesh firm, white throughout. Lamellae free, crowded, broad, white, with minutely hairy edges. Stipe 8–15 cm long, 0.2–0.3 cm wide, enlarging toward base, becoming bulbous at the base, white, covered with silky hairs. The only remains of the volva are 2 or 3 concentric rings above the bulb. Partial veil membranous, superior, often several centimeters long, white, persistent. Odorless. Do not taste.

Spores 8–11 x 6–8 µm elliptic, smooth, entire, thin-walled, nonamyloid. Spore print white.

Habit and distribution: Scattered or abundant under hardwoods and conifers. Widely distributed. Fruiting from spring to fall.

Comments: *Amanita frostiana* (Peck) Sacc. is an eastern species that has a thinner stipe; lacks the concentric rings above the bulb; and also has nonamyloid, almost globose spores 7.5–9.5 x 7–9 µm. It is apparently not toxic since we know mushroom hunters who have eaten large portions of *A. frostiana* without ill effects. In addition, certain areas have races of *A. muscaria* that seem to have less or different proportions of toxins than other areas. However, this is a dangerous fungus with Type 3 toxins and should be avoided. In some cases it has been eaten and characterized as a "pleasurable intoxication" (Spoerke and Rumack, 1994). *Amanita parcivolvata* (Peck) Gilb. is a close lookalike to *A. muscaria* but it has a powdery veil; leaves no ring; and the yellowish volval patches fall off readily. It is smaller in size; has spores of the same size; also no amyloid reaction; and its toxicity is unknown (Jenkins, 1986, Figs. 3 & 4). It is only reported from northeastern North America. We have collected the white form of *A. muscaria* under jack pine in Michigan, Virginia pine in Maryland, and aspen in Idaho, but it is not common. The orange to orange-red form *A. muscaria* var *formosa* and the red-capped *A. muscaria* var *muscaria* are common in New York and New England. A deep red pileus color is often found along the West Coast and Colorado. A faded light yellow-orange pileus color is typical of fruiting under northern Rocky Mountain conifers.

Amanita flavoconia G. F. Atk.
MAY BE POISONOUS

Pileus 3–8 cm broad, convex to nearly plane, viscid, bright orange to yellow but whole pileus is evenly colored with scattered yellow, often large, warts; margin faintly striate and at first often covered in volval remains. Flesh thin, firm, cream to buff near cap, remainder white. Lamellae free, close, white, with minutely hairy edges. Stipe 5–12 cm long, 0.5–1.5 cm wide, enlarging toward base to an almost oval basal bulb, pale yellow to white, dry, finely pruinose. Volva bright yellow, not persistent, breaking up around the basal bulb and often left in the soil. Partial veil membranous, whitish, leaving a persistent, superior ring with a buff margin. Odorless. Do not taste.

Spores 7.0–9.5 x 4.5–6.0 µm elliptic, smooth, entire, thin-walled, amyloid. Spore print white.

Habit and distribution: Single or several under hardwoods or occasionally conifers. Found in eastern and central United States and adjacent Canada. Fruiting in the summer and fall.

Comments: There is one report of unidentified cyclopeptides by Abdel-Malak (1974) but no known poison cases with this species. It is found commonly during most seasons. A rather rare closely related species is *A. flavorubescens* G. F. Atk., which has a strikingly yellow cap, partial veil, and red-stained flesh in the base of the stipe.

Amanita flavorubescens G. F. Atk
INEDIBLE

Pileus 6–12 cm broad, convex to plane in age, fibrous, slightly viscid, striate just at margin, deep even yellow with numerous orange warts of universal veil remains scattered over the surface which often fall or are washed off. Flesh firm, white except in stipe base, which is light red. Lamellae free, close to fairly well separated, white with pinkish stains in age. Stipe 5–18 cm long, 0.1–2.2 cm wide, enlarging toward base, which is bulbous, white to light yellowish with scanty hairs and sometimes with light pinkish tissue near the base. Volva deep yellow, quickly disintegrating in the soil around base. Partial veil membranous, same color as cap, but white above, leaving a superior, ragged, skirtlike ring. Odorless. Do not taste.

Spores 7.5–10.0 x 5.0–6.5 µm elliptic to almost globose, smooth, entire, thin-walled, amyloid. Spore print white.

Habit and distribution: Single or several under hardwoods or occasionally conifers. Found in eastern United States and Canada. Fruiting occasionally in spring usually in summer and early fall. Although not common Pomerleau (1966) reports it from Quebec, Huffman et al. (1989) from the central United States, Kimbrough (2000) from Florida, and we have recorded it in Maryland, North Carolina, and Virginia.

Comments: This species is also known as the "Yellow Blusher." *Amanita frostiana* Peck is very similar but has nearly globose, nonamyloid spores 7.0–9.5 x 7–9 µm and the pileus and warts are not intense yellow but whitish to buff.

Amanita brunnescens G. F. Atk.
NONPOISONOUS

Pileus (3-) 5–9 (-15) cm broad, convex, plane, viscid, dark brown or sometimes light tan to whitish, margin covered with white, cottony warts and patches, faintly striate. Flesh thin, white, staining reddish brown. Lamellae free, close, broad, white. Stipe 4–13 cm long, 0.8–2.0 cm wide, equal but with a large, oval, basal bulb up to 3.5 cm broad which is conspicuously split or cleft (Fig. 32) longitudinally, white, smooth above ring, hairy below and often stained brown near or over the base. Universal veil remains are in irregular patches on the basal bulb and sometimes form an obscure collar around top. Veil membranous, white, skirtlike or breaking irregularly to hang in shreds or patches as a superior ring or sometimes pulling free from the stipe altogether. Odorless. Do not taste.

Spores 7.0–9.5 (-11.0) µm globose, smooth, entire, thin-walled, amyloid. Spore print white.

Habit and distribution: Scattered and common under hardwoods, especially oaks and mixed woods. Found throughout eastern North America as far north as the boreal forest and west to Iowa, Kansas, and central Texas. Fruiting in summer and early fall.

Comments: This species is often called the "Cleft Foot Amanita." The less common A. *brunnescens* var *pallida* Krieger is very light tan or with a pure white pileus but is still easily diagnosed with the distinctive cleft bulb. It is known only from the eastern and central hardwood forests of North America. We have seen people eat this species but it has a metallic taste and again we do not recommend that anyone eat species of *Amanita*.

Amanita citrina (Schaeff.) Gray
POISONOUS

Pileus 4–10 cm broad, convex, sometimes with a broad umbo, viscid, citrine-green to light citrine-green with a whitish margin, covered with irregular, flattened, white, volval patches that are loose and may be washed off in wet weather, margin incurved at first, not striate. Flesh soft, white. Lamellae free, close, white, and with minutely hairy edges. Stipe 8–12 cm long, 0.8–1.5 cm wide, enlarging downward with a nearly round basal bulb, sometimes with a noticeable collar, white, smooth above and cottony below ring. Volva soft, flattened to bulb, sometimes free at the top, forming a collar. Veil fragile, membranous, white to buff, superior, somewhat persistent, hanging about or flattened down to the stipe, also seen surrounding the fruiting body on the ground. Odorless. Do not taste.

Spores 7–10 µm globose, smooth, entire, thin-walled, amyloid. Spore print white.

Habit and distribution: Single to scattered under conifers, hardwoods, or mixed woods. Found in eastern and central United States and Canada. Fruiting in late summer and fall.

Comments: This species has been called the "Citrine Amanita." *Amanita citrina* var *lavendula* Coker has a lavender-colored volva and is as widespread as the white variety. The olivaceous tint is usually present but may be weak. There are usually pines present with which it may be mycorrhizal. It contains the Type 3 toxin, bufotenin, which is a compound close to psilocin but is not centrally active in humans when taken orally (Spoerke & Rumack, 1994).

Amanita gemmata (Fr.) Gill.
POISONOUS

Pileus (2.5-) 4.0–7.0 (-12.0) cm broad, convex to plane or even slightly depressed in age, viscid to glutinous, smooth, dull yellow often with a pinkish cast, covered with whitish volval warts, sometimes tinted cinnamon in age, but readily washed off in wet weather; margin striate, often covered with sand, clay, and debris accumulated during expansion. Flesh soft, thin, white. Lamellae free, close, narrow, white. Stipe 5–14 cm long, 0.5–0.8 (-2.0) cm wide, equal, white, smooth above the ring, some fibrils on the surface, basal bulb with a narrow collar. Volva remains as patches clinging to the lower surface of the bulb or as pieces left in the soil. Partial veil fragile, membranous, forming a ragged, white, superior ring or absent at maturity. Odorless. Do not taste.

Spores 7.5–11.0 x 6–9 µm short elliptic to subglobose, smooth, entire, thin-walled, nonamyloid. Spore print white.

Habit and distribution: Single or several under mixed hardwood-conifer forests, especially pines. Widely distributed in North America. Fruiting from early summer to fall.

Comments: Spoerke & Rumack (1994) list Type 3 toxins, muscimol and ibotenic acid, and this species, like others in this group, are poisonous. We recommend again that no *Amanita* should be eaten in North America. *Amanita pantherina* var *multisquammosa* (Peck) D. J. Jenkins is similar but has a distinct collar around the bulb; a more persistent partial veil; and similar spores.

Amanita pantherina (DC.:Fr.) Secr.
POISONOUS

Pileus 5–12 cm broad, convex to nearly plane in age, viscid, often with soft, pyramid-like, white warts over a light to rich brown surface that is usually buff to yellowish just at the striate margin, which may have veil patches adhering to it. Flesh firm, white, buff just beneath pileus cuticle. Lamellae free, close to crowded, white, edges finely scalloped. Stipe 6–12 cm long, 1.0–2.5 cm wide, gradually enlarging to the ovoid basal bulb (Fig. 34), which has a roll or collar where stipe and bulb meet, white, nearly smooth above and hairy below the ring, occasionally with a single ring above the bulb. Universal veil tissue includes a cottony roll and a thin cottony layer on the bulb, which is inconspicuous and may rub off in the dirt. Partial veil an irregular superior, skirtlike, often ragged annulus or sometimes clinging to the margin of the pileus. Odorless. Do not taste.

Spores 9–12 x 6.5–8.0 µm elliptic, smooth, entire, thin-walled, nonamyloid. Spore print white.

Habit and distribution: Several to many under conifers or mixed woods. Widely distributed. Found in spring, summer, and fall.

Comments: This is the common, potentially deadly poisonous *Amanita* of the western conifer forests but it is widely distributed throughout North America. We know of examples where people have mistaken this species for *Amanita rubescens,* which is edible. It is usually not fatal but can cause serious toxic reactions described in Type 3 toxins. This example is a strong argument for avoiding all Amanitas in North America. There are several varieties of *A. pantherina,* all poisonous, one with a very light brown nearly white pileus well described by Jenkins (1986). Compare *Amanita gemmata,* which often looks similar. *Amanita aspera* (Fr.) Gray also looks similar but has yellow-gray warts on the pileus, yellow above the partial veil, and grayish yellow on the lower stipe.

Amanita francheti (Boud.) Fayod
POSSIBLY POISONOUS

Pileus 5–12 cm broad, broadly convex to plane in age, viscid, dark brown to orange-brown, with numerous warts from the universal veil, buff to yellowish or becoming grayish yellow, margin smooth without striations. Flesh firm, white. Lamellae narrowly free, close, white or tinted yellowish, especially at maturity. Stipe 6–13 cm long, 0.8–2.5 cm wide,equal or enlarging somewhat toward the base, cream to buff above the white to buff, flaring, persistent, superior annulus, white to yellowish below with floccose material from the universal veil especially over the clavate base. Odorless. Do not taste

Spores 7.5–12.0 x 5.5–8.0 μm elliptic, smooth, entire, thin-walled, amyloid. Spore print white.

Habit and distribution: Several under conifers or mixed conifer hardwood forests. Widely distributed in Pacific Northwest, Rocky Mountains, northern United States and Canada. Fruiting in the late summer and fall.

Comments: This species was commonly described in older works as A. aspera (Fr.) Gray. It could be confused with *A. pantherina*, which has a white universal veil; a striate margin; and nonamyloid spores. The two should be compared. However, McKenny et al. (1991) report that they should both be considered as poisonous and avoided.

Amanita rubescens (Pers.:Fr.) Gray
EDIBLE

Pileus 5–15 cm broad, convex or sometimes with an umbo, viscid to sticky, dull reddish brown shaded with buff or gray, covered with olive-gray to whitish or even pinkish irregular warts, often with some clustered along the obscurely striate margin. Flesh soft, white staining reddish when bruised. Lamellae nearly free, close, white, soon stained pinkish to red. Stipe 8–20 cm long, 0.8–4.0 cm wide, enlarging downward to a swollen, oval, basal bulb, tinged dingy pinkish above ring and usually with more reddish stains below. Universal veil not persistent, consisting of reddish pieces, some adhering to the bulb and some in the surrounding dirt. Partial veil membranous and pale white, staining reddish, fragile, leaving an irregular skirtlike or shredded white superior ring. Odorless. Do not taste.

Spores 7.5–10 x 5–7 μm elliptic, smooth, entire, thin-walled, darkly amyloid. Spore print white.

Habit and distribution: Solitary or in groups, under hardwoods and mixed woods. Found in eastern North America and under coastal oaks in California. Fruiting in summer and fall in the East, but California in the late winter and spring.

Comments: This species is known around the world as "The Blusher." Although it is rated excellent in many European guides and by North Americans who have eaten it, too many Amanitas are close look alikes to this one, to permit us to recommend it as edible. *Amanita pantherina*, which is poisonous and often confused with "The Blusher" should be compared.

Amanita ceciliae (Berk. & Broome) Bas
EDIBILITY UNKNOWN

Pileus 4–14 cm broad, ovoid to convex, plane with a low umbo in age, viscid, brown to dark brown over the center to brownish gray in age, covered with gray warts, margin striate. Flesh thin, soft, white. Lamellae free, close, with white, minutely hairy edges. Stipe 6–20 cm long, 1.0–2.5 cm wide, enlarging to a slightly larger base, white, covered with flattened to floccose gray hairs. Volva membranous, persistent, often clinging in patches to the base, white with gray hairs and often orange-brown stains in age. Partial veil absent. Odorless. Do not taste.

Spores 10–15 µm globose, smooth, entire, thin-walled, nonamyloid. Spore print white.

Habit and distribution: Single to several, usually under conifers. Widely distributed. Found in summer and fall.

Comments: This fungus has often been reported in the past as *Amanita inaurata* Secr. or *Amanitopsis strangulata* Fr. There are no reports of toxins nor of the edibility of this fungus but we recommend that no *Amanita* should be eaten.

Amanita excelsa (Fr.) Bertillon
NONPOISONOUS

Pileus 5–10 cm broad, convex, dry or tacky when moist, light to dark brown to reddish brown, many gray to grayish white warts from the universal veil becoming flocculose over the nonstriate margin, which is often lighter than the center. Flesh firm, white throughout. Lamellae free, close, broad, white. Stipe 5–10 cm long, 0.8–0.2 cm wide, with a clavate to bulbous base, dry, white to light gray cottony hairs to fibrillose scaly remains of the universal veil over the bulb. Partial veil superior, white, delicate membranous soon falling away or leaving a flaring annulus, warted beneath. Odor stale and unpleasant. Do not taste.

Spores 8.5–10.5 x 7.5–9.0 μm subglobose to broadly elliptic, smooth, entire, thin-walled, amyloid. Spore print white.

Habit and distribution: Single to several or occasionally in fairy rings, in mixed conifer and hardwood forests. Found from Quebec, New England and south to Texas. Fruiting from July to September.

Comments: There is a white form, *A. excelsa* var *alba* Coker. *Amanita excelsa* is also known under the name *A. spissa* (Fr.) P. Kumm. Dähncke & Dähncke (1979) report it as edible but there are too many closely related, poisonous species in North America and we recommend that no *Amanita* be eaten. Metzler et al. (1992) illustrates the young stage. It can be confused with *A. pantherina*, which has pure white warts; lacks gray floccose material at the stipe base; and has nonamyloid spores—and *A. porphyria*—which has flat gray patches of universal veil on the pileus; appressed gray fibrils on the stipe; and an abrupt rounded basal bulb. See young stages below.

Amanita porphyria (Alb. & Schwein.:Fr.)
Secr.
POISONOUS

Pileus 4–9 (-12) cm broad, convex to broadly
convex, viscid, fine radial hairs, deep drab-brown
to livid-brown with a few large, gray to pinkish
gray, flattened patches, margin incurved at first,
straight in age, nonstriate. Flesh firm, white,
unchanging when bruised. Lamellae free but
narrowly so and white. Stipe 6–10 cm long,
0.8–2.0 cm wide, enlarging slightly toward base,
terminating in a round to flattened bulb that has a
distinct collar, evenly gray to drab-brown above
and below ring from bands of flattened hairs.
Universal veil fragile, forming a collar several
millimeters high and adhering in scattered
patches to the bulb. Partial veil ashy gray
remaining as a hanging, superior ring. Odorless.
Do not taste.

Spores 7–9 (-10) µm globose, smooth, entire,
thin-walled, amyloid. Spore print white.

Habit and distribution: Solitary or several under
mixed hardwood-conifers and conifer stands.
Widely distributed. Found in summer and fall.

Comments: This species is sometimes called the
"Purple Brown Amanita." It contains Type 3
toxins. We have found a diminutive form of this
species with a pileus 2–3 cm in diameter along
the Oregon and California coasts. *Amanita spreta*
Peck is also gray, lacks a basal swelling but has a
thick white volva; larger spores 11–12 x 6–7 µm;
and it is found in eastern North America.

Amanita farinosa Schwein.
EDIBILITY UNKNOWN

Pileus 2–6 (-7) cm broad, nearly conic at first,
convex to plano-convex in age, dense dark gray,
grayish black to whitish gray, granulose, powdery
surface becoming nearly glabrous and grayish
white especially over the expanded margin which
is plicate-striate in age. Flesh soft, white, cottony
in stipe center. Lamellae free, subdistant, white,
finely granulose, margins minutely granulose.
Stipe 3–9 cm long, 0.3–0.9 cm wide, nearly equal
or slightly enlarged at the base, white, powdery
at first soon glabrous. Volva seen only as patches
on the stipe or ground beneath the fruiting body.
Partial veil powdery but soon disappearing.
Odorless. Do not taste.

Spores 6.0–9.5 x 4.5–7.5 µm globose to
subglobose, smooth, entire, thin-walled,
nonamyloid. Spore print white.

Habit and distribution: 2 to 4 fruiting bodies,
never common, under oaks in Virginia, or mixed
hardwoods and conifers, but associated with
conifers in Oregon and California according to
Thiers (1982) and personal observations. Also
found by the authors under hardwoods and
conifers in Japan and Korea.

Comments: This species is often called the
"Powdery Cap Amanita." It is one of the most
distinctive species of *Amanita*, however there is
no information concerning either toxins or
edibility. *Amanita cinereoconia* Atk. should be
compared with this species (see comments under
A. onusta.)

Amanita polypyramis (Berk. & M. A. Curtis) Sacc.
PROBABLY POISONOUS

Pileus robust 8–20 cm broad, convex, then plano-convex to plane in age, dry to sticky, chalk white with soft often powdery warts and small patches of the white universal veil over the surface, margin nonstriate with partial veil remains clinging to it. Flesh firm, white, not changing when bruised. Lamellae nearly free, close, white to yellowish white. Stipe 10–21 cm long, 1.0–3.5 cm wide, equal, dry, white with scattered or abundant fibrils, at base an ovoid bulb 3–7 x 2–6 cm tapering below but not rooting. Partial veil white, very soft and cottony clinging to the lamellae at first and then falling away or leaving a very loose fragile ring, often gone at maturity. Flesh firm, white not changing when bruised. Odor of strong "chloride of lime" or old tennis shoes! Do not taste.

Spores 9.0–13.5 x 5.5–9.0 µm elliptic to elongate, smooth, entire, thin-walled, amyloid. Spore print yellowish white.

Habit and distribution: Single to more often several on the ground under deciduous or mixed coniferous/deciduous forests, especially under oaks. Widely distributed and common in the oak forests of the eastern central and southern United States. Found in late summer and fall, later in the Deep South.

Comments: *Amanita chlorinosma* (Austin) Lloyd is often misidentified as this species. However, it is a more slender species with a smaller basal bulb; and smaller spores 8–11 x 5.5–6.5 µm, which are also amyloid. It has clamp connections, which are lacking in *A. polypyramis*. *Amanita chlorinosma* is much less frequently encountered and many collections are misidentified.

Amanita abrupta Peck
POSSIBLY POISONOUS

Pileus 5–10 cm broad, convex to plane in age, dry, shiny, white with pointed or conical white warts from the universal veil, margin becoming cottony but nonstriate. Flesh firm, white. Lamellae free, close to crowded, white. Stipe 8–14 cm long, 0.5–1.5 cm wide, nearly equal, with a round, abrupt basal bulb (Fig. 34), white throughout. Partial veil thick, white, cottony, leaving a thick annulus which often falls away usually striate above. Odorless. Do not taste.

Spores 7.0–9.5 x 5.5–8.5 µm globose to broadly elliptic, smooth, entire, thin-walled, amyloid. Spore print white.

Habit and distribution: Several in mixed conifer and deciduous forests throughout Midwest and eastern U.S. as far north as Vermont. Widely distributed. Fruiting in summer and early fall.

Comments: McIlvaine and Macadam (1973) report *A. abrupta* to be edible but caution about properly identifying it. We have found this species in the Dominican Republic under pure pine with which it must be associated as a mycorrhizal symbiont. *Amanita polypyramis* is similar and should be campared with it.

Amanita daucipes (Mont.) Lloyd
POISONOUS

Pileus 6–25 cm broad, conic to convex, white with powdery to granulose, orange or reddish brown universal veil over the surface, margin nonstriate. Flesh very firm, white. Lamellae free, crowded, narrow, white to yellowish white. Stipe 7.5–20.0 cm long, 0.8–2.5 cm wide, somewhat tapering toward the apex, with a large, rooting, basal bulb, white or some with pale orange, granulose universal veil material on the stipe and especially the bulb. Partial veil superior, soft soon falling away. Odor of old ham bones or soap. Do not taste.

Spores 8–12 x 5–7 µm elliptic, smooth, entire, thin-walled, amyloid. Spore print white.

Habit and distribution: Single to several in mixed conifer and hardwoods. Common in the Northeast, from Pennsylvania south to Texas. Fruiting in late August and through the fall.

Comments: The presence of toxins is not known but *A. daucipes* belongs to a group with many toxic species and no member of the amyloid species in the Subgenus *Lepidella* should be eaten.

Amanita atkinsoniana Coker
POSSIBLY POISONOUS

Pileus 6.0–12.5 cm broad, convex to plane in age, yellowish white, gray or orange-brown, covered with small reddish brown to gray-brown warts from the universal veil, with small patches near the margin and sometimes clinging remains of the veil. Flesh firm, white. Lamellae free, crowded, yellowish white sometime with a reddish stain. Stipe 8–20 cm long, 1.0–2.5 cm wide, equal or enlarging somewhat to the rounded, clavate, basal bulb, white, glabrous to floccose at the bulb which is covered with rings of reddish brown scales from the universal veil. Partial veil leaves a superior rather fragile yellowish white annulus collapsing in age. Odor of "chloride of lime." Do not taste.

Spores 9.0–12.5 x 5.5–8.0 µm elliptic, smooth, entire, thin-walled, amyloid. Spore print white.

Habit and distribution: Usually one to three in mixed conifer and hardwood/conifer forests. Found in northeastern, southeastern, and southern United States and eastern Canada. Fruiting in August and September.

Comments: *Amanita atkinsoniana* has a distinctive odor of "chloride of lime" lacking in *A. onusta*. Although there are no specific reports of toxins, this species, along with *A. onusta*, belongs to the Subgenus *Lepidella* where toxins are common. We strongly recommend species in the Subgenus be regarded as poisonous. Pomerleau (1980) reports and pictures *A. atkinsoniana* from Quebec.

Amanita onusta (Howe) Sacc.
POSSIBLY POISONOUS

Pileus 5–10 cm broad, broadly convex to plane in age, dry, with gray to brownish gray universal veil covering the entire pileus as raised to flattened, symmetrically arranged warts and often as hanging remains on the nonstriate margin. Flesh firm and white. Lamellae close, nearly free, medium broad, white to cream color. Stipe 5.5–12.0 cm long, 0.6–1.5 cm wide, equal or slightly larger at the apex, becoming narrowly club-shaped at the rooting base, white, sticky fibrils over the top half, gray or brownish, gray fibrils over the lower stipe, and gray or brownish gray, small, erect scales over the bulb from the universal veil. Partial veil with white, sticky fibrils over the upper surface often clinging to the margin of the pileus. Odor mild or slightly unpleasant. Do not taste.

Spores 8.0–11.5 x 5.0–6.6 µm elliptic, smooth, entire, thin-walled, amyloid. Spore print white.

Habit and distribution: One to several in mixed oak/hickory and chestnut forests. Widely distributed from southern New England to Texas (Metzler et al., 1982). Fruiting in late summer and fall.

Comments: *Amanita cinereoconia* lacks the universal veil warts on the pileus; is a small species; pileus 3–7.5 cm broad, with a brownish to silver-gray granular covering. The stipe has a white to pale grayish granular surface; a narrowly clavate, shallow rooting bulb; and distinct odor of chloride of lime (Metzler et al., 1982, p. 72 & Jenkins, 1986, Fig. 34).

Amanita ravenelii (Berk. & M. A. Curtis) Sacc.
POISONOUS

Pileus 8–17 cm broad, almost globose at first to convex or nearly plane in age, slightly viscid to dry, white to yellowish white with rather coarse, white warts from the universal veil, often in concentric rows to the margin, in age with a brownish orange hue, margin with warts but not striate. Flesh firm, white. Lamellae free, crowded, yellowish white. Stipe 10–25 cm long, 1–3 cm wide, white, dry with a large rooting basal bulb, surface with sticky white fibrils. Partial veil thick, appressed against the lamellae with numerous white warts on the underside, forming a thick, superior annulus which soon falls away. Universal veil left in soil around the bulb, white. Odor strong, of "chloride of lime" or old tennis shoes. Do not taste.

Spores 8–11 x 5.5–7.5 µm elliptic to ovoid, smooth, entire, thin-walled, amyloid. Spore print white.

Habit and distribution: Single to several in mixed hardwood and conifer forests. Reported from Maryland to South Carolina. Fruiting in late summer and fall.

Comments: The infrequently found *A. chlorinosma* has white, powdery universal veil remains on the pileus. *Amanita rhopalopus* Bas has brownish orange patches of universal veil on the pileus and a fusiform bulb that is deep rooting. *Amanita mutabilis* Beardslee has pink coloration on the pileus and stipe; the context turns pink when cut; and has a distinct odor of anise. All three species are infrequent and distributed in the southeastern and southern United States and all have amyloid spores. The first two have a strong odor of "chloride of lime."

Amanita cokeri (Gilb. & Kühner) Gilb.
POISONOUS

Pileus 6–15 cm broad, large, convex, plane or slightly depressed in age, viscid, shiny, ivory-white, covered with white to brownish orange, pyramidal, volval warts that often grade into dense, sticky hairs over and clinging to the margin especially when young. Flesh firm, white. Lamellae narrowly free or adnate, close together to fairly well separated in age, white or tinted yellow. Stipe 6–20 cm long, 1.5–3.0 cm wide, white, nearly smooth above the superior ring, loose sticky hairs below, widening to a basal bulb that has recurved scales arranged in several circles just above the short rooting bulb that often has pinkish brown stains as well as shallow cracks and splits. Volva adheres to the bulb, splitting into sticky, irregular patches. Partial veil white, fibrous, separating unevenly and leaving long strands attached in taffylike fashion to a wide area of the stipe, ring superior, hanging skirtlike. Odor mild. Do not taste.

Spores 10.0–13.5 x 7–9 µm elliptic, smooth, entire, thin-walled, amyloid. Spore print white.

Habit and distribution: Single, several or scattered under Virginia pine and mixed hardwood pine stands. Widely found in the southeastern and southern United States. Known in the West only from Marin and Santa Cruz Counties in California. Fruiting in the fall.

Comments: This species is also known as "Coker's *Amanita*." Following hard fall rains, this beautiful, stately fungus can become quite smooth and have only scattered warts. We have found it most commonly during September and October in North Carolina, Maryland, Texas, and Virginia. Like many of the species of *Amanita*, it contains Type 3 toxins, and is poisonous (Spoerke & Rumack, 1994). *Amanita silvicola* Kauffman has a pure white, floccose, viscid cap and amyloid, elliptical spores 9–12 x 5–6 µm; it is a similar species found in the Pacific Northwest under conifers.

LIMACELLA

Pileus convex to plane in age, covered with a slimy, glutinous layer, white to bright reddish brown. Lamellae free, white, trama divergent (Fig. 28). Stipe dry to slimy beneath the superior, glutinous to membranous annulus. Spores globose, subglobose to broadly elliptic, entire, thin-walled, nonamyloid. Universal veil forms a glutinous layer surrounding the button. The species are widely distributed in a variety of habitats in North America. Helen Smith (1954) includes 12 species in her monograph. The species of *Limacella* are placed in the Amanitaceae because of the presence of a universal veil.

Edibility: No toxins are recorded for the genus but the species are quite variable and we do not know who has actually tested the edibility of the species.

KEY TO LIMACELLA

1. Pileus white to creamy yellow, glutinous -- 2
1. Pileus light brown, orange-brown or red-brown, glutinous ---------------------------------- 3
   2. Partial veil glutinous, annular zone often barely visible ---------------------- *L. illinata*
   2. Partial veil a flaring, membranous annulus ----------------------------------- *L. solidipes*
                           (see comments under *L. illinata*)
3. Pileus glutinous, bright yellow-brown to reddish brown, glutin hanging from the margin; odorless --- *L. glischra*
3. Pileus glutinous, dark reddish brown, fading in age to pale pinkish brown; odor strongly farinaceous--- *L. glioderma*
                           (see comments under *L. glischra*)

Limacella illinata (Fr.) Murrill
EDIBILITY UNKNOWN

Pileus 2.5–8.0 cm broad, broadly convex, glutinous to slimy, white to creamy yellow in age, margin inrolled until mature. Flesh soft to firm, white. Lamellae nearly free, close, white. Stipe 3–10 cm long, 0.5–0.6 (-1.0) cm wide, equal or slightly larger toward the base, glutinous, white, cream color or with a trace of orange near the base. Odor farinaceous. Do not taste.

Spores 3.0–5.5 x 2.8–5.0 μm subglobose to short elliptic, smooth, entire, thin-walled, nonamyloid. Spore print white.

Habit and distribution: One to several under conifer or mixed conifer and deciduous forests. Widely distributed. Fruiting in summer and fall.

Comments: *Limacella solidipes* (Peck) H. V. Smith is a rare species with a white, viscid pileus; dry, white stipe; and a flaring, membranous annulus. It is widely distributed.

Limacella glischra (Morg.) Murrill
EDIBILITY UNKNOWN

Pileus 20–42 mm broad, convex, broadly convex with a low umbo in age, glutinous, smooth, yellow-brown to reddish brown, margin often with hanging pieces of gluten. Flesh soft, white, light reddish brown near pileus cuticle. Flesh firm, white. Lamellae free, close, broad, white to very pale cinnamon. Stipe 4–7 cm long, 0.8–1.2 cm wide, nearly equal, glutinous, pale to dull whitish or color similar to that of pileus. Universal veil glutinous leaving slime over pileus and stipe. Partial veil glutinous with a hairy veil beneath, pale pinkish cinnamon, leaving a glutinous, hairy ring and pieces hanging from the pileus margin. Odorless. Do not taste.

Spores 5.0–6.5 x 4.5–5.5 μm globose to subglobose, smooth, entire, thin-walled, nonamyloid. Spore print white.

Habit and distribution: Single or in small numbers, infrequent, under hardwoods and conifers. Widely distributed. Fruiting in the summer and fall often following wet weather.

Comments: *Limacella glioderma* (Fr.) Earle has a glutinous, dark brown pileus, lighter brown in age; partial veil a fibrillous zone and not viscid; stipe dry except for gluten from the pileus. More information on the North American species is available in the monograph of *Limacella* by H. V. Smith (1944).

LEPIOTACEAE

The Lepiotas have long been called the "Parasol Mushrooms." The free lamellae; long, thin stipes; and general stature remind one of the Amanitas. Among the white-spored agarics, they can be misidentified as an *Amanita*. However, the conic to convex pileus may have squamules or fibrils on the surface but, on close observation, they are part of the pileipellis and not remains of the universal veil as in *Amanita*. In fact a universal veil is absent in the Lepiotaceae. The lamellae are free, white, and, with the exception of *Chlorophyllum molybdites*, remain white and produce a white spore print. The stipe has a persistent, often moveable, partial veil. Spores are elliptic and thick-walled with an apical pore in *Chlorophyllum*, *Macrolepiota*, and *Leucoagaricus*. In *Lepiota* and *Cystolepiota*, they are thin-walled and entire. *Cystolepiota* has a pileipellis of round cells, while *Lepiota* has filamentous hyphae. Amyloid spores are unknown in the Lepiotaceae, while in a large number of species of *Amanita*, especially the deadly poisonous species, they are amyloid. In addition, the lamellar trama of the Lepiotaceae is interwoven (Fig. 27), and not divergent as in the Amanitaceae.

The Lepiotaceae are very closely related to the Agaricaceae and many mycologists place them in the Agaricaceae. However, to most accurately identify the genus and species, we have kept them separated.

Edibility: Both edible and poisonous species are found in the family. Young fruiting bodies of *Chlorophyllum molybdites* have pure white lamellae and are often misidentified as a *Macrolepiota*, leading to the most common toxicity in the family. The Type 8 toxins are present in some, and cause severe gastric upset including vomiting and diarrhea with impressive but not deadly results (Spoerke & Rumack, 1994). However, several small species including *Lepiota castanea* and *Lepiota subincarnata* are deadly poisonous and possess the Type 1 toxins including amanitins (cyclopeptides) found in *Amanita virosa* and related taxa. (See plate and description of *Lepiota castanea*), (Spoerke & Rumack, 1994). There are also some very good edible species, especially *Macrolepiota procera* and *M. rachodes*. Carefully read descriptions and be sure to obtain a spore print.

KEY TO THE LEPIOTACEAE

1. Large, robust fruiting body with a persistent partial veil, fringed outside and often movable on the stipe; spores thick-walled with an apical pore ------------------------------- 2

1. Very small to medium sized fruiting body; partial veil variable, often missing at maturity; spores thick or thin-walled, with or without an apical pore -------------------------- 5

   2. Lamellae white young, becoming gray-green in age and leaving a green spore print; fruiting in a complete or partial fairy ring ------------ *Chlorophyllum molybdites*

   2. Lamellae remaining white or buff; spore print white; fruiting singly or scattered ---- 3

3. Stipe 15–40 cm long, 0.8–2.0 cm wide with brown, cottony scales to the base; flesh unchanging when bruised; spores 12–18 x 8–13 μm ---------------- *Macrolepiota procera*

3. Stipe shorter (9–15 cm), thin or thicker without cottony scales; flesh bruising yellow, orange, red to reddish brown; spores smaller --- 4

   4. Pileus with cinnamon-brown scales; flesh bruising yellow to orange-red to red-brown; dries white or light gray -------------------------------- *Macrolepiota rachodes*

   4. Pileus with reddish brown scales; flesh quickly reddens where handled on pileus, stipe, and when dried--- *Leucoagaricus americanus*

   (see comments *under M. rachodes*)

5. Pileus conic to ovoid, convex in age, white, smooth to powdery and striate; spores thick-walled with an apical pore -- 6

5. Pileus convex to campanulate, yellow-brown, orange-brown to red-brown or with a very small pileus (0.8–1.8 cm) with a pinkish to cinnamon disc; spores thin-walled, without an apical pore --- 7

   6. Pileus large (4–12 cm), white, dry, smooth; spores thick-walled with an apical pore, red in Melzer's solution; usually in lawns or grassy areas ---- *Leucoagaricus naucinus*

   6. Pileus small (2.5–3.5 cm), white, dry, powdery with a striate margin; spores thick-walled with an apical pore, yellow-brown in Melzer's solution; fruiting usually in large clusters on compost--------------------------------- *Leucocoprinus caepestipes*

7. Pileus 0.8–1.8 cm, with minute granular (not scaly) surface on a white to pinkish background; spores small (4–5 x 2.5–3.0 μm)----------------------------- *Cystolepiota seminuda*

7. Pileus larger or not , surface not powdery, orange-brown to red-brown, with often pointed, dark brown, pyramidal warts or finely scaly--------------------------------------- 8

   8. Pileus 4–12 cm broad with a pale brown or cinnamon-brown surface with scattered to dense, dark brown, pyramidal warts ---------------- *Lepiota acutesquamosa*

8. Pileus smaller,1–5 cm broad; stipe 1.5–10.0 cm long, 0.1–0.4 cm wide; partial veil often missing or wooly, white, leaving annulus or pieces on margin of the pileus -- 9

9. Stipe with whitish to buff, wooly hairs; spores large 10–25 x 4–6 µm ------------------ 10

9. Stipe with red-brown to orange-brown squamules over lower half of the surface; spores smaller -- 11

    10.Pileus yellowish to light brown; spores 10–18 x 4–6 µm, elliptic to bean-shaped --- *Lepiota clypeolaria*

    10.Pileus light to dark brown; spores 12–25 x 4–6 µm, fusiform or spindle-shaped -- *Lepiota magnispora*
(see comments under *L. clypeolaria*)

11. Pileus with appressed, orange-brown squamules over white ground color; stipe with orange-brown fibrils; usually found in large troops -------------------------- *Lepiota cristata*

11. Pileus with dense, thick, red-brown to chestnut, small scales or fibrils, dense over the center; stipe with red-brown squamules over lower half ------------------------------------ 12

    12.Spores 7–14 x 3.0–4.5 µm, cylindric with a short spur -------------- *Lepiota castanea*

    12.Spores 6.0–7.5 x 3–4 µm, elliptic with a short spur ------------ *Lepiota subincarnata*
(see comments under *L. castanea*)

Chlorophyllum molybdites Massee
POISONOUS

Pileus 7–30 cm broad, conic, convex with an umbo to nearly plane in age, white with numerous, slightly raised scales tinted buff to cinnamon, dry. Flesh firm, white dingy reddish where bruised. Lamellae free, close, broad, white, becoming green in age, bruising yellow to brownish. Stipe 10–25 cm long, 1.0–2.5 cm wide, enlarging toward base, smooth, white with brownish stains over base. Partial veil a thick, white, superior ring with fringed edge and discoloring brownish beneath. Odorless. Taste mild (do not taste this species).

Spores 8–13 x 6.5–8.0 µm elliptic, smooth, thick-walled, with an apical pore. Spore print green.

Habit and distribution: Scattered or in partial or complete fairy rings in lawns and grasslands, during wet rainy periods. Widely distributed, but most common in grasslands and lawns everywhere. Fruiting in spring but mostly late summer and fall.

Comments: This species has been called the "Green Spored Lepiota." In older works it has been called *Lepiota morganii* Peck or *Lepiota molybdites* (Fr.) Sacc. Fruiting bodies, when young, have pure white lamellae which turn green only as the fruiting bodies mature. The distinctive characteristics should be known before other scaly-capped *Macrolepiota* species are eaten. Ingesting this species, which contains Type 8 toxins, causes severe gastric upset over several hours (Spoerke & Rumack, 1994). It is one of the common causes of mushroom poisoning since it is usually mistaken for *Macrolepiota rachodes* or *M. procera,* which are good edibles. Neither of these species grows in fairy rings, nor do either produce a green spore print. When in doubt take the oldest fruiting body and make a spore print.

Macrolepiota procera (Scop.:Fr) Singer
EDIBLE

Pileus 6–24 cm broad, ovoid, convex to broadly convex in age with a low umbo, white under a dense layer of flat to raised, reddish brown scales which appear to be in concentric rings, less dense near the margin, dry. Flesh soft, white, unchanging when bruised. Lamellae free, close, broad, even, white with minutely hairy edges. Stipe 15–40 cm long, 0.8–2.0 cm wide, enlarging gradually toward the base which forms a small bulb, with fine, silky, pinkish tan hairs above the ring but with brown cottony scales below, separating in ringlike fashion to reveal the white flesh beneath; basal bulb is covered with fine, white mycelium. Partial veil thick, soft, white, leaving an easily detached and moveable, collar-like, persistent, superior ring with an edge composed of two rows of hairs. Odor mild. Taste pleasant.

Spores 12–18 x 8–13 μm ovoid, with a minute, apical pore, smooth, thick-walled, purple-brown in Melzer's solution. Spore print white.

Habit and distribution: Several to gregarious in weeds, lawns, brush, or under hardwoods and conifers. Known from central and eastern North America. Fruiting in summer and fall.

Comments: This species is known as the "Parasol Mushroom." We have collected a very similar looking species, *Macrolepiota puellaris* (Fr.) M. M. Moser, on the Olympic Peninsula of Washington. It, however, has red staining when cut or bruised; lacks the rows of fibrils on the long stipe typical of "the parasol"; and has smaller spores. Note that the spores and lamellae are never green as in *Chlorophyllum molybdites,* the green spored lepiota. The parasol mushroom is one of the outstanding edible species. *Hope's Mushroom Cookbook* (H. H. Miller, 1993) has some recipes for this delicious species.

Macrolepiota rachodes (Vittad.) Quél.
EDIBLE

Pileus 6–12 (-20) cm broad, conic, rounded or blunt to convex in age, grayish to reddish gray, breaking up on expansion to form a ringed pattern of flat or slightly raised, small, cinnamon-brown squamules with white flesh between, dry. Flesh soft, white, pinkish beneath cuticle, when bruised stains orange-yellow to red-brown on the lower stipe, upper stipe has a hollow area in center. Lamellae free, close, broad, white to buff with occasional dark brown stains. Stipe 9–15 cm long, 1.5–3.0 cm wide, club- to spindle-shaped, white above ring to white below, with scattered brown hairs, stains yellow, yellow-orange to red-brown in age near the base. Partial veil soft, membranous, white, leaving a persistent, flaring ring in a wide belt with a flaring ring that has a red-brown, fringed margin. Odor pleasant. Taste is mild.

Spores 6–11 (-15) x 5–7 µm elliptic, smooth, thick-walled, with an apical pore, red-brown in Melzer's solution. Spore print white.

Habit and distribution: Several to large clusters in humus, grass, compost piles, wood chip mulch, and needle duff. Widely distributed but less frequent to rare in northern North America. Fruiting in early and late fall, except in California fruiting in February and March.

Comments: Though it is edible, some people have experienced gastric upset when ingesting this species. *Lepiota brunnea* Farl. & Burt has a darker brown pileus; smoky brown hairs on the stipe, and flesh "changing to reddish or slightly brownish when exposed to the air" and is darker than *M. rachodes*. It is less commonly collected and close to *M. rachodes* and we have collected and examined it in Virginia. Verlinga et al. (2003) has shown that *Chlorophyllum molybdites, Macrolepiota rachodes,* and *M. brunnea* belong in the same genus. *Leucoagaricus americanus* (Peck) Vellinga reddens where bruised or handled; has a reddish brown pileus; dries deep red. All the above species have spores, which are thick-walled with an apical pore. These species are edible except *Chlorophyllum molybdites,* but one must obtain a spore print to be sure they are white spored. See comments under *Chlorophyllum molybdites,* the poisonous "Green spored *Lepiota.*"

Leucoagaricus naucinus (Fr.) Singer
MAYBE POISONOUS

Pileus 4–12 cm broad, ovoid, convex in age with a low umbo, unpolished, white to dull white but sometimes with minute, flattened, gray squamules, dry. Flesh thick, white. Lamellae close, free, white. Stipe 6–12 cm long, 0.8–2.0 cm wide, nearly equal with an enlarged base, white, without hairs above but silky below the ring. Partial veil membranous, cottony, white, leaving a collar-like, superior ring, which has a double-fringed edge. Odor mild. Taste mild.

Spores 7.5–11.0 x 5.0–6.5 µm most ovoid, smooth, thick-walled, with a minute apical pore, red-brown in Melzer's solution. Spore print white.

Habit and distribution: Several to usually abundant in lawns, pastures, grassy areas, or less frequently under hardwoods and conifers, during wet, cool weather. Widely distributed. Fruiting in late summer and fall, or winter and spring on the West Coast.

Comments: We have often seen large troops in grass after rainy periods in the early fall. Although they have been judged edible by some, others have suffered severe gastric upset caused by Type 8 toxins. We caution those who have not tried this fungus to eat only a very small portion or not at all. However, this species does resemble the deadly white species such as *Amanita virosa*, *A. bisporigera*, and *A. ocreata*. These species have a volva or cup surrounding the base of the stipe and a skirt-like partial veil. See both illustrations and descriptions of these species of *Amanita*, page 29.

Leucocoprinus caepestipes
(Sowerby.:Fr.) Pat.
EDIBLE

Pileus 2.5–3.5 (-7.0) cm broad, conic to campanulate, powdery with small and or large scales, margin conspicuously striate, at first white but then light pinkish. Flesh white, soft, sometimes bruises straw-yellow near cuticle. Lamellae free, crowded, white, with even edges. Stipe 4–12 cm long, 0.3–0.6 cm wide, nearly equal with a small basal bulb, covered with fine short hairs (pubescent) to smooth and hairless, white or may be flesh-colored or straw-yellow where handled; arises from a dense mass of white mycelium and rhizomorphs. Partial veil hairy, leaving a well-developed, persistent, superior ring that can become detached. Odor mild. Taste mild.

Spores 6.5–10.0 x 6–8 µm broadly elliptic, smooth, thick-walled, with an apical pore, yellow-brown in Melzer's solution. Spore print white.

Habit and distribution: In large clusters on sawdust, wood chips, compost, rotten logs, and other rich humus. Found in eastern and occasionally western North America. Fruiting in spring, summer, and fall.

Comments: This species is also known as *Lepiota caepestipes* (Sowerby.:Fr.) P. Kumm. Its small size and soft tissue do not combine to make this a really desirable edible.

Cystolepiota seminuda (Lasch) M. Bon
EDIBILITY UNKNOWN

Pileus 0.8–1.8 cm broad, conic, convex to plane or upturned at margin with a low, broad umbo, dull white with a pinkish to cinnamon disc, dry, minutely granular surface but appearing smooth. Flesh very thin, white. Lamellae free, close, broad, white. Stipe 2.5–4.0 cm long, 0.1–0.2 cm wide, enlarging slightly toward base, dry, white above to light reddish brown below, clothed overall with minute white hairs. Partial veil white, fibrous, remaining as fibrils on the margin of the young pileus and as an obscure annular zone which soon disappears. Odorless. Taste mild.

Spores 4–5 x 2.5–3.0 µm elliptic, smooth, entire, thin-walled, pale brown in Melzer's solution. Spore print white.

Habit and distribution: Growing in groups on needle duff under conifers. Apparently widely distributed, known from Montana by the authors. Fruiting in summer and fall.

Comments: This species is also known as *Cystolepiota sistrata* (Fr.) Singer and *Lepiota seminuda* (Lasch) P. Kumm. This small distinctive *Lepiota* appears to be a *Mycena* at first glance, but on close inspection the typical free lamellae are observed. Moser (1983) has a key to the species of *Cystolepiota,* since there are several closely related taxa. It is placed in *Cystolepiota* since it has a pileus cuticle of dense, round cells called sphaerocysts. It is certainly too small to be considered an edible.

Lepiota acutesquamosa (Weinm.) P. Kumm.
EDIBLE

Pileus 4–12 cm broad, nearly conic to convex, or convex with an obscure umbo, pale brown or cinnamon-brown, covered with erect, often pointed, dark brown pyramid-like warts, dry. Flesh soft, white. Lamellae free, crowded, white, minutely hairy edges. Stipe 5–11 cm long, 0.8–1.5 cm wide, nearly equal with an obscure basal bulb, dingy white, dry, hairy. Partial veil cottony, fragile, membranous, leaving a superior, skirt-like ring which is not movable. Odor mild to fragrant. Taste mild.

Spores 7–11 x 2.0–3.5 µm long-elliptic, smooth, entire, thin-walled, pale yellow in Melzer's solution. Spore print white.

Habit and distribution: One to several on sawdust or rich humus under hardwoods or in mixed woods. Widely distributed in eastern North America, rare elsewhere. Fruiting in summer and fall.

Comments: This species is called the "Conical Warted *Lepiota.*" There are several closely related species including *L. eriophora* Peck, which has dense conical dark brown warts; lamellae subdistant, white; small spores (3.5–4.5 x 1.5–2.5 µm) which are dextrinoid in Melzer's solution. We have collected *L. eriophora* in Montana under or near conifers. This species closely resembles several species of *Amanita* and should therefore be avoided.

Lepiota clypeolaria (Bull.:Fr.) P. Kumm.
INEDIBLE

Pileus 2.5–7.0 cm broad, ovoid, convex, to convex with an umbo in age, dry, continuous yellowish to brownish tissue breaking up as it expands into numerous scales (ragged appearing) and hairy patches, even over the center, which remains intact the longest. Flesh soft, white. Lamellae free, close, broad, white. Stipe 3–10 cm long, 0.3–0.4 cm wide, nearly equal, white to buff, covered with whitish to buff, wooly hairs. Partial veil of white, cottony strands with pieces left on pileus margin, leaving a ring of fine wooly hairs that disappear at maturity. Odor mild. Taste mild.

Spores 10–18 x 4–6 µm elliptic or bean-shaped, smooth, entire, thin-walled, yellow-brown in Melzer's solution. Spore print white.

Habit and distribution: Single to numerous, most often under conifers. Widely distributed. Fruiting in late summer and fall.

Comments: There are a number of small species of *Lepiota* with scaly pilei and stipes. *Lepiota magnispora* Murrill with a somewhat darker pileus is very similar but has larger, fusiform spores 12–25 x 4–6 µm. Since there are look-alike species among the small *Lepiota* species and some are known to be deadly poisonous, **none of them should be eaten.** *Lepiota cristata* (Alg. & Schw:Fr.) P. Kumm. is usually somewhat smaller; not as "ragged" appearing; solid, reddish brown at center with reddish brown pileus scales; and a nearly smooth, hairless stipe. *Leucoprinus birnbaumii* (Corda) Singer (=*Lepiota lutea* (Bolt.) Quél.) is a small tropical species with soft, powdery, yellow hairs on the pileus and stipe and is most often found in greenhouses or in potted plants.

Lepiota cristata (Bolt.:Fr.) P. Kumm.
INEDIBLE

Pileus 1.0–5.0 cm broad, campanulate when young to broadly convex in age, dry, dense orange-brown over the disc, with well-spaced concentric orange-brown squamules over a white ground color to the margin. Flesh white in pileus and pinkish in the stipe. Lamellae free, crowded, white to cream. Stipe 1.5–3.5 (-5.5) cm long, 0.15–0.8 cm wide, equal, enlarging at the base, orange-brown, with orange-brown fibrils over lower surface, dry. Partial veil soft white, often missing, flaring upward one-third from the apex. Odor unpleasant. Taste mild or slightly acrid.

Spores 5.5–9.0 x 2.5–3.7 µm truncate, some with a spur, entire, slightly thick-walled, dextrinoid in Melzer's solution. Spore print white.

Habit and distribution: Usually in large troops, sometimes one or several, in needle litter or various kinds of humus. Widely distributed. Fruiting in summer and fall.

Comments: *Lepiota grangei* (Eyre) Kühner has a pileus with green to gray-green fibrils; is otherwise similar; found in the southeastern United States; and very rare. This is another in a series of closely related species that are hard to distinguish and some are deadly poisonous. Admire, but do not eat any of the species.

Lepiota castanea Quél.
DEADLY POISONOUS

Pileus 1.0–2.2 (-3.0) cm campanulate with an umbo, white, appearing moist, but with dry, dense, thick, deep red-brown to chestnut colored scales, very dense over the center in concentric rings over the margin. Flesh white in pileus; in stipe white to pale orange at the base. Lamellae free, close, moderately broad, white to pale pinkish buff. Stipe 2.0–6.5 cm long, 0.1–0.5 cm wide, equal, clavate at the base, appressed pinkish cream fibrils on upper half above the weak partial veil, below with irregular red-brown squamules. Partial veil white wooly, occasionally leaves an annulus on upper stipe. Odor not distinctive or pleasant. Taste not recorded; **don't taste.**

Spores 7–14 x 3.0–4.5 µm cylindric, with a short spur, smooth, entire, slightly thick-walled, dextrinoid in Melzer's solution. Spore print white.

Habit and distribution: Single to several in rich loam or humus, in hardwood or hardwood/conifer forests. Widely distributed. Fruiting in late summer and fall.

Comments: This species, along with *Lepiota subincarnata* J. Lange (= *L. josserandii* Bon & Boiffard), contains Type 1 toxins and are **deadly poisonous.** *Lepiota castanea* contains less amanitin than *L. subincarnata,* but all small species of *Lepiota* should be avoided. Both species are very similar in stature and color but *L. subincarnata* has smaller spores 6.0–7.5 x 3–4 µm elliptic without the short spur, but also dextrinoid in Melzer's solution (Noordeloos et al., 2001).

HYGROPHORACEAE

The fruiting bodies range from small, delicate, brightly colored species, to robust, fleshy species. The pileus ranges from sharply conic to plane, and the surface may be slimy, viscid to dry. The lamellae are thick, waxy, adnate to decurrent. The waxy feeling can be determined by rubbing a small amount of tissue between the fingers. It should feel as though you were rubbing candle wax. The spores are smooth, entire, thin-walled, nonamyloid, and white. The species are found in duff, grass, humus, but always on the ground. Fruiting occurs from early spring in the western mountains of the United States and Canada, to summer and fall.

There are two genera, *Hygrocybe* and *Hygrophorus*. The small, brightly colored species of *Hygrocybe* are decomposers of plant parts, such as grass or humus. They are dainty, conic to campanulate, brightly colored, red, orange, yellow, blue to white and have decurrent, distant, lamellae, a lesser number are adnate to adnexed and the partial veil absent. It would appear that most species of *Hygrophorus* are ectomycorrhizal, but this is based upon the occurrence of specific species with ectomycorrhizal trees such as pine. They are fleshy, often more robust, convex to plane, variously colored with more subdued colors, the lamellae are subdistant to distant, adnate to short decurrent, partial veil often present.

Edibility: There are no reports of poisonous species or toxins in the family. Several species in the genus *Hygrophorus* are edible, including *H. subalpinus, H. purpurascens* and *H. russula*. However, most are bland and have little flavor.

KEY TO THE SPECIES OF THE HYGROPHORACEAE

1. Fruiting body small, delicate, brightly colored (white, yellow, orange, green or red), conic to convex; stipe narrow 0.2–0.8 (-1.2) cm wide; lamellae white to yellow-olive --- *Hygrocybe*
1. Fruiting body medium to robust, fleshy, convex to plane, white, pinkish to bluish gray or greenish-blue --- *Hygropohorus*

KEY TO THE SPECIES OF HYGROCYBE

1. Pileus and stipe glutinous --- 2
1. Pileus viscid or dry; stipe moist but not viscid-- 3
    2. Pileus orange; stipe orange-yellow; odor fishy or skunklike-------------------- *H. laeta*
    2. Pileus green, yellow green; stipe green; odorless ------------------------- *H. psittacina*
3. Pileus scarlet, red, blood red to deep orange-red -- 4
3. Pileus white, yellow, orange to apricot --- 7
    4. Pileus conic; lamellae and stipe blacken where bruised or handled ------ *H. conica*
    4. Pileus convex; not blackening -- 5
5. Pileus convex to plane, dry, deep red to orange-red; lamellae decurrent,
    yellow--- *H. cantharellus*
5. Pileus conic to convex, dry to moist, bright blood red to scarlet --------------------------- 6
    6. Pileus convex, very small, brilliant scarlet ----------------------------------- *H. miniata*
    6. Pileus conic, medium size, bright red ---------------------------------- *H. coccinea*
7. Pileus viscid, plane in age, bright apricot-yellow; lamellae decurrent, pale yellow; stipe
    bright apricot-yellow-- *H. nitida*
7. Pileus white or lamellae not decurrent --- 8
    8. Pileus white, convex, moist not viscid; lamellae decurrent, white -------- *H. virginea*
    (Pileus white, viscid, see comments under H. virginea)
    8. Pileus orange to yellow, moist to viscid-- 9
9. Pileus conic to a narrow peak, orange to orange-yellow or yellow -------- *H. acuticonica*
                        (see comments under *H. conica*)
9. Pileus conic, soon convex to plane in age, moist to viscid; stipe round or compressed
    and fluted--- 10
    10. Pileus conic, convex in age with low umbo, yellow-orange; lamellae bright orange,
        not fading in age; stipe round, dry, pale yellow to buff ------------------ *H. marginata*
    10. Pileus convex, soon plane, viscid when fresh, bright orange-yellow; lamellae yel-
        low; stipe compressed or fluted-- *H. flavescens*
                (Stipe viscid-- see *H. chlorophana* under *H. flavescens*)

Hygrocybe laeta (Pers.:Fr.) P. Kumm.
NONPOISONOUS

Pileus 1.0–3.5 cm broad, convex to plane or slightly depressed, orange, orange-yellow to olive-orange, margin striate, glutinous. Flesh thin, light orange. Lamellae adnate to short decurrent, subdistant, pinkish to violet-gray. Stipe 3–5 cm long, 0.2–0.6 cm wide, equal, orange to orange-yellow, smooth, without hairs, glutinous. Partial veil absent. Odor fishy or skunk-like. Taste mild.

Spores 5–8 x 3–5 μm elliptic, smooth, entire, thin-walled, nonamyloid. Spore print white.

Habit and distribution: Scattered to numerous in moss and on the ground during wet weather. Widely distributed. Fruiting in spring, summer, fall, and into early winter.

Comments: We have collected *H. laeta* in October in the mountains of Idaho. The fruiting bodies froze over night and when thawed, in the laboratory, readily produced spores. Boertmann (2000) gives additional information about the alpine and northern distributions of this species.

Hygrocybe psittacina (Schaeff.:Fr.) P. Kumm.
EDIBILITY UNKNOWN

Pileus 1–3 cm broad, conic but soon convex, campanulate in age, rich grass green, in age infused with orange, yellow, buff or pink, glutinous to viscid. Flesh thin, concolorous with the pileus but more pale. Lamellae adnate, subdistant, light green to buff, waxy. Stipe 3–7 cm long, 0.2–0.5 cm wide, equal, green, glutinous. Partial veil absent. Odorless. Taste mild.

Spores 6.5–10.0 x 4–6 μm elliptic, smooth, entire, thin-walled, nonamyloid. Spore print white.

Habit and distribution: Scattered to numerous on the ground under hardwoods and conifers. Widely distributed. Fruiting in spring, summer, and fall.

Comments: This is a unique and beautiful green fungus but it often fades in age or in wet weather becomes orange, pale yellow to pinkish buff.

Hygrocybe conica (Fr.) Fr.
MAYBE POISONOUS

Pileus 2–9 cm broad, conic to a narrow point, scarlet, red to orange, usually more orange near margin, often tinted olive, hairless, tacky to viscid. Flesh thin, fragile, concolorous with the pileus, bruises black. Lamellae nearly free, close, white tinted yellowish to olive-yellow, bruise black, waxy. Stipe 4–12 cm long, 0.3–1.0 cm wide, equal, moist not viscid, appears twisted, hollow, base white, the rest concolorous with the pileus, but the surface blackens where handled or bruised when mature. Odorless. Taste mild.

Spores 8–12 x 4.5–6.5 µm elliptic, smooth, entire, thin-walled, nonamyloid. Spore print white.

Habit and distribution: Single, scattered to numerous, in meadows, open woods under conifers as well as hardwoods. Widely distributed. Fruiting in spring, summer, fall, and winter.

Comments: We have frequently found large fruitings following heavy rain or rainy periods in the late summer. *Hygrocybe persistens* (Britzelm.) Britzelm., known as *Hygrocybe acutoconica* (Clem.) A. H. Sm. in North America, looks very similar to *H. conica* but has larger spores (9–15 x 5–9 µm); the pileus tends to be more yellow to orange-yellow; it does not bruise black anywhere, although the base of the stipe may be turn black in age; and it is found in the same habitats (Hesler & Smith,1963).

Hygrocybe cantharellus (Schwein.)
Murrill
NONPOISONOUS

Pileus 1.0–3.5 cm broad, convex to plane with an umbo or depressed in center with an umbo, deep red to orange-red, smooth, without hairs, margin incurved and often wavy, dry. Flesh thin, reddish orange to yellow. Lamellae decurrent, distant, waxy, yellow to orange but lighter than pileus. Stipe 4–10 cm long, 0.15–0.4 cm thick, equal, dry, concolorous with the pileus or somewhat lighter, smooth, without hairs. Veil absent. Odorless. Taste mild.

Spores 7–12 x 4–6 µm elliptic, smooth, entire, thin-walled, nonamyloid. Spore print white.

Habit and distribution: Scattered to numerous on debris, humus and well-decayed logs. Found in eastern North America. Fruiting in summer and fall.

Comments: The distinctive, white, decurrent lamellae are definitely not like the ridges typical of a chanterelle despite the name. This feature clearly separates it from *H. miniata*, as well as other Hygrocybes.

Hygrocybe miniata (Fr.: Fr) P. Kumm.
NONPOISONOUS

Pileus 1–4 cm broad, broadly convex, brilliant scarlet, fading only in age, dry, glistening when moist, smooth, without hairs, margin incurved at first and striate, when moist. Flesh thin, scarlet to orange. Lamellae adnate to adnexed, subdistant, light orange or yellow, waxy. Stipe 3–5 cm long, 0.3–0.4 cm wide, equal, red, orange or yellow, dry, glistening when moist. Partial veil absent. Odorless. Taste mild.

Spores 6–10 x 4–6 µm elliptic, smooth, entire, thin-walled, nonamyloid. Spore print white.

Habit and distribution: Grows in groups, usually in moss or wood debris in hardwoods or mixed woods. Widely distributed. Fruiting from summer to late fall.

Comments: We have often found it almost buried in moss in various localities from New England, New York, Montana, and Alaska.

Hygrocybe coccinea (Schaeff.:Fr.) P. Kumm.
EDIBLE

Pileus 2–5 cm broad, conic often with an umbo in age, bright blood-red, sometimes with an orange hue or fading to whitish in age, moist to tacky but not viscid. Flesh soft, easily breaking, reddish to orange. Lamellae adnate, close, waxy, yellowish orange to orange-red, intervenose. Stipe 3–7 cm long, 0.3–0.8 cm wide, equal, often flattened and fluted, red to orange-red, yellowish just at base moist, smooth, without hairs. Partial veil absent. Odorless. Taste mild.

Spores 7–11 x 4–5 µm elliptic, smooth, entire, thin-walled, nonamyloid. Spore print white.

Habit and distribution: Scattered to numerous on soil under both hardwoods and conifers. Widely distributed. Fruiting in late summer and fall.

Comments: *Hygrocybe punicea* (Fr.:Fr.) P. Kumm. looks similar to *H. coccinea;* is found in similar habitats; has a viscid pileus; a fibrillose stipe that is seldom fluted and is more often white at the base. It is also somewhat larger, with a thicker stipe (1.0–1.5 cm wide); and pileus up to 7 cm broad. *Hygrocybe coccinea* may be edible, but is easily confused with *H. punicea* and Arora (1979) reports the latter species as inedible.

Hygrocybe nitida (Berk. & M. A. Curtis) Murrill
EDIBILITY UNKNOWN

Pileus 1–4 cm broad, convex, plane in age or slightly depressed, bright apricot-yellow to orange, smooth, without hairs, margin incurved, even, viscid. Flesh soft, yellowish. Lamellae decurrent, subdistant, pale yellow, waxy. Stipe 3–8 cm long, 0.2–0.5 cm wide, equal or slightly larger at top, dry, smooth, concolorous with the pileus. Partial veil absent. Odorless. Taste mild.

Spores 6.5–9.0 x 4–6 µm elliptic, smooth, entire, thin-walled, nonamyloid. Spore print white.

Habit and distribution: Scattered to numerous in low, wet, mossy areas under hardwoods. Found in eastern North America. Fruiting in summer and fall.

Comments: Few mushrooms can be mistaken for this bright orange-yellow species with viscid pileus and stipe and decurrent yellow lamellae. We have found it in oak forests in Maryland and Virginia often in great numbers. *Hygrocybe vitellina* (Fr.) P. Karst. is very similar, known from Europe, but not common, and has somewhat broader spores. *Hygrocybe laeta* (Fr.) Fr. is somewhat similar but has a glutinous stipe and a fishy to skunklike odor.

Hygrocybe virginea (Wülfen:Fr.) P. D. Orton & Watling
EDIBILITY UNKNOWN

Pileus 1.0–4.5 cm broad, convex, nearly plane in age, white, smooth, margin slightly striate in age, moist not viscid. Flesh soft, white. Lamellae decurrent, subdistant, white, waxy. Stipe 2–9 cm long, 0.2–0.8 cm wide, narrowing toward base, white, dry, smooth, without hairs. Odorless. Taste mild.

Spores 7–12 x 4.5–6.5 µm, elliptic, smooth, entire, thin-walled, nonamyloid. Spore print white.

Habit and distribution: Scattered to numerous under hardwoods and conifers. Widely distributed. Fruiting in summer and fall.

Comments: This species has been called *Hygrocybe borealis* Peck by American authors. However, there are several closely related species. *Hygrocybe nivea* Fr. is very similar; is also pure white but has a viscid cap. If a large, robust, white species is found near or under the edge of snowbanks in the Rocky Mountains, see *Hygrophorus subalpinus* A. H. Sm. *Hygrophorus piceae* Kühner & Romagn. has a white, viscid pileus; pale pinkish buff lamellae, dry stipe; and is often found under spruce.

Hygrocybe marginata (Peck) Murrill
NONPOISONOUS

Pileus 1–5 cm broad, ovoid, conic, convex in age with a low umbo, yellow to yellow-orange with an olive tint, smooth, hairless but occasionally with loose squamules or small scales, margin faintly striate, moist. Flesh thin, concolorous with the pileus, does not bruise black. Lamellae adnate to adnexed, subdistant, orange, yellow or yellow-orange, not fading in age, edges sometimes darker, intervenose, waxy. Stipe 4–10 cm long, 0.3–0.6 cm wide, round, equal or enlarging toward the base, pale buff to yellow, dry, smooth, without hairs. Veil absent. Odor mild. Taste mild.

Spores 7–10 x 4–6 μm elliptic, smooth, entire, thin-walled, nonamyloid. Spore print white.

Habit and distribution: Single to numerous on soil under hardwoods and conifers. Widely distributed. Fruiting in summer and fall.

Comments: *Hygrocybe marginata* does not have the tall conic pileus of *H. conica;* does not blacken when bruised; and the lamellae retain their color when other parts have faded. It is common in southeastern United States and eastern Canada.

Hygrocybe flavcescens (Kauffman) Singer
NONPOISONOUS

Pileus 2.5–7.0 cm broad, broadly convex, nearly plane in age, bright orange-yellow fading at margin to light orange-yellow, viscid, then soon dry. Flesh thin, yellowish. Lamellae adnexed, close, yellow, waxy. Stipe 4–7 cm long, 0.8–1.2 cm wide, equal, compressed or fluted, white, flushed with orange in center, moist but not viscid. Veil absent. Odorless. Taste not recorded.

Spores 7–9 x 4–5 μm elliptic, smooth, entire, thin-walled, nonamyloid. Spore print white.

Habit and distribution: Scattered to numerous under hardwoods and conifers. Found in eastern and central North America and on the West Coast. Fruiting in the spring, summer, and fall.

Comments: It is also known as *Hygrophorus flavescens* (Kauffman) A. H. Sm. & Hesler. *Hygrocybe chlorophana* (Fr.:Fr) Wünsche is very similar but has a viscid stipe and is also widely distributed (Hesler and Smith, 1963). If the specimens have a fishy or wet dog-fur odor, see *Hygrocybe laeta.*

KEY TO THE SPECIES OF *HYGROPHORUS*

1. Pileus and stipe white or with or without yellow fibrils on the pileus margin and upper stipe --- 2
1. Pileus and stipe colored --- 4
   2. Pileus and stipe with yellow fibrils on the pileus margin and upper stipe --- *H. chrysodon*
   2. Pileus and stipe pure white --- 3
3. Pileus robust, 5–25 cm broad; stipe dry; partial veil present; fruiting in spring in Rocky Mountains and Pacific Northwest -- *H. subalpinus*
   (see also *Hygrocybe virginea*)
3. Pileus medium size, 2–10 cm broad, viscid; stipe viscid; partial veil absent; widely distributed; fruiting in fall and early winter ------------------------------------- *H. eburneus*
   4. Partial veil fibrillose, thin, and a viscid band on the stipe------------------------ 5
   4. Partial veil absent -- 7
5. Pileus hairy, dark gray to brownish gray; veil thin, fibrillose, gray-brown --- *H. inocybiformis*
5. Pileus orange-red to bright yellow or streaked pinkish brown------------------------- 6
   6. Pileus orange-red to bright yellow, viscid; widely distributed under conifers --- *H. speciosus*
      (see *Hygrocybe* key for other orange-red to yellow species)
   6. Pileus streaked pinkish brown, viscid; in early spring under conifers --- *H. purpurascens*
      (see comments under *H. russula*)
7. Odor of bitter almonds or rancid meal-- 8
7. Odor absent or faintly of coal tar --- 9
   8. Pileus glutinous, ash-gray; odor of bitter almonds --------------------- *H. agathosmus*
   8. Pileus viscid, cream color, tinted blue or bluish green; odor of rancid meal -- *H. caeruleus*
9. Pileus drab gray, moist not viscid; lamellae tinted gray; odorless------------ *H. marzuolus*
9. Pileus pinkish brown streaked with reddish purple hairs, or pinkish buff to pale flesh color; odorless or faintly fragrant -- 10
   10. Pileus pinkish buff to pale flesh color, moist; lamellae distant; odor faintly fragrant --- *H. pudorinus*
   10. Pileus pinkish brown, streaked with reddish purple hairs ------------------------ 11

11. Lamellae close to crowded; most frequently found in eastern
   North America--- *H. russula*
11. Lamellae distant; most frequently under conifers in western
   North America --- *H. erubescens*

(see comments under *H. russula*)

Hygrophorus chrysodon (Fr.) Fr.
NONPOISONOUS

Pileus 3–8 cm broad, convex to convex with a low umbo in age, white flushed yellowish from yellow, minute hairs, which are especially dense over the margin, dry to viscid in wet weather. Flesh thick, soft, white. Lamellae decurrent, well-separated, white, waxy. Stipe 3–8 cm long, 0.6–1.8 cm wide, equal, viscid, white, except at apex, which is yellow from a thick or thin zone of yellow hairs. Partial veil absent. Odorless. Taste mild.

Spores 7–10 x 3.5–4.5 µm elliptic, smooth, entire, thin-walled, nonamyloid. Spore print white.

Habit and distribution: Scattered to numerous under conifers. Widely distributed. Fruiting in summer through late fall.

Comment: The taste of *H. chrysodon* is bland and, therefore, it is not considered an edible.

Hygrophorus subalpinus A. H. Sm.
EDIBLE

Pileus 5–25 cm broad, convex, soon plane, white, viscid, smooth, hairless. Flesh firm, white, thick. Lamellae decurrent, close, pale pink at first, then white, very waxy. Stipe 3–12 cm long, 1–4 cm wide, narrowing toward apex, dry, white, usually with a bulbous base. Veil white, leaving a thin, flaring partial veil in the stipe center. Odorless. Taste mild.

Spores 8–10 x 4.5–6.0 µm elliptic, smooth, entire, thin-walled, nonamyloid. Spore print white.

Habit and distribution: Single to numerous in deep needle litter under conifers, near or under melting snow banks. Found in the Rocky Mountains and Pacific Northwest. Fruiting in the very early spring or rarely in the late fall.

Comments: Only the waxy lamellae distinguish this species in the field from a *Russula*. *Hygrophorus ponderatus* Britzelm. is an uncommon winter species that grows under conifers and has a viscid stipe but is otherwise very similar (Largent, 1985). *Hygrophorus sordidus* Peck is a white species in eastern North America under hardwoods and California under oak. It has smaller spores than *H. subalpinus* and has a dry stipe. We have eaten *H. subalpinus* and it is bland and certainly not as good as many western edibles. It has good texture and would be a good substitute for bamboo shoots in stir-fry dishes.

Hygrophorus eburneus (Fr.) Fr.
EDIBILITY UNKNOWN

Pileus 2–10 cm broad, convex to nearly plane, often with a low umbo in age, pure white, viscid to glutinous, with minute, short hairs to smooth. Flesh thick, white. Lamellae short decurrent, subdistant, pure white, waxy. Stipe 4.5–18.0 cm long, 0.2–0.8 (-1.5) cm wide, nearly equal or smaller toward the base, pure white, glutinous, minute white scales at top, hollow in age. Partial veil absent. Odor not distinctive. Taste mild.

Spores 6–9 x 3.5–5 µm elliptic, smooth, entire, thin-walled, nonamyloid. Spore print white.

Habit and distribution: Scattered to numerous, usually under conifers but also noted under various hardwoods. Widely distributed. Fruiting in summer, fall, and early winter.

Comments: *Hygrophorus cossus* Fr. (*H. eburneus* var *cossus* of some authors) differs only in its pale pinkish buff pileus and lamellae, and a distinctive aromatic odor.

Hygrophorus inocybiformis A. H. Sm.
EDIBILITY UNKNOWN

Pileus 3–6 cm broad, conic, convex with a low umbo, drab to brownish gray, hairy, dry. Flesh thin, soft, white, gray just under pileus cuticle. Lamellae short decurrent, subdistant, pale white to olive-buff, waxy. Stipe 3–6 cm long, 0.5–1.2 cm wide, equal, dry, white and silky at apex but with scattered gray-brown hairs below. Veil fibrillose of thin gray-brown hairs. Odorless. Taste unknown.

Spores 9–14 x 5–8 µm elliptic, smooth, entire, thin-walled, nonamyloid. Spore print white.

Habit and distribution: Scattered under western conifers, especially Engelmann spruce and white fir. Found in United States and Canada. Fruiting in summer and fall.

Comments: This species resembles an *Inocybe* as well as a *Tricholoma*, but *Inocybe* has brown spores and *Tricholoma* has nonwaxy lamellae. *Hygrophorus olivaceoalbus* (Fr.) Fr. looks very similar; has a thick glutinous pileus and stipe with embedded, gray fibrils; and is widely distributed in eastern North America.

Hygrophorus speciosus Peck
NONPOISONOUS

Pileus 2–5 cm broad, convex, convex with a low umbo in some, smooth, bright yellow to orange-red to orange over the center and sometimes fading to yellowish orange over the margin, glutinous. Flesh soft, white to yellowish. Lamellae decurrent, subdistant, white to yellowish, waxy. Stipe 4–10 cm long, 0.4–1.0 cm wide, equal or enlarging toward base, glutinous, white or whitish with dull orange stains. Partial veil thin leaving a glutinous band on the stipe. Odorless. Taste mild.

Spores 8–10 x 4.5–6.0 μm elliptic, smooth, entire, thin-walled, nonamyloid. Spore print white.

Habit and distribution: Scattered, single to somewhat clustered, in needle duff and moist areas under or near conifers especially larch, pine, and fir. Widely distributed. Fruiting in late summer and fall.

Comments: *Hygrophorus speciosus* is usually found under larch, but we found it in abundance under subalpine fir at 6,000 to 8,000 feet in Washington state. It is listed as edible, but most species of *Hygrophorus* are bland and have little flavor.

Hygrophorus agathosmus Fr.
EDIBLE

Pileus 4–8 (-11) cm broad, convex, plane in age, ash-gray to drab, viscid to glutinous, smooth, hairless, margin inrolled at first. Flesh soft, white to grayish. Lamellae adnate to broadly adnate, close, white to dingy gray in age, waxy. Stipe 4–8 (-16) cm long, 0.6–1.4 (-2.5) cm wide, equal, whitish to pale gray in age, dry, smooth, without hairs. Partial veil absent. Taste mild. Odor fragrant, of bitter almonds.

Spores 7–10 x 4.5–5.5 μm elliptic, smooth, entire, thin-walled, nonamyloid. Spore print white.

Habit and distribution: Scattered to numerous under spruce, pine, and mixed conifers. Found most frequently in the western United States and Canada, occasionally found elsewhere in North America. Fruiting in late summer to late fall.

Comments: This species is rather common in the fall in Idaho and late fall along coastal California. It is listed as edible in McKenny et al. (1991) but "tasteless."

Hygrophorus caeruleus O.K. Mill.
EDIBILITY UNKNOWN

Pileus 5–9 cm broad, broadly convex, smooth, cream color with tints of blue, feltlike, moist but not viscid. Flesh dingy cream color tinted bluish green or bluish gray. Lamellae close, thick, short decurrent, bluish green, waxy. Stipe 2.5–5.0 cm long, 1.5–2.5 cm wide, equal or tapering just at the base, dry, cream color at the apex, rest smooth, with minute hairs, bluish green to dingy light brown with fine white rhizomorphs from the base. Partial veil absent. Odor of rancid meal, often very strong. Taste mild soon unpleasant.

Spores 7–9 x 4–5 µm elliptic, smooth, entire, thin-walled, nonamyloid. Spore print white.

Habit and distribution: Several together, often partially buried in needles, under Douglas fir, grand fir, and Engelmann spruce. Found in the Pacific Northwest and California. Fruiting in late June and early July.

Comments: Since the publication of this species (Miller, 1984), it has been found in Washington, and California and should be looked for in Oregon.

Hygrophorus marzuolus (Fr.) Bres.
EDIBILITY UNKNOWN

Pileus 4–8 cm broad, convex to nearly plane, slightly depressed, drab-gray, overall smoky-drab with fine radially arranged dark lines, viscid. Flesh firm, grayish white. Lamellae adnate to short decurrent, intervenose, subdistant, gray, very waxy. Stipe 4–8 cm long, 0.9–1.2 cm wide, equal, white at apex, pale gray, dry, silky with soft, fine hairs to smooth, without hairs near base. Partial veil absent. Odorless. Taste mild.

Spores 7–9 x 4.5–5.5 µm elliptic, smooth, entire, thin-walled, nonamyloid. Spore print white.

Habit and distribution: In clusters or groups near melting snow banks, under Engelmann spruce and subalpine fir. Found in the Rocky Mountains. Fruiting in the early spring.

Comments: *Hygrophorus camarophyllus* (Fr.) Dumée looks very similar but is found in summer and fall; is widely distributed; with white lamellae; is larger (up to 13 cm wide); with a slightly disagreeable odor. *Hygrophorus calophyllus* P. Karst. is also robust and similar, but with pale pinkish lamellae and is reported only from the Rocky Mountains and Pacific Northwest (Hesler & Smith, 1963).

Hygrophorus pudorinus (Fr.) Fr.
NONPOISONOUS

Pileus 5–12 cm broad, ovoid, convex to broadly convex with a broad umbo, hairless, smooth, viscid, pinkish, pinkish buff, pale flesh color, margin inrolled at first, slowly expanding in age. Flesh thick, firm, white or slightly pinkish. Lamellae adnate to short decurrent, distant, white, flushed with light pinkish buff or light salmon, intervenose, waxy. Stipe 4–9 cm long, 0.8–2.0 cm wide, equal or slightly smaller at base, tinted pinkish, areas near base staining yellow, dry, conspicuous minute white tufts of hair at top, rest with flattened hairs, tinted pinkish, areas near base staining yellow. Partial veil absent. Odor faintly fragrant. Taste unpleasant.

Spores 6.5–9.5 x 4.0–5.5 µm elliptic, smooth, entire, thin-walled, nonamyloid. Spore print white.

Habit and distribution: Scattered or in troops under or near conifers. Widely distributed. Fruiting in fall and early winter.

Comments: Smith and Hesler (1963) have described several forms and varieties of this variable species.

Hygrophorus russula (Fr.) Quél.
EDIBLE

Pileus 5–12 cm robust, broad, broadly convex, nearly plane in age, smooth, pink to dingy pinkish brown, streaked with reddish purple hairs, sometimes bruises yellow, dry, viscid at first or in wet weather. Flesh thick, firm, white to pinkish. Lamellae adnate to decurrent, close to crowded, pale pink, dingy purplish red stains in age, waxy. Stipe 2–7 cm long, 1.5–3.5 cm wide, nearly equal, dry, white at first but streaked with pink or even reddish brown in age. Partial veil absent. Odorless. Taste mild.

Spores 6–8 x 3–5 µm elliptic, smooth, entire, thin-walled, nonamyloid. Spore print white.

Habit and distribution: Scattered or in groups under oaks or hardwood-conifer forests. Widely distributed but most frequently seen in the East. We have collected it and seen it in quantity in western Massachusetts. Fruiting occurs in late summer and fall.

Comments: *Hygrophorus erubescens* Fr. is very similar but is under conifers and has distant lamellae. *Hygrophorus purpurascens* (Fr.) Fr., frequently found in early spring in the West nearly buried in conifer duff, has a partial veil, but is otherwise very similar. The latter has a very good flavor and our family has eaten it with pleasure. We have not eaten *H. russula,* but it is reported to have a good flavor.

RUSSULALES—RUSSULA AND LACTARIUS

The order Russulales contains two families: the Russulaceae and the Elasmomycetaceae. Genera of the latter family are secotioid (never open) and often hypogeous (fruit below ground), (Jülich, 1981), and are not covered here. Covered here are the Russulaceae, with two genera: *Russula* and *Lactarius.* The species are fleshy but typically brittle, with a convex pileus that is plane in age. The trama is composed of clusters of globose cells called sphaerocysts. In *Lactarius* a latex (milk-like) is produced when the lamellae and/or tissue is cut or broken. The latex varies from white, white changing to yellow on exposure to air, yellow, orange, red, and blue. Both genera have species which taste mild, bitter, very hot or strongly acrid. Odors range from fruity, bitter almonds, shellfish, camphor, or sweet clover. Both genera lack either a universal veil or a partial veil, but the pileus often remains appressed against the stipe as the fruiting bodies mature. Spores are globose, subglobose to elliptic, entire, with distinctive amyloid (dark blue) warts and ridges throughout the order. Spore prints range from white, buff, ochre to ochre-orange. All species in both *Russula* and *Lactarius,* grow in soil and are ectomycorrhizal with both conifers and hardwoods throughout North America and worldwide.

Edibility: There are many good edibles in both *Russula* and *Lactarius,* but there are also some species that contain Type 8 toxins and can cause gastrointestinal distress and should be avoided. The bitter tasting brown-, black-, and red-staining species, along with the very hot, peppery *Russula emetica* complex, are toxic. In *Lactarius,* the species that have a white latex that turns yellow or lilac on exposure to air are also toxic (Lincoff & Mitchel, 1977). In general the toxic reactions involve mild to severe gastric upset. Most species of *Russula* are not edible, however, *R. xerampelina* and *R. virescens* are exceptions and have very good flavor. In *Lactarius* the species that have latex colored orange, red, and blue are edible and include *L. deliciosus, L. salmoneus, L. paradoxus, L. rubrilacteus,* and *L. indigo.* In addition the species with white latex which slowly stain the lamellae brown are good edibles, such as *L. volemus* and *L. corrugis.*

KEY TO THE SPECIES OF RUSSULA

1. Pileus white to bright yellow, orange-yellow to orange----------------------------------- 2
1. Pileus red, brown, green, lilac, violet, or some other color---------------------------------- 9
   2. Pileus white, sometimes yellowish in center; not staining when bruised------------ 3
      (if dingy whitish and staining, see *R. nigricans, R. densifolia, R. albonigra*)
   2. Pileus bright yellow, orange-yellow to orange-- 5
3. Pileus robust 9–20 cm broad; very firm; taste mild or slightly acrid-- *R. brevipes complex*
3. Pileus smaller 5–7 cm broad, fragile; taste acrid; dry or viscid ---------------------------- 4
   4. Pileus white, often yellowish in center; dry ---------------------- ------- *R. albida*
      (see comments under *R. albidula*)
   4. Pileus white; viscid -- *R. albidula*
5. Flesh bruising gray to grayish black --- 6
5. Flesh not changing color when bruised or cut--- 8
   6. Pileus yellow-orange; lamellae cream; taste hot and peppery -------- *R. ochroleuca*
      (see comments under *R. claroflava*)
   6. Pileus lemon-yellow to reddish orange; lamellae white to pale yellow; taste mild -- 7
7. Pileus bright lemon-yellow, yellow-orange; lamellae white-------------------- *R. claroflava*
7. Pileus orange-red to reddish orange; lamellae pale yellow ------------------ *R. decolorans*
      (see comments under *R. claroflava*)
   8. Pileus and stipe bright chrome yellow to orange-yellow--------------------- *R. flavida*
   8. Pileus bright yellow; stipe white; often under birch ---------------------------- *R. lutea*
9. Pileus green, olivaceous or with scales or patches on the surface ----------------------- 10
9. Pileus some other color or without scales or patches on the surface -------------------- 12
   10.Pileus green, gray-green; smooth or with small irregular patches ----------------- 11
   10.Pileus covered with orange-brown to yellow-orange small scales -------- *R. ballouii*
11. Pileus gray-green with small irregular patches --------------------------------- *R. virescens*
11. Pileus green; glabrous; viscid when wet --------------------------------------- *R. aeruginea*
      (see comments under *R. virescens*)
   12. Pileus dingy white, blackening in age; flesh bruising black or red
      changing to black --- 13
   12.Pileus some other color; flesh not changing to either red or black ----------------- 15
13. Bruising red and then black; taste hot or slowly hot -------------------------------------- 14
13. Bruising directly to black; with distant lamellae --------------------------------- *R. albonigra*
      (see comments *under R. densifolia*)
   14.Pileus dingy white; lamellae distant; spores 6.3–8.0 x 5.5–7.0 µm------ *R. nigricans*
   14.Pileus dingy white; lamellae crowded; spores 7.0–10.0 x 6–8 µm------ *R. densifolia*

15. With a distinctive odor of fish, crab or lobster when fresh or dry -------- *R. xerampelina*
15. With a different odor or odorless -- 16
    16. Pileus ochre to yellow-brown; odor of bitter almonds, anise, foetid to spermatic -- 17
    16. Pileus bright red, purple-red, purple to lilac; odor different -------------------------- 19
17. Pileus with small yellow-brown, crustose patches; odor foetid to
    spermatic --- *R. granulata*
              (see comments under *R. laurocerasi*)
17. Pileus without crustose patches -- 18
    18. Pileus dark ochre to yellow-brown, viscid; odor of bitter almonds ---- *R. laurocerasi*
    18. Pileus yellow-brown, viscid; odor pleasant like anise --------------- *R. fragrantissima*
              (see comments under *R. laurocerasi*)
19. Pileus bright red to red, viscid; taste strongly acrid ---------------------------------- 20
19. Pileus purple, purple-red, reddish purple, violet to lilac; taste mild to acrid ----------- 21
    20. Pileus bright red, pink flesh under the pileus cuticle, viscid; spore print white; in
       deep moss or bogs under conifers; spore print white ----------------------- *R. emetica*
    20. Pileus red to reddish pink; white flesh under the pileus cuticle, viscid; spore print
       white; in woods under hardwoods and conifers, not in moss -------------- *R. silvicola*
             (see comments under *R. emetica*)
21. Pileus lilac to violet; white lamellae; spore print white; mild taste;
    under conifers -- *R. azurea*
            (see comments under *R. queletii*)
21. Pileus maroon, purplish red, reddish purple to purple; spore print white --------------- 22
    22. Pileus maroon; pale lavender tinted stipe; spore print white; mild taste; under
       hardwoods -- *R. rosea*
            (see comments under *R. sanguinea*)
    22. Pileus purplish to reddish purple to purple; acrid taste; usually under conifers ---- 23
23. Pileus deep purplish red, deep purple margin; lamellae light yellow; stipe purplish red to
    red: spore print cream to light yellow; acrid, often slowly; under conifers ------ *R. queletii*
23. Not with the above combination of characters -- 24
    24. Pileus purplish red to scarlet, viscid; stipe white tinted pink; taste slowly and
       slightly acrid; spore print yellow; under conifers especially pine ------ *R. sanguinea*
    24. Pileus purplish to violaceus, dark olivaceous brown to black in depressed center,
       viscid; stipe dry, white; spore print white; taste very hot to acrid; under conifers or
       hardwoods often in sphagnum bogs -- *R. fragilis*
           (Pileus with olive tints and dark olive-brown center, see *R. gracilis*)

Russula brevipes Peck
NONPOISONOUS

Pileus (5-) 9–20 cm broad, broadly convex, depressed in center, white, stained dull yellow or brown, dry, minutely tomentose, margin enrolled at first, not striate. Flesh firm, white. Lamellae decurrent, close to crowded and sometimes forked, with veins between, white, stained cinnamon to brown. Stipe 3–8 cm long, 2.5–5.0 cm thick, equal, dull white with brown stains, dry, smooth, hairless. Odor somewhat disagreeable. Taste slightly acrid.

Spores 8–11 x 6.5–8.5 μm elliptic with amyloid warts and ridges, entire, thin-walled. Spore print cream colored.

Habit and distribution: Usually several to many, often almost buried in duff under conifers or mixed conifer/hardwoods. Widely distributed. Fruiting in the summer and fall.

Comments: Some people eat this fungus, but it is not a very tasty mushroom. *Russula brevipes* var *acrior* Shaffer differs in having light green at the apex of the stipe and on the lamellae. *Russula cascadensis* Shaffer, found in the Pacific Northwest, is very similar but has a very acrid taste. *Russula delica* Fr. has nearly distant lamellae and has not been found in North America. The early reports of it must be referred to *R. brevipes* or the closely related species in the subsection *Lactarioideae* of *Russula* according to Shaffer (1964). *Russula vesicatoria* Burl. is similar but the lamellae frequently fork near the stipe. We have found this species under Virginia pine in the fall in Maryland and Virginia.

Russula albidula Peck
NONPOISONOUS

Pileus 2.5–10.0 cm broad, broadly convex, cream to white, smooth, hairless, viscid, margin faintly striate. Flesh fragile, white. Lamellae adnate, close, occasionally forking, white. Stipe 2.5–7.0 cm long, 1.0–2.3 cm wide, white, equal, dry, smooth, hairless, a fine white down at the base. Odorless. Taste acrid.

Spores 7–9 x 5.5–7.0 μm subglobose, with amyloid ridges, entire, thin-walled. Spore print pale yellow.

Habit and distribution: Single or several, found in mixed hardwoods and conifers, often under oak. Found in eastern North America. Fruiting in summer, fall, and early winter.

Comments: *Russula albida* Peck is white, dry, and yellowish in the center; found in mixed hardwood and conifers.

Russula claroflava Grove
EDIBLE

Pileus 5–10 cm broad, convex to plane in age, or depressed in center, bright yellow to lemon-yellow, dry, margin striate. Flesh soft, white, slowly gray on exposure to air. Lamellae adnate, close, narrow, white. Stipe 5–10 cm long, 0.9–2.0 cm wide, equal, dry, white, slowly bruising gray then grayish black. Odorless. Taste mild.

Spores 6.5–9.5 μm globose, with isolated amyloid warts, entire, thin-walled. Spore print ochre or pale ochre.

Habit and distribution: Solitary or several under hardwoods, especially birch or mixed woods. Widely distributed throughout North America. Fruiting in summer and fall.

Comments: *Russula decolorans* (Fr.) Fr. has an orange-red to reddish orange pileus; pale yellow lamellae; flesh that becomes gray when cut or bruised; and a mild taste. *Russula ochroleuca* (Pers.) Fr. also has a yellow-orange pileus and flesh that turns gray when exposed to air or cut, but the taste is hot and peppery. *Russula flavida* has white lamellae; a bright yellow to chrome yellow pileus and stipe; does not bruise gray; and is odorless. *Russula lutea* (Huds.:Fr.) Gray has a yellow to orange-yellow pileus; ochre lamellae; white stipe; and the odor of apricots.

Russula flavida Frost & Peck
EDIBLE

Pileus 3–10 cm broad, convex to plane in age, bright chrome yellow to cadmium yellow, lighter yellow at smooth margin, dry, with a light, frosted appearance. Flesh firm, white, gray in age. Lamellae adnate, thick, close, light yellow. Stipe 4–8 cm long, 1.0–2.0 cm wide, nearly equal or tapering slightly at the base, dry, concolorous with the pileus, with a similar frosted appearance, flesh not changing when bruised. Odorless. Taste mild.

Spores 5–8 x 5.5–8.5 µm subglobose, with weak amyloid reticulations, entire, thin-walled. Spore print cream color.

Habit and distribution: Single or several under oaks. Fruiting from New York, south and west to Texas. Fruiting in the summer.

Comments: This is a beautiful fungus (see Metzler et al., page 106, 1992) and is usually found in southern oak forests. See comments under *R. claroflava* to distinguish among the yellow-capped Russulas.

Russula lutea (Huds.:Fr.) Gray
EDIBLE

Pileus 2.5–7.0 cm broad, convex to plane or slightly depressed in center, clear bright yellow, smooth, hairless, viscid, with a striate margin in age. Flesh fragile, white, unchanging when cut. Lamellae adnexed, subdistant, narrow, yellow to ochre, often with veins between. Stipe 3–5 cm long, 0.5–2.0 cm thick, equal, white not bruising gray, dry, smooth, hairless. Odor sweet, reminds one of apricots. Taste mild.

Spores 7–10 x 6.5–8 µm broadly elliptic, amyloid warts, entire, thin-walled. Spore print white.

Habit and distribution: Scattered or in groups under hardwoods, especially paper birch. Widely distributed. Fruiting in summer and early fall.

Comments: We have always found *Russula lutea* in the western United States and Alaska wherever paper birch is found. See *R. claroflava* for comments on how to distinguish this species from other yellow-capped species of *Russula*.

Russula ballouii Peck.
NONPOISONOUS

Pileus 4–8 cm broad, broadly convex to plane in age, white to cream color with numerous orange-brown to yellow-orange, minute scales over the surface, dry. Flesh white, firm. Lamellae adnate, close, white, with few lamellulae. Stipe 3–6 cm long, 0.8–1.5 cm wide, nearly equal, dry, white over the upper one-half, below with light orange-brown scales arranged in rows almost to the base. Odor not distinctive. Taste hot and peppery or acrid to some.

Spores 7.0–9.5 x 5.5–8.0 µm elliptic, with amyloid warts and a partial reticulum (Fig. 12), entire, thin-walled. Spore print white.

Habit and distribution: Usually several under hardwoods. Distributed in eastern United States, mostly southeastern and southern United States. Fruiting in August and September.

Comments: We have collected this fungus in central Virginia and North Carolina almost every year. It appears to be mycorrhizal with oaks or hickories.

Russula virescens Fr.
EDIBLE

Pileus 5–12 cm broad, nearly round at first, convex to plane or somewhat depressed in age, green to gray-green, dry, surface broken up into many small irregular patches, margin not striate or very slightly so. Flesh firm, white, solid throughout. Lamellae nearly free, close, even, white, sometimes forked. Stipe 3–7 cm long, 1–2 cm thick, equal, white, dry, smooth, glabrous. Odorless. Taste mild.

Spores 6–8 µm subglobose, with amyloid warts and ridges, entire, thin-walled. Spore print white.

Habit and distribution: Solitary to scattered, under hardwoods or mixed conifer/hardwoods. Widely distributed in southern United States. Fruiting in summer or fall.

Comments: *Russula crustosa* Peck has more ochre to brownish coloration with greenish hues, has the small irregular patches, but a cream color spore deposit. *Russula aeruginea* Lindblad is darker green, smooth, and nearly viscid in wet weather, spores are cream-colored to a bit darker. The species above and *R. virescens* are generally reported as edible and good, but we have not tried them. *Russula redolens* Burl. is drab green to deep blue-green; smooth; with a disagreeable taste; and odor of parsley (Kibby & Fatto, 1990), but the edibility is not known to us.

Russula nigricans Bull.:Fr.
POISONOUS

Pileus 5–20 cm broad, convex to broadly convex or plane in age, depressed in center, dingy white, staining brown or black, moist soon dry. Flesh very firm, white, bruising reddish and then black. Lamellae adnexed, subdistant to distant, broad, staining red and black when handled or weathered. Stipe 2–8 cm long, 1–4 cm wide, equal, dull white, also staining like the pileus. Odor fruity. Taste slowly hot.

Spores 6.3–8.0 x 5.5–7.0 µm globose, with amyloid warts 0.8–1.4 µm high, entire, thin-walled. Spore print white.

Habit and distribution: Single to several under conifers and mixed hardwood/conifer stands. Widely distributed in North America, more common in the western United States and Canada but also in the eastern United States and Canada. Fruiting in late summer and fall.

Comments: Schalkwijk-Barendsen (1991) reports *R. nigricans* from western Canada and we have collected it in the western United States, as well as in Virginia and the eastern United States. Pomerleau (1980) reports it from Quebec. It contains Type 8 toxins. See *R. densifolia* with crowded, pale yellow lamellae in this closely related group of species.

Russula densifolia (Secr.) Gill.
POISONOUS

Pileus 5.5–12.0 (-20.0) cm broad, convex, convex-depressed, dingy white, soon smoky, gray or blackish, dry or slightly sticky to viscid in wet weather, margin striate. Flesh, firm, whitish turning red when bruised and then slowly to black. Lamellae adnate, crowded, thick, broad, whitish to pale yellow bruising red then black. Stipe 2–7 cm long, 1.8– 4.0 cm wide, equal, smooth, hairless, whitish streaked with brown to reddish brown stains, when bruised becoming red then slowly to brown. Odorless. Taste very hot.

Spores 7–10 x 6–8 µm, subglobose, warts 0.1–0.5 µm high, warts and ridges amyloid, entire, thin-walled. Spore print white.

Habit and distribution: Single or in groups under hardwood, conifer, or mixed forests. Widely distributed. Fruiting in the summer and fall.

Comments: We have found this species in the Northeast under eastern white pine and Virginia pine. *Russula albonigra* (Krombh.) Fr. is very similar but stains directly to black when bruised and tastes mild, like menthol. *Russula adusta* Fr. has crowded lamellae; a brown depressed pileus; bruises very slowly pink then to gray; and has a mild taste. *Russula nigricans* has distant lamellae; stains pink then promptly to black; and tastes slowly hot. These very firm species, which stain red to black, have Type 8 toxins and could cause severe gastric upset

Russula xerampelina Fr.
EDIBLE

Pileus 3–16 cm broad, broadly convex to convex-depressed, purplish red, carmine-red to maroon or lighter, even olive at the striate margin, viscid at first, soon dry and felty to touch. Flesh firm, white. Lamellae adnexed, close, thick, no lamellulae, cream color, yellow to orange-yellow, turning gray when dried. Stipe 3–8 cm long, 1.5–3.3 (-5.0) cm wide, clavate or even bulbous at the base, white flushed pinkish, wrinkled, grooved or even faintly reticulated, hollow in age. Odor of crab or lobster usually quite strong but stronger when dried. Taste mild.

Spores 8–11 x 6.0–8.5 µm, globose, with isolated amyloid warts, entire, thin-walled. Spore print yellow.

Habit and distribution: Scattered or in groups under conifer forests. Widely distributed. Fruiting in summer and fall.

Comments: The flesh turns deep green in 10% ferric sulphate. Other species also have the crab or lobster odor, including *R. elaeodes* Bres. which has an ochre-yellow pileus and is found under oak; *R. barlae* Quél. has an orange-red pileus with yellow in the center and is associated with mixed forests in the northeastern United States; while *R. faginea* Romagn., with a brownish red to cocoa-brown pileus and a crab smell in age, is found under hardwoods (Kibby & Fatto, 1990). A very small species, *R. chamiteae* Kühner, is found in alpine and Arctic tundra and also has a crab or lobster odor. Moser (1983) presents a key to the species in the complex. *R. xerampelina* is one of the best edibles in this genus.

Russula laurocerasi Melzer
NONPOISONOUS

Pileus 5–14 cm broad, broadly convex to convex-depressed, dark ochre to yellow-brown, smooth, hairless, margin deeply and widely striate, viscid to sticky in wet weather. Flesh thin, dingy white. Lamellae adnexed, close, broad, white to pale orange, often stained light brown, with veins between, and sometimes forked. Stipe 3–6 (-10) cm long, 1.0–2.5 cm wide, equal, smooth, hairless, dull white, staining brownish to yellowish in age. Odor of bitter almonds, in age slightly foetid. Taste very acrid.

Spores 7–9 x 6.0–9.5 μm subglobose, amyloid, with conic spines and ridges up to 1.0–2.5 μm high, entire, thin-walled. Spore print pale orange-yellow.

Habit and distribution: Scattered to occasionally numerous or in groups under conifers and hardwoods. Widely distributed. Fruiting in the summer and fall.

Comments: *Russula laurocerasi* is in the subsection *Foetentinae* of *Russula* according to Shaffer (1972). *Russula fragrantissima* Romagn. is large, also viscid and yellow-brown; odor of aniseed; pleasant taste; and a pale orange-yellow spore print. In addition *R. granulata* (Peck) Peck has small crustose patches on the pileus surface; smaller spores (5.7–8.0 x 4.4–6.3 μm); slightly foetid to spermatic odor; otherwise is very similar to the other species. *Russula foetens* (Pers.) Fr. has large fruiting bodies; large spores (7.5–10.5 x 6.7–8.7 μm); and unpleasant to slightly foetid odor. If present in North America, it is rare.

Russula emetica (Fr.) Pers.
POISONOUS

Pileus 2–12 cm broad, broadly convex to convex-depressed in age, bright red, fading in age, smooth, hairless, margin deeply striate in age, viscid. Flesh very soft, white, pink just under cap cuticle. Lamellae adnate, close, sometimes forked, white. Stipe 4–12 cm long, 1.0–2.5 cm wide, equal, dull white, hollow in age. Odor fruity or pleasant. Taste strongly acrid.

Spores 7–10 x 6.5–8.0 µm broadly elliptic, warts amyloid, entire, thin-walled. Spore print white.

Habit and distribution: Scattered or in groups on the ground or more commonly in deep moss, under conifers. Widely distributed. Fruiting in summer and fall.

Comments: This group of red Russulas has a white spore print; white lamellae; a hot taste; and contains Type 8 toxins. Other red Russulas with mild taste and/or yellowish spore prints are not treated here. A number of red or variously colored Russulas in North America are very hot to taste and often misidentified as *R. emetica*. *Russula silvicola* Shaffer is very similar; very hot; lacks the pink flesh just beneath the cuticle; and is found in mixed woods, usually not in moss. *Russula betularum* Hora is also hot and acrid; has a pale pink to yellowish pink pileus; white lamellae and stipe; and is found in deciduous woods often under birch. Lincoff and Mitchel (1977) report cases of poisoning by *R. emetica,* but the toxins are unknown.

Russula queletii Fr.
INEDIBLE

Pileus 2–8 cm broad, conic at first to convex and broadly convex in age, deep purplish vinaceous, reddish purple, deep purple, glabrous, margin smooth or with obscure striations, viscid but soon dry, glabrous. Flesh soft, gray. Lamellae adnate, close, narrow, forking near the stipe, white to very light yellow in age. Stipe 2–7 cm long, 1.5–3.0 cm wide, nearly equal or tapering somewhat toward the apex, dry, glabrous, mostly red to purple coloration similar to the pileus or some times lighter. Odor pleasant or fruity. Taste sometimes mild then acrid, or acrid at once.

Spores 7–10 x 6–9 µm subglobose, with isolated amyloid warts, entire, thin-walled. Spore print cream color.

Habit and distribution: Several to single under conifers especially pines and firs. Widely distributed in the western mountains and the northern United States and Canada. Fruiting in the summer and fall.

Comments: *Russula queletii* has no reaction when ammonia is applied to the flesh. *Russula sardonia* Fr. is very similar but has yellow lamellae; more brown coloration in the pileus; and the flesh turns red with ammonia. *Russula azurea* Bres. has a lilac to violet pileus; white lamellae and stipe; a mild taste; is also found under conifers, especially spruce and fir. This group of purple-, reddish purple- to violet-capped Russulas needs extensive study to clarify species concepts. It does not appear that any of the group above are edible.

Russula sanguinea Fr.
INEDIBLE

Pileus 3–10 cm broad, broadly convex, purplish red to scarlet, margin smooth, viscid. Flesh very firm, white, tinted rose under pileus cuticle. Lamellae adnate to short decurrent, close, cream color. Stipe 3–8 (-10) cm long, 1.0–2.5 cm wide, equal, or tapering toward the apex, smooth, dry, glabrous, white, tinted pink or more often pink to rose color overall. Odor pleasant. Taste slightly acrid to acrid.

Spores 7.0–9.5 x 6.0–8.5 µm short elliptic, with isolated, pointed, amyloid warts, entire, thin-walled. Spore print yellow.

Habit and distribution: Single to several, under conifers especially pines. Widespread in North America. Fruiting midsummer to October.

Comments: There are too many Russulas with red pilei to cover them all. However, *Russula rosea* Quél. has a maroon pileus; pale lavender tints on the stipe; cream-colored spores; mild taste; and is found under hardwoods. *Russula roseipes* (Secr.) Bres. has a pink to rosy red pileus; white tinted pink stipe; ochraceus spores; mild taste; and found in mixed woods or under conifers. *Russula vinacea* Burl. (= *R. krombholtzii* Shaffer) has a pileus that is vinaceous-purple to wine-red, blotched with ochre-yellow; a white stipe with rusty stains over the base; white spores; and mild to very acrid taste.

Russula fragilis (Pers.:Fr.) Fr.
POISONOUS

Pileus 2.5–6.0 cm broad, broadly convex to slightly depressed with a depressed center, purple to violaceus, usually olivaceous to dark olive-brown in the center with a pink margin, viscid. Flesh soft, white. Lamellae adnexed, subdistant, white to cream colored. Stipe 2–4 cm long, 0.5–1.0 cm thick, equal, dry, minutely wrinkled, white, often hollow. Odor fruity. Taste acrid or very hot.

Spores 6–8 x 5–7 µm subglobose, ridges amyloid, entire, thin-walled. Spore print white.

Habit and distribution: Solitary or in groups, on moist wet ground in conifers, hardwoods and mixed woods, often among moss in sphagnum bogs. Widely distributed. Fruiting in summer and early fall.

Comments: This species is rather common in eastern North America and reported from California by Thiers (1997) in a diverse series of habitats in western North America. It contains Type 8 toxins. An older name is *R. fallax* Cooke. *Russula atropurpurea* Krombh. is similar in color; is larger, 5–10 cm broad; and is also acrid. *Russula gracilis* Burl. has a pale lilac to pink margin often with olive hues and with a gray-green depressed center; an acrid taste; and is found in eastern North America.

KEY TO LACTARIUS

1. Latex orange, red, muddy red or blue -- 2
1. Latex white, white then yellow, or white staining tissue brown to gray or bluish gray -- 6
   2. Latex blue to deep indigo blue; pileus blue to gray-blue --------------------- *L. indigo*
   2. Latex some other color -- 3
3. Latex orange and unchanging --- 4
3. Latex muddy red or orange changing to muddy red ----------------------------------- 5
   4. Latex orange; pileus orange with green stains; widely distributed ---- *L. deliciosus*
   4. Latex bright orange; pileus white bruising orange to red; found in southern United
      States --- *L. salmoneus*
5. Latex blood-red to purple-red; pileus carrot colored ------------------------ *L. rubrilacteus*
   (see also *L. subpurpureus* under eastern hemlock)
5. Latex red, gradually staining green; pileus blue-green to olive-gray -------- *L. paradoxus*
   6. Latex white changing to yellow on exposure to air------------------------------------ 7
   6. Latex white, not changing to yellow, but can stain tissue --------------------------- 9
7. Stipe with polished, dark orange spots on stipe; pileus yellow to
   ochre-yellow --- *L. scrobiculatus*
7. Stipe without orange spots; pileus cinnamon to wine-red ---------------------------- 8
   8. Pileus pinkish cinnamon to cinnamon-buff; under hardwoods -------- *L. chrysorheus*
   8. Pileus wine-red; stains wine-red; under conifers ----------------- *L. vinaceorufescens*
      (see comments under *L. chrysorheus*)
9. Odor aromatic of camphor or sweet clover-- 10
9. Odor fishy, disagreeable or absent --- 11
   10. Pileus dark red-brown; spores heavily ornamented -------------------- *L. camphoratus*
   10. Pileus pale tan to cinnamon or light reddish gray -------------------------- *L. aquifluus*
11. Latex white, staining cut areas brown to lilac or bluish gray ---------------------------- 12
11. Latex white, not staining tissue or staining tissue pink ----------------------------------- 16
   12. Latex white, staining tissue lilac --- 13
   12. Latex white, staining tissue brown to bluish gray------------------------------------- 14
13. Pileus densely pubescent, orange to orange-buff-------------------------- *L. representaneus*
13. Pileus viscid, smooth, brownish gray to wine-colored------------------------------ *L. uvidus*
   14. Latex white, staining tissue bluish gray; pileus glutinous, gray-brown ---- *L. mucidus*
   14. Latex white, staining tissue brown --- 15
15. Pileus wrinkled to corrugated, dark red-brown ----------------------------------- *L. corrugis*
15. Pileus smooth, hazel brown to orange-brown----------------------------------- *L. volemus*

16. Pileus with olive-green hues; stipe with olivaceous-brown spots -------------------- 17

16. Stipe without spots --- 18

17. Pileus olive-brown, viscid with darker olive-brown spots on the stipe; usually under conifers -- *L. olivaceo-umbrinus*

17. Pileus yellow-brown, tinted olivaceous with a dry, felty surface; under conifer and hard-wood/conifer forests --- *L. sordidus*

18. Pileus velvety, blackish brown to dark brown; white latex staining tissue pink ---- 19

18. Pileus some other color; latex not staining tissues pinkish -------------------------- 22

19. Lamellae pure white, distant-- 20

19. Lamellae cream to pinkish, crowded --- 21

20. Pileus strikingly blackish brown; associated with pine; eastern North America --- *L. lignyotus*

20. Pileus brown; under hardwoods or mixed woods; eastern North America --- *L. gerardii*
(see comments under *L. lignyotis*)

21. Pileus dark, sooty brown; under western conifers-------------------------------------- *L. fallax*
(see comments under *L. lignyotis*)

21. Pileus smoky-white to smoky-brown, under conifer or hardwood/conifer forests; eastern North America; spores small, 6–8 µm globose -------------------------- *L. fumosus*
(see comments under *L. lignyotus*)

22. Pileus medium to large, 4–20 cm; taste strongly acrid------------------------------- 23

22. Pileus small,1–5 cm, taste mild to slightly acrid------------------------------------- 27

23. Pileus white with brown stains; margin with a thick cottony roll ----------- *L. deceptivus*
(see also *L. subvellereus* comments under *L. deceptivus*)

23. Pileus different; margin smooth -- 24

24. Pileus white, dry; with crowded, forked lamellae; taste very acrid ------ *L. piperatus*

24. Pileus yellow-brown, butterscotch to chestnut-brown -------------------------------- 25

25. Pileus red-brown to chestnut-brown; widely distributed ----------------------------- *L. rufus*

25. Pileus butterscotch to yellow-brown; latex white, copious; lamellae well separated; eastern North America -- 26

26. Pileus butterscotch brown, viscid; stipe viscid----------------------------------- *L. affinis*

26. Pileus yellow-brown, dry; stipe dry -------------------------------- *L. hygrophoroides*

27. Pileus grayish brown, grayish pink; taste milk to slightly acrid-------------------- *L. griseus*

27. Pileus orange-red, maroon red to reddish tan, often with a umbo; taste mild or becoming bitter with time -- *L. oculatus*

Lactarius indigo (Schwein.) Fr.
EDIBLE

Pileus 5–15 cm broad, convex, convex-depressed in age, margin inrolled, zoned blue to deep blue, indigo to gray in age and staining green, smooth, hairless, viscid. Flesh firm, indigo staining green. Latex deep indigo, slowly dark green on exposure to air. Lamellae short decurrent, close, light blue, staining green when bruised. Stipe 2–8 cm long, 1.0–2.5 cm wide, equal or narrowed at base, indigo blue, dry, hollow. Odorless. Taste mild or slightly bitter.

Spores 8–10 x 5.5–7.5 µm elliptic, warts and ridges amyloid, entire, thin-walled. Spore print yellow to orange-yellow.

Habit and distribution: Scattered or in groups under conifer and conifer/hardwood stands. Distributed in eastern Canada and the United States and into the Deep South. Fruiting in summer and fall, after periods of heavy rainfall.

Comments: *Lactarius indigo* var *diminutivus* Hesler & A. H. Sm. is a very small form with a pileus that is 3–4 cm wide, often seen in Virginia. Both species are very good edibles. *Lactarius paradoxus* Beardslee and Burl. has a grayish indigo pileus; pale orange gills; bluish flesh of pileus and stipe; and red latex when gills and stipe are cut. Found in eastern North America. This too is edible.

Lactarius deliciosus (Fr.) Gray
EDIBLE

Pileus 5–15 cm broad, convex to broadly convex, margin incurved, orange or carrot-colored mixed in various proportions with dingy green, usually more green with age, sometimes with several faint color zones, viscid to sticky in wet weather. Flesh very light orange, stained green in age. Latex carrot-colored, leaving green stains. Lamellae decurrent, close, bright orange, staining green in age or after injury. Stipe 2–6 cm long, 1.5–3.0 cm wide, equal, narrow just at base, dry, glabrous, light orange turning green when handled or in age. Odor not distinctive. Taste mild, in time slightly acrid.

Spores 8–11 x 7–9 µm subglobose to short elliptic, amyloid warts and ridges, entire, thin-walled. Spore print buff.

Habit and distribution: Single to scattered under conifer or mixed hardwood conifer forests. Widely distributed. Fruiting in late summer and fall.

Comments: *Lactarius deliciosus* var *areolatus* A. H. Sm. has cracks in the pileus surface; the young caps are dark red; and is known from central Idaho. *Lactarius thyinos* A. H. Sm. has an orange, sticky to viscid pileus that lacks green stains; a white stipe; orange latex that slowly stains tissues red; a mild taste; and is often found in northern cedar bogs in central to eastern North America. *Lactarius chelidonium* Peck is a rare, grayish green to yellow brown-capped species; staining bluish and then greenish; yellow to yellow-brown latex; a mild to slightly bitter taste; and is found in eastern North America. If blue stains are present, see *Lactarius rubrilacteus* and *L. paradoxus*.

Lactarius salmoneus Peck
EDIBLE

Pileus 2–4 (-6) cm broad, convex then convex depressed in age, pure white except light orange to red where bruised, dry or slightly sticky. Flesh soft, bright orange. Latex scanty, but bright orange. Lamellae short decurrent, subdistant, bright orange, irregularly green-stained in age. Stipe 0.7–2.5 cm long, 0.7–1.0 cm wide, equal or narrow at the base, dry, orange-buff to nearly white. Odorless. Taste mild and pleasant.

Spores 8–9 x 5–6 µm elliptic, with amyloid warts, entire, thin-walled. Spore print cream to white.

Habit and distribution: Several to many under hard pines. Found in southeastern and southern United States. Fruiting in summer to late fall.

Comments: Metzler et al. (1992) report this fungus from Texas and note that it often fruits following periods of heavy rain or flooding.

Lactarius rubrilacteus Hesler & A.H. Sm.
EDIBLE

Pileus 6–15 cm broad, convex, depressed in center with inrolled margin, carrot-colored zones alternating with pale zones, green stained in age, moist. Flesh brittle, pale buff to orange. Latex scanty, blood-red to purple-red. Lamellae adnate or short decurrent, close, orange-reddish, stained pale green in age. Stipe 2–8 cm long, 1–3 cm wide, narrow just at base, pale orange color, hollow, dry. Odorless. Taste mild.

Spores 7.5–10 x 6.5–8 µm elliptic, with amyloid ridges, entire, thin-walled. Spore print pale yellow.

Habit and distribution: Scattered or in groups under conifers. Found in the western United States. Fruiting in summer and fall.

Comments: In older works, including *Mushrooms of North America* (Miller 1977), this species is under the name *L. sanguifluus* Fr. Some western species and varieties of *L. deliciosus* display an orange latex that turns reddish brown, see Methven (1997). In eastern North America, *L. subpurpureus* Peck has scanty, muddy red latex and is closely associated with eastern hemlock. In Maryland and Virginia it appears in the fall and is often locally abundant. The pileus has clear zones of color, and pink with dingy green stains developing in age. It is also edible.

89

Lactarius paradoxus Beardslee & Burl.
EDIBLE

Pileus 4–8 cm broad, convex to broadly convex in age, blue-green, olive-gray to dull grayish blue, green stained where bruised, viscid. Lamellae adnate, subdistant, pale orange to reddish pink often with green stains. Flesh of pileus and stipe white tinted blue, deep red, only at the cutis of stipe and where lamellae are attached to the pileus. Latex red at first, gradually staining green. Stipe 1.5–3.5 cm long 0.8–1.3 cm wide, reddish brown to dull greenish stains, dry. Odorless. Taste mild or slightly bitter in age.

Spores 7–9 x 5.5–6.5 µm broadly elliptic, with an amyloid, partial reticulum, entire, thin-walled. Spore print buff to yellow.

Habit and distribution: Several often scattered, under pine. Fruiting in August to October in eastern United States and on into February in the Deep South.

Comments: We have found this species growing under both soft and hard pines in North Carolina, Maryland, Texas, and Virginia (Metzler et al., 1992). *Lactarius indigo* has blue latex and *L. rubrilacteus* a muddy red latex and lacks any blue coloration.

Lactarius scrobiculatus (Scop.:Fr.) Fr.
NOT EDIBLE, MAYBE POISONOUS

Pileus 5–15 (-22) cm broad, broadly convex, shallow to deeply depressed in age, pale yellow to ochre-yellow, even tawny-brown over the center, sometimes with color in zones, smooth, hairless in center to matted hairs extending beyond inrolled margin in young pilei, sticky to viscid. Flesh white, staining yellow. Latex scanty, white changing quickly to sulphur-yellow. Lamellae adnate to short decurrent, crowded, whitish to light yellow, staining dark yellow. Stipe 3–6 cm long, 1–3 cm wide, equal, concolorous with the pileus with polished, bright dark orange spots, hairless, dry, hollow in age. Odorless. Taste mild to slightly acrid.

Spores 7–9 x 6.0–7.5 µm broadly elliptic to subglobose, amyloid warts and ridges, entire, thin-walled. Spore print white.

Habit and distribution: Scattered or in groups under conifers. Widely distributed. Fruiting in summer and fall.

Comments: *Lactarius torminosus* (Fr.) Gray has white unchanging latex; the stipe is not as consistently covered with shiny spots; is also widely distributed but usually with birch. Note scrobiculate means spotted. *Lactarius resimus* Fr. resembles *L. scrobiculatus* but the pileus is very light, even white at first; the stipe does not have the depressed shiny spots; it is widely distributed. All species with white latex that change to yellow should be avoided.

Lactarius chrysorheus Fr.
POISONOUS

Pileus 4–10 cm broad, convex, plane to slightly depressed in age with an elevated margin, pinkish cinnamon to cinnamon-buff, sometimes darkening to reddish cinnamon, faintly zoned with bands near margin to totally lacking bands, wavy margin in some, subviscid to sticky in wet weather. Flesh firm, white, changing rapidly to yellow. Latex copious, white, changing to deep yellow. Lamellae adnate to decurrent, close, white to pale pinkish cinnamon, often with reddish brown stains in age. Stipe 4–7 cm long, 1.0–2.25 cm wide, equal, dry, with powdery, off-white to pale pink coating, often spotted or stained brownish purple. Odorless. Taste acrid, slowly increasing with time.

Spores 6–9 x 5–7 μm short elliptic, with netlike, amyloid ridges, entire, thin-walled. Spore print light buff.

Habit and distribution: Grows in groups under hardwoods and conifers. Found in eastern United States and Canada. Fruiting in late summer and fall.

Comments: In Virginia we have found it scattered throughout the surrounding native oak and Virginia pine woods. Section *Crocei,* in Hesler and Smith (1979), in which this fungus is placed, contains a very similar West Coast species, *L. xanthogalactus* Peck (Methven, 1997). *Lactarius vinaceorufescens* A. H. Sm., a conifer associate; has dark wine-red pileus; stains wine red; and has white latex that turns yellow on exposure to air. It is found in eastern North America. *Lactarius theiogalus* Fr., commonly associated with birch, has a pinkish cinnamon to orange-cinnamon pileus; white latex that very slowly changes to yellow; and is acrid like the other species in this group. All species in which the acrid white latex changes to yellow on exposure to air should be avoided. Gastrointestinal upset, sometimes severe, can occur when they are ingested, Type 8 toxins.

Lactarius camphoratus (Bull.: Fr.) Fr.
EDIBLE

Pileus 1.4–4.5 cm broad, convex, with an umbo in age, dark brownish red, lacking zones of color, smooth, without hairs, margin inrolled at first, dry. Flesh pale or same color as pileus. Latex white, unchanging. Lamellae short decurrent, close, white to yellowish or red-brown in age. Stipe 1–5 cm long, 0.3–0.8 (-1.1) cm wide, nearly equal, concolorous with the pileus, dry, smooth, without hairs or with slight powdery cover. Taste mild or slightly bitterish. Odor aromatic and fragrant, similar to sweet clover or fenugreek and very distinctive even when dried. Taste pleasant.

Spores 6.0–8.5 x 6.0–7.5 µm subglobose, with coarse, amyloid warts, entire, thin-walled. Spore print white.

Habit and distribution: Scattered or in groups on the ground or on very rotten wood often near or under conifers. Widely distributed in northern North America. Fruiting in summer and fall.

Comments: *Lactarius fragilis* (Burl.) Hesler & A.H. Sm. is also very aromatic even dried, but the lamellae are yellow, subdistant, and the spores more heavily ornamented. It is found in the southeastern United States. *Lactarius rimosellus* Peck is an eastern United States and Canadian species that is similar in every way except that the pileus is finely cracked and it is aromatic also when dried. In this complex of species, the dried material will be aromatic after years in the herbarium.

Lactarius aquifluus Peck
EDIBILITY QUESTIONABLE

Pileus (2-) 4–12 cm broad, convex, plane with a depressed center and a small umbo, pale tan to cinnamon or light reddish gray, nearly hairless, dry. Flesh white, soft. Latex white, watery. Lamellae decurrent, close, white to yellowish with a pink tinge. Stipe 4–8 cm long, 0.5–1.5 cm wide, concolorous with the pileus, pubescent, dry. Odor of camphor even when dried. Taste mild but then very slowly becomes acrid.

Spores 6.0–8.5 x 5–6 µm subglobose to short elliptic, amyloid warts and ridges, entire, thin-walled. Spore print white.

Habit and distribution: Scattered or in groups in moss in wet areas often under conifers in a wide variety of habitats. Found in eastern and western Canada and eastern North America as well as Montana and Idaho. Fruiting in summer and fall.

Comments: This species was referred to in early guides as *Lactarius helvus* (Fr.) Fr. *Lactarius aquifluus,* though not commonly reported from western North America, is illustrated and reported by Schalkwijk-Barendsen (1991) from western Canada and we have found it in Montana and Idaho. Methven (1997) does not include it from California, but does describe *L. alpinus* var *mitis* Hesler & A. H. Sm., a similar species that is odorless.

Lactarius representaneus Britzelm.
MAYBE POISONOUS

Pileus 7–15 (-20) cm broad, convex, broadly convex-depressed, center nearly solid orange, the rest buff with orange-buff hairs, pruinose with powdery surface to glabrous in the depressed center, the rest densely wooly with long hairs that are fringed along the inrolled margin, nearly flat in age, viscid. Flesh firm, white staining lilac. Latex white, staining cut portion lilac. Lamellae decurrent, close, light buff with conspicuous lilac stains when cut or bruised. Stipe 4–8 cm long, 2–3 cm wide, slightly larger at base, dry, light orange-buff, covered with slightly depressed, shiny, orange spots, hollow or with a soft pith. Odor slightly fragrant. Taste acrid.

Spores 9–11 x 7.5–9.0 µm short elliptic, amyloid warts and ridges, entire, thin-walled. Spore print white.

Habit and distribution: Scattered or in groups under conifers. Found in the northern United States, Rocky Mountains, West Coast, Canada, and Alaska. Fruiting in late summer and fall.

Comments: We have seen this species in quantity near Juneau, Alaska, under Sitka spruce and western hemlock, and near Fairbanks, Alaska, under aspen and spruce. *Lactarius scrobiculatus* is similar with orange spots on the stipe but the latex does not stain lilac. Both species can cause gastric upset or a burning sensation in the throat.

Lactarius uvidus (Fr.) Fr.
POISONOUS

Pileus 2.5–9.0 cm broad, convex, convex-depressed sometimes with a small umbo, brownish gray to pale lavender-brown, tinted lilac, without hairs, sometimes faintly zoned, margin inrolled at first smooth, viscid. Flesh white, staining lilac. Latex white, bruised or cut areas stain lilac. Lamellae short decurrent, close, white, bruising lilac. Stipe 2.5–6.0 cm long, 1.0–1.8 cm wide, slightly larger at base, white near apex with the rest light wine-colored gray, sticky to viscid. Odorless. Taste mild at first to acrid.

Spores 7–12 x 6–8 µm broadly elliptic, amyloid high warts and ridges, entire, thin-walled. Spore print white.

Habit and distribution: Scattered or in groups under northern conifers. Widely distributed. Fruiting in summer and fall.

Comments: This species contains Type 8 toxins, therefore we do not recommend eating it .

93

Lactarius mucidus Burl.
INEDIBLE

Pileus 2.5–8.0 cm broad, convex to broadly convex with a low umbo, often depressed in age, gray-brown in center, lacking color bands, gray over the margin, which is inrolled at first, smooth, hairless, viscid. Flesh soft, very thin, stipe sometimes hollow. Latex white but stains bruised areas bluish to greenish gray. Lamellae adnate, close, narrow, shiny white, also stains bluish gray when bruised. Stipe 2–6 cm long, 0.8–1.0 cm wide, nearly equal, concolorous with the pileus, sticky to viscid, smooth, hairless, sometimes wrinkled. Odorless. Taste very acrid.

Spores 7.5–10.0 x 6–8 µm short elliptic to subglobose, amyloid ridges, entire, thin-walled. Spore print white.

Habit and distribution: Scattered or in groups in needle duff under conifers. Widely distributed. Fruiting in summer and fall.

Comments: We have found this species frequently in northern Idaho. The acrid taste would make it undesirable as an edible. A similar species, *L. vietus* (Fr.) Fr. (= *L. varius* Peck), has a moist to sometimes sticky but not viscid pileus and latex which stains the lamellae olive-gray. Another species, *L. trivialis* (Fr.) Fr., has a gray pileus which is infused with purple or drab-gray; latex that dries olive-buff and hasa yellow spore print. It is found under conifers in the western mountains and Pacific Northwest and in the northern United States and Canada under birch.

Lactarius corrugis Peck
EDIBLE

Pileus 6–12 cm broad, convex, convex-depressed in age, dark red-brown, lacking color bands, velvety, wrinkled to corrugate overall but especially pronounced over the margin, dry. Flesh firm, white, with weak brownish stains. Latex white copious, gradually staining brown. Lamellae decurrent, close, cinnamon-yellow, cut or bruised areas staining brown. Stipe 6–10 cm long, 1.5–2.5 cm wide, equal, concolorous with the pileus or somewhat lighter, dry felty. Odor not distinctive. Taste mild.

Spores 9–12 µm globose, with amyloid spines, entire, thin-walled. Spore print white.

Habit and distribution: Solitary or several together under hardwoods. Found in eastern North America. Fruiting in late summer and early fall.

Comments: *Lactarius volemus* (Fr.) Fr. has a white latex that stains brown; does not have the wrinkled pileus and is also in eastern North America. Both species are very good edibles, with latex that stains brown.

Lactarius volemus Fr.
EDIBLE

Pileus 3–7 (-12) cm broad, convex, soon convex-depressed, colors vary from hazel-brown, orange-brown to light orange-buff, smooth, hairless, sometimes with minute cracks, dry, felty. Flesh firm, pale white, stains brown when cut or bruised. Latex white, plentiful, often drips readily when cut, in air changing slowly to brown. Lamellae adnate to decurrent, close, white to pinkish buff. Stipe 2.5–6.0 (-10.0) cm long, 0.1–0.2 cm wide, nearly equal, dry, pinkish buff to light orange often streaked or stained light reddish brown, sometimes hollow in age. Odor rather disagreeable, fishy or watermelon-like, stronger after collecting. Taste mild.

Spores 7–10 µm subglobose, amyloid netlike ridges, entire, thin-walled. Spore print white.

Habit and distribution: Single or in groups in hardwood or mixed conifer-hardwood forests. Found in eastern North America. Fruiting in summer to late fall.

Comments: See *L. hygrophoroides* for a comparison. Both species are edible, but *L. volemus* is the best.

Lactarius olivaceo-umbrinus Hesler & A. H. Sm.
INEDIBLE

Pileus 5–14 cm broad, broadly convex, umbilicate to convex-depressed in age, olive-brown, darker at center, lacking color bands, few hairs at center to hairy over the margin, which is inrolled at first, sticky to viscid. Flesh firm, dull white. Latex white, unchanging. Lamellae decurrent sometimes short, crowded, dull whitish to buff, bruising black or blackish brown. Stipe 2.5–6.0 cm long, 1.2–2.5 cm wide, equal, olive-buff at apex, the rest is olive-brown, usually with spots that are darker olive-brown, dry to sticky or viscid when moist, sometimes hollow. Odorless. Taste very acrid.

Spores 7–9 x 5.5–8.0 µm subglobose, amyloid warts and reticulate ridges, entire, thin-walled. Spore print buff.

Habit and distribution: Single or in small groups in conifer forests or sometimes mixed conifer/hardwood forests. Widely distributed in Canada, Alaska, Pacific Northwest and the Rocky Mountains. Fruiting in late summer and fall.

Comments: We have found this species in Idaho under old growth stands of western white pine, and also in Washington and Alaska. It is closely related to *L. necator* (Pers.:Fr.) P. Karst., also called *L. turpis* (Weinm.) Fr. in Europe. *Lactarius atroviridis* Peck is a closely related eastern North American species, distinguished primarily by the moist to dry, rough, scabrous surface of the pileus and moist to dry stipe. It occurs in both conifer and mixed hardwood/conifer forests.

Lactarius sordidus Peck
INEDIBLE

Pileus 5–10 cm broad, broadly convex to nearly plane and depressed in center in age, yellow-brown or dark olivaceous tinted in the depressed pileus center, moist to dry, with a felty surface. Flesh firm, white with a faint pinkish hue. Latex white and very acrid. Lamellae very short decurrent, close, white with brown stains in age. Stipe 4–8 cm long, 1.0–1.8 cm wide, equal or enlarging toward the base, dry, nearly white, with deep olivaceous brown shiny spots over the stipe. Odorless. Taste very acrid.

Spores 6–8 x 5.5–7.0 µm broadly elliptic, with a well-developed amyloid reticulum, entire, thin-walled. Spore print white to pale buff.

Habit and distribution: Several on the ground under conifers or occasionally hardwood/conifer forests. Widely distributed from North Carolina to Canada and west to Alaska, the Yukon, and British Columbia. Fruiting in late summer to fall.

Comments: See comments under *L. olivaceo-umbrinus* for the closely related species.

Lactarius lignyotus Fr.
NONPOISONOUS

Pileus 2–10 cm broad, convex to broadly convex, with an umbo, strikingly blackish brown, sometimes wrinkled, velvety, dry. Flesh brittle, white, staining rose to pink where bruised. Latex white, thin and watery, staining flesh pinkish. Lamellae attached or short decurrent, distant, white, bruising red, brown edges near stipe. Stipe 4–10 cm long, 0.4–1.5 cm wide, equal, concolorous with the pileus, dry, furrowed near apex, smooth, with a powdery, velvety cover below. Odorless. Taste slightly acrid or mild.

Spores 9–11 x 8–10 µm subglobose, amyloid ridges, entire, thin-walled. Spore print deep buff.

Habit and distribution: Several or in groups, often in moss, sometimes in bogs, under conifers, especially pine. Found in eastern North America. Fruiting in summer and fall.

Comments: We have seen this beautiful species under eastern white pine in New Hampshire in late summer. *Lactarius fallax* A. H. Sm. & Hesler is under conifers on the West Coast and is similar but has close to crowded lamellae (Methven, 1997). *Lactarius gerardii* Peck has well separated lamellae; a white spore print; and is found under hardwood and mixed woods in eastern North America. *Lactarius fumosus* Peck has a smoky white to smoky brown pileus; crowded lamellae; small round spores 6–8 µm with amyloid interrupted ridges; and is under conifers or mixed conifer hardwood forests in eastern North America. All of these species have pink to red stains when bruised.

Lactarius deceptivus Peck
INEDIBLE

Pileus 7–20 cm broad, robust, convex to plane or depressed in center in age, white with yellowish or brown stains, margin when young a thick cottony roll and inrolled. dry, glabrous. Flesh white, firm. Latex white, unchanging, slowly stains tissue brown. Lamellae adnate or short decurrent, crowded, white, soon cream color bruising dingy brown. Stipe 4–10 cm long, 1.0–3.5 cm wide dry, white, also stains brown in age. Odorless. Taste very acrid.

Spores 9–12 x 7.5–9.5 µm elliptic, isolated amyloid warts and spines, entire, thin-walled. Spore print white to pale buff.

Habit and distribution: One to several in conifer forests. Found in eastern North America. Fruiting from spring to fall.

Comments: *Lactarius subvellerius* Peck looks very similar but lacks the distinctive cottony roll on the pileus margin; has smaller spores (7.5–9.0 x 5.5–7.0 µm); also found in eastern North America. It is often very common in the fall in the Southeast. If no latex is found, especially in dry weather, or the lamellae show a green tint, one should compare it with *Russula brevipes* Peck (often incorrectly called *R. delica* Fr. in North America).

Lactarius piperatus (L.:Fr.) Gray
POISONOUS

Pileus 4–12 cm broad, convex-depressed to deeply depressed in age, dull white, smooth, hairless, azonate, margin inrolled at first but upturned in age, dry. Flesh thick, firm, white. Latex copious, white, unchanging. Lamellae decurrent, narrow, crowded, forked, white to cream in age. Stipe 2–6 cm long, 1–2 cm wide, equal or narrowed downward, white, dry, smooth, hairless. Odorless. Taste very acrid.

Spores 6.0–8.5 x 6.0–6.5 µm subglobose, amyloid warts and ridges, entire, thin-walled. Spore print white.

Habit and distribution: Scattered to numerous under hardwood forests. Found throughout eastern North America. Fruiting in summer and fall.

Comments: *Lactarius piperatus* var *glaucescens* (Cross.) Hesler & A. H. Sm. is identical, except that the latex dries olive-green. One must also be careful to compare this species with *L. vellereus* (Fr.) Fr., which has a wooly cap; distant gills that do not fork; and a white latex that stains the bruised or cut surface brown. Type 8 toxins have been reported, therefore we do not recommend eating these species.

Lactarius rufus (Scop.:Fr.) Fr.
POISONOUS

Pileus 5–10 cm broad, convex with an umbo to convex-depressed or plane with a depressed center, even red-brown to dark reddish chestnut, lacking bands of color, smooth, hairless, moist to dry. Flesh white with a pinkish tinge, hollow in stipe in age. Latex white, unchanging. Lamellae decurrent, close, light orange to pinkish salmon. Stipe 3–9 cm long, 0.8–1.5 cm wide, equal or slightly narrowed downward, salmon color to light red-brown, dry, smooth, hairless or sometimes with slight powdery surface. Odorless. Taste very acrid.

Spores 7–9 x 5–7 µm broadly elliptic, amyloid reticulations, entire, thin-walled. Spore print white.

Habit and distribution: Scattered or in groups in wet areas under conifers. Widely distributed. Fruiting in summer and fall.

Comments: Gastric upset could result from ingesting *L. rufus* or any other red-brown, very acrid species; see Type 8 toxins.

Lactarius affinis Peck
NONPOISONOUS

Pileus 5–15 cm broad, convex-umbilicate, rich yellow-brown, almost butterscotch color, lacking color bands, smooth, hairless, viscid, even slimy. Flesh firm to soft, white to cream, yellowish brown just under pileus cuticle. Latex white, copious, unchanging. Lamellae short decurrent or nearly adnate, subdistant, buff, staining brown. Stipe 2.5–8.0 cm long, 1.4–2.4 cm wide, equal, buff, often with stains the color of the pileus, smooth, hairless, viscid. Odorless. Taste strongly acrid.

Spores 8.5–11.0 x 7.0–8.5 µm subglobose to short elliptical, with amyloid warts and ridges, entire, thin-walled. Spore print white.

Habit and distribution: Scattered or in groups, sometimes abundant, under conifers (especially spruce), or mixed forests. Found in eastern North America. Fruiting in summer and fall.

Comments: *Russula laurocerasi* has a somewhat similar pileus and could be confused with this species, but it is aromatic, and has no latex (Hesler & Smith, 1979).

Lactarius hygrophoroides Berk. & M. A. Curtis
EDIBLE

Pileus 2.5–10.0 cm broad, convex, convex-depressed in age, yellowish to yellow-brown, lacking color bands, dry, appearing velvety. Flesh brittle, pale white, unchanging when bruised. Latex white, copious, unchanging in air. Lamellae short decurrent, subdistant, white to buff or cream color. Stipe 2–5 cm long, 0.8–2.0 cm wide, equal, concolorous with the pileus, often bright yellow near base, without fibrils. Odor mild. Taste mild.

Spores 7–10 x 6–7 µm broadly elliptic to subglobose, amyloid ridges, entire, thin-walled. Spore print white.

Habit and distribution: Single to scattered under hardwood forests. Found in eastern North America. Fruiting in summer and fall.

Comments: In this species the white latex drips copiously from the cut lamellae. It is edible, if found in sufficient quantity.

Lactarius griseus Peck
NONPOISONOUS

Pileus 0.9–3.0 (-5.0) cm broad, broadly convex to convex-depressed in age, grayish brown, grayish pink, pale gray to wine-red, squamulose in center, margin nearly smooth. Flesh firm, white, dry. Latex white, sparse, unchanging. Lamellae decurrent, close, buff to cream. Stipe 1.3–2.5 cm long, 0.2–0.6 cm wide, light pinkish to light cinnamon, equal, dry, minutely roughened to hairless. Odorless. Taste slightly acrid.

Spores 6–9 x 5–7 µm broadly elliptic to subglobose, amyloid warts and ridges, entire, thin-walled. Spore print white.

Habit and distribution: Scattered or in groups in moss or on well-decayed wood in wet areas under conifers. Found in eastern North America. Fruiting in summer and fall.

Comments: The latex in this species can dry yellowish or stain paper yellow. Only *L. cinereus* Peck may sometimes be as small, but it has a viscid pileus; white lamellae; and a dry, ashy-colored stipe.

Lactarius oculatus (Peck) Burl.
EDIBILITY UNKNOWN

Pileus 1.5–5.0 cm broad, convex to plane, and depressed in center in age, with a small umbo, orange-red, maroon-red to reddish tan, lacking bands of color, smooth, hairless, waxy and moist (may seem viscid). Flesh white, does not bruise. Latex white, unchanging. Lamellae short decurrent, close, buff to salmon or light flesh color. Stipe 1.2–4.0 cm long, 0.3–1.0 cm wide, equal, nearly white near apex to orange-brown, darker in age, smooth, hairless, often hollow. Odorless. Taste mild, acrid, or faintly acrid to bitter with time.

Spores 7–10 x 6–8 µm broadly elliptic, low amyloid warts, entire, thin-walled. Spore print buff.

Habit and distribution: Scattered or in groups, usually along the edges of wet areas or sometimes in bogs under conifers, less commonly under mixed conifers and hardwoods. Found in eastern North America. Fruiting in spring, summer, and fall.

Comments: *Lactarius subdulcis* (Bull.:Fr.) Gray is an older taxon and its presence in North America is in doubt, according to Hesler and Smith (1979). However, in the western North America, *Lactarius alpinus* Peck is a part of a complex of very similar species with a mild taste and a white spore print. We have found it under conifers in Idaho and Alaska. Methven (1997) records it under conifer/hardwood forests on the Pacific Coast and it is discussed by Arora (1986). Since it is a complex of species, edibility is questionable.

TRICHOLOMATACEAE, PLEUROTACEAE, AND ALLIES

Genera of the Tricholomataceae, Pleurotaceae, and Allies include species on the ground, humus, plant parts, wood, and stumps. The fruiting bodies range from centrally stipitate, eccentrically stipitate, or lack a stipe. The spores are white, buff, to light pinkish. They are globose, subglobose, elliptic, or fusiform, smooth or with warts or spines, and can be amyloid, dextrinoid to nonamyloid.

This is an artificial assemblage of agarics. They are composed of decomposers, parasites, and mycorrhizal fungi. They are presented as a group for the purpose of identification. In the white to buff-spored mushrooms, there are three families (Amanitaceae, Hygrophoraceae, and Lepiotaceae), one order (Russulales), and the Tricholomataceae, Pleurotaceae and Allies for a total of five white-spored groups. It is possible to diagnose each of these groups to arrive at the group in which your fungus belongs. The Amanitaceae and Lepiotaceae families have free lamellae; the Hygrophoraceae have waxy attached lamellae; and the Russulales have brittle flesh, no annulus, amyloid spore ornamentation, and latex in *Lactarius.* These three families, and one order, the Russulales, are almost always found growing on the ground. Therefore, any white-spored fungus that grows on wood, cones, or other mushrooms, or does not meets the criteria described above is a member of the Tricholomataceae.

Within the Tricholomataceae, Pleurotaceae and Allies, it is somewhat more difficult to distinguish the various genera. We have arbitrarily divided them into six groups. Each group includes species that can be recognized in some specific way. **Group I** includes the species on soil or that are mycorrhizal. **Group II** is species on conifer cones, magnolia cones, nut husks or parasitize mushrooms. **Group III** is species that have no stipe or have a short plug of tissue. **Group IV** has serrate edges of the lamellae. **Group V** is those on wood with a well-developed stipe. **Group VI** includes the small mushrooms with stipes and is all decomposers. It may be desirable to use the key to Group III, but if you are not satisfied with the key choices, try the Group V key. In this way characters such as the length or presence of a stipe in a given species can be searched out in two keys.

Edibility: There are many edible fungi in the Tricholomataceae, Pleurotaceae and Allies and very few species that are poisonous. Probably the most toxic species known in this group is *Clitocybe dealbata* (Type 6 toxins), although some species of *Tricholoma* are poisonous and can cause severe gastric upset (Type 8 toxins). Many genera, including *Tricholoma*, have not been thoroughly studied in North America. Some species of *Collybia* are known to cause severe gastrointestinal disturbances (see *Gymnopus dryophilus*), (Type 8 toxins). Many other species are too small, tough or bitter to be suited for the table. Species of *Pleurotus, Hypsizygus, Flammulina,* and *Lentinula* are very good edibles and some are grown commercially in North America and Asia (Stamets, 2000).

KEY TO TRICHOLOMATACEAE, PLEUROTACEAE AND ALLIES

1. Fruiting body on conifer cones, magnolia cones, nut husks, parasitizing mushrooms or on forest litter, wood, needles, leaves -- 2
1. Fruiting body on the ground, or soil --- Group I
  2. Mushrooms on conifer cones, magnolia cones, nut husks or parasitizing mushrooms --- Group II
  2. Mushrooms on wood, forest litter, needles or leaves ----------------------------------- 3
3. Stipe absent or a short plug of tissue or with serrate lamellae----------------------------- 4
3. Not as above --- 5
    4. Stipe absent or a short plug of tissue; lamellae not serrate, on wood ------ Group III
    4. Stipe absent or present; with serrate lamellae; on wood or plant debris---- Group IV
5. Large fleshy mushrooms, 3–40 cm broad; with thicker stipes, 0.4–2.5 cm wide; pileus convex, margin inrolled at first or not; not reviving when moistened-------------- Group V
5. Small mushrooms, 0.3–4.0 (occasionally up to 6.0 cm) broad; with thin stipes, 0.05–0.4 cm wide; pileus either opening umbrella-like or reviving when moistened------ Group VI

GROUP I
KEY TO THE GENERA IN THE TRICHOLOMATACEAE ON SOIL OR ARE MYCORRHIZAL

1. Partial veil double; pileus robust; spores elliptic to fusiform, amyloid ---- *Catathelasma*
1. Not as above --- 2

2. Lamellae pink, pinkish buff to light or dark purple; spores spiny, entire, nonamyloid-- *Laccaria*

2. Not as above--- 3

3. Pileus with an orange-brown to cinnamon-brown, fine granular surface; spores smooth, entire, amyloid or not --- *Cystoderma*

3. Not as above -- 5

    4. Pileus with bright yellow, mustard yellow to cinnamon-brown scales; partial veil cottony, white with a ragged ring; spores elliptic, smooth, amyloid--- *Floccularia albolanaripes*

    4. Not as above--- 6

5. Spores with amyloid warts; fruiting body with a tall, thin stipe; partial veil absent; cystidia lancelike, encrusted; clamp connections absent ------------------------- *Melanoleuca*

5. Not as above -- 6

    6. Fruiting body either robust and in dense clusters with round spores, or lamellae blue to black when bruised with the fingers --------------------------------- *Lyophyllum*

    6. Not as above --- 7

7. Pileus chalk white to brown; spores globose to elliptic, smooth or with amyloid warts; partial veil absent -- *Leucopaxillus*

7. Pileus dull white or variously colored; spores elliptic, nonamyloid; partial veil present --- *Tricholoma*

CATATHELASMA

There are two large North American species, 8–40 cm broad, with decurrent lamellae, and a robust stipe, 6–18 cm long and 3–8 cm wide. The partial veil is double with a membranous, outer veil and a soft, inner veil. Spores are elliptic to fusiform, smooth, entire, thin-walled, amyloid. They are terrestrial under conifers with which they are putatively ectomycorrhizal.

Edibility: The species are edible and good.

KEY TO CATATHELASMA

1. Pileus 15–40 cm broad, viscid when wet, cinnamon-buff, flushed olive to dark brown in age; spores 9.5–15.5 x 4.5–6.0 µm fusiform, smooth, entire, thin-walled, amyloid -- *C. imperialis*

1. Pileus 8–10 cm broad, dry, pale gray to ash-gray; spores 9.5–16.0 x 5.0–5.8 µm elliptic, smooth, entire, thin-walled, amyloid-------------------------------------- *C. ventricosa*

Catathelasma imperialis (Fr.) Singer
EDIBLE

Pileus 15–40 cm broad, convex, broadly convex to plane in age, somewhat cracked at the center, cinnamon-buff, sometimes flushed olive to dark brown in age, margin incurved at first, outer veil continuous with the margin in buttons, viscid when wet, soon dry. Flesh very thick, firm, white. Lamellae decurrent, close, broad, forked, buff to olive-gray. Stipe 12–18 cm long, 6–8 cm wide, tapering to a dull point at base, dull white. Partial veil double, outer veil membranous and attached to upper pileus margin, pinkish buff to brownish, inner veil softer, with clusters of hairs attached to lower margin of pileus, leaving a persistent, superior, double ring which flares upward at first. Odor not distinctive. Taste mild.

Spores 9.5–15.5 x 4.5–6.0 µm fusiform, smooth, entire, thin-walled, amyloid. Spore print white.

Habit and distribution: Single or several together under conifers, especially spruce and fir. Found in western North America, but most common in the western mountains. Fruiting in the summer and fall.

Comments: The buttons are often 15 centimeters (6 inches) thick and very robust. It is non-poisonous and some people eat it. In Alaska people have pickled this mushroom and canned it for use in the winter. We have eaten it and it is delicious prepared this way. The Alaskans have called it the "Potato Mushroom" because the flesh is so firm it reminds them of a raw potato.

Catathelasma ventricosa (Peck) Singer
EDIBLE

Pileus 8–10 cm broad, convex, broadly convex in age, pale gray to ash-gray, smooth, hairless, dry. Flesh firm, white. Lamellae decurrent, close to fairly well separated, often forked, pinkish buff. Stipe 6–8 cm long, 3–4 cm wide, tapering to a narrow base, dry, white above the ring, dull yellow-brown below. Partial veil pale white, tinted gray, with a white, hairy, inner veil, leaving a superior, persistent, double ring that flares upward at first. Odor not distinctive. Taste mild.

Spores 9.5–16.0 x 5.0–5.8 µm elliptic, smooth, entire, thin-walled, amyloid. Spore print white.

Habit and distribution: Solitary or several, under conifers. Found most commonly in western North America, occasionally found in eastern North America. Fruiting in late summer and fall.

Comments: Pomerleau (1980) reports this species from eastern Canada and we have collected it in Virginia, but it is rare. We have not eaten it but it is reported as good, and it is common in wet years in Idaho.

LACCARIA

The lamellae in *Laccaria* are adnate to short decurrent, pinkish buff, pink to violet or purple. The pileus is convex, often depressed in center and pinkish brown, red-brown, violet, dingy gray, brown to dull white. The spores are elliptic to globose with spines but smooth in one species, entire, thin-walled, nonamyloid. This is a widespread, ectomycorrhizal genus with more than 28 species and varieties that are found in a wide variety of habitats with both hardwoods and conifers (Mueller, 1992).

Edibility: The species of *Laccaria* are not toxic and several are listed as good edibles.

KEY TO THE GENUS LACCARIA

1. Pileus 4–13 cm broad, dull white; lamellae distant, purple; spores 8–10 µm globose, spiny -- *L. ochropurpurea*
1. Not as above --- 2
    2. Pileus 2.5–6.0 cm broad, dingy brown, covered with sand; lamellae pink to purple; spores smooth; in sand dunes or very sandy soil, eastern North America --- *L. trullisata*
    2. Not as above-- 3
3. Pileus 0.7–3.0 cm broad, very small, orange-brown, striate; lamellae pale flesh color; in Arctic tundra to boreal forest habitats; spores 10–16 x 9.5–14.5 µm subglobose, spiny -- *L. pumila*
3. Pileus larger; spores smaller; in different habitats --------------------------------------- 4
    4. Pileus 1–8 cm broad, pinkish brown, pinkish orange to orange-brown; lamellae orange-buff to pink; stipe smooth, pinkish brown with loose scales in age; spores 5–10 x 7–10 µm globose, spiny--------------------------------- *L. laccata* var *pallidifolia*
        (with violet basal mycelium, see *L. bicolor* under comments)
    4. Not as above--- 5
5. Pileus 1–3 cm broad, fibrillose, scaly, violet to violet-gray; lamellae violet gray; stipe violet to violet gray, fibrillose; spores 7–10 x 6.5–10.0 µm globose, spiny ---- *L. amethystina*
        (see comments under *L. laccata* var *pallidifolia*)
5. Pileus 1.5–8.0 cm broad, fibrillose to fibrillose-scaly, reddish brown to orange-brown; lamellae pinkish flesh color; stipe fibrillose, longitudinally striate; spores 8–10 x 7.0–8.7 µm broadly elliptic; found in spring and summer ----------------------- *L. proxima*
        (see comments under *L. laccata* var *pallidifolia*)

Laccaria ochropurpurea (Berk.) Peck
EDIBLE

Pileus 4–13 cm broad, convex, nearly plane in age, dull whitish to light gray, nearly hairless, dry. Flesh tough, dull whitish. Lamellae adnate, broad, distant, thick, light to dark purple. Stipe 5–19 cm long, 1.0–3.5 cm wide, equal or variable in shape, often curved, concolorous with the pileus, smooth, glabrous, dry. Partial veil absent. Odorless. Taste slightly acrid, disagreeable.

Spores 8–10 µm globose, spiny, entire, thin-walled, nonamyloid. Spore print pale lilac.

Habit and distribution: Single or several under hardwoods or in openings in forests. Widely distributed only in eastern North America. Fruiting in summer and early fall.

Comments: This large, coarse species is most likely a mycorrhizal associate of oaks. We have no personal information on its edibility.

Laccaria trullisata (Ellis) Peck
NONPOISONOUS

Pileus 2.5–6.0 cm broad, convex to broadly convex, flattened, small scales, dingy light brown, with dark brown spots and stains, always covered with sand, margin inrolled at first but straight and split in age, sometimes deeply, moist to tacky. Flesh firm, light brown. Lamellae adnate, well separated, thick, pink to purple. Stipe 3–8 cm long, 0.8–2.0 cm wide, enlarging toward base, curved, twisted, pinkish at first to dingy dull brown, covered with embedded sand particles. Mycelium around base is violet and also covered with sand. Partial veil absent. Odor and taste unknown.

Spores 16–21 x 6.0–7.5 µm long elliptic, slightly tapered at ends, smooth, entire, thin-walled, nonamyloid. Spore print white.

Habit and distribution: Single or several in one place, sometimes cespitose in clusters of two or three. Found in sand dunes or very sandy soil, after wet weather in eastern North America. Fruiting in summer and fall.

Comments: We have collected this species several years in a row in nearly pure sand near a log road in Maryland near the Patuxent River. The pileus is sometimes the only part of the fungus that shows and the rest is buried in the soft sand, which clings to all parts, including the lamellae. *Laccaria maritima* (Theodor.) Singer is in some marine habitats in eastern Canada; has elliptic, spiny spores; and white basal mycelium (Mueller, 1992).

Laccaria pumila Fayod
NONPOISONOUS

Pileus 0.7–1.5 (-3.0) cm broad, convex to plane in age, orange-brown to red-brown, with strong striations, smooth, hairless, dry. Flesh very thin, orange to reddish. Lamellae adnate, distant, thick, pale orange color. Stipe 1–3 (-6) cm long, 0.15–0.5 cm wide, orange to reddish orange as in the pileus, dry. Partial veil absent. Odorless. Taste mild.

Spores 10–16 x 9.5–14.5 µm subglobose to broadly elliptic, spines 0.5–1.4 µm, entire, thin-walled, nonamyloid. Spore print white. Basidia always 2-spored.

Habit and distribution: Several to many in Arctic and alpine tundra, and boreal forests under willows, birch and pines. Found in Alaska, Canada, and the Rocky Mountains. Fruiting in summer and fall.

Comments: *Laccaria pumila* is the only arctic and alpine tundra species with 2-spored basidia. *Laccaria montana* Singer is very similar in Arctic and Rocky Mountain tundra habitats, but it has 4-spored basidia (Mueller,1992). Both of these species are mycorrhizal with willow and dwarf birch in tundra and montane habitats.

Laccaria laccata (Fr.) Berk. & Broome var pallidifolia (Peck) Peck
NONPOISONOUS

Pileus 1–4 (-8) cm broad, convex, plane or with upraised margin in age, pinkish brown, pinkish orange to dark orange-brown, smooth, hairless, margin sometimes wavy and uneven, dry to moist. Flesh thin, color of pileus. Lamellae short decurrent, well separated, thick, orange-buff to pink. Stipe 2–10 cm long, 0.4–0.8 cm wide, nearly equal, dry, smooth, hairless, but with scattered loose scales in age, concolorous with the pileus. Partial veil absent. Odor not distinct. Taste mild.

Spores 7.5–10.0 x 7–10 µm globose, with minute, short spines, entire, thin-walled, nonamyloid. Spore print white.

Habit and distribution: Single, scattered to abundant, on damp soil, moss, and in extremely variable habitats, associated with birch, alder, beech, pine, and others. Widely distributed. Fruiting in spring, summer, and fall.

Comments: This variety of *Laccaria laccata* is one of the most common mushrooms in North America; fruiting from taiga in Alaska to deep southern hardwood/pine forests according to Mueller (1992). *Laccaria laccata* var *laccata* (Scop.:Fr.) Cooke is not commonly collected. *Laccaria proxima* (Boud.) Pat. has an orange-brown, scaly pileus; a fibrillose, longitudinally striate, orange-brown stipe; commonly found associated with pines; and is widely distributed. *Laccaria amethystina* (Bolton ex Hook.) Murrill is a small, similar species, but colored deep violet overall and a good edible. *Laccaria bicolor* (Maire) P. D. Orton is also similar, but often has mycelium over the violet base and a more roughened stipe. The edibility of *Laccaria laccata* var *pallidifolia* is rated as fairly good.

CYSTODERMA

These are small mushrooms with a granular to floccose or squamulose pileus (2–8 cm broad). A partial veil with sphaerocysts (large round cells) is always present. The stipe is granulose below the partial veil. Lamellae are adnate and not waxy. Spores are smooth, entire, thin-walled, and either amyloid or nonamyloid. Smith and Singer (1945) and Miller (1993) report 14 species in North America. *Cystoderma* appears to be related to *Lepiota*.

Edibility: There are no reports of toxic species in the genus. We have no reports on the edibility among the species

KEY TO CYSTODERMA

1. Pileus yellow-brown to orange-brown, radially rugulose and granulose; stipe granulose and orange-brown below the partial veil; spores 4.5–7.5 x 2.5–3.5 µm elliptic, amyloid; in moss under conifers -- *C. amianthinum*
1. Not as above -- 2
   2. Pileus dark rusty brown, with erect granulose scales; stipe granulose with a persistent, flaring partial veil; spores 3.5–5.0 x 2.8–3.6 µm elliptic, amyloid; in humus and duff under West Coast conifer forests--------------------------------------- *C. fallax*
                    (see comments under *C. amianthinum*)
   2. Pileus another color, not as above --- 3
3. Pileus orange-brown, densely granular, with small, sharp pointed scales; spores 3.5–5.0 x 2.5–3.5 µm elliptic, nonamyloid; odor farinaceous; on conifer duff; widely distributed --- *C. terreii*
3. Pileus yellowish to orange-cinnamon, conic, granular scales; spores 3.5–5.0 x 2.5–3.0 µm elliptic, nonamyloid; odor mild; on moss under hardwoods and conifers, widely distributed --- *C. granulosum*
                    (see comments under *C. terreii*)

Cystoderma amianthinum (Scop.:Fr.)
Fayod
NONPOISONOUS

Pileus 1.5–4.5 cm broad, convex to broadly
convex, yellow-brown to yellow-orange, radially
rugulose, granulose, often forming granular
scales, margin with conspicuous flaps of veil
tissue, dry. Flesh firm, white, thin. Lamellae
adnate to adnexed, close to crowded in age,
edges even, orange-yellow to buff. Stipe 2.5–6.0
cm long, 0.2–0.7 cm wide, equal or slightly
enlarged downward, has a powdery cover, pale
buff above ring, densely granulose below and
concolorous with the pileus. Partial veil silky
above, granulose below, fragile, soon breaking to
form a superior, poorly formed ring and leaving
pieces hanging from pileus margin. Odor weak to
that of geraniums. Taste unpleasant.

Spores 4.5–7.5 x 2.5–3.5 μm, elliptic, smooth,
entire, thin-walled, amyloid. Spore print white.

Habit and distribution: Single or in dense troops,
usually in moss, under conifers. Widely
distributed. Fruiting in summer and fall.

Comments: *Cystoderma fallax* A. H. Sm. & Singer
is a species found in western North America with
an upward flaring, persistent ring and a more
rusty pileus color.

Cystoderma terreii Berk. & Broome
NONPOISONOUS

Pileus 3–8 cm broad, ovoid, convex, often with a
broad umbo, orange-brown to cinnamon-brown,
densely granular and covered with small sharp-
pointed scales, dense at center, margin incurved
with hanging veil fragments at first, dry. Flesh
thin, pale buff near pileus cuticle, rest light
orange to light rusty brown. Lamellae adnate to
nearly free in age, close to crowded, thin, white,
edges minutely roughened. Stipe 3–6 cm long,
0.6–1.5 cm wide, nearly equal, with a powdery
cover above ring, covered below with granules
similar to and concolorous with the pileus. Partial
veil fragile, granulose leaving a thin ring that
soon disappears and hanging pieces on pileus
margin. Odor farinaceous. Taste mild.

Spores 3.5–5.0 x 2.5–3.5 μm elliptic, smooth,
entire, thin-walled, nonamyloid. Spore print
white.

Habit and distribution: In humus, needle duff, or
in well-decayed conifer wood in conifer or
hardwood stands. Widely distributed. Fruiting in
late summer and fall.

Comments: This species was previously known as
C. cinnabarinum (Alb. & Schwein.) Konrad &
Maubl. *Cystoderma granulosum* (Batsch.:Fr.) P.
Kühner also has nonamyloid spores; is similar in
size and shape, but small in stature; lacks the
farinaceous odor; and is dark reddish brown
(Miller, 1993).

FLOCCULARIA

The species of *Floccularia* have elliptic, smooth, entire, thin-walled, amyloid spores; a pileipellis of interwoven hyphae; and lack cystidia. They are terrestrial and most likely are mycorrhizal.

Edibility: Although they are listed as edible, we have not tried either species.

Floccularia albolanaripes G. F. Atk.
EDIBLE

Pileus 5–12 cm broad, convex, broadly convex to plane, sometimes with an obscure low umbo, margin viscid to moist over center, bright yellow to mustard-yellow with rich reddish to cinnamon-brown flattened scales and hairs over the center, which darken in age, margin inrolled somewhat at first and covered with ragged, pure white veil remnants. Flesh firm, white to yellow beneath cap cuticle. Lamellae adnexed, fairly well separated, broad, white to cream or yellowish in age, edges often toothlike. Stipe 3–8 cm long, 1.0–2.5 cm wide, equal, smooth, shiny white above cottony ring, covered with shiny, ragged, white scales below, staining yellowish or even dingy yellow-brown in age. Partial veil fragile, cottony, white leaving a ragged, short, superior ring that hangs skirtlike. Odorless. Taste mild.

Spores 5–7 x 3.0–4.5 µm elliptic, smooth, entire, thin-walled, amyloid. Spore print white.

Habit and distribution: Solitary to several under western conifers. Found in the Pacific Northwest and Rocky Mountains. Fruiting in the spring and summer.

Comments: This species was formerly put in the genus *Armillaria*. We have often found this species on hard ground beside roads or on road banks. It could be confused with *Floccularia straminea* var *americana* (Krombh.) Mitchel & A.H.Sm. (= *F. luteovirens* (A. & S.:Fr.) Pouz) which has yellow scales on the pileus but looks very similar (Evenson, 1997). We have not tried to eat it, but it is listed as an edible.

MELANOLEUCA

The genus is characterized by the tall, thin stipe, lack of an annulus or partial veil, combined with the convex, umbonate, wide pileus. Unlike *Leucopaxillus* the stipe and lamellae differ in that they are not chalky white. In fact many species of *Melanoleuca* have brown or gray brown fibrils on the stipe. Anatomically the genus does not have hyphae with clamp connections. The spores are usually elliptic with amyloid warts, entire, thin-walled, and the cystidia, when present, are fusiform, bottle-shaped to club-shaped, often with crystals at the apex and sometimes with secondary septa. They occur on the ground, in fields and woods. The only North American study of the genus is by Gillman and Miller (1977). *Leucopaxillus* has very similar spores; however it lacks cystidia and always has clamp connections on the hyphae (Fig. 25). The chalky white, thick stipe and decurrent lamellae and often farinaceous odor and/or taste are distinctive field characters.

Edible: However, there is not very much tissue to eat and few people actually eat these species.

KEY TO MELANOLEUCA

1. Pileus 3–10 cm broad, plane with a low umbo, dry, white, tinted pale yellow-brown; stipe thin, white to dingy white -- *M. alboflavida*
1. Not as above -- 2
　　2. Pileus 3–10 cm broad, orange-brown to gray-brown; stipe tinted light tan -- *M. cognata*
　　　　　　　(see comments under *M. melaleuca*)
　　2. Pileus brown to dark brown; stipe ochre-brown to dark brown ------------------------- 3
3. Pileus 3–7 cm broad, dark umber-brown to chestnut-brown; stipe dark brown to chestnut-brown over lower half--- *M. angelesiana*
　　　　　　　(see comments under *M. melaleuca*)
3. Pileus 2–8 cm broad; smoky brown; stipe white, tinted brown over lower half --- *M. melaleuca*

Melanoleuca alboflavida (Peck) Murrill
NONPOISONOUS

Pileus 3–10 cm broad, convex, in age plane sometimes with a low umbo and margin uplifted, whitish or tinted pale yellow brown, smooth, hairless, dry. Flesh firm white or tinted gray in the stipe. Lamellae adnate, medium broad, crowded, white or pale cream in age. Stipe 3.0–11.5 cm long, 0.4–1.1 cm wide, equal with a small basal bulb, white to dingy white with minute longitudinal striations, dry. Odor not distinctive. Taste mild.

Spores 7.5–9.0 x 4.0–5.5 µm elliptic, with small, amyloid warts, entire, thin-walled. Spore print white. Pleuro- and cheilocystidia fusiform to bottle-shaped, some with crystals at the apex.

Habit and distribution: Several in open ground, fields, or in mixed woods. Found in eastern and central North America as far north as Quebec. Fruiting in summer and early fall.

Comments: Also known as *Melanoleuca subalpina* (Britzelm.) Bresinsky & Stangl. *Melanoleuca evenosa* (Sacc.) Konrad is somewhat similar but has a white to cream-colored pileus; close lamellae which are tinted pink; and similar sized spores. However, it is found in conifer forests in the Rocky Mountains in the spring and early summer and in the northern boreal forests of Alaska and Canada (Gillman and Miller, 1977).

Melanoleuca melaleuca (Pers.:Fr.) Murrill
NONPOISONOUS

Pileus 2–8 cm broad, broadly convex, plane with a low umbo and upturned margin in age, smoky brown to dark brown, smooth, without hairs, margin wavy or straight, moist to dry. Flesh thin, white to tinted brown only in the lower stipe. Lamellae adnexed, close, broad in center, white. Stipe 2.5–12.0 cm long, 0.4–0.9 cm wide, equal or slightly swollen at the base, white or tinted brown, minutely hairy, appearing longitudinally striate, dry. Partial veil absent. Odorless. Taste mild.

Spores 6–8 x 4.0–5.5 µm elliptic, with amyloid warts, entire, thin-walled. Spore print white. Cystidia lancelike, incrusted at apex, forming a harpoonlike tip. Clamp connections absent.

Habit and distribution: Solitary or scattered in pastures and open woods. Widely distributed. Fruiting in summer in eastern North America, and both summer and fall in western North America.

Comments: *Melanoleuca melaleuca* is eaten in Europe and is probably edible in North America, but we have no specific information on it. *Melanoleuca cognata* (Fr.) Konrad & Maubl. has a convex, orange to red-brown pileus; deep ochre lamellae; a rancid odor; and large spores (7.5–10.0 x 5.0–6.5 µm). *Melanoleuca angelesiana* A.H. Sm. is smaller, with a dark brown pileus; white close lamellae; and a light brown stipe. It is found very commonly on the ground in spring often near melting snow banks in the Rocky Mountains (Bessette et al., 1995.)

LYOPHYLLUM

The fruiting bodies are fleshy, dry to moist, metallic gray to gray-brown with lamellae that are adnate to short decurrent, staining bluish to black or not staining at all. The stipe is brittle to fleshy and there is no partial veil. The spores are elliptic to subglobose, smooth, entire, thin-walled. The basidia have siderophilous granulations when treated as described in the glossary. Several species form dense cespitose clusters on the ground and are possibly mycorrhizal. Two other genera, *Calocybe* Kühner:Donk and *Tephrocybe* Donk, are closely related and have siderophilous granulations in the basidia. However, none are monographed in North America. Moser (1983) presents keys to the species in Europe.

Edibility: *Lyophyllum decastes* and *L. multiforme* are edible, while *L. infumatum* and *L. semitale* are not.

KEY TO SPECIES OF LYOPHYLLUM

1. Pileus large, 6–14 cm broad, gray to gray-brown; lamellae not staining; in cespitose clusters on the ground --- *L. decastes*
     (If pileus is nearly white, *L. multiforme,* see comments under *L. decastes*)
1.   Pileus smaller; lamellae stain blue to black; not in cespitose clusters -------------------- 2
    2. Pileus 1–6 cm broad, subviscid, gray to pinkish gray; lamellae white; bruising blue, soon turning black; odor and taste mild ------------------------------------- *L. infumatum*
    2. Pileus 2–5 cm broad, pinkish brown to beige-brown; lamellae cream color, slowly bruising directly to black; odor rancid; taste slightly rancid -------------- *L. semitale*
         (see comments under *L. infumatum*)

Lyophyllum decastes (Fr.) Singer
EDIBLE

Pileus 6–14 cm broad, broadly convex, plane, metallic gray to gray-brown, smooth, hairless, moist not viscid, margin lobed to crenulate, incurved at first, moist not viscid. Flesh firm, not thick, white, not staining when bruised. Lamellae adnate, subdistant, broad, uneven, white to pale buff in age. Stipe 3–6 cm long, 1.5–3.5 cm wide, equal or smaller toward base, white, sometimes with brownish stains near the base in age, smooth, hairless or with minute, scattered fibrils, moist to dry. Partial veil absent. Odorless. Taste mild.

Spores 5–7 x 5–6 µm broadly elliptic to subglobose, smooth, entire, thin-walled, nonamyloid. Spore print white.

Habit and distribution: Growing in often large, cespitose clusters on the ground, under or near conifers. Widely distributed. Fruiting in summer and fall.

Comments: We have observed this species in Alaska and the Yukon in late July and August. In Virginia it fruits in late November but always during cool moist weather. *Lyopohyllum multiforme* (Peck) H. E. Bigelow is also in cespitose clusters, with a white to white tinted brown pileus. The spores are 5–6 x 3.0–3.5 µm elliptic, smooth, entire, thin-walled, nonamyloid. Both species are good edibles but one must make sure they are in a cluster usually of six or more and the spore print is white and not pink as in *Entoloma*. Note also that the pileus is never chalky white, as in the poisonous *Clitocybe dilatata* Pers.:P. Karst., a western North American species that contains muscarine, Type 2 toxins, and grows in cespitose clusters on the ground.

Lyophyllum infumatum (Bres.) Kühner
INEDIBLE

Pileus 1–6 cm broad, convex to nearly plane, gray to pinkish gray, smooth, hairless, subviscid. Flesh firm, white at first, blue then black when bruised. Lamellae short decurrent, subdistant, dull white, bruising blue, but soon blackening irregularly when bruised. Stipe 2–5 cm long, 0.2–0.9 cm wide, equal, pale buff to very light gray, smooth, hairless, dry. Partial veil absent. Odor mild. Taste mild.

Spores 9–11 x 5–6 µm elliptic, smooth, entire, thin-walled, nonamyloid. Spore print white.

Habit and distribution: Single to several on ground under conifers. Widely distributed. Fruiting in early spring and summer.

Comments: Crush the lamellae near the margin to bruise them and observe the staining reaction. *Lyophyllum semitale* (Fr.) Kühner is similar. The pileus is beige-brown to pinkish brown; has cream-colored lamellae; the flesh bruises directly to black; odor and taste is rancid; and the spores are smaller (7–9 x 4.0–4.5 µm). Neither of these species is edible.

LEUCOPAXILLUS

These are large, fleshy mushrooms, with chalk white, adnate lamellae and stipe, and no partial veil. The spores are elliptic to globose, smooth or with amyloid warts, thin-walled and clamp connections are present. All species are found growing in soil and appear to be ecto-mycorrhizal with conifers and hardwoods. The base of the stipe and duff where they grow have dense, white mycelium.

Edibility: The species are bitter and should not be eaten.

KEY TO LEUCOPAXILLUS

1. Pileus 10–45 cm broad, deeply depressed in age, glabrous, cream to buff; lamellae decurrent, crowded, white; odor of fish meal; taste mild ---------------------- *L. giganteus*
1. Not as above -- 2
   2. Pileus 4–12 cm broad, dry, reddish brown; lamellae adnate, crowded, chalk white; odor unpleasant; taste bitter-- *L. gentianeus*
   2. Not as above-- 3
3. Pileus 4.0–7.5 cm broad, convex, bright yellow, dry; lamellae decurrent, close, light pink; odor and taste mild -- *L. subzonalis*
   (see comments under *L. gentianeus*)
3. Not as above -- 4
   4. Pileus 4–12 cm broad, convex with a low umbo, dull white; spores 3.5–5.5 x 3.5–4.5 µm globose with amyloid warts; under hardwoods; odor of meal; taste very bitter --- *L. laterarius*
   4. Pileus 5–20 cm broad, convex to flat, chalk white; spores 5.5–7.5 x 4.0–5.5 elliptic with dark amyloid warts; under conifers, especially pine, spruce, and fir; odor unpleasant; taste mild --- *L. albissimus*

Leucopaxillus giganteus (Fr.) Singer
NONPOISONOUS

Pileus 10–45 cm broad (usually 15–30 cm), broadly convex, plane or depressed to deeply depressed in age, cream to buff in age, light brown or light orange-brown in the center, glabrous, hairless, margin inrolled, sometimes striate, and finely downy at first, moist to dry. Flesh very firm, white. Lamellae decurrent, crowded, white to light buff, sometimes forked. Stipe 4.5–10.0 cm long, 2–5 cm wide, equal, smooth, hairless, concolorous with the pileus, dry. Partial veil absent. Odor farinaceous or like fish meal. Taste mild.

Spores 6.5–9.5 x 3.0–5.5 µm, elliptic, smooth, entire, thin-walled, weakly to strongly amyloid. Spore print white. Clamp connections always present.

Habit and distribution: Single, several together, or in a fairy ring, in grassy areas or open mixed woods, under conifers including spruce and fir. Widely distributed but uncommon. Fruiting in summer.

Comments: This species is also known as *Clitocybe gigantea* Fr. and is closely related to *Leucopaxillus candidus* (Bres.) Singer, which ranges from 6–20 cm broad at maturity, but is similar in all other aspects to *L. giganteus*. The plate illustrates large specimens (up to 40 cm diameter) near Harding Lake in Alaska. Not poisonous, but with poor flavor.

Leucopaxillus gentianeus (Quél) Kotl.
INEDIBLE

Pileus 4–12 cm broad, broadly convex, reddish brown with a pinkish, inrolled margin, smooth, hairless, dry. Flesh firm, white. Lamellae adnate, close to crowded, chalk white. Stipe 4–6 cm long, 0.8–4.5 cm wide, equal to bulbous, minutely powdered, white to dingy brownish over the base, which is surrounded by white mycelium. Partial veil absent. Odor unpleasant. Taste bitter.

Spores 4–6 x 3.5–5.0 μm subglobose, amyloid warts, entire, thin-walled. Spore print white. Cheilocystidia abundant. Clamp connections present.

Habit and distribution: Single to numerous under conifers, but under oak and conifers in the Pacific Southwest, infrequent elsewhere. Widely distributed. Fruiting in summer and fall.

Comments: This species is also known as *L. amarus* (Alb. & Schwein.:Fr.) Kühner. A number of forms have been described by Singer and Smith (1943). *Leucopaxillus subzonalis* (Peck) H. E. Bigelow is rare, but has a bright yellow pileus and small spores (3.6–4.5 x 3.2–4.2 μm) with dark amyloid spines. We have collected it in Virginia and it is reported from Michigan and New England.

Leucopaxillus laterarius (Peck) Singer & A. H. Sm.
NONPOISONOUS

Pileus 4–12 cm broad, broadly convex often with a low umbo, dull white with a tint of pink to buff, margin inrolled and sometimes striate, dry. Flesh firm, thick, white. Lamellae adnate to short decurrent, crowded, narrow, white to pale buff. Stipe 4–11 cm long, 0.6–2.0 cm wide, equal or enlarging toward base, smooth, hairless or minutely downy, dull chalk white, attached to leaves and ground by a mass of white mycelium. Partial veil absent. Odor of meal, often unpleasant. Taste very bitter.

Spores 3.5–5.5 x 3.5–4.5 µm globose to subglobose with amyloid warts, entire, thin-walled. Spore print white. Cystidia absent. Clamp connections present.

Habit and distribution: Single, scattered to numerous in leaves and debris under beech and oaks. Found in eastern North America. Fruiting in summer and fall.

Comments: The distribution in the eastern United States and occurrence under hardwoods is typical for this species. *Leucopaxilllus albissimus* is somewhat more robust and more widely distributed, but they are otherwise identical in appeerance.

Leucopaxillus albissimus (Peck) Singer
INEDIBLE

Pileus 5–9 (-20) cm broad, robust, convex, soon plane at maturity, dull chalk white to cream color, tinted orange in age, dry, leathery to touch. Flesh firm white. Lamellae adnate to short decurrent, broad, crowded, pure white. Stipe 3–8 cm long, 0.8–3.0 cm wide, often eccentric, enlarging somewhat at the base, chalk white, smooth. Partial veil absent. Odor unpleasant to pungent. Taste mild, becoming bitter and unpleasant with an aftertaste.

Spores 5.5–7.5 x 4.0–5.5 µm elliptic, dark amyloid, with amyloid warts, entire, thin-walled. Spore print white. Clamp connections present.

Habit and distribution: Single to several on the ground under conifers especially pine, spruce, and fir. Widely distributed. Fruiting in summer and fall.

Comments: Singer & Smith (1943) describes several varieties of this species with regional distributions including one uncommon variety under hardwoods. The bitter flesh is not edible.

TRICHOLOMA

The genus is characterized by fleshy, fruiting bodies. The pileus is convex to plane in age, dry or viscid often with radially arranged, appressed fibrils or scales. The lamellae are adnate to adnexed, non-waxy, and the stipe is brittle. A partial veil may be present. Spores are white, elliptic, smooth, entire, thin-walled, and nonamyloid. If the spores are amyloid, check *Floccularia*. The species are found on the ground, and are ectomycorrhizal worldwide. In the Northern Hemisphere, they are associated with trees in the Fagaceae (beech and oak families), Salicaceae (willow and poplar families), Betulaceae (birch family), and Pinaceae (pine, spruce, fir and hemlock). It helps to note the trees near where the collections are made. There are many species of *Tricholoma*, and the most common are included here.

Edibility: Several species are edible, especially *T. flavovirens, T. magnivelare* and *T. calligatum,* but others are difficult to identify and could be confused with inedible species. *Tricholoma magnivelare,* the "California matsutaki", is an excellent edible, and prized in its range along the West Coast and, to a lesser extent, in the Rocky Mountains. The related *T. calligatum,* in eastern North America, is also edible. *Tricholoma matsutake,* the Asian species, is one of the most highly prized edible mushrooms in the world (Hall et al., 2003). Several species are reported to be poisonous including *T. pardinum,* and those with disagreeable odors and bitter taste include *T. inamoenum, T. sulphureum, T. saponaceum,* and *T. bufonium* (Spoerke & Rumack, 1994). Poisoning usually involves Type 8 toxins resulting in severe gastric upset and often vomiting.

KEY TO TRICHOLOMA

1. Partial veil present, persistent or annular ring at maturity -------------------------------- 13
1. Partial veil absent, without an annular ring -- 2
  2. Odor of coal gas or tar--- 3
  2. Odorless or odor of meal (farinaceous) or soaplike -------------------------------------- 5
3. Pileus cream color to dingy pinkish -- *T. inamoenum*
3. Pileus yellow or violet-brown --- 4
  4. Pileus, lamellae, and stipe yellow --- *T. sulphureum*
            (see comments under *T. inamoenum*)
  4. Pileus violet-brown --- *T. bufonium*
            (see comments under *T. inamoenum*)
5. Pileus olive-gray to olive-brown; odor of soap; taste mild; stipe base often pink or tis-
    sue bruises pink -- *T. saponaceum*
5. Pileus colored differently; odorless or odor of meal (farinaceous) ------------------------ 6
  6. Odorless --- 11
  6. Odor of meal (farinaceous) --- 7
7. Pileus brownish red to orange-brown or yellow-brown; lamellae bright to
    dull yellow --- *T. flavovirens*
7. Not as above -- 8
  8. Pileus covered with small, gray-brown scales; stipe context buff to yellow at the
      base -- *T. pardinum*
  8. Not as above-- 9
9. Pileus viscid, radially streaked with yellow to olivaceous brown, radiating fibrils and
    dark brown over the center; lamellae yellow to yellow-gray ----------------- *T. sejunctum*
9. Pileus viscid, dark red-brown, red-brown to chestnut-brown------------------------------ 10
  10. Pileus viscid, dark red-brown, margin with red, round spots -------- *T. pessundatum*
  10. Pileus viscid, red-brown to chestnut-brown; blackens on handling ---------- *T. ustale*
            (see comments under *T. pessundatum*)
11. Pileus viscid, dull white; lamellae and stipe white ---------------------------- *T. resplendens*
            (for other white species, see comments under *T. resplendens*)
11. Not as above--- 12
  12. Pileus moist, not viscid, with radiating, flat, slate-gray, pale gray to purplish gray
      fibrils; lamellae light gray; stipe dull white ------------------------------------- *T. virgatum*

12. Pileus moist, gray with lilac tones to brownish gray; lamellae with black specks on the edges --- *T. sciodes*

(see comments under *T. virgatum*)

13. Partial veil leaving a persistent, superior, membranous ring ------------------------------ 14

13. Partial veil absent at maturity or leaving a thin, fibrillose ring or annular zone -------- 16

    14. Pileus white with flattened, brown scales over center, streaked brown over the margin; lamellae white, crowded, bruising pink to reddish brown; stipe with red-brown scales; with a spicy sweet odor ---------------------------------- *T. magnivelare*

    14. Not as above -- 15

15. Pileus viscid, radially streaked orange-brown with olivaceous tones; lamellae crowded, often with orange-brown stains; stipe orange-brown below partial veil -------- *T. focale*

15. Pileus dry, pale pinkish, covered with flattened, gray-brown to red-brown scales; lamellae close, white; stipe with brownish orange squamules and hairs -------------- *T. caligatum*

    16. Pileus sticky to viscid, flattened, fine scales orange-red to orange-brown with red-brown stains; lamellae white stained orange-brown; stipe orange-brown, fine scales below the superior, very thin, fibrillose ring or zone, white above --- *T. aurantium*

    16. Pileus dry, radially arranged, reddish brown fibrils with a wooly margin; lamellae cream color stained orange-brown in age; stipe with reddish brown scales; partial veil thin, white, soon gone --- *T. vaccinum*

Tricholoma inamoenum (Fr.) Quél.
POISONOUS

Pileus 1.5–4.5 cm broad, convex to broadly convex and plane in age, cream to dingy pinkish cream to tan over the center, dry. Flesh firm white. Lamellae adnate, subdistant, broad, white or with a light brownish hue in age. Stipe 2.5–7.0 cm long, 0.4–1.1 cm wide, equal or enlarged just at the base, dull white with brown stains over the base, dry. Partial veil absent. Odor strong of coal gas or tar. Taste disagreeable.

Spores 8.5–14.0 x 5.5–7.5 μm bean-shaped to broadly elliptic, smooth, entire, thin-walled, nonamyloid. Spore print white.

Habit and distribution: Several on the ground under conifer forests. Widely distributed. Fruiting in summer and fall.

Comments: *Tricholoma sulphureum* (Bull.:Fr.) P. Kumm. has the same coal gas odor, but has a yellow pileus, lamellae, and stipe; is found associated with conifers; and widely distributed. Both of these species are common in Virginia and North Carolina under conifer in the fall. A third species, *T. bufonium* (Pers.:Fr.) Gill., has a violet brown pileus, and also has the coal gas odor.

Tricholoma saponaceum (Fr.) P. Kumm.
POISONOUS

Pileus 3–9 cm broad, convex, hairless, color variable, grayish olive, yellowish olive shaded to olive-brown or deep olive-gray especially over the center, margin inrolled at first, hairless, sticky to viscid. Flesh thick, white often with pink just at the base of the stipe. Lamellae adnate, subdistant, white, cream to yellowish in age with a greenish tint, occasionally stained reddish near margin. Stipe 3–8 cm long, 0.7–2.5 (-3.5) cm thick, equal to enlarged at the base, white with brown stains in age, smooth, dry. Partial veil absent. Odor of soap sometimes pungent or mild. Taste mild or slightly sweet.

Spores 5.5–7.0 x 3.5–5.0 μm short elliptic, smooth, entire, thin-walled, nonamyloid. Spore print white. Trama has many clamp connections.

Habit and distribution: Single to several under hardwoods and conifers. Widely distributed. Fruiting in summer and fall.

Comments: It is not unusual to find large fruitings in the fall with hardwoods as well as conifers. The pileus coloration is variable, making the distinctive odor and pink flesh in the stipe base important to observe in fresh specimens. Clamp connections at almost every septum are unusual in *Tricholoma*, but is also true in *T. pardinum*. Can cause severe gastric upset, including diarrhea, nausea, and vomiting (Type 8 toxins).

Tricholoma flavovirens (Fr.) Lund.
INEDIBLE

Pileus 5–10 cm broad, convex, nearly plane in age, brownish to reddish brown or orange-brown, margin pale yellow, smooth, hairless, viscid. Flesh firm, white, yellowish beneath pileus cuticle. Lamellae adnexed, close, bright to dull yellow. Stipe 3–8 cm long, 1–2 cm wide, solid, equal to enlarged over the base, white to buff, with fine fibrils, dry. Partial veil absent. Odor and taste of new meal (farinaceous).

Spores 6–7 x 4–5 μm elliptic, smooth, entire, thin-walled, nonamyloid. Spore print white.

Habit and distribution: Single to scattered, sometimes in clumps on the ground under mixed conifers and mixed conifer/aspen stands. Widely distributed. Fruiting in late summer and fall.

Comments: Known also as *Tricholoma equestre* Fr., our variant of this species has more yellow in the pileus than is found in the European variety, but in other respects seems to be the same. We have often found it in sandy loam in late fall in Maryland and in Virginia pine-oak woods. The pileus often has a faint greenish tint over the yellow areas and is sometimes partially covered by sand and soil. There have been reports from France of 12 cases of severe toxicity, including three fatalities, following the ingestion of this species (Bedry et al. 2001). There have been no similar reports of poisoning in North America. *Tricholoma sulphureum* Fr. has a sulfur-yellow pileus and stipe, but it has a strong, disagreeable odor and is poisonous.

Tricholoma pardinum (Pers.) Quél.
POISONOUS

Pileus 5–10 cm broad, convex with a low, broad umbo, covered with gray-brown, small scales, white beneath, dry. Flesh firm, white. Lamellae adnexed, subdistant, white to cream color in age. Stipe 5.5–10.0 cm long, 1.0–2.5 cm wide, nearly equal or enlarged toward base, chalk white, smooth, hairless, sometimes brown to yellow stains at the base, dry. Partial veil absent. Odor and taste farinaceous.

Spores 7.5–10.0 x 5.5–6.5 µm short elliptic, smooth, thin-walled, nonamyloid. Spore print white. Cheilocystidia club-shaped to ovoid, sometimes abundant. Clamp connections in trama at almost every septum as in T. saponaceum (Fig. 25), and both species are poisonous.

Habit and distribution: Single to several under conifers or in mixed conifer/hardwoods. Widely distributed. Fruiting usually in the fall, but in January in California and the West Coast.

Comments: The white, gray to gray brown species of *Tricholoma* should be avoided. We have collected this species in Idaho, Montana, and eastern Washington, where it is common every fall. Ingestion can cause severe gastrointestinal upset from the Type 8 toxins. *Tricholoma terreum* (Schaeff.:Fr.) P. Kumm. is similar with a gray to brownish gray, a radially fibrillose pileus; white tinted gray lamellae; but the stipe is without brown to yellow stains; odor and taste are mild; and it is common in conifer forests. *Tricholoma myomyces* (Pers.:Fr.) J. E. Lange is also similar but has a very thin, fibrous partial veil; small spores (5–6 x 3.5–4.0 µm); and is also in northern conifer forests. Both species are smaller than *T. pardinum.*

Tricholoma sejunctum (Fr.) Quél.
INEDIBLE

Pileus 3.3–8.5 cm broad, convex, radially streaked with yellow to olivaceous brown, radiating fibrils, dark brown over the center, viscid. Flesh white firm. Lamellae adnate, subdistant, light yellow to yellow gray, brittle and easily broken. Stipe 3.3–10.0 cm long, 0.9–1.3 cm wide, white, often tinted yellowish, cylindric to narrowly clavate, base sometimes bulbous, dry. Partial veil absent. Odor of mildew or farinaceous. Taste mild or lightly farinaceous.

Spores 5–8 x 3.5–5.5 µm elliptic, smooth, entire, thin-walled, nonamyloid. Spore print white.

Habit and distribution: Single to several, on the ground under conifers and hardwoods. Widely distributed. Fruiting in the late summer and fall.

Comment: Some yellow color phases of *Tricholoma saponaceum* and *T. flavovirens* might be confused with this species, but neither species has radially streaked fibrils on the pileus with a dark brown center.

Tricholoma pessundatum (Fr.) Quél.
POISONOUS

Pileus 3–6 (-15) cm broad, convex to broadly convex to plane in age, dark red-brown, margin ringed with dark red, round spots over a pinkish buff margin (see photo below), viscid. Flesh firm white. Lamellae adnate, close, medium broad, white to light buff in age. Stipe 3.5–6.0 cm long, 0.9–2.5 cm wide, white, equal or enlarging to a broad base, dry, with small, light brown fibrils over the lower half. Partial veil absent. Odor of sour meal. Taste mild.

Spores 4–6 x 1.5–3.0 µm elliptic, smooth, entire, thin-walled, nonamyloid. Spore print white.

Habit and distribution: Several under conifers, sometime under willows or alder in conifer forests. Widely distributed. Fruiting in summer and fall.

Comments: This is one of a number of viscid, dark brown, poisonous species. Another common species is *Tricholoma ustale* (Fr.:Fr.) P. Kumm., which has a red-brown to chestnut-brown, viscid pileus; a dark brown stipe; and generally blackens on drying or handling. All of the species in this group have Type 8 toxins and can cause severe gastrointestinal upset and should be avoided.

Tricholoma resplendens Fr.
POISONOUS

Pileus 3.5–10.0 cm broad, convex, broadly convex in age, dull white with light brown spots in age, margin not inrolled but straight, viscid to slightly viscid in dry weather. Flesh firm, white. Lamellae adnate to adnexed, subdistant, white, tinted flesh color. Stipe 3–6 cm long, 1.0–1.8 cm wide, equal or slightly narrowed just at the base, white overall, lacking fibrils or sometimes downy near the apex, dry. Partial veil absent. Odorless. Taste mild.

Spores 6.0–7.5 x 3.5–4.5 µm elliptic, smooth, entire, thin-walled, nonamyloid. Spore print white.

Habit and distribution: Single, scattered, or occasionally numerous, in conifers and hardwoods. Found in eastern North America. Fruiting in summer and fall.

Comments: *Tricholoma columbetta* Fr. is also white; but has a moist to dry pileus often with yellow or blue stains. It is common in eastern North America, but we found it in Montana in 1975. *Tricholoma venenata* G. F. Atk. has a dry pileus; mild taste; and the lamellae and stipe bruise brown. Shanks (1997) reports it under conifers in the Sierra Nevada mountains in California, but it is also in eastern North America. This is a poisonous group of species that have Type 8 toxins and can cause severe gastrointestinal upset. Kauffman (1918) has accounts of all of the known white species of *Tricholoma*. The lamellae in this group of white Tricholomas are not waxy and not usually decurrent, which eliminates *Hygrophorus;* and there is no latex, which eliminates *Lactarius*. The spores are nonamyloid in Melzer's solution, which means that it could not be a *Russula*.

Tricholoma virgatum (Fr.) P. Kumm.
INEDIBLE

Pileus 2.5–7.0 cm broad, conic with an acute umbo, campanulate in age, with radiating, flattened fibrils, slate-gray, pale gray to purplish gray, with inrolled margin, dry to sticky. Flesh thin, white. Lamellae adnexed, close, broad, white young to light gray in age. Stipe 3.5–11.0 cm long, 0.6–1.8 mm wide, equal, white, smooth, hairless or with light fibrils, base sometime rounded, dry. Partial veil absent. Odorless. Taste acrid.

Spores 6.0–7.5 x 4.5–6.0 μm ovoid to short elliptic, smooth, entire, thin-walled, nonamyloid. Spore print white.

Habit and distribution: Single but usually in scattered groups in hardwood or conifer woods. Widely distributed. Fruiting in late summer and fall, however, on into winter on the California Coast.

Comments: *Tricholoma subacutum* Peck is another name for this fungus. *Tricholoma sciodes* (Pers.) Martin, which we have collected under live oak in Santa Barbara County, California, is similar. However, it has a pileus with a lavender-pink ground color and black specks on the edges of the lamellae. Both species are acrid to taste and not edible.

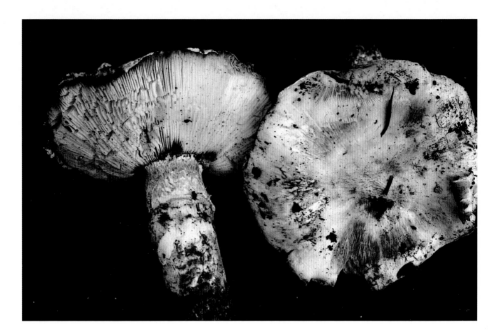

Tricholoma magnivelare (Peck) Redhead
EDIBLE AND CHOICE

Pileus 8–20 cm broad, broadly convex, plane in age, white with flattened brown scales developing over the center and streaked with brown hairs elsewhere, margin a narrow, white, inrolled flap, tacky to moist. Flesh firm, white. Lamellae adnexed, crowded, broad, white, bruising pinkish to reddish brown. Stipe 6–18 cm long, 2–4 cm wide, tapering somewhat toward base, smooth and white above the ring, below covered with reddish brown scales and hairs in age, sticky when wet to dry. Partial veil membranous, white, leaving a superior, persistent, skirtlike ring, soon stained reddish brown on the edge and outside. Odor spicy, with a sweet smell even in button stage. Taste pleasant.

Spores 5.5–7.0 x 4.5–5.5 μm broadly elliptic, smooth, entire, thin-walled, nonamyloid. Spore print white.

Habit and distribution: Scattered to abundant under mixed conifers. Widely distributed but abundant and common along the Pacific Coast and locally elsewhere. Fruiting in the fall, except along the West Coast, where it fruits from October to early February.

Comments: This species is also known as *Armillaria ponderosa* (Peck) Sacc. It is abundant and highly prized as a choice edible along the West Coast, where it is called the "American Matsutaki." *Tricholoma matsutaki* (S. Ito & S. Imai) Singer fruits under pines in Japan, Korea, and elsewhere in Asia where it is in high demand as a choice edible. We have occasionally collected the "American Matsutaki" in Idaho and Colorado in the fall, and it is known from scattered reports elsewhere in northern North America.

Tricholoma focale (Fr.) Ricken
EDIBLE

Pileus 6–12 cm broad, convex to broadly convex in age, margin inrolled when young, wavy in age, radially streaked orange-brown with olivaceous tones, shiny when dry, viscid. Flesh firm, white. Lamellae adnate, white, crowded young, close in age often with orange stains. Stipe 4.5–13.0 cm long, 1.0–3.0 cm wide, tapering toward the base, white above the partial veil, below with scattered fibrils, orange-brown over a white ground color. Partial veil white cottony, dense at first, leaving a ragged superior annulus. Odor farinaceous. Taste bitter, also farinaceous.

Spores 4.0–5.5 x 3–4 µm short elliptic, smooth, entire, thin-walled, nonamyloid. Spore print white.

Habit and distribution: Several on the ground in conifer woods or mixed woods. Found in western and northern North America. Fruiting in late summer and fall.

Comments: Formally known as *Armillaria zelleri* D. E. Stuntz & A. H. Smith and transferred to *Tricholoma zelleri* (D. E. Stuntz &. A. H. Sm.) Ovrebo & Tylutki, it is often abundant in the fall under conifers. Some people find this an excellent edible and others find it tasteless and slimy when cooked. We have not tried it ourselves. The highly prized *Tricholoma magnivelare* often fruits at the same time.

Tricholoma caligatum (Viv.) Ricken
EDIBLE

Pileus 4–15 cm broad, convex, broadly convex to plane, sometimes slightly depressed, center covered with flattened, radiating fibrils, reddish brown to grayish brown or brownish drab scales over pale pinkish cinnamon surface, margin silky white with few scales, dry. Flesh firm, white. Lamellae adnate, close, broad, white, sometimes veined. Stipe 4–9 cm long, 1.2–2.2 cm wide, equal or somewhat larger in center, smooth, white to light tan above ring, below brownish-orange squamules and hairs, dry. Partial veil soft, white, membranous, leaving a persistent, superior ring that flares upward at first, soon dingy brownish. Odor none or occasionally reported as unpleasant or spicy. Taste mild at first, soon bitter.

Spores 6–8 x 4.5–5.5 µm, elliptic, smooth, entire, thin-walled, nonamyloid. Spore print white.

Habit and distribution: Single, scattered to numerous under hardwoods or mixed hardwood and conifers. Found in eastern North America, on rare occasions under conifers along the Pacific Coast (Shanks, 1997). Fruiting in late summer and fall.

Comments: This species often fruits in large numbers under mixed conifers and hardwoods in the Northeast and under mixed oaks and pine in the Southeast. *Tricholoma magnivelare* is very closely related but is often more robust; and the pileus has more white ground color; it has a pleasant taste and fragrant odor; and is primarily found in western North America.

Tricholoma aurantium (Schaeff.:Fr.) Ricken
INEDIBLE

Pileus 4–7 cm broad, convex, plane in age, flattened scaly or scattered fibrils, orange-red to orange-brown with reddish brown stains, dry, sticky or viscid in wet weather. Flesh firm, pale buff to white. Lamellae adnexed, adnate to short decurrent, close, white, spotted or stained orange-brown, veined near stipe. Stipe 3–10 cm long, 0.8–2.0 cm wide, equal, enlarged near the base, bright white above the ring, orange-brown small flattened scales below, dry. Partial veil thin, sticky, fibrillose, colorless to white, leaving a very thin, fibrillose ring, usually not present at maturity. Odor disagreeable, strong, as old meal or corn silk. Taste disagreeable, rancid.

Spores 4.5–6.0 x 3–4 µm subglobose to short elliptic, smooth, entire, thin-walled, nonamyloid. Spore print white.

Habit and distribution: Single to scattered or in small groups under various conifers. Widely distributed. Fruiting in summer and fall.

Comments: We have found this fungus under pure Engelmann spruce in Alberta and under grand fir in Montana. *Tricholoma focale* is similar but has a persistent, flaring partial veil and a white stipe with orange-brown, loose scales.

Tricholoma vaccinum (Pers.:Fr.) P. Kumm.
INEDIBLE

Pileus 4–7 cm broad, convex, nearly plane or with a low umbo in age, reddish brown to light reddish brown, flattened, radially arranged fibrils, margin wooly, dry. Flesh thin, white to reddish beneath the pileus. Lamellae adnexed, close, white to cream, stained or spotted orange-brown in age. Stipe 5–8 cm long, 0.6–1.5 cm wide, with reddish brown scales, white at both apex and base, dry. Partial veil a thin, white cortina soon gone, leaving no annulus, but has an annular zone. Odor unpleasant. Taste unpleasant and bitter.

Spores 5.0–8.5 x 4.0–5.4 µm elliptic, smooth, entire, thin-walled, nonamyloid. Spore print white.

Habit and distribution: Scattered to numerous in needle duff under conifers. Widely distributed. Fruiting in summer and fall.

Comments: We have collected this species under spruce and fir in Idaho, and hard pines in Virginia. It is bitter and not edible.

GROUP II
KEY TO SPECIES OF THE TRICHOLOMATACEAE ON CONIFER CONES, MAGNOLIA CONES, NUT HUSKS OR PARASITIZING MUSHROOMS

1. Growing on dead and decaying mushrooms --- 2
1. Growing on conifer or magnolia cones or nut husks --- 4
   2. In clusters on the pileus of *Russula* or *Lactarius* ---------------------------------- 3
   2. In troops or dense clusters of very small mushrooms, on well-decayed mushrooms with small sclerotia present or absent --- 7
3. Pileus white, powdery, brown in age----------------------------- *Asterophora lycoperdoides*
3. Pileus pale silky gray and not powdery------------------------------ *Asterophora parasitica*
   (see comments under *A. lycoperdoides*)
4. Growing on the husks of hickory or walnut; pileus orange to pale yellow; stipe tall and thin--- *Mycena luteopallens*
4. Growing on conifer or magnolia cones --- 5
   5. Growing on magnolia "cones," southeastern and southern United States --- *Strobilurus conigenoides*
   5. Growing on the cones of conifers (pine, spruce, fir, Douglas fir) --------------------- 6
6. Lamellae close, pinkish buff; spores ovoid and amyloid -------------- *Baeospora myosura*
6. Lamellae subdistant to close, white; spores elliptic nonamyloid --- other *Strobilurus* species
   (see comments under *S. conigenoides*)
   7. Dense clusters of small, white to brown mushrooms with small red-brown to black-brown or yellow sclerotia at the base --- 8
   7. Dense clusters of small white mushrooms without sclerotia -------- *Collybia cirrata*
   (see comments under *C. tuberosa*)
8. Sclerotia red-brown to black-brown ----------------------------------- *Collybia tuberosa*
8. Sclerotia yellow to buff --- *Collybia cookei*
   (see comments under *C. tuberosa*)

Asterophora lycoperdoides (Bull.)
Ditmar: Gray
NONPOISONOUS

Pileus 1–2 cm broad, nearly globose, powdery, white becoming brown from the mature asexual spores on the surface, dry. Flesh firm, pale buff. Lamellae adnate, well separated, narrow, white. Stipe 2–3 cm long, 0.3–0.8 cm wide, equal, white stained brown in age, minutely downy. Odor and taste of fresh meal.

Basidiospores 4.8–6.0 x 2.5–3.2 µm elliptic, smooth, entire, thin-walled, nonamyloid. Spore print white. Chlamydospores on pileus 12–18 µm globose, spiny, brown in age.

Habit and distribution: Several together, parasitic on other mushrooms, especially *Russula* and *Lactarius*. Widely distributed. Fruiting in summer and fall, especially during wet weather.

Comments: Very often the agarics which have been parasitized are well rotted and beyond recognition. The pileus of *A. lycoperdoides* is covered with globose, thick-walled, warted chlamydospores, giving it the powdery appearance. *Asterophora parasitica* (Fr.) Singer is also parasitic on mushrooms, but the pileus is white to pale gray, silky and not powdery; basidiospores are 5–6 x 3–4 µm short-elliptic, hyaline, thin-walled, nonamyloid; lamellae soon break up into asexual, smooth, thick-walled chlamydospores. Both species are most common when late season rains produce an abundance of fleshy mushrooms.

Mycena luteopallens (Peck) Sacc.
NONPOISONOUS

Pileus 0.6–1.5 cm broad, conic with a shallow depression in center, orange over the center, margin striate, pale yellow, dry, appears shiny. Flesh very thin, yellowish. Lamellae adnate, subdistant, narrow, yellowish. Stipe 1.6–4.0 cm long, 0.1–0.15 cm wide dry, orange-yellow when young, to straw-yellow in age, with white mycelium over the base. Partial veil absent. Odor and taste not distinctive.

Spores 6–8 x 3.0–4.5 µm elliptic, smooth, entire, thin-walled, amyloid. Spore print white.

Habit and distribution: Single to several on the husks of hickory and walnut that are either buried or lying on the surface of the ground. Found in eastern North America. Fruiting in the fall to early winter in the Deep South.

Comments: The unusual occurrence on husks of hickory and walnut make this species most distinctive.

Strobilurus conigenoides (Ellis) Singer
EDIBILITY UNKNOWN

Pileus 1–5 mm broad, convex, minutely downy, tan, margin cream-colored and striate. Flesh thin, white, dry. Lamellae adnexed to nearly free, fairly well separated, white. Stipe 2–3 cm long, 0.05–0.1 cm wide, nearly equal, finely downy, white to tan with white mycelium over the base. Veil absent. Odor and taste not distinctive.

Spores 4–5 x 2–3 µm short elliptic, smooth, entire, thin-walled, nonamyloid. Spore print white. Cheilo- and pleurocystidia present.

Habit and distribution: Common, only on the cones of *Magnolia,* and noted on *M. fraseria* and *M. grandiflora* throughout the range of *Magnolia* in the southeastern and southern United States. Fruiting in summer and fall.

Comments: The habit on *Magnolia* cones, along with a minute tan pileus and stipe, is distinctive. Other species decompose conifer cones.

Strobilurus trullisatus (Murrill) Lennox has a white or tinted orange pileus; white, crowded lamellae; and is found on cones of pine, spruce, Douglas fir in western North America. *Strobilurus albipilata* (Peck) V. L. Wells & Kempton has a dark brown pileus; subdistant, white lamellae; fruits in the spring following snow melt in the Rocky Mountains; is often on buried conifer cones and elsewhere, in western and northeastern North America later in the season. *Strobilurus occidentalis* V. L. Wells & Kempton has a yellow-brown pileus; crowded, white lamellae; occurs on the cones of white spruce and Sitka spruce often in coastal forests and Alaska in western North America. These species are distinguished by microscopic characters, especially cystidia and spore size, see Redhead (1980) for details.

Baeospora myosura (Fr.) Singer
NONPOISONOUS

Pileus 5–20 mm broad, convex, nearly plane in age, pinkish brown to cinnamon-pink, margin slightly inrolled at first, striate, dry. Flesh soft, thin, white. Lamellae adnexed, close, light pinkish buff. Stipe 1.0–2.0 cm long, 0.1–0.2 cm wide, equal, cinnamon-pink, clothed with minute, white fibrils, attached to conifer cones by short, distinctive, white rhizomorphs, dry. Partial veil absent. Odor and taste not distinctive.

Spores 3.5–4.5 x 1.5–2.5 µm ovoid, smooth, entire, thin-walled, amyloid. Spore print white. Cheilocystidia club- to bowling-pin-shaped.

Habit and distribution: Numerous on conifer cones, especially Norway spruce, various pines, as well as Douglas fir. Widely distributed. Fruiting in the late summer and fall.

Comments: The fruiting bodies are attached to the conifer cones by short, white rhizomorphs (see color plate). The species of *Strobilurus* do not have amyloid spores. See discussion under *Strobilurus conigenoides* for other agarics that decompose cones. *Baeospora myriadophila* (Peck) Singer has pink lamellae; amyloid spores; and fruits on the rotten stumps of conifers.

Collybia tuberosa (Bull.:Fr.) P. Kumm.
NONPOISONOUS

Pileus 0.2–1.0 (-1.5) cm broad, convex, soon plane, sometimes with a small umbo, white, but often tinted yellowish to reddish, smooth, without fibrils, dry. Flesh very thin, white. Lamellae adnate, close, white. Stipe 0.4–2.0 cm long, 0.05–0.15 cm wide, nearly equal, dry, minutely downy, white tinted reddish brown, attached to a red-brown to blackish brown sclerotium, 0.2–0.4 cm diameter. Partial veil absent. Odorless. Taste unknown.

Spores 4.0–5.5 x 2–3 µm elliptic, smooth, entire, thin-walled, nonamyloid. Spore print white.

Habit and distribution: Small, dense clusters on decaying mushrooms, growing from a sclerotium. Widely distributed. Fruiting in summer and fall.

Comments: *Collybia cookei* (Bres.) A. D. Arnold is very similar; on dead mushrooms; but the sclerotium is yellow. *Collybia cirrata* (Schumach.:Fr.) P. Kumm. is also on decayed mushrooms; looks very similar; but lacks the sclerotia. Both of the above species also have nonamyloid spores, and are too small to be edible. They are very conspicuous during periods of prolific fruitings of mushrooms, and they fruit as the mushroom decline. See and compare to *Asterophora*.

GROUP III
KEY TO SPECIES OF THE TRICHOLOMATACEAE ON WOOD WITH STIPE ABSENT OR A SHORT PLUG OF TISSUE

1. Pileus very small (0.2–3.2 cm broad); stipe absent or a very short (0.6–1.2 cm long) and eccentric -- 2

1. Pileus much larger (2–30 cm broad); stipe absent or a very short plug of tissue -------- 5

  2. Pileus 0.2–0.6 cm broad, convex, grayish blue; stipe absent; spores globose 4–5 µm --- *Resupinatus applicatus*

  2. Not as above -- 3

3. Pileus 0.3–2.0 cm broad, shell-shpaed,pure white, covered with soft white haris; stipe absent; sproes 6–7 x 5.5–7.0 µm globose ---------------- *Cheimonophyllum candidissimus*

3. Not as above -- 4

  4. Pileus 1.2–3.2 cm long, tan to brown, with wooly hairs; stipe 0.6–1.2 cm long, a short, eccentric, white, hairy plug; occurring in large, imbricate clusters -- *Panellus stipticus*

  4. Pileus 0.9–3.0 cm long, densely hairy, whitish gray; stipe absent; lamellae split and very hairy, whitish gray ------------------------------------- *Schizophyllum commune*

5. Pileus light orange to orange-buff, tomentose; lamellae orange buff; stipe absent; with a strong disagreeable odor and taste --------------------------------- *Phyllotopsis nidulans*

5. Not with the above combination of characters --- 6

  6. Pileus fan-shaped, viscid, smooth, green, olive buff to olive-brown; lamellae pale orange to light yellowish tan ------------------------------------- *Panellus serotinus*

  6. Pileus white, pale pink to yellow-brown, gray-brown but not green; lamellae white to cream color or pale pink --- 7

7. Pileus petal-like to fan-shaped, pure white, very thin; with crowded white lamellae --- *Pleurocybella porrigens*

7. Not with the above combination of characters --- 8

  8. Pileus velvety from dense stiff hairs, pinkish tan to reddish brown; flesh tough; stipe absent --- *Panus rudis*

  8. Pileus glabrous, oyster-shell to fan-shaped, white, pale pink, light yellow-brown, gray-brown downy white hairs --------------------------------------- *Pleurotus ostreatus*

                    (see other species of *Pleurotus* in Group V)

Resupinatus applicatus (Fr.) Gray
EDIBILITY UNKNOWN

Pileus 0.2–0.6 cm broad, minute, cuplike to convex, grayish blue to grayish black, covered with fine, minute hairs, dry. Flesh firm, gelatinous. Lamellae fairly well separated, broad, whitish at first to gray sometimes very dark. Stipe absent. Partial veil absent. Odorless. Taste mild.

Spores 4–5 μm globose, smooth, entire, thin-walled, nonamyloid. Spore print white.

Habit and distribution: Scattered or often in great numbers on hardwoods including vines and shrubs. Widely distributed. Fruits in spring, summer and fall.

Comments: If the pileus is cut in two, a translucent, gelatinous layer can be seen, and this is diagnostic. These are too small to use as edibles.

Cheimonophyllum candidissimus
(Berk.& M. A. Curtis) Singer
EDIBILITY UNKNOWN

Pileus 0.3–2.0 cm broad, shell- to spatula-shaped, white, covered with soft white hairs, inrolled at first, dry. Flesh thin, white. Lamellae close, white, with minutely hairy edges, arising from a common point of attachment. Stipe absent. Veil absent. Odorless. Taste unknown.

Spores 6–7 x 5.5–7.0 μm globose to subglobose, smooth, entire, thin-walled, nonamyloid. Spore print white.

Habit and distribution: Usually several to numerous on dead twigs and branches of hardwoods and conifers. Widely distributed. Fruiting in the fall.

Comments: There are several small species with minute white pilei. *Panellus mitis* (Pers.:Fr.) Singer is very similar but has amyloid, sausage-shaped (allantoid) spores Fig. 7 (3.5–6.0 x 0.8–1.2 μm). These tiny fruiting bodies are too small to serve as edibles.

Panellus stipticus (Fr.) P. Karst.
NONPOISONOUS

Pileus 1.2–3.2 cm long, 1.2–2.5 cm wide, convex, orange-buff, tan to brown, covered with wooly hairs, dry. Flesh tough, firm, pinkish tan. Lamellae close, narrow, salmon to orange-buff, which glow in the dark. Stipe 0.6–1.2 cm long, 0.3–0.8 cm wide, eccentric, dull whitish, with clusters of hairs. Partial veil absent. Odorless. Taste very bitter.

Spores 3.0–4.6 x 1.2–2.2 µm allantoid (Fig. 7), smooth, entire, thin-walled, amyloid. Spore print white.

Habit and distribution: In large imbricate clusters on limbs, logs, and stumps on hardwoods and occasionally conifers. Widely distributed. Fruiting in the late summer and fall.

Comments: This common *Panellus* is one of the six species in North America (Miller, 1970). It is an important rot of fallen hardwood limbs. The lamellae of fresh specimens are luminescent. It requires several minutes in the dark to let the eyes adjust to the lower level of illumination. The luminescent glow gave rise to the term "fox fire" coined by early settlers in eastern and southern North America. They are too small and too bitter to be eaten.

Schizophyllum commune Fr.
NONPOISONOUS

Pileus 0.9–3.0 cm broad, fan-shaped, whitish gray when dry to brownish gray when moist, margin lobed, densely hairy, dry. Flesh tough, leathery, gray. Lamellae well separated, split and hairy, cuplike in cross section, white to gray. Stipe absent, pileus attached directly to the wood. Odor none. Taste mild.

Spores 3–4 x 1.0–1.5 µm cylindric, smooth, entire, thin-walled, nonamyloid. Spore print white.

Habit and distribution: Several or in dense clusters, sometimes from a common base on a wide variety of hardwood sticks, stumps, logs, and wood in service such as wooden steps or docks. Widely distributed. Fruiting in spring, summer, fall, and even warm spells in winter.

Comments: This very odd species, usually placed in the Aphylloporales, is not really in the Agaricales, but it does have what appear to be lamellae and readily keys out here. It has been used for many years for experimental genetics research. It fruits readily in culture in the laboratory, and we have identified it fruiting from the wood of commercial beer vats. It is too small and tough to be edible.

Phyllotopsis nidulans (Pers.:Fr.) Singer
NONPOISONOUS

Pileus 3–8 cm broad, 3–4 cm wide, broadly convex, light orange to orange-buff, margin inrolled at first, with dense, minute hairs over the surface, dry. Flesh duplex, upper layer orange-buff, lower layer very pale orange-buff. Lamellae close, narrow, orange-buff. Stipe reduced, a short plug of tissue. Partial veil absent. Odor often strong and disagreeable. Taste bitter and unpleasant.

Spores 5–7 x 2.0–2.5 µm elliptic to slightly sausage-shaped, smooth, entire, thin-walled, nonamyloid. Spore print light reddish cinnamon to pale pink.

Habit and distribution: In groups, on hardwoods, conifer logs, and stumps. Most commonly found in eastern North America, but widely distributed. Fruiting in early summer through fall.

Comments: We have found this strong decomposer on Coulter pine in California, aspen in Michigan, and maple in Maryland. It is not edible, and has an unpleasant taste and odor.

Panellus serotinus (Fr.) Kühner
EDIBLE

Pileus 2.5–6.0 cm broad, 2.0–3.5 cm wide, convex, fan-shaped to shell-shaped, green, yellowish green, olive-buff to olive-brown, smooth, lacking hair, margin wavy, viscid. Flesh thick, firm, white. Lamellae adnate, fairly well separated, pale orange to light yellowish tan. Stipe absent, attached by a basal plug covered with white, dense, wooly hairs. Partial veil absent. Odorless. Taste mild.

Spores 4.0–5.5 x 1.0–1.5 µm allantoid (Fig. 7), smooth, entire, thin-walled, amyloid. Spore print yellow. Cheilocystidia 40–60 x 6–12 µm, cylindric, thin-walled.

Habit and distribution: Solitary to overlapping on logs and sticks of hardwoods, occasionally on conifers, especially hemlock. Widely distributed. Fruiting in the fall.

Comments: *Panellus serotinus* has been transferred to *Sarcomyxa serotina* (Shrad.:Fr.) P. Karst. by various authors.

Pleurocybella porrigens (Pers.:Fr.) Singer
INEDIBLE

Pileus 5–10 cm broad, convex, petal-like to fan-shaped, white, minutely hairy, margin inrolled at first, dry. Flesh very thin, pliant, white. Lamellae long, crowded, narrow, white to cream color arising from a pluglike attachment to the host. Veil absent. Odorless. Taste mild and good.

Spores 5–7 x 4.5–6.5 μm subglobose, smooth, entire, thin-walled, nonamyloid. Spore print white.

Habit and distribution: In imbricate clusters, on logs and stumps of conifers. Widely distributed. Fruiting in late summer and fall.

Comments: The shiny white fruiting bodies attract attention against the somber browns of the forest floor and are responsible for the common name of "Angel Wings." *Pleurotus* has more fleshy species with broader lamellae that are not pliant. Reports of poisoning in Asia have changed our opinion of this species, and therefore we do not recommend eating it.

Panus rudis Fr.
EDIBLE

Pileus 1.5–7.0 cm broad, convex, pinkish tan to light reddish brown, velvety from dense, long, stiff hairs over the entire surface, margin inrolled, often irregularly lobed, dry. Flesh tough, thin, white. Lamellae decurrent, close, narrow, edges smooth (not serrate), white to pale pink. Stipe a lateral, short, stout plug of tissue, hairy and concolorous with the pileus. Partial veil absent. Odorless. Taste slightly bitter.

Spores 4.5–7.0 x 2.5–3.0 μm short elliptic, smooth, entire, thin-walled, nonamyloid. Spore print white. Cheilo- and pleurocystidia club-shaped, thick-walled.

Habit and distribution: Single fruiting bodies but usually of several together on logs and stumps of hardwoods. Widely distributed. Fruiting in spring, summer, and fall.

Comments: Also known as *Lentinus strigosus* (Schwein.) Fr., it is edible young, but very tough especially when mature.

Pleurotus ostreatus Fr.
EDIBLE

Pileus 2–30 cm broad, 0.8–8.0 cm wide, oyster-shell to fan-shaped to broadly convex, white, pale pink to light yellow-brown, sometimes lobed or wavy, smooth, hairless, moist. Flesh firm, thick, dull white. Lamellae long decurrent to the blunt point of attachment, fairly well separated, broad, thick, veined, white. Stipe usually absent; if present 0.5–1.5 cm long, 0.5–1.0 cm thick, eccentric, equal, dry, white, covered with a downy, often dense, white pubescence, with white hairs around base, dry. Odor of anise or fragrant and fruity. Taste mild and pleasant.

Spores 8–12 x 3.5–4.5 µm narrowly elliptic, smooth, entire, thin-walled, nonamyloid. Spore print white, buff to pale pink.

Habit and distribution: Rarely single, usually in large imbricate clusters on branches, logs, and stumps of hardwoods and conifers. Widely distributed, but most common in eastern North America. Fruiting during or following wet weather in spring and fall, often in late fall.

Comments: The "Oyster Mushroom" has been found almost any time conditions are right. We have actually found it on Dec. 19, during a warm spell in western Virginia. Two closely related species are known. *Pleurotus pulmonarius* (Fr.) Quél. is the most common species in western North America, on conifers and it can not be distinguished from *P. ostreatus* by field characters. *Pleurotus populinus* Hilber & O.K. Mill. is found on cottonwood and aspen in northern North America (Vilgalys et al., 1992). It has larger spores (9–15 x 3–5 µm), but is otherwise not easily distinguishable from the other two species. All three are good edibles. See Group V for other *Pleurotus* species.

GROUP IV
KEY TO SPECIES OF THE TRICHOLOMATACEAE WITH SERRATE LAMELLAE ON WOOD

1. Stipe absent; pileus depressed; flesh tough; taste bitter; spores <5 μm, small and amyloid --- 2

1. Stipe well developed, central; pileus not depressed; taste mild or disagreeable but not bitter; spores larger, nonamyloid -- 6

   2. Stipe present, 0.5–5.0 cm long or with fused stipes; pileus with a central depression --- 3

   2. Stipe absent; pileus broadly convex; often in imbricate clusters ---------------------- 4

3. Stipe single; pileus depressed, smooth, pinkish buff ------------ *Lentinellus omphalodes*

3. Stipe with fused stipes; pileus deeply depressed with a hairy surface -- *Lentinellus cochleatus*

       (see comments under *L. omphalodes*)

   4. Pileus brown, with dense, white to yellowish hairs; often on wounds of living trees --- *Lentinellus vulpinus*

       (see comments under *L. ursinus*)

   4. Pileus brown, with short hairs only near the point of attachment -------------------- 5

5. Widely distributed on hardwoods and conifers all season; amyloid tissue in the pileus -- *Lentinellus ursinus*

5. Restricted to spring, under and near melting snow on conifer logs --- *Lentinellus montanus*

       (see comments under *L. ursinus*)

   6. Pileus robust (5–40 cm broad) with pale cinnamon to wood brown scales; stipe robust (2.5–10.0 cm long x 3–5 cm wide); partial veil present or absent ------------ 7

   6. Pileus small to medium in size (2–6 cm broad), nearly glabrous or with flat, brown-tipped hairs; stipe 4-8 mm wide; partial veil present or absent ----------------------- 8

7. Pileus 5–12 cm broad; partial veil present; widely distributed ---- *Neolentinus lepideus*

7. Pileus 10–40 cm broad; partial veil absent; on conifer logs in the western U. S. --- *Neolentinus ponderosus*

       (see comments under *N. lepideus*)

   8. Pileus buff to light cinnamon with flat, brown-tipped hairs; often having a weak, annular zone, sometimes with tissue-covered lamellae; widely distributed -- *Lentinus tigrinus*

8. Pileus different; annulus not present; lamellae crowded ------------------------------ 9

9. Pileus with brown, shaggy fibrils; on hardwood logs and limbs; found in southern United States -- *Lentinus crinitus*

(see comments under *L. tigrinus*)

9. Pileus pale buff to tan with short, fine hairs; on Sitka spruce logs and limbs along the Pacific Coast from California to Alaska---------------------------------- *Lentinus kauffmanii*

(see comments under *L. tigrinus*)

Lentinellus omphalodes (Fr.) P. Karst.
INEDIBLE

Pileus 1–5 cm broad, broadly convex, nearly plane with a central depression in age, pinkish buff, cinnamon to wood-brown in age, smooth, hairless, moist. Flesh soft, white. Lamellae adnate, subdistant, edges serrate, pinkish cinnamon. Stipe 0.5–5.0 cm long, 0.1–0.4 cm wide, equal, sometimes slightly off center, red-brown above, wood-brown toward base, ridged and furrowed, smooth, hairless, dry. Partial veil absent. Odorless. Taste soon peppery.

Spores 5.0–6.5 x 3.5–4.5 µm short elliptic, with minute, amyloid warts, entire, thin-walled; tissue in pileus nonamyloid. Spore print buff.

Habit and distribution: Solitary or in small groups on wood debris, sticks or logs of conifers and hardwoods, or occasionally on litter on the ground. Widely distributed. Fruiting in summer and fall.

Comments: All the species in the genus are bitter and inedible. *Lentinellus cochleatus* (Fr.) P. Karst. is rarely found, but has several fused stipes; a deeply depressed pileus with conspicuous upraised hairs; and brown, thick-walled, asexual spores on the stipe. Miller (1971) illustrates this species.

Lentinellus ursinus (Fr.) Kühner
NONPOISONOUS

Pileus 2–10 cm broad, 2–5 cm wide, convex to nearly plane, dark brown to cinnamon, with sparse hairs to densely hairy, and stiff, rigid hairs over the center, margin incurved and minutely hairy, sometimes hairless, dry. Flesh firm, white to pinkish buff. Lamellae close, broad, coarsely toothed, often with ragged edges, light pink to pinkish buff. Stipe absent. Partial veil absent. Odor fruity. Taste strongly bitter.

Spores 3.0–4.5 x 2.0–3.5 µm subglobose, with minute, amyloid spines, entire; tissue in pileus with both amyloid and nonamyloid cells. Spore print white.

Habit and distribution: Several to overlapping clusters on logs and stumps of hardwoods and conifers during moist, cool periods. Widely distributed. Found in spring, fall, and winter.

Comments: *Lentinellus montanus* O. K. Mill. is similar, but has no amyloid tissue in pileus; larger spores (4.5–6.5 x 4–5 µm); and is always found fruiting on conifer logs and sticks, sometimes actually in water, in the spring, near melting snow at high elevations in the western mountains. *Lentinellus vulpinus* (Fr.) Kühner & Maire has dense white to yellowish hairs on the pileus; short fused point of attachment; and is often found on the wounds of living trees, especially elm. All the species of *Lentinellus* are too bitter to eat.

Neolentinus lepideus (Fr.) Redhead & Ginns
EDIBLE

Pileus 5–12 cm broad, convex, nearly plane in age, white to buff at first, soon breaking up into small scales, which are cinnamon to wood-brown and raised in age, margin incurved at first, straight in age, viscid when young, but soon dry. Flesh tough, white, except for stipe base, which is yellow to rusty brown. Lamellae adnexed, close, edges serrate, white to buff in age, rusty brown stains when bruised. Stipe 3–10 cm long, 1.0–1.5 cm wide, equal or tapering, white and minutely hairy above ring, recurved small scales develop below, white to reddish brown in age. Partial veil membranous, buff, leaving a usually persistent, superior white ring, but in age it may weather away. Odor fragrant, aniselike. Taste somewhat disagreeable.

Spores 7–15 x 4.0–6.5 µm long-elliptic, smooth, entire, thin-walled, nonamyloid. Spore print white to buff.

Habit and distribution: Single to several on logs and stumps of conifers, wood in service and occasionally hardwoods. Widely distributed. Fruiting in spring and fall, following but not during cool wet weather.

Comments: Also known as *Lentinus lepideus* Fr. Species of *Neolentinus* cause a brown rot of conifers and hardwoods. *Neolentinus ponderosus* (O. K. Mill.) Redhead & Ginns is similar, but lacks a partial veil; is larger (up to 41 cm broad); the pileus has more pinkish buff coloration; and it is known only from the western United States. Both species are tough, become woody and remain in place for a long time. They also require considerable cooking to soften them sufficiently before they can be eaten. We rate them both as good as long as one harvests the young specimens, but we prefer and use only the caps. White rotting species are still retained in the genus *Lentinus*.

Lentinus tigrinus (Bull.) Fr.
NONPOISONOUS

Pileus 2–6 (-10) cm broad, convex to convex with an umbo, sometimes a depressed umbo in age, buff to light cinnamon, with many small, flat, brown-tipped hairs, very dense at the center but less so near the incurved margin, dry. Flesh tough, white. Lamellae decurrent, close, edges toothed to finely serrate, buff to pinkish buff. Stipe 2–8 cm long, 0.4–0.8 cm wide, equal, dry, buff with small, brown scales that become a dense, short, almost complete hairy covering over the base, often with a long rootlike base that extends deep into the wood or ground. Partial veil white, fibrillose, sometimes leaving a weak annular zone. Odor pleasant, like resin. Taste mild.

Spores 6.5–12.0 x 2.5–3.5 µm narrowly elliptic, smooth, entire, thin-walled, nonamyloid. Spore print white. Cheilocystidia narrowly club-shaped, thin-walled. Pileocystidia thick-walled.

Habit and distribution: Single, but most often in densely cespitose clusters from a rooting base, occasionally in large clusters on hardwood logs, stumps or dead roots. Widely distributed in eastern North America. Fruiting in spring, summer, and fall.

Comments: It is also known as *Panus tigrinus* (Bull.: Fr.) Singer. *Lentinus tigrinus* var *squamosus* (also called *Lentodium squamulosum* Morgan) is a variety with abnormal lamellae covered with a dense tissue, and is frequently encountered. Species of *Lentinus* produce a white rot of conifers and hardwoods. *Lentinus crinitus* (L.:Fr.) Fr. has a shaggy brown pileus; very crowded, serrate, lamellae; and small, nonamyloid spores (5.7–8.5 x 2.4–3.5 µm). It is a tropical species found on hardwoods in the southern United States. *Lentinus kauffmanii* A. H. Sm. has a pale buff to tan pileus; short decurrent, finely serrate, crowded, white lamellae; and short elliptic, nonamyloid spores (4.5–6.7 x 2.5–3.5 µm). It is found on Sitka spruce along the Pacific Coast from California to Alaska.

GROUP V
KEY TO THE TRICHOLOMATACEAE ON WOOD WITH A WELL–DEVELOPED STIPE

1. Fruiting bodies often to always in cespitose clusters; on wood on buried roots; pileus brown, yellow-brown, yellow, buff, to bright orange --------------------------------------- 2
1. Not with the above combination of characters --- 3
   2. Pileus buff, clay-pink, yellow-brown, ochraceous to dark brown; partial veil usually present, loose, superior, membranous or persistent, flaring; if absent always in cespitose clusters; under oak; lamellac white to pinkish, not luminescent; with black rhizomorphs (cords) from the base or in wood beneath the fruiting bodies -- *Armillaria*
   2. Pileus bright orange to orange-yellow, dry; partial veil absent; lamellae yellow-orange, luminescent in the dark; without black rhizomorphs ---- *Omphalotus illudens*
3. Pileus salmon-orange to brick-red, covered with ridges and pits; on hardwoods in the Lake States and southern Ontario and Quebec ------------------------- *Rhodotus palmatus*
3. Not as above --- 4
   4. Pileus dull to bright white, pinkish cream or buff when young and fresh ------------ 5
   4. Pileus lilac, brick red, purplish red, reddish yellow, olivaceous to bright yellow ------ 8
5. Pileus 10–40 cm broad, white, covered with dense, stiff, hairs, yellowing in age; stipe covered with dense white, stiff, hairs; on wounds of living trees -------- *Pleurotus levis*
   (*Pleurotus dryinus* has a partial veil, see comments under *P. levis*)
5. Not as above --- 6
   6. Pileus 2–14 cm broad, glabrous, pinkish cream with distinctive darker water spots over the surface; stipe glabrous; spores subglobose, nonamyloid --- *Hypsizygus tessulatus*
   6. Not as above--- 7
7. Pileus cream to pinkish buff with fine flattened scales; spores 5–8 x 4–5 μm subglobose, nonamyloid; usually on wounds of living trees ---------------- *Hypsizygus ulmarius*
7. Pileus dull white with light brown squamules; spores 11 x 4–5 μm subfusiform (Fig. 5), nonamyloid; on wounds of living trees --------------------------------- *Pleurotus cystidiosus*
   (see *Pleurotus ostreatus* in Group III)
   8. Pileus 1.0–2.8 cm broad, bright yellow, yellow orange, dry, powdery; stipe covered with dense, wooly, orange fibrils------------------------------------ *Cyptotrama asprata*
   8. Pileus and stipe differently colored-- 9

9. Pileus reddish yellow to reddish brown; stipe appears black velvety with short dense dense hairs; in cespitose clusters on dead wood or living trees; usually in cold weather-- *Flammulina velutipes*

9. Pileus colored differently; stipe does not have black velvety hairs ----------------------- 10

   10. Pileus 0.9–4.0 cm broad, olivaceous yellow to gray, smooth; lamellae pale olivaceous; stipe olivaceous brown ------------------ *Callistosporium luteo-olivaceum*

   10. Not as above --- 11

11. Pileus 3–8 cm broad, yellow beneath gray to gray brown tipped fibrils; lamellae yellow; stipe yellow with gray fibrils --------------------------------- *Tricholomopsis decora*

11. Not as above-- 12

   12. Pileus 0.5–4.0 cm broad, buff brown with tints of gray or drab; lamellae orange yellow to apricot, subdistant; stipe yellow to orange-red ------ *Gerronema chrysophylla*

   12. Not as above --- 13

13. Pileus 3–8 cm broad, yellow beneath, often dense, brick red to purplish red fibrils; lamellae buff to yellow, crowded; stipe also yellow with red fibrils-- *Tricholomopsis rutilans*

13. Not as above-- 14

   14. Pileus 1.5–8.0 cm broad, glabrous, light lilac to reddish brown; lamellae decurrent, violet when young, fading to tan; stipe robust, tough, covered with fine violet tinted hairs -- *Panus conchatus*

   14. Not as above --- 15

15. Pileus 2.5–6.0 cm broad, covered with abundant rusty brown, pointed erect scales; lamellae white; stipe below annulus covered with rusty brown, erect scales; one to several on hardwood logs--- *Leucopholiota* decorosa

15. Pileus 1.5–3.5 cm broad, brown, appressed in center, radially fibrillose; stipe glabrous; numerous on conifer logs -- *Clitocybula abundans*

ARMILLARIA

The species have a convex pileus, plane in age, buff, clay-pink, yellow-brown, ochraceous to dark brown, glabrous to squamulose, dry to viscid. Lamellae close to subdistant, decurrent, less commonly adnate. Stipe fibrous, fleshy, with or without a partial veil, if present a loose membranous, persistent, sometimes flaring annulus, with black rhizomorphs and/or white mycelium at base. The role is either as a parasite or saprophyte, often occurring in cespitose clusters on both hardwoods and conifers. There are 10 North American species, but some are uncommon and difficult to identify (Shaw & Kile, 1991).

Edibility: The species covered here are all rated as edible. However, Kibby (1992) notes that they are "edible, when well-cooked," and our experience is that a slightly bitter taste disappears on cooking. Aside from *A. tabescens,* the 10 species are hard to identify and it may be especially difficult in some cases.

KEY TO ARMILLARIA

1. Partial veil absent-- *A. tabescens*
1. Partial veil present --- 2
    2. Pileus 3–12 cm broad, viscid with erect hairs over the center, honey-yellow; partial veil cottony, white to buff, leaving a persistent annulus; eastern North America --- *A. mellea*
    2. Pileus 4.0–25.0 cm broad, moist with dense reddish brown fibrils over entire surface, pinkish buff to pinkish tan; partial veil leaves a wooly, white to pinkish annulus; northern areas and across Canada --------------------------------------- *A. ostoyae*
        (*A. sinapina* has a yellow universal veil, see comments under *A. ostoyae*)

Armillaria tabescens (Scop.:Fr.) Singer
EDIBLE

Pileus 3–10 cm broad, convex, plane or slightly depressed in age, nearly yellow, honey-yellow to pinkish brown in age, with dense, minute, erect hairs in center, with the rest flattened hairs, dry. Flesh thick near center, white to tinted or stained brown in age, brown at stipe base. Lamellae decurrent, subdistant, white to light pinkish, stained brown in age. Stipe 5–20 cm long, 0.4–1.6 cm wide, equal or tapering toward base, silky white near apex gradually darkening to brown over the base, with rhizomorphs, dry. Veil absent. Odor pleasant. Taste mild.

Spores 6–8 x 5.0–5.5 μm broadly elliptic, smooth, entire, thin-walled, nonamyloid. Spore print white.

Habit and distribution: Grows in dense large clusters attached to the base of living and dead hardwood trees, roots, stumps, or on the ground from buried wood or roots. Often found as a parasite on oaks and other trees in eastern North America. Fruiting in summer and fall.

Comments: The dense cespitose clusters and lack of a partial veil are the characters that separate *A. tabescens* from all other species of *Armillaria*. Like the other *Armillaria* species, rhizomorphs are formed in nature as well as in laboratory cultures. It has also been called *Clitocybe monadelpha* Morgan and *Clitocybe tabescens* Bres. in earlier American publications. Like *A. mellea,* it is a choice edible.

Armillaria mellea (Vahl.:Fr.) P. Kumm.
EDIBLE

Pileus 3–12 cm broad, convex, convex with an umbo variable in color from yellow to honey-yellow, fine, erect hairs over the center, very finely striate on the margin, sticky to viscid or even glutinous in wet weather. Flesh thin, white with brown to rusty brown discoloration in age. Lamellae adnate to short decurrent in age, subdistant, white to dingy cream color with rusty brown to pinkish brown stains in age. Stipe 4–15 cm long, 1.0–2.0 cm wide, nearly equal, enlarging slowly toward apex, white with downy, flattened hairs above ring, white to buff, becoming brown to cinnamon-pink with yellow fibrils below the ring, dry. Partial veil cottony, with clusters of hairs, white to buff or mustard-yellow, leaving a white, persistent ring on the upper surface, which is dry, but in wet weather often has a yellow, viscid margin. Odor mild. Taste pleasant.

Spores 6.0–9.5 x 5–6 µm elliptic, smooth, entire, thin-walled, nonamyloid. Spore print white.

Habit and distribution: Small or large cespitose clusters around the base of living and dead trees or on soil from buried wood. Widely distributed, most common in eastern North America. Fruiting in summer and fall.

Comments: This is commonly called the "Honey Mushroom" and often fruits year after year from the same log or stump. Recently studies have revealed at least 10 biological species in North America alone, all of which went under the name of *A. mellea*. Shaw and Kile (1991) have edited a handbook yielding recent information on the species. The name "Shoestring Root Rot" is often used to label the parasitic species, which are characterized by rhizomorphs proliferating from the base of the stipe that blacken with age. Economic loss to commercial and shade trees is great from some of the *Armillaria* species, but *A. mellea* is primarily a decomposer. Also see comments under *A. ostoyae*.

Armillaria ostoyae (Romagn.) Herink
EDIBLE

Pileus 4.5–25.0 cm broad, convex to broadly convex or even upturned in age, pinkish buff to pinkish tan young, to darker brown in age, dense reddish brown fibrils over the center extending to the margin, moist Flesh white, firm. Lamellae adnate, close, even, light ochraceous-buff darkening to cinnamon in age. Stipe 7–15 cm long, 0.9–2.5 cm wide, equal or wide in the center, expanding toward the base or narrowing at the base in cespitose clusters, pinkish cinnamon to cinnamon, with floccose patches. Partial veil leaves a wooly annulus near the lamellae, white with a pinkish hue. Odor mild. Taste mild.

Spores 8–11 x 5.5–7.0 µm elliptic, smooth, entire, thin-walled, nonamyloid. Spore print white.

Habit and distribution: Single, several, but most commonly in cespitose clusters at the base of conifers and aspen. Widely distributed in northwestern North America. Fruiting in summer and fall.

Comments: *Armillaria ostoyae* is an important pathogen of conifers causing a root disease. We have observed it on western red cedar and western white pine. *Armillaria gemina* Bérube & Dessur. is identical, but occurs infrequently on hardwoods in eastern North America. *Armillaria sinapina* Bérube & Dessur. is also similar to *A. ostoyae,* but has a yellow universal veil that leaves yellow warts on the pileus and a yellow, fibrous annulus (Burdsall & Volk, 1993). It is most common on hardwoods in the Pacific Northwest. It is also a very good edible.

Omphalotus illudens (Schwein.) H. E. Bigelow
POISONOUS

Pileus 7–11 cm broad, convex to plane, depressed in center, often with a shallow umbo, bright orange to orange-yellow, smooth, streaked with flat fibrils, margin inrolled, nearly even in age, dry. Flesh thin, firm, white, tinted orange. Lamellae decurrent, close, yellow-orange, luminescent in the dark. Stipe 5–18 cm long, 0.5–2.3 cm wide, tapering to a narrow base, light orange, minutely downy or somewhat scaly in age, even, dry. Odor unpleasantly sweet. Taste not recorded.

Spores 3–5 μm globose, smooth, entire, thin-walled, nonamyloid. Spore print creamy white.

Habit and distribution: Large dense cespitose clusters at the base of hardwood stumps or on the ground from buried roots (very often oak). Found in central and eastern North America. Fruiting in the fall.

Comments: The luminescent lamellae give rise to the name "Jack-O'Lantern Fungus." The old name in most books is *Clitocybe illudens* Schwein. The luminescence of the lamellae will often last 40-50 hours after collecting. It may be seen after sitting in the dark, facing the lamellae for about 2-4 minutes, sometimes 5 if the fruiting body is old. It is usually bright enough to enable one to see the lamellae clearly. *Omphalotus subilludens* (Murrill) H. E. Bigelow is found in the southeastern and southern United States but is distinguished only by using microscopic characters. The orange color and distribution in the eastern North America distinguishes this fungus from *Omphalotus olivascens* H. E. Bigelow, O. K. Mill. & Thiers, which has a brownish orange pileus and is found only in western North America. The three species are all poisonous and contain Type 8 toxins (atromentin, illudin M and S) (Kirchmair, et al., 2002). *Omphalotus olearius* (DC.:Fr.) Singer is distributed in Europe, and very closely related to our species. Is also poisonous.

Rhodotus palmatus (Bull.:Fr.) Maire
EDIBILITY UNKNOWN

Pileus 2–5 cm broad, broadly convex, covered with ridges and pits, pink, salmon-orange, brick-red to flesh color, margin smooth, dry. Flesh firm, pinkish buff. Lamellae adnate, close, broad, veined, pink. Stipe 1.5–3.0 cm long, 0.4–0.6 cm wide, off-center, enlarging slightly toward base, light pinkish, dry. Partial veil absent. Odorless. Taste unknown.

Spores 5–7 x 4.5–6.5 μm globose, tuberculate, entire, thin-walled, nonamyoid. Spore print cream color.

Habit and distribution: Single or several on logs and branches of hardwoods (on elm, basswood, and maple) during cool, wet weather. Found in eastern North American, rare in the southern Appalachians and southeastern United States. Fruiting in spring, summer, and fall.

Comments: We personally have never collected *R. palmatus* from Virginia, North Carolina, Tennessee, on south to Texas, but have in Kansas and Maryland. Pomerleau (1980) records it from southern Quebec, and Huffman et al. (1989) from the central United States. Since it is rare, there is no information on the edibility.

Pleurotus levis (Berk. & M.A.Curtis) Singer
EDIBLE

Pileus 10–40 cm broad, broadly convex, depressed in center, white, cream to buff, turning mustard-yellow when dry, covered with dense, short, stiff hairs (0.1–0.2 cm long), margin inrolled with fine, dense hairs, dry. Flesh tough, thick, yellowish. Lamellae decurrent, subdistant, thick, broad, white to lilac-brown with tints of gray or yellow when dried; edges smooth, not serrate. Stipe 2–15 cm long, 2–4 cm wide, enlarging toward base, eccentric to lateral, similar to the pileus. Veil absent. Odorless. Taste mild and pleasant.

Spores 10–13 x 3–4 μm nearly oblong (Fig. 4), smooth, entire, thin-walled, nonamyoid. Spore print white. Cheilo- and pleurocystidia, narrowly cylindric to club-shaped, thin-walled.

Habit and distribution: Solitary or several together from wounds on various living hardwoods, often up in the tree. Found in eastern North America as far north as southern Quebec but also on Arizona walnut in Cochise County, Arizona. Fruiting in the late summer and fall.

Comments: It is also known as *Panus strigosus* (Berk. & M.A.Curtis). *Pleurotus dryinus* is also white; has dense hairs on the pileus; but has a partial veil which leaves a weak annulus on the stipe. The spores are similar in size, but there are no cystidia. It is also found on the wounds of living hardwoods and conifers. Both species are infrequently found and edible only when young and soft. See comments under *Pleurotus ostreatus* in Group III.

Hypsizygus tessulatus (Bull.:Fr.) Singer
EDIBLE

Pileus 2–14 cm broad, convex, nearly plane at maturity, pinkish cream with distinctive, darker, round, water spots over the center, smooth, hairless, moist. Flesh firm but not tough, white to pinkish buff with a soft cottony stipe center. Lamellae adnexed with a thin line on the upper stipe, subdistant, broad, veined, buff to pinkish buff. Stipe 4–22 cm long, 0.4–2.0 cm wide, nearly equal or gradually tapering toward base, often lateral, curved or bent, white down near the apex, white and smooth, hairless over the rest, except the base, which has white stiff hairs. Veil absent. Odorless. Taste mild.

Spores 4.0–5.5 x 3.5–4.5 µm subglobose (Fig. 2), smooth, entire, thin-walled, nonamyloid. Spore print buff.

Habit and distribution: Usually cespitose to occasionally single, on logs and limbs of hardwood trees or shrubs. Found in eastern North America and northern Canada and Alaska. Fruiting in late summer and fall.

Comments: Early guides referred to it as *Pleurotus elongatipes* Peck and *Hypsizygus marmoreus* (Peck) H. E. Bigelow. This is a circumboreal species called "Shimeji" by mushroom growers in Asia and North America. It is commonly marketed in Japan and rated as delicious (Stamets, 2000). Recently it is being cultivated in North America. Compare with *Hypsizygus ulmarius.*

Hypsizygus ulmarius (Bull.:Fr.) Redhead
EDIBLE

Pileus 7–12 cm broad, broadly convex to shallow depressed, cream to pinkish buff covered with very fine, flattened scales, dry. Flesh firm, hard, tough, white throughout. Lamellae adnexed to adnate, fairly well separated, broad, white to cream. Stipe 6–9 cm long, 1.5–2.5 cm wide, centered or eccentric, equal or swollen near base, white, pinkish in age with longitudinal, ropelike cords of tissue revealing a white flesh beneath, minute hairs at apex, rest smooth, hairless, dry. Partial veil absent. Odor mild. Taste mild.

Spores 5–8 x 4–5 µm subglobose (Fig. 2), smooth, entire, thin-walled, nonamyloid. Spore print buff to white.

Habit and distribution: Single to several on hardwoods, on living trees in wounds or decayed branch stubs, often high up in the tree. Found in eastern North America. Fruiting in fall and early winter.

Comments: Formally called *Pleurotus ulmarius* (Fr.) P. Kumm. and, incorrectly, *Hypsizygus tessulatus* (Bull.:Fr.) Singer (Redhead, 1986). It is tough and would have to be very young or cooked thoroughly before eating. It is much tougher than other edible species such as *P. pulmonarius* or *P. ostreatus,* which are typically in imbricate clusters and do not have globose spores.

Pleurotus cystidiosus O.K. Mill.
EDIBLE

Pileus 3.0–7.5 (-11) cm broad, 3–8 cm wide, broadly convex, inrolled at first, dull white with small light brown squamules, very light in center, dry. Flesh firm, white, yellowing in age. Lamellae decurrent, subdistant, medium broad, white, to buff at maturity. Stipe 5–11 cm long, 0.5–2.0 cm wide, eccentric, white with a white pubescence, tapering to a smaller base, often covered with distinctive, tiny, white pegs with black heads, dry. Partial veil absent. Odor musty. Taste mild.

Spores 11–17 x 4–5 µm subfusiform (Fig. 2), smooth, entire, thin-walled, hyaline, nonamyloid. Cheilocystidia 23–30 x 8.5–12 µm pear-shaped to clavate, thin-walled, hyaline. Spore print white.

Habit and distribution: Single or several on wounds of living hardwood trees. Found in eastern North America. Fruiting in summer and fall.

Comments: The common name of this fungus is "Miller's Oyster Mushroom" and it is very similar to *Pleurotus ostreatus*. The difference is the presence of distinctive, tiny, white pegs with black heads at the base of the fruiting body or appearance in pure culture. In North America these pegs are only produced by *P. cystidiosus*. An almost identical species *P. abalonus* or "Abalone Mushroom," is found in Asia and both are important commercial edible species in Asia (Stamets, 2000).

Cyptotrama asprata (Berk.) Redhead & Ginns
INEDIBLE

Pileus 1.0–2.8 cm broad, convex to broadly convex in age, bright yellow-orange, powdery, netlike or pitted, dry. Flesh firm, pale yellow. Lamellae adnate, subdistant, thick, often fused together, buff to white. Stipe 1.0–6.0 cm long, 0.2–0.4 cm wide, somewhat larger at the base, dry, covered with dense, wooly, orange fibrils, thicker and longer over the base. Partial veil cortinous with pale buff remains on the pileus margin, but soon gone. Odor mild. Taste mild.

Spores 6.5–14.0 µm lemon-shaped to broadly elliptic, smooth, entire, thin-walled, nonamyloid. Spore print white. Cheilocystidia numerous to infrequent, long and narrowly clavate, thin-walled, hyaline.

Habit and distribution: Single or several on decayed conifer and hardwood logs and limbs. Found in eastern North America. Fruiting in late summer and fall.

Comments: It is also known as *Xerulina chrysopepla* (Berk. & M. A. Curtis) Singer, and *Collybia chrysopepla* (Berk & M. A. Curtis) Pers. (Redhead & Ginns, 1980). We have found it many times in Virginia. It has no taste.

Flammulina velutipes (Fr.) Singer
EDIBLE

Pileus 1.5–10.0 cm broad, convex, nearly plane in age, reddish yellow, reddish orange to reddish brown, margin often irregular, viscid. Flesh thick, white to yellowish. Lamellae adnexed, subdistant, broad, cream color to yellow, edges minutely hairy. Stipe 2–8 cm long, 0.3–1.2 cm wide, slightly narrowed at base, yellowish at apex, rest dense, velvety, with short, brown to blackish brown hairs, tough, hollow in age. Partial veil absent. Smell pleasant. Taste mild.

Spores 7–9 x 3–4 µm narrowly elliptic, smooth, entire, thin-walled, nonamyloid. Spore print white.

Habit and distribution: Single but most often in cespitose clusters on dead wood or living trees. Widely distributed. Fruiting in cold weather in winter, spring, and late fall.

Comments: Also known as *Collybia velutipes* Fr., the "Winter Mushroom" or "Velvet Foot" often fruits in late winter after warm spells. We have found this cold-loving species in every month of the year from Alaska to New Hampshire, but it always favors cool periods of weather. A thaw of any length during the winter is a good time to look for this species, especially in southern exposures. It is widely cultivated as food, especially in Asia, as Enokitake (Enoki). Stamets (2000) reports that the slender white stipe with the round white head is achieved using elevated levels of carbon dioxide and by excluding light. The inset plate shows a typical cluster ready for commercial use. This species tastes quite good, but in the wild, the stipe is extremely tough and should be discarded.

Callistosporium luteo-olivaceum (Berk. & M. A. Curtis) Singer
INEDIBLE

Pileus 0.9–4.0 cm broad, broadly convex, sometimes slightly depressed in age, olivaceous yellow, olivaceous gray, olive gray-brown, to brown, minutely hairy but soon smooth, moist to dry. Flesh thin, pale yellow gray. Lamellae adnate to adnexed, fairly well separated, buff to pale olivaceous sometimes with brown to blackish brown edges or tinted yellow-brown overall. Stipe 1.2–3.6 cm long, 0.1–0.4 cm wide, equal, dry, color of the pileus or darker olivaceous brown, with scattered patches of frosted, white fibrils, base surrounded by white mycelium. Partial veil absent. Odor and taste not distinctive.

Spores 5.0–8.0 x 3.0–4.5 µm elliptic, smooth, entire, thin-walled, nonamyloid, many with reddish brown pigment in the spores. Spore print white.

Habit and distribution: Scattered to numerous on needles, leaves, most often on well-decayed stumps, and logs. Widely distributed. Fruiting in spring, summer, and fall.

Comments: This species has variable coloration in the pileus and stipe but does have olivaceous hues. The pigment in the spores as seen in 3% KOH is typical of this species. We have collected this species in Idaho, Montana, Virginia, and elsewhere. Bessette et al., (1997) describes and illustrates *Callistosporium purpureomarginatum* Fatto & Bessette, which is purplish red with reddish purple edges to the lamellae; on oak logs; from eastern North America.

Tricholomopsis decora (Fr.) Singer
NONPOISONOUS

Pileus 3–8 cm broad, convex, often depressed in center, yellow beneath gray to gray-brown tipped fibrils, dense over the depressed center, dry. Flesh firm buff. Lamellae adnate, close, even, yellow. Stipe 4–8 cm long, 0.5–1.0 cm wide, equal or slightly larger over the base, dry, yellow with gray fibrils. Partial veil absent. Odor mild. Taste mild.

Spores 6.0–7.5 x 4.2–5.2 μm elliptic, smooth, entire, thin-walled, nonamyloid. Spore print white. Cheilocystidia abundant, clavate to saclike, thin-walled. Spore print white.

Habit and distribution: Several to numerous on conifer logs and stumps, especially hemlock. Widely distributed. Fruiting in the fall.

Comments: *Tricholomopsis sulfureoides* (Peck) Singer has a pale yellow pileus with sparse brown fibrils on both pileus and stipe, that are never gray; and a thin partial veil that soon disappears. We have found it only on eastern hemlock. Both species are inedible.

Gerronema chrysophylla (Fr.) Singer
EDIBILITY UNKNOWN

Pileus 0.5–4.0 cm broad, convex depressed to plane, buff-brown with tints of gray or drab, margin incurved at first, minutely hairy, scaly, dry to moist. Flesh thin, pliant, reddish orange. Lamellae decurrent, subdistant, orange-yellow to apricot. Stipe 2–4 cm long, 0.15–0.3 cm thick, equal, often curved, yellow to smoky orange-red, smooth, hairless, or with a few scattered hairs, moist. Partial veil absent. Odorless. Taste mild.

Spores 8.5–15.5 x 4.5–6.0 μm elliptic, smooth, entire, thin-walled, nonamyloid. Spore print yellow.

Habit and distribution: Numerous on well decayed conifer logs. Widely distributed. Fruiting in spring, summer, and fall.

Comments: Also known as *Omphalina chrysophylla* (Fr.) Murrill or *Chrysomphalina chrysophylla* (Fr.) Clémençon. We have frequently observed it in Montana and Idaho fruiting in abundance on decayed logs.

Tricholomopsis rutilans (Fr.) Singer
EDIBLE

Pileus 2–15 cm broad, convex to plane with a low umbo, covered with brick-red to purplish red fibrils, yellow underneath, which shows through and between the fibrils. Flesh thick, firm, pale yellow. Lamellae adnate buff to yellow, crowded, edges roughened, yellow. Stipe 4–10 cm long, 0.8–2.0 cm wide, equal or enlarged toward the base, covered with red hairs over a pale yellowish ground color, staining yellow when bruised, dry to moist. Partial veil absent. Odor mild. Taste faintly radishlike.

Spores 5–6 x 3.5–4.5 µm elliptic, smooth, entire, thin-walled, nonamyloid. Cheilocystidia abundant, club-shaped. Spore print white.

Habit and distribution: Single but usually several on conifer logs and stumps. Widely distributed. Fruiting in summer and fall.

Comments: We have seen very large specimens on conifer logs under Sitka spruce near Juneau, Alaska. It is very common on conifer logs and stumps, especially Norway spruce, in New Hampshire. Smith (1960) has included 19 species in a monograph of the Western Hemisphere species.

Panus conchatus (Bull.:Fr.) Fr.
EDIBLE

Pileus 1.5–8.0 cm broad, broadly convex, somewhat depressed in center in age, color variable, tan, often with a light lilac hue to reddish brown, smooth, glabrous, margin inrolled, minutely downy at first, dry. Flesh firm, leathery, white. Lamellae decurrent, subdistant, edges even, violet at first fading to tan or buffy tan. Stipe 2–6 cm long, 2–3 cm wide, off center, thick, stout, tough, covered with fine violet-tinted hairs. Partial veil absent. Odorless. Taste mild.

Spores 5.0–7.5 x 2.5–3.0 µm elliptic, entire, thin-walled, nonamyloid. Spore print white. Cheilo- and pleurocystidia narrowly club-shaped.

Habit and distribution: Several to cespitose clusters on hardwood stumps and logs. Widely distributed. Fruiting in spring, summer, fall, an winter on the West Coast.

Comments: This species is also known as *P. torulosus* Fr. Some eat it, but it should be very young since it is tough in age. We would rate it as inedible.

Leucopholiota decorosa (Peck) O.K.
Mill., Volk, & Bessette
EDIBLE

Pileus 2.5–6.0 cm broad, conic to convex then nearly plane in age, dry, covered with abundant rusty brown pointed, erect scales, dry. Flesh firm white. Lamellae adnexed, close, white edges finely scalloped. Stipe 2.5–7.0 cm long, 0.6–1.2 cm wide, equal or enlarging toward the base, white at apex, below the superior annular zone sheathed with rusty brown recurved, erect scales and coarse fibrils. Partial veil of coarse, rusty brown fibrils that flare upward as an annulus. Odor and taste not distinctive.

Spores 5.5–6.0 x 3.5–4.0 µm elliptic, smooth, entire, thin-walled, amyloid. Spore print white.

Habit and distribution: Single to cespitose on decaying stump and logs of hardwoods, eastern North America. Fruiting in late summer and fall.

Comments: This beautiful fungus was previously called *Armillaria decorosa* (Peck) A. H. Sm. and *Tricholoma decorosa* (Peck) Sacc., however neither genus has species with amyloid spores. The genus *Floccularia* has amyloid spores, but the species are putative mycorrhizal associates of higher plants and not decomposers (Miller et al., 1996). McIlvaine and MacAdam (1900) remark that "it is of good consistency and flavor, having a decided mushroom taste." We have not eaten it.

Clitocybula abundans (Peck) Singer
NONPOISONOUS

Pileus 1.5–3.5 cm broad, convex, depressed in center, with a small umbo, brown in center, with radially appressed fibrils, light brownish gray on the margin, dry. Flesh firm white. Lamellae adnate, narrow, close, white. Stipe 1.5–3.0 cm long, 0.2–0.4 cm wide, cylindric, white, with fine, white hairs over the surface, dry. Partial veil absent. Odor and taste not distinctive.

Spores 4.5–6.5 x 3.5–5.5 µm elliptic, smooth, entire, thin-walled, amyloid. Spore print white. Cheilocystidia large, clavate to nearly cylindric.

Habit and distribution: Numerous on conifer logs and stumps. Widely distributed. Fruiting in spring, summer, and fall.

Comments: One of the key characters to look for are the numerous fruiting bodies on conifer logs. In addition, the amyloid spores and large cystidia define the species. *Clitocybula lacerata* (Scop.:Pollini) Métrod is light grayish white; without cheilocystidia; and widespread on hardwood and conifer logs (Bigelow, 1973). See *Clitocybula familiae*, under comments under *Gymnopus acervatus* in Group VI, page 179.

GROUP VI
KEY TO SPECIES IN THE TRICHOLOMATACEAE WHICH ARE SMALL MUSHROOMS WITH STIPES

1. Fruiting body not reviving when moistened; with fleshy or brittle stipes ------------------ 2
1. Fruiting body revives when moistened; with stiff, erect stipes ---------------------------- 7
   2. Fruiting body opens umbrella-like, small with brittle stipes; in troops or clusters; on litter, humus, and well decayed wood -- *Mycena*
   2. Not as above-- 3
3. Lamellae long or short decurrent; stipe thin, fragile (0.05–0.25 cm wide) to thicker and/or fleshy (0.6–7.0 cm wide--- 4
3. Lamellae adnate to adnexed -- Collybioid Fungi
   4. Stipe thin and fragile (0.05–0.25 cm wide) --- 5
   4. Stipe thicker and/or fleshy (0.6–7.0 cm wide)---------------------------------- *Clitocybe*
5. Pileus 0.3–0.8 cm broad, convex-depressed with inrolled margin and orange with a red center; stipe 0.05 cm wide; always in beds of moss ---------------------- *Rickenella fibula*
5. Not as above -- 6
   6. Pileus deeply depressed in center, straw to yellowish, fading to white, margin striate; surrounded by minute, round, green algae on moss covered rotten logs; widely distributed; odorless--- *Lichenomphalia umbellifera*
   6. Pileus dark red-brown, shallow central depression, margin striate to the center; gregarious on hardwood limbs and litter; eastern North America; sour cabbage odor --- *Micromphale foetidum*
7. Pileus with erect, thick-walled hairs (setae); on wood---------------------------- *Crinipellis*
7. Not as above -- 8
   8. Pileus convex, depressed in center, honey-yellow to orange-brown, margin striate; spores elliptic, amyloid; on logs, stumps and wood debris ------------ *Xeromphalina*
   8. Pileus campanulate, plane with a shallow depression in center, white, orange-yellow to dark red-brown, margin striate; spores elliptic to teardrop-shaped, non-amyloid; in grass, leaves, needles, twigs and wood debris ---------------- *Marasmius*

MYCENA

The Mycenas are small, with a conic to companulate pileus and thin, brittle stipe. The pileus margin is striate and, at first, appressed against the stipe and then opening much like an umbrella. *Collybia, Rhodocollybia, Gymnopus,* and *Omphalina* are similar, but either have inrolled margins or decurrent lamellae. The Mycenas are found single, in troops, or even densely cespitose on leaves, needles, humus or wood. In addition, they are fleshy and fragile and do not revive when moistened like species of *Xcromphalina, Marasmius, Marasmiellus* or *Crinipellis.* There are more than 230 species of *Mycena* in North America (Smith, 1947). A selection of the common species is included here.

Edibility: The edibility of *Mycena* is either unknown or not recommended. *Mycena pura* contains muscarine (Type 2 toxins), and therefore should not be eaten. The genus is made up of small fruiting bodies that render them as too small to eat anyway.

KEY TO MYCENA

1. Pileus and stipe both viscid --- 2
1. Pileus viscid or dry; stipe dry or viscid -- 3
    2. Pileus mustard-yellow often with greenish tones; lamellae white; stipe glabrous, white to lemon-yellow -- *M. epipterygia*
    2. Pileus bright orange to orange-red; lamellae orange; stipe orange ------ *M. leaiana*
3. Pileus dry, yellowish white; stipe with a thick glutinous, transparent sheath---- *M. rorida*
3. Pileus and stipe dry --- 4
    4. Pileus bright red, scarlet, pink to orange or orange-yellow---------------------------- 5
    4. Pileus not as above-- 7
5. Pileus 0.5–1.4 cm broad, bright red to scarlet; lamellae pinkish white; stipe white; spores < 5 µm-- *M. adonis*
5. Pileus pink, orange or orange-yellow; spores >7 µm----------------------------------- 6
        (see comments under *M. adonis*)
    6. Pileus pink; lamellae and stipe tinted rose; spores 7–9 x 4–5 µm, amyloid -- *M. rosella*
        (see comments under *M. adonis*)

   6. Pileus orange to yellow-orange; lamellae and stipe white; spores 7–8 x 3.5–4.0 μm, nonamyloid -- *M. aurantiidisca*

                   (see comments under *M. adonis*)

7. Cut flesh of stipe exuding a red to white latex -- 8

7. Cut flesh of stipe not exuding a latex --- 10

   8. Cut flesh of stipe exuding a red latex --- 9

   8. Cut flesh of stipe exuding a white latex -------------------------------------- *M. gallops*

                  (see comments under *M. haematopus*)

9. Lamellae with dark red-brown edges -- *M. sanguinolenta*

                  (see comments under *M. haematopus*)

9. Lamaellae whitish to grayish red, edges not red-brown -------------------- *M. haematopus*

   10. Growing in melting snow banks in the Western mountains; stipe covered with dense, white, cottony hairs -- *M. overholtzii*

   10. Growing in other habitats, not in melting snow; stipe not as above ---------------- 11

11. Odor strong, radishlike; taste radishlike -- 12

11. Odor different or mild; taste different -- 13

   12. Pileus rosy red, purplish, light lilac-gray; lamellae bluish to lilac ------------ *M. pura*

   12. Pileus buff-brown to clay-color; lamellae grayish violet with dark purplish margins-- *M. pelianthina*

                  (see comments under *M. pura*)

13. Pileus brown to gray-brown, at first covered with a white fuzz; odor strongly alkaline; several but not in cespitose clusters -- *M. stipata*

13. Odor and taste rancid to farinaceous; in dense cespitose clusters ----------------------- 14

   14. Lamellae white, stained with reddish spots or entirely reddish in age--- *M. maculata*

                  (see comments under *M. stipitata*)

   14. Lamellae white, tinted light-gray to pink -- 15

15. Pileus reddish brown, margin striate, light pinkish white --------------------- *M. inclinata*

15. Pileus buff-brown to cinnamon-brown, margin striate, splitting in age, gray -- *M. galericulata*

Mycena epipterygia (Fr.) Gray
EDIBILITY UNKNOWN

Pileus 0.8–2.0 cm broad, conic, broadly conic with an umbo in age, mustard-yellow in center, often with faint greenish tone, smooth, hairless, margin straight, striate, whitish, viscid. Flesh thin, yellowish. Lamellae adnate, fairly well separated, white to buff. Stipe 6–8 cm long, 0.1–0.2 cm wide, equal, pliant, smooth, white to lemon-yellow, viscid, base with a few coarse hairs. Partial veil absent. Odor farinaceous or rancid. Taste mild or slightly bitter.

Spores 8–10 x 5–6 µm elliptic, smooth, entire, thin-walled, amyloid. Spore print white. Cystidia club-shaped and covered with short fingerlike projections.

Habit and distribution: Scattered to many in humus or occasionally on wood, under conifers in northern conifer forests. Widely distributed. Fruiting in the fall.

Comments: *Mycena epipterygia* var *lignicola* A.H. Sm. is very similar but occurs on wood (A. H. Smith, 1947).

Mycena leaiana (Berk.) Sacc.
NONPOISONOUS

Pileus 1–4 cm broad, broadly convex, campanulate in age, bright orange to orange-red, bright orange to orange-red, fading in age, eventually whitish, smooth, hairless, shining, viscid, margin slightly striate when moist. Flesh soft, watery, white. Lamellae adnate, close, salmon, which bruise orange-yellow, edges reddish orange. Stipe 3–7 cm long, 0.2–0.4 cm wide, equal or enlarging below, orange, viscid, covered with fine hairs, and a densely hairy base. Veil absent. Odor somewhat farinaceous. Taste mild.

Spores 7–10 x 5–6 µm elliptic, smooth, entire, thin-walled, amyloid. Spore print white. Cheilo- and pleurocystidia variously shaped.

Habit and distribution: In cespitose clusters on hardwood logs and limbs. Found in eastern North America. Fruiting in spring, summer, and fall.

Comments: We have found this colorful species every year in Virginia.

Mycena rorida (Fr.) Quél.
EDIBILITY UNKNOWN

Pileus 0.5–1.5 cm broad, broadly convex, often depressed in the center, brownish to yellowish white, margin striate, dry. Flesh thin, pale buff. Lamellae adnate, decurrent in age, subdistant, white. Stipe 2–5 cm long, 0.1 cm wide, equal, covered with a thick, glutinous, transparent sheath, beneath the gluten, bluish black near apex, turning whitish overall in age, gluten sliding to base in age. Partial veil absent. Odor and taste not distinctive.

Spores 8–10 x 4–6 μm elliptic, smooth, entire, thin-walled, darkly amyloid. Spore print white. Cheilocystidia fusiform to cylindric, thin-walled.

Habit and distribution: Several to numerous on needles or conifer wood. Widely distributed. Fruiting in spring, summer, and fall.

Comments: The extremely thick, translucent, gelatinous sheath makes this one of the most distinctive of all Mycenas.

Mycena adonis (Bull.:Fr.) Gray
INEDIBLE

Pileus 0.5–1.4 cm conic to campanulate in age, bright red, scarlet fading in age to pinkish white, dry. Flesh firm, pinkish to orange. Lamellae adnate, subdistant, pinkish white. Stipe 2–4 cm long, 0.1–0.2 cm wide, white sometimes tinted pink, pruinose at apex, base dingy yellow to brownish, darkening in age. Partial veil absent. Odor and taste not distinctive.

Spores 6–7 x 3.0–3.5 μm narrowly elliptic, smooth, entire, thin-walled, nonamyloid. Spore print white. Cheilocystidia fusiform with a long neck, abundant.

Habit and distribution: Single or several together under conifer forests. Found in western North America. Fruiting in spring and fall.

Comments: *Mycena rosella* (Fr.) Quél. is somewhat similar with a pink pileus; lamellae and stipe tinted rose; and amyloid spores 7–9 x 4–5 μm. However, it is often found in large troops under conifer forests in North America in the same habitats as *Mycena adonis. Mycena aurantiidisca* Murrill, also under conifers on the needles, is very similar to *M. adonis* but has an orange to yellow-orange pileus, not bright red; and somewhat longer, nonamyloid spores, 7–8 x 3.5–4.0 μm.

Mycena haematopus (Fr.) Quél.
INEDIBLE

Pileus 1–4 cm broad, conic to campanulate in age, red-brown center, reddish gray margin, covered at first by a frosted, white downiness, margin striate, straight, often torn and ragged, moist. Flesh thin, grayish red, exuding a blood-red latex when cut. Lamellae adnate, close, whitish to grayish red, with a blood-red latex visible when bruised or broken. Stipe 3–8 cm long, 0.1–0.2 cm wide, equal, covered with dense minute hairs, pale cinnamon, exuding a blood-red latex when broken, brittle, and hollow, dry. Veil absent. Odorless. Taste mild or faintly radishlike.

Spores 8–11 x 5–7 µm elliptic, smooth, entire, thin-walled, amyloid. Spore print white. Cheilocystidia fusiform, abundant.

Habit and distribution: Single but most often in cespitose clusters on well-decayed wood. Widely distributed. Fruiting in spring, summer, and fall.

Comments: *Mycena sanquinolenta* (Fr.) Quél. is very similar; also exudes a red latex; has dark red-brown edges on the lamellae; and is usually found on the ground in litter and not on wood. A number of species of *Mycena* have a white or colored latex. They are too numerous to be included here, but they are well described and illustrated by A. H. Smith (1947) in section Lactipedes. *Mycena gallops* (Fr.) Quél. has a light grayish brown pileus with a dark orange-brown center and exudes a white latex when broken. The latex should be checked by breaking the stipe near the base in one of the specimens in each collection when they are first collected.

Mycena overholtzii A. H. Sm. & Solheim
NONPOISONOUS

Pileus 1.5–5.0 cm broad, conic at first with a striate margin, campanulate to convex with an umbo in age, brown, brownish gray to gray, margin with minute radial ridges in age, smooth, hairless, moist. Flesh soft, white. Lamellae adnate to short decurrent, almost distant, light gray. Stipe 4–15 cm long, 0.3–1.0 cm wide, enlarging toward base, light pinkish brown and smooth near the apex, dry, lower part covered with dense, cottony, white hairs. Partial veil absent. Odor and taste not distinctive.

Spores 5.0–7.5 x 3.5–4.0 µm elliptic, smooth, entire, thin-walled, amyloid. Spore print white.

Habit and distribution: In large clusters on rotten conifer logs and stumps in melting snowbanks. Found in the Rocky Mountains and Cascade Range. Fruiting in early spring (late May to early August depending upon elevation) as the mountain snowbanks are melting.

Comments: This large *Mycena* is found where deep snow at high elevations results in the slow melting of the snowbanks. This happens into July and early August at the highest elevations. These mushrooms mature under the snow and as the snowbanks melt away; the large cespitose clusters fruiting from decayed conifer logs are revealed. Below freezing temperatures at night keep the snowbanks from melting too quickly and so the spores will be dispersed by the afternoon into the moist soil.

Mycena pura (Fr.) Quél.
POISONOUS

Pileus 2–5 cm broad, conic, broadly convex with a broad, low umbo in age, smooth, hairless, color quite variable, rosy-red, purplish, light lilac-gray to nearly white, margin straight, sometimes yellowish to white, striate, moist. Flesh firm, purplish to lilac fading to whitish in age. Lamellae adnate to adnexed, close, broad, veins between, bluish to lilac. Stipe 3–10 cm long, 0.2–0.6 cm wide, equal or enlarged below, sometimes twisted, whitish or color of pileus, striate, dry, smooth, hairless, hollow. Partial veil absent. Odor disagreeable of radish. Taste radishlike.

Spores 6–10 x 3.0–3.5 μm narrowly elliptic, smooth, entire, thin-walled, amyloid. Spore print white. Cheilocystidia abundant, 40–100 x 10–25 μm, flask-shaped with long necks.

Habit and distribution: Single to several on humus under hardwoods and conifers. Widely distributed. Fruiting in spring to early fall.

Comments: This small fungus is variable in size and color and is found in great abundance throughout Canada and the United States. *Mycena pelianthina* (Fr.) Quél is very similar, also with a radishlike odor, but has grayish violet lamellae with purple black margins. *Mycena pura* contains muscarine Type 2 toxins (Spoerke & Rumack, 1994) and should not be eaten. The pileus and lamellae are bioluminescent when fresh.

Mycena stipata Maas Geest. & Schwöbel
NONPOISONOUS

Pileus 0.5–3.0 cm broad, conic, campanulate in age, covered at first with a white fuzz, brown to gray-brown, margin white to pale buff, straight, lightly striate, dry. Flesh thin, white to grayish. Lamellae adnate, close, narrow, white to grayish, staining red-brown in age. Stipe 1.5–11.0 cm long, 0.1–0.3 cm wide, enlarging toward base, brittle, also covered with a white bloom at first, brown to gray-brown, dry. Partial veil absent. Odor strongly alkaline. Taste mildly acrid.

Spores 7.5–11.0 x 4.5–7.0 µm elliptic, smooth, entire, thin-walled, amyloid. Spore print white. Cheilo- and pleurocystidia abundant, flask-shaped with long necks.

Habit and distribution: Grows in groups, often in cespitose clusters, on decaying conifer logs and stumps. Widely distributed. Fruiting spring, summer, and fall.

Comments: This species is also known as *Mycena alcalina* (Fr.) Quél. (Breitenback & Kränzlin 1991). *Mycena leptocephala* (Pers.:Fr.) Gill. has a alkaline or nitrous odor; is always on the ground in litter; has tenpin-shaped cheilocystidia; and the pileus is more gray than *M. stipata*. The odor should be noted immediately after collecting or when collection is unwrapped. Crushing a small amount of tissue will enhance the odor. We have collected these species in Montana, Idaho, Maryland, and Virginia.

Mycena inclinata (Fr.) Quél.
NONPOISONOUS

Pileus 1.0–4.5 cm broad, conic at first to convex with a low umbo or campanulate, center reddish brown, margin light pinkish white and striate, moist not viscid. Flesh very thin, white, tinted yellow-orange in the stipe. Lamellae adnate, subdistant, broad, white, tinted light gray, or pink in age. Stipe 4.8–7.5 cm long, 0.1–0.3 cm wide, equal or tapering slightly toward the base, white at apex, yellow-orange becoming reddish brown with white specks in age. The base is surrounded by white, strigose hairs, also darkening in age, dry. Partial veil absent. Odor strong rancid to farinaceous. Taste also farinaceous.

Spores 7–9 x 5.0–6.5 μm elliptic, smooth, entire, thin-walled, strongly amyloid. Spore print white. Cheilocystidia clavate with irregular projections at the apex (difficult to see).

Habit and distribution: Found in dense large cespitose clusters on decaying hardwood logs and stumps. Found in eastern North America but occasionally on oak on the West Coast. Fruiting in summer and fall.

Comments: *Mycena maculata* P. Karst. is very similar to *M. inclinata,* as well as to *M. galericulata*. However, *M. maculata* is common on decayed hardwood and conifer wood in both eastern and western North America. The white lamellae are stained with reddish spots or totally reddish in age. The spores are 7–9 x 4–5 μm and also amyloid. For closer microscopic comparisons see Smith (1947) or Breitenbach & Kränzlin (1991).

Mycena galericulata (Fr.) Gray
INEDIBLE

Pileus 2–4 cm broad, conic, campanulate in age, buff-brown, dingy cinnamon-brown, margin gray, striate, often splitting in age, moist to greasy feeling but not viscid. Flesh thick, gray. Lamellae adnexed, close, veined, grayish white to pale pink. Stipe 5–10 cm long, 0.2–0.4 cm wide, equal, smooth, without hairs, twisted-striate, pale grayish white, dark brown in age, often with a rootlike base penetrating the host, dry. Partial veil absent. Odor mildly rancid. Taste rancid to farinaceous.

Spores 8–10 x 5.5–8.0 μm elliptic, smooth, entire, thin-walled, amyloid. Spore print white. Cheilocystidia, club-shaped with fingerlike projections at the top.

Habit and distribution: Single or in cespitose clusters on decayed logs and stumps of hardwoods especially oak. Found in eastern North America and the Pacific Coast. Fruiting in spring and fall.

Comments: *Mycena galericulata* is a large species, most often in cespitose clusters and is bioluminescent. *Mycena elegantula* Peck is somewhat similar but the pileus is blackish brown to red-brown and it is widely distributed on decayed conifer wood. If the lamellae are white with red spots, see comments under *M. inclinata*. None of these is considered to be edible.

COLLYBOID FUNGI

The classical concept of Collybias has adnate but never decurrent lamellae. The pileus is broadly convex to plane but inrolled at first, with thin flesh; and the stipe is pliant, not brittle. The spores are smooth, entire and nonamyloid. The genus *Collybia* is now confined to the very small species that grow from sclerotia on rotting mushrooms (see Group II). *Rhodocollybia* includes those species with pink to orange tinted spore prints. *Gymnopus* includes species with white spore prints but never form sclerotia (Antonin et al., 1997). *Xerula* has a distinctly deep-rooting base and distant lamellae. The genera above all appear collybioid and were once put in the genus *Collybia*. *Megacollybia* has abundant cheilocystidia and large, nonamyloid spores. *Clitocybula* is included here, even though it has small, amyloid spores, but like *Gymnopus acervatus* it occurs in dense clusters on conifer wood.

Edibility: There are both edible and poisonous species in this group. Check each description for the important edibility information.

KEY TO THE SPECIES OF COLLYBOID FUNGI

1. Stipe deeply rooting, narrow; pileus 2–12 cm broad, orange-brown, viscid; lamellae adnate, distant; partial veil absent ------------------------------------- *Xerula megalospora*
1. Not as above --- 2

   2. Pileus 5–20 cm broad, dry, convex, blackish brown, gray to whitish gray; lamellae broadly adnate, distant, white; spores large (7–10 x 4.5–7.0 µm) broadly elliptic, smooth, entire, nonamyloid, thin-walled---------------------- *Megacollybia platyphylla*

   2. Not as above; typically smaller; spores <7 µm- --- 3

3. Pileus 3–15 cm broad, dry, white to cream color with yellow stains; lamellae adnate, crowded, white tinted pink in age; stipe white, with brown spots in age; spores 5–7 x 4–5 µm elliptic, smooth, entire, thin-walled, nonamyloid-------- *Rhodocollybia maculata*
3. Not as above --- 4

   4. Pileus 2–8 cm broad, with a broad umbo, yellow-brown to red-brown, greasy to dry; lamellae adnate, crowded, white stained lilac in age; stipe twisted, striate, whitish to buff; spores 5–7 x 3.0–3.4 µm elliptic, smooth, entire, nonamyloid, thin-walled-- *Rhodocollybia butyracea*

   4. Not as above --- 5

5. Pileus 1.8–5.0 cm broad, convex, reddish brown to grayish pink, dry; lamellae free, crowded, white; stipe pinkish white, often grooved or ridged, clothed in dense, grayish white, short hairs; in clusters, on ground; spores 4–6 x 3–4 µm teardrop-shaped, smooth, entire, thin- walled, nonamyloid ----------------------------- *Gymnopus confluens*
5. Not as above --- 6

   6. Pileus 2.5–6.0 cm broad, orange to reddish brown, dry; lamellae adnate, crowded, white; stipe glabrous, white to yellow-brown at the base; spores 5–7 x 2.5–3.5 µm -- *Gymnopus dryophilus* (if pileus yellow to ochraceous-buff, see *G. subsulphureus* under comments)

   6. Not as above; usually in dense, cespitose clusters, on wood ------------------------ 7

7. Pileus 2–5 cm broad, convex, light reddish brown; lamellae nearly free, close, white; stipe glabrous, reddish brown to wine-brown, dry; spores 5–7 x 2–3 µm elliptic, smooth, entire, thin-walled, nonamyloid; in dense clusters, on wood--- *Gymnopus acervatus*
7. Pileus 1.5–4.5 cm broad, convex to plane, grayish white; lamellae nearly free, crowded, white; stipe dry, grayish white; spores 3.5–4.5 x 3.5–4.5 µm globose, smooth, entire, thin-walled, amyloid, on wood ------------------------------------- *Clitocybula familia* (see comments under *G. acervatus*)

Xerula megalospora (Clem. & Pound) Redhead, Ginns & Shoemaker
EDIBLE

Pileus 2–8 cm broad, conic to convex and plane in age, wrinkled to rugulose, light orange-brown, margin with translucent, light orange striations on a white ground color, viscid in wet weather. Flesh thin, white. Lamellae adnate, distant, white. Stipe 6–13 cm long, 0.2–0.6 cm wide, expanding to 0.3–1.0 cm at base, white, glabrous, often appears twisted, with a deeply rooting base, dry. Partial veil absent. Odor of geraniums. Taste mild.

Spores 18–23 x 10–15 µm lemon-shaped to bean-shaped, with one large oil body, smooth, entire, thick-walled, nonamyloid. Spore print white. Cheilocystidia numerous, capitate, thin-walled, forming a sterile margin, 90–120 x 10–22 µm. Pileocystidia large, ventricose, thin-walled.

Habit and distribution: Single to several, on the ground in hardwood forests. Found in eastern North America. Fruiting in summer and fall.

Comments: *Xerula furfuracea* (Peck) Redhead, Ginns & Shoemaker is smaller, 3–12 cm broad, smoky brown, margin wrinkled to rugose, dry to moist; spores 14–17 x 9–11 µm, broadly elliptic. Cheilocystidia numerous, narrowly fusoid to clavate, forming a sterile margin. It is also distributed in eastern North America. *Xerula longipes* (Bull.:Fr.) Maire is a smaller species, with a light gray pileus 3–7 cm broad; small spores, 8–11 x 6–8 µm, and is distributed in the western mountains in hardwood litter, but uncommon. The long, radicating "root" often extends 9–12 cm into the soil. None of these species are poisonous but there is little flesh to eat (Redhead et al., 1987).

Megacollybia platyphylla (Pers.) Kotlaba & Pouzar
INEDIBLE

Stipe 5–12 (-20 cm) broad, convex, plane or slightly depressed in age, blackish brown, gray or whitish gray, radial appressed hairs, margin inrolled at first, with short faint striations when wet, dry to moist. Flesh thin, pliant, white to gray. Lamellae adnate to adnexed, distant, very broad, veined, white to gray. Stipe 6–12 cm long, 1–3 cm wide, equal or enlarging toward base, white to grayish white, smooth, hairless, or with flattened hairs, hollow in age, with white rhizomorphs from the base, dry or moist. Partial veil absent. Odor fungal, fresh earth. Taste mild or slightly bitter.

Spores 7–10 x 4.5–7 μm broadly elliptic, smooth, entire, thin-walled, nonamyloid. Spore print white. Cheilocystidia pear-shaped to club-shaped, abundant.

Habit and distribution: Single to scattered on wood or ground from buried wood, well-decayed logs, stumps, or boards of hardwoods and conifers. Widely distributed. Fruiting following wet cool weather from early spring to fall.

Comments: This species is also known as *Tricholomopsis platyphylla* (Fr.) Sing. and *Collybia platyphylla* (Fr.) P. Kumm. We have found this species most commonly in New England, New York, and generally in the eastern hardwood region, but we also encounter it almost every season somewhere in western North America. Some people have experienced gastric upset after eating this fungus due to Type 8 toxins.

Rhodocollybia maculata (Fr.) Singer
NONPOISONOUS

Pileus 3–8 (-15) cm broad, convex, broadly convex to nearly plane in age, dry, smooth, hairless, felty to touch, white to cream color with mustard-yellow to yellow stains to brown spots which usually develop in age, margin inrolled at first to wavy in age, dry. Flesh firm, thick, white. Lamellae attached at first to adnate and appearing almost free, crowded, white to buff, sometimes tinted light pinkish in age with red-brown spots. Stipe 4–15 cm long, 0.6–1.2 cm wide, equal, white, sometimes with mustard-yellow stains or brown spots over the base which is clothed in a dense white mycelium, dry. Veil absent. Odor sweet. Taste slightly bitter.

Spores 5–7 x 4–5 µm broadly elliptic, smooth, entire, thin-walled, nonamyloid. Spore print pinkish buff. Cheilocystidia numerous, cylindric with coralloid appendages.

Habit and distribution: Single or in small clusters on rich humus, wood debris, or even well-decayed logs. Widely distributed. Fruiting in spring, summer, and fall.

Comments: Also known as *Collybia maculata* (Fr.) Quél. Though nonpoisonous, this species does not taste good.

Rhodocollybia butyracea (Bull.:Fr.)
Lennox
NONPOISONOUS

Pileus 2–8 cm broad, broadly convex with a broad umbo, yellow-brown to red brown, dry, moist to greasy when wet, feltlike to touch, glabrous. Flesh soft, white. Lamellae adnate, adnexed to almost free, crowded, thin, toothed or ragged edges, white in age stained lilac to buff. Stipe 3–12 cm long, 0.4–1.2 cm wide, enlarging slightly at base, dry, striate, sometimes twisted, dull white to light tan, covered with downy, white mycelium over the base, often brown stained in age with white mycelium just at the base. Veil absent. Odor mild. Taste mild or slightly bitter.

Spores 5–7 x 3.0–3.4 µm short elliptic, smooth, entire, thin-walled, nonamyloid. Spore print white to light pinkish buff. Cheilocystidia small, coralloid.

Habit and distribution: Scattered to numerous, in needle duff or in hardwood litter. Widely distributed. Fruiting in late summer and fall.

Comments: The fruiting bodies of this species are quite variable in shape and size at maturity. See notes under *Gymnopus dryophilus* to distinguish it from *Rhodocollybia maculata*.

Gymnopus confluens (Pers.:Fr.) Atonin, Halling, & Noordel
NONPOISONOUS

Pileus 1.8–5.0 cm broad, convex, plane sometimes with a small central depression, dry, smooth, hairless, reddish brown when moist, fading to grayish pink, margin faintly striate. Flesh thin, tough, pliant, white. Lamellae free, crowded, narrow, white. Stipe 5–10 cm long, 0.2–0.5 cm wide, tough, pliant, equal or slightly larger toward base, pinkish to reddish under a dense covering of grayish white, very short hairs, sometimes grooved or ridged, drys. Partial veil absent. Odorless. Taste unknown.

Spores 4–6 x 3–4 μm teardrop-shaped, smooth, entire, thin-walled, nonamyloid. Spore print white.

Habit and distribution: Found in dense cespitose clusters among fallen leaves and debris on the ground of either hardwoods or conifers. Widely distributed. Fruiting in summer and fall.

Comments: Also known as *Collybia confluens* (Pers.:Fr.) P. Kumm. or *Marasmius confluens* (Fr.) Pers. by many authors. *Gymnopus polyphyllus* (Peck) Halling (= *Marasmius polyphyllus* Peck) is somewhat similar; not as common, and has the odor and taste of garlic.

Gymnopus dryophilus (Bull.:Fr.) Murrill
POISONOUS

Pileus 2.5–6.0 cm broad, convex, flat in age, pliant, color variable from orange-brown to reddish brown or chestnut, usually one color overall, smooth, hairless, dry to moist when fresh, margin often upturned in age, sometimes wavy. Flesh thin but pliant, watery, white. Lamellae adnate to adnexed, narrow, crowded, white to dull white. Stipe 3–8 (-11) cm long, 0.2–0.6 cm wide, equal or nearly so, smooth, white with a tint of yellow below to yellow-brown or even reddish brown toward the base, which is covered with white mycelium, often in strands. Veil absent. Odorless. Taste mild.

Spores 5–7 x 2.5–3.5 µm elliptic, smooth, entire, thin-walled, nonamyloid. Spore print white. Cheilocystidia clavate to coralloid.

Habit and distribution: Several to numerous in deep humus or leaf litter usually under hardwoods, mixed woods, or alder and willow, but under conifers in western North America. Widely distributed. Fruiting in spring, summer, and fall during or after wet periods.

Comments: Also known as *Collybia dryophila* (Bull.:Fr.) P. Kumm. *Gymnopus subsulphureus* (Peck) Murrill has a yellow to ochraceous buff pileus; buff to yellow lamellae; and a light yellow stipe especially when young, but is otherwise very similar (Vilgalys & Miller, 1983). The stipe is not twisted striate or grooved, nor is it as fleshy as in *Rhodocollybia maculata.* It also does not form the dense, large, cespitose clusters typical of *Gymnopus acervatus* (Fr.) P. Kumm. or *Clitocybula familia* Peck. This species can caused severe gastrointestinal disturbance (Type 8 toxins), and we do not recommend eating it.

Gymnopus acervatus (Fr.) Murrill
INEDIBLE

Pileus 2–5 cm broad, convex to broadly convex in age, smooth, without hairs, dry, light reddish brown, slightly striate over the margin when wet. Flesh thin, whitish to dull pinkish. Lamellae adnexed to nearly free, close, narrow, white sometimes tinged pinkish. Stipe 4–10 cm long, 0.3–0.6 cm wide, equal, dry, reddish brown to wine-brown, usually darker than the pileus, base usually covered with a dense white mycelium. Veil absent. Odor and taste not distinctive.

Spores 5–7 x 2–3 µm, elliptic to teardrop-shaped, smooth, entire, thin-walled, nonamyloid. Spore print white. Cheilocystidia cylindric, clavate to coralloid.

Habit and distribution: Several to more frequently in large, dense, cespitose clusters on well decayed conifer logs and sticks or from buried wood. Widely distributed. Fruiting in late summer and fall.

Comments: Also known as *Collybia acervata* (Fr.) P. Kumm. *Collybia erythropus* (Pers.:Fr.) P. Kumm., also called *Collybia marasmoides* (Britzelm.) Bresinsky & Stangl., is very similar but decomposes hardwoods and is separated by microscopic characters (J. Breitenback & F. Kränzl., 1991). *Clitocybula familia* (Peck) Singer also occurs in dense clusters on conifer wood; has a gray pileus 1.5–4.5 cm broad; grayish white stipe and globose, amyloid spores (3.5–4.5 x 3.5–4.5 µm).

CLITOCYBE

This is a large genus with 226 species monographed by Bigelow (1982, 1985). The species are fleshy, small to robust, most have decurrent lamellae, and white, elliptic, smooth or minutely warted, nonamyloid spores. They are decomposers of a wide variety of plant substrates. Some appear to be restricted to hardwood or conifer forests or in some cases to the litter under particular trees.

Edibility: *Clitocybe dealbata* has typical symptoms of Type 2 toxins, as does *C. dilatata.* Both are white, on the ground, and should be avoided. *Clitocybe clavipes* should not be consumed with alcohol, since it appears to possess Type 6 toxins similar to disulfram, much the same as *Coprinus atramentarius* (Lincoff and Mitchel, 1977). There are also many species that have never been tested and one is wise to consider them inedible. However, there are several very good edible species, including *C. nuda, C. irina,* and *C. tarda,* all of which we have eaten and enjoyed. These species have minutely warted spores, which have very light pinkish spore prints and belong in Section Verraculosae (Bigelow, 1982), and have been separated out in the genus *Lepista* by some mycologists.

KEY TO CLITOCYBE

1. Pileus 1.5–15.0 cm broad, gray to chalky white; in dense cespitose clusters on the ground; western North America --- *C. dilatata*
1. Pileus colored or white; single or several, not in cespitose clusters, on humus, litter or leaves --- 2

   2. Pileus bluish green to pale bluish green; odor of anise ----------------------- *C. odora*
   2. Pileus some other color; odor not of anise --- 3

3. Pileus violet to violet-gray to cinnamon; lamellae pale violet; stipe pale violet to dull lavender --- *C. nuda*
3. Pileus some other color; lamellae white to pale cream or buff, stipe some other color --- 4

   4. Pileus 1.5–3.3 cm broad, buff to dull white; lamellae decurrent, close, dull white; stipe glabrous, white; in partial or total fairy rings in grass --- *C. dealbata* ssp *sudorifica*
   4. Not as above-- 5

5. Pileus 2–9 cm broad, slightly depressed in center, olive-brown; lamellae decurrent, close, pale cream; stipe clavate and hollow with pale ash-colored hairs ---- *C. clavipes*
5. Not as above --- 6

   6. Pileus 3–9 cm broad, deeply depressed at maturity, pinkish tan, glabrous; lamellae decurrent, crowded, white; stipe equal, base enlarged and densely wooly-- *C. gibba*
   6. Pileus, at most, with a shallow depression; lamellae adnate to short decurrent ---- 7

7. Pileus 4–13 cm broad, convex, dingy buff to pale cinnamon, margin inrolled at first; lamellae short decurrent, crowded, pale pinkish; in groups or in fairy rings under conifer or mixed woods -- *C. irina*
7. Pileus 9–15 cm broad, robust, convex, plane, gray to drab squamules; lamellae short decurrent, white; stipe robust 8–10 cm long, 2.5–4.0 cm wide, white ------ *C. nebularis*

                          (If pure white, see *C. robusta* under comments)

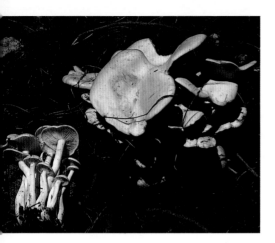

Clitocybe dilatata Pers.:P. Karst.
POISONOUS

Pileus 1.5–15.0 cm broad, convex, plane in age, gray at first, soon mostly chalky white, with fine matted hairs, margin inrolled at first, smooth, dry to moist. Flesh thick, white to gray. Lamellae adnate to short decurrent, close, narrow, sometimes forked, buff to pinkish buff. Stipe 5–12 cm long, 0.7–2.8 cm wide, equal or slightly larger at base, dull white, somewhat fibrous, dry. Partial veil absent. Odorless. Taste sour.

Spores 4.5–6.5 x 3.0–3.5 µm elliptic, smooth, entire, thin-walled, nonamyloid. Spore print white.

Habit and distribution: In dense, cespitose clusters on hard soil from buried wood, along logging roads. Found in the Pacific Northwest, Rocky Mountains, western Canada, and Alaska. Fruiting usually after cool, wet weather in early summer to early fall.

Comments: This fungus is often seen in wet fall weather at every turn along dirt roads. The pilei are often misshapen from being crowded together in large clusters. *Lyophyllum decastes* (Fr.: Fr.) Singer looks similar, but has a short, wider stipe and a gray-brown to brown pileus. In general the white *Clitocybe* species should be avoided and *C. dilatata* is reported to contain Type 2 toxins (Spoerke & Rumack, 1994).

Clitocybe odora (Fr.) P. Kumm.
EDIBLE

Pileus 3–10 cm broad, convex, broadly convex in age, bluish green, pale bluish green to white with a buff hue, covered with a whitish cast when young, radially streaked with hairs, moist. Flesh thin, soft, white to pale buff. Lamellae adnate to decurrent, close, whitish to pale buff to bluish green. Stipe 2–9 cm long, 0.4–1.6 cm wide, equal enlarged just at base, white to buff, appressed hairs, moist. Partial veil absent. Odor of anise, strong and fragrant. Taste mild.

Spores 5–9 x 3.5–5.5 µm elliptic, smooth, entire, thin-walled, nonamyloid. Spore print pinkish to pinkish cream.

Habit and distribution: Scattered or several under hardwoods or mixed conifer/hardwood stands. Widely distributed. Found in summer and fall.

Comments: *Clitocybe odora* var *pacifica* Kaufmann found in northwestern North America, has bluish green to dark green lamellae that are white to pale buff elsewhere. We have not eaten this species. See *Hygrophoropsis morganii* (Peck) H. E. Bigelow, which is a small, dull orange-colored fungus, has a strong, fragrant odor, and is uncommon.

Clitocybe nuda (Fr.) H. E. Bigelow & A. H. Sm.
EDIBLE, CHOICE

Pileus 4–15 cm broad, broadly convex, plane with uplifted margin in age, sometimes with a low umbo, smooth, hairless, various shades of violet to violet-gray to cinnamon with buff color in age, margin inrolled at first, dry. Flesh usually firm, light lilac-buff. Lamellae adnexed, pale violet, pale lilac to sometimes brownish in age. Stipe 3–6 (-10) cm long, 1.0–2.5 cm wide, equal, often with an oval basal bulb, pale violet, dull lavender covered below with scattered white hairs, dry. Partial veil absent. Odor pleasant, faintly fragrant. Taste mild.

Spores 5.5–8 x 3.5–5 µm elliptic, roughened, entire, thin-walled, nonamyloid. Spore print pinkish buff.

Habit and distribution: Single but more often numerous, occasionally cespitose in needle duff or deep leaf litter under hardwoods and conifers or even in piles of leaves, lawn grass, or around compost piles. Widely distributed. Fruiting in summer and fall.

Comments: This species is also known also as *Tricholoma nudum* (Fr.) P. Kumm., *Lepista nuda* (Fr.) M. C. Cooke, and the name *T. personatum* (Fr.:Fr.) P. Kumm. has also been used for some color variants of this species. This is a delicious edible fungus and is often found in great quantity. *Clitocybe saeva* (Fr.) H. E. Bigelow & A. H. Sm. is closely related but has a brown to pinkish brown pileus. *Clitocybe tarda* Peck (*Lepista sordida* (Fr.) Singer) is also very similar but is somewhat smaller and has a thinner stipe. Also see comments under *C. irina*.

Clitocybe dealbata (Sowerby.: Fr.) P. Kumm. **ssp. sudorifica** (Peck) H. E. Bigelow
DEADLY POISONOUS

Pileus 1.5–3.3 cm broad, convex to plane, depressed in center in age, pale buff to dull white, smooth, hairless, margin incurved, nearly even in age, dry. Flesh thin, whitish. Lamellae decurrent, close, narrow, dull white to nearly buff. Stipe 1–5 cm long, 2.0–6.0 cm wide, equal or slightly larger at apex, dull white, concolorous with the pileus, smooth, glabrous to minutely downy, sometimes curved. Partial veil absent. Odorless. Taste not recorded.

Spores 4–5 x 2.5–3.0 µm short elliptic, smooth, entire, thin-walled, nonamyloid. Spore print white.

Habit and distribution: Single, scattered, or numerous, sometimes in partial or complete fairy rings, in lawns and grass, on leaves in open woods. Widely distributed. Fruiting in late summer and fall.

Comments: This small, deadly poisonous *Clitocybe* may be found growing among edible species in lawns or occasionally in mushroom beds. It is, therefore, important to be aware of the decurrent, close lamellae and dull white overall appearance. The North American subspecies has no odor and a smooth pileus. Spoerke and Rumack (1994) report the presence of substantial muscarine, Type 2 toxins, in this species. Small white agarics, especially *Clitocybe* species with decurrent lamellae, should not be eaten and should be avoided in all cases (Bigelow, 1982). In Europe *Clitocybe dealbata* (Fr.) P. Kumm. is very similar, also poisonous, but has a strong farinaceous odor, and a lightly furrowed pileus surface.

Clitocybe clavipes (Fr.) P. Kumm.
EDIBLE WITH CAUTION

Pileus 2–9 cm broad, convex, soon plane with a slightly depressed center, often with a low, pointed umbo, moist, gray-brown to olive-brown, margin lighter. Flesh thick, watery, whitish, stipe hollow. Lamellae decurrent, close, often forked with veins between, pale cream. Stipe 3.5–6.0 cm long, 0.4–1.0 cm wide, equal then abruptly widening to a clavate, basal bulb, olive-buff to pale ash-colored hairs over a white stipe, moist. Partial veil absent. Odor often fragrant. Taste mild.

Spores 6–10 x 3.5–5.0 µm elliptic, smooth, entire, thin-walled, nonamyloid. Spore print white.

Habit and distribution: Single, scattered to abundant, usually on needles, under conifers or in mixed woods. Widely distributed. Fruiting in summer and fall.

Comments: This is a most common and often very abundant *Clitocybe*, which is usually long lived and does not decay readily. It is edible and, according to reports, has a good flavor, but should not be consumed with alcohol because it contains Type 6 toxins.

Clitocybe gibba (Fr.) P. Kumm.
EDIBLE

Pileus 3–9 cm broad, plane to shallow depressed, soon deeply depressed (infundibuliform), pinkish tan, smooth, hairless, margin inrolled at first, sometimes striate, moist. Flesh thin, white, fragile. Lamellae decurrent, crowded, forked, narrow, white to pale buff. Stipe 3–7 cm long, 0.4–1.2 cm wide, equal, hairless, sometimes with an enlarged base, white, dry, smooth, densely wooly over the base, dry. Odorless. Taste mild.

Spores 5–10 x 3.5–5.5 µm elliptic, smooth, entire, thin-walled, nonamyloid. Spore print white.

Habit and distribution: Single to scattered on humus under woods of all kinds. Common in eastern North America, less so in western North America. Fruiting in summer and fall, April in California.

Comments: This species is also called *C. infundibuliformis* (Fr.) Quél. in many mushroom books. The small amount of flesh requires many fruiting bodies to make a meal. We prefer *C. nuda* or *C. irina,* which are large, fleshy, and usually appear in quantity.

Clitocybe irina (Fr.) H. E. Bigelow & A. H. Sm.
EDIBLE, CHOICE

Pileus 4–13 cm broad, broadly convex, plane with a broad, low umbo, whitish but soon dingy buff to pale cinnamon-pink with a white, cottony margin that is inrolled at first, smooth, sticky but soon dry. Flesh thick, soft, white or tinted pinkish. Lamellae adnate to short decurrent, crowded, white at first to pale pinkish in age. Stipe 4–8 cm long, 1.0–2.5 cm wide, equal or even thicker in the middle, thin, hairy, dull whitish, sometimes dingy in age, dry. Partial veil absent. Odor very faintly fragrant. Taste mild.

Spores 7–10 x 4–5 μm long elliptic, minutely roughened, but some smooth, entire, thin-walled, nonamyloid. Spore print pale pinkish buff.

Habit and distribution: Grows in groups, often in fairy rings, in duff, under conifers or mixed hardwoods. Widely distributed. Fruiting in late summer and fall.

Comments: *Lepista irina* (Fr.) H. E. Bigelow, *Tricholoma irinus* (Fr.) P. Kumm., and *Rhodopaxillus irinus* (Fr.) Métrod are all synonyms. Bigelow (1982) reports this fungus from Alaska, Idaho to Tennessee. We have enjoyed this good edible and have canned it, and enjoy eating it in various casseroles, on meat, or in turkey stuffing throughout the winter months. Many authors accept *Lepista* as the genus for the ornamented-spored species of *Clitocybe*.

Clitocybe nebularis (Fr.) P. Kumm.
EDIBLE FOR SOME

Pileus 9–15 cm broad, robust, convex, plane, with incurved margin and a shallow depression, gray to drab, with radiating, flat squamules, dry. Flesh tough, thick, white. Lamellae adnate to short decurrent, close, whitish. Stipe 8–10 cm long, 2.5–4.0 cm wide, equal with enlarged base, curved, sometimes eccentric, silky, white, covered with scattered buff-brown hairs. Partial veil absent. Odor and taste disagreeable.

Spores 5.5–8.0 x 3.5–4.5 µm elliptic, smooth, entire, thin-walled, nonamyloid. Spore print pale yellow.

Habit and distribution: Solitary, sometimes several in humus and soil under conifers. Found in northern and western North America. Fruiting in summer and fall.

Comments: *Clitocybe robusta* Peck (also called *C. alba* [Bat.] Singer) is also a robust species but the pileus 5–17 cm broad, is white; the stipe white to buff without buff-brown hairs; and is distributed throughout North America. It also has a disagreeable odor and taste. *Clitocybe nebularis* is sometimes found with the mushroom parasite *Volvariella surrecta* (J. A. Knapp) Singer growing from its pileus. Some people have gastric upset from eating *C. nebularis* so tasting a small portion is advisable when first trying it. There may be some Type 8 toxins.

Rickenella fibula (Bull.:Fr.) Raithelh.
NONPOISONOUS

Pileus 3–8 mm broad, conic soon convex depressed with an inrolled margin, orange to reddish orange, with a dark center, and finely striate margin, dry to moist. Flesh thin, whitish. Lamellae decurrent, close, narrow, white to buff. Stipe 2–5 cm long, 0.05 cm wide, equal, white tinted yellow, minutely downy, tough, dry. Veil absent. Odorless. Taste not distinctive.

Spores 5–6 x 2–3 µm elliptic, smooth, entire, thin-walled, nonamyloid. Spore print white.

Habit and distribution: Single but most often groups in moss beds in moist areas in hardwood and hardwood conifer forests. Widely distributed. Fruiting in spring, summer, and fall.

Comments: This is a very common species, which is also known as *Omphalina fibula* Fr., and is found in a wide variety of habitats but always in moss beds.

Lichenomphalia umbellifera (L.:Fr.) Redhead, Lutzoni, Moncalvo & Vilgalys
NONPOISONOUS

Pileus 0.5–2.0 cm broad, plane, deeply depressed in center, light brown at first, soon straw to yellowish or fading to whitish in age, with a slightly incurved, deeply striate, wavy margin, moist to dry. Flesh very thin, pliant, concolorous with the pileus. Lamellae decurrent, subdistant, at times veined, pale yellowish. Stipe 1.0–3.0 cm long, 0.1–0.2 cm wide, equal, often curved, light reddish brown at apex to light brown below, fading to pale yellowish in age, with fine, white mycelium over the base, smooth, hairless, dry. Partial veil absent. Odorless. Taste unknown.

Spores 7–9 x 4–6 µm elliptic, smooth, entire, thin-walled, nonamyloid. Spore print white.

Habit and distribution: Scattered in low moss and algae, on wood and stumps, often on moss-covered, conifer logs along the Pacific Coast. Widely distributed in temperate and arctic regions. Fruiting in summer and fall.

Comments: Also known as *Omphalina ericetorum* (Fr.) M. Lange and *Phytoconis ericetorum* (Pers.:Fr.) Redhead & Kuyper. This is a basidiolichen and the small, bright green, round lichen, *Botrydina vulgaris* Breb,. is usually clustered around the fruiting bodies and can be easily seen with a hand lens. Other basidiolichens include *Omphalina luteovitellina* (Pilát & Nannf.) M. Lange, which has a bright yellow pileus and stipe, is found in tundra communities in the arctic regions of Alaska and Canada and the lichen associate is *Botrydina vulgaris*. *Omphalina hudsoniana* (H. S. Jenn.) H. E. Bigelow is bright orange-yellow and associated with a small leaf-like lichen, *Coriscium viride* (Ach.) Vain. in alpine and arctic tundra habitats. *Omphalina luteicolor* Murrill is similar, completely orange, and is found on conifer logs and stumps in the Pacific Northwest.

Micromphale foetidum (Sow.:Fr.) Singer
INEDIBLE

Pileus 1.5–2.5 cm broad, broadly convex, plane in age, with a shallow dark red-brown central depression, and red-brown striation from the center to the margin, striate-sulcate, moist but not viscid. Flesh very thin, light pinkish. Lamellae short decurrent, narrow, subdistant, thick, pinkish buff. Stipe 1.5–2.5 cm long, 0.15–0.25 cm wide, thin, equal or slightly thicker at apex, pinkish brown at apex rest dark red-brown to black-brown over the lower one half, dry, with minute, short, white hairs. Partial veil absent. Odor of sour cabbage, strongly disagreeable. Taste disagreeable.

Spores 7–10 x 2.6–3.2 µm narrowly elliptic, smooth, entire, thin-walled, nonamyloid. Spore print white.

Habit and distribution: Gregarious on hardwood limbs and litter. Found in eastern North America. Fruiting in late summer and fall.

Comments: *Micromphale perforans* (Hoffm.:Fr.) Gray is found on needles; has a long, red-brown stipe, black-brown at the hairy base; a pinkish brown, radially grooved pileus; and also has the strongly disagreeable odor of sour cabbage. We have found it in needle duff in Montana, but it is widely distributed.

189

CRINIPELLIS

Crinipellis appears to be similar to *Marasmius,* but the pileus is covered with thick-walled, erect fibrils that are dextrinoid in Melzer's solution. The stipe is covered with fine hairs or granules. All species revive when moistened as in *Marasmius* or *Xeromphalina.* The spores are elliptic, smooth, entire, thin-walled, and nonamyloid. The species are decomposers of needles, leaves, and wood in hardwood and conifer forests. There are five species in North America according to Redhead (1986).

Edibility: They are inedible.

KEY TO CRINIPELLIS

1. Pileus 1–4 cm broad, with dense, erect, red-brown to light brown, stiff hairs arranged in zones; spores 4.8–7.0 x 3.8–5.0 µm elliptic -- *C. zonata*
1. Pileus smaller, hairs not arranged in zones; spores larger ----------------------------------- 2
     2. Pileus 0.2–0.6 cm broad, orange to brown, center glabrous, rest with fibrils; stipe 1.8–3.2 cm long; spores 7.5–9.0 x 3.3–4.2 µm; in Stika spruce needles ---- *C. piceae*
     2. Pileus 0.2–0.7 cm broad, dark chestnut center; stipe 2.9–8.5 cm long; spores 6–8 x 3–4 µm; in eastern hardwood or mixed forests ------------------------------- *C. setipes*
                    (see comments under *C. piceae*)

Crinipellis zonata (Peck) Pat.
NONPOISONOUS

Pileus 1–4 cm broad, broadly convex to plane in age, with a shallow depression, covered with dense erect red-brown to pale, light brown, stiff hairs arranged in zones, most dense in the center over a light orange-buff ground color, dry. Flesh firm, white. Lamellae free, narrow, close white. Stipe 2–6 cm long, 0.1–0.3 cm wide, equal, with dense red-brown hairs and rhizomorphs from the base, pliant, dry. Partial veil absent. Odorless. Taste mild.

Spores 4.8–7.0 x 3.8–5.0 μm elliptic, smooth, entire, thin-walled, nonamyloid. Spore print white. Cheilocystidia long, narrow, thick-walled, and dextrinoid. Hairs on the pileus deeply dextrinoid.

Habit and distribution: One to several on dead wood, in hardwood forest. Found in eastern North America. Fruiting in late summer and fall.

Comments: Redhead (1986) reports a second population of this species in eastern North America, which has longer spores (7–12 x 3.8–5.0 μm).

Crinipellis piceae Singer
INEDIBLE

Pileus 0.2–0.6 cm broad, broadly convex, with a central small, smooth orange to brown papilla. (See photo for the tiny projection in the center of the pileus), rest with radiating orange to brown fibrils over a white ground color. Lamellae adnexed, close, narrow, white. Stipe 2.5–4.5 cm long, 0.05–0.1 cm wide, equal, minutely hairy, light brown at apex to gray-brown over the base, rhizomorphs absent, dry. Partial veil absent. Odorless. Taste mild.

Spores 7.5–9.0 x 3.3–4.2 μm elliptic, smooth, entire, thin-walled, nonamyloid. Spore print white. Cheilocystidia short with multiple fingers. Pileocystidia capitate to swollen, thick-walled, dextrinoid.

Habit and distribution: Several to many in troops on the needles of Sitka spruce. Found in coastal forests of western North America. Fruiting in late summer and fall.

Comments: *Crinipellis setipes* (Peck) Singer is also minute. Its pileus is 0.2–0.7 cm broad, with a dark chestnut center, which is radially fibrillose; it has a long, very thin stipe (2.8–8.5 cm long); and is found in eastern hardwoods or mixed forests (Redhead, 1986).

XEROMPHALINA

The species are small, with a smooth, usually striate pileus, decurrent lamellae, which are well spaced, and thin stipes. They are often found in troops on well decayed wood, or several on the ground in humus and organic debris. The fruiting bodies revive when moistened as in *Marasmius* and *Crinipellis*. Unlike the latter two genera, *Xeromphalina* has elliptic, smooth, entire, thin-walled, amyloid spores. There are 11 North American species (Miller, 1968).

Edibility: They are small, often bitter tasting, and have no value as edibles. There are no toxins in the genus.

KEY TO XEROMPHALINA

1. On seeds, needles and twigs of conifer or on aspen leaves; taste mild ---- *X. cauticinalis*
1. On logs and stumps -- 2
   2. Pileus dull orange-brown; on conifer wood; taste bitter-------------------- *X. brunneola*
                  (see comments under *X. campanella*)
   2. Not as above-- 3
3. Pileus red-brown, hairs over the center; only on redwood logs ---------------- *X. orickiana*
                  (see comments under *X. campanella*)
3. Pileus light yellow-brown, margin striate; on other wood ----------------------------------- 4
   4. Growing on well-decayed conifer logs and stumps --------------------- *X. campanella*
   4. Growing on well-decayed hardwood logs and stumps ------------------ *X. kauffmanii*
                  (see comments under *X. campanella*)

Xeromphalina cauticinalis (Fr.) Kühner
NONPOISONOUS

Pileus 0.5–2.5 cm broad, convex, slightly depressed in center, nearly plane in age, honey-yellow, margin faintly striate, moist. Flesh pliant, thin, pale buff, turns red in 3% KOH. Lamellae decurrent, subdistant, veined, pale yellow. Stipe 3–8 cm long, 0.1–0.25 cm wide, equal, pliant, tough, straight, yellow-brown to dark brown at the base. Partial veil absent. Odor and taste not distinctive.

Spores 4–7 x 2.5–3.5 µm elliptic, smooth, entire, thin-walled, amyloid. Spore print white.

Habit and distribution: Solitary or several, occasionally in groups on conifer seeds, needles, sticks, or sometimes on aspen leaves. Widely distributed. Fruiting in summer and fall.

Comments: The fresh flesh turns red in 3% KOH. If a collection from western North America is bitter tasting, it is no doubt *X. cauticinalis* var *acida* O. K. Mill. (Miller, 1968). For additional information see comments under *X. campanella*.

Xeromphalina campanella (Fr.) Kühner & Maire
NONPOISONOUS

Pileus 0.3–2.5 cm broad, convex to broadly convex with a central depression, smooth, glabrous, yellow-brown to orange-brown, margin striate, inrolled at first, moist. Flesh thin, pliant, yellowish. Lamellae decurrent, subdistant with veins between, yellowish to dull orange. Stipe 1–4 cm long, 0.05–0.2 cm wide, equal, pliant, tough, yellowish at apex, red-brown at base, surrounded by yellow-brown tufts of hair, usually curved from the host. Partial veil absent. Odorless. Taste mild.

Spores 5–9 x 3–4 µm elliptic, smooth, entire, thin-walled, amyloid. Spore print buff. Cheilocystidia present, thin-walled, tapering at each end.

Habit and distribution: Several, small groups to large cespitose clusters on decayed conifer wood. Widely distributed. Fruiting in summer and fall, into early winter.

Comments: *Xeromphalina kauffmanii* A. H. Sm. has a yellow pileus; smaller spores (4–5 µm long); yellow hairs around stipe base; and is found on hardwood logs and stumps. *Xeromphalina brunneola* O. K. Mill. has a dull orange pileus; disagreeable taste; and grows on western conifers and in northern North America. *Xeromphalina orickiana* (A. H. Sm.) Singer has a red-brown pileus with hairs over the central portion, and grows only on redwood logs.

GENUS MARASMIUS

The species of *Marasmius* are small, rather tough with rigid, hard, but often flexible stipes. Wilted fruiting bodies will absorb moisture and revive to look fresh and, in many cases, continue to produce spores. Species of *Mycena* will not behave in this manner. *Marasmius* spores are elliptic to pip-shaped, smooth, entire, thin-walled, and nonamyloid. *Xeromphalina* and *Crinipellis* also revive when moistened and have similar tough fruiting bodies. *Xeromphalina* has amyloid spores and *Crinipellis* has distinctive pileocystidia. *Marasmius* species are decomposers of grass, needles, leaves, and twigs.

Edibility: Many of the species of *Marasmius* are too small and have too little flesh to be considered good edibles, however, *Marasmius oreades* is edible and choice. We have eaten it many times and recommend it.

KEY TO MARASMIUS

1. Pileus 2–6 cm broad, campanulate, light tan; odor fragrant; taste mild; forming fairy rings on lawns, pastures, and golf courses -- *M. oreades*
1. Not as above, generally smaller --- 2
    2. Pileus convex, plicate, white, radially striate; lamellae joined to a collar that encircles the stipe; in troops, on twigs and leaves ---------------------------- *M. rotula*
    2. Not as above-- 3
3. Pileus reddish brown, wrinkled; stipe glabrous, light orange-yellow; odor of garlic; taste of bitter garlic; in troops, on conifer needles ------------------------- *M. scorodonius*
(stipe with fine, velvety hairs and garlic odor, *M. coplandii*-see comments *M. scorodonius*)
3. Not with garlic odor or taste -- 4
    4. Pileus 0.4–1.2 cm, minute, reddish to pinkish brown; lamellae white, subdistant; stipe 0.1 cm long, 0.3 cm wide, shiny black; in large troops on conifer needles--- *M. androsaceus*
    4. Not as above, pileus larger--- 5
5. Pileus 1.3–3.5 cm broad, campanulate, bright reddish brown; stipe glabrous, reddish brown to dark reddish brown; odor and taste mild; western North America --- *M. plicatulus*
5. Pileus 1.0–2.7 cm broad, campanulate, striate almost to the disc; stipe glabrous, white above, dark brown at the base; odor and taste mild to farinaceous; eastern North America --- 6
    6. Pileus rose colored to light pink; odor mild ------------------------------------ *M. siccus*
    6. Pileus hazel-brown to reddish brown; odor farinaceous---------- *M. fulvoferrugineus*
        (see comments under *M. siccus*)

Marasmius oreades Fr.
EDIBLE, CHOICE

Pileus 2–6 cm broad, convex, campanulate in age, light tan, light brown to reddish brown usually faded in age, smooth, hairless, margin somewhat striate in age, dry, Flesh thin, watery, white. Lamellae adnexed, nearly free, fairly well separated, veined, broad, light buff. Stipe 3–7 cm long, 0.3–0.5 cm wide, equal, tough, buff at apex to reddish brown at base, minute hairs especially dense over the base, dry. Partial veil absent. Odor fragrant. Taste mild and pleasant.

Spores 7–11 x 4–7 µm teardrop to pip-shaped, smooth, entire, thin-walled, nonamyloid. Spore print white to buff. Cystidia absent.

Habit and distribution: Grows in partial or complete fairy rings on lawns, pastures, golf courses, and grasslands of various kinds. Widely distributed. Fruiting in spring, summer, and fall.

Comments: The fairy rings increase in size each year as the mycelium grows out to decompose the dead parts of new grass. The fungus dies within the circle, leaving an advancing ring of mycelium from which the fruiting bodies arise. It is a very good edible with a flavor that enhances vegetables or gravies. "Marasmius Cookies" are also enjoyed by mushroom fanciers (H. H. Miller, 1993). Use caution in eating those that grow along interstate highways because they often contain lead, cadmium, or other car exhaust compounds. We have seen multiple fairy rings following heavy summer thunder storms on range land in Montana.

Marasmius rotula (Scop.:Fr.) Fr.
NONPOISONOUS

Pileus 0.3–1.8 cm broad, convex, with a central, navel-like depression, radially striate, plicate, white, margin wavy. Flesh very thin, membranous, white. Lamellae joined to a collar which encircles the stipe, well separated, broad, white. Stipe 1.2–8.0 cm long, 0.05–0.15 cm wide, tough, equal, shiny black, smooth, hairless, hollow, black rhizomorphs often present. Partial veil absent. Odorless. Taste soon bitter.

Spores 7–10 x 3–5 µm teardrop or pip-shaped, smooth, entire, thin-walled, nonamyloid. Spore print white. Cystidia absent.

Habit and distribution: Several or in troops on twigs, leaves, and debris of hardwoods on the ground. Found in eastern North America especially in New England, on west to the Great Lake states, uncommon elsewhere. Fruiting in spring, summer, and fall.

Comments: The common name for this fungus is the "Horse Hair Fungus."

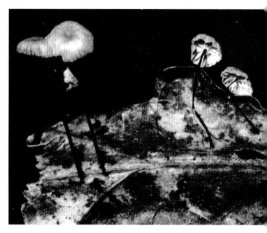

Marasmius scorodonius Fr.
NONPOISONOUS

Pileus 0.5–3.0 cm broad, dry, convex, then plane, pliant, brown but tinted reddish, margin whitish, wrinkled, wavy. Flesh very thin, whitish. Lamellae adnate, close, narrow, whitish. Stipe 2–6 cm long, 2.0–3.5 cm wide, tapering toward base, yellowish buff to light orange-yellow at apex, reddish to blackish brown below, tough, smooth, glabrous. Partial veil absent. Odor of strong garlic when pileus is crushed. Taste of bitter garlic.

Spores 5.5–9.5 x 2.8–4.2 μm elliptic to teardrop-shaped, smooth, entire, thin-walled, nonamyloid. Spore print white. Cheilocystidia clavate with small apical fingers (diverticulate). Pileus with oval to clavate, thick-walled cells.

Habit and distribution: Grows in groups on conifer needles, twigs, and debris usually under forest trees, common in eastern North America, less common in the western North America and rare on the Pacific Coast. Fruiting in spring, summer and fall.

Comments: On the West Coast, *Marasmius coplandii* Peck is often misidentified as *M. scorodonius* and is very similar, also with a garlic odor (Desjarden, 1987). However, it has a stipe with fine velvety hairs, larger spores and (13–17 x 3–4 μm), and usually grows on hardwood litter. Rated as edible but too small with too little flesh to be of use.

Marasmius androsaceus (L.) Fr.
NONPOISONOUS

Pileus 0.2–1.2 cm broad, conic, broadly convex, depressed in center, smooth, hairless, dry, brown to reddish brown with a pinkish tint, margin striate to radially wrinkled. Flesh very thin, dull white. Lamellae adnate, subdistant, whitish to flesh color. Stipe 2–5 cm long, 0.1–0.3 cm wide, equal, pale buff at apex, rest shiny black, tough, dry, hairless, hollow. Brown to black rhizomorphs from the base. Partial veil absent. Odorless. Taste mild.

Spores 6–9 x 3.0–4.5 μm broadly elliptic, smooth, entire, thin-walled, nonamyloid. Spore print white. Cheilocystidia clavate with fingers at apex. Pileus with similar clavate cells with fingers at apex.

Habit and distribution: Grows in groups, often in great numbers on conifer debris and needles, rarely hardwood debris, during wet periods. Widely distributed. Fruiting in spring, summer and fall.

Comments: We have often seen fruiting in large numbers during and following heavy rain in the West.

Marasmius plicatulus Peck
NONPOISONOUS

Pileus 1.3–3.5 cm broad, conic to campanulate in age, dry, obscurely striate over the margin, strikingly reddish brown to dark reddish brown in age. Flesh very thin, buff. Lamellae adnexed, distant, broad, white. Stipe 6.0–8.5 cm long, 0.2–0.3 cm wide, equal or enlarging somewhat toward the base, dry, hairless, pinkish just at the apex rest reddish brown to dark reddish brown over the lower one-third, with white mycelium and stiff hairs surround the base. Partial veil absent. Odorless. Taste mild.

Spores 12–16 x 4.5–6.5 μm bean-shaped to narrowly elliptic, smooth, entire, thin-walled, nonamyloid. Spore print white. Cheilo- and pleurocystidia clavate cells with fingers (diverticulate cells).

Habit and distribution: Several to many in a cluster, under willows, cottonwoods, oak or conifer debris. Found in the Rocky Mountains and western North America. Fruiting from July to April.

Comments: This beautiful deep reddish brown *Marasmius* with white lamellae is both distinctive and common according to Desjardin (1987) and Arora (1986) on the West Coast especially California, and we find it in Idaho following summer rains. It is not an edible mushroom.

Marasmius siccus (Schwein.) Fr.
NONPOISONOUS

Pileus 1.0–2.7 cm broad, convex, campanulate, often depressed in center, striate almost to the top, dry, rose colored, darker at center. Flesh very thin, white. Lamellae adnexed to free, well separated, white. Stipe 3–8 cm long, 0.02–0.1 cm wide, equal, dry, white at apex, brown to dark brown at the base, which is covered with white mycelium, tough, smooth, hairless, dry, hollow. Partial veil absent. Odorless. Taste mild.

Spores 13–18 x 3.0–4.5 μm tear-drop or pip-shaped, smooth, entire, thin-walled, nonamyloid. Spore print white.

Habit and distribution: Several or numerous on leaves, twigs, and debris. Found in northeastern North America. Fruiting in summer and early fall.

Comments: In southeastern and southern North America *Marasmius fulvoferrugineus* Gilliam is very similar but has a hazel brown to reddish brown pileus and the odor is weakly farinaceous as is the taste (Gilliam, 1976). We also found it commonly in Virginia and North Carolina. There is no reason to eat these tiny species.

PLUTEACEAE

This is a very distinctive family with a convex to plane pileus, free lamellae, smooth, elliptic, thin-walled spores and a deep pink spore print. Many species also have metuloids, which are a type of cystidia that is thick-walled, often with two hornlike projections at the apex. Lastly, the lamellar trama is convergent (Fig. 29), which is a family character. The species are primarily on sticks, logs, and stumps of hardwoods and conifers. They are decomposers, except for *Volvariella surrecta,* which parasitizes other mushrooms. *Pluteus* has the most species, and lacks both a volva and partial veil. *Chamaeota* is rare, has a partial veil and a persistent annulus, unlike *Pluteus. Volvariella* has a well-formed, membranous volva but no partial veil. The family is distributed worldwide.

Edibility: *Pluteus salicinus* (Pers.:Fr.) P. Kumm. and *P. cyanopus* (Quél.) Métrod are both hallucinogenic containing Type 4 toxins, and are characterized as moderately active by Stamets (1996). They both have grayish green to bluish green stipes. *Pluteus salicinus* has spores 7.0–8.5 x 5–6 μm, while the spores are 6–7 x 5–6 μm in *P. cyanopus* according to Moser (1983). Both are widely disbributed but not commonly collected (Bessette, et al., 1997; Arora, 1986; Pomerleau, 1980).

Pluteus cervinus is edible and good when fresh and firm. *Volvariella volvacea* (Bull.:Fr.) Singer, the "Paddy Straw Mushroom", is widely cultivated in Asia. They are harvested when still embryonic buttons (the egg stage) and used in Asian soups and stir fry dishes. They are often canned and sold in many markets in North America (Hall, et al., 2003; Stamets, 2000). However, if collected in nature, the buttons could be confused with those of the deadly poisonous *Amanita virosa.*

KEY TO PLUTEACEAE

1. Partial veil present or absent; volva absent -- 2
1. Partial veil absent; volva present -- 10
   2. Partial veil present; rare--------------------------------------- *Chamaeota sphaerospora*
   2. Partial veil absent -- 3
3. Pileus yellow, olive-buff, scarlet to orange-red --- 4
3. Pileus white, grayish to dark brown -- 6
   4. Pileus scarlet to orange-red ----------------------------------- *Pluteus aurantiorugosa*
   4. Pileus yellow, olive-buff to light olive brown--- 5
5. Pileus yellow--- *Pluteus admirabilis*
5. Pileus olive-buff to light olive brown-- *Pluteus lutescens*
   (see comments under *P. admirabilis*)
   6. Pileus white to grayish white with brown fibrils over the center --------------------- 7
   6. Pileus dark brown to drab-brown -- 8
7. Pileus white --- *Pluteus pellitus*
   (see comments under *P. cervinus*)
7. Pileus grayish white with brown fibrils over the center------------------ *Pluteus petasatus*
   (see comments under *P. cervinus*)
   8. Pileus dark brown to drab-brown, smooth to slightly wrinkled ---- *Pluteus cervinus*
   8. Pileus dark brown in center, pinkish brown margin, or dark brown and radially
      veined --- 9
9. Pileus dark brown in center, pinkish brown margin ------------------------- *Pluteus plautus*
9. Pileus dark brown and radially veined----------------------------------- *Pluteus thompsonii*
   (see comments under *P. plautus*)
   10. Fruiting body in cespitose clusters on robust mushrooms-------- *Volvariella surrecta*
   10. Fruiting on mulch, litter, logs, stumps, wounds or decayed areas on
       living trees -- 11
11. Fruiting bodies very small; pileus 0.8–3.0 cm broad, gray with
    matted fibrils --- *Volvariella pusilla*
11. Fruiting bodies larger; pileus color different --- 12
    12. Pileus 5–20 cm broad, white to dingy yellow, covered with fine
        fibrillose hairs -- *Volvariella bombycina*
    12. Pileus 5–15 cm broad, viscid to dry, glabrous, white, light gray, gray brown to
        black-brown -- 13
13. Pileus viscid, glabrous, white to light gray or brownish gray -------- *Volvariella speciosa*
13. Pileus dry, gray-brown to black-brown ---------------------------------- *Volvariella volvacea*
    (see comments under *V. speciosa*)

Chamaeota sphaerospora (Peck) Kauffman
EDIBILITY UNKNOWN

Pileus 3–6 cm broad, conic to campanulate in age, appressed fibrils, bright yellow-orange, umbo darker orange-brown, dry. Flesh thin white. Lamellae free, crowded, white becoming pink in age. Stipe 3–8 cm long, 0.4–0.8 cm wide, enlarging somewhat toward the base, white, buff over the lower half, smooth, dry. Partial veil white to buff in age, remains as an inferior, membranous annulus. Odorless. Taste unknown.

Spores 5–6 µm globose to subglobose (Fig. 2), smooth, entire, thin-walled, nonamyloid. Spore print pink. Cheilocystidia numerous, slender, thin-walled.

Habit and distribution: Single or several, on decayed hardwood limbs and debris. Found in eastern North America. Fruiting in warm summer weather.

Comments: This is a rare species known from locations in the Midwest including Missouri and Michigan. Most species in the genus have yellow pigment and must have a partial veil, unlike *Pluteus,* which has no partial veil.

Pluteus aurantiorugosus (Trog) Sacc.
NONPOISONOUS

Pileus 2.5–8.0 cm broad, conic, convex to convex umbonate, scarlet, orange-red to orange, smooth or wrinkled, dry. Flesh firm, white to yellow in the stipe. Lamellae free, crowded, white to pale pink in age. Stipe 3–8 cm long, 0.2–0.8 cm wide, dull white, buff, to yellow just at the base. Partial veil absent. Odorless. Taste bitter.

Spores 5–7 x 3.5–5.0 µm elliptic to subglobose, smooth, entire, thin-walled, nonamyloid. Spore print pinkish brown. Cheilocystidia clavate to spherical, abundant.

Habit and distribution: Several often in a cluster on hardwood stumps and logs. Found in eastern North America. Fruiting in summer and fall.

Comments: This is a most beautiful species, which is also known as *Pluteus caloceps* G. F. Atk. or *P. coccineus* (Massee) J. Lange. It is not common, although we have collected it several times in Virginia. In age, the pileus sometimes fades to yellow.

Pluteus admirabilis (Peck) Peck
NONPOISONOUS

Pileus 13–40 mm broad, campanulate to broadly convex with a low umbo, dark yellow, sometimes olive-yellow, hairless, wrinkled over the center, with a striate margin when fresh, moist. Flesh thin, dull whitish. Lamellae free, close, broad, buff becoming pinkish in age. Stipe 2–6 cm long, 0.2–0.4 cm wide, equal, very thin, clear yellow, hairless, moist. Odorless. Taste mild.

Spores 5.5–6.5 x 5–6 µm subglobose, smooth, entire, thin-walled, nonamyloid. Spore print salmon to pink.

Habit and distribution: Single or more often in small groups on new to very decayed logs or woody debris of hardwoods. Found in eastern North America. Fruiting in spring, summer, and fall.

Comments: *Pluteus lutescens* (Fr.) Bres. has an olive-buff to light brown pileus but also a bright yellow stipe. It is also found throughout North America on hardwood sticks, logs, and debris.

Pluteus cervinus (Schaeff.:Fr.) P. Kumm.
EDIBLE

Pileus 5–14 cm broad, conic, broadly convex to campanulate in age, dark brown to drab-brown, usually lighter brown in age, flattened hairs over the center, rest smooth, hairlesss, often slightly wrinkled, moist but not viscid. Flesh thick, soft, white. Lamellae free, crowded when young to close, broad in age, white at first, soon pink from the maturing spores. Stipe 5–12 cm long, 0.6–1.5 cm wide, enlarging evenly at base, dry, white with tinted brown or dull whitish hairs, sometimes nearly erect. Odorless. Taste mild.

Spores 5.5–7.0 x 4–6 µm elliptic, smooth, entire, thin-walled, nonamyloid. Spore print salmon to pink. Cystidia present, walls thickened, apex with hornlike projections (metuloids).

Habit and distribution: Single or several closely positioned on decaying wood of hardwoods and conifers. Widely distributed. Fruiting in cool damp weather usually in spring and fall.

Comments: The soft flesh soon spoils in warm weather. Fresh material must be refrigerated as soon as possible. A striking white species with abundant cystidia, *P. pellitus* (Pers.:Fr.) P. Kumm., is occasionally encountered by us in the Pacific Northwest. Another white to grayish white species, *P. petasatus* (Fr.) Gill, has brown fibrils over the center of the pileus and very few cystidia. It is found on hardwood stumps in North America and occasionally on conifer stumps in western North America. These species are edible when young and fresh. *Pluteus longistriatus* Peck has the general coloration of *P. cervinus* but the pileus is radially striate to the margin, often squamulose just at the center, and is also on hardwood logs and debris.

Pluteus plautus (Weinm.) Gill
NONPOISONOUS

Pileus 1–5 cm broad, convex to plane in age, dark brown in center to pinkish brown over the margin, but extremely variable in color, rugose in center to sulcate over the margin, surface smooth young to granular in age and squamulose in center, dry but appears moist. Flesh soft white to gray or brownish gray, brown in the stipe. Lamellae free, crowded, white to gray or sordid pink in age. Stipe 2–6 cm long, 0.3–0.7 cm wide, equal with an abrupt, flattened, basal bulb, dry, white over the apex to yellow brown below, clothed in minute brownish squamules, dry. Partial veil absent. Odor mild. Taste mild or slightly unpleasant.

Spores 5.0–8.5 x 4.5–7.0 µm subglobose to globose, smooth, entire, thin-walled, nonamyloid. Spore print pinkish brown. Cheilocystidia numerous, fusiform to clavate, thin-walled.

Habit and distribution: Single to several on hardwoods and conifers. Widely distributed. Fruiting in summer to late fall.

Comments: *Pluteus plautus* is a highly variable species but recently it has been determined that *Pluteus granulatus* Bres. is a form of this species. Vellinga (1990) has done an in-depth study of the Pluteaceae. *Pluteus thompsonii* (Berk. & Broome) Dennis has a dark brown pileus that is radially veined over the center (pictured in Roody, 2003).

Volvariella surrecta (J. A. Knapp) Singer
EDIBILITY UNKNOWN

Pileus 3–8 cm broad, convex, broadly convex with an umbo in age, fibrillose, gray, often brown over the center in age. Flesh thick, white. Lamellae free, close, broad, white but soon pink. Stipe 3–9 cm long, 0.4–1.0 cm wide, enlarging toward the base, white to gray, fibrillose. Universal veil a soft, white volva surrounding the base. Partial veil absent. Taste and odor mild.

Spores 5.4–7.0 x 3–5 µm elliptic, smooth, entire, thin-walled, nonamyloid. Spore print pinkish brown. Cheilocystidia fusiform with a long neck.

Habit and distribution: In cespitose clusters on *Clitocybe nebularis* or other robust, mushrooms with lamellae. Widely distributed. Fruiting in summer and fall.

Comments: *Volvariella surrecta* is parasitic on gilled mushrooms and is infrequently encountered, but most often found on *Clitocybe nebularis* (Fr.) P. Kumm. We have no information on its edibility.

Volvariella pusilla (Pers.:Fr.) Singer
NONPOISONOUS

Pileus 0.8–3.0 cm broad, ovoid to conic, convex in age, mouse gray, with thick, matted fibrils, weakly striate just at the margin, dry. Flesh white, very thin. Lamellae free, thick, close, white at first soon pink. Stipe 1–3 cm long, 0.1–0.5 cm wide, equal, white, enlarged just at the stipe base, which is surrounded by the fibrillose, mouse gray, persistent, lobed, deep, membranous volva. Partial veil absent. Odor and taste not distinctive.

Spores 5.2–8.0 x 3.5–5.7 µm short elliptic, smooth, entire, thin-walled, nonamyloid. Spore print pink to pinkish brown. Cystidia broadly fusiform to clavate, thin-walled.

Habit and distribution: Single to several, in moist damp locations, along streams, gardens and lawns. Widely distributed. Fruiting in the summer.

Comments: *Volvariella hypopithys* (Fr.) Shaffer is somewhat larger, fibrillose, pure white, with a white volva, and widely distributed.

205

Volvariella bombycina (Schaeff.:Fr.) Singer
EDIBLE

Pileus 5–20 cm broad, ovoid, campanulate to convex in age, yellowish to dingy yellow, silky, fibrillose in age, margin white and fringed with fine hairs, dry. Flesh thin, soft, white. Lamellae free, crowded, broad, white at first becoming pink. Stipe 6–20 cm long, 1–2 cm wide, enlarging or even bulbous at the base, white, hairless, dry. Universal veil present, volva as a thick, deep cup around the stipe base, dull whitish to dingy yellowish, persistent. Odorless. Taste mild and pleasant.

Spores 6.5–10.5 x 4.5–6.5 µm elliptic, smooth, entire, thin-walled, nonamyloid. Spore print salmon-pink.

Habit and distribution: Solitary or several together on hardwood logs, sticks, and stumps. Widely distributed but most frequently found in eastern North America. Fruiting in late summer and fall.

Comments: We have collected and photographed *V. bombycina* in both Denver, Colorado, and Hawaii. However, it is not common and one must keep in mind that *Amanita* species do not grow on wood, are not parasitic on other agarics, nor have they a pink spore print. The salmon-pink spore print and free gills, combined with the volva, and the lack of a partial veil clearly indicate species of *Volvariella*. There are 18 species in North America, but most are very rarely encountered. Many of the other species reported by Shaffer (1957) are found on soil or humus under forest stands.

Volvariella speciosa (Fr.:Fr.) Singer
NONPOISONOUS

Pileus 5–15 cm broad, conic to convex in age, white to light gray or brownish gray, obscurely striate just at the margin, glabrous, viscid. Flesh firm, white. Lamellae free, close to crowded, white with roughened edges. Stipe 9–24 cm long, 0.5–2.0 cm wide, enlarging toward the base, white, glabrous over the top half, fine hairs over the lower half, dry. Universal veil remains as a soft, white, persistent volva surrounding the base. Partial veil absent. Odor and taste unpleasant.

Spores 11–20 x 7–12 µm broadly elliptic to ovoid, smooth, entire, nonamyloid, thin-walled. Spore print pinkish brown. Cystidia broadly fusiform to clavate, thin-walled, hyaline.

Habit and distribution: Single to numerous, in mulch, rich loam, wood chips, gardens, grasslands, and in greenhouses. Widely distributed. Fruiting in spring, summer, and fall.

Comments: *Volvariella volvacea* (Bull. ex Fr.) Singer is similar and found on soil or compost in the Deep South or in green houses. The pileus, however, is dry and gray-brown to blackish brown. It is known as the "Paddy Straw Mushroom" in Asia, and is raised commercially for use in soups, stir fry, and other dishes. Many of the other similar species reported by Shaffer (1957) are found on soil or humus under forest stands.

ENTOLOMATACEAE

The family has pink spores and distinctive angular to longitudinally stri-ate spores (Fig. 13). The lamellae are attached and not free like the Pluteaceae. The species, with the exception of *Claudopus,* are not on wood but on the ground or in humus or grass. The fruiting bodies vary from very fragile to fleshy and robust. The genera included here are *Leptonia, Alboleptonia, Pouzarella, Nolanea, Entoloma, Claudopus, Rhodocybe* and *Clitopilus.* They are distinguished as follows. *Leptonia:* dainty and fragile; pileus umbilicate margin striate, often colored green, yellow to blue or purple; lamellae adnexed to adnate; stipe tall and thin; spores angular, 4- to 6-sided (Fig. 14); in grass and mulch. *Alboleptonia:* small to medium; pileus conic to convex, white to yel-lowish; lamellae adnate to decurrent; stipe thin to thick; white, spores angular, 4- to 6-sided (Fig. 14); in humus in disturbed areas. *Pouzarella:* medium size; pileus convex with dense fibrils, brown; lamellae adnate to adnexed; stipe equal narrow fragile; spores angular, 5- to 9-sided; on ground or humus. *Nolanea:* small to large; pileus conic to campanu-late, pinkish, cinnamon to reddish brown; lamellae adnexed to adnate; stipe slender, glabrous to pruinose; spores angular, four to six sided (Fig. 14); in grass communities. *Entoloma:* medium to large; pileus convex to plane red brown to gray brown; lamellae adnexed to adnate; stipe narrow to broad, equal or larger at base; spores angular, 4- to 6-sided (Fig. 14); on ground and/or mycorrhizal. *Claudopus:* small sessile; pileus conchate, light to dark brown, spores angular, 4- to 6-sided (Fig. 14), on wood. *Rhodocybe:* medium size; pileus convex plane in age or depressed; lamellae adnate to decurrent; stipe straight to flexuous, firm equal or enlarged at base; spores warted to pustulate, elliptic; in litter and humus. *Clitopilus:* medium size, fleshy; pileus convex, fleshy, dry; lamellae decurrent; stipe equal; spores elliptic with longitudinal ridges (Fig. 13); in grass.

Edibility: *Clitopilus prunulus* is edible and so is *Entoloma abortivum.* However, *Entoloma lividum* (Bull.) Quél. is known to be poisonous with Type 8 toxins. There are reports of some toxins causing mild liver damage (Ammirati et al., 1985). Lincoff and Mitchel (1977) provide a list of reported or suspected toxic Entolomas. It is best to leave this pink-spored family in the field, unless one is sure of the identification.

KEY TO ENTOLOMATACEAE

1. Fruiting body either lacking a stipe or with a short, minute, lateral stipe -- *Claudopus byssisedus*
1. Fruiting body with a central stipe --- 2
  2. Fruiting body white; pileus tinted buff; lamellae adnate, slowly pink as spores mature; odor and taste mild -- *Alboleptonia sericella*
  2. Fruiting body colored or lamellae decurrent --- 3
3. Pileus dark brown, covered with dense, erect fibrils; spores 12–19 x 7–9 µm, 7- to 9-sided --- *Pouzarella nodospora*
3. Not as above --- 4
  4. Pileus 1.2–2.5 cm broad, bright green to greenish yellow, bruising blue; stipe yellow-orange, bruising blue; odor of wet mouse fur------------------ *Leptonia incana*
  4. Not as above--- 5
5. Fruiting body dark blue to bluish gray; stipe dark blue over upper half-- *Leptonia serrulata*
5. Not as above --- 6
  6. Pileus conic with a pointed apex or an acute papilla at the apex--------------------- 7
  6. Pileus more convex, without a pointed apex --- 8
7. Pileus 2–4 cm broad, brownish orange; lamellae white, salmon-pink in age --- *Nolanea quadrospora*
7. Pileus 1–4 cm broad, with an acute papilla, straw-yellow; lamellae pale yellow --- *Nolanea murraii*
  8. Pileus 5–10 cm broad, dry, felty, white to ash-gray; lamellae decurrent; odor and taste farinaceous; spores longitudinally striate; common in grassy areas-- *Clitopilus prunulus*
  8. Not as above--- 9
9. Pileus smoky gray with concentric zones; lamellae decurrent; spores finely warted; odor farinaceous; taste very bitter; spores angular -------------------- *Rhodocybe mundula*
9. Not as above--- 10
  10. Pileus 2–7 cm broad, fragile, convex with a low umbo, campanulate in age, brown to gray-brown; common in spring; spores 9–13 x 7–9 µm, five to six-sided --- *Entoloma strictius*
  10. Not as above -- 11
11. Pileus 4–10 cm broad, gray-brown; lamellae decurrent, pale gray; usually accompanied by aborted fruiting bodies --- *Entoloma abortivum*
11. Pileus 5–9 cm broad, robust, dark brown to yellow-brown; lamellae adnexed, white to pink in age; normal fruiting bodies ------------------------------------- *Entoloma lividoalbum*

Claudopus byssisedus (Pers.:Fr.) Gillet
NONPOISONOUS

Pileus 0.5–7.5 cm broad, 0.5–4.5 cm wide, petaloid, glabrous, with a dense cover of appressed, white to grayish fibrils over a dark brown ground color. Flesh very thin, white. Lamellae adnexed, close to subdistant, grayish white. Stipe, if present, short lateral 0.3–0.5 cm long, 0.1–0.4 cm wide, with a densely appressed, dull white, fibrillose covering. Partial veil absent. Odor and taste farinaceous.

Spores 7.0–10.5 x 5.5–6.5 um angular, 5- to 6-sided, entire, thin-walled, nonamyloid. Spore print pinkish brown.

Habit and distribution: Single to several on humus, rotten logs of conifers and hardwoods. Widely distributed. Fruiting in late summer and fall.

Comments: *Claudopus depluens* (Batsch: Fr.) Hesler is similar, but has cheilocystidia and *C. parasiticus* (Qúel.) Ricken is occasionally encountered on old fruiting bodies of *Cantharellus subalbidus* according to Largent (1994).

Alboleptonia sericella (Fr.) Largent & R. G. Benedict
INEDIBLE

Pileus 0.6–6.0 cm broad, broadly convex to plane in age, sometimes with a central papilla, white tinted buff or pinkish, fibrillose to squamulose in age, dry. Flesh thin, white, fragile. Lamellae adnate, subdistant, white slowly pinkish as the spores mature. Stipe 2.5–6.5 cm long, 0.15–0.4 cm wide, equal or enlarging toward the base, white to light yellowish in age, finely fibrillose, dry. Partial veil absent. Odor and taste mild.

Spores 7–12 x 9–10 µm angular, 4- to 5-sided, entire, thin-walled, nonamyloid. Spore print pink.

Habit and distribution: Several to gregarious, in leaf litter, humus, grass, in open areas or hardwood to conifer forests. Widely distributed. Fruiting in late summer and fall.

Comments: This small, common fungus, also known as *Entoloma sericellum* (Fr.:Fr.) P. Kumm., is one of just a few white or nearly white species in the Entolomataceae. See *Clitopilus prunulus* for comparisons.

Pouzarella nodospora (Atk.) Mazzer
NONPOISONOUS

Pileus 1–5 cm broad, convex, broadly convex in age, light brown, dark brown over the center, with dense tufts of erect fibrils, and a striate margin, dry. Flesh soft, thin, dull white. Lamellae adnexed to adnate, broad, subdistant, grayish very young to dark brown with a slight pinkish hue at maturity. Stipe 2–7 cm long, 0.1–0.3 cm wide enlarging upward, with dense tufts of dark brown, erect fibrils over a white ground color, dry. Partial veil absent. Odor and taste mild.

Spores 12–19 x 7–9 μm long elliptic, angular, 7- to 9-sided, entire, nonamyloid, thin-walled. Spore print cinnamon-brown. Cheilocystidia cylindric to bottle-shaped. Pleurocystidia absent. Fibrils on pileus large tapering and incrusted.

Habit and distribution: 2 to 3 on the ground, in leaf litter, and humus. Found in eastern North America. Fruiting in summer and fall.

Comments: The brown lamellae and pileus fibrils appear similar to an *Inocybe,* but the spore color and morphology are those of the Entolomataceae. It is the most distinctive member of the family and not infrequent in Virginia in the fall. Also known as *Entoloma babingtonii* (Bloxam) Hesler (Hesler, 1967).

Leptonia incana (Fr.) Gillet
INEDIBLE

Pileus 1.2–2.5 cm broad, convex, may be depressed in center, bright green to greenish yellow, bruising blue, radially fibrillose in age, dry. Flesh soft, thin, yellowish. Lamellae adnate, close, white, bruising blue, becoming pink in age. Stipe 2–7 cm long, 0.15–0.4 cm wide, equal, dry, bright yellow-orange with an olivaceous hue, base clothed in white mycelium, blue stains where handled or bruised. Partial veil absent. Odor of wet mouse fur, unpleasant. Taste mild, then unpleasant.

Spores 8.5–13.0 x 7.0–9.5 μm elliptic, angular, 6- to 7-sided, entire, thin-walled, nonamyloid. Spore print pink.

Habit and distribution: Several to gregarious in leaf mold, humus, and grassy areas. Widely distributed. Fruiting in spring, summer, and fall.

Comments: Also known as *Entoloma incanum* (Fr.) Hessler. Noordeloos (1987) reports this species from Europe.

Leptonia serrulata (Fr.:Fr.) P. Kumm.
NONPOISONOUS

Pileus 0.5–3.0 cm broad, convex to broadly convex, dark blue to bluish gray, with fibrils over the center, glabrous over the margin, dry. Flesh soft, light blue. Lamellae adnexed, close, bluish gray but soon pink from the maturing spores. Stipe 2.5–6.0 cm long, 0.15–0.35 cm wide, slightly larger at base, blue to bluish gray over the upper half to nearly white over the base from a covering of minute fibrils, dry. Partial veil absent. Odor mild. Taste somewhat farinaceous.

Spores 8–12 x 5.5–9.0 um angular, 5- to 7-sided, entire, thin-walled, nonamyloid. Spore print pinkish brown. Cheilocystidia cylindric, thin-walled, numerous.

Habit and distribution: Solitary or several in grassy areas, humus, and leaf litter. Widely distributed. Fruiting in early spring in the western mountains and fall elsewhere.

Comments: Largent (1994) presents many of the western North American species and Hesler (1967) described many species now placed in the genus *Leptonia*. Hesler retained them in the genus *Entoloma,* but he covered many of the species in eastern North America.

Nolanea quadrospora Largent & O. K. Mill.
INEDIBLE

Pileus 2–4 cm broad conic with pointed apex to campanulate in age, yellow-brown to brownish orange, minutely felted, moist but not viscid. Flesh thin, orange-gray. Lamellae adnexed, subdistant, broad, white at first salmon pink in age. Stipe 2.5–4.0 cm long, 0.2–0.3 cm wide equal, or slightly larger at base, longitudinally striate and slightly twisted, pale gray brown, dry, white mycelium at base. Taste mile. Odor none.

Spores 7–9 x 6–9 µm 4-sided, entire, thin-walled, nonamyloid. Spore print salmon pink.

Habit and distribution: Several to gregarious on soil, under hardwood and hemlock. Found in southeastern North America. Fruiting in spring and early summer.

Comments: *Nolanea quadrata* Berk. & M. A. Curtis. is similar but has a salmon orange pileus and salmon-pink lamellae, a longer stipe (5–10 cm) and larger 4-sided spores 10–12 um. It fruits in late summer and fall and is distributed in eastern North America.

Nolanea murraii (Berk & M. A.Curtis) Sacc.
INEDIBLE

Pileus 1–4 cm broad, conic with an acute papilla at the apex, campanulate in age, straw-yellow, mustard-yellow to light orange, dry. Flesh thin, pale yellow. Lamellae adnate, close, broad, pale yellow sometimes tinted pinkish. Stipe 5–12 cm long, 0.2–0.5 cm wide, equal or slightly larger at the base, whitish to light orange, striate, often appears twisted, dry. Partial veil absent. Odor and taste mild.

Spores 9–12 x 8–10 µm angular, 4- to occasionally 5-sided, entire, thin-walled, nonamyloid. Spore print pinkish cinnamon.

Habit and distribution: Single to several on wet soil, swamps, and marshland. Found in eastern North America. Fruiting in summer and fall.

Comments: Also known as *Entoloma murraii* Berk & M. A. Curtis. It is very similar to *N. quadrata*. We have collected both of these distinctive species routinely in southeastern and northeastern United States.

Clitopilus prunulus (Fr.) P. Kumm.
EDIBLE

Pileus 5–10 cm broad, broadly convex, plane or edges upturned in age, felty, dull white to ash-gray, margin even and wavy in age, dry. Flesh firm, white. Lamellae decurrent, close, white to pale pink in age. Stipe 4–8 cm long, 0.4–1.5 cm wide, central or eccentric, nearly equal, dull white, without hairs, dry. Partial veil absent. Odor and taste farinaceous or mealy.

Spores 9–12 x 4–7 µm elliptic, with longitudinal ridges or striations, best seen in end-view, entire, thin-walled, nonamyloid. Spore print salmon-pink.

Habit and distribution: Scattered, in open woods, disturbed ground or in grassy areas. Widely distributed. Fruiting in summer and fall.

Comments: This species is considered to be a choice edible. *Clitopilus orcellus* (Fr.) Quél. is considered to be a synonym. Be sure to obtain a spore print, since *Clitocybe dealbata* grows in the same habitat, looks similar, but is white, has smooth, white spores and is poisonous.

Rhodocybe mundula (Lasch) Singer
INEDIBLE

Pileus 2–11 cm broad, convex, often with a low umbo at first, margin often split, in age upraised and depressed in center, nearly white to smoky gray, darker just in the center, concentric zones often split at the margin, dry. Flesh soft, dull white tinted buff. Lamellae decurrent, narrow, crowded, pale cream color with a grayish cast. Stipe 1–4 cm long, 0.5–1.5 cm wide, equal or enlarged at the base in age, white to buff, often covered with a fine white pubescence, dry. Partial veil absent. Odor farinaceous. Taste instantly bitter.

Spores 5.0–5.6 x 4–3 μm subglobose, finely warted, entire, thin-walled, nonamyloid. Spore print pinkish salmon.

Habit and distribution: Scattered to gregarious on decaying debris of hardwoods. Found in eastern North America. Fruiting in summer and fall.

Comments: Occasionally the pileus and lamellae will blacken on handling. The characteristic concentric zones on the pileus are not found in other pink spored agarics. It is too bitter to be considered an edible. This is a cosmopolitan species according to Baroni (1981).

Entoloma strictius (Peck) Sacc.
NONPOISONOUS

Pileus 2–7 cm broad, convex with a low umbo, campanulate in age, dark brown to gray-brown, smooth, hairless, silky appearing, margin with very short striations, wavy in age, dry to moist. Flesh thin, white to brown when water-soaked. Lamellae adnexed, medium broad, close, grayish white to pinkish gray in age. Stipe 5–10 cm long, 0.2–0.4 cm wide, enlarged toward base, grayish brown, with fine silky fibrils and often appearing twisted, dry. Partial veil absent. Odor and taste mild.

Spores 9–13 x 7–9 μm broadly elliptic, angular, 5- to 6-sided, entire, thin-walled, nonamyloid. Spore print deep salmon-pink.

Habit and distribution: Solitary, several and usually abundant in grassy areas or open woods. Widely distributed. Fruiting in the early spring to early summer, also in mid-November on the West Coast, late fall in the Rocky Mountains, and in July in Alaska.

Comments: Also known as *Nolanea stricta* (Peck) Largent, it is one of the most common early spring agarics. It often fruits during rainy periods, unlike many ground fungi that fruit on the drying cycle. However, there are a large number of species of *Entoloma* that resemble each other, all having the general appearance of the one described here. There are somewhat similar species in the *Entoloma sinuatum* complex that are poisonous (Lincoff & Mitchell, 1977). These species of *Entoloma* should not be eaten.

Entoloma abortivum (Berk. & M.A. Curtis) Donk
EDIBLE

Pileus 4–10 cm broad, convex, plane in age, gray-brown, lacking hairs, margin even at first, lobed in age, dry. Flesh soft, fragile, white. Lamellae short decurrent, close, pale gray to pink or dull salmon in age. Stipe 3–10 cm long, 0.5–1.2 cm wide, equal, grayish white, minutely fibrillose, dry. Veil absent. Odor and taste farinaceous or mealy.

Spores 8–10 x 5–7 µm elliptic-angular, nonamyloid, thin-walled. Spore print salmon-pink.

Habit and distribution: Several or in large groups around stumps or on rotten limbs. Found in eastern North America. Fruiting in the fall.

Comments: Often found with contorted to oval, white, aborted fruiting bodies that result from the growth of a species of *Armillaria* and *Entoloma abortivum* together. These are often found where no normal fruiting body can be located. They have been tested and are edible. *Clitopilus abortivus* Berk. & M. A. Curtis is another name for this curious fungus. We have found it in abundance in the mountains of Virginia and North Carolina. The novice should compare this with *Entoloma lividum,* which is poisonous.

Entoloma lividoalbum (Kühner & Romagn.) Kubicka
INEDIBLE

Pileus 5–9 cm broad, convex to broadly convex often with a low umbo, dark brown to yellow-brown, shiny at first, glabrous, margin incurved at first, moist. Flesh dull white to grayish. Lamellae adnexed, subdistant, broad, white turning pink as the spores mature. Stipe 4.5–12 (-20) cm long, 1.0–2.4 cm wide, equal or wider in the middle, white, longitudinally striate sometimes twisted, dry. Partial veil absent. Odor mild to farinaceous. Taste farinaceous.

Spores 7–12 x 5.0–10.5 µm angular, 5- to 6-sided, entire, thin-walled, nonamyloid. Spore print salmon-pink.

Habit and distribution: Several to often gregarious, under oak, aspen and willow but also western conifers. Found along the California Coast. Fruiting in late summer, fall to winter and midwinter.

Comments: This robust, often abundant *Entoloma* is very likely an ectomycorrhizal associate with a broad host range and is widely distributed in western North America. We have collected it in quantity under a mixed stand of aspen and Engelmann spruce. *Entoloma lividoalbum* f. *inodoratum* Largent lacks the farinaceous odor (Largent, 1994).

GOMPHIDIACEAE

The Gomphidiaceae is found only in the Northern Hemisphere and forms mycorrhizae with conifers in the Pinaceae. The thick, decurrent lamellae with smoky-gray to black, entire, subfusiform spores (Fig. 5) are typical of all the species. The genus *Gomphidius* has a gelatinous pileus with white flesh that is nonamyloid and yellow flesh in the stipe base. *Chroogomphus* has a dry or viscid or tacky pileus with amyloid hyphae, pink to salmon-colored flesh, and the stipe base is not yellow. Both genera have long elliptic to subfusiform, nonamyloid spores and long cylindric cystidia protruding above the basidia (Miller, 2003). The pileipellis is composed of interwoven, filamentous hyphae and is not cellular. Recent studies have revealed that the family is closely related to two mycorrhizal genera, *Suillus,* a bolete, and *Rhizopogon,* a false truffle (Bruns, et al.,1998).

Edibility: All of the species in the family are edible. We would not rate them as choice but in certain areas, such as the Pacific Northwest, large fruitings of many of the species could yield quantities of table food. When cooked, the flesh turns maroon in color and the texture is somewhat slimy, but would add interest to casseroles.

KEY TO GOMPHIDIACEAE

1. Pileus dry to viscid; flesh light orange to salmon color --------------------------------------- 2
1. Pileus slimy to glutinous; flesh white; base of stipe yellow -------------------------------- 6
   2. Pileus dry, with fine areas of tomentum to downy fibrillose; western
      North America -- 3
   2. Pileus viscid, glabrous; widely distributed --- 5
3. Pileus 2–6 cm broad, downy fibrillose, light orange to
   orange-buff --- *Chroogomphus tomentosus*
3. Not as above --- 4
   4. Pileus 6–12 cm broad, convex, robust, with fine areas of tomentum, reddish orange
     to ochre-red over disc, margin pale orange-ochraceous, uncommon, pileus trama
     dark amyloid; uncommon ------------------------------- *Chroogomphus pseudovinicolor*
                  (see comments under *C. vinicolor*)

4. Pileus 2.5–9.0 cm broad, convex and broadly umbonate, coarsely fibrillose, ochraceous-orange, margin gray with ochraceous-salmon fibrils; pileus trama with very reduced amyloid tissue ---------------------------------- *Chroogomphus leptocystis*
(see comments under *C. tomentosus*)

5. Pileus 1–12 cm broad, conic with a pointed or papillate umbo, convex in age, dark red-brown; cystidia long, thick-walled ----------------------------------- *Chroogomphus vinicolor*

5. Pileus 1.5–12 cm broad, convex, sometimes with a small pointed umbo, ochraceous-orange to reddish brown; cystidia long, thin-walled ------------ *Chroogomphus ochraceus*

   6. Pileus 1.5–8.5 cm broad, convex, glutinous, cinnamon to reddish brown; stipe white at apex, below with purplish black hairs, becoming black when handled; always under larch -- *Gomphidius maculatus*

   6. Not as above; without purplish black hairs; not blackening when handled ---------- 7

7. Spores small 10.5–13.5 x 4.2–5.5 µm fusiform; pileus salmon-buff to reddish brown; often in cespitose clusters --- *Gomphidius oregonensis*
(see comments under *G. glutinosus* var *glutinosus*)

7. Spores larger 15–29 x 4.5–8.5 µm subfusiform; not cespitose ----------------------------- 8

   8. Spores large 18–29 x 6.0–8.5 µm; pileus 1-4 cm broad -------- *Gomphidius flavipes*

   8. Spores 15–20 x 4.5–6.0 µm; pileus larger, 2-10 cm broad ----------------------------- 9

9. Pileus 2–5 cm broad, pink to deep red -------------------------------- *Gomphidius subroseus*

9. Pileus 2–10 cm broad, gray-brown, cinnamon-buff, dark purple to orange -------------- 10

   10. Pileus orange; western North America ------ *Gomphidius glutinosus* var *salmoneus*
(see comments under *G. glutinosus* var *glutinosus*)

   10. Pileus gray-brown, cinnamon-buff, purple-gray to dark purple ----------------------- 11

11. Pileus dark purple, western North America -------- *Gomphidius glutinosus* var *purpureus*
(see comments under *G. glutinosus* var *glutinosus*)

11. Pileus gray-brown, cinnamon-buff to light purple gray; widely distributed -------------------------------------- *Gomphidius glutinosus* var *glutinosus*

Chroogomphus tomentosus (Murrill) O. K. Mill.
EDIBLE

Pileus 2–6 cm broad, broadly convex, plane in age, light orange to orange-buff, downy fibrillose, dry. Flesh firm, light orange. Lamellae decurrent, well separated, yellow-orange to smoky at maturity. Stipe 4–17 cm long, 0.9–1.4 cm wide, tapering to a narrow base, smooth, orange-buff, with scattered fibrils, dry. Partial veil orange-buff, thin, hairy, leaving a few fibrils on the stipe but no annulus. Odor not distinctive. Taste mild and pleasant.

Spores 15–25 x 6–9 µm long elliptic, smooth, entire, thick-walled, nonamyloid. Spore print smoke gray to black. Cystidia long cylindric, thick-walled, conspicuous above basidia. Pileus tissue is strongly amyloid.

Habit and distribution: Single to numerous or scattered under western conifers (especially western hemlock). Found in western North America. Fruiting in late summer and fall.

Comments: This attractive orange mushroom stands out in the dark green hemlock forests of the western mountains. *Chroogomphus leptocystis* (Singer) O. K. Mill. is a reddish brown, dry, hairy-capped species with reduced amyloid tramal tissue but also found in the same habitats as *C. tomentosus*.

Chroogomphus vinicolor (Peck) O.K. Mill.
EDIBLE

Pileus 1–12 cm broad, conic, convex to broadly convex in age, orange-brown to dark red- brown, appressed fibrillose, viscid. Flesh firm, orange-buff to pale salmon. Lamellae decurrent, subdistant, dingy orange, buff to smoky brown in age. Stipe 5–10 cm long, 0.6–2.0 (-6.0) cm wide, equal or narrowing at the base, orange-buff to buff. Partial veil fibrillose, orange-buff, without an annulus or scanty fibrils on the upper stipe. Smell and taste not distinctive.

Spores 15.5–23.0 x 4.5–7.0 µm elliptic to subfusiform, smooth, entire, thick-walled, nonamyloid. Spore print smoky brown. Cystidia nearly cylindric to fusiform, thick-walled, often amyloid. Trama light yellow-brown with amyloid cell walls.

Habit and distribution: Several to many under various pines, hemlock, Douglas fir, and spruce. Widely distributed. Fruiting in late summer and fall except in coastal California from late July to April.

Comments: *Chroogomphus vinicolor* ssp. *californicus* Singer is a large subspecies but otherwise similar. However, *C. pseudovinicolor* O.K. Mill. is a large species with a dry, orange-buff to ochre-red pileus, with an appressed, fibrillose, annular zone near the stipe apex and often cespitose. It is found under Douglas fir and Ponderosa pine in the central Rocky Mountains (Miller, 1966).

Chroogomphus ochraceus (Kauffman) O. K Mill.
EDIBLE

Pileus 1.5–12.0 cm broad, convex, convex with a small, pointed umbo, ochraceous-orange to reddish brown, smooth, margin incurved at first, viscid. Flesh firm, light salmon to pinkish near the cuticle to light yellowish near stipe base. Lamellae decurrent, subdistant, broad, buff to dull cinnamon. Stipe 3.5–10.0 (-18) cm long, 0.5–2.5 cm wide, tapering toward base, covered in center with thin fibrils, orange-buff flushed reddish, dry to moist. Partial veil fibrous, dry, leaving a thin, superior, annular zone of hairs that soon disappears. Odor not distinctive. Taste pleasant.

Spores 14–22 x 6.0–7.5 µm long elliptic, smooth, entire, thick-walled, nonamyloid. Spore print smoke gray to black. Cystidia long cylindrical, thin-walled, conspicuous above basidia. Pileus tissue amyloid.

Habit and distribution: Single to abundant only under conifers, especially pines. Widely distributed in North America. Fruiting in summer and fall.

Comments: Also known as *Chroogomphus rutilus* (Fr.) O. K. Mill., a European species now considered not to occur in North America (Miller, 2003). The pileus ranges in color from salmon to reddish brown and is viscid when fresh. *Chroogomphus* species are all rated as a good edibles.

Gomphidius maculatus (Scop.:Fr.) Fr.
EDIBLE

Pileus 1.5–8.5 cm broad, convex, broadly convex to plane in age, light cinnamon to reddish brown, appearing streaked and dingy, smooth, hairless, or sometimes with fine flattened hairs, glutinous. Flesh firm, white tinted wine color near pileus cuticle and dingy reddish to yellow just at stipe base. Lamellae decurrent, well separated, sometimes forked, intervenose, white to smoky gray in age. Stipe 3–8 cm long, 0.3–3.5 cm wide, tapering somewhat toward base, white above, covered below with dark ochre to purplish black hairs, yellowish brown to bright yellow over the base, becoming black on the lower stipe upon handling. Partial veil absent. Odor mild. Taste mild.

Spores 14–22 x 6–8 µm fusiform, smooth, entire, thick-walled, nonamyloid. Spore print black. Cystidia cylindric to fusiform, thin-walled, protruding conspicuously above the basidia.

Habit and distribution: Single to numerous under mixed conifer stands, but always in the presence of larch. Widely distributed in northern North America. Fruiting in summer through late fall.

Comments: *Gomphidius maculatus* is associated with larch worldwide. Only *G. nigricans* Peck, associated with eastern white pine, has similar characteristics, but it is infrequently encountered and has a partial veil (Miller, 1971).

Gomphidius flavipes Peck
NONPOISONOUS

Pileus 1–4 cm broad, broadly convex, pinkish red to orange-vinaceous, weakly striate margin, moist. Flesh firm pale pinkish, yellow in stipe base. Lamellae decurrent, distant, broad, pale salmon becoming grayish in age. Stipe 3.5–6.0 cm long, 0.4–0.6 cm wide equal, white at apex, to buff and then yellow over the lower one third, dry to moist. Partial veil not observed. Odor and taste not distinctive.

Spores 18–29 x 6.0–8.5 µm subfusiform to elliptic, smooth, entire, thick-walled, nonamyloid. Spore print grayish black. Cystidia cylindric to fusiform, thin-walled, protruding conspicuously above the basidia. Center of trama with scattered amyloid cells.

Habit and distribution: Single to several in northern bogs. Found under black spruce, larch, and hemlock, in eastern North America, and under red spruce in the Appalachian mountains of North Carolina Fruiting in August to October.

Comments: Also known as *Chroogomphus flavipes* (Peck) O. K. Mill. *Gomphidius pseudoflavipes* O.K. Mill. & Camacho from California has the longest spores (18–40 x 6.0–9.5 µm) in the Gomphidiaceae. It is a rarely collected species under pine and firs (Miller et al., 2002).

Gomphidius subroseus Kauffman
EDIBLE

Pileus 2–5 (-7) cm broad, convex, plane in age with upturned margin, pink to deep red, smooth, glutinous. Flesh thick, firm, white. Lamellae decurrent, subdistant, broad, white to smoky gray in age. Stipe (2.2-) 3.5–7.0 cm long, 0.4–1.8 cm wide, tapering somewhat toward base, white and silky above ring, cream to yellow below, deep yellow at base. Partial veil glutinous, thin, leaving a superior, colorless, glutinous ring, which is soon blackened from the spores. Odorless. Taste pleasant.

Spores 15–21 x 4.5–7.0 µm subfusiform, smooth, entire, thick-walled, nonamyloid. Spore print dark brown to black. Cheilo- and pleurocystidia long, thin-walled, cylindric to narrowly fusiform, hyaline, protruding above the basidia.

Habit and distribution: Solitary but more often abundant, always under or near conifers. Widely distributed. Fruiting in spring, summer, fall and into winter in California coastal areas.

Comments: This is a rather small species with a red to rose-red pileus and should be compared to *G. glutinosus*, which is larger, and has a differently colored pileus. *Gomphidius subroseus* is a good edible, but like other species of *Gomphidius* the glutinous cuticle must be removed for the best taste. *Gomphidius nigricans* Peck is similar with a pinkish pileus, but the stipe blackens when handled. It is found in eastern North America under eastern white pine. *Gomphidius smithii* Singer has a grayish red pileus, the lower stipe, which is covered with gluten, blackens upon handling; while the context in the base of the stipe is pinkish. It is found in the western United States under conifers.

Gomphidius glutinosus var glutinosus (Schaeff.:Fr.) Fr.
EDIBLE

Pileus 2–10 cm broad, broadly convex to plane with an upturned margin in age, gray-brown, purple-gray or cinnamon-buff, often spotted or stained blackish, glabrous, smooth, glutinous. Flesh thick, soft, white with a pinkish tint near the pileus cuticle, yellow in the stipe base. Lamellae decurrent, close, pale drab to smoky gray in age. Stipe 4–10 cm long, 0.7–2.0 cm wide, tapering toward base, shiny white above glutinous ring, yellow over the lower part. Partial veil a thin, glutinous, outer layer with a white hairy inner layer leaving a superior ring in the form of a glutinous band which soon darkens from the spores. Odor mild. Taste pleasant.

Spores 15–21 x 4.0–7.5 μm subfusiform, smooth, entire, thick-walled, nonamyloid. Spore print smoke-gray to blackish. Cystidia long, thin-walled, cylindric to narrowly fusiform, hyaline, protruding above the basidia.

Habit and distribution: Seldom solitary, usually abundant under many different conifers. Found throughout North America, but most abundant in the West. Fruiting in summer and fall, but on the West Coast in late fall and winter.

Comments: There are two closely related varieties: *G. glutinosus* var *salmoneus* O. K. Mill. which has an orange-colored pileus, and *G. glutinosus* var *purpureus* O. K. Mill. with a dark purple pileus. Both are found only in western North America, and at first glance seem to have no relationship to *G. glutinosus* var *glutinosus*. *Gomphidius oregonensis* Peck has a salmon-buff to reddish brown pileus, a yellow stipe base, is usually cespitose, and has small spores 10.5–13.0 x 4.2 5.5 μm. It is found in western North America under conifers. *Gomphidius largus* O. K. Mill. is a robust western species, with a pileus up to 21 cm broad, which is dull pinkish brown to dingy reddish drab. It is known from the southwestern United States under conifers, especially pine. All these species and varieties are edible.

COPRINACEAE

In the Coprinaceae, the pileus is most often conic to campanulate, and the stipe is thin and fragile to thick and fleshy. The lamellae are usually free, adnate, to adnexed, and deliquescent in age or not. The family has black to dark purple-brown, thick-walled spores with an apical germ pore (Fig. 6). The pileipellus is cellular, with only a few exceptions in which it is filamentous. The species are common saprophytes on grass, dung, humus, and wood often in disturbed areas.

The family has six genera: *Coprinus, Coprinopsis, Parasola, Coprinellus, Panaeolus* and *Psathyrella. Coprinus:* pileus fleshy, narrowly cylindric, campanulate in age, with scales; partial veil present, leaving a weak annulus; stipe thick; lamellae deliquescence; pileipellus of filamentous cells. *Coprinopsis:* pileus thin fleshed, conic to campanulate (Fig. 36), smooth to scaly; partial veil membranous leaving an annulus; stipe thin to thick; lamellae deliquescent; pileipellus of radially arranged, elongate cells. *Parasola:* pileus very delicate, plane to upturned, deeply plicate-striate to center; partial veil absent; stipe very thin; lamellae very slowly deliquescent; pileipellis of clavate (hymeniform) cells. *Coprinellus:* pileus fragile, conic, margin striate (Fig. 36); partial veil absent; stipe thin; lamellae not deliquescent; pileipellis of round cells (a cystoderm). Previously, these four genera were in the genus *Coprinus.* As a result of recent research they are now separate genera. *Panaeolus:* pileus thin fleshed, conic, nonstriate, annulus and partial veil absent except in one species; stipe tall and thin; lamellae not deliquescent; pileipellis of round cells; usually on dung or one on grass. *Psathyrella:* pileus fleshy, convex to plane in age, margin not striate; partial veil present or absent, stipe variable in size and shape; lamellae not deliquescent; pileipellis of round cells; on grass, humus, wood, and plant products.

Edibility: Toxins are found in the genus *Panaeolus,* where at least six species have hallucinogenic compounds, Type 4 toxins. The genus *Psathyrella* has no known poisonous species. However, *Coprinellus* and *Coprinopsis* have several species with Type 6 toxins. *Coprinopsis atramentaria* is reported to be incompatible with alcohol (Type 6 toxins) (Spoerke & Rumak, 1994). There are also very good edible species in the family. *Coprinus comatus* is a very well-known edible species and for information on its preservation and preparation see H. Miller (1993). Other species, including *Coprinellus micaceus* and *Coprinopsis atramentaria,* are also collected for the table.

KEY TO THE GENERA OF THE COPRINACEAE

1. Lamellae black and inky in age and/or pileus with deep, marginal, plicate striations, often folded as an umbrella --- 2
1. Lamellae purple-brown, gray-brown, or mottled black-brown but not inky in age ------ 5
    2. Pileus large, 5–15 cm broad, with flattened, red-brown to gray-brown scales; lamellae black and inky mature; partial veil present, leaving an annulus ---------- *Coprinus*
    2. Not as above--- 3
3. Pileus small, 0.2–2.0 cm broad, narrowly conic, plicate-striate almost to the disc; lamellae black turning to ink; partial veil absent ----------------------------------- *Parasola*
3. Pileus larger, or if small, lamellae black but not turning to ink ---------------------------- 4
    4. Pileus 0.6–1.0 cm broad, conic to campanulate, margin striate; lamellae black turning to ink or not; partial veil absent --- *Coprinellus*
    4. Pileus 1–9 cm broad, narrowly conic to campanulate, universal veil remains on surface, margin wrinkled, split or striate; lamellae black, inky in age; partial veil present or absent --- *Coprinopsis*
5. Pileus conic to campanulate; with tall, thin, rigid stipe; on dung or grass; single to numerous but not cespitose --- *Panaeolus*
5. Pileus campanulate to convex; with a fleshy stipe; usually on humus or wood; often numerous or cespitose -- *Psathyrella*

COPRINUS, PARASOLA, COPRINELLUS, COPRINOPSIS

These genera were all previously species in the very large genus *Coprinus*. Many are plicate-striate and fold like an umbrella. However, recent molecular studies have indicated that there are four distinct groups or genera (Moncalvo et al., 2002). The disposition of the *Coprinus* species has been detailed by Redhead et al., 2001. However, in general the species in these four genera all have black to brownish black, thick-walled spores with an apical pore. A majority of the species also have deliquescent lamellae and a cellular pileipellis. They are all decomposers of dung, as well as plant parts.

KEY TO COPRINUS, PARASOLA, COPRINELLUS, COPRINOPSIS

1. Pileus pure white; on cow or horse dung--- 2
1. Pileus colored or with colored scales; on wood, humus, ground, rarely on dung ------ 3
    2. Partial veil present, leaving a faint, hairy ring; pileus pure white -- *Coprinopsis nivea*

    2. Partial veil absent; white fibrils rub off, revealing a grayish black
surface -- *Coprinopsis narcoticus*

(see comments under C. nivea)

3. Pileus 0.6–1.5 cm broad, conic to campanulate, margin plicate-striate; lamellae black
but not inky; in large, numerous troops ---------------------------- *Coprinellus disseminatus*
3. Not as above --- 4

    4. Pileus small 0.2–1.0 cm broad, deeply plicate-striate, almost to pileus center;
lamellae attached to a collar or directly to the stipe------------------------------------- 5
    4. Pileus larger and not as above -- 6

5. Pileus 0.5–1.0 cm broad, orange-brown in center; lamellae attached to a collar and
slowly turning to ink; on grass or humus ------------------------------------ *Parasola plicatilis*
5. Pileus 0.2–1.0 cm broad, covered with fragile, white hairs; lamellae adnate, without a
collar, black in age; on dung--- *Parasola miser*

(see comments under P. plicatilis)

    6. Typically in dense clusters or cespitose on ground, logs, stumps, or from buried
wood-- 7
    6. Typically single to several or in troops on ground, mulch or wood chips ---------- 10

7. Pileus with shaggy, reddish brown to grayish brown scales; partial veil leaving a ring -- 8
7. Pileus without large scales; partial veil absent or inferior ---------------------------------- 9

    8. Pileus 5–15 cm broad, narrowly cylindric, campanulate in age, covered with
reddish brown scales; lamellae crowded, white young, very inky in age;
on ground --- *Coprinus comatus*
    8. Pileus 2.5–8.0 cm broad, conic, white, floccose with light brown to grayish brown
scales from the universal veil; lamellae free, white, crowded, slowly inky black at
maturity; on logs and stumps--------------------------------------- *Coprinus quadrifidus*

9. Partial veil inferior and near base of stipe; pileus smooth to slightly scaly,
light gray-brown; in grass, on ground from buried wood or in wood
debris --- *Coprinopsis atramentaria*
9. Partial veil absent; pileus reddish brown, covered at center with glistening, white particles, margin plicate-striate --- *Coprinellus micaceus*

    10. Odor of tar or gas; pileus 5–9 cm broad, light to dark brown with patches of white,
universal veil over the surface, margin striate -------------------- *Coprinopsis picacea*
    10. Odorless; pileus 1–3 cm broad, conic, gray to bluish gray with fine, white powdery
remains of the universal veil; very fragile ------------------------- *Coprinopsis lagopus*

Coprinopsis nivea (Pers.:Fr.) Redhead, Vilgalys, & Moncalvo
NONPOISONOUS

Pileus 1–3 cm tall, 1–2 cm broad, narrowly conic, campanulate in age, white, covered with pure white, soft hairs, margin splitting and recurving in age, dry. Flesh soft, white, and thin. Lamellae adnexed, nearly free, crowded, narrow, white, then black and inky (deliquescent) in age. Stipe 3–8 cm long, 0.4–0.9 cm wide, equal or enlarged toward the base, white, hollow, covered with fine fibrils, fragile, dry. Partial veil hairy and mealy, sometimes leaving a faint fibrous, superior ring. Odorless. Taste mild.

Spores 15–17 x 8–11 µm elliptic, smooth, thick-walled, with an apical pore, nonamyloid. Spore print black. Cheilocystidia pear-shaped to subglobose, thin-walled, numerous.

Habit and distribution: Single or several on manure and compost, usually cow and horse dung. Widely distributed. Fruiting in the summer and fall.

Comments: *Coprinopsis narcotica* (Batsch.:Fr.) Redhead, Vilgalys, & Moncalvo is also on cow and horse dung; is white but the powdery tufts of hairs rub off, revealing a grayish black surface; and has a strong smell of coal gas similar to *Tricholoma sulphureum*. *Coprinopsis radiata* (Bolton:Fr.) Redhead, Vilgalys, & Montcalvo is a minute species with a white, soon dark gray pileus 0.2–0.6 cm; common on dung; spores 11–14 x 6–7 µm; (Orton & Watling, 1979). Species of *Coprinopsis* were previously placed in *Coprinus* (Redhead et al., 2001).

Coprinellus disseminatus (Pers.:Fr.) J. E. Lange
NONPOISONOUS

Pileus 0.6–1.5 cm broad, conic, campanulate, yellow-brown to gray-brown, striate, with folds over the margin, dry. Flesh soft, thin, pale buff. Lamellae attached, distant, narrow, white, gray to black in age but not becoming inky. Stipe 2.5–4.0 cm long, 0.1–0.2 cm wide, equal, curved, white, hairless, hollow. Partial veil absent. Odor and taste not distinctive.

Spores 7–10 x 4–5 µm elliptic, smooth, thick-walled, with an apical pore, nonamyloid. Spore print black.

Habit and distribution: Gregarious in dense troops curving out from well-decayed wood debris or buried wood. Widely distributed, but most common in eastern North America. Fruiting in spring, summer, and fall.

Comments: Known as *Coprinus disseminatus* (Pers.:Fr.) Gray and *Pseudocoprinus disseminatus* (Pers.:Fr.) P. Kumm., the fruiting bodies dry out, instead of deliquescing.

Parasola plicatilis (M. A. Curtis:Fr.)
Redhead, Vilgalys & Hopple
NONPOISONOUS

Pileus 0.5–2.0 cm tall, 0.5–1.0 cm broad, narrowly conic, plane to upturned in age, center reddish to orange-brown, margin light brown but soon gray, deeply plicate-striate, very fragile, dry. Flesh fragile, white, very thin. Lamellae free but attached to a collar, distant, gray to black, lamellae slowly deliquesce and turn inky black. Stipe 4–7 cm long, 0.1–0.2 cm wide, equal, with a small basal bulb, white, hairless, brittle, hollow. Partial veil absent. Odorless. Taste mild.

Spores 10–12 x 7.5–9.5 µm broadly elliptic, smooth, thick-walled, with an apical pore, nonamyloid. Spore print black.

Habit and distribution: Troops in grass or humus usually during wet cool weather. Widely distributed. Fruiting in spring, summer, and fall.

Comments: *Parasola miser* (Mont.) Redhead, Vilgalys & Hopple is found on dung and is very small (0.2–1.0 cm broad), with a narrowly conic pileus that is covered with fragile white hairs, especially dense over the center. Its spores measure 11–14 x 6–7 µm. *Coprinus cordispora* Gibbs is also similar, but very small with a pileus 0.1–0.7 cm broad, center pinkish brown; white universal veil when young; lamellae do not deliquesce; and it is found on rodent dung. There are a number of other small fragile species found on grass, humus, and dung. *Parasola miser* and *P. plicatilis* were formerly placed in *Coprinus*.

Coprinus comatus (Müll.:Fr.) Gray Edible, CHOICE

Pileus 5–15 cm broad, narrowly cylindric, expanding to campanulate, white, covered with flattened, reddish brown scales which recurve in age, dry. Flesh soft, white. Lamellae adnexed, crowded, white young, soon becoming black and inky as the lamellae deliquesce in age. Stipe 8–20 cm long, 1.0–2.5 cm wide, equal, white, smooth, dry. Partial veil fibrous and soon free, leaving an inferior, often movable ring. Odorless. Taste pleasant.

Spores 11–18 x 7.0–8.5 µm elliptic, smooth, thick-walled, with an apical pore, nonamyloid. Spore print black.

Habit and distribution: Scattered or more often in groups on hard ground or grassy areas growing from buried wood, often along roadsides. Widely distributed. Fruiting in cool, wet weather, most commonly in early spring and late fall.

Comments: Commonly called the "Shaggy Mane," it is one of the most delightful of all edible mushrooms. It matures quickly and, when the spores begin to mature, the lamellae turn black starting from the margin of the pileus extending upwards toward the stipe. The blackened flesh soon becomes bitter and so the young buttons should be prepared for the table as quickly as possible after being collected. Fruiting often occurs in the same place for several years from decomposing buried wood. *Coprinus sterquilinus* (Fr.) Fr. is similar but occurs on dung, is smaller and less scaly; and has larger spores, 17–22 x 10–13 µm.

Coprinus quadrifidus Peck
NONPOISONOUS

Pileus 2.5–8.0 cm broad conic becoming convex in age, white, floccose, with light brown to grayish brown scales of the universal veil, soon loosening and flaking off. Flesh soft white. Lamellae free, white, crowded, slowly blackening and inky at maturity. Stipe 5.0–12.5 cm long, 0.6–1.2 cm wide, equal or larger at the base, white, fibrillose to scaly, with brown rhizomorphs extending from the base. Partial veil leaving a scaly annulus near the base. Odorless. Taste mild.

Spores 7.0–10.5 x 4.0–5.5 μm elliptic, smooth, thick-walled, with an apical pore, nonamyloid. Spore print black.

Habit and distribution: In dense clusters on logs, stumps, and debris of hardwoods, especially elm, ash, cottonwood. Widely distributed. Often in riparian habitats in western North America. Fruiting in spring, summer, and early fall.

Comments: We have collected it in Big Fork, Montana, and Laramie, Wyoming; it is reported from Alberta, as well as eastern North America. There are reports of gastric upset from eating this species. We would not recommend it. It is also known as *Coprinus variegatus* Peck.

Coprinopsis atramentaria (Bull.: Fr.)
Redhead, Vilgalys & Montcalvo
EDIBLE

Pileus 2–8 cm broad, conic, campanulate in age, light gray-brown, margin striate to wrinkled, hairless to scaly over the central portion, dry. Flesh thin, pale buff. Lamellae nearly free, crowded, broad, white, gray to black and inky in age. Stipe 4–10 cm long, 0.6–1.0 cm wide, equal or enlarged toward base, white, covered with minute, flattened, white hairs, dry. Partial veil membranelike, leaving an inferior, fibrous ring. Odorless. Taste mild.

Spores 8–12 x 4.5–6.5 μm elliptic, smooth, thick-walled, with an apical pore, nonamyloid. Spore print black.

Habit and distribution: In tight clusters of three or more in grass, on wood debris, or from buried wood. Widely distributed. Fruiting in summer and fall.

Comments: Also known as *Coprinus atramentarius* (Bull.:Fr.) Fr. The lamellae become inky as they deliquesce and the spores mature. It should not be eaten along with, or followed by, alcoholic drinks. The toxic reaction is a flushed hot feeling, nausea, and gastrointestinal disturbance as described in Type 6 toxins.

Coprinellus micaceus (Bull.:Fr.) Redhead, Vilgalys & Moncalvo
EDIBLE

Pileus 2–6 cm broad, conic, campanulate in age, reddish brown, covered with glistening white particles that disappear in age, margin plicate-striate, dry. Flesh soft, watery, pale buff. Lamellae adnexed, crowded, white, maturing to black in age and becoming inky. Stipe 1.5–10.0 cm long, 0.3–0.6 cm wide, equal, silky, white, hollow. Partial veil not seen. Odor and taste mild.

Spores 7–10 x 3.5–5.0 μm elliptic, smooth, thick-walled, with an apical pore, nonamyloid. Spore print blackish brown. Pileipellis has large, globose, thin-walled cells that glisten in the light.

Habit and distribution: In dense cespitose clusters often in great numbers, on wood debris or around old stumps on buried wood. Widely distributed. Fruiting during cool, moist weather in spring, summer, and fall.

Comments: Also known as *Coprinus micaceus* (Bull.:Fr.) Fr. This good edible is worth collecting but it must be prepared for the table very quickly because it matures and becomes inky very quickly. Be sure to collect the youngest specimens, with white to very light gray lamellae for the table.

Coprinopsis picacea (Bull.:Fr.) Redhead, Vilgalys & Montcalvo
INEDIBLE

Pileus 5–9 cm broad, conic to campanulate in age, light brown to dark brown to blackish in age, with patches of the white universal veil over the surface, margin striate and split in age. Flesh soft, gray-brown. Lamellae crowded, white, clay-brown to black in age. Stipe 9–30 cm long, 0.6–1.5 cm wide enlarging toward the base up to 3 cm wide, white, floccose, but smooth in age, base with stiff, white fibrils, dry. Partial veil absent. Odor of tar or gas, unpleasant. Taste unpleasant.

Spores 12–17 x 10–12 µm broadly elliptic, smooth, thick-walled, with a large apical pore, nonamyloid. Spore print black. Cheilocystidia clavate to broadly clavate, thin-walled.

Habit and distribution: Single to occasionally several, on soil in humus. Widely distributed. Fruiting in summer, fall, and late winter in southern California.

Comments: This species causes digestive upset and should be avoided. It is also known as *Coprinus picaceus* (Bull.:Fr.) Gray. We have collected this species in southern California during the rainy season in March.

Coprinopsis lagopus (Fr.:Fr.) Redhead, Vilgalys & Moncalvo
NONPOISONOUS

Pileus 1.0–3.0 cm broad, conic, expanding to plane, recurved in age, covered with fine white powder, scales, and strands of the universal veil, soon gone revealing a gray to bluish gray ground color, intensely plicate-striate almost to the center of the pileus, margin split in age. Flesh soft, thin, gray. Lamellae free, thin, distant, grayish, soon black, somewhat inky. Stipe 6–7 (-13) cm long, 0.4–0.6 cm wide, equal, pure white, dry, minute white fibrils over the base with a few white rhizomorphs. Partial veil not present. Odorless. Taste mild.

Spores 11–13 x 6–7 µm elliptic, broad in center, thick-walled, with a large apical pore, nonamyloid. Spore print violet-black. Cheilocystidia pear-shaped to ovoid, thin-walled, numerous. Universal veil in chains of broad, elongate cells.

Habit and distribution: Several to troops, in humus, mulch, and sticks (not on dung). Widely distributed. Fruiting in summer and fall.

Comments: We have observed *Coprinopsis lagopus* initiating fruiting in the evening, expanding to full maturity during the night (see inset), and discharging spores by 7:00 A.M. the next day. *Coprinopsis lagopides* (P. Karst.) Redhead, Vilgalys & Montcalvo is similar; usually on burned soil, charred wood, or humus; but has smaller, subglobose to ovoid spores (6–9 x 5–7 µm), and deliquesces more quickly and completely. Both species were formerly placed in *Coprinus*, mature quickly, and are not edible.

PANAEOLUS

The pileus is conic to campanulate in age, gray-brown to red-brown and the margin is not striate. The lamellae are deep purple-brown to black at maturity, often mottled as they mature. The stipe is thin and rigid, and only *P. separatus* has an annulus. The purple-black spores are smooth or warted, thick-walled, with an apical pore, nonamyloid and do not discolor in concentrated sulphuric acid. The species are decomposers of grass, plant parts and dung, especially horse and cow dung.

Edibility: They are not edible. *Panaeolus foenisecii* and others described under it are hallucinogenic and contain Type 4 toxins.

KEY TO PANAEOLUS

1. Partial veil leaving a persistent annulus at stipe middle; pileus conic, viscid, dull grayish white; on horse and cow dung --- *P. separatus*
1. Partial veil absent or not leaving an annulus -- 2
    2. Growing on horse or cow dung; stipe and flesh turn blue on handling or unchanging --- 3
    2. Growing on lawns and grassy areas; stipe and flesh unchanging on handling ---- 4
3. Stipe and flesh unchanged; pileus gray-brown, tinted olive; partial veil soft, white, leaving pointed remnants on the margin ------------------------------------- *P. papilionaceus*
3. Stipe and flesh turn blue; pileus pale gray to nearly white; partial veil absent --- *P. cyanescens*
(see comments under P. foenisecii)

    4. Spore print gray-black to black --- *P. castaneifolius*
(see comments under P. foenisecii)

    4. Spore print dark purple-brown --- *P. foenisecii*

Panaeolus separatus (L.) Gill.
NONPOISONOUS

Pileus 0.8–4.5 cm broad, ovoid, conic to campanulate in age, light gray to dull grayish white, smooth, margin turned in at first, often splitting in age, viscid. Flesh thin, soft, white. Lamellae adnate, close, broad, gray, mottled blackish brown, nearly black in age. Stipe 7–18 cm long, 0.2–0.6 cm wide, nearly equal, enlarged just at base, smooth or somewhat striate above ring, smooth whitish below. Partial veil membranous leaving a persistent ring near the middle of the stipe, soon blackened by falling spores. Odorless. Taste mild.

Spores 15–20 x 8–11 µm elliptic, smooth, thick-walled, with an apical pore, nonamyloid. Spore print black. Cheilocystidia cylindric to clavate with yellowish contents.

Habit and distribution: Single or several on horse and cow dung during cool, moist weather. Widely distributed. Fruiting in spring, summer, and fall.

Comments: Also known as *P. semiovatus* (With.:Fr.) Wünsche or *Anellaria separata* (L.:Fr.) P. Karst., this fungus is the only large *Panaeolus* with a persistent ring. *Panaeolus antillarum* Berk. & Broome (= *P. solidipes* Peck) is larger and also on manure, but has a scaly to wrinkled pileus, (4–10 cm broad), no ring, and a frequently twisted, striate stipe. *Panaeolus antillarum* fruits in the cool, moist, Yukon and Alaskan summers. Both of these species are nonpoisonous but are not desirable edibles.

Panaeolus papilionaceus (Bull.:Fr.) Quél.
INEDIBLE

Pileus 0.8–4.0 cm broad, conic, narrowly campanulate in age, gray-brown to yellowish gray-brown, often with a tint of olive, hairless, margin white at edge with small toothlike, white, hanging veil remnants when young, dry. Flesh soft, white. Lamellae adnate, close, broad, gray, speckled dark purple-brown with white edges at maturity. Stipe 4–11 cm long, 0.1–0.3 cm wide, equal, brittle, rigid and straight, enlarged somewhat at base, light gray and striate at apex, rest reddish brown to gray-brown. Partial veil soft, white, not leaving a ring, but margin with white, pointed remnants of veil. Odorless. Taste mild.

Spores 14–18 x 8–13 µm broadly elliptic, smooth, thick-walled, with an apical pore, nonamyloid. Spore print black. Cheilocystidia cylindric, thin-walled, hyaline.

Habit and distribution: Single or several on horse or cow dung, following moist weather. Widely distributed. Fruiting in spring, summer, and fall.

Comments: Also known as *Panaeolus campanulatus* (Bull.:Fr.) Quél. *Panaeolus retirugis* (Fr.) Quél. and *P. sphinctrinus* (Fr.) Quél. are both synonyms but for many years were regarded as separate species. Stamets (1996) reports this species as not hallucinogenic and we would support this conclusion from what we know.

Panaeolus foenisecii (Pers.:Fr.) Schröt.
POISONOUS (HALLUCINOGENIC)

Pileus 1.0–3.0 cm broad, narrowly conic, campanulate in age, dry, hairless, dark smoky brown to reddish brown when moist and fresh, soon drying in sun to tan or light gray-brown, margin smooth or faintly striate in age. Flesh thin, watery, tan to light brown. Lamellae adnate, close, broad, deep purple-brown to chocolate, often mottled with whitish edges. Stipe 3.5–10.0 cm long, 0.15–0.3 cm wide, nearly equal or slightly enlarged toward base, brittle, whitish to pinkish brown, minute hairs at apex, rest hairless. Partial veil absent. Odor pleasant. Taste mild.

Spores 11–18 x 6–9 µm broadly elliptic, ornamented with warts, thick-walled, with an apical pore, nonamyloid. Spore print dark purple-brown, not black. Cheilocystidia 10-pin-shaped, thin-walled, hyaline.

Habit and distribution: Scattered to abundant on lawns and grassy areas, in the dew of cool early mornings, wilted and gone by midday. Widely distributed. Fruiting most frequently in spring and early summer, but also in summer and fall.

Comments: The presence of low levels of psilocybin and psilocin (Type 4 toxins) has been reported by Ola'h (Spoerke & Rumack, 1994). Stamets (1996) reports that some strains may be hallucinogenic. *Panaeolus castaneifolius* (Murrill) Ola'h is also widely distributed and closely related. It is reported by Stamets (1996) to contain small amounts of psilocybin. It may be distinguished from *P. foenisecii* by the purple gray-black spore print. The warted spores are difficult to see but present in both species. *Panaeolus cyanescens* Berk. & Broome is distributed in the deep southern areas of North America, on cow and horse dung, and is a potent producer of psilocybin. The flesh and stipe turn blue when handled (Stamets, 1996).

PSATHYRELLA

The pileus is convex to plane in age, smooth to hairy or with squamules, and whitish, pale tan to dark brown, dry to moist. The stipe ranges from very thin and long to fleshy and short, shiny, white, often brittle. The lamellae are adnate to adnexed and the spores are purple-brown, thick-walled, with an apical pore, nonamyloid. In addition, the spores discolor to red or dingy blue in the presence of concentrated $H2SO_4$ (sulphuric acid). *Psathyrella* also has a cellular pileipellis. There are 414 species in the monograph by A. H. Smith (1972). Many species are small with few visible field characters. They are decomposers of plant parts worldwide.

Edibility: Spoerke & Rumack (1994) indicate that there are no toxins known in the genus. Two of the species described here are edible, but we do not recommend eating species in this very large genus, where many are untested.

KEY TO PSATHYRELLA

1. Stipe thin and tall (3–12 cm long, 0.1–0.5 cm wide); never cespitose -------------------- 2
1. Stipe fleshy, more robust; often in cespitose clusters----------------------------------- 4
    2. Membranous, white, flaring, partial veil; known from the Pacific Northwest --- *P. longistriata*
    2. Not as above--- 3
3. Fruiting on charred wood or burned ground ------------------------------------ *P. pennata*
3. Fruiting on soil under aspen, alder, cottonwood or other hardwoods----------- *P. gracilis*
    4. Pileus whitish to light brown with small white scales and hanging veil remnants; in lawns and grass communities --- *P. candolleana*
    4. Pileus light brown to dark brown; in various habitats ---------------------------------- 5
5. Pileus covered with dense, dark brown hairs; partial veil white, leaving a weak, superior annulus; single to several --- *P. velutina*
5. Pileus glabrous, light to dark brown or red-brown; in cespitose clusters ------------------ 6
    6. Pileus light to dark brown; spore print purple-brown; in cespitose clusters at the base of or on hardwood stumps and logs ----------------------------------- *P. hydrophila*
    6. Pileus deep red-brown; spore print red-brown; in cespitose clusters at the base of or on hardwood and conifer stumps, logs, or debris ----------------------- *P. spadicea*
              (see comments under *P. hydrophila*)

Psathyrella longistriata (Murr.) A. H. Sm.
EDIBILITY UNKNOWN

Pileus 4–9 cm broad, conic, convex to broadly convex in age, glabrous, dark brown to reddish brown, with thin, scattered patches of white veil at first, moist. Flesh soft, pale white to buff. Lamellae adnate, close, medium broad, pale buff young, to purple brown in age. Stipe 3–10 cm long, 0.5–1.0 cm wide, equal or slightly enlarged toward the base, glabrous, white above the annulus, white and often scaly below, especially in age, dry. Partial veil in middle, membranous, flaring, white. Odor and taste mild.

Spores 6.5–9.0 x 4.0–4.5 µm elliptic, smooth, apical pore present but hard to see, thick-walled, nonamyloid. Spore print dull vinaceous brown. Cheilo- and pleurocystidia ovoid, thin-walled.

Habit and distribution: Several to gregarious under conifers or conifer/hardwoods. Found in the Pacific Northwest and northern California. Fruiting usually in fall, occasionally in spring.

Comments: There are only a few species of *Psathyrella* with the distinctive, flaring, partial veil.

Psathyrella pennata (Fr.) A. Pearson & Dennis
INEDIBLE

Pileus 2–6 cm broad, conic to convex, broadly convex to plane in age, brown to dark brown covered at first by patches of white veil, margin with the shaggy white remains of the partial veil, dry. Flesh thin, white, tinted brown. Lamellae adnate, close, medium broad, brown becoming dark purple-brown as the spores mature. Stipe 3–7 cm long, 0.2–0.5 cm wide, minute white fibrils above the white annular zone, scattered white floccules below over a pale brown surface, white mycelium over the base. Partial veil white, cottony, leaving a white annular zone and white remains on the margin of the pileus. Odorless. Taste mild.

Spores 6.0–8.5 x 3.0–4.5 µm elliptic, smooth, thick-walled, apical pore very small, nonamyloid. Spore print dark purple-brown. Cheilocystidia pear-shaped to ovoid, thin-walled, numerous.

Habit and distribution: Cespitose and gregarious, often in great numbers on charcoal and burned ground. Widely distributed in northern North America. Fruiting during spring to fall into winter in California.

Comments: Also known as *Psathyrella carbonicola* A.H. Sm., it is often accompanied in burned areas by *Pholiota highlandensis* (Peck) Hesler & A. H. Sm. and *Pholiota molesta* Hesler & A. H. Sm. The cinnamon-brown spore print, red to reddish brown pileus, and lack of the abundant white flocculose veil material distinguish these species from *P. pennata*.

Psathyrella gracilis (Fr.) Quél.
INEDIBLE

Pileus 1.0–5.3 cm broad, campanulate to plane or recurved somewhat in age, smooth, clay color to light cinnamon-brown, margin striate to deeply sulcate in age, moist. Flesh soft light brown to yellowish. Lamellae adnate, subdistant, light grayish brown or tinted pink at the margin becoming dark chocolate-brown in age. Stipe 5–12 cm long, 0.1–0.3 cm wide, cylindric, dull whitish, white mycelium just at the base. Partial veil absent. Odorless. Taste mild.

Spores 10–14 x 6.5–8.0 μm elliptic, smooth, thick-walled, with a large apical pore, nonamyloid. Spore print dark chocolate-brown. Cystidia fusiform to 10-pin-shaped, thin-walled, hyaline.

Habit and distribution: Several to gregarious on soil and debris under aspen, alder, cottonwood, and other hardwoods. Found in northern North America. Fruiting in summer and fall.

Comments: This is one of a complex of species with long, very thin stipes, conic caps, that decompose various types of litter. *Psathyrella uliginicola* McKnight & A. H. Sm. is gray, more robust, and also under aspen in western North America. Smith (1972) describes a number of species in this complex that are difficult to identify. Species of *Conocybe* appear similar, but the spore print is cinnamon-brown. Some species of *Hypholoma,* which have a purple-brown spore print, also appear similar.

Psathyrella candolleana (Fr.:Fr.) Maire
EDIBLE

Pileus 2–8 cm broad, convex, broadly convex in age, whitish to light brown, pale cinnamon or honey-yellow, with scattered small white scales at first, margin at first with hanging veil remnants, dry. Flesh thin, fragile, white. Lamellae adnate, close to crowded, white, grayish to purplish brown in age. Stipe 2–5 cm long, 0.2–0.4 cm wide, equal, smooth, shiny-white, minute fibrils at the apex, hollow. Partial veil membranous, white, rarely leaving ring. Odor fungoid. Taste mild.

Spores 6.5–8.0 x 4–5 μm elliptic, smooth, thick-walled, with an apical pore, nonamyloid. Spore print purple-brown. Cheilocystidia clavate to broadly cylindric, thin-walled, hyaline.

Habit and distribution: Single to scattered or numerous in grassy areas, lawns, or forest openings. Widely distributed. Fruiting in spring, summer, and fall.

Comments: Also known as *Psathyrella appendiculata* (Fr.) Maire and *Hypholoma incertum* Peck, it is one of the few members of the genus that is edible. However, there is not really much flesh and a large number would be required for a meal, although the flavor is reported to be excellent.

Psathyrella velutina (Pers.:Fr.) Singer
EDIBLE

Pileus 2–5 cm broad, convex, to convex with an umbo in age, dry, covered with dense dark brown hairs, sometimes with an olive hue, margin lighter to pinkish buff. Flesh firm, brownish. Lamellae adnexed to nearly free, light brown to dark brown, mottled, edges white, minutely hairy. Stipe 3.0–8.5 cm long, 0.4–1.7 cm wide, equal, dry, with hairs and whitish above ring, light brown flattened hairs below, white mycelium at the base, dry. Partial veil fibrous, white leaving an obscure, superior, hairy ring. Odorless. Taste unpleasant.

Spores 8.5–12.0 x 5.5–7.0 µm elliptic, warted, thick-walled, with an apical pore, nonamyloid. Spore print dark purple-brown to blackish brown. Cheilocystidia narrowly club-shaped, thin-walled, numerous.

Habit and distribution: Several to abundant on lawns, grassy areas, mulch beds or humus. Widely distributed. Fruiting in spring, summer, and fall.

Comments: Also known as *Lacrymaria lacrymabunda* (Bull.:Fr.) Pat., it is reported as edible, but we have no personal information on it and don't recommend it.

Psathyrella hydrophila (Fr.) Maire
NONPOISONOUS

Pileus 1.5–4.0 cm broad, convex to broadly convex with low umbo, hairless, light brown to dark brown, margin faintly striate, moist but not viscid. Flesh thin, fragile, light brownish. Lamellae adnate to adnexed, close, narrow, brown to purple-brown. Stipe 2–8 cm long, 0.2–0.5 cm wide, equal or enlarging toward base, shiny-white, streaked with inconspicuous hairs, hollow, dry. Partial veil usually not seen, delicate, thin, soon disappears. Odor mild. Taste mild.

Spores 5–7 x 3.0–3.5 µm kidney-shaped, smooth, thick-walled, with an apical pore, nonamyloid. Spore print purple-brown.

Habit and distribution: In cespitose clusters, often in great numbers, on well-decayed hardwood stumps and logs. Found commonly in northern North America. Fruiting in summer and fall.

Comments: Not enough is known about closely related species of *Psathyrella* to recommend these as edibles. In addition they have relatively little flesh. *Psathyrella spadicea* (Schaeff.: Fr.) Singer looks similar but lacks a veil, the pileus is deep red-brown, has larger spores (8–9 x 3.5–4.5 µm), and a reddish to red-brown spore print. *Psathyrella spadicea* is a northern species, which we have encountered in Alaska and in the Yukon Territory of Canada in abundance, but it is infrequent further south.

239

STROPHARIACEAE

The Strophariaceae are decomposers of wood, grass, humus, dung, and other plant material. The species have a central stipe and are single, or in cespitose clusters. The pileus is dry to viscid, of interwoven to parallel, filamentous hyphae; the lamellae are adnate, not free; and the spore print is purple-brown to brown in all genera, except orange-brown to yellow brown in *Phaeolepiota* and *Pholiota*. There are five genera, *Hypholoma*, *Stropharia*, *Psilocybe*, *Pholiota*, and *Phaeolepiota*, which are distinguished as follows. *Hypholoma:* pileus convex, convex with an umbo, dry to greasy; stipe without a ring or annulus, not staining blue; spore print purple-gray to purple-brown, smooth, entire, thick-walled, nonamyloid; chrysocystidia present; on wood, humus, peat or in moss. *Stropharia:* pileus convex, dry to viscid; stipe with a partial veil that leaves a ring on the stipe, not staining blue; spores purple-brown, smooth, entire, thick-walled, nonamyloid; cheilocystidia and chrysocystidia present; on ground, humus, wood or dung. *Psilocybe:* pileus convex to campanulate, dry to sticky; stipe without a ring or annulus, often bruising or staining blue; spore print purple-brown, smooth, thick-walled, with an apical germ pore (Fig. 6), nonamyloid; cheilocystidia 10-pin-shaped, chrysocystidia absent; on dung, manured grass, grass or humus. *Pholiota:* pileus convex, fibrils or scaly, dry to viscid; stipe with ring or annulus or scaly, not staining blue; spores ochre brown to brown, smooth, thick-walled, with or without an apical germ pore, nonamyloid; cheilo- and chrysocystidia present; on wood or buried wood. *Phaeolepiota:* pileus large (5–30cm), convex-umbellate; stipe with a ragged annulus; spores orange-buff, smooth, entire, thick-walled, nonamyloid; on ground.

Edibility: There are both edible and poisonous species in the family. Many of the species of *Psilocybe* are hallucinogenic and contain psilocybin and psilocin, Type 4 toxins, that are well known. However, very often the species, which contain these toxins, are not well known. Misidentification has led to severe toxification by debilitating toxins. In general, hallucinogenic toxins such as those in *Psilocybe cubensis* are not life threatening, except in young children, but should be avoided.

Some species of *Stropharia* can cause severe gastrointestinal upset, Type 8 toxins, and are discussed under the individual species. There are relatively few edible species; however, *Stropharia rugosoannulata* is an excellent edible and is raised and marketed in Europe by commercial growers.

KEY TO STROPHARIACEAE

1. Partial veil does not leave an annulus; single or often in clusters, on stumps, logs, wood debris, or adjacent to stumps; spore print purple-brown ---------------- *Hypholoma*
1. Not as above -- 2
   2. Partial veil present or absent; with or without blue stains on pileus and stipe; spore print purple-brown; cheilocystidia ten-pin shaped, on dung, manured ground or moss -- *Psilocybe*
   2. Not with the above combination of characters -- 3
3. Spore print purple-brown; partial veil present as an annulus; not bruising or staining blue; spores with an obvious apical germ pore; cheilocystidia and often chrysocystidia present; on ground, humus, or dung --- *Stropharia*
3. Spore print yellow, orange-brown to brown; partial veil present or scaly; not bruising or staining blue; spores with or without an apical pore; cheilocystidia and chrysocystidia present or absent; often in clusters on wood or from buried wood --- *Phaeolepiota* and *Pholiota*

HYPHOLOMA

The species of *Hypholoma* have previously been included in the genus *Naematoloma* and a monograph was published by A. H. Smith (1951). The species are often cespitose or in troops, on conifer and hardwood logs, stumps, and debris. The partial veil is present but does not leave an annulus. The spores are thick-walled, have an apical pore (Fig. 6), and the spore print is purple-brown.

Edibility: *Hypholoma fasciculare* is intensely bitter and can cause severe gastric upset (Type 8 toxins). However, *H. capnoides* is edible, but does not have much flavor. *Hypholoma sublateritium* is bitter to taste, and we have not tried eating it. Other species have little flesh and are not edible.

KEY TO HYPHOLOMA

1. Pileus conic, moist, yellowish to dingy olive; stipe 6–10 cm long, 0.2–0.5 cm wide; spores 7–11 x 4–5 μm elliptic, with an apical pore; single or in troops, not cespitose, in humus and mulch -- *Hypholoma dispersum*
1. Pileus convex; stipe shorter and fleshier; spores smaller; in cespitose clusters -------- 2
   2. Pileus citrine-yellow to orange-yellow; lamellae sulphur-yellow to greenish yellow; taste intensely bitter; cespitose on wood ---------------------- *Hypholoma fasciculare*
   2. Not as above; lamellae not sulphur-yellow --- 3
3. Pileus brick-red, margin buff-pink; cespitose, on or around hardwood stumps and logs --- *Hypholoma sublateritium*
3. Pileus orange to reddish orange, margin pale yellow; cespitose, on or around conifer stumps or logs --- *Hypholoma capnoides*

Hypholoma dispersum (Fr.) Quél.
POSSIBLY POISONOUS

Pileus 1–4 cm broad, conic, convex in age, waxy, with an umbo in age, tawny to orange-tawny, yellowish to dingy olive over the margin, glabrous over the central portion, thinly silky over the margin, moist. Flesh thin, dingy white. Lamellae adnate, close, broad, white dingy olive, purplish brown in age with whitish edges. Stipe 6–10 cm long, 0.2–0.5 cm wide, equal, pruinose (with a powdery cover) and buff to whitish above the obscure, hairy, annular zone, below with scattered hairy patches, reddish brown over the base, dry. Partial veil thin, hairy, buff, having a superior, often nearly absent, hairy zone. Odorless. Taste bitter and unpleasant.

Spores 7–11 x 4–5 μm elliptic, smooth, thick-walled, with a small apical pore, nonamyloid. Spore print purple-brown. Cheilocystidia cylindric, thin-walled, numerous. Pleurocystidia modified as chrysocystidia, fusiform with an apical umbo.

Habit and distribution: Single but more often in troops or numerous on conifer debris, sawdust, wood chips mixed with dirt. Found in northern California, the Pacific Northwest, Rocky Mountains, and adjacent Canada. Fruiting in late summer and fall.

Comments: Also known as *Naematoloma dispersum* (Fr.) P. Karst. We have encountered massive fruitings along newly constructed roads during wet weather in Idaho and Alaska. The non-cespitose habit and the long slender stipes separate it from the other species treated here. *Hypholoma udum* (Pers.:Fr.) Kühner is very similar but has larger, punctate spores (14–20 μm long) and is found in eastern North America and at high elevations in western North America. There are a group of closely related species with slender stipes described by Smith (1951), and we would not recommend any of these as edibles, since severe gastric upset could occur, Type 8 toxins.

Hypholoma fasciculare (Huds.:Fr.) P. Kumm.
POISONOUS

Pileus 1–8 cm broad, conic, soon broadly convex to nearly plane in age, with a broad umbo at times, citron-yellow to orange-yellow over center, sometimes tinted olive, hairless or silky over the margin, which is incurved at first with hanging veil remains, moist. Flesh very thin, yellowish, bruising dingy brown. Lamellae adnate, crowded, narrow, sulphur-yellow to greenish yellow. Stipe 5–12 cm long, 0.3–1.0 cm wide, narrow, tapering toward base, white to light buff above, brown to rusty-brown below, usually darkening in age, hairless above ring, flattened hairs below, moist to dry. Partial veil hairy, light buff to cream color leaving a superior, hairy ring zone. Odorless. Taste very bitter.

Spores 6.5–8.0 x 3.5–4.0 µm elliptic, smooth, thick-walled, with a small apical pore, nonamyloid. Spore print purple-brown. Cheilocystidia and pleurocystidia ten-pin shaped to clavate, some modified as chrysocystidia, thin-walled.

Habit and distribution: In large or small cespitose clusters on logs and stumps of hardwoods and conifers. Widely distributed. Fruiting in spring and fall and on the West Coast in the winter.

Comments: Also known as *Naematoloma fasciculare* (Huds,:Fr.) P. Karst. We have seen large fruitings of sterile populations in Montana. The green lamellae yield no spore print and no fertile basidia can be seen with microscopic observation. Most fruitings are not sterile and yield a deep purple-brown spore print. The intense bitter taste makes this species totally inedible and has been reported to cause severe gastric upset, Type 8 toxins.

Hypholoma sublateritium (Fr.) Quél.
INEDIBLE

Pileus 2–10 cm broad, convex to broadly convex with a low obtuse umbo at times, brick-red over the center, margin buff to buff-pink, inrolled at first, covered with scattered patches of yellowish hairs, the rest glabrous, moist. Flesh thick, pale brownish, sometimes staining yellow when bruised. Lamellae adnate, close, white sometimes yellowish, rarely with a faint olive tint, soon gray to dingy purple from the spores. Stipe 5–9 cm long, 0.5–1.5 cm wide, equal, smooth and white above annular zone, gray, eventually dull brown and flattened hairs below, often staining yellowish over base. Partial veil hairy, buff, leaving a thin, superior ring. Odorless. Taste mild to bitter.

Spores 6.0–7.5 x 3.5–4.0 µm elliptic, smooth, thick-walled, with a small apical pore, nonamyloid. Spore print purple-gray. Cheilocystidia and pleurocystidia fusiform to broadly clavate, modified as chrysocystidia, numerous.

Habit and distribution: In densely cespitose clusters on hardwood stumps and logs, common. Found in eastern North America. Fruiting in late summer and fall.

Comments: Also known as *Naematoloma sublateritium* (Fr.) P. Karst., or the "Brick-Cap" for its pileus coloration, it is bitter and not edible.

Hypholoma capnoides (Fr.:Fr.) P. Kumm.
EDIBLE

Pileus 2–7 cm broad, convex, soon broadly convex, nearly plane in age, sometimes with a low umbo, reddish orange, orange to cinnamon, smooth, hairless, or with scattered buff fibrils, margin inrolled at first and pale yellow with buff patches of adhering veil remnants, moist but not viscid. Flesh thick, white to pale buff. Lamellae adnate, close, white to gray finally purple-brown. Stipe 5–10 cm long, 0.4–1.0 cm wide, equal, yellowish above a faint ring, tan to rusty brown below, scattered hairs to hairy at base, dry. Partial veil hairy, white to buff, leaving a thin to obscure, superior annulus. Odorless. Taste mild.

Spores 6.0–7.5 x 3.5–4.5 µm elliptic, smooth, thick-walled, with a small apical pore, nonamyloid. Spore print purple-brown. Cheilocystidia and pleurocystidia fusiform with an apical umbo, modified as chrysocystidia, numerous.

Habit and distribution: Large cespitose clusters, often abundant as decomposers of conifer wood. Widely distributed. Fruiting in late summer and fall.

Comments: Also know as *Naematoloma capnoides* (Fr.) P. Karst., the lamellae do not have the greenish coloration of *H. fasciculare,* and the pileus is not the brick-red color of *H. sublateritium,* which occurs on hardwood logs and stumps. An edible, but not a favorite of most people.

PSILOCYBE

Species of *Psilocybe* have conic to campanulate pilei; rather long, thin, central stipes; sometimes with adnate lamellae; and a purple-brown spore print. The spores are smooth, thick-walled, with an apical pore (Fig. 6), nonamyloid. Many of the species have blue stains of the pileus, flesh and stipe. This amounts to about 16 or 17 species in the United States and Canada (Stamets, 1996). The blue-staining reaction is correlated with the presence of the hallucinogenic compounds, psilocybin and psilocin, Type 4 toxins, but not all active species bruise or stain blue when handled. The greatest concentration of hallucinogenic species is found within the coastal regions of California, Oregon, Washington, and Vancouver, Canada. A second area is the southeastern and southern United States from South Carolina, Florida to Texas. All of the species are decomposers, or in the case of *Psilocybe montana*, a weak parasite. Favored substrates are on the dung of ungulates, rich manured soil, mulch beds, gardens, moss and grass communities (Guzmán, 1983).

Edibility: Some species of *Psilocybe* contain psilocybin and psilocin, Type 4 toxins, and therefore the species are considered not edible and should be avoided (Spoerke & Rumack, 1994; Stamets, 1996). Possession of the fruiting bodies is illegal since psilocybin and psilocin are classified as Schedule One drugs by the United States Federal Government. Those species of *Psilocybe* that do not contain toxins are also not good edibles.

KEY TO PSILOCYBE

1. Pileus minute 0.5–1.5 cm conic to convex, red-brown, striate margin; blue stains absent; grows in *Polytrichum* moss -- *Psilocybe montana*

1. Not as above --- 2

    2. Pileus 1.5–9.0 cm broad, yellow-brown, viscid; partial veil a membranous, leaving a superior ring; with blue stains on stipe, pileus and flesh; on dung; spores 10–17 x 7–10 µm --- *Psilocybe cubensis*

    2. Not as above-- 3

3. On horse or cow dung --- *Psilocybe coprophila*

3. On grass, mulch, sawdust or rotten wood --- 4

    4. Pileus acutely conic, campanulate in age, margin striate; found only west of the Cascade Mountains; usually with blue stains ---------------- *Psilocybe semilanceata*

    4. Not as above--- 5

5. Pileus conic; stipe very thin and tall (6–8 cm long, 0.1–0.25 cm wide)-- *Psilocybe pelliculosa*

        (see comments under *P. cyanescens*)

5. Pileus convex to convex-umbonate; stipe thicker; West Coast only ----------------------- 6

    6. Stipe quickly staining blue; partial veil falls away ------------- *Psilocybe cyanescens*

    6. Stipe not staining blue; partial veil superior ring, white ------------ *Psilocybe stuntzii*

        (see comments under *P. cyanescens*)

Psilocybe montana (Pers.:Fr.) P. Kumm.
INEDIBLE

Pileus 0.5–1.5 cm broad, conic to convex with a low umbo, dark red-brown with lighter striate lines over the margin, moist. Flesh thin, brown. Lamellae adnate, fairly well separated, light brown to red-brown in age. Stipe 0.2–0.4 cm long, 0.1–0.2 cm wide, slightly larger toward base, reddish brown, smooth or with a few scattered hairs, dry. Partial veil very thin, leaving no ring. Odor pleasant. Taste mild.

Spores 5.5–8.0 x 4–5 µm short elliptic, smooth, thick-walled, with an apical pore, nonamyloid. Spore print purple-brown to blackish violet gray. Cheilocystidia club-shaped with a rounded head, abundant.

Habit and distribution: Several to numerous, sometimes in a fairy ring usually in deep *Polytrichum* moss, sometimes buried almost to the pileus. Found across northern North America and the western mountains. Fruiting spring, summer, and fall.

Comments: This minute agaric is also known as *Psilocybe atrorufa* (Fr.) Quél. We have observed it to form fairy rings in *Polytrichum* moss beds creating a dead (necrotic) zone in which the fruiting bodies are located. However, we have observed it fruiting among healthy stands of *Polytrichum* as well. Guzmán (1983) lists a number of genera of Bryophytes (mosses) associated with fruiting bodies of *P. montana*. It does not contain toxins, but is too minute and tasteless to be edible. *Psilocybe semistriata* (Peck) Guzmán is very similar, but has larger spores (6.6–9.0 x 5.5–8.0 µm) is also widely distributed in northern North America.

Psilocybe cubensis (Earle) Singer
POISONOUS, HALLUCINOGENIC

Pileus 1.5–9.0 cm broad, conic, to campanulate and convex in age, smooth, whitish to pale yellow to light brownish young, brownish yellow in center in age with a white margin, stains bluish especially at the margin and in age, viscid. Flesh firm, white bruises blue. Lamellae adnate to adnexed, close, light gray young to violet-gray in age with white edges, dark violet old. Stipe 4–15 cm long, 0.4–1.4 cm wide, enlarging somewhat toward the base, white staining blue when bruised or on handling, smooth, dry. Partial veil white, leaving a superior membranous ring. Odorless. Taste mild.

Spores 10–17 x 7–10 µm elliptic to oval in side view, smooth, thick-walled, with a large apical pore, nonamyloid. Spore print purple-brown. Cheilocystidia 10-pin or club-shaped with rounded heads.

Habit and distribution: Several or in groups on cow dung, horse dung, on manured soil. Known from South Carolina, on south to Florida and eastern Texas.

Comments: This species has been called *Stropharia cubensis* Earle and *Stropharia cyanescens* Murrill. Stamets (1996) rates the levels of psilocybin and psilocin, Type 4 toxins, as "moderately potent." The ease with which this fungus can be grown in pure culture has resulted in widespread fruiting of it indoors and the use of it as a hallucinogen. It does not grow and fruit naturally in cold climates, which restricts its distribution as indicated above. The fruiting bodies we have seen in Texas and elsewhere in nature are often quite variable in size from very slight to robust. We regard psilocybin and psilocin as toxins. Therefore this species should not be eaten.

Psilocybe coprophila (Bull.:Fr.) P. Kumm.
INEDIBLE

Pileus 1–3 cm broad, convex, gray-brown to dark brown, smooth with fine hairs over the margin, tacky to viscid. Flesh thin, brown, not staining. Lamellae adnate, fairly well separated, gray-brown to deep purple-brown in age. Stipe 2–6 cm long, 0.1–0.3 cm wide, nearly equal, yellow to yellowish brown with scattered fibrils, dry. Partial veil absent. Odorless. Taste of fresh meal.

Spores 11–15 x 6.5–10.0 μm broadly elliptic, smooth, thick-walled, with an apical pore, nonamyloid. Spore print dark purple-brown. Cheilocystidia cylindric to 10-pin-shaped with a long neck, thin-walled.

Habit and distribution: Several or in groups on horse or cow dung. Widely distributed. Fruiting in spring, summer, and fall.

Comments: *Stropharia semiglobata* (Fr.) Quél. is similar, also occurs on dung; has a yellow, viscid pileus; and a persistent ring from the partial veil; the stipe is viscid, yellowish; and its spores are also much larger (17–23 x 9–12 μm). There are no toxins in *P. coprophila* and none in *S. semiglobata*, but they are not good edibles.

Psilocybe semilanceata (Fr.) P. Kumm.
POISONOUS, HALLUCINOGENIC

Pileus 0.5–2.8 cm broad, acutely conic, striate when young, to campanulate and plane in age, smooth, cream-buff over the apex to yellow-brown, gray-brown often with olivaceous hues, margin inrolled, blackening in age, viscid when moist. Flesh soft, thin, dull white. Lamellae adnexed, close, narrow, light brownish soon purple-brown. Stipe 4–10 cm long, 0.15–0.3 cm wide, equal, white to cream, smooth, moist, sometimes bruising dull bluish green especially over the lower half. Partial veil very thin, soon gone, without an annular zone. Odor mild to unpleasant. Taste mild.

Spores 11–15 x 6–8 (-9) μm elliptic, smooth, thick-walled, with an apical pore, nonamyloid. Spore print purple-brown. Cheilocystidia thin-walled, fusiform to 10-pin-shaped, often with a long narrow neck.

Habit and distribution: Several to gregarious in grass, gardens, fields but not on dung. Found west of the Cascades in the United States and Canada. Fruiting in the fall, winter, on into the spring.

Comments: It is very common in many habitats in Europe, but confined to the West Coast in North America. It contains moderately active hallucinogens, Type 4 toxins, but Stamets (1996) reports that some populations can have a very high psilocybin content. Again this is a toxic species and should be avoided.

Psilocybe cyanescens Wakef.
POISONOUS, HALLUCINOGENIC

Pileus 2–5 cm broad, convex to convex-umbonate, reddish brown, margin striate in age, smooth, viscid when moist. Flesh firm light reddish brown, bruising blue. Lamellae adnate, close, medium broad, cinnamon-brown, soon nearly black brown with blue staining. Stipe 5–8 cm long, 0.25–0.6 cm wide, enlarging slightly toward the base, white with fine appressed fibrils, readily staining blue, with white rhizomorphs from the base, dry. Partial veil white, cortinous, falls away leaving, if anything, an obscure annular zone. Odorless. Taste not recorded.

Spores 9–13 x 5.0–8.5 µm long elliptic, smooth, thick-walled, with a large apical pore, nonamyloid. Spore print dark purple-brown. Cheilocystidia fusiform, 10-pin-shaped, thin-walled, with a long neck.

Habit and distribution: Several to usually gregarious on mulch, sawdust, rotten wood. Known from the coastal areas of Vancouver, Canada and Washington, Oregon, and California. Fruiting from October to January.

Comments: This species contains Type 4 toxins. According to Arora (1986), it is "extremely potent, especially raw." Stamets (1969) reports levels of psilocybin that reach as much as 1.68%. Recreational collectors should be aware of the possibilities of a strong toxic reaction in some populations. Several other hallucinogenic species also occur in the range of this species. *Psilocybe stuntzii* Guzmán & Ott has a chestnut-brown, viscid pileus, and striate margin. The partial veil is white, forming a fragile but persistent annulus. It is weakly hallucinogenic. *Psilocybe pelliculosa* (A. H. Sm.) Singer & A.H. Sm. has a conic, dark reddish to orange-brown pileus, white partial veil that does not leave an annulus. Stamets (1969) comments that it resembles *Hypholoma dispersum* and we agree. It has relatively low psilocybin content and is distributed and fruits in the same pattern as *Psilocybe cyanescens*. These are all toxic and difficult to identify in the field and we recommend the use of the monographs by Stamets (1996) and Guzmán (1983).

STROPHARIA

Stropharia is a genus with medium- to large-sized species, with a convex pileus that is nearly plane in age, with adnate lamellae, a fleshy, central stipe, and an annulus or flaring, membranous partial veil. The spore print is purple-brown and the spores are thick-walled with an apical pore. They are decomposers of grass, wood, and other plant parts.

Edibility: *Stropharia rugosoannulata,* "The King Stropharia", is a good edible and raised commercially in Europe (Stamets, 2000). Under cultivation, specimens can weigh as much as 5 pounds. However, *S. coronilla* can cause severe gastric upset, with Type 8 toxins (Lincoff & Mitchel, 1977). Other species of *Stropharia* have not been tested, and we recommend not eating any of the species, except *S. rugosoannulata.*

KEY TO STROPHARIA

1. Pileus bright green to yellowish green; stipe greenish blue ------ *Stropharia aeruginosa*
1. Not as above -- 2
   2. Pileus large 5.5 to 25.0 cm broad, robust, dark red-brown to purple-red; membranous partial veil, white with white cogs on the underside; and a flaring, persistent annulus --- *Stropharia rugosoannulata*
   2. Not as above-- 3
3. On the dung of horses, cows, buffalo, or sheep -------------------- *Stropharia semiglobata*
3. On other substrates -- 4
   4. On lawns, meadows, under open woods; pileus viscid in wet weather, glabrous; annulus white, persistent --- *Stropharia coronilla*
         (see also *S. ambigua*)
   4. On other substrates, and/or pileus with fibrils or light brown scales ---------------- 5
5. Pileus reddish orange, viscid, covered with small, white scales; dense, buff scales below the fragile, superior annulus --------------------------------------- *Stropharia thrausta*
5. Not as above -- 6
   6. Pileus viscid, cinnamon-gray to reddish brown, partial veil a white, superior annulus that flares upwards, scaly below; in conifer needles and litter--- *Stropharia hornemannii*
   6. Not as above-- 7

7. Pileus viscid, smooth, light yellow-brown; stipe smooth, partial veil weak, soon disappearing; in litter in western North America ----------------------------- *Stropharia ambigua*

    (see comments under *S. hornemannii*)

7. Not as above --- 8

    8. Pileus dry, yellow-brown, covered with small, light brown scales; stipe with cream-colored, recurved scales; spores 6–8 x 4.0–4.5 μm, apical pore not visible; found in western North America --- *Stropharia kauffmanii*

    8. Pileus moist, yellow-brown, covered with cinnamon to reddish scales; stipe smooth; spores 6–9 x 3–5 μm with an apical pore; southeastern United States --- *Stropharia hardii*

    (see comments under *S. kauffmanii*)

Stropharia aeruginosa (M. A. Curtis:Fr.) Quél.
INEDIBLE

Pileus 1–5 cm broad, convex, convex-campanulate in age, bright green, yellowish green in age, viscid. Flesh soft, white often tinted bluish. Lamellae adnate, close, broad, gray, lilac to violet-gray in age, edges minutely hairy, white. Stipe 3–8 cm long, 0.3–1.0 cm wide, equal, smooth, white above ring, greenish blue to blue below, moist. Partial veil soft, membranous, leaving fragile, superior ring, which may disappear in age. Odor fungoid. Taste mild.

Spores 7–10 x 4–5 μm elliptic, smooth, thick-walled, with an apical pore, nonamyloid. Spore print purple-brown. Cheilocystidia club-shaped with an elongated neck.

Habit and distribution: Single or several in grassy areas, gardens, humus, or in damp areas in forests. Widely distributed but infrequently encountered. Fruiting late summer and fall.

Comments: This species is also known as *Psilocybe aeruginosa* (M. A. Curtis:Fr.) Noordel. There is no evidence or reports of poisonings by this species in North America. *Stropharia caerulea* Kreisel is very similar, but has only a fibrous annular zone, and the cheilocystidia are chrysocystidia (Watling, 1987).

Stropharia rugosoannulata Farl.:Murrill
EDIBLE

Pileus 5.5–25 cm broad, robust, convex to plane in age, dark red, red-brown to purple-red, light brownish red in age, viscid. Flesh firm, white. Lamellae adnate, close, broad, white to gray but soon purple in age. Stipe 7–14 cm long, 1.4–3.5 cm wide, equal to clavate, white above the superior annulus, below smooth, white, dry. Partial veil a superior, white, flaring membranous annulus, which soon becomes starlike, with conspicuous white cogs on the under surface. Odor pleasant, faintly farinaceous. Taste mild.

Spores 9.5–14.5 x 7–9 μm elliptic, smooth, thick-walled, with an apical pore, nonamyloid. Spore print dark violet-brown. Cheilocystidia clavate to 10-pin-shaped, thin-walled.

Habit and distribution: Several to gregarious in mulch, cultivated beds, gardens, and cultivated areas. Widely distributed. Fruiting from spring to fall.

Comments: This choice edible, frequently referred to as "King Stropharia," is found throughout North America in mulch beds and areas under some sort of cultivation. It is not found in natural habitats in North America. It can be very robust, and is grown commercially in Europe. The very characteristic partial veil and red pileus make identification easy.

Stropharia semiglobata (Batsch:Fr.) Quél.
INEDIBLE

Pileus 0.5–4.5 cm broad, conic to ovoid, convex in age, smooth, yellow to orange-brown at first, to reddish brown or brownish orange in age, slimy to viscid. Flesh soft, whitish to buff. Lamellae adnate, distant, broad, buff soon tinted purple to purple-brown in age, edges minutely fimbriate, white. Stipe 1.5–11.0 cm long, 0.1–0.35 cm wide, equal, white with fine white fibrils, white mycelium over the base, dry to viscid when moist. Partial veil a white, very thin, superior annulus soon purple from the spores. Odorless. Taste mild.

Spores 14–20 x 8.5–10 μm elliptic, smooth, thick-walled, with an apical pore, nonamyloid. Spore print purple-brown. Cheilocystidia fusiform with a long neck, thin-walled, hyaline. Pleurocystidia infrequent to frequent, sometimes as chrysocystidia.

Habit and distribution: Several to many on manured soil or dung of horses, cows, buffalo, sheep, and other ungulates. Widely distributed. Fruiting following wet weather in spring, summer, and fall.

Comments: This is a highly variable species also known at *Psilocybe semiglobata* (Batsch:Fr.) Noordel. *Stropharia stercoraria* (Huds.) Murrill and *S. umbonatescens* (Peck) Sacc. are both considered variants of *S. semiglobata* and there are many intermediate forms. McIlvaine and Macadam (1973) report it as a good edible. Most people don't desire a food grown directly on dung, and it could be confused with an inedible species!

Stropharia coronilla (Bull.:Fr.) Quél.
POISONOUS

Pileus 1–5 cm broad, convex, broadly convex in age, buffy tan, yellowish brown to straw-yellow, hairless, slimy, viscid to nearly viscid in wet weather. Flesh firm, thick, white. Lamellae adnate, close, broad, light purple to brownish violet or purple-black in age. Stipe 3–4 cm long, 0.3–0.7 cm wide, equal, white, minute fibrils above ring, shiny with longer fibrils below, dry. Partial veil membranous, white, leaving a usually persistent annulus, striate above, about in the middle of stipe, soon colored purple-brown above from the spores. Odor slightly disagreeable. Taste mild.

Spores 7.0–9.5 x 4–5 μm ovoid, smooth, thick-walled, with an apical pore, nonamyloid. Spore print purple-brown. Cheilocystidia clavate to fusiform, modified as chrysocystidia.

Habitat and distribution: Several to abundant on lawns, meadows, under open stands of trees. Widely distributed. Fruiting in late summer and fall.

Comments: This species is poisonous and can cause severe gastric upset, Type 8 toxins (Spoerke & Rumack, 1994). We have found this in great numbers on lawns in central Idaho. *Stropharia hardii* Atk. is larger, has small spores (6–7 x 3–4 μm, usually under hardwoods in litter, and is found in southeastern and southern United States. Little is known about *S. hardii* and no toxic studies have been done, so avoid both species.

Stropharia thrausta (Schulz apud Kalchbr.) Sacc.
NONPOISONOUS

Pileus 3–6.5 cm broad, convex, broadly convex in age, red-brown to reddish orange surface that is covered with small white hairy scales, viscid. Flesh firm, white. Lamellae adnate, fairly well separated, buff to violet-brown with white, minutely hairy margins. Stipe 7–12 cm long, 0.6–0.8 cm wide, equal or enlarging somewhat toward base, white with minute white scales above annulus, below white to orange with dense buff to orange-buff small scales, base surrounded with long, often stiff, orange-buff hairs, dry. Partial veil fragile, membranous, buff, leaving a superior annulus that hangs, often torn, around the stipe. Odorless. Taste unpleasant.

Spores 11–15 x 6–8 μm broadly elliptic, smooth, thick-walled, with an apical pore, nonamyloid. Spore print purple-brown. Cheilocystidia with a swollen base and a long narrow neck, thin-walled, hyaline.

Habit and distribution: Single or several on buried wood, wood chips of hardwoods. Widely distributed, especially common in eastern North America. Fruiting in late summer and fall.

Comments: *Stropharia squamosa* (Pers.:Fr.) Quél. has an orange-brown to yellow-orange pileus, but in all other ways resembles *S. thrausta*. Both species have also been placed in *Psilocybe*. They are not poisonous but not good tasting. We have no further information on the edibility of this species.

Stropharia hornemannii (Fr.) Lund. & Nannf.
INEDIBLE

Pileus 2–14 cm broad, convex, broadly convex often with a broad low umbo, smooth, cinnamon-gray, reddish brown to light purple-brown with white cottony fibrils over the margin at first, slimy, viscid. Flesh firm, white, light yellowish near stipe base. Lamellae adnate, close, broad, whitish young, light gray to smoky violet in age. Stipe 5–15 cm long, 0.7–2.5 cm wide, equal, silky, smooth, white above ring, below with cottony, abundant, soft, pure white scales. Partial veil soft, white, leaving a persistent, superior annulus that flares upward at first, later hanging skirtlike around stipe. Odorless. Taste disagreeable.

Spores 10.5–13.0 x 5.5–7.0 μm elliptic, smooth, thick-walled, with an apical pore, nonamyloid. Spore print purple-brown. Cheilocystidia cylindric to clavate, thin-walled, numerous.

Comments: Single to several, sometimes numerous, in needles and litter under conifers or on well-decayed conifer wood. Widely distributed. Fruiting in late summer and fall.

Comments: *Stropharia ambigua* (Peck) Zeller is similar in size but has a light yellow-brown pileus, a weak annulus which soon disappears, slightly smaller spores (11–14 x 3–4 μm), and is most abundant in similar habitats in western North America. We have conflicting reports of poison cases in *Stropharia*. We do not recommend either of these species as edible.

Stropharia kauffmanii A.H. Sm.
INEDIBLE

Pileus 6–15 cm broad, convex to broadly convex in age, yellowish covered with small, light brown scales, with remains of the partial veil along the margin, dry. Flesh firm white. Lamellae adnate, close, grayish brown, but violaceus gray at maturity. Stipe 6–10 cm long, 1.5–3.0 cm wide, white, fibrillose above the superior partial veil, below cream color with recurved scales to the base. Partial veil white, weak, membranous leaving an annulus near the lamellae. Odor unpleasant. Taste unpleasant.

Spores 6–8 x 4.0–4.5 µm elliptic, smooth, thick-walled, apical pore not visible, nonamyloiid. Spore print dark purple-brown. Cheilocystidia fusiform, modified as chrysocystidia, thin-walled with yellow contents.

Habit and distribution: Single to several, in litter and debris under hardwoods. Found in western North America. Fruiting in spring, summer, and fall.

Comments: Smith (1941) reports finding this species under alder, cottonwood, and maple along the coast of Washington. In Montana we have found it under aspen and alder in the early summer. *Stropharia hardii* in the southeastern United States also has a yellow-brown pileus covered with cinnamon to reddish scales, and has a white, smooth stipe with a white superior annulus. The spores are similar 6–9 x 3–5 µm elliptic, thick-walled, but with an apical pore. Both species are inedible and not common.

PHOLIOTA AND PHAEOLEPIOTA

Pholiota is the only genus in the Strophariaceae with a yellow-brown, orange-brown or dark brown spore print. The species are dry to viscid, usually with scales or fibrils on the pileus surface. The partial veil is present and leaves an annulus or loose remains on the margin of the pileus. Lamellae are adnate. The stipe below the annulus has fibrils or scales. The spores are thick-walled but the apical pore though present is not readily visible with the light microscope, nonamyloid. Cheilocystidia and/or pleurocystidia and chrysocystidia are routinely present, thin- or thick-walled. Fruitings range from single, several, gregarious, to more often in cespitose clusters on limbs, logs, stumps, wood debris to wounds on living trees. (Smith & Hesler, 1968). *Phaeolepiota,* once placed in *Pholiota,* is presented here to more easily reach it in the keys. Recent studies indicate strongly that it is not closely related to *Pholiota* (Moncalvo et al., 2002).

Edibility: *Phaeolepiota aurea* is reported to have caused gastric upset in several cases, Type 8 toxins. *Pholiota squarrosa,* especially taken in conjunction with alcohol, has caused general severe gastric upset (Type 6 toxins) according to Lincoff and Mitchel (1977). We have records of gastric upset by others eating it without alcohol, Type 8 toxins. Many other species are bitter or have no taste. *Pholiota mutabilis* is eaten by people here and especially in Europe. However, it resembles *Galerina autumnalis,* which is deadly poisonous, Type 1 toxins, but *Pholiota mutabilis* has scales on the stipe below the partial veil. These two species are close enough so that we recommend not eating either of them. We generally recommend leaving Pholiotas in the woods to decompose woody substrates.

KEY TO PHOLIOTA AND PHAEOLEPIOTA

1. Pileus dry to viscid, bright yellow, orange or red; spore print orange-buff to brown or dark brown --- 2
1. Pileus dry or viscid, but not as above --- 5
    2. Pileus 5–30 cm broad, dry, convex-umbonate, orange to golden-yellow, granulose; partial veil leaves an orange-buff, persistent annulus; spores 9–13 x 4–6 µm elliptic -- *Phaeolepiota aurea*
    2. Not as above --- 3

3. Pileus 3–8 cm broad, viscid, bright yellow; spore print brown -------- *Pholiota flammans*

3. Pileus viscid, bright orange or red; spore print yellow-brown to dark brown ----------- 4

    4. Pileus 2–4 cm broad, viscid, bright orange; lamellae light yellow to yellow-orange; spore print yellowish brown--- *Pholiota astragalina*

        (see also *Pholiota aurivella*)

    4. Pileus 3–7 cm broad, viscid, red to orange-red with scattered loose squamules; lamellae buff; spore print dark brown ---------------------------------- *Pholiota lubrica*

5. Abundant, on burned wood and debris ------------------------------- *Pholiota highlandensis*

5. Not as above -- 6

    6. Pileus 8–20 cm broad, robust, viscid, whitish, creamy to light brown with large, white patches of the universal veil on the pileus and margin; in cespitose clusters on cottonwood and aspen, especially along streams -------------- *Pholiota destruens*

    6. Not as above-- 7

7. Pileus 1.5–6.0 cm broad, viscid, convex, smooth, cinnamon-brown, fading in center to light buffy brown; stipe below partial veil covered with sparce, cinnamon-brown scales --- *Pholiota mutabilis*

7. Not as above -- 8

    8. Pileus 2.5–8.0 cm broad, glutinous, deep red-brown with cottony remains of partial veil on the margin; solitary to several, on stumps, logs, and living hardwoods, in eastern North America --- *Pholiota albocrenulata*

    8. Pileus dry to viscid, buff, cinnamon-buff to yellow-orange; not as above; usually cespitose --- 9

9. Pileus 3–12 cm broad, dry, yellow-brown, covered with buff scales; lamellae yellow, often tinted green; cespitose clusters on wood of hardwoods and conifers-- *Pholiota squarrosa*

9. Not as above-- 10

    10. Pileus 2.5–11.0 cm broad, cinnamon-buff in center, rest whitish, viscid with dry, yellow-brown scales; lamellae white to rusty brown in age; cespitose on hardwoods --- *Pholiota squarrosoides*

    10. Not as above -- 11

11. Pileus 4–16 cm broad, convex, viscid, orange with wine-red, appressed, triangular scales; flesh yellow; lamellae light yellow; spores 8.5–10.2 x 5.0–6.5 µm ------ *Pholiota aurivella*

11. Similar in every way but spores smaller, 6.5–9.2 x 3.7–5.6 µm-------- *Pholiota limonella*

    (see comments under *P. aurivella*)

Phaeolepiota aurea (Fr.) Konrad & Maubl.
NOT RECOMMENDED

Pileus 5–20 (-30) cm broad, convex, convex-umbonate, granulose, golden yellow to golden orange-brown, margin with ragged, hanging pieces of the veil, dry. Flesh firm, thick, yellowish. Lamellae adnate to adnexed, close, yellowish orange to cinnamon. Stipe 5–15 (-25) cm long, 1–3 (-6) cm wide, enlarging toward the base, hairless above ring, granular surface below, buff overall. Partial veil membranous, dark buff, leaving a large, superior, upward flaring, persistent ring. Odorless. Taste mild.

Spores 9–13 x 4–6 µm elliptic, smooth to slightly roughened, thick-walled, apical pore not visible, nonamyloid. Spore print pale orange-buff. Cheilocystidia absent.

Habit and distribution: Single to numerous, often under or near alder, vine maple or under old growth Douglas fir. Found in the Pacific Northwest and Alaska. Fruiting in the fall.

Comments: Known also as *Pholiota aurea* (Fr.) P. Kumm. and *Togaria aurea* (Fr.) W. G. Smith, this is a very distinctive species. It resembles a *Pholiota*, but is not closely related to it. We have seen it in the West and in Europe. The pileus is reported to be edible, but there are also reports of Type 8 toxins, which cause gastrointestinal disturbances from eating it; hence we don't recommend it.

Pholiota flammans (Fr.) P. Kumm.
NONPOISONOUS

Pileus 3–8 cm broad, conic, convex in age with a low umbo, brilliant yellow beneath a dense covering of small, lemon-yellow to orange scales, margin fringed with yellow pieces of the partial veil, viscid. Flesh firm, yellow. Lamellae adnate, close, yellow staining dingy brown in age. Stipe 5–10 cm long, 0.5–1.0 cm wide, equal or enlarged at base, silky and yellow above ring, covered with dense yellow scales below. Partial veil yellow, membranous, leaving a superior, yellow, fibrillose ring that may disappear in age. Odor mild. Taste mild.

Spores 3.4–5.0 x 2.2–3.0 µm elliptic, smooth, thick-walled, apical pore absent, nonamyloid. Spore print brown. Pleuro- and cheilocystidia present. Cheilocystidia clavate to broadly clavate, thin-walled, intermixed with clavate chrysocystidia. Pleurocystidia clavate, modified as chrysocystidia.

Habit and distribution: Single or in small cespitose clusters on conifer logs (especially western hemlock) and stumps. Widely distributed. Fruiting in summer and fall.

Comments: This brilliant yellow fungus is distinguished at once by its color. We have found it commonly under hemlock and Sitka spruce along the southeastern Alaskan coast.

Pholiota astragalina (Fr.) Singer
NONPOISONOUS

Pileus 2–4 cm broad, conic soon convex umbonate, plane or recurved in age, bright orange to orange-red, fading in age, glabrous, viscid. Flesh soft, pale yellow to yellow-orange. Lamellae adnexed to nearly free, close, moderately broad, light yellow to yellow-orange. Stipe 5–9 cm long, 0.4–0.8 cm wide, equal, white above to dull orange over the lower half with orange to yellow fibrils over the surface. Partial veil white, fibrillose with some gluten from the pileus. Odor mild. Taste bitter.

Spores 5.0–7.5 x 3.8–4.5 µm short elliptic, smooth, thick-walled, apical pore minute, not readily visible, nonamyloid. Spore print yellowish brown. Cheilocystidia cylindric, narrowly fusiform, thin-walled. Pleurocystidia modified as chrysocystidia, 10-pin-shaped to clavate with an umbo.

Habit and distribution: Several on logs, stumps, and conifer debris. Widely distributed. Fruiting in late summer through fall.

Comments: The bright orange to orange-red lamellae and dull orange stipe are distinctive characters, but it has a bitter taste and is not edible.

Pholiota lubrica (Pers.:Fr.) Singer
INEDIBLE

Pileus 3–7 cm broad convex, plane in age, red to orange-red, scattered loose squamules in the slime, margin buff when young, white veil sometimes attached, glabrous, slimy, viscid. Flesh cream to buff in the stipe. Lamellae adnate, subdistant, broad, buff becoming brown in age. Stipe 2–7 cm long, 0.2–0.8 cm wide, equal or tapering toward the base, dry, buff fibrils above the superior annular zone, below orange-red to brownish red squamules over a dull white ground color, darker toward the base. Partial veil white fibrous, soon falling away leaving an indistinct annulus. Odor pleasant. Taste mild.

Spores 6.3–8.0 x 3.6–4.8 µm elliptic, smooth, thick-walled, minute apical pore not always visible, nonamyloid. Spore print dark brown.

Habit and distribution: Several to gregarious on logs, stumps, and snags of conifers. Found in western North America. Fruiting in spring, summer, and fall.

Comments: A. H. Smith (1968) describes a group of very similar species in section *Lubrica* that have a somewhat wider distribution, but are on conifer wood. *Pholiota spumosa* (Fr.) Singer is similar but has a viscid, olive-brown pileus, yellow green flesh, is found on both conifer and hardwood logs and debris, and is more widely distributed. Edibility has not been tested in most of these species and so they are not recommended.

Pholiota highlandensis (Peck) A.H. Sm. & Hesler
INEDIBLE

Pileus 1–4 cm broad, convex to plane in age, orange-brown, reddish brown to deep chestnut-brown in age, glabrous, viscid. Flesh white, light yellowish in the stipc. Lamellae adnate, close, broad, pale cream to buff, maturing to dark brown in age. Stipe 1.5–5.0 cm long, 0.2–0.5 cm wide, equal, apex white to light buff, below annulus brown with yellow-brown tufts of fibrils to the base. Partial veil pale yellow to cinnamon, thin, leaving a superior fibrillose partial veil soon brown from the spores. Odor mild. Taste mild with a slightly unpleasant aftertaste.

Spores 6–8 x 4.0–4.5 µm elliptic, smooth, thick-walled, with a small apical pore, nonamyloid. Spore print cinnamon-brown. Cheilo- and pleurocystidia fusiform, thin-walled.

Habit and distribution: Gregarious, often very abundant on burned wood and debris. Widely distributed. Fruiting from early spring until early winter.

Comments: Also known as *Flammulina carbonaria* (Fr.) P. Kumm. and *Pholiota carbonaria* (Fr.) Singer, large populations develop in burn sites and show considerable variation in pileus color, veil development, and size. This is partially due to substrate and climatic variation. We have not eaten this species since the taste is not pleasant. *Pholiota subangularis* A. H. Sm. & Hesler has larger, angular spores 8.0–11.5 x 7–9 µm and is also on burned areas in the western mountains.

Pholiota destruens (Brond.) Gillet
NONPOISONOUS

Pileus 8–20 cm broad, robust, convex, broadly convex in age, whitish, creamy, light brown in age, scattered whitish to buff scales, margin with hanging pieces of white, partial veil, viscid. Flesh firm, thick, white. Lamellae adnate to adnexed, close, white to cinnamon in age. Stipe 5–18 cm long, 1–3 cm wide, equal or enlarged at base, silky white above ring, covered with scales below, white to brownish in age, tough. Partial veil shaggy, fibrous, superior, leaving a loose ring that is very near the lamellae, sometimes absent in age. Odorless. Taste unpleasant.

Spores 7.0–9.5 x 4.0–5.5 µm elliptic, smooth, thick-walled, with an apical pore, nonamyloid. Spore print brown. Cheilocystidia cylindric to clavate, thin-walled, numerous.

Habit and distribution: Single or more often in cespitose clusters on logs, limbs and dead wood of cottonwood, aspens, and balsam poplar. Widely distributed. Fruiting in fall.

Comments: Also known as *Pholiota populnea* (Pers.:Fr.) Kuyper & Tjall. This is a large, robust, distinctive species of *Pholiota* that is found along river bottom habitats (riparian habitats) where the three North American species of cottonwood grow. Australian quarantine officials sent us, for identification, specimens that fruited on cottonwood crates in an American ship. It does not taste good and is not edible.

Pholiota mutabilis (Fr.) P. Kumm.
EDIBLE WITH CAUTION

Pileus 1.5–6.0 cm broad, convex to convex-umbonate, smooth, cinnamon-brown, fading in center to light buffy brown (hygrophanous) gradually spreading toward the margin, viscid. Flesh soft, thin, white. Lamellae adnate to short decurrent, close, medium broad, warm buff to light brown in age. Stipe 2.5–8.0 cm long, 0.4–0.7 cm wide, narrowing toward the base, dry, cream color at the apex, lower two-thirds increasingly dark red-brown toward the base and covered with cinnamon-brown scales. Partial veil weak, white, membranous soon breaking up leaving pieces on the pileus margin or as a weak annulus soon covered by the brown spores. Odor weakly spicy. Taste mild.

Spores 5.5–7.5 x 3.5–4.5 µm elliptic, thick-walled, with an apical pore, nonamyloid. Spore print cinnamon-brown. Cheilocystidia cylindric to fusoid often with a small, round head, numerous.

Habit and distribution: Usually cespitose to gregarious, on hardwood logs and stumps. Widely distributed. Fruiting in spring and fall.

Comments: This species is edible but could be misidentified by the inexperienced collector. It is critical to note the scales on the lower stipe and hygrophanous pileus; both distinguish it from *Galerina autumnalis* (Peck) A. H. Sm. & Singer and *G. marginata* (Fr.) Kühner, which are both **deadly poisonous** and have larger spores. *Pholiota vernalis* (Peck) A.H. Sm. & Hesler is very abundant following snow melt on conifer wood in northern North America. The pileus is viscid, butterscotch to pale yellow, and the stipe is covered by silky grayish fibrils. It is also not edible.

Pholiota albocrenulata (Peck) Sacc.
NONPOISONOUS

Pileus 2.5–8.0 cm broad, conic to convex, orange-brown to red-brown, with light brown, cottony remains of the partial veil on the margin, smooth, glutinous. Flesh firm, pale buff. Lamellae adnate to adnexed, close, white to gray in age, with white uneven edges, often covered with drops of liquid. Stipe 3–10 cm long, 0.5–1.5 cm wide, equal, pale buff above, cinnamon-brown, cottony squamules below ring. Partial veil cottony, fragile, forming a superior ring, sometimes absent. Odorless. Taste mild, slowly bitter.

Spores 10–18 x 5.5–8.0 µm elliptic, not equilateral, smooth, thick-walled, nonamyloid. Spore print brown. Cheilocystidia cylindric to clavate, thin-walled, numerous.

Habit and distribution: Single or several on stumps, logs, and living hardwoods especially elm and maple, rarely on conifers. Found in eastern North America, on cottonwood and pine in the Southwest. Fruiting in late summer and fall.

Comments: The stipe of this striking decomposer often curves from its host. We have no information on its edibility.

Pholiota squarrosa (Fr.) P. Kumm.
NOT RECOMMENDED

Pileus 3–12 cm broad, convex, broadly convex in age, yellow-brown, covered with scales, margin incurved and covered, at first, with hanging pieces of veil, dry. Flesh firm, pale yellowish. Lamellae adnate to adnexed with fine lines on stipe, close to crowded, yellowish sometimes with a greenish tint to dingy brown in age. Stipe 4–12 cm long, 0.4–1.2 cm wide, equal, with yellow-brown scales, dry. Partial veil membranous, superior, sometimes absent in age. Odor mild or faintly onion-like especially in age. Taste mild.

Spores 5–8 x 3.5–4.5 µm elliptic, smooth, thick-walled, with an apical pore, nonamyloid. Spore print brown. Cheilocystidia clavate to fusiform, thin-walled. Pleurocystidia modified as chrysocystidia, clavate with an apical umbo.

Habit and distribution: In cespitose clusters at the base or on the wood of hardwoods and conifers or on wounds of living trees. Widely distributed in North America. Fruiting in late summer and fall.

Comments: Some reported Type 8 toxins resulting in digestive upset should rule this out as an edible. See *Pholiota squarrosoides* for comparison. *Pholiota terrestris* Overh. has a dry, brown to cinnamon-brown pileus, is usually found on the ground in large, cespitose clusters, not directly on logs and stumps. Found commonly in the mountains of western North America, but is widely distributed. None are edible.

Pholiota squarrosoides (Peck) Sacc.
EDIBLE

Pileus 2.5–11.0 cm broad, conic, convex in age, whitish at first, soon cinnamon-buff, viscid with dry, yellow-brown scales that are often pointed and erect. Flesh firm, white. Lamellae adnate to adnexed, close, white to rusty brown. Stipe 5–10 cm long, 0.5–1.5 cm wide, equal, white at apex with recurved buff to rusty-brown scales below, dry. Partial veil hairy, ring superior, often absent. Odor mild. Taste mild.

Spores 4–6 x 2.5–3.5 μm elliptic, smooth, thick-walled, apical pore not visible. Spore print brown. Cheilo- and pleurocystidia clavate to fusiform, abundant.

Habit and distribution: Rarely single, usually in large cespitose clusters on hardwoods. Widely distributed. Fruiting in late summer and fall.

Comments: This fungus is particularly common on birch, beech, and maple. See *Pholiota squarrosa* for comparison.

Pholiota aurivella (Fr.) P. Kumm.
INEDIBLE

Pileus 4–16 cm broad, convex to broadly convex in age, sometimes with a broad umbo, orange with large appressed triangular, wine-red scales, viscid. Flesh firm, yellow. Lamellae adnate to adnexed, close, light yellow to brown in age. Stipe 5–8 cm long, 0.5–1.5 cm wide, equal, yellowish brown, hairy above, to scaly below, dry. Partial veil hairy, which is sometimes absent, leaving a thin, superior ring. Odor mild. Taste mild.

Spores 8.5–10.2 x 5.0–6.5 μm elliptic, smooth, thick-walled, with an apical pore, nonamyloid. Spore print brown.

Habit and distribution: Solitary or several on living trunks and logs of hardwoods and conifers. Widely distributed. Fruiting in spring and fall.

Comments: *Pholiota limonella* (Peck) Sacc. is very similar but has smaller spores (6.5–9.3 x 3.7–5.6 μm). Both species are mating incompatible and therefore distinct species (Farr et al., 1977). Both species are inedible and can cause gastric upset (Type 8 toxins).

BOLBITIACEAE

The Bolbitiaceae have spore print colors that range from yellow-brown, cinnamon-brown to earth brown, and the spores are thick-walled with an apical pore (Fig. 6), nonamyloid. The pileipellis has clavate or round cells (cellular), and many species in *Bolbitius* and *Conocybe* have a plicate-striate pileus, typical of species in the Coprinaceae, which are very similar but have black to dark purple-black spores. There are three genera; *Conocybe, Bolbitius,* and *Agrocybe. Conocybe:* pileus small, conic; stipe fragile tall and very thin; veil absent, with a cinnamon brown spore print; fruiting in grass or humus. *Bolbitius:* pileus small to medium, conic to campanulate, margin striate; stipe shorter, very thin; veil absent, with a yellow spore print, typically fruiting on manured ground or dung. The species closely resemble species of *Coprinopsis. Agrocybe:* pileus large fleshy, convex to plane; stipe equal to clavate, thick; partial veil present leaving a ring or absent, with an earth brown spore print. All of the species in the family are decomposers of dung, humus, and plant parts.

Edibility: Two species, *Conocybe cyanopus* (Atkins) Kühner and *C. smithii* Watling, contain Type 4 toxins, and are hallucinogenic. They are seldom collected and very small (Stamets, 1996). *Conocybe filaris* (Fr.) Kühner contains the potentially fatal amatoxins, Type 1 toxins, and usually fruits in rich, moist soil or wood debris during or following wet weather (Spoerke & Rumack, 1994). It is uncommon but reported from the Pacific Coast (Arora, 1986). *Agrocybe praecox* and several other species are potentially edible, but we find that they have no flavor. There are no toxins in *Bolbitius,* but they are inedible and too small to be considered.

BOLBITIACEAE

1. Stipe tall, very thin (0.1–0.3 cm wide); pileus white, yellow or reddish brown, narrowly conic; lamellae cinnamon-brown to crust-brown; very fragile ------------------------------ 2
1. Stipe fleshy; lamellae earth brown; not fragile -- 5
    2. Pileus dry; spores cinnamon-brown --- 3
    2. Pileus viscid; spores rusty brown --- 4
3. Pileus pure white, margin striate; stipe thin, dry, white ------------------ *Conocybe lactea*
3. Pileus reddish to yellow-brown; stipe thin, dry, dark reddish brown ---- *Conocybe tenera*
    4. Pileus bright yellow, plicate-striate, viscid-------------------------- *Bolbitius vitellinus*
    4. Pileus reddish brown, striate, reticulate veined, viscid ---------- *Bolbitius reticulatus*
5. Pileus small, 1.0–3.5 cm broad, ochre-yellow to light orange, viscid; in lawns and grassy areas -- *Agrocybe pediades*
5. Not as above --- 6
    6. Pileus 3–9 cm broad, convex to plane in age, white to cream, viscid; in lawns, grassy areas, and pastures--- *Agrocybe molesta*
    6. Not as above-- 7
7. Black sclerotium with white context present at base of stipe; pileus dark brown; stipe white fibrillose --- *Agrocybe arvalis* (see comments under *A. firma*)
7. Not as above --- 8
    8. Pileus dark yellow-brown; stipe with a well-formed, superior annulus--- *Agrocybe acericola* (see comments under *A. praecox*)
    8. Not as above-- 9
9. Pileus felty, dry, rich dark brown to black-brown; stipe white at apex, rest red-brown with loose, white fibrils; partial veil absent---------------------------------- *Agrocybe firma*
9. Pileus glabrous, dry, light tan to light brown; stipe white at apex, rest pinkish gray; partial veil membranous, leaving a superior annulus or annular zone ------ *Agrocybe praecox*

267

Conocybe lactea (J. E. Lange) Métrod
INEDIBLE

Pileus 1.2–3.0 cm broad, 1.5–3.5 cm tall, narrowly conical, campanulate in age, pure white to pale cinnamon-pink or very light tan in age, irregular folds or wrinkles often over center, striate from margin one-half distance to center, moist but soon dry. Flesh thin, water-soaked, dull white. Lamellae nearly free, narrow, uneven, close, cinnamon to reddish cinnamon. Stipe 5–12 cm long, 0.15–0.3 cm wide, enlarging toward base, white with scattered minute, white hairs, hollow, small white or slightly yellowish basal bulb, dry. Partial veil absent. Odor mild. Taste mild.

Spores 11–14 x 6.5–9.0 µm broadly elliptic to ovoid, smooth, thick-walled, with an apical pore, nonamyloid. Spore print red-brown. Cheilocystidia with a bulbous top. Pileipellis of round to club-shaped cells.

Habit and distribution: Scattered in grass, often in great numbers. Widely distributed. Fruiting in late spring to fall.

Comments: Also known as *Galera lateritia* Fr. and *Conocybe lateritia* (Fr.) Kühner. The pileus expands in the early morning in dew-laden grass and in sunny areas but usually wilts and is gone by midday. The long white "dunce cap," which is often wrinkled, along with the long delicate stipe, identifies it at once.

Conocybe tenera (Schaeff.:Fr.) Fayod
INEDIBLE

Pileus 0.8–2.2 cm broad, 0.8–1.6 cm high, narrowly conic, campanulate in age, dark reddish to yellow-brown, becoming lighter in age, striate almost to the center, dry. Flesh thin, watery, brown. Lamellae free or nearly so, subdistant, narrow, clay-brown to cinnamon-brown. Stipe 4.0–8.5 cm long, 0.15–0.2 cm wide, equal, rigid, straight, color of the pileus, fine longitudinal striations, base not appreciably enlarged. Partial veil absent. Odorless. Taste mild.

Spores 10–14 x 5–7 µm, elliptic, smooth, thickened wall, with an apical pore, nonamyloid. Spore print red-brown. Cheilocystidia ten-pin shaped, thin-walled, numerous. Pileus cuticle of broadly, clavate to pear-shaped, thin-walled cells.

Habit and distribution: Scattered to abundant on lawns, grassy areas or under forest stands. Widely distributed. Fruiting in spring and summer, occasionally in the fall.

Comments: This species was also known as *Galera tenera* Fr. A number of species of *Conocybe* all have the same tall, slender growth habit. At least one species of *Conocybe* contains the deadly Type 1 toxin, amatoxin, and species are difficult to distinguish. In additiion, *C. cyanopus* contains Type 4 toxins. Therefore, do not test these for eating. Watling (1982) and Britenback & Kranzlin (1995) should be consulted if critical identification is desired.

269

Bolbitius vitellinus Fr.
NONPOISONOUS

Pileus 2–5 cm broad, conic, campanulate in age, bright yellow, hairless, margin striate, plicate or grooved in age, viscid. Flesh soft, very thin. Lamellae attached, free in age, close to fairly well separated in age, narrow, reddish gray with minute hairy edges. Stipe 6–12 cm long, 0.2–0.4 cm wide, equal or slightly enlarged toward base, shiny white often tinted yellow, minutely hairy at apex. Partial veil absent. Odorless. Taste mild.

Spores 10–13 x 6.0–7.5 μm elliptic, smooth, thick-walled, with an apical pore, nonamyloid. Spore print bright rusty orange. Pileus cuticle composed of round or pear-shaped cells.

Habit and distribution: Several to abundant on dung, most often cow dung, manured soil or fertilized grass. Widely distributed. Fruiting in spring, early summer, and fall.

Comments: This fungus resembles a small yellow *Coprinus* but, of course, there is no deliquescence of the lamellae and the spore print is not black. *Bolbitius callistus* (Peck) Watling is bright blue, soon becoming olive-brown, and is on well decayed wood. Uncommon, in eastern North America (Watling & Miller, 1987).

Bolbitius reticulatus (Pers.:Fr.) Ricken
INEDIBLE

Pileus 1–4 cm broad, convex, grayish brown to reddish brown over the center, with veinlike wrinkles or reticulations over the center, margin striate, viscid. Flesh soft and white. Lamellae adnate, close, white soon gray to rusty brown in age. Stipe 3–7 cm long, 0.2–0.6 cm wide, white, with white tufts of fibrils, enlarging toward base. Partial veil absent. Odorless. Taste mild.

Spores 8–12 x 5–6 μm elliptic, smooth, thick-walled, with a small apical pore, nonamyloid. Spore print rusty-brown.

Habit and distribution: Several to troops, on mulch, decayed wood, and manure rich soil. Widely distributed. Fruiting in spring, summer, and early fall.

Comments: Watling (1982) has provided additional information on this species and the genus *Bolbitius* in general.

Agrocybe pediades Fr.
EDIBLE BUT NOT RECOMMENDED

Pileus 1.0–3.5 cm broad, convex, campanulate, ochre-yellow, light orange to dull yellowish, light reddish brown in age, hairless, viscid. Flesh firm, pale buff. Lamellae adnate, subdistant, whitish soon light yellowish brown, dark brown in age. Stipe 4–7 cm long, 0.5–1.5 cm wide, equal or slightly larger at base, whitish to light brown, scattered minute hairs, dry. Partial veil present at first, but seldom seen in age. Odor mealy. Taste mealy and disagreeable.

Spores 11–13 x 7–8 μm elliptic, smooth, thick-walled, with an apical pore, nonamyloid. Spore print dark tobacco-brown. Cheilocystidia club-shaped with bulbous apex. Pileus cuticle of pear-shaped cells.

Habit and distribution: Several to numerous in lawns and grassy areas. Widely distributed. Fruiting in spring, summer, and fall.

Comments: Also known as *Agrocybe semiorbicularis* (Bull.:St.-Amans) Fayod, this species could be confused with *Agrocybe paludosa* (J. E. Lange.) Kühner & Romagn., which is slender, has a similar pileus coloration, and is found in grass habitats. However, it has smaller spores (7.5–10.5 x 5.4–7.0 μm). Both species could be mistaken for a poisonous *Hebeloma* and other small brown mushrooms, and are not recommended edibles.

Agrocybe molesta (Lasch) Singer
EDIBLE

Pileus 3–9 cm broad, convex, plane in age, white to cream, smooth or slightly wrinkled margin often with fragments of the white, partial veil, viscid. Flesh firm, white. Lamellae adnate, close, white, tinted pinkish gray becoming brown as the spores mature. Stipe 4–10 cm long, 0.5–1.5 cm wide, equal, white, fibrils on lower surface, rhizomorphs at base. Partial veil thin, fragile, white and superior. Odor fungoid. Taste mild with an after taste.

Spores 11–14 x 6.5–8.0 μm broadly elliptic, smooth, thick-walled, with an apical pore, nonamyloid. Spore print dark brown. Cheilocystidia ovoid, swollen fusiform, thin-walled. Pileipellis of clavate to ovoid, thin-walled cells.

Habit and distribution: Several to gregarious in lawns, grassy areas, and pastures. Widely distributed. Fruiting in warm, summer weather.

Comments: Also known as *Agrocybe dura* (Bolton) Singer, it can be confused with *A. praecox* and *A. acericola*. Our experience is that it is typically in lawn, grassy areas, more often than in humus and litter, like the species described above. It is also edible, but not choice.

Agrocybe firma (Peck) Kühner
INEDIBLE

Pileus 1–5 cm broad, convex, plane in age, felty, rich dark brown to black-brown usually darker in the center, margin inrolled when young, dry. Flesh firm, pale white, darkening in age. Lamellae adnate, close, medium broad, light brown to brownish orange, edges minutely fimbriate. Stipe 1.5–5.0 cm long, 0.2–0.5 cm wide, enlarging somewhat toward the base, white near the apex, rest brown, with small, loose, white to brown fibrils over the surface, dense white mycelium over the base, dry. Partial veil not seen. Odor farinaceous. Taste mild then bitter and unpleasant.

Spores 5.4–7.0 x 3.6–4.4 µm elliptic, smooth, thick-walled, with an apical pore, nonamyloid. Spore print dark brown. Cheilocystidia broadly clavate to fusiform, thin-walled. Pileipellis of clavate cells with protruding cystidia.

Habit and distribution: Several to gregarious, often in clusters on hardwood mulch, and debris. Widely distributed, most common in eastern North America. Fruiting in early spring and again in the fall.

Comments: *Agrocybe arvalis* (Fr.) Singer (= *A. tuberosa* (Henn.) Singer) also has a brown pileus, is similar in stature, but has a smooth, white stipe, and grows from a buried, black sclerotium which is white inside. We have found it occasionally in Virginia and North Carolina. Both species are bitter to taste and inedible.

Agrocybe praecox Fr.
EDIBLE

Pileus 1–7 cm broad, convex, nearly plane in age, cream color to light tan or light brown, hairless, dry. Flesh soft, thick, white. Lamellae adnate to adnexed, close, whitish at first to light brown in age. Stipe 4–10 cm long, 0.4–1.0 cm wide, equal, white above, pinkish gray below the partial veil, streaked brown from the spores, white mycelium over the base with white rhizomorphs, hairless, dry. Partial veil membranous, white, leaving a superior, weak annulus. Odor mild to fungoid. Taste farinaceous

Spores 8–13 x 5.5–7.0 µm elliptic, smooth, thick-walled, with an apical pore, nonamyloid. Spore print dark rich brown. Cheilocystidia ovoid, inflated, thin-walled. Pileipellis of pear-shaped to round cells.

Habit and distribution: Solitary to scattered in lawns, mulch beds, humus, and grassy areas. Widely distributed. Fruiting in spring and early summer.

Comments: Spring can bring very large fruitings in humus and litter. It is edible but has very little flavor. A very similar species, *Agrocybe acericola* Peck, has a dark yellow-brown pileus, a persistent annulus, and is found on rotten logs and stumps or on buried wood. It is common in areas which have been logged in western North America. Neither *A. praecox* nor *A. firma* have the persistent, well-formed annulus.

AGARICACEAE

This is a family of fleshy mushrooms with white, orange, pinkish to brown ground color with flattened or raised squamules or fibrils, and a dry to moist surface. The pileipellis or stipe cuticle may or may not stain yellow or red, the flesh within stains yellow, reddish, red-brown, or not at all. The lamellae are free, white, gray, grayish white to bright pink at first, but dark chocolate-brown in age from the maturing spores. The spores are elliptic, smooth, thick-walled, with or without an apical pore, spore print is chocolate-brown. The stipe is fleshy, with the remains of a partial veil, at least when young. The partial veil is either single or double and usually white, membranous to cottony. The pileipellis is always filamentous. The species grow on the ground, rarely on well-decayed wood, and are decomposers of plant material. Some species are typically on lawns, meadows, and grassy areas, while others favor forest habitats under hardwoods or conifers. Kerrigan (1986) treats the western North American species and presents only 38 species. There are many more species for North America as a whole, but there is no such treatment for them. Kimbrough (1986) treats the species from Florida. The Lepiotaceae are very closely related and many mycologists have combined the two families. For more practical reasons, they are easier to identify if left as two families.

There is a second genus, *Melanophyllum* with one North American species, *M. echinatum* (Roth:Fr.) Singer. It is not treated here since it is only occasionally encountered. It has bright red lamellae, a red stipe, is very small, and widely distributed.

Edibility: There are both excellent edible and poisonous species in this very large genus. The species to be avoided have flesh (not just the cuticle) that is yellow to red or bruises yellow to red, and include *A. xanthoderma, A. silvaticus,* and *A. placomyces.* They contain Type 8 toxins and cause severe gastric upset. They often have a phenolic or coal-tar odor. The "Mushroom of Commerce," *A. brunnescens* Peck, is grown and marketed as the "Button Mushroom," "Portabello," or "Crimini." It has its origin in Europe (Stamets, 2000). However, it is closely related to *A. campestris,* the "Meadow Mushroom." Other species of *Agaricus* that do not stain, are edible, as well as those that only stain yellow on the pileipellis or stipe cuticle. In the suburbs of many of our cities, such as Philadelphia, New York City, and Boston, *A. brunnescens* has escaped from cultivation and can be found in lawns and meadows. It has basidia that are 2-spored, in contrast to the 4-spored basidia of *A. campestris,* the "Wild Meadow Mushroom." See *Hope's Mushroom Cookbook* (H. Miller, 1993) for recipes for these good edibles.

KEY TO AGARICUS

1. Flesh of pileus and stipe, when cut and bruised, yellow, pinkish, orange or red -------- 2
1. Flesh of pileus and stipe not staining yellow or red; cuticle of stipe or pileipellis surface may stain yellow but not the flesh inside --- 4
    2. Flesh, especially in base of stipe, yellowish to bright yellow; lamellae pink when young; pileus 7–10 cm broad, white to tan in age ------------ *Agaricus xanthoderma*
    2. Not as above-- 3
3. Pileus 4–12 cm broad, pale white with pinkish brown scales, bruising red; flesh white, slowly to instantly bruising red --- *Agaricus silvaticus*
3. Pileus 4–15 cm broad, covered with densely arranged, gray-brown to blackish brown scales; flesh white, bruising yellow to dull pinkish or orange-red -- *Agaricus placomyces*
    4. Partial veil white, double, leaving a flaring, double ring ---------- *Agaricus bitorquis*
    4. Partial veil single, flaring or leaving a small annulus ---------------------------------- 5
5. Partial veil membranous, thick, lower layer with a characteristic coglike pattern; pileipellis or stipe cutis stains yellow, pileus white to yellowish-------------------------- 6
5. Partial veil simple, lower layer without a coglike pattern; pileus some other color ---- 7
    6. Spores 7.0–9.2 x 4.4–5.5 µm elliptic; in meadows and fields ---- *Agaricus arvensis*
    6. Spores 5.0–6.5 x 3.5–4.4 µm elliptic; in humus, hardwood and conifer litter in forests --- *Agaricus silvicola*
                    (see comments under *A. arvensis*)
7. Pileus 2–7 cm broad, small, pinkish infused with orange, sometimes bruising slightly yellowish with light brown surface fibrils; lower stipe orange to orange-buff-- *Agaricus semotus*
7. Pileus larger; fruiting body more fleshy and robust or a different color -------------------- 8

8. Pileus 10–25 cm broad, robust, yellow-brown covered with dense, hazel-brown scales, bruising yellow; partial veil membranous, with raised cottony patches underneath, leaving a superior, soft, skirtlike ring; in mulch or litter in woods -- *Agaricus augustus*

8. Not as above --- 9

9. Pileus up to 35 cm broad, robust, white, with thick, raised scales, white, darkening to dark brown in age; spores 8–16 x 6–8 μm elliptic; in meadows, roadsides in western North America --- *Agaricus crocodilinus*

(see comments under *A. augustus*)

9. Not as above--- 10

10. Pileus 7–22 cm broad, large, reddish brown to lilac, tinted gray-brown; partial veil white, membranous, flaring to skirtlike; not in fairy rings---- *Agaricus subrutilescens*

10. Pileus 2–10 cm broad, white, often obscure, light brown to cinnamon-brown, appressed scales; partial veil white, smooth, leaving a small annulus; often forming fairy rings in lawns and meadows ----------------------------- *Agaricus campestris*

Agaricus xanthoderma Genev.
POISONOUS

Pileus 7–10 (-20) cm broad, convex to broadly convex, in age plane, even slightly depressed in center, white, becoming light tan in age, glabrous to appressed fibrillose sometimes with fine cracks in the surface, often yellow when bruised, dry. Flesh firm, white, when bruised staining yellow especially in the stipe base. Lamellae free, close, broad, white, soon pink to black-brown in age. Stipe 5–12 cm long, 1–2 cm wide, base somewhat larger to 3 cm, white, above the superior annulus, white with fine fibrils below, staining yellow when bruised, dry. Partial veil membranous, white, flaring to skirtlike, or sometimes falling away especially in age. Odor of phenol. Taste unpleasant.

Spores 4.5–6.0 x 3.2–4.5 μm elliptic, smooth, thick-walled, apical pore absent, nonamyloid. Spore print chocolate-brown.

Habit and distribution: Several to gregarious in lawns, grassy areas or under open hardwood forests. Widely distributed, especially common in western grasslands and along the West Coast. Fruiting in summer and fall.

Comments: This species is often mistaken for the meadow mushroom, *Agaricus campestris,* which grows in lawns and grassy areas and looks very similar. The meadow mushroom does not stain yellow or have a yellow context nor does it have a phenolic odor, and is edible. *Agaricus albolutescens* Zeller is very similar, but has an almond to anise odor, tastes mild, but does stain yellow when bruised on the pileus and in the context of the stipe. It also resembles *A. silvicola,* which has the same odor but does not stain yellow in the context of the pileus and stipe. Unlike *A. silvicola,* both *A. xanthoderma* and *A. albolutescens* are not edible and can cause severe gastric upset, Type 8 toxins.

Agaricus silvaticus Schaeff.:Fr.
NOT RECOMMENDED

Pileus 4–12 cm broad, convex to broadly convex in age, nearly white with obscure scales or covered with dense pinkish brown scales, bruising red, margin only slightly inrolled, straight in age, dry. Flesh thick, firm, white, slowly to instantly bruising red to reddish brown. Lamellae free, crowded, grayish pink to dark reddish brown in age. Stipe 6–11 cm long, 1–2 cm wide, enlarging toward base, white, nearly smooth, scattered fibrils above and below the superior annulus, turning dingy pink to pinkish brown in age, sometimes with a bulbous base, dry. Veil membranous, cottony beneath, with raised buff patches, leaving a superior, persistent flaring ring. Odorless. Taste mild.

Spores 5–7 x 3–4 μm broadly elliptic, smooth, thick-walled, apical pore not visible, nonamyloid. Spore print chocolate-brown. Cheilocystidia club-shaped, thin-walled, numerous.

Habit and distribution: Scattered to numerous under conifers and occasionally hardwoods. Widely distributed. Fruiting in spring and summer but most often in the fall.

Comments: There appear to be a number of closely related species which range in pileus color from nearly white to those covered with brown squamules and with varying degrees of staining (Smith, 1949). *Agaricus haemorrhoidarius* Schulzer is smaller, with brown scales, and quickly stains deep red. Related species are discussed by Pilát (1951), but no North American study of these variants has been done. There are varying reports of gastric upset with those that are considered edible. We recommend avoiding this complex.

Agaricus placomyces Peck
POISONOUS

Pileus 4–8 (-15) cm broad, oval, convex, nearly plane in age, sometimes with a low umbo, covered with densely arranged, gray-brown to blackish brown hairy scales, margin incurved and wrinkled at first but soon straight, dry. Flesh firm, white, or dull pinkish in age, staining yellow, especially in the base of the stipe, then changing to dull reddish brown. Lamellae free, close, pink, dark chocolate-brown in age. Stipe 3–9 (-15) cm long, 0.7–2.0 cm wide, slender, forming a small bulb, dull white changing to pinkish brown or dingy brown to yellowish in the base in age, dry. Partial veil membranous, with white cottony patches underneath, leaving a persistent, often flaring, superior ring. Odor disagreeable of coal tar or phenol. Taste mild.

Spores 4.5–6.0 x 3.5–4.5 µm broadly elliptic, smooth, thick-walled, without an apical pore, nonamyloid. Spore print chocolate-brown. Cheilocystidia abundant, thin-walled, club-shaped.

Habit and distribution: Several to numerous under hardwoods or conifers. Widely distributed. Fruiting in late summer and fall.

Comments: This species causes gastrointestinal upset (Type 6 toxins) and is one of a group of poisonous species with yellow or orange-red staining context tissue, especially in the stipe, and a coal-tar or phenol odor. *Agaricus meleagris* Schaeff. is generally considered to be a synonym, but the western collections that we have studied are larger and more robust. The stipe tissue turns dull orange-red when bruised (see photo) but it also has the strong coal-tar odor. The pileus of *A. placomyces* has gray hairs with no sign of the red-colored fibrils typically seen in *A. silvaticus*. Do not eat any species with the characters described above.

Agaricus bitorquis (Quél.) Sacc.
EDIBLE

Pileus 5–12 cm broad, broadly convex, to nearly plane in age, dull white with dingy yellow to yellow-brown or even grayish stains, flattened hairs but often appearing smooth and hairless, surface finely cracked in age, margin inrolled, dry. Flesh firm, white, does not change color when bruised. Lamellae nearly free, close, pale pink, pinkish brown to deep blackish brown in age. Stipe 2–8 cm long, 1.5–3.0 cm wide, equal or narrowed at base, white, hairless above and below ring. Partial veil membranous, wooly, white, double, leaving a double ring that flares outward at first in the middle of the stipe. Odor pleasant, faintly almond. Taste mild.

Spores 4.0–6.5 x 4–5 μm elliptic, smooth, thick-walled, apical pore absent, nonamyloid. Spore print chocolate-brown. Cheilocystidia clavate, thin-walled, numerous.

Habit and distribution: Single to numerous in lawns, on hard-packed soil, frequently around barnyards. Widely distributed, most common in eastern North America and on the West Coast. Fruiting in spring, summer, and fall. On the West Coast also in winter and spring.

Comments: This species is also known as *A. edulis* Vitt. or *Psalliota rodmanii* Peck. *Agaricus bitorquis* is thick, fleshy, and extremely good eating and closely resembles *A. campestris*, which is widely cultivated throughout the world (Hall et al., 2003).

Agaricus arvensis Fr.:Schaeff.
EDIBLE, CHOICE

Pileus 8–20 cm broad, oval, convex to plane in age, white, creamy white to yellowish brown, smooth, hairless, with small scales over the center in age, margin sometimes covered with hanging veil remnants, cuticle bruises yellow, darkening to dingy yellowish brown, dry. Flesh thick, firm, white, unchanging when bruised or slowly tinged yellowish. Lamellae free, crowded, whitish but soon grayish pink, blackish brown in age. Stipe 5–20 cm long, 1.0–3.0 cm wide, equal enlarging somewhat toward the base, shining and smooth above the cottony, white ring, small scales below, cuticle unchanged when bruised or slowly bruising yellow, dry. Partial veil membranous, white, thin, double before breaking, the lower layer with a characteristic coglike pattern around the stipe leaving a superior, skirtlike annulus. Odor of anise. Taste mild.

Spores 7.0–9.2 x 4.4–5.5 µm elliptic, smooth, thick-walled, apical pore absent, nonamyloid. Spore print purplish brown to blackish brown.

Habit and distribution: Several to numerous in meadows and fields. Widely distributed. Fruiting in summer and fall.

Comments: This species is commonly known as the "Horse Mushroom." *Agaricus abruptibulbus* Peck is very similar, but is not robust, has a thin stipe with an abrupt basal bulb, odor of anise, and smaller spores (5.9–7.6 x 4–5 µm). *Agaricus silvicola* (Vittad.) Sacc. is very similar; found in woodlands; has smaller spores (5.0–6.5 x 3.5–4.4 µm); in other respects is indistinguishable. We have recorded it under conifers in the Yukon, Montana, Idaho, Virginia, and in many other locations. This complex contains species that are all edible and very good. There is one species in this complex with the characteristic yellow staining cuticle, however, it is white with a pale orange hue. It smells like coal-gas and can cause gastric upset, Type 8 toxins; and should be avoided.

Agaricus semotus Fr.
INEDIBLE

Pileus 2–7 cm broad, convex, plane in age with a low umbo, light pinkish at first with light brown fibrils, infused with orange in age, bruising yellow, margin may have some white veil remains, dry. Flesh white, soft, bruising very slightly yellowish. Lamellae free, close, white then pink to dark black-brown in age. Stipe 4–7 cm long, 0.4–0.8 cm wide, enlarging to 0.6–1.2 cm at base, white, smooth at apex, below annulus with loose appressed fibrils becoming orange to orange-buff. Partial veil soft, white, forming a skirtlike annulus, often falling away in age. Odor of anise or almonds. Taste mild.

Spores 4.0–5.6 x 3–4 μm elliptic, smooth, thick-walled, no apical pore visible, nonamyloid. Spore print dark purple-brown.

Habit and distribution: Single to several, infrequently gregarious. Widely distributed. Fruiting in late summer and fall.

Comments: There are several small species of *Agaricus*. Kerrigan (1986) describes *Agaricus diminutivus* Peck, another very small species that also bruises yellow that is part of an unexplored complex. We have collected and seen *A. semotus* in various locations throughout North America. Edibility is unknown.

Agaricus augustus Fr.
EDIBLE

Pileus 10–25 cm broad, large, ovoid with a flattened top, convex to plane with a low umbo, yellow-brown, covered with dense hazel-brown scales, bruising yellowish, margin only slightly recurved, soon straight, dry. Flesh thick, white or becoming very slowly yellowish in age. Lamellae free, close, pink to chocolate-brown at maturity. Stipe 8–20 cm long, 1.5–3.0 cm wide, equal or enlarged near base, white, above ring densely hairy, with erect, white scales below, nearly hairless, white to brownish in age, sometimes bruising yellow, dry. Partial veil membranous, white above, with raised, cottony patches underneath, leaving a superior, soft, skirtlike ring. Odor of anise. Taste mild and pleasant.

Spores 8–11 x 5–6 μm elliptic, smooth, thick-walled, no apical pore visible, nonamyloid. Spore print chocolate-brown.

Habit and distribution: Scattered to numerous under conifers or in grassy areas in or near forest cover. Widely distributed. Fruiting in spring, summer, or fall.

Comments: A giant, closely related, western species is *A. crocodilinus* Murrill. It has a short, stout stipe; a white pileus, up to 35 cm broad, covered with raised scales that only darken to brown in age; and spores 8–16 x 6–8 (-16) μm. It is found in open grasslands, in Idaho onto the West Coast and in the Southwest and is also edible. Compare both of these species with *A. arvensis* which also grows in open grasslands.

Agaricus subrutilescens (Kauffman) Hotson & D. E. Stuntz
EDIBLE

Pileus 7–22 cm broad, convex to broadly convex to nearly plane in age, reddish brown to lilac, tinted gray-brown, fibrillose scales and hairs over the surface, sometimes with white patches of the partial veil clinging to the margin, dry. Flesh soft, white. Lamellae free, crowded, narrow, white young, soon pink, changing to dark reddish brown. Stipe 8–20 cm long, 1–3 cm wide at apex, flaring to 3–5 cm at the base, white, smooth above the superior annulus, white floccose scales below to the base, rooting into the litter, dry. Partial veil white membranous, flaring or skirtlike, silky above, cottony below. Odor mild even fruity. Taste mild and pleasant.

Spores 4.5–6.0 x 3–4 µm elliptic, smooth, thick-walled, no apical pore visible, nonamyloid. Spore print chocolate-brown.

Habit and distribution: Solitary, several to gregarious, in litter, under conifers, less frequently under hardwoods in Washington, Oregon, and northern California. Fruiting in the fall and winter.

Comments: Kerrigan (1986) indicates that 3% KOH stains the pileus green, which is unique in western North America. It is generally considered to be an excellent edible, but Arora (1986) indicates that some people experience gastric upset.

Agaricus campestris L.: Fr.
EDIBLE

Pileus 2–10 cm broad, convex, nearly plane in age, usually white at first often becoming light brown, cinnamon-brown, or even dingy brown in age, occasionally remaining nearly white, smooth, glabrous, sometimes with flattened scales, dry. Flesh thick, firm, white or tinted reddish brown. Lamellae free, crowded, narrow, pink at first, becoming chocolate-brown in age. Stipe 2–6 cm long, 1–2 cm wide, equal, white and smooth, smooth above the annulus, white with loose fibrils below, slowly discoloring dingy reddish brown, dry. Partial veil white smooth leaving a small annulus, soon brown from the spores. Odor pleasant. Taste mild.

Spores 5.5–8.0 x 4–5 µm elliptic, smooth, thick-walled, with a minute, obscure, apical pore, nonamyloid. Spore print dark chocolate-brown. Cystidia absent.

Habit and distribution: Several to abundant on lawns, grassy areas, and meadows, often forming fairy rings. Widely distributed. Fruiting in spring and fall or during periods of cool moist weather at other times.

Comments: This is the common, delicious "Meadow Mushroom" or "Pink Bottom" found on lawns and fields throughout North America. One must note the characteristic pink, free gills that soon turn chocolate-brown from the maturing spores. *Agaricus bisporus* (J. E. Lange) Imbach (also known as *A. brunnescens* Peck), the "Commercial Mushroom," looks very similar. However, it has basidia with 2 spores, while *A. campestris* has 4 spores on each basidium; the spores are similar (7–9 x 4.5–5.5 µm); and it is found where it has escaped in grass or on well-manured ground, usually around big cities where it has been sold for many years. The stipe context is not nor does it turn yellow or orange in the stipe or at the base when cut open and bruised (see *Agaricus xanthoderma*). Species that have yellow, orange or red contexts are generally poisonous. There are many good recipes for preparing the "Meadow Mushroom" for the table (Miller, H. H., 1993).

CREPIDOTACEAE

This family is represented here by a single genus, *Crepidotus*. For additional information on the genera within the Crepidotaceae, (see Aime 2005 and Moncalvo et al. 2002). The species of *Crepidotus* are wood-inhabiting fungi largely without stipes; they are generally small, convex to fan-shaped, with thin flesh; the brown spores are smooth (Figs. 2 & 3), or minutely spiny (Fig. 10), thick-walled, and entire. There are approximately 125 species in North America (Hesler & Smith, 1965).

Edibility: These are bitter or bland and are not suitable for the table. There are no toxins reported in the genus.

KEY TO CREPIDOTUS

1. Pileus covered with hairy brown squamules or fibrils --- 2
1. Pileus hairless or with white fibrils -- 3
    2. Pileus flesh gelatinous; spores elliptic, smooth ---------------------- *Crepidotus mollis*
    2. Pileus flesh not gelatinous; spores globose, spiny ---------- *Crepidotus crocophyllus*
3. On conifer logs, near melting snow ----------------------------------- *Crepidotus lanuginosus*
                 (see comments under *C. applanatus*)
3. On hardwood logs or herbaceous material ------------ *Crepidotus applanatus* and others

Crepidotus mollis (Fr.) Staude
INEDIBLE

Pileus1.5–4.0 (-8.0) cm broad, 2.0–2.5 cm wide, convex, buff ground color covered with dark brown, small, fibrous scales, beneath which is a thin, gelatinous layer. Flesh soft, thin, white. Lamellae close to subdistant, narrow, brown to red-brown. Stipe absent, merely a short basal plug covered with minute hairs. Partial veil absent. Odorless. Taste mild.

Spores 7–10 x 5–7 μm short elliptic, smooth, entire, thick-walled, nonamyloid. Spore print yellow-brown. Cheilocystidia flask-shaped to clavate, thin-walled.

Habit and distribution: Grows in groups to nearly imbricate on the bark of dead hardwoods and sometimes conifers. Widely distributed. Fruiting in spring, summer, and fall.

Comments: There is too little flesh to consider these edible.

Crepidotus crocophyllus (Berk.) Sacc.
EDIBILITY UNKNOWN

Pileus 0.5–6 cm broad, convex, color variable, ranging from buff to yellow to orange ground color, covered with dark brown fibrils, dry. Flesh soft, thin, not gelatinous. Lamellae close to crowded, broad, color variable, similar to the pileus, but eventually becoming brown from spores. Stipe absent. Partial veil absent. Odorless. Taste mild.

Spores 5–7 μm globose, minutely spiny, entire, thick-walled, nonamyloid. Spore print brown. Cheilocystidia clavate to cylindric, sometimes capitate, thin-walled.

Habit and distribution: Scattered to gregarious on decorticated hardwoods or woody hardwood litter, rarely on conifer litter. Widely distributed. Fruiting from spring to fall.

Comments: The color of this species is variable and ranges from buff to bright orange on both pileus and lamellae; the amount of brown fibrils on the pileus can vary from a light sprinkling to a dense brown cover. The combination of spiny, globose spores 5–7 μm distinguish it from other commonly collected species of *Crepidotus*. It can sometimes be confused with *Crepidotus mollis*, which has a gelatinous layer in the pileus and smooth spores.

Crepidotus applanatus (Pers.) P. Kumm.
INEDIBLE

Pileus 1–4 cm broad, petal-like to fan-shaped, dull cinnamon or brownish, hygrophanous and dull white in age, hairless to minutely downy, margin inrolled, faintly striate, moist. Flesh firm, thin, white. Lamellae close, narrow, white but soon brown, edges minutely hairy. Stipe absent, replaced by a short, white, hairy plug. Partial veil absent. Odorless. Taste with an unpleasant after taste.

Spores 4.0–5.5 µm globose, minutely spiny, entire, thick-walled, nonamyloid. Spore print brown to cinnamon-brown. Cheilocystidia present, thin-walled, narrowly club-shaped. Clamp connections present.

Habit and distribution: Abundant, shelving, and sometimes appearing overlapping, usually on hardwood limbs, logs, and stumps. Widely distributed. Fruiting in spring and fall.

Comments: Two other common species of *Crepidotus* can be found in herbaceous matter and litter, more infrequently on decaying hardwood. Both resemble *C. applanatus* but are distinguished by their sessile habit. *Crepidotus herbarum* (Peck) Sacc. has small spores (6–8 x 3–4 µm) that are pip-shaped, smooth, and very pale yellow. *Crepidotus versutus* (Peck) Sacc. has large spores (7–11 x 4.5–6.0 µm) that are elliptic and appear wrinkled under the microscope. *Crepidotus lanuginosus* Hesler & A. H. Sm. is a minute (3–15 mm broad), wooly, white, western species with minutely spiny, elliptic spores; and fruits as the snow melts on conifer logs in the spring.

PAXILLACEAE

This is a small family, with only one genus, *Paxillus,* and only five species in North America. Two species are sessile, and the other three have long decurrent lamellae, which are often intervenose. The family is characterized by having a clay-brown to yellow-brown spore print, and short elliptic to elliptic (Fig. 3), smooth, thick-walled, nonamyloid spores. The pileus is dry, often matted, and the margin is inrolled. The fresh tissue is green in 3% ferric sulphate. First apply several drops of alcohol followed by the ferric sulphate. Three species occur on wood and two are mycorrhizal, and occur on the ground under conifers and hardwood forests.

Edibility: *Paxillus* species should not be eaten because they have Type 8 toxins and cause gastrointestinal upset which can be severe.

KEY TO PAXILLUS

1. Stipe absent; fruiting bodies often imbricate on conifer logs ------------------------------- 2
1. Stipe present -- 3
    2. Lamellae intervenose, corrugate, and anastomosing --------------------- *P. corrugatus*
             (see comments under *P. panuoides*)
    2. Lamellae not intervenose or anastomosing -------------------------------- *P. panuoides*
3. Stipe lateral, covered with dense black-brown hairs -------------------- *P. atrotomentosus*
3. Stipe central, smooth light brown -- 4
    4. Pileus dry, light reddish brown to yellow-brown, margin cottony at first and deeply inrolled; spore print clay-brown to yellow-brown --------------------------- *P. involutus*
    4. Pileus dry, dingy buff to light chamois, staining red-brown, margin not deeply inrolled and soon even; spore print vinaceous-brown ----------------------- *P. vernalis*

Paxillus panuoides Fr.
POISONOUS

Pileus 3–8 cm broad, sessile, petal-like to fan-shaped, ochraceous-buff, brownish yellow to light buff or tinted olive, minutely downy, soon glabrous, margin lobed or wavy, dry. Flesh thin, soft, white. Lamellae radiate from point of attachment, close, some are forked, intervenose, pale yellow or pale yellow-orange. Stipe absent. Partial veil absent. Odorless or pleasant. Taste pleasant.

Spores 4.0–6.0 x 3.0–4.5 µm short elliptic, entire, smooth, dextrinoid in age in Melzer's solution. Spore print pale brown to yellowish-brown.

Habit and distribution: Several to many overlapping on limbs, logs, and stumps of conifers, or on wood products in service. Widely distributed. Fruiting in spring, summer, and fall.

Comments: This species is also known as *Tapinella panuoides* (Fr.:Fr.) Gill. *Paxillus corrugatus* Atk., also placed in *Tapinella* by some mycologists, is very similar but has an intervenose, almost poroid or corrugate, yellow-brown hymenium. The spores are 3.0–4.0 x 1.5–2.5 µm elliptic, thin-walled, dextrinoid in Melzer's solution. *Phyllotopsis nidulans* (Pers.:Fr.) Singer is also similar; has a foul smell; a densely hairy cap; and pink, allantoid (sausage-shaped) (Fig. 7) spores, which are hyaline in Melzer's solution.

Paxillus atrotomentosus (Batsch: Fr.) Fr.
POISONOUS

Pileus 6–22 cm broad, convex, plane to depressed somewhat in center at maturity, light to rusty brown or dark brown, tomentose, margin inrolled, dry. Flesh firm, thick, white. Lamellae short to long decurrent in age, close, narrow, forked to sometimes nearly poroid at the stipe, mustard-yellow to yellow-brown. Stipe 2.5–10 cm long, 0.8–4.0 cm wide, equal, lateral, robust, densely hairy, dark brown to blackish brown, with a root-like base. Partial veil absent. Odor and taste not distinctive.

Spores 4.4–7.0 x 3.0–4.0 µm short elliptic, smooth, entire, yellowish to dextrinoid in Melzer's solution. Spore print clay-color to mustard-yellow.

Habit and distribution: Single to several or in clusters on conifer stumps, logs and limbs, sometimes partially buried wood. Widely distributed. Fruiting in summer and fall.

Comments: The black-brown wooly stipe clearly sets this species apart from all other species of *Paxillus*. Ingestion causes gastrointestinal upset, sometimes severe (Type 8 toxins).

Paxillus involutus (Batsch:Fr.) Fr.
POISONOUS

Pileus 4–15 cm broad, convex, plane with a central depression in age, light reddish brown, tinged with olive, to yellow-brown, covered with matted, soft hairs, sometimes obscurely zoned or spotted, margin inrolled until late age, dry. Flesh thick, dingy yellowish, bruising brownish. Lamellae decurrent, crowded, broad, sometimes anastomosing and intervenose near stipe, yellowish olive bruising brown. Stipe 4–10 cm long, 1.4–2.0 cm wide, equal or enlarged toward the base, central, yellowish brown, streaked or stained darker brown, glabrous, dry. Partial veil absent. Odor pleasant. Taste mild to unpleasant.

Spores 7–9 x 4–6 μm elliptic, smooth, entire, yellowish to dextrinoid in Melzer's solution, thick-walled. Spore print clay-brown to yellowish brown.

Habit and distribution: Single or several, on ground under conifer or hardwood forest including aspen and birch. Widely distributed. Fruiting in summer and fall.

Comments: This is an ectomycorrhizal fungus with a broad host range. Ingestion of this fungus can result in severe gastrointestinal upset (Type 8 toxins).

Paxillus vernalis Watling
PROBABLY POISONOUS

Pileus 5–20 cm broad, broadly convex soon plane, pale dingy buff to light chamois, staining red-brown, margin inrolled at first soon expanding, minutely tomentose, dry. Flesh firm, nearly white to buff, red-brown to wine-colored in the stipe. Lamellae decurrent, close, narrow, sometimes forking, dingy buff staining red-brown on bruising, dingy cinnamon-brown in age. Stipe 3–10 cm long, 0.5–3.0 cm wide, equal or enlarging slightly toward base, cinnamon-brown becoming dark brown in age, dry. Partial veil absent. Odor and taste mild to acidulous.

Spores 6.5–9.0 x 5.0–6.5 μm elliptic, smooth, entire, ochraceous-tawny in Melzer's solution, thick-walled. Spore print vinaceous-brown.

Habit and distribution: Single to several on ground in mixed conifer/hardwoods, especiallly aspen and birch. Found in central, northeastern, and southeastern North America. Fruiting in summer and early fall.

Comments: Paxillus vernalis differs from P. involutus in the vinaceous-brown spore print; pale pileus coloration; lighter colored stipe; and larger size. We have no information on the possible toxins, but with toxins distributed throughout the family, we do not recommend eating any Paxillus, including this one.

CORTINARIACEAE

This is a large and diverse family with both decomposers and mycor-rhizal species. The species in the family all have dark spores that range from pale yellow-brown to rusty brown and dark cinnamon brown. They are entire, either smooth and thin-walled, or smooth, thick-walled and rugose, nodulose or tuberculate, nonamyloid. Cystidia are critical to the identification of *Inocybe* and *Hebeloma,* but are seldom found in *Cortinarius.* The partial veil is most frequently a cortina or spiderweb-like veil, which leaves stringlike remains on the stipe, tinted brown from the spores. Only *Rozites* has a membraneous partial veil.

The three decomposer genera covered here are found primarily on wood, leaf litter, and moss. These include *Gymnopilus, Tubaria,* and *Galerina.* The mycorrhizal genera include *Rozites, Inocybe, Hebeloma,* and *Cortinarius.* There are many mycorrhizal species in a wide variety of habitats throughout North America. *Cortinarius* contains the greatest number of species among the agaric genera in North America.

Edibility: Only *Rozites caperata* is commonly collected and eaten by a wide number of people. There are many toxic species, including *Galerina autumnalis,* which contains deadly poisonous Type I toxins. Two species of *Gymnopilus* are hallucinogenic, Type 4 toxins. Many species of *Inocybe* and *Hebeloma* have muscarine, Type 2 toxins, or cause severe gastric upset caused by Type 8 toxins. In *Cortinarius,* several uncommon species contain the deadly poisonous Orellanine Type 7 toxins, but a larger number of species cause gastric upset, Type 8 toxins. Knowing the genera and species in the Cortinariaceae is knowing what to avoid!

KEY TO THE GENERA OF THE CORTINARIACEAE

1. On wood, sometimes buried wood, moss, leaf litter, or mulch ----------------------------- 2
1. On the ground, not on wood -- 4
    2 . On leaf litter or mulch; spore print yellow-brown ------------------------------- *Tubaria*
    2. On logs, stumps sometimes buried wood or on moss ------------------------------------ 3
3. Spore print bright rusty orange to bright rusty brown; on wood or
    buried wood --- *Gymnopilus*
(See also *Pholiota*)

3. Spore print dull brown; on wood or on moss -- *Galerina*
   4. Stipe deep rooting; partial veil absent ------------------------------------ *Phaeocollybia*
   4. Stipe not deep rooting; partial veil present or absent ---------------------------------- 5
5. Partial veil membranous; pileus orange, with a white bloom when
   young --- *Rozites caperata*
5. Partial veil cortinous or long rusty hairs on stipe, sometimes absent --------------------- 6
   6. Pileus small, dry, conic to campanulate, often matted with radial, appressed fibrils;
      spores nodulose to smooth, brown; lamellae with clavate cheilocystidia, usually
      thick-walled; odor of green corn -- *Inocybe*
   6. Not as above--- 7
7. Pileus viscid to greasy; veil present or absent; stipe always dry; spores brown;
   cheilocystidia long cylindric to narrowly clavate; odor radishlike---------------- *Hebeloma*
7. Pileus dry, viscid to glutinous; stipe dry to viscid; spores rusty-brown; cheilocystidia
   usually absent, if present 10-pin-shaped -- *Cortinarius*

TUBARIA

Tubaria is a small genus of less than a dozen species. The pileus is small, brown to orange-brown, moist to dry; the lamellae are adnate to short decurrent and light brown. The stipe is dry, brown, often clothed in white hairs at first, with or without an annulus. The spores are elliptic, thin-walled (often collapsed when viewing through the microscope), entire, and the spore print light to yellow-brown. They are decomposers of leaves, plant litter, and mulch, often fruiting in troops.

Edibility: They are nonpoisonous, but have no taste and therefore inedible.

KEY TO TUBARIA

1. Pileus moist, dark brown, glabrous with striate margin; often fruits in winter or during
   spring --- *T. heimalis*
1. Pileus dry, covered with downy white fibrils, without striate margin; fruiting in spring,
   summer, and fall -- 2
   2. Pileus with white hairs, usually in a fringe around the margin of the pileus; stipe
      brown, clothed with appressed white hairs ------------------------------ *T. furfuracea*
   2. Pileus clothed in dense hairs, often clinging to the margin; stipe covered with white
      floccules --- *T. conspersa*
            (see comments under *T. furfuracea*)

Tubaria heimalis Romagn.:Bon
INEDIBLE

Pileus 0.9–3.5 cm broad, convex to broadly convex, sometimes depressed in center, dark brown with distinct brown striations over the margin, which is orange-buff, hygrophanous, drying to light brown, moist not viscid. Flesh firm white to orange-buff, stipe center cottony white. Lamellae adnate to broadly adnate, subdistant, narrow, pinkish brown to cinnamon-buff. Stipe 1.1–2.5 (- 4.5) cm long, 0.2–0.6 cm wide, equal or slightly larger at the base, brown, smooth with a superior, fragile, annular zone often missing in age, dry. Partial veil fibrous, white, clinging to the margin of the pileus at first sometimes leaving a weak annulus. Odor not distinctive. Taste mild.

Spores 7–10 x 3–5 µm long elliptic, smooth, entire, thin-walled, nonamyloid. Spore print pale yellow-brown to pinkish brown. Cheilocystidia long cylindric (40–55 x 5.0–7.5 µm) often with a capitate head (5–8 µm wide).

Habit and distribution: Gregarious or in troops, in mulch or hardwood debris. Widely distributed but common in eastern North America. Fruiting during the winter months generally from February to April.

Comments: This is truly a winter mushroom that appears during midwinter periods with warming trends. We have observed *T. heimalis* every spring in mulch beds on the Virginia Tech campus. It has no taste, but is not poisonous.

Tubaria furfuracea (Pers.:Fr.) Gill.
INEDIBLE

Pileus 1.2–3.3 cm broad, convex to plane in age, light orange-brown, covered in part with white downy fibrils, at first veil remains as small patches near the margin and white fibers clinging to the margin, dry. Flesh cream color, becoming dull brown in age. Lamellae adnate, broad mature, subdistant, light orange to brown in age. Stipe 1.8–5.0 cm long, 0.2–0.4 cm wide, equal, brown clothed in white hairs, light brown to darker over the lower one half, dry. Partial veil absent. Odor mild. Taste mild.

Spores 7.0–9.5 x 4.5–5.5 µm elliptic to nearly teardrop-shaped, smooth, entire, thin-walled, nonamyloid. Spore print yellow-brown. Cheilocystidia 35–60 x 6–10 µm cylindric, narrowly clavate to irregular, thin-walled, numerous.

Habit and distribution: Several to gregarious on hardwood leaves especially aspen, alder, and willow. Widely distributed. Fruiting during wet periods in the spring, summer, and fall.

Comments: *Tubaria conspersa* (Pers.:Fr.) Fayod is very similar but has floccules on the stipe from the partial veil; often dense remains clinging to the pileus margin; and the spores are more bean-shaped. However, the habitat and substrate are the same. Both are too small and tasteless to be considered edibles.

GYMNOPILUS

The pileus is convex to plane in age, dry to moist, yellowish to brownish or rarely greenish, and smooth to squamulose. The lamellae are adnate to adnexed or short decurrent, and yellowish to rusty brown at maturity. The stipe is centrally stipitate, mostly concolorous with the pileus, sometimes bruising brown on handling. The partial veil, when present, is fibrillose to cortinous. The spores are 3.5–12.5 μm elliptic, warted, (Fig. 11) entire, dextrinoid or not in Melzer's solution, thick-walled, nonamyloid. The spore print rusty-brown or rusty-yellow. Most species are often in cespitose clusters, on limbs, logs, or stumps, but some are terrestrial from buried wood (Hesler, 1969).

Edibility: Most species are bitter tasting and none are edible. However, *Gymnopilus spectabilis* and *G. aeruginosus* are hallucinogenic having Type 4 toxins. The toxins range from very active to mild (Stamets, 1996). We recommend you avoid all species of *Gymnopilus*.

KEY TO GYMNOPILUS

1. Pileus lilac, dull green with bluish green bloom; on conifer wood, Pacific Northwest and California -- *G. punctifolius*
(see comments under *G. sapineus*)
1. Pileus colored differently; distributed more widely -- 2
 2. Pileus small (1.0–3.3 cm broad), orange-buff, orange-brown to deep red-brown ---- 3
 2. Pileus typically larger, up to 18 cm broad; often cespitose ----------------------------- 4
3. Pileus 1.0–2.5 cm broad, orange-brown to dark orange-brown;
spores 3.5–5.5 x 2.8–3.5 μm --- *G. bellulus*
3. Pileus 1–4 cm broad, deep red-brown; spores 7.0–9.5 x 4.5–6.0 μm ---------- *G. picreus*
(see comments under *G. bellulus*)
 4. Pileus robust, 5–18 cm broad, yellow-orange; veil yellow, annulus present; often
 cespitose on ground from buried wood -------------------------------------- *G. spectabilis*
 4. Pileus smaller or differently colored --- 5
5. Pileus robust, variegated green and yellow to dull bluish gray, glabrous; partial veil yellow, leaving a weak, superior zone or annulus -------------------------------- *G. aeruginosus*
(see comments under *G. spectabilis*)
5. Pileus 3–9 cm broad, golden yellow to bright salmon, minute fibrils on surface; not
forming an annulus; single to cespitose, but on wood not on ground -------- *G. sapineus*
(If pileus is glabrous; partial veil white, see *G. penetrans* in comments under *G. sapineus*)

Gymnopilus bellulus (Peck) Murrill
INEDIBLE

Pileus 1.0–2.5 cm broad, convex, broadly convex in age, glabrous, orange-brown to dark orange-brown, moist not viscid. Flesh thin, pale orange. Lamellae adnate, close, bright yellow young, becoming rusty brown in age. Stipe 1.2–3.3 cm long, 0.15–0.3 cm wide, equal, light brown at apex to dark brown below, in age deep reddish brown, minutely hairy, dry. Partial veil absent. Odorless. Taste bitter.

Spores 3.5–5.5 x 2.8–3.5 µm elliptic, entire, distinctly warted (Fig. 9), thick-walled, nonamyloid. Spore print bright rusty yellow. Cystidia fusiform to clavate with a long neck and capitate apex, thin-walled.

Habit and distribution: Several to many on conifer stumps and logs. Found in northern North America south to Tennessee. Fruiting from June to January.

Comments: *Gymnopilus picreus* (Fr.) P. Karst. is also very small, on conifer wood, similar in color (chestnut-brown), but has larger, warted spores (7.0–9.5 x 4.5–6 µm). *Gymnopilus liquiritiae* (Pers.:Fr.) P. Karst. is somewhat larger (2–8 cm broad), pileus orange-buff to orange-brown, with larger, warted spores (7–10 x 4.0–5.5 µm), and is psychoactive (Type 4 toxins) (Stamets, 1996). Hesler (1969) has more details on this hard to distinguish group of small species of *Gymnopilus*.

Gymnopilus spectabilis (Fr.) A. H. Sm.
POISONOUS HALLUCINOGENIC

Pileus 5–18 cm broad, convex, nearly plane in age, buff, yellow to yellow-orange, hairless, to hairy in age, dry. Flesh firm, pale yellow, red-brown in 3% KOH. Lamellae adnate to short decurrent, crowded, mustard-yellow to orange-buff, edges minutely hairy. Stipe 3–20 cm long, 0.8–1.0 (-3.0) cm wide, equal or club-shaped, with scattered hairs, concolorus with the pileus above and below ring, brownish near base, dry. Partial veil membranous, persistent, superior, yellowish. Odorless. Taste very bitter.

Spores 7–10 x 4.5–6.0 µm elliptic, roughened, entire, thin-walled, nonamyloid. Spore print orange or rusty orange. Cheilocystidia long, narrow, thin-walled.

Habit and distribution: Single but most often in cespitose clusters on ground from buried wood, stumps and logs of hardwoods and conifers. Widely distributed. Fruiting in spring, summer, fall to early winter on the West Coast.

Comments: *Gymnopilus spectabilis* is often referred to as the "Laughing Mushroom" with Type 4 toxins, but the hallucinogens vary in different populations of the species. They range from inactive to very active from one population to another. Stamets (1996) cites a number of cases of hallucinogenic reactions after ingesting this species. *Gymnopilus aeruginosus* (Peck) Singer is also widely distributed, has a variegated green and yellow to dull bluish gray pileus, smaller spores, grows on stumps and logs, and is also psychoactive according to Stamets (1996). *Gymnopilus ventricosus* (Earle) Hesler has no toxins, a red-brown pileus, but is otherwise very close to *G. spectabilis* and misidentifications could explain the apparent lack of toxins in some populations. Hesler's (1969) monograph should be consulted for additional information.

Gymnopilus sapineus (Fr.) Maire
NONPOISONOUS

Pileus 1–9 cm broad, convex, sometimes with a low umbo, golden-yellow to bright salmon color or orange, with scattered patches of hairs, dry. Flesh firm, yellow. Lamellae adnate, close, yellow to rusty yellow in age, minutely hairy edges. Stipe 3–7 cm long, 0.4–1.2 cm wide, equal, buff darkening to yellow-brown below the usually missing annulus, dry. Partial veil hairy, fragile, superior, yellow. Odor not distinctive. Taste often very bitter.

Spores 7–10 x 4.0–5.5 µm elliptic, minutely roughened, entire, thin-walled, nonamyloid. Spore print bright rusty brown. Cheilocystidia abundant, thin-walled, narrow, with rounded heads.

Habit and distribution: Single to cespitose clusters on conifers and hardwoods. Widely distributed. Fruiting in summer and fall.

Comments: *Gymnopilus penetrans* (Fr.:Fr.) Murrill is closely related but has a glabrous pileus and white veil. *Gymnopilus punctifolius* (Peck) Singer has a bluish green to lilac pileus, is on conifer wood, found in the Pacific Northwest and California in the fall, is also bitter to taste; has small spores (4.0–5.5 x 3.5–5.0 µm), but, like all other species in the genus, is not edible.

GALERINA

These small brown mushrooms are most often distinguished by the usually striate, brown, moist, conic pileus, with a very thin brittle stipe, and attached lamellae. They are very similar to *Mycena* or *Conocybe*. However, the brown spores have a roughened surface and a flattened depression called a plage, which is found near the apiculus. The species are typically decomposers on mosses, logs, limbs, decayed wood, or wood debris. Smith and Singer (1964) include 199 species in their North American monograph, and Horak and Miller (1992) give an account of the specific mosses, which are decomposed by individual species. These small species are very difficult to identify, seldom encountered, and one must use a microscope for a complete identification. Only the deadly poisonous species are covered in this guide.

Edibility: *Galerina autumnalis* and related taxa contain the deadly poisonous Type 1 toxins, also found in *Amanita.* They should be totally avoided. In fact it is wise to avoid all small mushrooms that occur in grass, moss, or on wood and have thin, brittle stipes.

Galerina autumnalis (Peck) A. H. Sm. & Singer
DEADLY POISONOUS

Pileus 2.5–5.0 cm broad, convex, with or without a small discreet umbo, light tan in dry weather, dark brown when moist, glabrous, margin faintly striate, viscid, Flesh thick, light brown, watery. Lamellae adnate, close, broad, rusty-brown. Stipe 1.5–6.0 cm long, 0.3–0.7 cm wide, equal, brown, streaked with white fibrils, dry. Partial veil fibrous, leaving a thin, superior, white annulus. Odor mealy. Taste mealy (don't taste it!).

Spores 8.5–10.5 x 5.0–6.5 μm elliptic, rugose (Fig. 11), entire, some with an indistinct plage, thick-walled, nonamyloid. Spore print rusty brown. Cheilocystidia bottle-shaped to fusiform, thin-walled.

Habit and distribution: Scattered to abundant on well-decayed, often moss-covered, hardwood and conifer logs. Widely distributed. Fruiting in fall or sometimes in the early spring.

Comments: The **deadly poisonous** phallotoxins and amatoxins (Type 1 toxins) have been isolated and identified in this species and in *Galerina marginata* (Fr.) Kühner, which is very similar but often loses the annulus as it matures. *Galerina venenata* A.H. Sm. has somewhat larger spores (8.7–11.0 x 5–7 μm), is also poisonous, but is rare, and known only from Oregon. Smith (1964) has an involved discussion of this poisonous group of species, but all little brown mushrooms on wood should be avoided!

Phaeocollybia kauffmanii A.H. Sm.
INEDIBLE

Pileus 3–15 up to 19 cm broad, conic with a small papilla when young, broadly companulate with a low umbo in age, orange-brown, center often reddish, margin inrolled, glabrous, viscid. Flesh firm, pale cream to pinkish. Lamellae free or narrowly adnate, crowded young to close in age, ventricose, pale buff to golden brown in age. Stipe 4–11 cm long, 1.0–3.7 cm wide at the apex, tapering to a long rooting base below ground, orange-brown to reddish orange, nearly glabrous with appressed fibrils. Partial veil scattered fibrils on stipe or patches of fibrils. Odor weakly or strongly farinaceous. Taste farinaceous to bitter.

Spores 7.5–10.0 x 4–6 μm lemon-shaped, minutely warted, entire, slightly thick-walled, nonamyloid. Spore print cinnamon-brown. Cheilocystidia numerous, cylindric to narrowly clavate, thin-walled. Clamp connections absent.

Habit and distribution: Several to gregarious in the ground under coniferous-hardwood forests. Found in western North America. Fruiting in the late summer and fall.

Comments: Norvell (1999) has presented four additional species that are similar. Norvell & Redhead (2000) recognize two vernal species from the West Coast. In the eastern United States, three species are recorded. The most common, *P. christinae* (Fr.) Heim, is a much smaller species, pileus 1–5 cm broad, with an acute umbo, olive-brown, and is found under conifers in sandy soil. See Bessette et al. (1997). The species are bitter and not edible.

Rozites caperata (Fr.) Michx.
EDIBLE

Pileus 5–10 cm broad, nearly oval to campanulate in age, straw-colored to orange-brown, covered at first with minute, white hairs that give a frosted appearance, margin wrinkled and inrolled at first, dry. Flesh thick, firm, white. Lamellae adnate to adnexed in age, close, dull whitish to rusty-colored in age. Stipe 6–12 cm long, 1–2 cm wide, enlarging toward base, dingy white, without hairs. Partial veil membranous, white, leaving a superior, persistent, membranous ring. Odorless. Taste pleasant.

Spores 11–14 x 7–9 μm elliptic, finely warted, entire, thick-walled, nonamyloid. Spore print dingy-rusty to yellowish brown.

Habit and distribution: Several to numerous in mixed conifer-hardwood or conifer stands. Widely distributed. Fruiting in late summer to early fall.

Comments: We have collected "The Gypsy" in quantity in many places along the East Coast, near our home in Idaho and in Alaska. *Rozites caperata* resembles a *Cortinarius* with a membranous, instead of fibrillose or cobweblike, veil. Recent research has shown that it will most likely be transferred to *Cortinarius*. The presence of a membranous veil is not enough to create a separate genus. The flavor is excellent and we enjoy it very much.

INOCYBE

This is a large and common group of small brown mushrooms. There is no general work on *Inocybe* for North America, but Stangl (1989) describes 138 species for southern Germany, an area with a much less complicated flora than in North America. The pileus is conic to convex, dry, and typically radially fibrillose with brown lamellae. The stipe is smooth to hairy sometimes with a fibrous annulus. Spores are usually elliptic, smooth (Fig. 3) to angular or tuberculate (Fig. 10), thick-walled, nonamyloid. The cheilocystidia are usually 10-pin to pear-shaped, thick-walled. Odors include green corn, spermatic, fishy, to that of geraniums. The species are found under hardwood and conifer trees with which they form mycorrhizae. They are also found in alpine and Arctic tundra, where they form mycorrhizae with dwarf willows and birches.

Edibility: Many species of *Inocybe* have been studied and, almost without exception, found to have muscarine (Type 2 toxins) (Spoerke and Rumack, 1994). Both humans and dogs have been severally poisoned by species of *Inocybe,* and they should be strictly avoided.

KEY TO INOCYBE

1. Pileus, lamellae, and stipe lilac to violaceous or stipe base bluish green ---------------- 2
1. Not with the above combinations of colors --- 3
2. Pileus brown, scaly; stipe base bluish green ---------------------- *Inocybe calamistrata*
2. Pileus, lamellae, and stipe lilac to violaceous -------- *Inocybe geophylla* var *lilacina*
(see comments under *I. geophylla*)
3. Pileus and stipe white --- *Inocybe geophylla*
3. Pileus and stipe colored -- 4
4. Strong odor of geraniums --- *Inocybe pelargonium*
4. Odorless or some other odor -- 5
5. Pileus brown, convex, campanulate in age, sometimes with a small umbo, fibrillose-scaly; odor weak; spores long, slightly angular, 11–15 x 4.8–6.0 μm ---- *Inocybe lacera*
5. Pileus not as above; spores smaller -- 6
6. Pileus conic-pointed to campanulate, with radially appressed , yellow-brown fibrils; odor strongly of green corn; spores smooth,
9–13 x 5–7 μm -- *Inocybe fastigiata*
6. Pileus convex to convex with a blunt umbo, wooly or with densely tufted to raised or pointed scales -- 7
7. Pileus with erect, dense, dark brown tufts; spores tuberculate; cystidia thick-walled -- *Inocybe lanuginosa*
7. Pileus with appressed, raised or pointed scales; spores smooth -------------------------- 8
8. Pileus ochre, wooly or with appressed scales; cystidia thin-walled -- *Inocybe dulcamera*
8. Pileus with dark brown, point, erect scales on a white ground color; cystidia thick-walled -- *Inocybe hystrix*

Inocybe calamistrata (Fr.:Fr.) Gillet
POISONOUS

Pileus 1–3 cm broad, convex, dark brown, with small scales becoming somewhat recurved in age, dry. Flesh white, reddening when cut, darkening to brown and blue-green in the base. Lamellae adnate, close, white at first to cinnamon-brown in age. Stipe 2.5–7.0 cm long, 0.2–0.6 cm wide, equal, light brown at the apex, darker brown over the lower surface with blue green at the base and with scattered fibrils, dry. Partial veil cortinous, white, soon gone. Odor weak green corn to fishy. Taste mild (don't taste).

Spores 9.5–13.5 x 5.0–6.5 µm elliptic, smooth, entire, thick-walled, nonamyloid. Spore print yellow-brown. Cheilocystidia narrowly clavate, thin-walled, numerous. Pleurocystidia absent or rare.

Habit and distribution: Single to numerous, under hardwood and conifer forests. Widely distributed. Fruiting in summer to late fall.

Comments: The bluish green stipe base separates it from other species of *Inocybe* with scaly pilei. *Inocybe tenebrosa* Quél. has a more radially fibrous pileus, bluish green stipe base, and thick-walled cystidia.

Inocybe geophylla (Sowerby:Fr.) P. Kumm.
POISONOUS

Pileus 1–3 cm broad, conic to campanulate with a small umbo, white, covered with flattened hairs, white, margin upturned in age and often split, dry. Flesh thin, except in center, white. Lamellae adnate to adnexed, close, broad, white to grayish white to clay-color in age. Stipe 2–6 cm long, 0.2–0.4 cm wide, equal, white to grayish white, minutely hairy with a weak annular zone, white to grayish white. Partial veil hairy, white, rarely leaving a faint annulus. Odor of green corn to disagreeable. Taste mild (don't taste).

Spores 7–10 x 4.5–6.0 µm elliptic, smooth, entire, thick-walled, nonamyloid. Spore print dull clay-brown. Cheilo- and pleurocystidia common, club-shaped, thick-walled.

Habit and distribution: Several to abundant under hardwoods and conifers. Widely distributed. Fruiting from early summer to fall.

Comments: *Inocybe geophylla* var *lilacina* (Peck) Gillet has a lilac-colored pileus, partial veil, young lamellae, and stipe. It grows throughout the range of the white variety (Kuyper, 1986). Other white species are separated microscopically or by odor (Cripps, 1997). Spoerke and Rumack (1994) list muscarine (Type 2 toxins) as one of the toxins in *I. geophylla*, but all species of *Inocybe* should be avoided.

Inocybe pelargonium Kühner
POISONOUS

Pileus 1.5–3.3 cm broad, conic with a pointed umbo, with small, loose, light brown squamules radially arranged over a pale brown ground color, dry. Flesh thin, white in pileus, light brown in stipe. Lamellae adnate, subdistant, white at first to gray-brown to brown in age, edges minutely fringed. Stipe 3–5 cm long, 0.3–0.5 cm wide, equal, with a small bulb at the base, tinted pinkish brown, with fine white fibrils, dry. Partial veil white fibrillose, no annulus. Odor of geraniums. Taste mild (don't taste).

Spores 6.5–10.0 x 4.0–5.5 µm broadly elliptic, smooth, entire, slightly thick-walled, nonamyloid. Spore print brown. Cheilocystidia fusiform to clavate, thick-walled, with apical incrustations. Pleurocystidia absent.

Habit and distribution: Several under hardwoods and conifers often on limestone soils. Widely distributed. Fruiting in summer and fall.

Comments: *Inocybe pelargonium* is not common, but we have found this mushroom with its distinctive odor of geraniums in Glacier National Park under aspen. *Inocybe pyriodora* (Pers.:Fr.) Quél. has flesh that reddens when cut and a pungent fruity smell. Like all species of *Inocybe*, it should not be eaten.

Inocybe lacera (Fr.:Fr.) P. Kumm.
POISONOUS

Pileus 1.2–3.4 cm broad, conic, often with a small umbo, campanulate in age, with radially arranged, dark brown, matted hairs especially dense over the umbo, dry. Flesh firm white in pileus, light brown in the stipe. Lamellae adnate, subdistant, light brown darkening in age with lighter edges. Stipe 1.6–4.5 cm long, 0.1–0.5 cm wide, equal, light brown at apex to dark brown below, covered with pale longitudinal fibrils, dry. Partial veil cortinous, dull white, not leaving an annulus. Odor none, fungoid or faintly of green corn. Taste mild (don't taste).

Spores 11–15 x 4.8–6.0 µm broadly to narrowly elliptic, slightly irregular or angular, entire, thick-walled, nonamyloid. Spore print dark brown. Cheilo- and pleurocystidia fusiform, thick-walled with apical crystals.

Habit and distribution: Several to gregarious under both hardwood and conifers, often in disturbed areas and acid soils. Widely distributed. Fruiting in summer and fall.

Comments: This species is found in very diverse habitats from deep woods to recently vegetated mine spoils. Like all species of *Inocybe* it is mycorrhizal but has a very broad host range. See the discussion under *I. lanuginosa* for related species.

Inocybe fastigiata (Schaeff.:Fr.) Quél.
POISONOUS

Pileus 2–6 cm broad, sharply conic, campanulate, yellow-brown, with radially appressed fibrils, margin splitting in age, dry. Flesh thin, white but soon dingy yellowish. Lamellae adnexed, close, white, soon tinged olive-yellow, brown in age. Stipe 4–10 cm long, 0.2–0.8 cm wide, equal or enlarged downward, whitish to very light brownish, finely hairy, twisted-striate, dry. Partial veil absent. Odor of green corn or spermatic. Taste mild (don't taste.)

Spores 9–13 x 5–7 μm elliptic, smooth, entire, thick-walled, nonamyloid. Spore print dull brown. Cheilocystidia, abundant, club-shaped, thin-walled. Pleurocystidia absent.

Habit and distribution: Several to numerous under hardwoods and conifers. Widely distributed. Fruiting in summer and fall.

Comments: Also known as *Inocybe rimosa* (Bull.:Fr.) P. Kumm. This is a variable species that contains large concentrations of muscarine (Type 2 toxins), and serious poisoning can occur if any quantity of this fungus is eaten. There are many similar species of *Inocybe* and like all members of the genus, they should be avoided.

Inocybe lanuginosa (Bull.:Fr.) Quél.
POISONOUS

Pileus 1.5–3.5 cm broad, conic to convex with a blunt umbo, rich dark brown, densely tufted hairs that are matted, raised, or erect, margin flat or slightly raised in age, dry. Flesh watery, light brown. Lamellae adnate to adnexed, fairly well separated, white at first, soon dull brown. Stipe 2.5–8 cm long, 0.2–0.7 cm wide, equal, pale buff with a covering of dark brown hairs. Partial veil buff, hairy, soon gone leaving no ring, dry. Odor weakly green corn. Taste mild (don't taste).

Spores 6.5–10.0 x 4.5–7.0 μm elliptic, tuberculate, entire, thick-walled, nonamyloid. Spore print yellow-brown. Cheilocystidia numerous, broadly club-shaped, with thickened walls.

Habit and distribution: Several together in small groups in wood debris, on the ground, or on very rotten wood, in both conifer and hardwood forests. Widely distributed. Fruiting in summer and fall.

Comments: This species, like all species of *Inocybe*, has Type 2 toxins and should be avoided. This is one of the few Inocybes associated with wood. See *I. hystrix*, *I. lacera*, and *I. calamistrata* for comparison.

Inocybe dulcamera (Alb & Schwein.:Pers)
P. Kumm.
POISONOUS

Pileus 1.2–5.5 cm broad, convex, soon broadly
convex often with a low umbo, orange-brown to
brownish orange, with radially appressed to
somewhat raised, wooly scales, dry. Flesh firm
white to light buff, stipe cotton-stuffed to hollow.
Lamellae adnate, subdistant, white at first,
darkening to orange-pink, brown in age. Stipe
1.5–4.0 cm long, 0.3–0.8 cm wide equal, white at
apex, longitudinally streaked with light brown
fibrils, dry. Partial veil dense, white, cortinous
soon gone, leaving no annulus. Odor mostly fishy
to faintly radishlike. Taste mild or slightly sweet
(don't taste).

Spores 6.1–10.5 x 3.8–6.0 μm elliptic to bean-
shaped, smooth, entire, thick-walled, nonamyloid.
Spore print brown. Cheilocystidia thin-walled,
clavate to ovoid cells, without thick-walled
incrusted cells.

Habit and distribution: Single, several to
gregarious under alder, willows, birch and other
hardwood as well as conifers. Widely distributed.
Fruiting in spring, summer, and fall.

Comments: *Inocybe terrigena* (Fr.) Kuyper is very
close, but has squamules on the stipe and more
of an annular zone.

Inocybe hystrix (Fr.) P. Karst.
POISONOUS

Pileus 0.8–3.5 cm convex, without an umbo,
discrete, dense, dark brown, pointed scales on a
buff to cream-colored ground color, several
individual scales converge to form the pointed
scales, covering the entire surface, dry. Flesh thin,
white. Lamellae adnate, close, white young to
light brown in age. Stipe 2–6 cm long, 0.3–0.8 cm
wide, equal or slightly larger below, white or
tinted brown just at apex, rest covered with
wooly dark brown scales, dry. Partial veil
cortinous, white, soon gone, often leaving a
fibrous annulus near the apex. Odor disagreeable.
Taste unpleasant (don't taste).

Spores 7.5–12.5 x 5.0–6.5 μm elliptic to bean-
shaped, smooth, entire, thick-walled, nonamyloid.
Spore print dark brown. Cheilo- and pleurocystidia
fusiform, thick-walled, yellow-brown with apical,
encrusted material.

Habit and distribution: Solitary to several under
hardwood and conifer trees. Widely distributed.
Fruiting in summer and fall.

Comments: Unlike the other Inocybes with scaly
caps, the scales are like the connivent fibrils
found in puffballs (see *Lycoperdon umbrinum*),
and is a unique character in *Inocybe*.

HEBELOMA

This is a large genus with many species in North America. Smith et al. (1983) includes 112 veiled species from western North America alone. They are very difficult to distinguish by macroscopic study, and microscopic examination is essential. Establishing the genus is not so difficult. The pileus is convex, always viscid fresh, usually cream color to red-brown. The lamellae are adnate to adnexed and frequently covered with minute water drops. In cross-section, the lamellae have parallel hyphae (Fig. 26). The stipe is fleshy, dry, and has a fibrous annulus in some species. The spores are finely rugose to rarely smooth, similar to *Cortinarius,* but clay-brown in color. The most important characters are the long cylindric to club-shaped cheilocystidia, which are always numerous. These cystidia do not exist in *Cortinarius,* which is closely related. Lastly, they often smell of radishes and are bitter to taste. The species of *Hebeloma* are on the ground and form mycorrhizae with various shrubs and forest trees throughout North America. Miller and Evenson (2001) have reported on the alpine tundra species in Colorado.

Edibility: All species of *Hebeloma* tested so far are very poisonous with many records of poisonings. The toxin may be hebelomic acid, but the connection between it and the severe gastrointestinal upset that occurs has not been shown as yet (Spoerke & Rumack, 1994). However, severe diarrhea, vomiting and stomach cramps, typical of Type 8 toxins, occur following ingestion of *Hebeloma* species.

KEY TO THE SPECIES OF HEBELOMA

1. Stipe white, with distinctive dull white scales;
   spores large 12–15 x 6.5–7.5 µm --- *H. insigne*
1. Stipe without scales; spores smaller 8.5–12.5 x 5.5–7.5 µm -------------------------------- 2
   2. Pileus 1–4 cm broad, viscid to slimy, dark brown in center; stipe clothed in longitudinal, white fibrils -- *H. mesophaeum*
   2. Pileus 4–9 cm broad, viscid, cream, pale orange-tan to orange-gray; stipe glabrous, dull white -- *H. crustuliniforme*

Hebeloma insigne A. H. Sm., V. S. Evenson
& Mitchel
POISONOUS

Pileus 3.5–9.0 cm broad, convex to broadly
convex, pinkish buff to cinnamon-buff, margin
with partial veil remains at first, viscid. Flesh firm
dull white. Lamellae adnexed, close, medium
broad, clay-color to cinnamon-buff. Stipe 4–7 cm
long, 0.1–0.4 cm wide, equal, sometimes with a
small, abrupt, basal bulb, white, with well-spaced
zones of dull white scales, dry. Partial veil white
scanty soon gone. Odor fungoid strong. Taste
mild.

Spores 12–15 x 6.5–7.5 µm elliptic, rugose,
entire, thick-walled, nonamyloid. Spore print
reddish brown. Cheilocystidia numerous, narrowly
clavate, thin-walled, hyaline.

Habit and distribution: Single to several on the
ground under hardwoods (birch, aspen, oak) as
well as conifers (especially spruce and fir). Found
in western North America. Fruiting in summer and
fall.

Comments: *Hebeloma sinapizans* (Paul.:Fr.) Gill.,
common in Europe, is very similar and both can
be found under spruce and fir, and have clamp
connections. Like other species of *Hebeloma*,
severe gastrointestinal upset can result from
eating either species, Type 8 toxins.

Hebeloma mesophaeum (Pers.:Fr.) Quél.
POISONOUS

Pileus 1–4 cm broad, convex to broadly convex in
age, with a broad umbo, dark brown over the
center, gray-brown to cream color over the
margin, which is incurved at first, viscid to slimy.
Flesh firm, dull white tinted brown, stipe brown.
Lamellae adnate to adnexed, close, broad, white
at first to brownish or gray-brown in age, margins
minutely hairy. Stipe 2.0–8.5 cm long, 0.3–0.5 cm
wide, slender, equal, with longitudinal white
fibers, changing gradually to brown toward the
base, dry. Partial veil cortinous leaving a superior,
fibrous annulus often with remnants on the pileus
margin. Odor of radish. Taste unpleasant, radishlike.

Spores 8–11 x 4–6 µm broadly elliptic, finely
rugose, entire, thick-walled, nonamyloid. Spore
print yellow to olive-brown. Cheilocystidia
numerous, cylindric, long and narrow, thin-walled,
hyaline.

Habit and distribution: Several to gregarious,
sometimes cespitose, under conifers. Widely
distributed. Fruiting in summer and fall.

Comments: As in all species of *Hebeloma*, severe
gastrointestinal upset can result from ingestion,
Type 8 toxins. This species is especially common
in the northern boreal forest.

Hebeloma crustuliniforme (Bull.:St.-Amans) Quél.
POISONOUS

Pileus 4–9 cm broad, convex, broadly convex with a low umbo in age, glabrous, cream color to orange-tan over the incurved margin to grayish-orange, brown or red-brown in age at the center, viscid. Flesh firm, white, pale brown in age. Lamellae adnate to adnexed, close to crowded, narrow, white to gray, when moist or young covered with fine water drops, (see insert) edges minutely hairy. Stipe 3–8 cm long, 0.3–1–0 (-2.3) cm wide, equal but often enlarging to form a clavate base, dull white, sometimes light yellowish tan over the base, minute tufts of fibrils over the apex, nearly smooth toward base, dry. Partial veil absent. Odor of radishes usually strong. Taste very bitter.

Spores 8.5–12.5 x 5.5–7.5 µm broadly elliptic to almond-shaped, finely rugose, entire, thick-walled, nonamyloid. Spore print yellow-brown to brown. Cheilocystidia numerous, cylindric to narrowly clavate, thin-walled, hyaline. Pleurocystidia absent.

Habit and distribution: Single or several in open areas under hardwood and conifer forests. Widely distributed. Fruiting in the summer and fall.

Comments: The water spots on the lamellae usually leave yellowish to brown spots on drying. Severe gastrointestinal upset can occur from eating this species (Type 8 toxins). All species of *Hebeloma* are poisonous. *Hebeloma hiemale* Bres. is a small but similar species (pileus 2–4 cm broad) without the radishlike odor.

CORTINARIUS

There are over 360 species of *Cortinarius* described for North America, but there is little doubt that the total will exceed 500 species. They are mycorrhizal and particularly numerous in association with conifers, but are also found, in smaller numbers, with hardwoods throughout North America. They are fleshy, with conic to convex pilei, rusty-brown to cinnamon-brown spores, and a typical spiderweb-like (cortinous) veil. If a cortinous annulus, colored rusty-brown from the spores, is not present, the long rusty-brown partial veil hairs can often be seen on the stipe. The spores are subglobose to elliptic, rugose to warted (Figs. 9 & 11), entire, thick-walled, nonamyloid. The viscid pileate species of *Cortinarius* have rusty-brown spores and no cheilocystidia, which distinguishes them from species of *Hebeloma*.

Six subgenera have been recognized. The subgenus *Cortinarius* has a dry, tomentose, violet pileus and stipe, the colors don't fade, and pleurocystidia are present. Subgenus *Myxacium* includes all the species with a viscid pileus and stipe. Subgenus *Phlegmacium* has a viscid pileus but the stipe is equal to club-shaped. Subgenus *Telamonia* has a dry to moist, brown or violaceus brown pileus, a thin, dry stipe, and the colors fade as it grows older or dries. Subgenus *Dermocybe* has a dry, red, red-brown to orange-brown pileus and maroon, red to orange-brown lamellae, while the subgenus *Sericeocybe* has a silky to shiny, dry pileus. Lastly, subgenus *Leprocybe* has a fibrillose-scaly to tomentose, red, orange, green to olive-brown pileus, and mostly sub-globose to broadly elliptic spores. Smith et al., (1979) has keys to many of the North American species and Breitenbach & Kränzlin (2000) treat over 430 species, many of which are also in North America.

Edibility. There are several North American species that contain the deadly Orellanine, Type 7 toxins. They are *C. gentilis* (Fr.:Fr.) Fr., *C. rainierensis* A. H. Sm. & D. E. Stuntz and *C. speciosisimus* Kühner & Romagn. which are rarely encountered and found in the northern boreal forests and in western North America (Thorn & Malloch, 1993). A number of species cause gastrointestinal upset (Type 8 toxins) and should be avoided. Many species have never been either tested or eaten. Some of the very distinctive identifiable species can be eaten safely but caution is advised.

KEY TO SPECIES OF CORTINARIUS

1. Pileus dry, silky or moist and slightly sticky -- 2
1. Pileus glutinous to slimy-viscid --- 15
   2. Fruiting body under the duff or partially exposed; with a persistent, dense, cortinous partial veil covering the lamellae------------------------------------- *C. bigelowii*
   2. Not as above-- 3
3. Pileus dark violet; lamellae also violet; under hardwoods ---------------------- *C. violaceus*
3. Pileus and lamellae some other color -- 4
   4. Stipe surface with squamulcs, chevron bands, scales or covered by dense, white or lilac-colored fibrils; lamellae lilac, pale brown, ochre, rusty brown ----------------- 5
   4. Stipe surface not as above; lamellae clay brown, bright yellow, orange, red, dark cinnamon--- 1
5. Stipe circled by several rusty-red zones of veil tissue; pileus orange-brown to red-brown; found in eastern North America ------------------------------------ *C. armillatus*
5. Stipe not as above --- 6
   6. Stipe and pileus with red scales and squamules; stains yellow where handled; eastern North America --- *C. bolaris*
   6. Stipe and pileus not as above -- 7
7. Stipe scales and squamules pale lilac, lilac to dark brown, stipe 0.8–3.0 cm wide ---- 8
7. Stipe scales, squamules or fibrils white, stipe usually very thin ------------------------- 10
   8. Stipe below annulus with dark brown scales over a white to buff ground color; pileus with dark brown squamules--- *C. pholideus*
   8. Stipe below annulus with a lilac, fibrillose covering------------------------------------ 9
9. Flesh thin, light violaceus; partial veil fibrillose; pileus pale lilac, tinted white; under mixed conifers and hardwoods; taste mild ---------------------------------- *C. alboviolaceus*
9. Flesh thick, tinted yellowish; partial veil dense, fibrillose, white tinted lilac; pileus pale lilac, fibrillose; under conifers; taste bitter --- *C. traganus*
   10. Pileus acutely conic, covered until mature with dense, dull white, veil fibrils; stipe also covered with fine white fibrils --- *C. acutus*
   10. Pileus conic, campanulate in age, waxy, dark brown; stipe with dense, white bands or chevrons, nearly to the base --- *C. flexipes*
11. Lamellae strikingly blood-red or clay-brown -- 12
11. Lamellae yellow-brown, cinnamon to orange-brown -------------------------------------14

12. Lamellae strikingly blood-red; stipe equal-- 13

12. Lamellae clay-brown to cinnamon-brown in age; stipe with a thick,
    clavate base --- *C. crassus*

13. Pileus deep blood-red --- *C. phoeniceus* var *occidentalis*

13. Pileus yellowish cinnamon -- *C. semisanguineus*

14. Pileus bright red-brown --- *C. cinnabarinus*

14. Pileus cinnamon-buff, margin light yellow-brown--------------------- *C. cinnamomeus*

15. Stipe viscid to glutinous--- 16

15. Stipe dry or moist--- 19

16. Pileus purple, viscid to slimy-viscid --- *C. iodes*

16. Pileus yellow-brown, orange-brown to orange-buff, viscid to glutinous,
    smooth to corrugated --- 17

17. Pileus viscid, yellow-brown, roughly corrugated ------------------------------- *C. corrugatus*

17. Pileus not as above-- 18

18. Stipe with a thick gluten, white tinted, pale bluish------------------------- *C. collinitus*

18. Stipe with tufted, light yellow bands over a gelatinous, white,
    ground layer --- *C. trivialis*

19. Pileus viscid, glabrous, bright yellow to orange-yellow ----------------------- *C. percomus*

19. Pileus viscid, cinnamon to red-brown, or tinted lilac-gray--------------------- *C. glaucopus*

Cortinarius bigelowii Thiers & A. H. Sm.
INEDIBLE
Subgenus Sericeocybe

Pileus 4.0–6.4 cm broad, broadly convex, plane in age, light yellow-brown, sticky very young, soon dry. Flesh firm, white in pileus, lilac in stipe. Lamellae adnate, close, medium broad, yellowish at first, tinted lilac-gray to rusty brown in age. Stipe 1.5–3.4-cm long, 1.2–2.3 cm wide with an abrupt, depressed, basal bulb, dull white, dry. Partial veil dense, cortinous-membranous, buff with olivaceous hues, soon deep rusty brown from the spores, often remaining as a cover over the lamellae. Odor and taste mild.

Spores 9–11 x 6–7 µm elliptic, rugose, entire, thick-walled. Spore print dark rusty brown.

Habit and distribution: Single to several, under the duff or just breaking through at maturity, with conifers at high elevations in the western United States. Fruiting in summer and fall.

Comments: Smith and Thiers (1969) have described several species that fruit beneath the duff and have the dense cortinous partial veil. All are found under conifers in western North America. We have collected this species in Alberta, Canada, and in Idaho. We have no information on its edibility.

Cortinarius violaceus (Fr.) Gray
INEDIBLE
Subgenus Cortinarius

Pileus 5–12 cm broad, convex, often with an umbo, dark shining violet, covered with hairs in erect tufts over the center, dry. Flesh thick, firm, grayish violet, not bruising. Lamellae adnate, fairly well separated, broad, dark violet concolorous with the pileus. Stipe 7–16 cm long, 1.0–2.5 cm wide, enlarging downward, also dark violet, flattened hairs, dry. Partial veil hairy, violet, leaving a superior, fibrillose annulus. Odor mild. Taste slightly peppery.

Spores 12–17 x 8–10 µm, elliptic, minutely roughened to rugose, entire, thick-walled, nonamyloid. Spore print rusty brown. Pleurocystidia present.

Habit and habitat: Single or scattered on ground in northern hardwood forests. Widely distributed. Fruiting in the fall.

Comment: *Cortinarius hercynicus* (Pers.) M. M. Moser is very similar but is found in conifer woods. It is interesting that both species have large cystidia, which is unusual for species of *Cortinarius*.

Cortinarius armillatus (Fr.) P. Kumm.
EDIBLE
Subgenus Telamonia

Pileus 5–12 cm broad, convex, campanulate in age, orange-brown to reddish brown, with radially appressed hairs, rusty veil pieces adhering to the margin, moist when fresh. Flesh thick, soft, pale buff. Lamellae adnate, subdistant, broad, cinnamon to rusty brown in age. Stipe 7–15 cm long, 1.0–2.5 cm wide, enlarging toward base, dry, dull brownish, circled by several rusty red zones of veil tissue. Partial veil white, cortinous, nearly membranous, collapsing upon expanding to form the rusty red concentric rings. Odor, if present, radishlike. Taste mild.

Spores 10–12 x 5.0–6.5 µm elliptic, strongly rugose, entire, thick-walled, nonamyloid. Spore print rusty brown.

Habit and distribution: Single to several under mixed conifer/hardwood forests, especially birch. Widely distributed but common in eastern North America. Fruiting in summer and fall.

Comments: This species is uncommon in western North America, but we have seen it. It is easy to spot because of the concentric, rusty red rings on the stipe. It is edible, but not choice.

Cortinarius bolaris (Fr.) Fr.
POISONOUS
Subgenus Telamonia

Pileus 2–7 cm broad, convex, plane in age, with appressed red scales dense over the apex, separated over the margin revealing a light yellow ground color, dry. Flesh firm, white, bruising yellowish. Lamellae adnate, medium broad, subdistant, orange-yellow to rusty brown in age. Stipe 3–10 cm long, 0.5–1.3 cm wide, equal, buff at apex, below with red scales and squamules to the base, staining yellow where handled, dry. Partial veil cortinous, leaving a superior, red, fibrillose zone. Odor and taste mild, not distinctive.

Spores 6–8 x 4.5–6.0 µm subglobose, rugose, entire, thick-walled, nonamyloid. Spore print rusty brown.

Habit and distribution: Single to several, found in hardwood/conifer forests in eastern North America. Fruiting in late summer and early fall.

Comments: This species is generally regarded as poisonous, but the Type 8 toxins are unknown.

Cortinarius pholideus Fr.
INEDIBLE
Susbgenus Sericeocybe

Pileus 4–8 cm broad, conic, convex in age, covered with dark brown small squamules on a light brown surface, margin inrolled until mature, dry. Flesh firm, dull white with a hint of brownish red. Lamellae adnate, narrow, violet at first, soon rusty brown. Stipe 5–10 cm broad, 0.8–1.3 cm wide, enlarging somewhat toward the base, white at apex, below the fibrillose annulus covered with dark brown scales over a light whitish to buff ground color, dry. Partial veil, a dense cream-colored cortina, which usually leaves a superior fibrous annulus, soon brown from the spores. Odor and taste mild.

Spores 6.7–8.6 x 5.0–6.5 μm subglobose, rugose, entire, slightly thick-walled, nonamyloid. Spore print rusty-brown.

Habit and distribution: Single to several on ground under mixed pine/hardwood forests. Found in eastern North America. Fruiting in late summer and fall.

Comments: It is unusual for a *Cortinarius* to have raised squamules on the stipe, which reminds one of a *Pholiota*. However, the rugose spores are typical of a *Cortinarius*.

Cortinarius alboviolaceus (Fr.) P. Kumm.
POISONOUS
Subgenus Sericeocybe

Pileus 3–7 cm broad, campanulate, convex to nearly plane with an umbo, silvery white, pale lilac tinted white, with flattened silky hairs, margin incurved until mature, dry. Flesh thin, light violaceous. Lamellae adnate, close, broad, pale violet to grayish violet, cinnamon-brown in age. Stipe 4–9 cm long, 0.5–2.0 cm wide, enlarging to a club-shaped, basal bulb, white, tinted the color of the pileus, silky fibrillose, dry. Partial veil fibrillose, white, leaving a superior, fibrillose ring. Odor mild. Taste mild.

Spores 7–10 x 4–6 µm elliptic, roughened, entire, thick-walled, nonamyloid. Spore print rusty brown.

Habit and distribution: Single to several under mixed conifers and hardwoods. Widely distributed. Fruiting in late summer and fall.

Comments: There are conflicting reports concerning its edibility, so we recommend not eating it. It would appear to form mycorrhizae with many trees, both hardwoods and conifers.

Cortinarius traganus (Fr.:Fr) Fr.
POISONOUS
Subgenus Sericeocybe

Pileus 4–10 cm broad, convex, nearly plane, sometimes with a low, broad umbo in age, pale lilac overall, with flattened hairs, sometimes cracked in age, dry. Flesh thick, firm, tinted yellowish. Lamellae adnexed, subdistant, broad, pale lilac, but soon yellow-brown. Stipe 4–6 cm long, 1–3 cm wide, enlarging to a club-shaped bulb, pale lilac above and below annulus, fibrillose, dry. Partial veil dense and fibrillose, white tinted lilac soon streaked brown from the spores, leaving a superior, hairy ring that may disappear in time. Odor pungent and disagreeable. Taste bitter.

Spores 7.5–10.0 x 5–6 µm elliptic to almond-shaped, coarsely rugose, entire, thick-walled, nonamyloid. Spore print rusty brown.

Habit and distribution: Several to numerous in old-growth conifer woods, often in deep moss. Widely distributed, especially in northern and western North America. Fruiting in summer and fall.

Cortinarius acutus (Pers.:Fr.) Fr.
POISONOUS
Subgenus Telamonia

Pileus 1.0–1.5 cm broad, acutely conic, campanulate in age, covered with dense, dull white, veil material at first, later glabrous and orange-brown, margin weakly striate, moist. Flesh firm, dull white. Lamellae adnexed, close, gray with a pink cast. Stipe 0.4–0.8 cm long, 0.2–0.4 cm wide, equal, at first covered with fine white fibrils over an orange-brown ground color, dry. Partial veil dense, white. Odor of iodine. Taste mild.

Spores 7.0–10.0 x 4.5–6.5 μm elliptic, minutely rugose, entire, thick-walled, nonamyloid. Spore print rusty brown. Cheilocystidia clavate to ovoid, thin-walled.

Habit and distribution: Several to gregarious under conifers. Found in western North America. Fruiting in summer and early fall.

Comments: One of only a few distinctive species in the subgenus *Telemonia*. See additional comments under *C. flexipes*. We do not recommend eating any *Cortinarius* species.

Cortinarius flexipes (Pers.:Fr.) Fr.
POISONOUS
Subgenus Telamonia

Pileus 0.8–4.0 cm broad, conic, campanulate with an umbo in age, dark brown with small white fibrils when young, but soon smooth, waxy, moist. Flesh soft dark brown. Lamellae adnate, close, light brown. Stipe 2.2–6.0 cm long, 0.4–1.5 cm wide, equal, white thin covering of hyphae over a brown surface at apex, below bands of dense white fibrils of the partial veil arranged in a spiral or as chevrons nearly to the base, dry. Odor strong of geraniums. Taste mild.

Spores 6.5–10.0 x 4.5–6.5 μm elliptic, minutely rugose, entire, slightly thick-walled, nonamyloid. Spore print rusty brown.

Habit and distribution: Several to gregarious under hardwood and conifer forests. Widely distributed. Fruiting in summer and fall.

Comments: The subgenus *Telemonia* in *Cortinarius,* where *C. flexipes* belongs, contains a number of closely related and very difficult species to distinguish. They are mycorrhizal with conifers such as pine, fir, and spruce and hardwoods such as birch and beech. There are a number of seldom collected and unstudied species. Therefore, we recommend that no one eat these species.

Cortinarius crassus Fr.
POISONOUS
Subgenus Phlegmacium

Pileus 5–11 cm broad, robust, broadly convex, with or without a low umbo, deep ochre to red-brown somewhat lighter over the margin, dry to slightly sticky. Flesh firm white, stipe soft in center and often hollow near base, yellow in 3% KOH. Lamellae emarginate, broad, close, clay-brown to cinnamon-brown in age. Stipe 4–8 cm long, 1.5–2.5 cm wide, expanding to a clavate base 1.9–2.8 cm wide, white just a apex, rest red-brown from the spores, glabrous, dry. Partial veil cortinous, white, leaving a weak superior annular zone or none. Odor none. Taste mild.

Spores 6.5–11.5 x 4.5–6.5 µm elliptic, rugose (Fig. 11), entire, thick-walled, nonamyloid. Spore print rusty brown. Cheilocystidia narrowly fusiform, with yellow contents.

Habit and distribution: Single to several on ground under conifers. Found in western and northern North America. Fruits in late summer and fall.

Comments: In Europe, this large species is considered poisonous. We have collected it in Idaho, but have no information on edibility. *Cortinarius balteatus* (Fr.) Fr. is similar but the lamellae are violaceus gray at first and not white. It also has a northern distribution, but is most often found under hardwoods, especially oak (Smith et al., 1979). Both species are large and fleshy, but neither is known to be edible.

Cortinarius phoeniceus var occidentalis A. H. Sm.
EDIBILITY UNKNOWN
Subgenus Dermocybe

Pileus 2–8 cm broad, convex to broadly convex in age, deep blood red, appressed fibrillose, margin enrolled at first, dry. Flesh firm, red near the pileipellis, rest light brown. Lamellae adnate, subdistant, narrow, bright red. Stipe 4–8 cm long, 0.6–1.2 cm wide, dry, equal, yellow-brown, dry. Partial veil dense white to buff, cortina soon fading, leaving scattered hairs on the upper stipe. Odor and taste mild.

Spores 6.0–8.0 x 4.0–5.5 μm elliptic, roughened, rugose, slightly thick-walled, nonamyloid. Spore print rusty brown.

Habit and distribution: Several to occasionally gregarious, under conifers. Found in northwestern North America. Fruiting in late summer to fall.

Comments: The trama is dark red in 3% KOH. It is the most commonly encountered species with red lamellae on the Pacific Coast according to Ammirati (1989). *Cortinarius cinnabarinus* Fr. has a red-brown pileus, reddish cinnamon lamellae and larger spores, but is found most commonly under hardwoods in eastern North America. We don't recommend eating *Cortinarius* species in the subgenus *Dermocybe*, because we have little knowledge of their edibility.

Cortinarius semisanguineus Fr.
POISONOUS
Subgenus Dermocybe

Pileus 2–5 cm broad, convex, nearly plane with a low umbo in age, yellowish cinnamon, smooth to minutely hairy, dry. Flesh firm, whitish buff. Lamellae adnate, crowded, strikingly blood-red. Stipe 3–6 cm long, 0.3–0.6 cm thick, equal, yellow, hairy. Partial veil hairy, leaving an indistinct superior, hairy ring. Odor unpleasant. Taste bitter.

Spores 5–8 x 3–5 μm elliptic, coarsely rugose (Fig. 11), thick-walled, nonamyloid. Spore print rusty brown.

Habitat and distribution: Several to gregarious in moist woods, often in deep moss under hardwoods and conifers. Widely distributed. Fruiting in summer and fall.

Comments: A very common mycorrhizal species with many tree hosts. Look for the very striking blood-red lamellae and yellowish stipe. Gastrointestinal upset (Type 8 toxins) has been reported in the subgenus *Dermocybe*, of which this species is a member.

Cortinarius cinnabarinus Fr.
POISONOUS
Subgenus Dermocybe

Pileus 2.5–4.0 cm broad, convex, convex with a low umbo, bright red-brown, felty to touch, dry. Flesh firm, water-soaked, brown. Lamellae adnate, subdistant, cinnamon to reddish cinnamon. Stipe 2–6 cm long, 0.3–0.8 cm wide, equal or enlarged toward base, concolorus with the pileus or slightly lighter, often curved, streaked with hairs, shining, hollow. Partial veil cortinous also reddish, sometimes leaving an obscure, superior, ring zone. Odor of radish or mild. Taste mild.

Spores 7–9 x 4.5–5.5 µm elliptic, rugose, entire, thick-walled, nonamyloid. Spore print rusty brown.

Habitat and distribution: Several to numerous at times under hardwoods and conifers. Widely distributed. Fruiting in summer and fall.

Comments: Most often observed in oak or beech woods in eastern North America. Listed as poisonous in Europe.

Cortinarius cinnamomeus (Fr.) Gray
POISONOUS
Subgenus Dermocybe

Pileus 1.5–4.0 cm broad, convex to broadly convex, sometimes with a low umbo, cinnamon-buff, brown or reddish brown, smooth to finely fibrillose, margin lighter yellow brown, dry. Flesh firm, yellow to cinnamon-yellow. Lamellae adnate, close, bright cinnamon to orange brown. Stipe 2–5 cm long, 0.3–0.8 cm wide, equal, yellow-brown to orange-yellow, darker reddish brown in age, finely fibrillose, dry. Partial veil cortinous, yellow, soon gone, leaving a superior fibrillose zone, soon brown from the spores. Odor none. Taste mild, not distinctive.

Spores 5.5–7.5 x 4–5 µm elliptic, minutely rugose, entire, thick-walled, nonamyloid. Spore print rusty brown.

Habit and distribution: Several to gregarious, under conifers throughout North America. Often fruiting in the spring in western North America, but usually in the fall elsewhere.

Comments: We have found it fruiting in June under pure lodgepole pine near snow and again in September in similar habitats. It fruits under pure hemlock in Virginia, under white bark pine and subalpine fir in western Oregon. It is one of the most common among the western species in the subgenus *Dermocybe* with yellow to orange-yellow lamellae (Ammirati & Smith, 1977). We do not recommend eating species of *Cortinarius*.

Cortinarius iodes Berk. & M. A. Curtis
POISONOUS
Subgenus Myxacium

Pileus 2.5–5.5 cm broad, convex to broadly convex with a low umbo, purple often with mottled pale yellow spots, viscid to slimy in wet weather. Flesh soft, pale violet. Lamellae adnate, close, pale lilac to violet. Stipe 3.5–8.0 cm long, 0.5–1.7 cm wide, equal, enlarging somewhat to the base, violet to nearly white in age, glabrous, viscid. Partial veil cortinous, white tinted violet, leaving scattered fibrils on the stipe surface. Odor and taste mild.

Spores 8–10 x 5–6 µm elliptic, minutely rugose, entire, thick-walled, nonamyloid. Spore print rusty brown.

Habit and distribution: Usually several, under hardwoods especially oaks and beech. Found in eastern North America. Fruiting in the summer and fall.

Comments: In Subgenus *Myxacium, Cortinarius iodioides* Kauffman is very similar, but the pileipellis is bitter to taste. It is found in the Great Lake states and Schalkwijk-Barendsen (1991) report it from western Canada. Although *C. iodes* is reported as edible, we know of no one who has eaten it.

Cortinarius corrugatus Peck
INEDIBLE
Subgenus Myxacium

Pileus 5–10 cm broad, broadly convex to campanulate, yellow-brown to reddish brown, hairless, roughly corrugated, viscid. Flesh thin, firm, white. Lamellae adnate, close, broad, violet young to purplish and finally rusty cinnamon. Stipe 6–10 cm long, 0.5–1.5 cm wide, enlarging somewhat toward base and terminating in a basal bulb, yellowish with a tint of brown, scattered yellow-brown hairs, with a viscid annular zone. Partial veil hairy with a thin, glutinous layer leaving a viscid ring zone. Odor pleasant. Taste mild.

Spores 10–13 x 7–9 µm elliptic, rugose, entire, slightly thick-walled, nonamyloid. Spore print rusty brown.

Habit and distribution: Single to several, often in clumps under moist hardwoods. Found in eastern North America. Fruiting in summer and fall.

Comments: Like many other species of *Cortinarius* it is not edible, but is easily identified by the radially corrugated pileus. It is mycorrhizal with hardwoods.

Cortinarius collinitus Fr.
POISONOUS
Subgenus Myxacium

Pileus 3–12 cm broad, convex to nearly plane in age, rich ochre-brown to orange-brown, margin faintly striate, whitish or light brown at first, glutinous. Flesh firm, white. Lamellae adnate, nearly distant, pinkish buff to rusty brown in age. Stipe 6–12 cm long, 0.6–1.5 cm wide, equal or narrowing toward the base, dull white, with a thick gluten, which is white with a tint of pale bluish to very light yellowish brown in age, with flattened hairs beneath. Partial veil of pure white hairs with a thin, superior, glutinous layer over them, often, light brown from the spores. Odor not distinctive. Taste mild.

Spores 10–15 x 6–8 μm almond-shaped, minutely roughened or rugose, entire, thick-walled, nonamyloid. Spore print rusty brown.

Habit and distribution: In troops under conifers and hardwoods. Widely distributed. Fruiting in the fall.

Comments: Also known as *C. muscigenus* Peck, we have often found *C. collinitus* in great quantity, in the Southeast in the fall. Pileus colors are quite variable, and so are the subtle hues of stipe color in age. *Cortinarius vanduzerensis* A. H. Sm. & Trappe is similar but has purple stipe hues and is found along the West Coast. *Cortinarius mucosus* (Bull.:Fr) J. J. Kickx does not have the pale bluish tint to the glutinous stipe surface and is also more commonly associated with northern conifer forests.

Cortinarius trivialis J. E. Lange
POISONOUS
Subgenus Myxacium

Pileus 6.0–8.0 cm broad, convex to plane in age with an indistinct umbo, maroon at the center, rest orange to light buff just at the striate margin, glutinous, glabrous, when young the slimy cortinous partial veil is joined to the stipe. Flesh soft, dull white. Lamellae adnate, subdistant, white tinted lilac when young, becoming rusty brown as the spores mature. Stipe 5–9 cm long, 0.8–1.6 cm wide, equal or tapering toward the base, with a dense fibrillose superior annulus with an ivory gelatinous ground color and a series of tufted, light, yellow-brown bands almost to the base. Partial veil glutinous, white, with an embedded cortina leaving a superior glutinous band. Odorless. Taste mild.

Spores 10–15 x 6.5–8.0 μm almond-shaped, rugose, entire, thick-walled, nonamyloid. Spore print yellow-brown.

Habit and distribution: Several on the ground under hardwoods, especially aspen and oak in northern and western North America. Widely distributed. Fruiting in late summer and fall.

Comments: Pomerleau (1980) and Schalkwijk-Barendsen (1991) report it as edible, but it is listed as poisonous in Europe.

Cortinarius percomus Fr.
POISONOUS
Subgenus Phlegmacium

Pileus 4–9 cm broad, convex to broadly convex in age, bright yellow to orange-yellow, tinted brown in age, margin inrolled at first, glabrous, viscid. Flesh yellow often tinted olive. Lamellae adnate, medium broad, subdistant, yellow to olive-yellow, rusty yellow in age. Stipe 4.0–8.5 cm long, 1.0–1.6 cm wide equal, light yellow, brown over the base in age, glabrous, dry. Partial veil a dense cream colored cortina, collapsing, leaving a fibrillose zone, sometimes very scanty on the upper surface. Odor pleasant and sweet. Taste mild.

Spores 9–12 x 3.5–5.5 µm elliptic, minutely rugose, entire, slightly thick-walled, nonamyloid. Spore print rusty brown. Cheilocystidia clavate, thin-walled, hyaline.

Habit and distribution: Several, on the ground under confers. Found in western North America. Fruiting in the fall.

Comment: We have collected *C. percomus* in old-growth conifer forests in Idaho.

Cortinarius glaucopus (Schaeff: Fr.) Fr.
POISONOUS
Subgenus Phlegmacium

Pileus 3.5–8 cm broad, convex, broadly convex in age, cinnamon to red-brown, tinged sometimes with lilac-gray, with flattened hairs, viscid. Flesh thick, white to buff. Lamellae adnate, close together, lavender to violet-gray, rusty brown in age. Stipe 3–8 cm long, 1.5–2.5 cm wide, enlarging downward to a basal bulb, streaked with flattened hairs, pale lilac to pale lavender, or mostly brown, obscure annular zone turns brown from the spores, dry. Partial veil hairy, leaving an obscure, superior ring of scattered hairs. Odor earthlike or weakly farinaceus. Taste weakly farinaceous.

Spores 7–9 x 4–5 µm elliptic, rugose (Fig. 11), entire, thick-walled, nonamyloid. Spore print rusty brown.

Habit and distribution: Several to numerous under hardwoods and conifers. Widely distributed. Fruiting in spring, summer, and fall.

Comments: Fruiting has usually been observed near snowbanks in the Rocky Mountains in the early spring. The immature specimens have lilac to violet lamellae, a viscid pileus, and a bulbous, usually lavender stipe. However, there is considerable variation in pileus and stipe coloration and the intensity of the pigment in the lamellae. We recommend that *Cortinarius* species not be eaten.

CANTHARELLACAE

These highly prized edibles, commonly known as the Chanterelles, range in shape from vaselike and deeply depressed in the center, to that of a regular mushroom. A pileus is present, even though it may be deeply depressed. The spore-bearing surface (hymenium) is used to differentiate between genera. *Craterellus* has a smooth to slightly wrinkled hymenium and white to pale orange-buff spores. *Cantharellus* is nearest to a mushroom with lamellae, but with blunt ridges instead and white to buff spores. *Gomphus* differs from both by its wrinkled and irregularly ridged hymenium, which is almost poroid at times. It has minutely ornamented, light orange-red spores. *Polyozellus* has only one species, which is deep violet-black with roughend tuberculate spores (Fig. 9). Chanterelles are mycorrhizal with specific trees and therefore tend to reappear in the same locality, if not the same area, each year.

Edibility: The species of *Cantharellus* comprise one of the truly delicious groups of edible mushrooms. Most species have an excellent flavor and only a few in the genus *Cantharellus* do not taste good. *Cantharellus cibarius,* the "Golden Chanterelle" of the French, "Pfifferling" in Germany, or "Kantarellas" in Scandinavia, has long been a highly regarded edible in Europe. It is widespread in North America. A large western species, *C. subalbidus,* the "White Chanterelle," has the same flavor, but is larger and has thicker flesh than *C. cibarius. Polyozellus multiplex* is also a good edible, but not as commonly encountered. *Gomphus* species cause gastrointestinal upset (Type 8 toxins) and should be approached with caution. Some people can eat specific species of *Gomphus,* but we prefer species of *Cantharellus* and *Craterellus fallax.*

KEY TO THE CANTHARELLACEAE

1. Fruiting body in deep purple, gray-black to blue-black, cespitose clusters; under conifers; spores tuberculate-warted (Fig. 9) --------------------------- *Polyozellus multiplex*

1. Not as above --- 2

  2. Fruiting body robust, trumpet-shaped to deeply depressed in center --------------- 3

  2. Fruiting body not robust and/or not deeply depressed--------------------------------- 6

3. Hymenium light purple-brown to purple-gray; pileus glabrous, slightly depressed--- *Gomphus clavatus*

3. Hymenium white to cream or buff; pileus deeply depressed with appressed or raised scales --- 4

  4. Pileus with raised, block-like, yellow-orange scales with orange-red tips; under conifers in western North America ------------------------------------ *Gomphus bonarii*

  4. Pileus not as above--- 5

5. Pileus with small, appressed or slightly raised, buff, yellowish to pale orange scales; widely distributed under conifers--- *Gomphus floccosus*

5. Pileus with slightly raised clay-colored to tawny-olive scales; found in western North America--- *Gomphus kauffmanii*
(see comments under *G. floccosus*)

  6. Hymenium smooth or with well-spaced, very low ridges ------------------------------- 7

  6. Hymenium with blunt ridges interspersed with veins, usually forked --------------- 8

7. Pileus blackish brown, tubular, radially fibrillose; hymenium smoky-gray brown --- *Craterellus fallax*

7. Pileus yellow-orange, usually deeply depressed; hymenium yellow-orange, smooth or with well-spaced, low ridges --- *Cantharellus lateritius*

  8. Pileus gray to grayish olive or orange-brown to yellow-brown; hymenium low, with multi-forked, lamellae-like ridges; on decayed wood, dead snags, moss or humus -- 9

  8. Not as above; on ground or soil -- 10

9. Pileus gray to grayish olivaceous; on moss, especially *Polytrichum* moss-- *Cantharellula umbonata*

9. Pileus orange-yellow to brownish orange; on decayed wood or dead snags --- *Hygrophoropsis aurantiaca*

  10. Pileus dark brown, orange-brown to yellow-brown ----------------------------------- 11

  10. Pileus white, orange to bright cinnabar-red --------------------------------------- 12

11. Pileus dark brown to yellow-brown; hymenium light gray to orange-gray--- *Cantharellus tubaeformis*

11. Pileus dark orange-brown; hymenium orange-pink to orange-yellow--- *Cantharellus lutescens*

(see comments under C. tubaeformis)

12. Pileus 1.2–4.0 cm broad, bright cinnabar-red to reddish orange; hymenium of pink to light red, blunt ridges; stipe bright cinnabar-red ------ *Cantharellus cinnabarinus*

12. Not as above -- 13

13. Pileus small, 0.5–3.0 cm broad, intense yellow-orange; eastern North America --- *Cantharellus minor*

13. Not as above-- 14

14. Pileus robust, white, scaly in age; hymenium white -------- *Cantharellus subalbidus*

14. Not as above--- 15

15. Pileus smaller 1–7 cm broad, pale orange-yellow, glabrous or with a few scales; hymenium light pinkish buff to pale grayish orange; eastern North America --- *Cantharellus ignicolor*

15. Pileus fleshy, orange, orange-yellow, cinnamon-brown, yellow or brownish------------ 16

16. Pileus 3–17 cm broad, glabrous, orange to orange-yellow; hymenium pale orange; widely distributed--- *Cantharellus cibarius*

16. Pileus 1–5 cm broad, fibrillose, cinnamon-brown; hymenium pale yellow-orange; eastern and central North America ----------------------- *Cantharellus appalachiensis*

(see comments under C. cibarius)

Polyozellus multiplex Murrill
EDIBLE

Pileus 2–10 cm broad, flat, smooth, deep purple, violet-black or blue-black; incurved margins, densely grouped together in large cespitose clusters. Fruiting body in clusters 5–18 cm high. Flesh soft, thick, blue-black. Hymenium decurrent with low ridges and many veins, similar to pores at times, pale violet. Stipe 1.0–4.0 cm long, 1.0–2.5 cm wide, mostly grown together and fused, violet-black. Odor not distinctive. Taste mild and pleasant.

Spores 5.5–8.5 x 5.5–7.5 µm, globose to subglobose, tuberculate warted (Fig. 9), thin-walled, nonamyloid. Spore print white.

Habit and distribution: Cespitose clusters under conifers (especially spruce and fir), often in blueberry patches. Found in northern North America. Fruiting in summer and fall.

Comments: We have found it in the Payette National Forest in Central Idaho under pure Engelmann spruce and as far south as Colorado at high elevations under conifers. In Korea we have seen quantities collected under pine to be eaten. They are frequently sold in the markets or along the road.

GOMPHUS

The fruiting bodies are trumpet-shaped with a deeply depressed pileus, that grows deeper in age, and has flattened to erect scales. They have a hymenium with narrow blunt ridges with anastomosing veins; spores which are minutely wrinkled; and characteristic fruiting in partial fairy rings. The species are mycorrhizal with conifer and hard-wood trees and the associated forest types are given with each species.

Recent studies reveal that *Gomphus* is not as closely related to *Cantharellus,* as previously assumed. *Polyozellus multiplex* has rough, turberculate spores (Fig. 9), but is the only species in the genus.

Edibility: The species of *Gomphus* can cause intense gastric upset (Type 8 toxins) and, with the possible exception of *G. clavatus,* should be eaten only with extreme caution.

Gomphus clavatus (Fr.) Gray
EDIBLE

Pileus 3–15 cm broad, plane to depressed, yellowish, buff to light purplish gray, hairless to minutely scaly, usually cespitose, margin lobed to deeply lobed, dry. Flesh firm, white or tinged cinnamon. Hymenium decurrent on stipe to the base, blunt, thick, interconnected by veins, frequently forked or almost poroid, light purple to light purplish brown to purple-gray (see inset). Stipe 1–8 cm long, 1–2 cm wide, often arising from a compound base, blending at once into the funnel-shaped pileus, purple-drab, base covered with white mycelium. Odor none. Taste mild.

Spores 10–13 x 4–6 μm elliptic, wrinkled, entire, thick-walled, nonamyloid. Spore print yellowish orange.

Habit and distribution: Cespitose, often many in one cluster, under conifer forests. Widely distributed. Fruiting in late summer and fall.

Comments: *Gomphus pseudoclavatus* (A. H. Sm.) Corner is a smooth-spored, similar species, which occurs under hardwoods and is known from the Central States and westward. *Gomphus clavatus* is widely eaten, but some people experience gastric upset.

Gomphus bonarii Morse
INEDIBLE

Pileus 9–16 cm broad, convex depressed, deeply depressed in age, broken into blocklike, raised scales, margin light yellow-orange, with orange scales or dark orange-red at the tips, filling the center depression, dry. Flesh very firm white, bright green in 10% $FeSO_4$. Hymenium of decurrent, narrow, low ridges often fusing with low veins, white, dingy white in age with pinkish brown stains on handling. Stipe 4–9 cm long, 2.2–4.1 cm wide, white, below hymenium base is glabrous and dry. Odor none. Taste mild to slightly unpleasant.

Spores 10.0–13.5 x 4.5–6.3 µm elliptic to broadly elliptic, minutely wrinkled, entire, thick-walled, nonamyloid. Spore print white to buff.

Habit and distribution: In clusters or troops, or partial fairly rings, often numerous, under conifers. Found in western North America. Fruiting in early summer to fall.

Comments: This species as well as *G. floccosus* and *G. kaufmanii* cause gastrointestinal upset in many people (Type 8 toxins). Some people eat these species without any harmful effect. However, we do not recommend eating them.

Gomphus floccosus (Schwein.) Singer
POISONOUS

Pileus 5–15 cm broad, depressed to funnel-like or trumpet-shaped when mature, surface dry, clothed with flattened, then erect and even recurved, relatively small scales, buff, yellowish to pale orange scales usually darker. Flesh fibrous white. Hymenium decurrent, of narrow, low, blunt ridges that form or give rise to irregular veins, buff to yellow. Stipe not distinct from the hymenium, whole fruiting body stands 8–20 cm high, which is buff colored and hollow from the deep trumpet-shaped pileus. Odor and taste mild.

Spores 11.5–17.0 x 6–8 µm elliptic, minutely wrinkled, entire, nonamyloid, thick-walled. Spore print ochre.

Habit and distribution: Sometimes solitary but usually in cespitose clusters under conifers at all elevations. Widely distributed. Fruiting in summer and fall.

Comments: *Gomphus kauffmanii* (A.H. Sm.) Corner is a closely related, large, western species, infrequent elsewhere. It is distinctive with clay-colored to tawny olive scales on the pileus and hymenium cream color, with dense, blunt, frequently forking ridges, and spores that are similar and also wrinkled (Bigelow, 1978). These species cause strong to severe gastrointestinal upset and should be avoided (Type 8 toxins).

CANTHARELLUS AND CRATERELLUS

The species look very much like the Agarics, with a hymenium that resembles lamellae. However, the ridges are blunt with anastomosing veins extending between the ridges. In some species the ridges are greatly reduced. *Craterellus* typically has a smooth to only slightly wrinkled hymenium. In contrast to *Gomphus* and *Polyozellus,* the spores are smooth and not ornamented. However, both *Cantharellus* and *Craterellus* are mycorrhizal with forest trees and so a knowledge of which tree hosts a given species is associated with is necessary to successfully find them. *Hygrophoropsis aurantiacus* is included here because of its cantharelloid hymenium and because it keys out here best. Its inclusion here is not an indication of its relationship to *Cantharellus.*

Edibility: None of the species are poisonous, but some certainly taste better than others. *Cantharellus cibarius,* often called the "Golden chanterelle," is eaten by many people and featured in restaurants throughout North America and Europe.

Craterellus fallax A.H. Sm.
EDIBLE

Fruiting body 4–15 cm tall. Pileus 2–8 cm broad, with a hollow, tubular depression (infundibuliform), radially fibrillose, brown to blackish brown in age, dry. Flesh very thin, brown. Hymenium decurrent, almost to the base, smooth or nearly so, smoky gray-brown. Stipe very short, hollow, brown. Odor pleasant. Taste mild and pleasant.

Spores 12–17 (-20) x 7–10 µm broadly elliptic, smooth, entire, nonamyloid, thin-walled. Spore print orange-buff.

Habit and distribution: Gregarious and often cespitose, on ground in mixed conifer/hardwoods or under hardwoods. Widely distributed. Fruiting from early summer to early fall.

Comments: *Craterellus cornucopioides* Pers. is very similar, but has a white or faintly buff spore print. It is common in Europe but also occurs in North America, where its distribution is unclear (Bigelow, 1978). Both species are choice edibles that we enjoy, but it takes a large number of these delicate fruiting bodies to make a meal.

Cantharellus lateritius (Berk.) Singer
EDIBLE

Pileus 3–14 cm broad, deeply depressed to funnel-shaped, yellow-orange to orange, glabrous to wooly, margin thin, inrolled at first. Flesh thin (0.5–0.9 cm), white to tinted yellow-orange. Hymenium nearly smooth or with well-spaced low ridges, and incomplete veins, light yellowish, tinted pink. Stipe 2.5–10 cm long, 0.5–2.5 cm thick, tapering toward base, cream color or color of hymenium, usually solid, glabrous, dry. Odor fragrant, fruity. Taste mild.

Spores 5.5–10.5 x 3.5–6.5 µm elliptic, smooth, entire, nonamyloid, thin-walled. Spore print pinkish yellow.

Habit and distribution: Several or in clusters under hardwoods. Found in eastern North America. Fruiting in late summer and fall.

Comments: This species is also known as *Craterellus cantharellus* (Schw.) Fr. The reduced veins, fragrant odor, thin consistency and pinkish coloration separates *Cantharellus lateritius* from the fleshy, orange-colored, thick-veined *Cantharellus cibarius*, which it otherwise resembles. *Cantharellus odoratus* (Schwein.) Fr. is very similar; single but often in dense clusters, very thin flesh and a hollow stipe. We have seen large clusters in North Carolina. Both species are choice edibles.

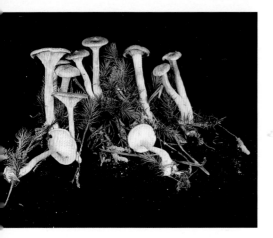 

Cantharellula umbonata (Fr.) Singer
EDIBLE

Pileus 1.2–4.5 cm broad, convex with a small umbo, gray to gray with an olive tinge, margin inrolled at first upturned in age, glabrous or minutely fibrous, dry to moist. Flesh thin, white. Hymenium decurrent, narrow, lamellae, crowded, highly forked, white tinted gray. Stipe 6–9 cm long, 0.4–0.8 cm wide, equal, thickening just at base, pinkish buff staining reddish brown over the base, moist. Partial veil absent. Odor none. Taste mild.

Spores 8–14 x 3–5 µm narrowly elliptic, smooth, entire, thin-walled, thin-walled, nonamyloid. Spore print white

Habit and distribution: Single to scattered, almost always in *Polytrichum* moss. Found in eastern North America. Fruiting in summer and fall.

Comments: Also known as *Cantharellus umbonatus* Fr. and *Geopetalum carbonarium* (Fr.) Pat. This rather distinctive fungus is always associated with *Polytrichum* or other mosses in the southeastern United States, where we have found it in quantity every fall. It is not related to the Chanterelles, but will key out here because of the highly forked narrow lamellae. It is reported to be a good edible when young and fresh.

Hygrophoropsis aurantiaca (Wulfen:Fr.) Maire
POISONOUS

Pileus 2.5–9.0 cm broad, convex, plane to depressed in age, minutely hairy with a velvety appearance, orange-yellow to brownish orange, margin often lobed, inrolled at first, but elevated in age, dry. Flesh thin, soft, whitish to buff or tinted orange. Hymenium decurrent, crowded, forking repeatedly, very narrow, bright orange to orange-yellow. Stipe 2.5–9.0 cm long, 0.5–2.0 cm wide, enlarging toward the base, sometimes eccentric, sometimes curved or twisted, minutely wooly, orange to orange-brown, often color of pileus margin, dry. Odor and taste not distinctive.

Spores 5–7 x 3–4 µm elliptic, smooth, entire, thin-walled, yellow to rusty brown in Melzer's solution. Spore print white.

Habit and distribution: Single or several on the ground or on partially decayed wood, even on standing dead snags, under hardwoods and conifers. Widely distributed. Fruiting in summer and fall.

Comments: Known also as *Cantharellus aurantiacus* Fr., this colorful orange fungus has narrow, crowded, forked lamellae, which remind one of a *Cantharellus*. Some people report serious digestive upset (Type 8 toxins), so it should be avoided. It could be confused with *Cantharellus cibarius*, which does not grow on wood and has ridges with veins in between. Compare both species in this guide.

Cantharellus tubaeformis Fr.
EDIBLE

Pileus 1.5–4.5 (-7.0) cm broad, convex, plane to depressed, margin wavy, dark brown to yellow-brown, glabrous, dry. Flesh soft pale buff, stipe stuffed, becoming hollow. Hymenium well spaced with blunt ridges with veins between, orange-gray to light gray. Stipe 1.5–5.0 cm long, 0.3–1.2 cm wide, equal, somewhat fluted, yellow-gray, orange-gray to gray, glabrous, dry. Odor none. Taste mild and pleasant.

Spores 8–12 x 6–8 µm elliptic, smooth, entire, thin-walled, nonamyloid. Spore print white to buff.

Habit and distribution: Several or gregarious in deep moss, very well decayed logs or mulch. Found in eastern and northern North America. Fruiting in summer and fall.

Comments: *Cantharellus lutescens* Fr. has a dark orange-brown pileus, but the hymenium and stipe are orange-yellow to orange-pink These are edible species with good flavor.

Cantharellus cinnabarinus Schwein.
EDIBLE

Pileus 1.2–4.0 cm broad, convex-depressed, lobed and irregular margin, bright cinnabar-red to reddish orange, hairless, dry. Flesh very thin, white. Hymenium with blunt, lamellae-like ridges, decurrent, forked, veined, and narrow, pinkish to light red. Stipe 2.0–4.0 cm long, 0.4–0.9 cm wide, equal or slightly smaller toward base, bright cinnabar-red. Odor mild. Taste mild and pleasant.

Spores 7–11 x 4.0–5.5 µm elliptic, smooth, entire, thin-walled, nonamyloid. Spore print pink.

Habit and distribution: Usually several to gregarious on ground under hardwoods. Found in eastern North America. Fruiting in summer and fall.

Comments: It is often found in large numbers, which are needed since it has a rather small fruiting body. It is a desirable edible, which we have often enjoyed.

Cantharellus minor Peck
EDIBLE

Pileus 0.5–3.0 cm broad, conic to convex, margin inrolled, plane and deeply depressed in age, intense yellow-orange to orange, glabrous, waxy when moist. Flesh soft orange. Hymenium decurrent, close in age subdistant, blunt ridges with veins between, orange. Stipe 1.6–3.8 cm long, 0.3–0.7 cm wide, equal, furrowed, often curved, deep chrome, dry. Odor mild. Taste mild and pleasant.

Spores 6–10 x 3–7 µm elliptic, smooth, entire, thin-walled, nonamyloid. Spore print light yellow-orange.

Habit and distribution: Several, occasionally gregarious, on ground under hardwoods or mixed hardwood/conifer forests. Found in eastern North America. Fruiting summer and fall.

Comments: This minute species is very common in August in southwestern Virginia under oak and beech forests.

Cantharellus subalbidus A.H. Sm. & Morse
EDIBLE

Pileus 5–14 cm broad, convex soon plane and slightly depressed, white, scaly in age. Flesh firm, white. Hymenium long-decurrent blunt ridges, close, forked, with veins, white bruising yellow. Stipe 2–5 cm long, 1–4 cm wide, equal, white, stains yellow or brown from soil or handling, dry. Odor mild. Taste pleasant.

Spores 7–9 x 5–6 µm elliptic, smooth, entire, thin-walled, nonamyloid. Spore print white.

Habit and distribution: Single to several on the ground under conifers and hardwoods. Found along the West Coast and western North America. Fruiting in the late summer and fall.

Comments: This is a robust, very good, edible species, which we have found and eaten in Idaho and Montana. Note the blunt ridges so typical of a chanterelle.

Cantharellus cibarius Fr.
EDIBLE

Pileus 3–17 cm broad, depressed with recurved margin at first to deeply depressed in center in age, orange, orange-yellow to whitish yellow, sometimes tinted pink, glabrous, dry. Flesh firm, thick, light yellowish. Hymenium decurrent, blunt, lamellae-like ridges, veins between, often forked, pale orange, or concolorous with the pileus (see inset). Stipe 2–8 cm long, 0.5–2.5 cm wide, somewhat smaller at base, glabrous, light to dark orange, glabrous, dry. Odor mild to fruity. Taste pleasant and mild.

Spores 8–11 x 4.0–5.5 µm elliptic, smooth, entire, thin-walled, nonamyloid. Spore print pale yellow.

Habit and distribution: Solitary, scattered, numerous to sometimes in cespitose clusters, under hardwoods and mixed woods. Widely distributed. Fruiting in summer and fall.

Comments: Known the world around as the "Golden Chanterelle," it is one of the truly well known and delicious, edible, wild mushrooms. It is mycorrhizal with trees, and therefore cannot be grown in artificial culture. *Cantharellus appalachiensis* R. H. Petersen is very similar, but is smaller with a fibrillose, cinnamon-brown pileus and a pale yellow-orange hymenium. It is found in eastern North America and southern central United States. *Cantharellus formosus* Corner, from western coastal forests, is also similar to *C. cibarius*, but has a dull yellow to brownish pileus, and a pink to salmon-colored hymenium, along with *C. subalbidus*. These are all very good edibles.

Care must be taken not to mistake *C. cibarius* for the "Jack-O'Lantern Fungus," *Omphalotus illudens*, which is poisonous and grows in large cespitose clusters on buried roots or on stumps (page 154).

Cantharellus ignicolor R. H. Petersen
EDIBLE

Pileus 1.0–7.0 cm broad, convex, inrolled, then convex depressed in center, dull orange to pale yellow-orange, glabrous or with a few fibrillose scales, dry. Flesh soft, dull orange fading to nearly white. Hymenium decurrent, blunt ridges with veins between, light pinkish buff, pale grayish orange. Stipe 3–6 cm long, 0.2–1.0 cm wide, equal, base slightly larger, orange-yellow to yellow-orange, glabrous, dry, white mycelium just at the base. Odor mild or slightly like citrine. Taste mild.

Spores 9–13 x 6–9 µm broadly elliptic, smooth, entire, thin-walled, nonamyloid. Spore print salmon to orange-pink.

Habit and distribution: Several to gregarious on the ground under hardwoods and occasionally conifers. Found in eastern North America. Fruiting in July and August to early September.

Comments: The very light yellow-orange pileus and size separates this species from *C. tubaeformis* and *C. lutescens*. It is much larger than *C. minor*.

CLAVARIACEAE—CORAL FUNGI

The family consists of species with erect, fingerlike fruiting bodies, with the spore-bearing surface over the upper half of the fruiting bodies. The fruiting bodies may be single or many branched appearing bushlike. There is no pileus present and the spores are forcibly discharged, so that a spore print may be obtained by placing the fruiting body on its side on white paper. Covering the paper and specimen with a bowl or wrapping them in wax paper will preserve moisture and increase the chances of a thick spore print.

The spores range from elliptic to subglobose (Figs. 2 & 3), and are white, cream or even brown. The surface is smooth to ornamented and a few species have amyloid walls in Melzer's solution. The flesh may be soft and brittle to leathery and tough.

Ferric sulphate ($FeSO_4$) mixed to 10% in water (e.g., 10 grams in 90 mls of water) will turn the flesh of the brown-spored genus *Ramaria* green. Other genera, such as *Ramariopsis,* are white spored and will not stain green using ferric sulphate.

There are many coral fungi in North America, and we have included the common, interesting, and edible species. Broad studies of the family have been published by Coker (1923) and Corner (1967), and detailed monographs exist for *Clavulinopsis* by Petersen (1968), *Ramaria* by Marr & Stuntz (1973), Petersen (1988), and *Clavariadelphus* by Methven (1990). However, there is no comprehensive treatment of the entire family for North American.

Edibility. *Ramaria formosa* and *R. gelatinosa* can cause gastric upset including diarrhea (Type 8 toxins). Generally, those that stain black when bruised, or have translucent, gelatinous tissue in the base and major branches should be avoided. Other species, such as *R. magnipes,* are edible, but some individuals can experience gastric upset which usually involves stomach cramps and diarrhea (Spoerke & Rumack, 1994, page 360).

KEY TO THE CLAVARIACEAE—CORAL FUNGI

1. Fruiting body single, several, branched or not; spore print white --------------------------- 2

1. Fruiting body branched from a stout, often robust base, large, fleshy; spore print yellow-orange, cinnamon-brown to brown -- 14

   2. Fruiting body single, unbranched or rarely with short branches which may form a cespitose cluster --- 3

   2. Fruiting body branched, either tough or very brittle and breaking easily on handling -- 10

3. Fruiting body 0.4–1.0 cm tall; single, numerous, fruiting on a wet to soggy, green algal mat --- *Multiclavula mucida*

3. Fruiting body larger; not fruiting on an algal mat -- 4

   4. Fruiting body cylindric; pure white; cespitose -------------------- *Clavaria vermicularis*

   4. Fruiting body pigmented yellow, orange, red, lilac, violet to purple ------------------ 5

5. Fruiting body violet, amethyst, purple to lilac --- 6

5. Fruiting body not colored as above-- 7

   6. Fruiting body purple, blue to lilac; white mycelium at base; single or cespitose; spores large (6–10 µm long); large cystidia present ---------------- *Clavaria purpurea*

   6. Fruiting body deep violet to amethyst; clustered or cespitose; spores small (4–7 µm long); cystidia absent -- *Clavaria zollingeri*

7. Fruiting body single, bright yellow; in dense clusters, tapering to a narrow base -- *Clavulinopsis fusiformis*

7. Not as above -- 8

   8. Fruiting body club-shaped with a broad, sometimes flattened apex that often ruptures at apex -- *Clavariadelphus truncatus*

   8. Fruiting body not with a broad apex, cylindric to narrowly club-shaped-------------- 9

9. Fruiting body large (7–30 cm tall), rugose to wrinkled, with occasional short branches at apex; pink to light orange-red to brownish red -------------- *Clavariadelphus pistillaris*

9. Fruiting body smaller (2–10 cm tall), not rugose, not branched, salmon color to orange-buff -- *Clavariadelphus ligula*

   10. Fruiting body tough, flexible, or even bending double, branch tips acute or cristate (with tiny spines) --- 11

   10. Fruiting body with brittle branches, not as above -------------------------------------- 13

11. Fruiting body 1.5–5.0 cm tall, very tough, bending double; on decayed wood, cones, plant parts; spores 10–15 µm long, basidia 4-spored ------------------ *Lentaria byssiseda*

11. Fruiting body up to 10 cm tall, firm, white, tinted yellow to smoke gray or bluish gray on ground; basidia 2-spored --- 12

    12. Fruiting body white tinted yellowish ----------------------------------- *Clavulina cristata*

    12. Fruiting body smoke gray to bluish gray ------------------------------ *Clavulina cinerea*

13. Fruiting body with dichotomous branching, tan to pale pinkish ---- *Clavicorona pyxidata*

13. Fruiting body with a dense cluster of erect, terminal, fine pointed tips, pure white -- *Ramariopsis kunzii*

    14. Fruiting body with translucent, gelatinous, jellylike tissue in the context --- *Ramaria gelatinosa* var *oregonensis*

    14. Fruiting body lacking a translucent, jellylike context ----------------------------------- 15

15. Fruiting body turning red when bruised on exposure to air, especially over the base, eventually becoming black -- *Ramaria bataillei*

15. Fruiting body not as above -- 16

    16. Fruiting body cinnamon-brown to darker brown, base turning green in age or on handling --- *Ramaria abietina*

    16. Not as above --- 17

17. Fruiting body pink, with deep pink branch tips ----------------------------- *Ramaria botrytis*

17. Not as above -- 18

    18. Fruiting body bright pink to red overall -- 19

    18. Fruiting body not colored as above --- 20

19. Found in eastern North America -- *Ramaria subbotrytis*

19. Found in western North America ----------------------- *Ramaria araiospora* var *araiospora*
                (see comments under *R. subbotrytis*)

    20. Fruiting body arising from a dense cluster, with dichotomous branches and narrow pointed tips; often on well-decayed hardwood logs and stumps ---- *Ramaria stricta*

    20. Not as above --- 21

21. Fruiting body robust, white with yellow upper branches; deeply seated in conifer duff; in western North America, in spring --------------------------------------- *Ramaria magnipes*

21. Fruiting body not deeply seated, orange-yellow to yellow-orange: under conifers and hardwoods in summer and fall -- *Ramaria aurea*

Multiclavula mucida (Fr.) R.H. Petersen
NONPOISONOUS

Fruiting body 0.4–1.0 cm tall, 0.1– 0.2 cm wide, cylindric to narrowly clavate with a blunt apex, white, but soon buff to yellow, moist, darkening on drying or exposure to direct sun. Flesh firm, flexible, white. Odor and taste not distinctive.

Spores 5.5–7.0 x 2–3 µm narrowly elliptic, smooth, entire, thin-walled, hyaline, nonamyloid. Spore print white.

Habit and distribution: Gregarious, on wet and soggy ground or decorticated rotting wood which is always covered with green algae. Widely distributed. Fruiting most often in late summer and fall following wet weather.

Comments: Also known as *Clavaria mucida* Fr. and *Lentaria mucida* (Fr.) Corner, this minute species is associated with a green alga. We have found it on the ground many times.

Clavaria vermicularis Fr.
NONPOISONOUS

Fruiting body 6–12 cm tall, simple, cylindric, usually cespitose, pure white and tips often yellowing in age. Flesh soft, brittle, white, hollow in age. Odor vaguely of green corn. Taste mild.

Spores 4.4–7.0 x 3–4 µm subglobose, smooth, entire, thin-walled, nonamyloid. Spore print white. Cystidia absent.

Habit and distribution: Several to occasionally many cespitose clusters, on the ground, in grass, moss, or in humus under forest trees. Widely distributed. Fruiting in summer and fall.

Comments: The picture is in a hardwood forest in Virginia. Compare with the complicated branching of *Ramariopsis kunzii* (Fr.) Donk, which is also pure white.

Clavaria purpurea Fr.
NONPOISONOUS

Fruiting body 2.5–10.0 cm tall, single, round to somewhat flattened, often cespitose, tapering somewhat at the apex, purple, bluish, fading to buff tinted lilac, base white with white mycelium, dry. Flesh soft, white becoming hollow in age. Odor and taste mild.

Spores 6–10 x 3.5–5.0 μm elliptic to oblong (Fig. 4), smooth, entire, thin-walled, nonamyloid. Spore print white. Cystidia large, protruding, thin-walled.

Habit and distribution: Several to numerous, cespitose or not, on ground under conifers. Widely distributed. Fruiting in spring, summer, and early fall.

Comments: Corner (1967) lists a number of synonyms for this species and indicates that some collections have giant spores (8.5–15.0 x 3.5–5.0 μm). It is indicated as edible by some authors, but there is very little flesh to eat!

Clavaria zollingeri Lév.
INEDIBILE

Fruiting body 2–8 cm tall, 0.2–0.5 cm wide, round to somewhat flattened, rarely branched, deep violet to amethyst, cylindric, clustered or cespitose, smooth, nearly pointed at top and abruptly narrowed at base. Flesh brittle, pale violet. Odor mild. Taste somewhat disagreeable.

Spores 4–7 x 3–5 μm subglobose, smooth, entire, thin-walled, nonamyloid. Spore print white. Basidia mostly 4-spored.

Habit and distribution: In a dense cluster on the ground under hardwood or mixed hardwood/conifer forests. Widely distributed. Fruiting in summer and fall.

Comments: A similar appearing species *Clavulina amethystina* (Fr.) Donk is lilac, branched, not brittle and has 2–spored basidia. *Clavaria vermicularis* Fr. is a closely related, pure white, brittle species; usually 6–12 cm high; with the same growth habit; and white, elliptical spores 5–7 x 3–4 μm.

Clavulinopsis fusiformis (Fr.) Corner
NONPOISONOUS

Fruiting body 3–15 cm tall, growing in a dense cluster, cylindric to somewhat flattened, pale to bright yellow, the narrow tips becoming reddish to brown in age, white at the base, dry. Flesh solid at first becoming hollow in age, green with ferric sulphate. Odor mild. Taste slightly bitter.

Spores 5.0–7.5 x 4.5–6.5 μm globose to subglobose (Figs. 1 & 2), smooth, entire, thin-walled, hyaline, nonamyloid. Spore print buff. Cystidia absent.

Habit and distribution: In clusters, on ground in grass, humus, in fields or under hardwoods and conifers. Widely distributed. Fruiting in summer and fall.

Comments: *Clavulinopsis helveola* (Fr.) Corner is very similar but has strongly warted spores 5.2–7.2 x 4.5–7.5 μm, and is found in northeastern North America (Petersen, 1968).

Clavariadelphus truncatus (Quél.) Donk
EDIBLE

Fruiting body 6–15 cm tall, 2–9 cm wide, club-shaped, with a broad or even flattened apex that may rupture, revealing the hollow interior, smooth at base to wrinkled or veined near the top, bright yellow, golden yellow to orange-yellow, pinkish brown to yellow-brown below with a white, hairy covering over the base. Flesh white, thin, hollow at top, turns green in ferric sulphate solution. Odor pleasant. Taste sweet.

Spores 9–13 x 5.0–7.5 µm elliptic, smooth, entire, thin-walled, nonamyloid. Spore print pale orange-red.

Habit and distribution: Scattered to several under conifers in needle litter. Widely distributed. Fruiting in summer and fall.

Comments: *Clavariadelphus pistillaris* (Fr.) Donk is not as yellow and the apex is never as wide as *C. truncatus.*

Clavariadelphus pistillaris (Fr.) Donk
var americana Corner
EDIBLE

Fruiting body 7–30 cm tall, 2–6 cm wide, narrowly club-shaped, sometimes a few short branches, longitudinally rugose to wrinkled, flesh colored, pink to light orange-red, brownish red, tinted yellowish, white, with a fine down just over the base. Flesh firm, whitish, hollow in age. Odor none. Taste bitter.

Spores 10–16 x 5–10 µm elliptic, smooth, entire, thin-walled, nonamyloid. Spore print white to buff.

Habit and distribution: Single to many in hardwoods in eastern North America and mixed hardwoods and conifers in western North America. Fruiting in spring and fall.

Comment: The flesh is very thin and there is usually not enough to bother with, as an edible.

Clavariadelphus ligula (Fr.) Donk
EDIBLE

Fruiting body 2–10 cm tall, 0.3–1.2 cm wide, cylindric, narrowly club-shaped to flattened, surface roughened, salmon color to orange-buff, fine white downy base. Flesh firm, not brittle, white, green in ferric sulphate solution. Odor none. Taste slightly bitter.

Spores 8–15 x 3–6 µm elliptic, smooth, entire, thin-walled, nonamyloid. Spore print white. Basidia 4-spored.

Habit and distribution: Gregarious in clusters or even cespitose, in conifer duff, under many different conifers. Widely distributed. Fruiting in summer and fall.

Comments: *Clavariadelphus sachalinensis* (Imai) Corner is very similar, but has an ochre spore print and larger spores 16–24 x 5.0–5.5 µm. We have collected it in Alaska, where it was reported by Wells and Kempton (1968).

Lentaria byssiseda (Pers.) Corner
INEDIBLE

Fruiting body 1.5–5 cm tall, 0.5–4.5 cm wide, white to very light pinkish at the acute tips, cespitose with dense, very thin branches, base with rhizomorphs. Flesh tough, bends double without breaking, dull white. Odor none. Taste mild but disagreeable.

Spores 10–15 x 3.0–4.4 µm oblong, curved somewhat, smooth, entire, thin-walled, nonamyloid. Spore print white to cream. Basidia 4-spored. Cystidia absent.

Habit and distribution: Several to gregarious on well-decayed wood, cones, plant parts, under both hardwoods and conifers. Widely distributed. Fruiting in late summer and fall.

Comments: Corner (1967) describes several species, all of which appear to be decomposers of plant material. They are all equally tough and very flexible fruiting bodies.

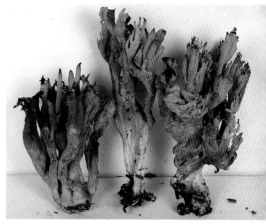

Clavulina cristata (Fr.) J. Schröt.
EDIBLE

Fruiting body 2.5–8.5 cm tall, 0.2–0.4 cm wide, dainty, fine branches with fine tips (cristate), white tinted yellowish in age, base with a white pubescence. Flesh not brittle, very firm, will almost bend on itself without breaking. Odor none. Taste mild.

Spores 7–11 x 5–7.5 µm subglobose, smooth, entire, slightly thick-walled, smooth, nonamyloid. Spore print white. Basidia club-shaped, 2-spored.

Habit and distribution: Single, several to gregarious in fields and under hardwoods and conifers. Widely distributed. Fruiting in summer, fall, and early winter.

Comments: It is said to be a good edible, but we have not tried it.

Clavulina cinerea (Fr.) Schröt.
EDIBLE

Fruiting body 2.5–10.0 cm tall, 2–6 cm thick, medium sized, smoke gray, sometimes bluish gray or even brownish in age, densely covered with short, often irregular, thin branches, whitish just at the base. Flesh firm, grayish white. Odor mild. Taste mild.

Spores 6.5–11.0 x 7–10 µm subglobose, smooth, entire, thin-walled, nonamyloid. Spore print white. Basidia club-shaped, 2-spored. Clamp connections present.

Habit and distribution: Scattered to very abundant on the ground, in moss, or needle duff, under conifers or mixed conifers and hardwoods. Widely distributed. Fruiting in late summer and fall.

Comments: The gray coloration separates this from the very similar white *Clavulina cristata*, which also has delicate, very fine, terminal branches.

Clavicorona pyxidata (Fr.) Doty
EDIBLE

Fruiting body 8–13 cm tall, 6–10 cm wide, pliant, tan to pale pinkish with slender, dichotomous, yellow, candelabra-like branching, crownlike tips, pubescent, whitish to pinkish brown over the base. Flesh tough, white. Odor not distinctive. Taste mild.

Spores 3.5–5.5 x 2–3 µm elliptic, smooth, entire, thin-walled, nonamyloid. Spore print white.

Habit and distribution: Single, gregarious or in cespitose clusters on dead and decayed wood (especially poplar and willow). Widely distributed. Fruiting in the spring and summer.

Comments: The distinctive dichotomous branching pattern of equal pairs of branches sets this growth habit apart from other members of the coral fungi. Only very occasionally does one find enough for a meal.

Ramariopsis kunzii (Fr.) Donk
NONPOISONOUS

Fruiting body 2–12 cm tall, 3–6 cm wide, branching into a dense cluster of erect, pure white, terminal, fine-pointed tips, bright white throughout sometimes becoming yellowish or pinkish white over the base. Flesh fragile and very brittle, negative in 10% ferric sulphate. Odor none. Taste mild.

Spores 3.0–5.5 x 2.5–4.5 µm short elliptic, with minute spines, entire, thin-walled, nonamyloid. Spore print white.

Habit and distribution: Several to gregarious, on ground, in wood debris, humus, in pastures, fields, and woods. Widely distributed. Fruiting in summer and fall.

Comments: *Ramariopsis pulchella* (Boud.) Corner is a very small, violet species with very small, subglobose, warted spores, 3.0–4.5 x 2.5–3.5 µm, which could be mistaken for a very small *Clavaria zollingeri*.

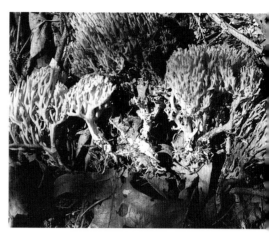

Ramaria gelatinosa (Coker) Corner **var oregonensis** Marr & D. E. Stuntz
INEDIBLE

Fruiting body 5–15 cm tall, 5–14 cm wide, light orange, tinted gray or yellowish, base 4–7 cm wide, giving rise to numerous branches, culminating in short, round tips. Flesh base translucent jellylike, very firm, arms with translucent central core, green in ferric sulphate. Odor unpleasant. Taste mild.

Spores 7.5–10 x 4.5–6 μm elliptic, with numerous warts, entire, slightly thick-walled, ncnamyloid. Spore print light buff to orange-buff.

Habit and distribution: Single to several on the ground under both conifers and hardwoods. Widely distributed. Fruiting in fall.

Comments: This is a complex of closely related taxa including *R. gelatinosa* var *gelatinosa* (Coker) Corner, which also has translucent gelatinous flesh. All species with gelatinous flesh should be avoided since they cause gastric upset, Type 8 toxins.

Ramaria bataillei (Maire) Corner
POISONOUS

Fruiting body 7–25 cm tall, 3–8 cm thick, pinkish buff to light yellow-orange, base 0.3–1.5 cm wide, white, then bruising wine-red, giving rise to narrow branches 0.3–0.6 cm wide, with compact, usually blunt, whitish buff to light yellow, branched tips. Flesh firm, white bruising wine-red then brown to black. Odor mild and pleasant. Taste faintly bitter unpleasant with an aftertaste.

Spores 8–15 x 4–6 μm oblong-elliptic, minutely roughened, entire, slightly thick-walled, nonamyloid. Spore print red-brown.

Habit and distribution: On humus or in soil under hardwoods or occasionally conifers. Widely distributed. Fruiting in late summer and fall.

Comments: *Ramaria testaceo-flava* (Bres.) Corner and *R. formosa* (Fr.) Quél. are two more in a group of species with flesh that turns wine-red on exposure to air, eventually changing to black as shown in the color plate. These species cause gastrointestinal distress and diarrhea (Type 8 toxins), and should be regarded as poisonous.

Ramaria abietina (Pers.:Fr.) Quél.
INEDIBLE

Fruiting body 3–10 cm tall, 2–8 cm wide, base 0.3–1.4 cm wide, with short branches from the base, cinnamon to darker brown, turning greenish in age or when handled, with white rhizomorphs. Flesh tough, white, green in ferric sulphate. Odor strong. Taste bitter.

Spores 5.5–10.5 x 3–5 µm short elliptic, teardrop-shaped, with small warts, entire, thin-walled, nonamyloid. Spore print light brown.

Habit and distribution: Several to gregarious under conifers and sometimes hardwoods. Found in northern North America. Fruiting in the summer and fall.

Comments: Also known as *Ramaria ochraceo-virens* (Jungh.) Donk, it is too bitter to be considered an edible. However, its green coloration is distinctive in *Ramaria*.

Ramaria botrytis (Fr.) Ricken
EDIBLE WITH CAUTION

Fruiting body 7–20 cm tall, 10–30 cm wide, pink, cauliflower-like, robust, with thick, numerous branches, and deep pink tips, arising from a large, whitish to tan, fleshy base 2–5 cm wide. Flesh somewhat brittle, white, green in ferric sulphate. Odor and taste pleasant.

Spores 12–17 x 4–7 µm elliptic, with fine, longitudinal striations (Fig. 13), smooth, entire, thin-walled, nonamyloid. Spore print light orange-brown.

Habit and distribution: Scattered to abundant under hardwoods and conifers. Widely distributed. Fruiting in the summer and early fall.

Comments: Some people experience a laxative effect but others are unaffected, Type 8 toxins. *Ramaria subbotrytis* is bright pink to reddish overall; spores 7–9 x 3–3.5 µm. It is uncommon, but the most colorful of our coral fungi. Only small amounts of a new edible should be consumed at first to establish an individual's reaction to this new food.

Ramaria subbotrytis (Coker) Corner
EDIBLE

Fruiting body 7.5–10.0 cm tall, 5.5–10.0 cm wide, bright pink to red, robust, with short, branches giving rise to short, dichotomous, small, rounded, terminal branches, base 3–5 cm wide. Flesh firm, also pink, green in ferric sulphate. Odor none. Taste mild.

Spores 7.0–9.3 x 3.0–3.8 μm elliptic, low warts, entire, slightly thick-walled, nonamyloid. Spore print light yellow-brown.

Habit and distribution: Single to several on the ground under mixed hardwoods and conifers. Found in eastern North America. Fruiting in late summer and fall.

Comments: In western North America *Ramaria araiospora* var *araiospora* Marr & D. E. Stuntz and *R. araiospora* var *rubella* Marr & D. E. Stuntz are both very similar, and also edible.

Ramaria stricta (Pers.:Fr.) Quél.
INEDIBLE

Fruiting body 4–10 cm tall, 2–7 cm wide, pale yellow to orange-gray, branches 0.2–1.2 cm wide, tapering, dichotomous to the narrowly pointed tips and arising from within the woody substrate. Flesh tough and elastic, dull white to light brownish. Odor slightly garlic to radishlike. Taste bitter.

Spores 7.5–10.0 x 3.8–5.0 μm elliptic, minutely warted, entire, slightly thick-walled, nonamyloid. Spore print yellowish.

Habit and distribution: Single to several on ground or commonly from dead, very decayed hardwood. Widely distributed. Fruiting in summer and fall.

Comments: A dense white mycelium and rhizomorphs proliferate into the dead wood as described by Coker (1923) and observed by us. *Ramaria apiculata* (Fr.) Donk is similar, but is found on well-decayed conifer wood, and is smaller, tougher, and acrid tasting.

Ramaria magnipes Marr & Stuntz
EDIBLE

Fruiting body 8–27 cm tall, 10–23 cm wide, robust, cauliflower-like, with several stout, white branches, with dense, short, stout, yellow tips, arising from a white base, 2–8 cm wide. Flesh very firm, white, green in ferric sulphate. Odor mild. Taste mild and pleasant.

Spores 9.5–13.5 x 3–5 μm narrowly elliptic, smooth, entire, slightly thick-walled, nonamyloid. Spore print light brown.

Habit and distribution: Several to gregarious, deeply seated in soil in conifer duff under well-developed often older conifers, especially grand fir, Engelmann spruce, and Douglas fir. Found in western North America. Fruiting from very early spring to early summer.

Comments: Often in large fruitings, this spring *Ramaria* is a good edible, but in some people it acts as a strong laxative. Start by eating only a small amount the first time to be sure you are not affected. It is the most abundant spring coral near our home in McCall, Idaho. Petersen (1988) presents information on several edible spring corals in the Pacific Northwest.

Ramaria aurea (Schaeff.:Fr.) Quél.
EDIBLE

Fruiting body 8–12 cm tall, 10–20 cm wide, orange-yellow, arising cauliflower-like, with repeated branching, with dense, closely packed, yellow to orange-yellow tips, from a white, bulbous base. Flesh firm to tough, white, green in 10% ferric sulphate. Odor musty. Taste slightly bitter.

Spores 9–13 x 4.0–5.5 μm elliptic, with minute warts, entire, slightly thick-walled, nonamyloid. Spore print yellow.

Habit and distribution: Single to several on ground in conifer and occasionally hardwood forests. Widely distributed. Fruiting in summer and fall.

Comments: *Ramaria flava* (Schaeff.:Fr.) Quél. is very similar, but somewhat paler in color with somewhat larger spores, 12–14 x 4.5–6.4 μm. Both species are edible.

THE BOLETES—BOLETALES

The boletes are fleshy mushrooms that have a pileus, central stipe, and the spore-bearing surface beneath the pileus is composed of very small pores. The pores are actually tubes usually 5–20 mm long. These tubes contain the spores, which are forcibly discharged; and one can therefore obtain a spore print by placing a pileus on white paper the same as one would do for the lamellate agarics. The spore color is also important in the boletes to distinguish among genera and species. The spores may be smooth, elliptic to subfusiform (Figs 3 & 5), warted, ornamented with a reticulum (Fig. 12), pitted, or may have longitudinal ridges (Fig 13). Many boletes stain blue when cut or bruised, while others stain red or green and these reactions should be noted from fresh specimens. Description of the flesh includes the pileus and stipe. Odor and taste may be of importance and should be noted. Boletes are mycorrhizal with certain hardwoods such as oak, beech, birch, willow, and poplar (or aspen), as well as conifers including, fir, spruce, pine, hemlock, and larch. Specific boletes are associated with certain trees. For example, *Suillus pictus* is a mycorrhizal associate only of eastern white pine and *Suillus sibericus* only with western white pine. Therefore, it is very desirable to note the trees in the immediate vicinity of a fruiting bolete at the time of collection.

Boletus is the largest genus with large species. The pores are circular, never boletinoid; the stipe may be reticulate; some stain blue when cut or bruised; the spores are smooth; and the spore print yellow to dark brown. *Boletellus* is similar to *Boletus,* but the spores are ornamented with longitudinal ridges (Fig. 13), or appear partially striate. *Phylloporus* has yellow lamellae with veins in between them or are almost poroid; the flesh often stains blue when cut or bruised. *Gyrodon* has very shallow tubes (3–5 mm deep), which are decurrent and yellowish; they are found near or under ash trees. *Pulveroboletus* is a small genus with a bright yellow pileus that is powdery from the distinctive granular universal veil; the spores are smooth; and the spore print, olive-brown. *Gastroboletus* is a small western genus found buried deep in the duff with contorted pores; some stain blue when cut or bruised; and the spores are smooth but no spore print is obtainable.

Austroboletus is also a small genus, with tall slender species with reticulate stipes; they never stain blue; and have spores that are pitted; the spore print is pinkish brown to reddish brown. *Chalciporus* has small fruiting bodies; pores that are yellow-brown to cinnamon-brown; a stipe without reticulations, scabers, or glandular dots; some stain blue; the spores are smooth, and cinnamon brown in mass. *Gyroporus* has a yellow spore print and ovoid to elliptic, smooth, entire spores; has a stipe without reticulations, glandular dots, or scabers. *Strobilomyces* has a fibrillose to scaly pileus that is gray to purplish gray; the flesh stains orange-red; and has globose spores that are warted to reticulate; and a black-brown spore print. *Tylopilus* has pink pores and the spore print is pink to reddish brown.

"North American Boletes" by Bessette, Roody, and Bessette (2000) is an excellent source for additional information on the 300 or more species of boletes in North America. Smith and Thiers (1971) have also contributed to the general work on the boletes. Lastly, Snell and Dick (1970) produced a well-illustrated work on the boletes of northeastern North America.

Edibility: Each section treats the edible, inedible, and poisonous species

KEY TO THE BOLETALES

1. Pores arranged like lamellae (boletinoid) or lamellate with veins between ------------- 2
1. Pores circular or angular but not arranged as above------------------------------------ 4
   2. Lamellate with veins between the lamellae ---------------- *Phylloporus rhodoxanthus*
   2. Not above, boletinoid -- 3
3. Pores very thin (3–6 mm deep); always under or near ash ---------- *Gyrodon merulioides*
3. Pores thicker; mostly under conifers, oaks and other hardwoods ------------------- *Suillus*
   4. Spores print pale to bright yellow; stipe hollow------------------------------ *Gyroporus*
   4. Not as above-- 5
5. Stipe with usually black to blackish brown scabers-------------------------------- *Leccinum*
5. Not as above --- 6
   6. Pores pink; spore print pink to reddish brown ---------------------------------- *Tylopilus*
   6. Pores not pink; spore print not pink -------------- See key to *Boletus* and its relatives

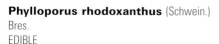

Phylloporus rhodoxanthus (Schwein.) Bres.
EDIBLE

Pileus 2–9 cm broad, convex, brown to red-brown, often developing cracks exposing the yellow flesh, felty to touch, dry. Flesh firm, buff to yellow. Lamellae decurrent, subdistant, with veins sometimes nearly poroid, yellow to lemon-yellow, bruising blue or sordid brown. Stipe 2–6 cm long, 0.5–2.0 cm wide, widest at apex, tapering toward base, dry, buff, but stained dingy-reddish most often over the lower two-thirds. Partial veil absent. Odor none. Taste mild.

Spores 11–15 x 4.5–6.0 µm narrowly elliptic, smooth, entire, thick-walled, nonamyloid. Spore print orange-brown to yellowish brown.

Habit and distribution: Single or several under conifers or in mixed conifer-hardwood forests. Widely distributed. Fruiting in spring, summer, and fall.

Comments: Recent studies have confirmed the placement of the genus *Phylloporus* in the Boletales. There are 6 species in the genus with *P. rhodoxanthus,* a common and widely distributed mycorrhizal associate of both hardwoods and conifers. It is edible, but not usually found in quantity. *Phylloporus boletinoides* A.H. Sm. & Thiers is found in eastern North America; has a strong poroid hymenium with uneven veins and ridges between the lamellae; and bruises gray with a tint of greenish blue. We have collected it in Georgia under loblolly pine.

Gyrodon merulioides (Schwein.) Singer
EDIBLE

Pileus 5–25 cm broad, nearly plane to slightly depressed, dull yellow-brown to red-brown, felty, dry. Flesh yellow, sometimes slowly becoming bluish green. Tubes very shallow, 1–2 mm deep, mouths long, 2–3 mm wide, radial and nearly lamellate with uneven cross walls, bright yellow to dull, dingy yellow in age, bruises slightly blue-green. Stipe 1–6 cm long, 1.0–3.0 cm wide, lateral, partially reticulate at apex, yellow at first, stained reddish over lower part in age, dry. Partial veil absent. Odor not distinctive. Taste acidic, unpleasant.

Spores 7–11 x 5.0–7.5 µm broadly elliptic, smooth, entire, nonamyloid. Spore print brownish red to yellowish ochre.

Habit and distribution: Single to scattered, always under or near white ash. Found in eastern North America. Fruiting in summer and fall.

Comments: It is also known as *Boletinellus merulioides* (Schwein.) Murrill. In the soil surface surrounding the fruiting bodies there are sclerotia. These are small, black, elliptical knots of fungal tissue (1–6 mm wide), which are attached to the mycelium (Cotter and Miller, 1985). These sclerotia can overwinter, germinate, and grow a new mycelium.

SUILLUS

The species of *Suillus* are found on the ground and usually under conifer trees, with just a few associated with hardwoods. The pileus varies from dry and fibrillose to viscid or glutinous, white, yellow, brown to intensely bright red. The pores at maturity are radially aligned (boletinoid), and yellow, gray, olive-brown to brown in age. The stipe is smooth or has small glandulae on the surface. A partial veil is either absent or, if present, often left as cottony or viscid marginal remains, and soon gone as the fungus matures. The spores are elliptic (Fig. 3) and the spore print is light to dark brown or reddish brown. Smith and Thiers (1964) describe 46 species in North America, and they are all mycorrhizal with conifers, except for possibly 3 species with hardwoods. Species with a reddish brown spore print have been placed in *Fuscoboletinus* in the past and separated from *Suillus,* however recent research does not support this, and we place these species in *Suillus.*

Edibility: Although many of the species of *Suillus* covered here are eaten and enjoyed, there are some cautions which must be observed. There are reports of gastric upset eating *Suillus granulatus,* which may be the result of a toxin in some strains or an individual allergy to this species. *Suillus tomentosus* has caused gastric upset including diarrhea and vomiting (Type 8 toxins). *Suillus luteus,* which is not native to North America, has caused severe gastric upset even when the glutinous pileipellis has been removed in preparation for the table. This includes severe diarrhea and vomiting. However, we find *Suillus brevipes* a very good edible and have served it to our mycology classes in Montana. Other species, such as *Suillus americanus,* are coarse and do not taste good. A new edible should be carefully identified as a *Suillus* before eating and should always be tried in small amounts at first, and wait at least one day, in order to be sure you do not have a personal allergy to the fungus.

KEY TO THE SPECIES OF SUILLUS

1. Partial veil absent --- 2
1. Partial veil present, annulus present or absent --- 5
   2. Stipe smooth, without glandulae -- *S. brevipes*
   2. Stipe with tan to red-brown glandulae -- 3
3. Pileus cinnamon to pinkish gray -- *S. granulatus*
3. Pileus orange-brown to orange-yellow --- 4
   4. Flesh stains blue or blue-green; western North America ------------- *S. tomentosus*
   4. Flesh does not stain blue; eastern North America ------------------------- *S. hirtellus*
               (see comments under *S. tomentosus*)
5. Pileus dry, with matted hairs or with scales -- 6
5. Pileus viscid to glutinous --- 8
   6. Pileus covered with thick, red scales; only with eastern white pine -------- *S. pictus*
   6. Pileus with dense, pink to cinnamon-brown fibrils or scales; only with eastern or
      western larch --- 7
7. Pileus with dense, pink fibrils, reddish zone beneath pileipellis; with western larch,
   western North America--- *S. ochraceoroseus*
7. Pileus with cinnamon-brown scales; stipe hollow; with western and eastern larch;
   widely distributed --- *S. cavipes*
   8. Partial veil leaves no annulus or a very weak annular zone -------------------------- 9
   8. Partial veil leaves a sticky to gelatinous annulus or a membranous, dull white,
      annular zone --- 11
9. Partial veil leaves a thick, cottony roll on pileus margin; under eastern white pine in
   eastern North America--- *S. americanus*
9. Not as above-- 10
   10. Pileus viscid to gelatinous, orange-brown to reddish brown; under pines in western
      North America--- *S. albivelatus*
   10. Pileus dry, fibrillose, cinnamon-buff to reddish cinnamon; under hardwood and
      conifer forests in southeastern and southern United States -------------- *S. decipiens*
11. Associated with western or eastern larch; pileus glutinous, bright yellow, orange-red,
   deep chestnut-red , nearly white to smoky gray --------------------------------------- 12
11. Not as above-- 13
   12. Pileus bright yellow, orange-red to rich chestnut-red; not staining
      when bruised --- *S. grevillei*

12. Pileus nearly white, smoky gray to brown; staining blue-green when exposed to air or bruised --- *S. aeruginascens*

13. Pileus tacky, reddish to orange-brown scales; stipe flesh stains blue-green; under conifers in western North America -- *S. lakei*

13. Not as above--- 14

14. Pileus yellow to deep reddish brown, glutinous layer; partial veil leaving a pink to purplish annulus; usually under plantations of imported conifers------------ *S. luteus*

14. Not as above --- 15

15. Pileus convex-umbonate, olive-buff to olive-gray; pores yellow, large, radially aligned; annulus thin, whitish, flaring, gelatinous; northern and western North America -- *S. flavidus*

15. Not as above-- 16

16. Pileus broadly convex, clay-color to cinnamon-buff; pores very small, light orange; annulus thick, light buff, gelatinous, leaving a viscid, cottony roll at margin edge; eastern North America --- *S. salmonicolor*

16. Pileus olive-brown; pores olive-buff; annulus thin, white, viscid; western North America --- *S. subolivaceus*

(see comments under *S. salmonicolor*)

Suillus brevipes (Peck) Kuntze
EDIBLE

Pileus 5–10 cm broad, convex, nearly plane in age, dark reddish brown to yellow-brown, often lighter in age, glutinous. Flesh white, yellowish in age, unchanged when cut or bruised. Tubes about 4–10 mm deep, mouths small (1–2 per mm), radial near stipe, yellow. Stipe 2–5 cm long, 1–3 cm wide, equal, dry, white to pale yellow, without glandular dots. Partial veil absent. Odor none. Taste mild.

Spores 7–10 x 2.5–3.5 µm elliptic, smooth, entire, thick-walled, nonamyloid. Spore print cinnamon.

Habitat and distribution: Several to numerous or even in cespitose clusters under pines. Found throughout most of North America. Fruiting in summer, fall and early winter on the West Coast.

Comments: We really enjoy the flavor of this species and have served it to mycology classes in Montana. A very similar species *Suillus albivelatus*, has a veil and sometimes an annular zone and is also found associated with pines.

Suillus granulatus (Fr.) Kuntze
EDIBLE

Pileus 5–15 cm broad, convex, broadly convex in age, mottled cinnamon to pinkish gray, darker when young, viscid to glutinous. Flesh white becoming yellowish when cut or bruised, with a watery green line above the tubes. Tubes about 10 mm deep, mouths small (2 per mm), radially arranged in age, pale honey-yellow to dark mustard yellow, brownish in age. Stipe 3.5–8.0 cm long, 1.0–2.5 cm wide, equal, dry, yellow at apex, white covered with tan to red-brown glandular dots, cinnamon over the base. Partial veil absent. Odor none. Taste mild.

Spores 7–10 x 2.5–3.5 µm elliptic, smooth, entire, thick-walled, nonamyloid. Spore print dingy cinnamon to red-brown.

Habit and distribution: Single to several or gregarious on ground under pines, especially 5-needle white pines. Widely distributed. Fruiting in late spring, summer and fall.

Comments: Occasionally, gastric upset has resulted from eating *S. granulatus,* but it is widely used as an edible. One should remove the gelatinous pileipellis before eating it. It is mycorrhizal with pines, both 5-needle and 2- to 3-needle, hard pines, worldwide. *Suillus placidus* (Bonord.) Singer is similar but with an ivory white pileus. It is found under pines in eastern North America, especially eastern white pine but rarely reported elsewhere. *Suillus pungens* Thiers & A.H.Sm. is associated with Monterey pine *(Pinus radiata)* in California. It has a gray pileus often with yellow or white patches or completely white. *Suillus subaureus* (Peck) Snell has a yellow, viscid pileus, beneath finely flattened, wooly hairs and develops glandular dots on the stipe. It is, however, found under oak and, in some cases, pure aspen according to Smith and Thiers (1964) in central North America.

Suillus tomentosus (Kauffman) Snell, Singer & E. A. Dick
EDIBLE WITH CAUTION

Pileus 5–15 cm broad, convex to broadly convex in age, orange-brown to orange-yellow, coarsely tomentose (wooly) at first, nearly hairless in age, sticky to viscid. Flesh pale buff to yellow usually bruising blue or greenish blue. Tubes 10–20 mm deep, mouths minute at first, 2 per mm in age, adnate or short decurrent, somewhat reddish in age, dark brown to dingy yellow in age, staining blue when bruised. Stipe 3–12 cm long, 1–3 cm wide, equal or club-shaped, yellow-orange to orange and covered with red-brown, glandular dots, dry. Partial veil absent. Odor none. Taste mild.

Spores 7–12 x 3–4 μm elliptic, smooth, entire, thick-walled, nonamyloid. Spore print dark olive-brown.

Habit and distribution: Occurs alone or in groups, frequently under lodgepole pine or other two-needle pines. Found in north central to western North America. Fruiting in summer and fall.

Comments: Very common in pine stands in western North America and found less commonly in the Lake States under jack pine. *Suillus hirtellus* (Peck) Kuntze is very similar but does not stain blue when bruised. It is found in eastern North America under conifers including pines. *Suillus punctipes* (Peck) Singer, also found in eastern North America, has an almondlike odor; gray-brown scales on the pileus; and does not stain blue. Some people experience gastric upset.

Suillus pictus (Peck) A. H. Smith & Thiers
EDIBLE

Pileus 3–12 cm broad, conic, convex to nearly plane in age, covered with thick, red scales, yellow flesh beneath, as scales separate in age more flesh is exposed, dry. Flesh firm, yellow, slowly changing to reddish when cut or bruised. Tubes 4–8 mm deep, mouths large and angular, 0.5–5 mm wide, radially arranged, often short decurrent on upper stipe, yellow to brownish in age, staining reddish brown where injured. Stipe 4–12 cm long, 0.8–2.0 cm wide, equal or somewhat larger toward the base, yellow above ring, whitish below with zones and patches of dull red hairs. Partial veil dry, fibrous, whitish, leaving a superior, white, annular zone. Odor not distinctive. Taste mild.

Spores 8–12 x 3.5–5.0 μm elliptic, smooth, entire, thick-walled, nonamyloid. Spore print olive-brown.

Habit and distribution: Solitary to scattered only under eastern white pine. Found in eastern North America. Fruiting in summer and fall.

Comments: This species is also known as *Boletinus pictus* Peck and *Suillus spraguei* (Berk. & M. A. Curtis) Kuntze. It is very abundant during wet weather throughout the range of eastern white pine.

Suillus ochraceoroseus (Snell) Singer
EDIBLE

Pileus 8–25 cm broad, broadly convex, plane in age, dense, pink fibrils with white beneath, darkening in age, margin sometimes yellow with the white remains of the veil tissue adhering, dry. Flesh yellow, strong pink just beneath the pileipellis, turns slightly bluish green when bruised or cut. Tubes decurrent, radially aligned, 3–6 mm deep, mouths 1–2 mm wide, yellow, straw-yellow to dingy-brown in age. Stipe 3–5 cm long, 1–3 cm wide, netlike ridges on upper surface, base often enlarged, straw-yellow, white near base, dry. Partial veil fibrous, white, leaving ragged patches on margin of pileus and sometimes a weak annulus. Odor and taste none.

Spores 7.5–9.5 x 2.5–3.5 μm long cylindric, smooth, entire, thick-walled, nonamyloid. Spore print dark reddish brown.

Habit and distribution: One to several on the ground under western larch. Found in western North America. Fruiting from early summer until late fall.

Comments: Also known as *Fuscoboletinus ochraceoroseus* (Snell) Pomerl. & A.H. Sm. It is very common in central Idaho as an obligate mycorrhizal species with larch. It is sometimes confused with *Suillus lakei*, which has more orange coloration on the pileus, and an olive-brown spore print.

Suillus cavipes (Opat.) A.H. Sm. & Thiers
EDIBLE

Pileus 3–12 cm broad, convex to broadly convex, plane or with a low umbo in age, dense cinnamon-brown scales over the entire surface, tips often white, margin with torn remains of the partial veil, dry. Flesh soft, white to buff not changing when bruised, stipe base hollow. Tubes 3–6 mm deep, mouths 0.5–1.0 mm wide when mature, decurrent, strongly radially aligned, bright yellow, Stipe 3–9 cm long, 0.6–2.0 cm wide, enlarging somewhat toward the base, yellow above the annulus, below covered with scales concolorous with the pileus, dry. Partial veil white, fibrous, leaving a cinnamon-brown annulus. Odor none. Taste mild.

Spores 7–10 x 3.5–4.0 μm elliptic to subfusiform (Fig. 5), smooth, entire, slightly thick-walled, nonamyloid. Spore print olive-brown.

Habit and distribution: On the ground under either eastern or western larch. Widely distributed. Fruiting in late summer and fall.

Comments: Also know as *Boletinus cavipes* (Opat.) Kalchbr. The hollow foot (*cavipes* in Latin) and the mycorrhizal association only with larch, clearly distinguishes this species from other species of *Suillus*.

Suillus americanus (Peck) Snell
NONPOISONOUS

Pileus 4–11 cm broad, convex with a low umbo, pale buff to cinnamon, streaked with reddish hairs, margin with a white to buff, soft, cottony, hanging veil, disappearing only at maturity, viscid. Flesh very narrow, yellow to orange-yellow, staining brown when bruised. Tubes 4–6 mm deep, mouths large 1–2 mm broad, short decurrent, mustard-yellow to yellow-brown in age. Stipe 3–10 cm long, 0.4–1.2 cm wide, nearly equal, often crooked, lemon-yellow, densely covered with cinnamon, red, or red-brown glandular dots, dry. Partial veil cottony, thick, no annulus but pieces may remain on pileus margin. Odor none. Taste mild

Spores 8–11 x 3–4 µm subfusiform, smooth, entire, thick-walled, nonamyloid. Spore print dull cinnamon.

Habit and distribution: Gregarious, on ground under eastern white pine. Found in northeastern North America. Fruiting in late summer and early fall.

Comments: This species is only found as a mycorrhizal associate of eastern white pine. The distribution of the white pine limits the distribution of *S. americanus*. *Suillus sibiricus* (Singer) Singer has brown spots on the pileus; is darker or more dingy yellow; has a thicker stipe; is associated only with western white pine (*Pinus monticola* Doug.:D. Don) and is a closely related species. Neither of these is a very good tasting species.

Suillus albivelatus A.H. Sm., Thiers, O.K. Mill.
NONPOISONOUS

Pileus 4–12 cm broad, convex to broadly convex, smooth, orange-brown to reddish brown inrolled margin, with white remains of the partial veil often until maturity, glutinous. Flesh firm, white to buff. Tubes 4–10 mm deep, mouths 1-2 per mm at maturity, depressed around the stipe, buff to orange-buff, radially arranged at maturity. Stipe 1–4 cm long, 1.4–3.3 cm wide, smooth, glabrous, white to yellow just beneath the tubes, dry. Partial veil white, membranous, clinging to the margin of the pileus but no annulus is formed. Odor pleasant. Taste mild and good.

Spores 6.4–8.4 x 2.6– 4.2 µm elliptic, smooth, entire, slightly thick-walled, nonamyloid. Spore print cinnamon-buff.

Habit and distribution: Several to gregarious under conifers especially Ponderosa pine. Found in western North America. Fruiting in late summer and early fall.

Comments: *Suillus albivelatus* reminds one of *Suillus brevipes* with a partial veil. At times, it is abundant in Idaho. We have collected it in the Dominican Republic under pine, although its distribution in southwestern United States and Mexico is unknown.

Suillus decipiens (Berk. & M. A. Curtis) Kuntze
EDIBILITY UNKNOWN

Pileus 4–8 cm broad, convex, broadly convex to plane in age, cinnamon, cinnamon-buff to reddish cinnamon, margin incurved until fully mature, fibrillose with appressed scales, dry. Flesh firm yellow to pinkish buff, sometimes reddish when exposed or bruised. Tubes adnate, mouths 3–6 mm deep, 0.5–1.0 mm wide, honey yellow to mustard yellow, light brown when bruised. Stipe 4–8 cm long, 0.7–1.6 cm wide, uneven, orange-yellow to yellow-brown, dry. Partial veil fragile, fibrous, whitish gray leaving a weak annular zone near the apex. Odor none. Taste mild to slightly acidic.

Spores 8.5–12.0 x 3.5–4.5 μm cylindric to subfusiform (Figs. 5 & 8), smooth, entire, slightly thick-walled, nonamyloid. Spore print light brown.

Habit and distribution: Several to gregarious, on ground in mixed hardwood/conifer forests. Found in the southeastern and southern United States. Fruiting in late summer and into late fall.

Comments: This species is most likely a mycorrhizal associate of the southern hard pines. Also known as *Boletinus decipiens* (Berk & M. A. Curtis) Peck.

Suillus grevillei (Klotzch) Singer
EDIBLE

Pileus 5–15 cm broad, convex to broadly convex, bright yellow with a yellow margin, orange-red to deep, rich chestnut-red in age, especially in western material, glabrous, glutinous. Flesh pale lemon-yellow, dingy pinkish or not changing when bruised, sometimes yellow-green just at base of stipe. Tubes about 6–15 mm deep, mouths 1–2 per mm, attached or slightly depressed, radial arranged, yellow, dingy in age, bruising brown. Stipe 4–10 cm long, 1.0–3.0 cm wide, nearly equal, somewhat enlarged at base, yellow above the annulus, streaked reddish brown below, but without glandular dots, dry. Partial veil forming a pale lemon-yellow to red annulus, gelatinous in wet weather. Odor and taste mild.

Spores 8–11 μm x 3–4 μm elliptic, smooth, entire, thick-walled, nonamyloid. Spore print olive-brown.

Habit and distribution: Several to abundant, often cespitose under or near larch. Widespread where larch grows. Fruiting from early summer to late fall.

Comments: *Suillus grevillei* is mycorrhizal only with species of larch and is found under or near eastern or western larch. *Suillus luteus* looks very similar to the chestnut-red western form of *S. grevillei,* but has glandular dots above the annulus and is not found under or near larch trees. Remove the glutinous pileipellus before preparing it to be eaten. *Fuscoboletinus spectabilis* (Peck) Pomerl. & A.H. Sm. has a viscid, red pileus with gray veil patches and is found in eastern larch bogs.

Suillus aeruginascens (Secr.) Snell
NONPOISONOUS

Pileus 3–12 cm broad, convex to plane in age, nearly white, smoky gray to wood-brown, dry, sticky to glutinous in wet weather. Flesh white, staining blue-green when exposed or bruised or in contact with white paper. Tube 4–15 mm deep, mouths 1–3 mm wide when mature, radially arranged, white, gray to brown in age, with flesh-colored staining. Stipe 4–6 cm long, 0.8–1.2 cm wide, nearly equal, with reticulate ridges, white above ring, smoke-gray to brownish gray below, viscid. Partial veil membranous, cottony hairs, white, leaves a flattened ring. Odor none. Taste mild.

Spores 8–12 x 4–5 μm subfusiform, smooth, entire, thick-walled, nonamyloid. Spore print reddish brown.

Habit and distribution: Scattered to numerous under larch. Widely distributed. Fruiting in late summer and fall.

Comments: Also known as *Fuscoboletinus aeruginascens* (Secr.) Pomerl. & A.H. Sm., *F. laricinus* (Berk. & Broome) Roody & Bessette, and *Suillus laricinus* (Berk.) Kuntze. *Suillus serotinus* (Frost) Kretzer & Bruns is very similar, but has a dark red brown, glutinous pileipellis, and is also an obligate mycorrhizal associate of larch.

Suillus lakei (Murrill) A. H. Sm. & Thiers
EDIBLE

Pileus 3.5–9.5 (- 20) cm broad, convex, plane in age, tacky to viscid beneath a layer of small, dark reddish to orange-brown scales, yellow ground color, margin inrolled somewhat even in age. Flesh firm, yellowish with a pinkish cast, unchanged when cut or bruised, in age the base of stipe stains blue-green. Tubes 5–10 mm deep, mouths small at first, but up to 2 mm wide in age, radially arranged, orange-brown to nearly salmon color, in age dingy brown and staining brown when bruised. Stipe 6–13 cm long, 1–4 cm thick, equal or narrowed somewhat at the base, yellow and smooth above ring sometimes with glandular dots, yellow, but staining brown to greenish blue over lower half. Partial veil dry, membranous, leaving a dull white superior ring. Odor none. Taste mild.

Spores 7–10 x 3–4 μm elliptic, smooth, entire, thick-walled, nonamyloid. Spore print cinnamon-brown to olive-brown.

Habit and distribution: Solitary to scattered on ground under mixed conifers, especially Douglas fir and western hemlock. Found in western North America. Fruiting in spring, summer, and fall.

Comments: *Suillus lakei* fruits abundantly in the early spring and summer and is one of the most common boletes encountered in northwest Montana and Idaho. *Suillus caerulescens* A.H. Sm. & Thiers is similar; also in western North America; but stains blue when the stipe base is bruised.

Suillus luteus (Fr.) Gray
EDIBLE

Pileus 4–17 cm broad, convex to broadly convex in age, brown shading to yellow-brown or deep reddish brown, glabrous, viscid to glutinous, forming a layer that can be peeled off. Flesh white to pale yellow. Tubes about 3–7 mm deep, mouths 3 per mm, adnate, radial in age, white at first to pale or deep yellow with a brownish tint in age. Stipe 4–11 cm long, 1.0–2.5 cm wide, equal, yellow, with pink to pinkish brown glandular dots above the partial veil, pale yellow to nearly white and glandular dotted below. Partial veil white, membranous, persistent, with a purplish zone on the underside, gelatinous in humid weather. Odor not distinctive. Taste mild and pleasant.

Spores 6–11 x 2.5–4.0 µm elliptic, smooth, entire, thick-walled, nonamyloid. Spore print dull cinnamon.

Habit and distribution: Occurs scattered to numerous in plantations under Scotch pine and Austrian pine. Found wherever these species are planted. Fruiting in summer and fall.

Comment: Common in Europe, it has been introduced into North American plantations of European Scotch pine (*Pinus sylvestris* L.) and Austrian pine (*Pinus nigra* Arnold). *Suillus borealis* A.H. Sm., Thiers, & O.K. Mill. is a very similar species in western North American associated with western white pine. The purple-brown partial veil does not form an annulus. Both species are edible, but the pileipellis must be removed.

Suillus flavidus (Fr.) Singer
EDIBLE

Pileus 3–9 cm broad, conic to convex-umbonate, olive-buff, olive-gray to tan, appearing streaked, viscid to glutinous. Flesh pale yellow, bruising dingy cinnamon. Tubes short decurrent, 4–6 mm deep, mouths 1–2 mm broad, radial, yellow to yellow-green, flesh colored stains. Stipe 3–9 cm long, 0.4–0.8 cm wide, equal, pale yellow above the flaring gelatinous ring, whitish below, covered with pale buff to yellow glandular dots. Partial veil a whitish gelatinous layer clasping the stipe leaving a flaring, gelatinous, dingy pink to cinnamon annulus and marginal gelatinous veil remains on the pileus. Odor none. Taste unpleasant.

Spores 7–10 x 3.5–4.5 µm elliptic, smooth, entire, thick-walled, nonamyloid. Spore print dull cinnamon-brown.

Habit and distribution: Scattered, often in moist areas in sphagnum or various mosses, associated with hard pines (for example, lodgepole pine in the West and jack pine in the East). Widespread in northern and western North America. Fruiting in late summer and fall.

Comments: Also known as *Suillus umbonatus* Snell & E. A. Dick We have collected this distinctive species in Alaska, Alberta, Idaho, and in Glacier National Park, Montana. It is undoubtably mycorrhizal with other conifers not observed by us. We have not eaten it, but would remove the pileipellis to try it. Bessette et al, (2000) records it from eastern Canada and New York.

Suillus salmonicolor (Frost) Halling
EDIBLE

Pileus 3.0–9.5 cm broad, convex, broadly convex to nearly plane in age, smooth, clay-color, cinnamon-buff, to pale pinkish cinnamon, shiny in dry weather, glutinous. Flesh firm, cinnamon to clay-color, darkest near apex of stipe. Tubes 7–12 mm deep, cinnamon-buff to light orange, minute, 3-4 per mm, in age 1-2 per mm. Stipe 3.3–8.5 cm long, 0.6–2.2 cm wide, pinkish buff with cinnamon glandulae above and below the annulus. Partial veil thick, glutinous, forming a cottony roll where it clasps the stipe, light buff to concolorous with the pileus, parting to form a thick, gelatinized annulus. Odor mild. Taste mild.

Spores 7–10 x 2.5–3.5 µm elliptic, entire, slightly thick-walled, nonamyloid. Spore print light brown.

Habit and distribution: Several to gregarious under 2- and 3-needle hard pines. Found in eastern North America. Fruiting in late summer and fall.

Comments: Also known as *Suillus cothurnatus* Singer, *S. pinorigidus* Snell & E. A. Dick, and *Boletus subluteus* Peck. Both (1993) has clarified the status of this confusing complex of species. We have often collected and described this species from the southeastern and southern United States, and choose to recognize only one taxon. *Suillus salmonicolor* has a broad host range among the many species of hard pines in eastern North America. It is edible but not our choice. *Suillus subolivaceus* A.H. Sm. & Thiers found only in the Pacific Northwest and Rocky Mountains is similar; has an olive-brown glutinous pileus; thin, white, partial veil and annulus, with pinkish brown glandulae on the stipe. It is most often found associated with western white pine.

GYROPORUS

The genus *Gyroporus* is distinguished from other boletes by the yellow spore print and the nearly ovoid to elliptic spores. The pileus is always dry, and the stipe is smooth and lacks either reticulations, glandular dots, or scabers.

Edibility. We have not found a sufficient quantity to make a meal of these boletes, but they both are eaten in Europe.

KEY TO GYROPORUS

1. Pileus dry, white; stipe white; flesh stains instantly blue -------------------- *G. cyanescens*
1. Pileus dry, brown; stipe carrot-color to pale cinnamon; flesh white, bruises brown -- *G. castaneus*

Gyroporus cyanescens (Bull.:Fr.) Quél.
EDIBLE

Pileus 4.5–12.0 cm broad, broadly convex, cottony with small scales or hairy patches, margin incurved at first, whitish to yellowish, dry. Flesh white, but instantly blue when bruised or cut. Tubes 3–7 mm deep, mouths small 1–2 per mm, depressed at stipe, white at first to yellow in age, turn blue instantly when bruised. Stipe 5–10 cm long, 1.5–3.5 cm wide, irregular in shape and swollen, concolorous with the pileus, instantly deep blue when bruised, felty, hollow with a soft pith. Partial veil absent. Odor none. Taste mild.

Spores 7–11 x 4–6 µm elliptic to ovoid-elliptic, thick-walled, smooth, nonamyloid. Spore print pale yellow. Cheilocystidia fusiform to narrowly clavate, thin-walled.

Habit and distribution: Single or scattered on gravel or sandy soil under hardwoods, sometimes under mixed hardwood-conifers. Found in eastern North America. Fruiting in summer and early fall.

Comments: We have not eaten it, but it is reported to be a very good edible in Europe (Dähncke & Dähncke, 1979).

Gyroporus castaneus (Bull.:Fr.) Quél.
EDIBLE

Pileus 3–10 cm broad, convex to plane in age, orange-gray to rusty-red or chestnut-brown, minutely wooly, dry. Flesh of pileus white, bruising brown, stipe interior hollow, or filled with a cottony, fragile pith. Tubes 3–7 mm deep, mouths 1-3 per mm, depressed and not attached to stipe, white to light yellow in age. Stipe 3–8 cm long, 0.6–2.2 cm wide, enlarged somewhat toward base, uneven with a band of pure white beneath tubes, the rest is carrot-color, light orange to reddish brown, dry. Partial veil absent. Odor not distinctive. Taste mild, slightly acidic.

Spores 7.0–12.5 x 4.5–6.0 µm elliptic, smooth, entire, thick-walled, nonamyloid. Spore print light yellow. Cheilocystidia numerous, fusoid, thin-walled.

Habit and distribution: Single to several under hardwoods, especially oak. Widely distributed, but rare under live oak in western North America. Fruiting in summer and fall.

Comments: The very uneven, hollow stipe resembles a common carrot root. We have not found enough at one time to make a meal, but it is reported to be edible.

LECCINUM

The conspicuous brown to blackish brown scabers on the stipe separate *Leccinum* from the other bolete genera. The pileus is usually dry or viscid when wet, and a narrow sterile margin without pores is present in some species around the outer margin of the pileus. The pore mouths are various shades of yellow, yellow-brown to olive-brown but never red and not radially arranged. The flesh ranges from unchanged when bruised to bruising pink, wine red, gray or blue.

The spores are elliptic, oblong to subfusiform (Figs. 3–5), and thick-walled. There are more than 40 species with combinations of characters, which need to be recorded when fresh. The species are mycorrhizal with both hardwoods and conifers and most species have specific hosts that are indicated under "Habit and distribution." Only the most common, obvious species are included here. Smith et al. (1966), Snell and Dick (1970) and Bessette et al. (2000) provide more information on the species. Smith and Smith (1973) provide an extensive key to the species.

Edibility: Marilyn Shaw, consultant on mushrooms to the Colorado Poison Center, has handled a number of cases of gastrointestinal upset involving vomiting and diarrhea (Type 8 toxins), following the ingestion of *Leccinum*. We do know that at least some of the species involved stained pinkish or wine-red becoming blue on standing. In general, the species of *Leccinum* are edible. However, one should try a small amount of a species eaten for the first time and wait at least a day before eating a large portion. We have eaten *Leccinum scabrum,* which does not stain red or blue, and enjoyed it.

KEY TO LECCINUM

1. Pileus with coarse, brown to red-brown scales; under mixed conifers in western North America --- *L. fibrillosum*
1. Not as above -- 2
    2. Flesh, when cut or bruised, unchanging or very slightly bruising brown or very slowly light pink--- 3

    2. Flesh, when cut or bruised, becoming pink, pinkish blue to fuscus, or
         spotted green -- 6

3. Pileus smooth, white, cinnamon-drab to dull yellow-brown -------------------------------- 4

3. Pileus wrinkled, white to gray; flesh often stains very light pink; usually associated
    with birch -- *L. rotundifoliae*
              (see comments under *L. scabrum*)

    4. Pileus smooth, cinnamon-drab to dull yellow-brown ----------------------- *L. scabrum*

    4. Pileus smooth, white; flesh not staining to staining light pink------------------------- 5

5. Pileus smooth or slightly pitted, white; flesh not staining; under oak
    and hardwoods--- *L. albellum*
              (see comments under *L. scabrum*)

5. Pileus smooth, white; flesh staining slowly pink; under or near birch in northern
    North America -- *L. holopus*
              (see comments under *L. scabrum*)

    6. Pileus wrinkled to pitted; under hardwoods, especially oaks ------------------------- 7

    6. Pileus smooth; under aspen, birch and conifers--- 8

7. Pileus mustard-yellow, with white cracks and a sterile flap of tissue ------ *L. rugosiceps*

7. Pileus yellow-brown to olive-brown, without a sterile flap of tissue ------------ *L. carpini*
              (see comments under *L. rugosiceps*)

    8. Pileus bright rusty red to orange-red; tissue bruising wine-red, fading to blue-gray;
         with aspen or mixed aspen and pine, widely distributed, especially in eastern
         North America --- *L. aurantiacum*

    8. Not as above-- 9

9. Associated with yellow birch, beech or mixed hardwoods and pine, in eastern
    North America; flesh pink to rose in pileus and upper stipe, lower stipe with
    green stains --- *L. snellii*

9. Not as above-- 10

    10. Associated with aspen, or mixed aspen-conifer forests; found in northern North
        America and western United States --- *L. insigne*

    10. Associated with birch or conifer-birch forests in northern
        North America--- *L. versipelle*
            (see comments under *L. aurantiacum*)

Leccinum fibrillosum A H. Sm., Thiers, & Watling
EDIBLE WITH CAUTION

Pileus 8–25 cm broad, convex, broadly convex in age, brown to red-brown, with a sterile, narrow, marginal flap of hanging veil tissue, matted hairs concentrated into coarse, small scales, dry. Flesh firm, pale buff staining reddish then purplish drab. Tubes 10–20 mm deep, mouths 1-2 per mm, depressed to nearly free at the stipe. Stipe 4–12 cm long, 2–5 cm wide, sometimes even but very often enlarged at center and tapering toward both ends, white but covered with dense, long, black scabers and coarse scales, dry. Odor none. Taste mild.

Spores 14–20 x 4–5 µm narrowly fusiform, smooth, entire, thick-walled, nonamyloid. Spore print olive-brown.

Habit and distribution: Scattered to locally common under mixed western conifers, often in dense huckleberry brush. Found in western North America. Fruiting in late summer and early fall.

Comments: We have collected this distinctive *Leccinum* in Idaho, Montana, and British Columbia. It is edible, but caution should be taken. We have not eaten it, but have no negative reports on its edibility.

Leccinum scabrum (Bull.: Fr.) Gray
EDIBLE

Pileus (4-) 7–12 (-20) cm broad, convex to broadly convex, cinnamon-drab, gray-brown to dull yellow-brown, fine cracks near the margin, which is free of hanging veil remains, glabrous, tacky to viscid in wet weather. Flesh firm, white, not staining when bruised. Tubes 8–15 mm long, mouths small 2-3 per mm, deeply depressed at the stipe, a very narrow sterile margin, white, then tan with a pinkish tint in age, do not stain when bruised or becomes faintly yellow. Stipe 7–15 cm long, 0.7–1.5 cm wide, enlarging toward the base, pale buff to whitish with dark brown to black scabers (see inset), which, when numerous, makes the stipe appear almost reticulate, dry. Veil inconspicuous, no ring or marginal patches. Odor none. Taste pleasant.

Spores 15–19 x 5–7 µm subfusiform (Fig. 5), smooth, entire, thick-walled, nonamyloid. Spore print olive-buff.

Habit and distribution: Several to numerous under birch and aspen. Widely distributed. Fruiting in the summer and fall.

Comments: *Leccinum holopus* (Rostk.) Watling has a pure white pileus; scabers on the stipe; and the context may stain light pink when bruised. It is also mycorrhizal with birch; we have collected it in New Hampshire and New York, and it is restricted to northeastern North America. *Leccinum albellum* (Peck) Singer also has a white, smooth to lightly pitted pileus and thin stipe with very few scabers. It is found in eastern North America, but most frequently in southern United States. It does not change when bruised. *Leccinum rotundifoliae* (Singer) A.H.Sm., Thiers, & Watling is closely related to *L. scabrum*, but has a wrinkled, white to gray pileus; the flesh is unchanging or slowly pinkish when bruised; and it is found in northern North America usually under birch (Bessette et al., 2000). All four species are edible.

Leccinum rugosiceps (Peck) Singer
EDIBLE, WITH CAUTION

Pileus 6–15 cm broad, convex, wrinkled to pitted, orange-yellow, mustard-yellow often with white cracks, with a sterile flap of tissue at the margin, dry. Flesh firm, white staining vinaceous to vinaceous-purple. Tubes 6–12 mm deep, mouths small 0.5-1.5 per mm, recessed around the stipe, light yellowish to olive-brown in age. Stipe 7–15 cm long, 1.2–2.5 cm wide, equal or enlarging somewhat toward the base, yellow ground color with orange-brown scabers often almost reticulate, dry. Partial veil absent. Odor none. Taste mild.

Spores 12–21 x 4.5–6.0 µm subfusiform (Fig. 5), smooth, entire, thick-walled, nonamyloid. Spore print ochraceous-brown.

Habit and distribution: Single to several under hardwoods, especially oaks. Found in eastern North America. Fruiting in summer to early fall.

Comments: The mycorrhizal hosts appear to be oaks. This is unique for two species of *Leccinum*. *Leccinum rotundifoliae* (Singer) A. H. Sm., Thiers, & Watling also has a wrinkled pileus and is similar, but is associated with birch in northern North America (see comments under *Leccinum scabrum*). *Leccinum carpini* (Schulzer) M. M. Moser also has a pileus that is wrinkled and pitted and the flesh stains pink to reddish. It is associated with oak, especially in southeastern and southern United States.

Leccinum aurantiacum (Fr.) Gray
EDIBLE WITH CAUTION

Pileus 5–20 cm broad, robust, convex to broadly convex, with flattened hairs to minutely wooly, brown, bright rusty red, orange-red, red to reddish brown, at first with marginal veil tissue that remains in patches, dry to sticky in wet weather. Flesh firm, thick, white, bruises wine-red, with gray or faded blue-gray overtones. Tubes 10–20 mm deep, mouths round, small, 3-5 per mm, depressed at stipe, white, olive-gray to olive-brown in age or when bruised. Stipe 10–20 cm long, 1.0–3.5 cm wide, slender, enlarging at the base, pale buff to white and covered with light brown scabers almost to the base, dry. Partial veil dull white, remains only as marginal tissue on the pileus. Odor none. Taste mild.

Spores 13–18 x 3.5–5.0 µm subfusiform (Fig. 5), smooth, entire, thick-walled, nonamyloid. Spore print yellow-brown.

Habit and distribution: Scattered to numerous usually under aspen and pines. Widely distributed especially in eastern North America. Fruiting in summer and fall.

Comments: *Leccinum insigne* is closely related, but the pileus is orange-cinnamon not bright rusty red; the stipe more robust; the scabers darker; and stains very quickly to fuscus or livid. *Leccinum versipelle* (Fr.) Snell (also known as *Leccinum testaceoscabrum* (Secr.) Singer) has an orange-yellow dry pileus; black scabers on the stipe; and the flesh stains pink and slowly to bluish when bruised. It is associated with birch in northern North America. We have collected *L. insigne* and *L. versipelle* in Alaska and the Rocky Mountains for the table. Gastsrointestinal upset is reported by some for these species.

Leccinum snellii A.H. Sm., Thiers, & Watling
EDIBLE WITH CAUTION

Pileus 4–12 cm broad, broadly convex, with matted, appressed, fine fibrils, orange-brown, dark brown to black-brown, often fine cracks in the surface, dry, sticky in wet weather. Flesh firm, stains pink to rose, soon fuscus in the pileus and upper stipe, lower stipe with irregular green stains, just at the base. Tubes 8–12 mm deep, mouths 2-3 per mm, depressed at stipe, white young but soon yellow to olive-brown in age, often bruising yellow. Stipe 6–11 cm long, 1–3 cm wide, enlarging somewhat toward the base, dull white with dense, black scabers to the base, dry. Partial veil absent. Odor none. Taste mild.

Spores 13–22 x 5.0–7.5 µm subfusiform (Fig. 5), smooth, entire, thick-walled, nonamyloid. Spore print light brown.

Habit and distribution: Single to several under yellow birch, beech, or mixed hardwood pine forests. Found in eastern North America. Fruiting from spring to late fall.

Comments: The pink staining on the upper stipe and green spots at the stipe base can be seen in the photo. Often a deep rose coloration will develop in the pileus and upper stipe. It is one of the few species of *Leccinum* found from southern Canada and the Lake States, south to the southeastern United States, where it appears to be mycorrhizal with yellow birch (*Betula alleghaniensis* Britt.). Reported as edible; we have not eaten it.

Leccinum insigne A. H. Sm., Thiers, & Watling
EDIBLE WITH CAUTION

Pileus 5.5–20.0 cm broad, convex to broadly convex, orange-cinnamon sometimes with olive tones, sterile flap of tissue on the margin, which results in hanging pieces of tissue in age, dry to sticky when wet. Flesh firm, white, staining to reddish gray when bruised, then to bluish gray, resulting in a livid stain. Tubes 15–20 mm deep, mouths 2-4 per mm, depressed at the stipe, pinkish buff, light cinnamon-drab to olive-brown in age. Stipe 7–14 cm long, 1.0–4.1 cm wide, robust, enlarging toward the base, whitish or tinted brown with dense brown scabers in tufts, which blacken at maturity, dry. Partial veil dull white, absent at maturity or leaving sparse appendiculate remains on the pileus margin. Odor none. Taste mild

Spores 13–16 x 4.0–5.5 μm subfusiform (Fig. 5), smooth, entire, thick-walled, nonamyloid. Spore print dark yellow-brown.

Habit and distribution: Common and often abundant under pure stands of aspen, or in mixed stands of aspen with conifers (jack pine, lodgepole pine, and white spruce). Found in northern North America and western United States. Fruiting in spring, summer, and fall, under cool moist conditions.

Comments: *Leccinum insigne* is especially common in Alaska and the Rocky Mountains where large aspens stands are found. We have collected and eaten this species in Alaska. *Leccinum discolor* A. H. Sm., Thiers, & Watling is similar; also under aspen but is smaller; stains slowly wine-red changing to gray; and is distributed in northwestern North America. See also *Leccinum aurantiacum,* which is very similar. The wine-red to blue staining species of *Leccinum* frequently cause digestive upset, and one should sample small amounts at first in a new collecting area.

TYLOPILUS

The species of *Tylopilus* are usually robust boletes with minute to small pores, which turn pink as the spores mature and yield a pink, brownish pink, to reddish brown spore print. The spores are elliptic, oblong, to subfusiform, smooth (Figs. 3–5). The pores are never radially aligned as in *Suillus*. Only one species, *T felleus,* has a reticulate network over the entire stipe. One other species, *T. chromapes,* has scabers like a *Leccinum,* but has a unique, bright yellow stipe base. A majority of the species are found associated with hardwoods and conifers in eastern North America, and several species are also in western North America, but also associated with oaks and hardwoods. A majority of the species have a bitter taste. They are all mycorrhizal associates of trees such as oaks, beech, hemlock. and pine. There are about 30 species included by Bessette et al. (2000) in North America, but there is no technical monograph.

Edibility: None, except *T. chromapes,* of the species of *Tylopilus* is edible.

KEY TO THE SPECIES OF TYLOPILUS

1. Stipe with a distinct, reticulate network almost to the base --------------------- *T. felleus*
1. Stipe without reticulations or with a few just at the apex near the pores --------------- 2
  2. Stipe base yellow; context of base also yellow --------------------------- *T. chromapes*
  2. Stipe base never yellow-- 3
3. Flesh, when cut or bruised, greenish blue, finally turning black-brown -- *T. pseudoscaber*
3. Flesh not as above --- 4
  4. Flesh bruising pinkish buff, lilac to reddish-- 5
  4. Flesh unchanging when bruised --- 6
5. Pileus bright orange to orange-red; flesh bruising pinkish buff to lilac brown -- *T. ballouii*
5. Pileus dark gray to blackish gray; flesh bruising pink to reddish ---------------- *T. alboater*
  6. Stipe violaceus to violaceus brown; pileus brown, tinted violaceus to dark cinnamon --- *T. plumbeoviolaceus*
  6. Stipe brown or tinted vinaceous brown; pileus light brown to reddish brown --- *T. rubrobrunneus*

Tylopilus felleus (Bull.:Fr.) P. Karst
INEDIBLE

Pileus 8–30 cm broad, broadly convex, tan to crust-brown, nearly hairless, dry, but feels slimy in wet weather. Flesh soft, white, slightly pink where bruised. Tubes 10–20 mm deep, mouths small 1–2 per mm, often depressed at stipe, white at first, but soon deep pink. Stipe 4–15 cm long, 1.5–2.5 cm wide, enlarged below or sometimes bulbous, strongly reticulate, pale buff to pale brown, dry. Partial veil absent. Odor not distinctive. Taste very bitter.

Spores 9–15 x 3–5 μm long elliptic, smooth, entire, thick-walled, nonamyloid. Spore print pinkish brown to rose-brown. Cystidia numerous, fusiform, often with a pointed or narrow apex.

Habit and distribution: Single or scattered on or near rotten conifer stumps or buried wood. Found in eastern North America. Fruiting in summer and fall.

Comments: The closely related *Tylopilus plumbeoviolaceus* (Snell) Snell & E. A. Dick has a smooth stipe with netlike ridges only at the apex and violet coloration on the pileus and stipe, at least when young. *Tylopilus alboater* (Schwein.) Murrill is an eastern bolete growing under oak; has a black to grayish brown pileus; flesh that stains dingy pink to black; and a bluish purple to nearly black, partially reticulate stipe. This species is very bitter to most people but some are non-tasters and do not experience the bitterness.

Tylopilus chromapes (Frost) A.H. Sm. & Thiers
NONPOISONOUS

Pileus 5–15 cm broad, convex to broadly convex in age, pinkish brown to reddish brown, minutely fibrillose, dry, tacky in wet weather. Flesh firm white, lower one third of stipe bright yellow. Tubes 5–12 mm deep, mouths 2-3 per mm, depressed at stipe, white at first to buff or yellowish finally pinkish brown in age. Stipe 5–14 cm long, 1.0–2.5 cm wide, equal, white to buff and bright yellow over the base, surface with dense reddish brown scabers, dry. Partial veil absent. Odor none. Taste slightly bitter.

Spores 11–17 x 4.0–5.5 μm subfusiform (Fig. 5), smooth, entire, slightly thick-walled, nonamyloid. Spore print pinkish brown. Cystidia numerous, broadly clavate with a pointed to narrow apex.

Habit and distribution: Single to several under oaks, aspen, mixed hardwoods and conifers. Found in eastern North America. Fruiting in summer and fall.

Comments: Known also as *Boletus chromapes* Frost and *Leccinum chromapes* (Frost) Singer. The presence of the pinkish brown spore print is a character of *Tylopilus*, so it has now been placed in that genus. McIlvaine and Macadam (1973) report it to be an excellent edible. We have not tried it.

Tylopilus pseudoscaber (Secr.) A. H. Sm. & Thiers
EDIBILITY UNKNOWN

Pileus 6–15 cm broad, convex to nearly plane in age, dark olive-brown to dark red-brown, minutely fibrillose, dry. Flesh firm, white, when cut bruising or turning bright blue then darkening to black-brown. Tubes 9–16 mm deep, mouths 2-3 per mm, olive-gray, when bruised greenish blue, olive-brown in age. Stipe 5–12 cm long, 1–3 cm wide, equal or enlarging somewhat toward the base, olive-brown, often with obscure to distinct, longitudinal ridges, lighter just at the base, which slowly stains to blue on exposed to air, dry. Partial veil absent. Odor antiseptic-like. Taste bitter with an aftertaste.

Spores 10–18 x 5–7 µm elliptic, smooth, entire, slightly thick-walled, nonamyloid. Spore print reddish brown.

Habit and distribution: Single to several under conifers (spruce, fir, hemlock, pine, etc.) in northern North America. Fruiting in summer and early fall.

Comments: It is also known as *Porphyrellus pseudoscaber* (Secr.) Singer. We have collected it in Glacier National Park under hemlock and spruce. Compare it with *Tylopilus alboater,* which has a dark gray pileus; bruises pink to reddish; and has smaller spores.

Tylopilus ballouii (Peck) Singer
NONPOISONOUS

Pileus 5–12 cm broad, convex to broadly convex in age, bright orange to orange-red, fading in age to pale orange or light cinnamon-brown, dry. Flesh white, when bruised pinkish buff to lilac-brown. Tubes 4–10 mm deep, mouths 1-2 per mm, white, becoming brown to smoky-brown in age. Stipe 3–12 cm long, 0.7–2.5 cm wide, equal or slightly enlarged toward the base, partially reticulate just at apex, white tinted yellowish to dull orange, staining brown when bruised, dry. Partial veil none. Odor chlorinelike, unpleasant. Taste mild to slightly bitter.

Spores 5–11 x 3–5 µm elliptic, smooth, entire, slightly thick-walled, nonamyloid. Spore print cinnamon-buff to pale yellow. Cystidia, numerous, fusiform, some with a long narrow apex, thin-walled, hyaline.

Habit and distribution: Solitary to several under hardwood pine forests. Found in northeastern, southeastern to southern United States. Fruiting in summer and early fall.

Comments: We have found this in Texas, where it is often under pine but also oaks. It does not taste good, and is not edible (Metzler et al., 1992).

Tylopilus alboater (Schwein.) Murrill
NONPOISONOUS

Pileus 4–15 cm broad, convex to plane in age, dark gray to blackish gray, minutely granular, dry. Flesh firm, white tinted gray, bruising pink to reddish. Tubes 5–10 mm deep, mouths 2 per mm, white tinted light gray, soon light pink as the spores mature. Stipe 4–12 cm long, 2–4 cm wide, nearly equal or enlarging somewhat toward the base, pale gray to dark gray, bruising reddish changing to black, dry. Partial veil absent. Odor none. Taste mild.

Spores 7–11 x 3.5–5.0 μm ovoid to oblong (Fig. 4), smooth, entire, thin-walled, nonamyloid. Spore print pink to pinkish red. Cystidia oval with a long neck, thin-walled, hyaline.

Habit and distribution: Several to numerous under hardwoods especially oaks. Found in eastern North America. Fruiting in late summer and early fall.

Comments: Snell and Dick (1970) report it as "edible and good" and illustrate the reddish staining. Compare it with the dark olive-black *Tylopilus pseudoscaber*, which has pale grayish brown tubes and is more widely distributed.

Tylopilus plumbeoviolaceus (Snell & E. A. Dick) Singer
INEDIBLE

Pileus 5–16 cm broad, broadly convex to plane in age, brown tinted violaceous at first to drab or dark cinnamon in age, minutely fibrillose to glabrous, dry. Flesh firm, white, unchanging. Tubes 10–20 mm deep, mouths 1-2 per mm, white at first slowly pinkish to dark reddish, drab mature. Stipe 4–12 cm long, 1–4 cm wide, equal or enlarging somewhat toward the base, with a white bloom at first, violaceus to soon violaceous brown, white at the base, dry. Partial veil absent. Odor none. Taste very bitter.

Spores 10–15 x 3–5 µm fusiform, smooth, entire, slightly thick-walled, nonamyloid. Spore print vinaceous. Cystidia numerous, fusoid with a pointed tip, thin-walled.

Habit and distribution: Single, several to cespitose under oaks, hemlocks, or mixed hardwood conifer forests. Found in eastern North America. Fruiting in late summer to early fall.

Comments: For more information, see comments under *T. felleus*.

Tylopilus rubrobrunneus Mazzer & A.H. Sm.
INEDIBLE

Pileus 8–30 cm broad, broadly convex, plane in age, light brown, brown to reddish brown, dry. Flesh firm, white, unchanging. Tubes 10–20 mm deep, mouths 1–2 mm, dull white to light brown, becoming vinaceous brown in age or staining brown when bruised or handled. Stipe 8–20 cm long, 1–5 cm wide, equal or enlarging somewhat toward the base, brown or tinted vinaceous brown, white at the base, dry. Partial veil absent. Odor none. Taste very bitter.

Spores 10–15 x 3.0–4.5 µm oblong to subfusiform (Figs. 4–5), smooth, entire, slightly thick-walled, nonamyloid. Spore print wine-red. Cystidia numerous, clavate with a narrow apex, thin-walled.

Habit and distribution: Several to numerous under hardwoods especially oaks. Found in eastern North America. Fruiting in summer and early fall.

Comments: It is very common in Virginia and North Carolina, and the central Midwest, in the late summer. See also comments under *Boletus affinis. Austroboletus gracilis* (Peck) C. B. Wolfe is very similar, but has punctate spores.

BOLETUS AND ITS RELATIVES

There are 125 species of *Boletus* known in North America. The other five genera in this section include *Austroboletus, Chalciporus, Gasteroboletus, Pulveroboletus,* and *Strobilomyces.* They each have a small number of species. A description of each is provided under the general section for the Boletales (pages 351–53).

Edibility: Gastrointestinal irritants (Type 8 toxins) are present in a number of species of *Boletus.* Most of those have red tube mouths, bruise blue or both. Several species have low levels of muscarine (Type 2 toxins). These include *Boletus luridus, B. pulcherrimus, B. satanus,* and *B. calopus.* Others, including *Boletus bicolor, B. frostii, B. subvelutipes,* and *Tylopilus felleus,* are gastrointestinal irritants (Type 8 toxins) (Spoerke & Rumack, 1994). In addition, *Gastroboletus turbonatus* and other species are infrequently found and their edibility is unknown. *Chalciporus piperatus* contains Type 8 toxins, and other species of *Chalciporus* should be avoided until they are thoroughly tested.

In addition, *Strobilomyces* has edible species, along with *Austroboletus betula, Pulveroboletus ravenelii,* and *Boletellus russellii* are edible and good. However, most boletes are fleshy, provide a good quantity of food, and many have rather distinctive flavors. Those with a glutinous or slimy pileus are much better if the cuticle is removed. In some species the pores can be removed in older specimens, since they become slimy when cooked. However, the spores and pores have the nutrients in them, and they should be eaten with the rest of the fruiting body. We have always kept a supply of dried *Boletus edulis,* and enjoy it in many recipes.

KEY TO BOLETUS AND ITS RELATIVES

1. Pores bright red, orange-red to rusty red --- 2
1. Pores yellow, olive-yellow, gray to olive-brown-- 7
   2. Flesh not changing to blue when cut or bruised--- 3
   2. Flesh changing or bruising blue when cut --- 4
3. Flesh buff to pink near tubes; taste hot and peppery; stipe base
   bright yellow -- *Chalciporus piperatus*
3. Flesh bright yellow; taste mild; stipe base not bright yellow------ *Chalciporus rubinellus*
   (see comments under *Chalciporus piperatus*)
   4. Stipe bright red, lacerate-reticulate to the base; pileus bright red -- *Boletus frostii*
   4. Stipe not as above -- 5
5. Pileus olive-gray to buff-brown; pores deep blood-red; under or near oaks
   in California --- *Boletus satanus*
5. Not as above -- 6
   6. Pileus reddish brown to olive-brown; stipe with dark red reticulations;
      under western conifers --- *Boletus pulcherrimus*
      (see comments under *Boletus satanus*)
   6. Pileus deep maroon, bright red to orange-red; stipe with reticulations
      only on upper half or just at apex; under eastern hardwood and
      conifer forests --- *Boletus subvelutipes*
7. Pileus covered with downy, blackish brown to greyish black scales; stipe shaggy and
   colored like the pileus-- 8
7. Pileus not as above -- 9
   8. Pileus with downy, soft, blackish gray scales; spores 9–16 x 8–12 µm subglobose
      to globose, reticulate --- *Strobilomyces floccopus*
   8. Pileus with more grayish, erect, stiff, spinelike hairs; spores 10–12 x 9.5–10.5 µm
      globose, warted -- *Strobilomyces confusus*
      (see comments under *Strobilomyces floccopus*)
9. Flesh not staining blue when cut, handled or bruised ------------------------------------- 10
9. Flesh staining blue slowly or instantly when cut, handled or bruised -------------------- 19
   10. Stipe without reticulations or reticulate just at the apex ----------------------------- 11
   10. Stipe reticulate, upper half or completely to the base ------------------------------- 13
11. Fruiting body joined together with the "earth ball" Scleroderma; known from eastern
    North America --- *Boletus parasiticus*
11. Not as above-- 12
   12. Pileus viscid, bright golden-yellow; stipe bright yellow and viscid ---- *Boletus curtisii*

12. Pileus sticky when wet, olive-brown to yellowish brown; stipe white, streaked brown to reddish brown -- *Boletus affinis*

13. Stipe tall and thin, deeply reticulate; pileus relatively small; known from eastern North America -- 14

13. Stipe reticulate, not tall and thin; pileus not small in relation to the stipe; found in eastern and western North America -- 16

14. Pileus viscid, maroon-red to yellow-orange; stipe reticulate to the base, bright yellow; spores reticulate --- *Austroboletus betula*

14. Pileus dry, not as above -- 15

15. Pileus dry, scaly, yellow-brown; stipe with shaggy reticulations, yellow-brown; spores longitudinally ridged -- *Boletellus russellii*
(see comments under *Austroboletus betula*)

15. Pileus dry, gray-brown to yellow-brown; stipe with long, ornamented, reticulate ridges; spores smooth, thick-walled --- *Boletus projectellus*
(see comments under *Austroboletus betula*)

16. Pileus dry, orange-yellow to smoky gray; stipe bright orange-yellow, with raised, elongated reticulations; found in eastern North America ---------- *Boletus ornatipes*

16. Not as above --- 17

17. Pileus dry, densely wooly to hairy, red-brown to purple-red; flesh sulphur yellow; fruiting from well decayed conifer stumps and logs, under conifers; found in western North America--- *Boletus mirabilis*

17. Pileus dry to slight viscid in wet weather, glabrous; flesh white; more widely distributed-- 18

18. Pileus yellow-brown, cinnamon-brown to red-brown; stipe with fine, white reticulations nearly to the base -- *Boletus edulis*

18. Pileus cream colored with a pinkish hue; stipe with fine, white reticulations to the base; southwestern North America------------------------------------ *Boletus barrowsii*
(see comments under *Boletus edulis*)

19. Pileus bright yellow, covered with a yellow powder; stipe bright sulphur yellow; copious yellow partial veil -- *Pulveroboletus ravenelii*

19. Not as above-- 20

20. Stipe without reticulations or with reticulations just at apex ----------------------- 21

20. Stipe reticulate at least one-half or more --- 24

21. Tubes twisted and contorted, yellow to sometimes orange-red, bruises instantly dark blue; deep in duff under conifers in western North America ---- *Gastroboletus turbinatus*

21. Not as above-- 22

22. Pileus wooly, red to purple-red; pores bright yellow, instantly turning blue when bruised -- *Boletus bicolor complex*

22. Not as above --- 23

23. Pileus dark brown to blackish brown, dry, with a white bloom or powdered; known only from western North America-- *Boletus zelleri*

23. Pileus olive-brown to reddish brown, pink flesh shows in cracks; widely distributed --- *Boletus chrysenteron*

24. Pileus gray to pinkish buff, dry; stipe light gray; lightly reticulated over the upper half; under hardwoods; eastern North America ----------------------- *Boletus pallidus*

24. Not as above --- 25

25. Pileus robust (up to 25 cm broad), dry, brown to dark brown, bruising lilac; flesh yellow, instantly bruising blue; mostly under western conifers ---- *Boletus calopus* var *frustosus*

25. Not as above--- 26

26. Pileus dry, tomentose, olive-brown to yellow-brown; flesh white; stipe base cherry red; widely distributed -- *Boletus subtomentosus*

26. Pileus viscid in wet weather, red-brown to olive brown; flesh white to light pink or yellowish; stipe base not cherry red; central and eastern North America -- *Boletus badius*

Chalciporus piperatus (Bull.) Bat.
POISONOUS

Pileus 2–8 cm broad, convex, orange-brown to reddish brown, hairy or felted on margin, rest glabrous, viscid when wet. Flesh firm, buff, pink near tubes, not blue when cut or bruised. Tubes 3–8 mm deep in age, mouths angular 1-3 per mm, adnate or short decurrent, radial near stipe, cinnamon, deep red to rusty red. Stipe 2–8 cm long, 0.4–0.8 cm wide, thickest at apex, narrowing gradually toward base, yellowish to rusty brown, base bright yellow, felted to glabrous, dry. Partial veil absent. Odor none. Taste very hot and peppery.

Spores 7–10 x 3–4 µm short elliptic, smooth, entire, thick-walled, nonamyloid. Spore print cinnamon to brown.

Habit and distribution: Solitary to several, rarely numerous, under various conifers. Widely distributed. Fruiting in summer and fall.

Comments: Also known as *Boletus piperatus* Fr., it is much too bitter to serve as an edible. *Chalciporus rubinellus* (Peck) Singer (also known as *Boletus rubinellus* Peck) is very small, (pileus 2–5 cm broad); with bright red pores; bright yellow flesh; and a mild taste. We have collected this small species in Maryland and Virginia in hardwood-pine forests. This is so bitter that no one would eat it, and it does contain Type 8 toxins.

Boletus frostii A. W. Russell
NONPOISONOUS

Pileus 6–15 cm broad, convex to plane in age, entirely blood-red, smooth, viscid. Flesh firm yellowish, bruising blue. Tubes 7–10 mm deep, mouths round, 2-3 per mm, adnate or depressed at the stipe, deep red, exuding yellow drops when young, bruising dingy blue. Stipe 4–11 cm long, 1.0–3.0 cm wide, enlarging downward, blood-red with distinct, lacerate, reticulations overall, occasionally yellow just at base, dry. Partial veil absent. Odor sweet. Taste mild to somewhat acrid.

Spores 12–17 x 4–6 µm oblong-elliptic, smooth, entire, thick-walled, nonamyloid. Spore print yellow-brown.

Habit and distribution: Scattered to several in oak woods. Found in eastern North America. Fruiting in summer and early fall.

Comments: This is one of the distinctive species in a group of confusing red-tubed species that bruise blue. Although it is listed by some as edible, a thorough knowledge of the species that have red pores and stain blue is recommended before specific species are collected for the table.

Boletus satanus Lenz
POISONOUS

Pileus 6–25 cm broad, convex, robust, pale olive-gray to buffy brown or light olive-brown, minutely fibrillose, dry. Flesh very thick (2–5 cm), yellow tinted olive, bruising blue at once when young, more slowly in age. Tubes 10–20 mm deep, mouths small, 2 per mm or less, depressed at the stipe, reddish brown young to deep blood-red at maturity, blue when bruised. Stipe 6–12 cm long, 3.5–7 cm wide, conspicuously bulbous (up to 14 cm broad) and reticulate over the upper part, which is pink, rest concolorus with the pileus, dry. Partial veil absent. Odor none. Taste mild.

Spores 12–15 x 4–6 µm elliptic, smooth, entire, thick-walled, nonamyloid. Spore print olive-brown.

Habit and distribution: Single to gregarious, under or near oaks. Found along the California Coast, especially the Santa Cruz Peninsula (Thiers, 1975). Fruiting in the late fall and winter.

Comments: *Boletus pulcherrimus* Thiers & Halling (known also as *B. eastwoodiae* (Murrill) Sacc. & Trotter) is closely related; has a stipe that is strongly reticulate and red over the lower half; and the pileus is reddish brown to olive-brown with red tube mouths. It is found occasionally in conifer woods in western North America and reported from Canada by Schalkwijk-Barendsen (1991). *Boletus satanus* is also widely reported in Europe, where we have collected it. Both of these species have caused severe gastrointestinal upset and should be avoided (Type 8 toxins).

Boletus subvelutipes Peck
POISONOUS

Pileus 4.5–14.0 cm broad, convex, color variable, deep maroon, bright red, orange-red to dark fuscus brown, staining blue when handled or bruised, felty to minutely tomentose, dry, subviscid when wet. Flesh yellow but instantly deep blue when cut or bruised. Tubes 8–15 mm deep, mouths 2-3 per mm, depressed at stipe, yellow-orange young, soon deep red staining instantly blue when bruised or handled. Stipe 3.5–10.0 cm long, 1.2–2.7 cm wide, nearly equal, with reticulations over the upper surface or just at the apex, yellow at apex with orange and red below to dingy or bright red over the base, which has red hairs, blue where handled or cut. Partial veil absent. Odor none. Taste mild.

Spores 9.5–17.0 x 4–7 µm elliptic, smooth, entire, thick-walled, nonamyloid. Spore print olive-brown.

Habit and distribution: Several to gregarious under hardwoods especially oak or mixed hardwood/ pine and hemlock. Found in eastern United States. Fruiting in summer and fall.

Comments: *Boletus luridus* Schaeff., uncommon in North America, has red reticulations on the stipe and is found in eastern North America. *Boletus erythropus* (Fr.) Kromh. is associated with the western coastal oak forests; has a cinnamon to reddish brown pileus; deep red pores; a smooth orange-brown stipe and reddish brown below. It also stains blue quickly when cut or bruised; spores 13–16 x 4.5–5.5 µm. *Boletus amygdalinus* (Thiers) Thiers, also in the same habitats as *B. erythropus,* has a red pileus; a smooth, yellowish stipe only streaked with red fibrils; and wider spores 11–16 x 5.2–8 µm. For western red-pored boletes with reticulations on the stipe, see *Boletus satanus* and the comments under that species. There are reports of poisoning attributed to these species in North America. Boletes with red tube mouths that stain instantly blue apparently can contain either muscarine (Type 2 toxins) or cause severe gastrointestinal upset (Type 8 toxins). A safe bet is to avoid these boletes.

Strobilomyces floccopus (Vahl.:Fr.) P. Karst
EDIBLE

Pileus 4–15 cm broad, convex, covered with downy, blackish brown to gray-black scales, becoming coarse in age, with veil pieces hanging from margin, dry. Flesh white, staining red when bruised and finally black. Tubes 10–15 mm deep, with large angular mouths, 1-2 per mm, white then gray, when bruised staining red then black. Stipe 5–14 cm long, 0.5–2.0 cm wide, nearly equal, shaggy, same color as pileus. Partial veil white to gray, cottony. Odor none. Taste mild.

Spores 9–16 x 8–12 µm subglobose to globose (Figs. 1-2), strongly reticulate (Fig. 12), thick-walled, with an apical pore, nonamyloid. Spore print black. Cystidia numerous, oval with long narrowed tips, thin-walled.

Habit and distribution: Occurs alone or in small numbers, on the ground, or on well rotted wood under hardwoods or mixed hardwoods and conifers. Found in eastern North America and southwestern United States. Fruiting in summer and early fall.

Comments: Also known as *Strobilomyces strobilaceus* (Scop.:Fr.) Berk., the "Old Man of the Woods" is very distinctive, but its taste is not outstanding. It does not rot easily and may be found still standing in the fall and covered with a green mold. *Strobilomyces confusus* Singer is closely related, but has short elliptic to globose, warted spores, 10–12 x 9.5–10.5 µm, and acute, erect, spines on the pileus. It is found in eastern North America.

Boletus parasiticus Fr.
NONPOISONOUS

Cap 4–7 cm broad, convex, yellow-brown to olive in age. Flesh white, yellowish, does not bruise blue, felty, sometimes cracked, dry. Tubes 5–10 mm deep, mouths large, 1-2 per mm, short decurrent, yellow to olive in age. Stipe 2.5–10.0 cm long, 0.5–2.0 cm wide, equal, brownish yellow, glabrous. Partial veil absent. Odor none. Taste mild.

Spores 12–18 x 4.0–5.5 µm nearly elliptic, smooth, entire, thick-walled, nonamyloid. Spore print dark olive-brown.

Habit and distribution: One to three fruiting bodies next to each *Scleroderma citrinum* (a earthball), under hardwoods especially oak. Found in eastern North America. Fruiting in summer and early fall.

Comments: Also known as *Xerocomus parasiticus* (Bull.:Fr.) Quél., it actually is growing in close proximity to the *Scleroderma*, and they are both mycorrhizal with the host tree, which is often an oak. They are too rarely collected to be considered for the table, however the *Scleroderma* is poisonous. We have collected this species in Europe, as well as in North America.

Boletus curtisii Berk.
UNKNOWN

Pileus 3–9 cm broad convex to plane in age, often uneven, bright golden yellow, to yellowish brown in age, with a sterile, narrow band at the margin, glabrous, viscid. Flesh firm, white to cream, unchanging. Tubes adnate or slightly depressed at the stipe, 8–20 mm deep, 2-3 per mm, white, flesh colored to yellowish brown in age. Stipe 4–12 cm long, 0.6–1.5 cm wide, enlarging somewhat toward the base, white to buff at the apex, yellow to bright yellow below, white mycelium at the base, glabrous, viscid. Partial veil absent. Odor none. Taste mild.

Spores 10–15 x 4.3–6.5 µm long elliptic to subfusiform (Figs. 3 & 5), smooth, entire, thick-walled, nonamyloid. Spore print olive-brown to rusty brown.

Habit and distribution: Several to gregarious under hardwoods and conifers, usually pines. Found in eastern North America. Fruiting from late summer to late fall.

Comments: Also known as *Pulveroboletus curtisii* (Berk.) Singer, the viscid, bright yellow pileus and stipe is very distinctive for the genus *Boletus*. We have collected it in August in Virginia and late September in Texas. There is no information on its edibility.

Boletus affinis Peck
EDIBLE

Pileus 5–11 cm broad, convex, olive-brown to yellowish brown, glabrous, dry, sticky when wet. Flesh soft, white, slightly pinkish in stipe. Tubes 5–15 mm deep, mouths small, 2-3 per mm, depressed at stipe, white to dingy yellowish in age. Stipe 4–8 cm long, 1.0–2.5 cm wide, nearly equal or enlarged at apex, reticulate only at stipe apex, white, streaked brown to reddish brown. Partial veil absent. Odor none or slightly farinaceous. Taste mild or farinaceous.

Spores 10–16 x 3–4 µm elliptic, smooth, entire, thick-walled, nonamyloid. Spore print bright rusty-red.

Habit and distribution: Scattered to numerous under hardwoods. Found in eastern North America. Fruiting in summer and fall.

Comments: Also known as *Xanthoconium affinis* (Peck) Singer. *Boletus affinis* Peck var *maculosus* Peck has conspicuous white spots over the pileus surface. It is also distributed in eastern North America in similar habitats. Both are edible, but we have not eaten them. *Austroboletus gracilis* (Peck) Wolfe has a reddish brown pileus and pinkish pores, with a smooth reddish brown stipe. It is also found under hardwoods in eastern North America. The spores are similar in size, but pitted, not smooth.

Austroboletus betula (Schwein.) E. Horak
EDIBLE

Pileus 3–10 cm broad, convex, dark maroon-red to orange-red, or even yellow-orange, smooth, glabrous, viscid. Flesh orange-yellow, yellow sometimes tinted olive. Tubes 10–20 mm deep, mouths large, 1 or more per mm, depressed just at stipe, bright yellow becoming tinted olive then olive-brown. Stipe 10–27 cm long, 0.5–2.3 cm wide, equal, tall and thin, deeply reticulate, bright yellow, becoming reddish stained over the lower half in age, with white mycelium at the base. Partial veil absent. Odor none. Taste mild.

Spores 15–19 x 6–10 µm elliptic, with a loose reticulate surface, thick-walled with an apical pore, nonamyloid. Spore print brown.

Habit and distribution: Several to numerous under mixed hardwoods and pine. Found in southeastern and southern North America. Fruiting in late summer and fall.

Comments: Also known as *Boletellus betula* (Schwein.) Gilb. It is mycorrhizal with pines and probably oaks and beech as well. *Boletellus russellii* (Frost) Gilb. looks very similar, but has a dry, yellow-brown, scaly pileus; a long, thin stipe with coarse, shaggy reticulations; strongly longitudinally ridged spores (Fig. 13); and is distributed in the eastern and southwestern United States. *Boletus projectellus* Murrill has a grayish brown to yellow-brown pileus; a long, thin stipe with long, ornamented reticulate ridges; thick-walled, smooth, and longer elliptic spores (20–32 x 6–12 µm); and is under pine in eastern North America. The three species are all edible.

Boletus ornatipes Peck
INEDIBLE

Pileus 3–10 cm broad, convex to plane in age, orange-yellow, smoke-gray to brownish olive, margin with a narrow sterile band of tissue, smooth, felty, dry. Flesh firm, dull buff to yellowish tinted reddish under the pileipellis, not blue when bruised. Tubes 5–15 mm deep, 3–5 per mm, honey yellow, brownish olive, to dark brown in age. Stipe 6–12 cm long, 0.7–3.0 cm wide, slightly larger at the base, bright yellow to orange-yellow with coarse, raised, elongate reticulations usually extending to the stipe base, staining dark orange-yellow when bruised, dry. Partial veil absent. Odor mild, fungoid. Taste usually bitter.

Spores 9–13 x 3–5 µm subfusiform (Fig. 5), smooth, entire, thick-walled, nonamyloid. Spore print olive-brown.

Habit and distribution: Single to several under hardwoods, especially oak. Found in eastern North America. Fruiting in late summer and fall.

Comments: Typical specimens we have examined from Virginia and North Carolina, have no yellow powder on the pileus as described for *Boletus retipes* Berk. & M. A.Curtis (also known as *Pulveroboletus retipes* (Berk. & M. A. Curtis) Singer). We consider *B. ornatipes* to be a distinct species.

Boletus mirabilis Murrill
EDIBLE

Pileus 5–16 cm broad, robust, convex, dark red-brown to purple-red, margin with a white flap of tissue when young, densely wooly to hairy, dry. Flesh firm, lemon-yellow, not staining blue but sometimes reddish when bruised. Tubes 10–30 mm deep, mouths angular, 0.5–1.0 per mm, depressed just at stipe, bright sulphur-yellow, mustard-yellow in age. Stipe 12–22 cm long, 2–8 cm wide, club-shaped to bulbous, widest near base, variable, large, dark red-brown with white reticulations that darken in age over apex or entire surface in some, whitish just at base. Partial veil very reduced, forming a white flap of marginal pileus tissue. Odor none. Taste mild and pleasant.

Spores 14–24 x C.5 9.0 µm nearly elliptic, smooth, entire, thick-walled, nonamyloid. Spore print olive-brown.

Habit and distribution: Single to several often fruiting from well decayed conifer logs and stumps (especially on western hemlock). Found in western North America. Fruiting in summer and fall.

Comments: This is a very distinctive bolete, but never found in abundance and commonly associated with old-growth trees. However, it is rated as a choice edible species. We have not eaten it.

Boletus edulis Bull.:Fr.
EDIBLE

Pileus 8–37 cm broad, broadly convex, yellow-brown, cinnamon-brown to red-brown, glabrous but often uneven, dry, moist to slippery feeling or slightly viscid in wet weather. Flesh firm, white, sometimes reddish just under the pileus, unchanging when bruised. Tubes 10–40 mm deep, mouths small, 2-3 per mm, depressed just at stipe, white at first, slowly yellow, yellowish olive to olive-brown in age. Stipe 10–25 cm long, 2–6 cm wide, equal or an enlarged bulbous base, whitish to yellow or yellow-brown, with fine, white, reticulations overall or nearly to the base, see inset photo, dry. Partial veil absent. Odor none. Taste mild and pleasant.

Spores 12–21 x 4–6 µm nearly elliptic, smooth, entire, thick-walled, nonamyloid. Spore print olive-brown.

Habit and distribution: Solitary to gregarious under conifers, mixed conifer-hardwoods, or hardwoods. Widely distributed. Fruiting from spring, summer, and fall.

Comments: Perhaps one of the most sought after edible mushrooms, it is called the "Penny Bun" in England, "Cepe" in France, "Steinpilz" in Germany, and "Porcini" in Italy. The shape of the stipe and color of the pileus vary a great deal throughout North America. In general, populations in western North America form a bulbous stipe. The equal or club-shaped stipe is most often encountered in eastern North America. A form with a very brown or even light brown pileus is often seen in the Rocky Mountains. Regardless of shape and color there is no blue staining of any tissue and the tubes and reticulations are white at first. It is mycorrhizal with both hardwoods and conifers, but in North America more commonly with conifers. We have collected it in Italy under chestnut. A very similar species, *Boletus barrowsii* A.H.Sm., has a cream-colored pileus with a pinkish hue. It is most common under conifers in the southern part of western North America. We have collected it in Idaho on one occasion. *Boletus variipes* Peck also has a dry, cream-colored tinted yellowish pileus, an equal, light grayish brown, reticulate stipe but is associated with hardwoods or mixed hardwood/conifer stands in eastern North America. *Boletus nobilis* Peck is a robust eastern North American species with a reddish brown pileus; light reticulations over the upper stipe; and is found under or near oaks. These closely related species are edible and fully described and illustrated by Snell & Dick (1970) and Bessette et al. (2000).

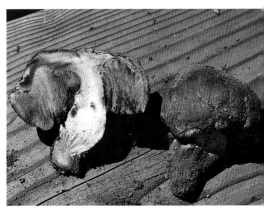

Pulveroboletus ravenelii (Berk. & M. A. Curtis) Murrill
EDIBLE

Pileus 3–12 cm broad, convex, nearly plane in age, covered with a yellow powder at first, dry, soon bright yellow, appressed fibrillose becoming orange-red and subviscid when moist. Flesh firm white to buff or yellowish, slowly staining blue when cut or bruised. Tubes 4–12 mm deep, 2–4 per mm, depressed at stipe, yellow at first, yellow-gray to yellow-brown in age, greenish blue fading to dingy brown when bruised. Stipe 4–14 cm long, 0.4–1.5 cm wide, narrowing toward the base, bright sulphur-yellow, with minute fibrils, white mycelium at the base, viscid to dry in age. Partial veil copious, membranous and powdery, leaving an appressed fibrillose annular zone, often gone in age. Odor pleasant. Taste mild but soon unpleasant.

Spores 8–11 x 4–5 µm subfusiform (Fig. 5), smooth, entire, thick-walled, nonamyloid. Spore print olive-brown.

Habit and distribution: Single to several under mixed conifers and hardwoods including oak as well as pine. Found in eastern North America, and under oak and manzanita along the California Coast. Fruiting summer, fall, and during the winter, rainy season on the West Coast.

Comments: Also known as *Boletus ravenelii* Berk. & M.A. Curtis. There is no information on the quality of this fungus as an edible. We have collected it under pine in Belize.

Gastroboletus turbinatus (Snell) A. H. Sm. & Singer
EDIBILITY UNKNOWN

Pileus 2–8 cm broad, convex, blackish brown, golden brown to red with orange tints, felty, dry. Flesh firm, yellow to pinkish, blue when cut or bruised. Tubes 10–20 mm deep, mouths round when visible, up to 1 per mm, twisted and contorted, yellow to orange-red in some, instantly blue when bruised. Stipe 1–7 cm long, 0.8–2.0 cm thick, short, marbled yellow, orange-yellow to red, bruising blue, dry. Partial veil absent. Odor not distinctive. Taste mild.

Spores 10–18 x 5.5–9.5 µm elliptic, smooth, entire, thick-walled, nonamyloid. No spore deposit since spores are not discharged.

Habit and distribution: Scattered under western conifers (often hemlock and fir), often deep in the duff with only the pileus showing. Found in western North America, rare elsewhere. Fruiting in summer and fall.

Comments: This is one of 10 known species in the genus *Gastroboletus*. Bessette et al. (2000) describes and illustrates 6 species, but the one described here is the most frequently encountered.

Boletus bicolor Peck
EDIBLE

Pileus 4.5–16.0 cm broad, convex to plane in age, red to purple-red sometimes stained yellow, glabrous to finely wooly, dry, perhaps sticky in wet weather. Flesh yellow, often red near the stipe base, staining slowly blue when bruised but fading again to yellow. Tubes 5–14 mm deep, mouths seldom up to 1–2 per mm, usually adnate, bright yellow to olive in age, bruising blue. Stipe 4–15 cm long, 1.0–3.5 cm wide, nearly equal, even, deep red, slowly bruising blue, apex yellow, glabrous, if reticulate only at the apex. Partial veil absent. Odor radish-like. Taste mild.

Spores 8.5–12.0 x 3.5–4.5 µm narrowly elliptic, smooth, entire, thick-walled, nonamyloid. Spore print olive-brown.

Habit and distribution: Single or several under hardwood (especially oaks). Found in eastern North America. Fruiting in summer and early fall.

Comments: There are a number of species with nonreticulate stipes that exhibit blue staining when bruised. *Boletus miniato-olivaceus* Frost has a more yellow pileus often with olive tints; a yellow non-reticulate, smooth stipe with red stains; and a much faster change to blue when bruised. It is also considered poisonous (see Type 8 toxins) and should be avoided. A small species, *B. fraternus* Peck, is often found in similar habitats; and has yellow pores; stains blue; but has larger spores 12–15 x 4.5–7.0 µm. *Boletus pulverulentus* Opat. has yellow flesh that stains blue instantly, and a stipe with raised longitudinal ridges. *Boletus speciosus* Frost is similar; has a reticulate mostly yellow stipe; and is also edible. For other species with yellow pores that stain blue, see Bessette et al. (2000) and Snell & Dick (1970). It is easy to get confused and misidentify species which are not edible. We strongly recommend consulting an expert if in doubt about the identity of a species in this group.

Boletus zelleri (Murrill) Murrill
EDIBLE

Pileus 4–12 cm broad, convex to plane in age, deep brown, blackish brown to dark chestnut-brown, finely powdered at first, dry. Flesh firm, buff to yellow, slowly changes to blue when bruised or not at all. Tubes 5–15 mm deep, mouths large, 1–2 per mm, depressed at stipe, yellow, olive-yellow in age. Stipe 5–10 cm long, 1–3 cm wide, equal, red to brownish red, may be yellow just at base, glabrous, dry. Partial veil absent. Odor none. Taste mild.

Spores 9–15 x 4–6 µm elliptic, smooth, entire, thick-walled, nonamyloid. Spore print olive-brown.

Habit and distribution: Several to gregarious under western conifers. Found in western North America. Fruiting in late summer and fall.

Comments: Also known as *Xerocomus zelleri* (Murrill) Snell. *Boletus chrysenteron* (Bull.) Fr. is similar, but the brown pileus develops cracks which expose the reddish tissue beneath. Both are mycorrhizal with conifers and common. They are both edible.

Boletus chrysenteron Fr.
EDIBLE

Pileus 3–11 cm broad, convex to plane in age, finely cracked to deeply cracked or rimose in age, olive-brown to red just along margin with pink flesh showing in the cracks, wooly, dry. Flesh white to stained red near the cuticle of pileus and stipe base, slowly blue or blue-green when bruised. Tubes 4–8 mm deep, mouths angular, 1–2 per mm, adnate or short decurrent, pale yellow, yellow-brown, bruising greenish blue. Stipe 3–9 cm long, 1.5–2.4 cm wide, nearly equal, often curved, dull yellow sometimes with red streaks and red over the base, sometimes blue when bruised or handled, not reticulate, dry. Partial veil absent. Odor none. Taste mild.

Spores 9–15 x 4–5 µm nearly elliptic, smooth, entire, thick walled, nonamyloid. Spore print olive-brown.

Habit and distribution: Single to several or gregarious under hardwoods or conifers, especially grand fir in Idaho. Widely distributed. Fruiting in spring, summer, and fall.

Comments: Also known as *Xerocomus chrysenteron* (Bull.: St.Amans) Quél. Compare this species with *B. subtomentosus* Fr. and see comments under *B. zelleri*. It is edible but not choice.

Boletus pallidus Frost
NONPOISONOUS

Pileus 5–15 cm broad, convex, smooth, gray, buffy gray to pinkish buff. Flesh white, yellow near the tubes, light blue when bruised in some, felty, dry. Tubes 8–15 mm deep, mouths angular 0.5-2 per mm, adnate or depressed at stipe, white, olive-gray to olive-buff in age, staining blue when bruised. Stipe 5–15 cm long, 0.7–2.5 cm wide, enlarged slightly toward base, white to light grayish brown in age, lightly reticulate over upper half, dry. Partial veil absent. Odor none. Taste faintly bitter.

Spores 9–12 x 3.5–5.0 µm subfusiform to elliptic (Fig. 5 & 3), smooth, entire, thick-walled, nonamyloid. Spore print olive-brown.

Habit and distribution: Single to several under hardwoods especially oak. Found in eastern North America. Fruiting in summer and fall.

Comments: It is probably mycorrhizal with oak and extends throughout the range of oaks in eastern North America. It is bitter in taste, and not usually collected for the table.

Boletus calopus var frustosus (Snell & E. A. Dick) O. K. Mill. & Watling
POISONOUS

Pileus 5–25 cm broad, convex, robust, brown to dark brown, finely cracked in age, bruising blue, dry. Flesh firm, pale yellow, bruising instantly blue. Tubes 5–20 mm deep, mouths small, 2–3 per mm, round, depressed at stipe, pores yellow, lemon-yellow with a greenish cast, instantly bruising blue when bruised. Stipe 5–9 cm long, 3.5–8 cm wide, robust, nearly equal or swollen in center, reticulate at maturity, straw-yellow with red stains at the base. Partial veil absent. Odor none. Taste bitter.

Spores 10–16 x 4–5 µm nearly elliptic, smooth, entire, thick-walled, nonamyloid. Spore print ochre-brown. Septa in pileus trama have unique, amyloid cross-walls.

Habit and distribution: Single or several under conifers, especially western hemlock, grand fir, and Douglas fir. Found in western North America and rarely northeastern North America. Fruiting in summer and fall.

Comments: Smith and Thiers (1971) were unable to find a correctly identified specimen from the Great Lake states. One small button that we examined from Maine has the typical amyloid septa. Pomerleau (1980) does not list it from Quebec. We conclude that it is very rare in eastern North America. In Europe, it is listed as causing severe illness, Type 8 toxins. *Boletus smithii* Thiers is a similar western bolete under conifers but the upper stipe is red; the flesh stains blue slowly or erratically; and it is mild tasting.

Boletus subtomentosus Linne
EDIBLE

Pileus 4–15 cm broad, convex to broadly convex in age, olive-brown to yellow-brown becoming cracked in age, minutely tomentose, dry. Flesh firm, white, except stipe base, which is cherry-red, bluing when bruised. Tubes 10–25 mm deep, mouths 6–20 per mm when mature, mustard-yellow, bruising blue. Stipe 4.5–10.0 cm long, 0.8–2.5 cm wide, equal or tapering toward the base, yellowish with orange-brown stains over the top half, with a broken reticulum over the apex. Partial veil absent. Odor none. Taste mild.

Spores 10–15 x 3.5–5.0 µm subfusiform, smooth, entire, thick-walled, nonamyloid. Spore print olive-brown.

Habit and distribution: Single to several hardwood and conifer forests. Widely distributed. Fruiting from early summer to late fall.

Comments: Known also as *Xerocomus subtomentosus* (Linne) Quél. It is closely related to *Boletus spadiceus* Fr., which has a more reddish brown pileus. Both stain reddish brown when a drop of NH_2OH is applied, but *B. spadiceus* becomes quickly and fleetingly green first. They are both edible, but we have not eaten them.

Boletus badius Fr.
EDIBLE

Pileus 3.5–11.0 cm broad, convex to plane at maturity, minutely, red-brown, dark brown to olive-brown, felty, viscid in wet weather. Flesh white to light pink or yellowish, sometimes bruising light blue near the tubes. Tubes 7–15 mm deep, mouths 0.5-1 per mm, adnate or somewhat depressed at stipe, light greenish yellow, dull blue-green when bruised. Stipe 4–10 cm long,0.8–2.5 cm wide, equal or enlarged toward base, reddish brown over a yellow ground color dry, reticulate and whitish just at apex, below finely powdered. Partial veil absent. Odor none. Taste mild.

Spores 10–14 x 3.5–5.0 µm narrowly elliptic, smooth, entire, thick-walled, nonamyloid. Spore print olive to olive-brown.

Habit and distribution: Single to scattered, often growing in rotten wood under conifers, and mixed hardwoods and conifers. Found in central and eastern North America. Fruiting in summer and fall.

Comments: Also known as *Xerocomus badius* (Fr.) Kühner:Gilb. It is reported as edible.

THE FUNGI WITH SPINES

The fungi included in this section are not related, but included here because the hymenium is composed of spines or teeth. The *Hydnaceae* have a pileus and stipe, but in place of either lamellae or tubes under the pileus, the hymenium is composed of fine spines. The spores are smooth or warted with fine spines (Fig. 9). They are found on the ground, usually near or under their hosts. Unlike the other fungi with spines, they are mycorrhizal associates of conifers and hardwoods. The other species in this section are decomposers of wood and pine cones. Their fruiting bodies are found on logs, stumps, dead snags, or living trees.

Edibility: There are some very good edible species described here, including *Hydnum repandum* and *Hydnum albidum,* and several species of *Hericium.* However, most species are too woody to eat or are so bitter they would be rejected at once. There are no toxins reported.

KEY TO THE FUNGI WITH SPINES

1. Fruiting body with a pileus; spines beneath the pileus; a stipe, usually centrally located; growing on the ground--- *Hydnaceae*
1. Fruiting body not as above; growing on wood or cones------------------------------------- 2
   2. Fruiting body small; growing from pine, fir, Douglas fir, or spruce cones; erect, tough, brown stipe clothed in brown hairs; pileus lateral to eccentric, dark brown-- *Auriscalpium vulgare*
   2. Not as above; not on cones --- 3
3. Fruiting body a single, white, fleshy mass, with long, pendant spines up to 3.5 cm long; on hardwood tree trunks -- *Hericium erinaceus*
3. Not as above --- 4
   4. Fruiting body highly branched, white with sharp, pendant, delicate spines; attached to wood --- 5
   4. Not as above-- 6
5. Branches delicate, with spines that arise in tufts at the branch tips --- *Hericium americanum*

5. Branches delicate, with spines growing along the branches but not at
   the tips --- *Hericium coralloides*
   (see comments under *Hericium americanum*)

   6. Fruiting body a black-brown, woody conk, with a rusty-red context; spines stout,
   gray, with blunt ends; growing directly from the living conifer host; found in western North America -- *Echinodontium tinctorium*

   6. Not as above; in eastern North America --- 7

7. Fruiting body a single, large cluster up to 50–80 cm long, 10–30 cm wide; on living
   hardwoods, especially sugar maple ------------------------------ *Climacodon septentrionale*

7. Fruiting body single to several, 2–8 cm broad, concentrically zoned; with or without a
   stipe; on hardwood limbs, logs, and stumps ------------------------ *Mycorraphium adustum*

HYDNACEAE

The fruiting bodies consist of a pileus; spinose hymenium beneath; and a stipe. The species grow from soil or on very well-decayed wood, on the ground. The spores are nonamyloid, subglobose to short ellip- tic, smooth to warted or with fine spines from the warts (Figs. 2, 3, 9, 10). Spore prints are white to brown. The species in the Hydnaceae are mycorrhizal associates with various species of hardwoods and conifers throughout North America (Harrison, 1961; Baird, 1986).

Edibility: *Hydnum repandum* and *Hydnum albidum* are choice edible species. Both have soft tissue and smooth, white spores. *Sarcodon imbricatus* is edible after cooking, but far less desirable. It has warted spores and a brown spore print. Species in *Hydnellum* and *Phellodon* have tough flesh and are not edible. Other species are bitter or have no taste.

KEY TO THE HYDNACEAE

1. Fruiting body of soft flesh; easily broken --- 2

1. Fruiting body of tough flesh, very hard to cut or break -------------------------------------- 6

   2. Pileus smooth, glabrous, bright orange, orange-buff to white; spores subglobose,
   smooth, spore print white -- 3

   2. Pileus with raised or flattened scales, light to dark brown or light yellow-brown;
   found with matted needles and embedded debris ------------------------------------ 4

3. Pileus orange to orange-buff -- *Hydnum repandum*

3. Pileus white to cream color --- *Hydnum albidum*

    4. Pileus with raised or flattened scales, brown to red-brown; spores strongly warted; spore print brown -- 5

    4. Pileus light yellow-brown to reddish brown, embedded with matted needles and/or debris; spore print white --- *Bankera fuligineo-alba*

5. Pileus with brown, raised scales -- *Sarcodon imbricatus*

5. Pileus with reddish brown, appressed scales --------------------------- *Sarcodon scabrosus*

                       (see comments under *S. imbricatus*)

    6. Flesh tough, two-layered, lower layer black; spore print white --- *Phellodon niger* var *alboniger*

    6. Flesh tough, with light and dark brown zoned; spore print brown -------- *Hydnellum*

Hydnum repandum L.:Fr.
EDIBLE

Pileus 3–10 cm broad, convex, broadly convex in age, buff to orange or faded orange, margin wavy, glabrous, dry. Flesh thick, soft, brittle, light yellowish. Spines 4–8 mm long, various lengths intermixed, cream color. Stipe 2–8 cm long, 0.6–2.0 cm wide, equal or enlarged at base, white, sometimes with pale orange or buff tinges, solid, glabrous, dry. Odor none. Taste delicious.

Spores 6.5–9.0 x 6.5–8.0 μm subglobose (Fig. 2), smooth, entire, thin-walled, nonamyloid. Spore print white.

Habit and distribution: Solitary to numerous, under hardwoods or conifers. Widely distributed. Fruiting in summer and fall.

Comments: Also known as *Dentinum repandum* Fr., it is edible and delicious. *Hydnum umbilicatum* Peck is a small species, with a darker pileus, and is usually found in swamps and bogs. We have collected it in lodgepole pine bogs near Juneau, Alaska. It is also edible.

Hydnum albidum Peck
EDIBLE

Pileus 1–7 cm broad, convex, soon plane, white to creamy, felty, dry. Flesh soft, white, light orange when cut or bruised. Spines 4–7 mm long, white, decurrent. Stipe 2–5 cm long, 0.8–2.0 cm wide, white, glabrous. Odor none. Taste mild.

Spores 4.0–5.5 x 3.5–4.0 μm ovoid, smooth, entire, thin-walled, nonamyloid. Spore print white.

Habit and distribution: Single to several under conifer and hardwood forests. Widely distributed. Fruiting in summer and fall.

Comments: We have collected this species the same day we also collected *Hydnum repandum*, and they are equally good to eat.

Bankera fuligineo-alba (J. C. Schmidt:Fr.)
Pouzar
INEDIBLE

Pileus 4–15 cm broad, convex to plane in age, sometimes depressed in center, light yellow-brown to dark or reddish brown, surface often covered and incorporated with matted needles and organic debris, dry. Flesh soft and brittle, light reddish brown to dark brown when bruised. Spines 4–5 mm long, crowded, white at first gray to light brown or cinnamon-brown in age. Stipe 2–5 cm long, 1–2 cm wide, equal, white at apex, rest dull reddish brown, dry. Odor slight or of fenugreek or curry. Taste mild.

Spores 3.5–5.5 x 3.0–3.6 µm subglobose to short elliptic (Figs. 2 & 3), smooth, entire, thin-walled, nonamyloid, with minute spines. Spore print white.

Habit and distribution: Several, rarely more, under pines. Widely distributed, but not common. Fruiting in summer and fall.

Comments: Both *Bankera* and *Phellodon* have white spores with fine spines. However, the tissue in *Phellodon* is tough, while the flesh in *Bankera* is soft and easily breakable. We don't consider the species in these genera edible.

Sarcodon imbricatus (L.:Fr.) P. Karst.
EDIBLE

Pileus 8–30 cm broad, convex with a depressed center, covered with coarse, raised, brown scales, dry. Flesh easily breaking but not soft, white to very light brown, does not turn black in 3% KOH solution. Spines decurrent, 5–15 mm long, brown. Stipe 4–10 cm long, 1.5–3.0 cm wide, enlarging toward base, light brown, smooth, dry. Odor none. Taste somewhat bitter.

Spores 6–8 x 5–7 µm subglobose, strongly warted (Figs. 2 & 9), entire, thick-walled, nonamyloid. Spore print brown.

Habit and distribution: Single to several, under conifer or mixed conifer/hardwood forests. Widely distributed. Fruiting in summer and fall.

Comments: Known also as *Hydnum imbricatum* L.:Fr. The largest specimens we have collected have been found in Alaska. *Sarcodon scabrosus* (Fr.) P. Karst. is similar, but the pileus scales are appressed and not raised, and it has more red coloration; the stipe base is bluish to black. It is very bitter and the flesh blackens in 3% KOH solution (Baird, 1986). Reported as edible, but we have not tried it.

Phellodon niger (Fr.) P. Karst. **var alboniger** Peck
INEDIBLE

Pileus 2.5–8.5 cm broad, tomentose, whitish gray to brownish gray, sometimes margin lightly tinted orange or blue, dry. Flesh tough, two layers, top layer white to orange-gray, lower layer black, Spines 2.0–3.5 mm long, dull white to light gray, dark brown at maturity. Stipe 4–7 cm long, 1.0–2.0 cm wide, glabrous over apex, tomentose below, white mycelium surrounds the base. Odor none. Taste mild.

Spores 4.0–4.7 x 3.8–4.2 µm subglobose, with fine spines (Figs. 2 & 10), entire, thin-walled. Spore print white.

Habit and distribution: Several to numerous, under hardwood and conifer forests. Found in eastern North America, rare elsewhere. Fruiting in the late summer and fall.

Comments: It is important to obtain a spore print, since *Phellodon* is white spored and *Hydnellum,* also with tough flesh, is brown spored. *Phellodon melaleucus* (Fr.) P. Karst. has a dark brown pileus and a very thin stipe (0.3–1.0 cm wide). It is under conifers in northern North America (Harrison, 1961).

403

HYDNELLUM

There are about 30 species in the genus *Hydnellum* in North America. They grow on the ground; are solitary to several, and sometimes are joined together or with embedded needles and debris. They form ecto-mycorrhizae with both hardwoods and conifers. The flesh is woody, tough, often zoned, and usually light to dark brown. Spores are subglobose to short elliptic, warted (Figs. 2 & 9) , with a brown spore print. They are found under hardwoods, conifers, or mixed forests and are widely distributed.

Edibility: They are all tough, woody, and/or bitter. They are not edible.

KEY TO HYDNELLUM

1. Stipe indigo-blue to bluish black; odor penetrating, aromatic, of wintergreen; taste mild-- *Hydnellum suaveolens*
1. Not as above ------------- --- 2
    2. Pileus exudes blood-red droplets over a white to cream-color surface ------------- 3
    2. Pileus not as above--- 4
3. Odor sweetish, pungent -- *Hydnellum diabolus*
3. Odor not noticeable or not as above --- *Hydnellum peckii*
                                      (see comments under *H. diabolus*)
    4. Pileus blue at first, tinted blue in age and brown in center; odor heavy, unpleasant, aniselike --- *Hydnellum caeruleum*
    4. Not as above--- 5
5. Stipe dingy orange-brown, felty, firm, and tough; found under conifers, especially pine--- *Hydnellum aurantiacum*
5. Stipe dark brown, fibrillose, swollen and spongy feeling; found under hardwoods in eastern North America --- *Hydnellum spongiosipes*
                             (see comments under *H. aurantiacum*)

Hydnellum suaveolens (Scop.:Fr.) P. Karst.
INEDIBLE

Pileus 5–14 cm broad, convex to plane in age, white to gray or dingy brown in age, tomentose, dry. Flesh tough, zoned brown or brown tinted blue to bluish black. Spines up to 6 mm long, decurrent, crowded, light to dark brown. Stipe 1–5 cm long, 1–2 cm wide, strikingly indigo blue to grayish blue, smooth, dry. Odor very penetrating aromatic, of wintergreen. Taste mild.

Spores 4–5 x 3–4 µm irregular, angular, warted, entire, thick-walled, nonamyloid. Spore print brown.

Habit and distribution: Several to numerous under conifers, especially spruce and hemlock. Widely distributed. Fruiting in summer and fall.

Comments: We have had to remove specimens from the working area because of the penetrating odor of this species. It appears to be mycorrhizal with hemlock and spruce.

Hydnellum diabolus Banker
INEDIBLE

Pileus 2–15 cm broad, white soon reddish to grayish brown, exuding red drops on the surface when young, minutely hairy, dry. Flesh tough, lightly zonate, light to dark brown. Spines 3–8 mm long, white at first to brown in age. Stipe 6–8 cm long, 1.5–3.0 cm wide, white to dingy brown, white mycelium at the base, felty, dry. Odor sweetish, pungent. Taste acrid, sometime slowly.

Spores 4.5–5.5 x 3.5–4.5 µm subglobose, warted (Figs. 2 & 9), entire, thick-walled, nonamyloid. Spore print brown.

Habit and distribution: Single or several, under conifers especially pines. Widely distributed. Fruiting in summer and fall.

Comments: *Hydnellum peckii* Banker is very similar, also has the red drops on the pileus but does not have the sweetish pungent odor.

Hydnellum caeruleum (Hornem.:Pers.) P. Karst.
INEDIBLE

Pileus 3–11 cm broad, broadly convex, sometimes slightly depressed, white, tinted blue or blue at the margin when young, fading to light brown in center, brown in age, surface dry, pitted and irregular. Flesh tough, zoned at first white with blue bands, soon darkening with orange-brown in the stipe. Spines 3–5 mm long, decurrent, light bluish gray becoming dark brown in age. Stipe 1–4 cm long, 0.8–2.0 cm wide, smooth, orange-brown to dark brown, often with much clinging debris. Odor heavy and unpleasant, aniselike. Taste mild but slightly unpleasant.

Spores 4.5–6.0 x 4.5–5.5 µm subglobose, irregularly warted (Figs. 2 & 9), entire, thick-walled, nonamyloid. Spore print brown.

Habit and distribution: Several, under conifers, especially pine. Widely distributed. Fruiting in late summer and fall.

Comments: The color plate shows the blue pileus pigment in the young fruiting bodies of *H. caeruleum*.

Hydnellum aurantiacum (Batsch:Fr.) P. Karst.
INEDIBLE

Pileus 5–15 cm broad, plane to depressed in age, white but soon orange to brown, uneven with knobs and lumps, blackens when bruised, surface velvety, dry. Flesh tough and fibrous, zoned, dull brown. Spines 3–4 mm long, fine, brown, with light tips. Stipe 1.5–5.0 cm long, 0.8–2.0 cm wide, equal, dingy orange-brown, felty. Odor disagreeable. Taste mild or slightly unpleasant.

Spores 5.5–7.5 x 5–6 µm subglobose, strongly warted (Figs. 2 & 9), entire, thick-walled, nonamyloid. Spore print brown.

Habit and distribution: Single to several under conifers. Widely distributed. Fruiting in summer and fall.

Comments: This species is a common mycorrhizal partner with conifers especially hemlock and pine. The tough tissue and unpleasant taste make this an inedible species. *Hydnellum spongiosipes* (Peck) Pouzar is similar, but has a dark reddish brown, fibrillose stipe, which is spongy feeling and swollen as the name suggests. It is found in eastern North America under hardwoods.

Auriscalpium vulgare Gray
INEDIBLE

Pileus 0.5–2.0 cm diameter, broadly convex to plane, eccentric, covered with dense, dark brown hairs, dry. Flesh firm, light brown. Spines very fine, needlelike, dense, light brown. Stipe 1.5–8.0 cm long, 0.1–0.2 cm wide, ridged, attached at one side, clothed in dark brown hairs. Odor none. Taste unknown, too tough.

Spores 5–6 x 4–5 µm subglobose, with minute, amyloid spines (Figs. 2 & 10), entire, thin-walled. Spore print white.

Habit and distribution: Single, several or in cespitose clusters, on pine cones, occasionally on spruce, Douglas fir, and fir cones. Widely distributed. Fruiting in summer and fall.

Comments: This diminutive fungus is often called the "Pine Cone Fungus," and is too small and tough to be considered as an edible. It is a decomposer of conifer cones.

Hericium erinaceus (Bull.) Pers.
EDIBLE

Fruiting body 5–41 cm broad, 5–24 cm wide, oval, solid, white, dingy yellowish in age, with long white spines up to 3.5 cm long, crowded below, attached to the substrate by a solid white cord. Flesh firm, somewhat spongy, white. Odor fungoid. Taste mild and pleasant.

Spores 5.0–6.5 x 4.0–5.5 µm subglobose (Fig. 2), smooth, entire, thin-walled, amyloid. Spore print white. Trama with thick-walled, amyloid cells.

Habit and distribution: Single, from wounds on hardwood tree trunks, often high up. Widely distributed. Fruiting in late summer and fall.

Comments: This is a very good edible species which we have often enjoyed in different recipes. *Hericium erinaceus* ssp *erinaceo-abietus* Burds., O. K. Mill. & Nakasone is similar in growth form, but has small, very short, white spines. It is frequently found in southern and central southern United States. It fruits on decaying hardwood logs, limbs and stumps (Sundberg & Richardson, 1980). *Hericium abietis* (Weir:Hubert) K. A. Harrison is very similar when young, branching in age, and more massive; salmon buff; and found on conifer trunks in western North America.

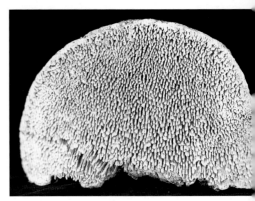

Hericium americanum Ginns
EDIBLE

Fruiting body large, 10–25 cm broad, many branches, with delicate, long, white spines, which arise at the branch tips and hang downward, pure white to yellowish in age, attached to wood by a stout, thick stipe. Flesh fibrous, white. Odor mild. Taste nutty.

Spores 6.5–7.0 x 6–7 μm subglobose (Fig. 2), smooth, entire, thin-walled, amyloid. Spore print white.

Habit and distribution: On the logs of hardwoods and conifers. Widely distributed. Fruiting in late summer and fall.

Comments: *Hericium coralloides* (Scop.:Fr.) Pers., also known as *H. ramosum* (Bull.) Letellier, is similar, but has spines along the branches not just at the end. It has amyloid spores, 6–7 x 4.5–5.5 μm subglobose to elliptic. It is also widely distributed on the wood of both hardwoods and conifers. Both of these species are very good edibles.

Echinodontium tinctorium Ellis & Everh.
INEDIBLE

Fruiting body woody, perennial, large, 10–25 cm broad, hoof-shaped, surface cracked, rough, dingy blackish brown, with no stipe. Flesh tough, zoned, bright cinnamon to rusty red. Spines stout, gray, with blunt ends, brittle and dry. Odor and taste none.

Spores 5.5–7.0 x 3.5–4.5 μm elliptic, minutely spiny, entire, nonamyloid. Spore print white.

Habit and distribution: Single to several on living western conifers, especially western hemlock and grand fir. Known only from the Rocky Mountains and Cascade Range in western North America.

Comments: This fungus has been known by its common name "Indian Paint Fungus" because it was used as a source of dye by the Indians of the Pacific Northwest. The presence of fruiting bodies, which are large conks on a tree, indicates that extensive heart rot of the stem below and just above the conk has taken place. The fruiting bodies soon die on downed trees.

Climacodon septentrionale (Fr.) P. Karst.
INEDIBLE

Fruiting body large, 50–80 cm long, 10–30 cm wide, with multiple shelflike pilei one above the other, from a common fleshy base, nearly white young, dingy buff to yellow-brown in age, densely hairy, dry. Flesh 2–4 cm thick, white, zoned, tough. Spines 5–20 mm long, narrow, dull white, pliant. Odor of ham when dried. Too tough to taste.

Spores 4.0–5.5 x 2.5–3.0 µm elliptic, smooth, entire, thin-walled, nonamyloid. Spore print white.

Habit and distribution: Large single clusters on wounds of living hardwoods especially sugar maple in the North and green ash in Shelterbelts in the Great Plains (Sinclair, 1987). Found in eastern North America. Fruiting in late summer and fall.

Comments: Known also as *Hydnum septentrionale* Fr. and *Steccherinum septentrionale* (Fr.) Banker. It is too tough to eat and looks like a polypore, until one examines the hymenium and observes the spines. It produces a spongy heart rot of both shade and commercial trees.

Mycorrhaphium adustum (Schwein.) Maas Geest.
INEDIBLE

Fruiting body 2–8 cm, perennial, broad, plane or depressed in center, faintly concentrically zoned, dull cream-color to light brown. Flesh tough, flexible, dull white. Spines 1–3 mm long, white tips becoming pinkish in age, with brownish bases. Stipe when present 0.6–3.0 cm long, 0.8–1.5 cm wide, dull light brown to darkening in age, dry. Odor none. Taste mild.

Spores 3–4 x 1.0–1.2 µm cylindric (Fig. 8), smooth, entire, thin-walled, nonamyloid. Spore print white.

Habit and distribution: Single to several on hardwood limbs, logs, and stumps, especially oak Found in eastern North America.

Comments: Also known as *Steccharinum adustum* (Schwein.) Banker, it is variable, sometimes growing on wood, without a stipe and with single or several fused fruiting bodies. It is tough and inedible.

THE POLYPORES

Only the boletes and polypores have a spore-bearing surface composed of tubes oriented down, which open by pores. However, the boletes are centrally stipitate, fleshy, and the tubes are easily separated from the pileus. They are always on the ground or in very rotten wood because they are a mycorrhizal group of mushrooms. By comparison the polypores are seldom centrally stipitate and, if so, they are usually tough and woody or found growing directly on wood. Some polypores also have annual fruiting bodies like the boletes, but many species have perennial fruiting bodies often referred to as "conks" as they are commonly called. They may be seen season after season on limbs, stumps, or on old or dying trees. The abundant, imbricate (shelflike) fruiting bodies of some species can literally cover stumps, old logs, and snags. The annual species usually grow during the summer months and reach maturity in the fall. Some of them are fleshy, at least when they are young, but most are tough to fibrous. Only one species, *Cryptoporus volvatus,* has a partial veil. In most cases, the polypore fruiting body is woody to tough and fibrous and is listed as inedible. The spores range from subglobose, elliptic, oblong, allantoid to cylindric (Figs. 2, 3, 4, 7 & 8) in most species. *Ganoderma* species are truncate at one end, with fine, internal spines. *Bondarzewia* has amyloid, reticulate spores (Fig. 12). Spore prints range from white to brown.

Polypores are very important as saprophytes on dead logs, limbs, and stumps. Some, such as *Phellinus pini,* are important saprophytes on the dead vascular tissue in the center of living trees and are called heart-rotting fungi. *Phaeolus schweinitzii* causes a heart rot of conifer roots, causing wind throw of trees. A few, such as *Heterobasidion annosum* and *Inonotus tomentosus,* can become deadly parasites and attack and kill living roots of forest trees. In some areas widespread mortality of forest and shade trees has resulted from these parasitic root rots. Some polypores are found on the ground, such as species of *Albatrellus* and are mycorrhizal with forest trees. Others including *Coltricia perennis* are suspected of being mycorrhizal, but their role has not been determined.

The classical work of Overholts (1953) gives much detail and illustrations of 371 species of polypores. Gilbertson and Ryvardin (1986; 1987) published an excellent two-volume series with illustrations of microscopic details and current information and concepts in the family. Generic concepts presented here follow their work.

Edibility: Several species are excellent edibles. Perhaps the two outstanding edibles are *Grifola frondosa* and *Laetiporus sulphureus*. *Polyporus squamosus* is also a good edible when young. *Fistulina hepatica* is also an edible, but not a true polypore. Older specimens should be soaked and the water discarded. Most other polypores are to woody or tough or are tasteless or bitter. We have no knowledge of any toxins in the polypores.

KEY TO THE POLYPORES

1. Fruiting body with a central or eccentric stipe or short point of attachment-------------- 2
1. Fruiting body without a stipe or with a lateral stipe --------------------------------------- 18
    2. Fruiting body with a central or eccentric stipe; with a single pileus ----------------- 3
    2. Fruiting body with a short point of attachment; several to many, often imbricate pilei in a rosette --- 14
3. Fruiting body on the ground or very well decayed soil and duff---------------------------- 4
3. Fruiting body on limbs, logs, stumps or wood debris-- 12
    4. Fruiting body tough, brown; pileus zonate, shades of brown to grayish brown ---- 5
    4. Flesh firm but easily broken, white to buff --- 8
5. Pores at margin but displaced by circular lamellae -------------------- *Coltricia montagnei*
                     (see comments under *Coltricia perennis*)
5. Pores 2-4 per mm, without lamellae--- 6
    6. Pileus zonate--- 7
    6. Pileus not zonate, 3–18 cm broad; under conifers especially spruce --- *Inonotus tomentosus*
7. Pileus with a velvety sheen, reddish brown; under hardwoods -- *Coltricia cinnamomea*
                     (see comments under *Coltricia perennis*)
7. Pileus dull colored, grayish brown to brown; under conifers ------------ *Coltricia perennis*
    8. Fruiting body bolete-like; pileus convex, white with gray tinges, with an incurved margin -- *Boletopsis subsquamosa*

8. Pileus not bolete-like, pileus not incurved, often orange-brown tinted blue and deeply cracked or even fused with other fruiting bodies ------------------------------ 9

9. Pileus and pores blue to blue-gray --------------------------------- *Albatrellus caeruleoporus*
(see comments under *Albatrellus confluens*)

9. Pileus blue, tinted blue in part, or dull white; pores not blue ----------------------------- 10

10. Pileus white, cream to orange-brown, without blue colors; under conifers -- *Albatrellus ovinus*

10. Not as above -- 11

11. Pileus with partially blue to completely blue coloration ------------------ *Albatrellus flettii*
(see comments under *Albatrellus confluens*)

11. Pileus pinkish buff to light orange-brown, sometimes with tints of blue --- *Albatrellus confluens*

12. Pileus 1–3 cm broad, convex to depressed, with hairs on the margin -- *Polyporus arcularius*

12. Pileus with a smooth margin, without hairs -- 13

13. Pores 0.5–2.0 mm wide, angular to diamond-shaped; stipe base white --- *Polyporus alveolaris*

13. Pores 5–8 per mm, circular; stipe base black ------------------------------- *Polyporus badius*

14. Pores greenish yellow; flesh spongy, watery; pileus hairy, rusty brown to orange-brown; under conifers --- *Phaeolus schweinitzii*

14. Not as above --- 15

15. Fruiting body a circular cluster of overlapping, orange-yellow pilei; pores white; growing from soil or buried wood, under hardwoods, especially oak -------- *Laetiporus cincinnatus*
(see comments under *Laetiporus sulphureus*)

15. Not as above -- 16

16. Fruiting body very large, 25–70 cm broad, several pilei, in circular cluster; pores when bruised exude white latex; spores with amyloid ridges; under hardwoods in eastern North America -- *Bondarzewia berkeleyi*

16. Not as above; spores nonamyloid; no latex -- 17

17. Fruiting body in a large, circular cluster of small pilei, 2–8 cm broad; flesh firm, white, unchanging when bruised --- *Grifola frondosa*

17. Fruiting body large, 40–80 cm broad; pilei 8–20 cm broad, flesh firm, white, slowly bruising black --- *Meripilus giganteus*

18. Fruiting body a woody, perennial, shelflike to hooflike conk; on snags, logs, stumps, and occasionally wounds on living trees --- 19

18. Fruiting body annual, tough, fibrous to fleshy --- 27

19. Pileus shelflike, surface when wet appears shellacked, bright red to reddish orange to
gray or gray-brown, surface easily dented with a finger nail, spores with internal
spines, nonamyloid -- 20

19. Not as above -- 23

20. Pileus sessile, 30–75 cm broad, gray to gray-brown, pores white, bruising brown
when handled or scratched ------------------------------------- *Ganoderma applanatum*

20. Pileus sessile, 20–100 cm broad, red to reddish orange ------------------------------- 21

21. Pileus very large up to 100 cm broad and 20 cm thick; western North America on
conifer snags and stumps -- *Ganoderma oregonense*

21. Pileus smaller; in eastern North America, on conifers and hardwoods ------------------ 22

22. On conifers, especially hemlock and fir ------------------------------ *Ganoderma tsugae*
(see comments under *Ganoderma oregonense*)

22. On hardwoods, especially oak and beech -------------------------- *Ganoderma lucidum*
(see comments under *Ganoderma oregonense*)

23. Fruiting body a hoof-shaped conk; on trunks, logs, and stumps of living and dead hardwoods or conifers-- 24

23. Fruiting body nearly plane; at or under the duff of living trees, on the trunk and roots of
conifers and less frequently hardwoods --------------------------- *Heterobasidion annosum*

24. Fruiting body shelflike, 5–40 cm broad, zoned with a distinctive red zone near the
margin on wood of conifers and hardwoods----------------------- *Fometopsis pinicola*

24. Not as above -- 25

25. Fruiting body hoof-shaped to shelflike, 5–20 cm broad; on living and
dead conifers--- *Phellinus pini*

25. Not as above-- 26

26. Fruiting body hoof-shaped, 5–15 cm broad; on living hardwoods, especially aspen
and birch--- *Fomes fomentarius*

26. Fruiting body semicircular 3–20 cm broad; on living and dead
conifers --- *Daedalea quercina*

27. Fruiting body fleshy, flesh marbled white and red, oozing red juice; tubes separate, not
joined, like a series of straws clustered tightly together ---------------- *Fistulina hepatica*

27. Not as above-- 28

28. Spore bearing surface at least partially lamellate, pores at margin ---------------- 29

28. Spore bearing surface with pores --- 31

29. Pileus zoned, rusty red to yellowish red; on conifer stumps, logs, and wood
in service -- *Gloeophyllum sepiarium*

29. Pileus zoned, white to gray, brown to gray-brown --- 30

30. Fruiting body with deep, thick lamellae; pileus with white to grayish zoned; on
hardwood -- *Lenzites betulina*
(see comments under *Gloeophyllum sepiarium*)

30. Fruiting body with shallow, irregular lamellae and pores at margin;
pileus with brown to gray-brown zonations; on hardwoods and wood
in service ------------ -- *Gloeophyllum trabea*
(see comments under *Gloeophyllum sepiarium*)

31. Fruiting body round, 1.5–5.0 cm broad; on trunks of living or recently dead conifers;
pores protected by a thick volva --- *Cryptoporus volvatus*

31. Not as above--- 32

32. Pileus overlapping, orange to orange-yellow; pores bright sulphur-yellow; on
stumps, logs or wounds on trees -------------------------------- *Laetiporus sulphureus*

32. Not as above -- 33

33. Fruiting body semicircular, dull white; on birch with a short lateral point
of attachment --- *Piptoporus betulinus*

33. Fruiting body sessile; on stumps, logs and limbs of hardwoods and conifers ---------- 34

34. Pileus red, coral-red to orange-red, azonate; pores orange to
orange-red -- *Pycnoporus cinnabarinus*

34. Not as above --- 35

35. Pileus 2–5 cm broad, colorfully zoned white, yellow, green to bluish green; pores
minute, 3–5 per mm, bright white --------------------------------------- *Trametes versicolor*

35. Not as above--- 36

36. Fruiting body overlapping, light gray to whitish buff; pores violet to purple; on hardwoods --- *Trichaptum biforme*

36. Fruiting body overlapping, gray; pores bright purple, fading to
ochraceus --- *Trichaptum abietinum*
(see comments under *Trichaptum biforme*)

Inonotus tomentosus (Fr.) Teng
INEDIBLE

Fruiting body annual, central to laterally stipitate, pileus 3–18 cm broad, yellow-brown, mustard-yellow to caramel-brown, dry, minutely hairy, sometimes weakly zoned, often with embedded needles or plants, red then black in 3% KOH. Flesh duplex, top spongy below firm tough, yellowish brown. Tubes 4–5 mm deep, pores 2–4 per mm angular, decurrent, white tinted buff brownish in age. Stipe 3–4 cm long, 0.5–2.0 cm wide, central, off-center to lateral, concolorous with the pileus, dry. Odor fragrant. Taste mild.

Spores 5–6 x 3–4 µm elliptic, smooth, entire, thin-walled, nonamyloid. Spore print whitish buff. Cystidia are pointed thick-walled setae.

Habit and distribution: Single, several to gregarious sometimes anastomosing, under conifers, especially spruce. Widely distributed. Fruiting in summer and fall.

Comments: Also known as *Polyporus tomentosus* Fr., it is found under many different species of conifers but known as a root pathogen on spruce. *Inonotus circinatus* (Fr.) Gilb. differs in having curved setae and usually is sessile on the trunk of conifers. Both cause a white pocket rot.

Coltricia perennis (Fr.) Murrill
INEDIBLE

Fruiting body annual, centrally stipitate, pileus 1.5–5.5 cm broad, circular, with zones of varying shades of brown, rusty brown, to grayish brown in age, tomentose, dry. Flesh tough, brown. Tubes 1.5–3.0 mm deep, 2-4 pores per mm, round or somewhat angular, decurrent, cinnamon to dark brown. Stipe central, 2–5 cm long, 2–5 mm wide, dark brown, tomentose, dry. Odor none. Taste mild.

Spores 6–9 x 3.5–5.0 µm elliptic, smooth, entire, thick-walled, nonamyloid. Spore print brown.

Habit and distribution: Single to gregarious on the ground, under conifer or mixed conifer-hardwood forests. Widely distributed. Fruiting in summer and fall.

Comments: Also known as *Polyporus perennis* Fr., it is very possibly a mycorrhizal species but so far without conformation. *Coltricia cinnamomea* (Pers.) Murrill is very similar but has a velvety sheen and is reddish brown. It has larger spores (6–10 x 4.5–7.0 µm) and is common in hardwood forests. *Coltricia montagnei* (Fr.) Murrill (also known as *Cyclomyces greenei* Berk) is also similar; larger but has very distinctive circular lamellae. It is found in eastern North America.

Boletopsis subsquamosa (Fr.) Kotl. & Pouzar
NONPOISONOUS

Fruiting body annual, fleshy, cental stipe, pileus 5–15 cm broad, light brown, tinted olivaceous, nearly white at the incurved margin, smooth or obscurely scaly, dry. Flesh firm, white, darker just above the tubes. Tubes 7–10 mm deep, 1–3 pores per mm, white to slightly olivaceous, decurrent. Stipe 3–8 cm long, 1.5–2.8 cm wide, central or eccentric, dull white, tinted brown, glabrous, dry. Odor none. Taste mild or slightly bitter.

Spores 5–7 x 3.5–5.0 µm subglobose, angular (Figs. 2, 14), entire, thin-walled, nonamyloid. Spore print white.

Habit and distribution: On the ground, single to several under conifers especially spruce and fir. Widely distributed. Fruiting in summer and early fall.

Comments: Also known as *Polyporus griseus* Peck and *Boletopsis leucomelaena* Pers., it is a mycorrhizal associate of conifers especially spruce, but, unlike *Albatrellus,* it has warted, angular spores. Although it is eaten in Asia, we know of no one who eats it in North America.

Albatrellus ovinus (Fr.) Murrill
EDIBLE

Fruiting body annual, centrally stipitate, pileus 4–15 cm broad, white, cream-color to light orange-brown, minutely tomentose, dry. Flesh firm, breakable, cream to buff with a dark layer next to the pores. Tubes 1–2 mm deep, 3–5 pores per mm, decurrent, cream-color, pinkish to pinkish brown. Stipe 3–8 cm long, 1–3 cm wide, central or eccentric, white, bruising light pinkish brown, dry. Odor pleasant even aromatic. Taste mild.

Spores 4–5 x 3.0–3.5 µm subglobose to very short elliptic, smooth, entire, thin-walled, nonamyloid. Spore print white.

Habit and distribution: Single to several, on the ground under conifer forests especially spruce and fir. Widely distributed. Fruiting in late summer and fall.

Comments: Known also as *Polyporus ovinus* Schaeff.:Fr. Those who have eaten it do not consider it first rate (Arora, 1986). *Albatrellus cristatus* (Pers.:F.) Kotl. & Pouzar is yellow-brown to olive-brown, with weakly amyloid, smooth spores, 5–7 x 4–5 µm. It is solitary or in clusters, on the ground under hardwood/conifer forests, in eastern North America. Both species are mycorrhizal with conifers.

Albatrellus confluens (Alb. & Schwein.:Fr.) Kotl. & Pouzar
INEDIBLE

Fruiting body annual, pileus 4–11 cm broad, often fused together, cream color, buff, pinkish buff to light orange-brown in age sometime with blue tints, cracked especially in age, revealing buff flesh, dry. Flesh firm, but easily broken, white at first cream to buff in age. Tubes 2–5 mm deep, 3–5 pores per mm, pure white young to straw-yellow or mustard-yellow in age, often decurrent. Stipe 2.5–6.5 cm long, 0.9–2.4 cm wide, central to eccentric, ovoid to plane and irregular, white to buff in age, glabrous sometime orange-brown at the base, dry. Odor pleasant even fragrant. Taste mild.

Spores 4.2–5.5 x 2.5–4.5 μm subglobose to short elliptic, smooth, entire, slightly thick-walled, weakly amyloid or nonamyloid. Spore print white.

Habit and distribution: Single to cespitose or with fused pilei, on the ground in conifer duff, under a wide variety of conifers. Widely distributed. Fruiting in summer and fall.

Comments: Known as *Polyporus confluens* Alb. & Schwein.:Fr. The species of *Albatrellus* are mycorrhizal with conifers and *A. confluens* has a broad host range with many conifer species. *Albatrellus flettii* Morse & Pouzar is very similar, but the pileus has much more blue coloration or it is entirely blue with white to buff pores. It is also mycorrhizal in the same habitats. *Albatrellus caeruleoporus* (Peck) Pouzar is found only in eastern North America, also has a blue to blue-gray pileus, but has blue pores and is easily distinguished from *A. flettii*. We have collected all three species in Virginia. These species are either bitter or without flavor.

Polyporus arcularius Batsch:Fr.
INEDIBLE

Fruiting body annual, pileus 1–3 cm broad, convex to convex-depressed just in center, yellow to dark brown, appressed-fibrillose to fibrillose-scaly, with a row of marginal hairs, dry. Flesh thin, white, tough. Tubes large, hexagonal, 2 mm deep, 1–2 pores per mm wide, white, decurrent. Stipe 2–6 cm long, 2–4 mm broad, central, yellow to dark brown, hairless, dry. Odor none. Taste mild.

Spores 7–11 x 2–3 μm cylindric (Fig. 8), smooth, entire, thin-walled, nonamyloid. Spore print white.

Habit and distribution: Several, usually close together on hardwood sticks, logs, or stumps. Widely distributed. Fruiting in summer and fall.

Comments: *Polyporus brumalis* Pers.:Fr. is similar, but has smaller pores (2–3 per mm) and marginal pileus hairs are rare. *Polyporus elegans* Bull.:Fr. has a tan pileus; minute pores (4–5 per mm); and a distinctive black stipe base. It is a white rot of hardwoods, especially willow and alder.

Polyporus alveolaris (D.C.: Fr.) Bondartsev & Singer
EDIBLE WHEN YOUNG

Fruiting body 1–8 cm broad, cream, orange, reddish buff to brick-red, convex or fan-shaped, dry. Flesh tough, thin, white. Tubes large, 4–5 mm deep, pores 0.5–2.0 mm wide, angular, diamond-shaped to hexagonal, white to buff. Stipe short, lateral, white. Odor none. Taste mild.

Spores 9–11 x 3.0–3.5 μm nearly elliptic, smooth, entire, thin-walled, nonamyloid. Spore print white.

Habit and distribution: Single to several on limbs and twigs of hardwoods. Widely distributed. Fruiting in the summer and fall.

Comments: Also known as *Favolus canadensis* Klotzsch. The hexagonal, nearly diamond-shaped, large pores give this species its most distinctive field characteristic. Edible when young. *Polyporus squamosus* Huds.:Fr. has a much larger pileus, 6–30 cm broad, with large brown appressed scales; the pores are large (1.0–2.5 mm wide) and also somewhat angular, and it is tough in age but edible when young.

Polyporus badius (Pers.:Gray) Schwein
INEDIBLE

Fruiting body annual, pileus 4–15 cm broad, azonate, orange-brown, red-brown to black-brown, margin often wavy, glabrous, dry. Flesh tough, flexible when fresh, 5–15 mm thick. Tubes 0.5–2.0 mm deep, pores 5-8 per mm, white to pale buff. Stipe 2–5 cm long, 0.5–2.0 cm wide, narrowing toward base, brown over upper half, base black, dry. Odor none. Taste mild.

Spores 6–9 x 3.3–5.0 µm cylindric (Fig. 8), smooth, entire, thin-walled, nonamyloid. Spore print white.

Habit and distribution: Single to several on limbs, logs, and stumps of hardwood and conifers. Widely distributed. Fruiting in the summer and fall.

Comments: Also known as *Polyporus picipes* Fr. *Polyporus elegans* Bull.:Fr. is very similar; also has a black stipe base; is smaller; and the pileus is light brown to nearly white. Both species are white rots of the hardwood and conifer hosts.

Phaeolus schweinitzii (Fr.) Pat.
INEDIBLE

Fruiting body annual, a centrally stiped series of fused pilei 15–43 cm broad, densely hairy, rusty brown to orange-brown. Flesh tough spongy, watery, yellow-brown. Cherry-red turning black where touched with 3% KOH. Tubes 5–10 mm deep, 1–3 pores per mm, mustard-yellow to greenish yellow. Stipe central very short, protrudes 1–3 cm from the ground. Odor none. Taste unknown.

Spores 5.5–8.0 x 4–5 µm elliptic, smooth, entire, thin-walled, nonamyloid. Spore print white.

Habit and distribution: Solitary to several on the ground, from roots, lower tree trunk, near the ground, or on the ground from buried roots of living and dead conifers. Widely distributed. Fruiting in the early summer to early fall.

Comments: Known also as *Polyporus schweinitzii* Fr., this fungus causes a brown cubical rot of the heartwood and roots. It is a major butt rot of living conifers. The strength of the root system is impaired, and the trees are often wind-thrown. See also the root rot pathogen *Inonotus tomentosus* in conifer forests.

Bondarzewia berkeleyi (Fr.) Bondartsev &
Singer
INEDIBLE

Fruiting body annual, very large, stipitate, pileus
25–70 cm broad, often obscurely zonate with
shades of brown, fibrillose, several imbricate
pilei, dry. Flesh firm, 2–3 cm thick, white. Tubes
1–2 mm deep, 1-2 pores per mm, thick walls,
white when young and fresh, exudes a white
latex when cut or bruised. Stipe 4–10 cm long,
3–5 cm wide, dry, dull white. Odor none. Taste
bitter.

Spores 7–9 x 6–8 µm globose to subglobose,
with strongly amyloid, short ridges, entire, thick-
walled. Spore print yellow-orange.

Habit and distribution: Solitary on ground from
an underground sclerotium, under hardwood trees
especially oaks, hickory and chestnuts. Found in
eastern North America. Fruiting in late summer
and fall.

Comments: Also known as *Polyporus berkeleyi*
Fr., and is often found under old growth trees. We
have collected it a number of times in Virginia
and observed the white latex on the cut pores.
Recent studies have placed it in the Russulales
near where latex and spores with amyloid
ornamentation are the chief characters. However,
unlike the mycorrhizal Russulales, *B. berkeleyi*
forms a white rot of hardwood roots.
Bondarzewia montana (Quél.) Singer is smaller,
has an orange-brown to purplish brown, azonate
pileus; spores with amyloid ridges; and is found
under conifers in western North America.

Grifola frondosa (Dicks.:Fr.) Gray
EDIBLE

Fruiting body large, fleshy, up to 60 cm broad,
with many small overlapping pilei, 2–8 cm broad,
dull white, cream color to gray in age, glabrous to
minutely fibrillose, dry. Flesh firm, fleshy, white.
Tubes 4–5 mm deep, 1–3 pores per mm, small,
white to yellowish in age. Stipe large, compound,
white, short. Odor mild. Taste pleasant.

Spores 5–7 x 3.5–5.0 µm short elliptic, smooth,
entire, thin-walled, nonamyloid. Spore print
white.

Habit and distribution: Usually solitary on the
ground from buried roots and wood near but not
on stumps and snags of oaks or other hardwoods.
Found in eastern, southeastern, and midwestern
North America, and rarely in the Pacific
Northwest. Fruiting in late summer and fall.

Comments: Known also as *Polyporus frondosus*
Dicks.:Fr., this is one of the truly delicious edibles,
and its bulk makes it a prize find. *Polyporus
umbellatus* Fr. is also in a large clusters; is also
edible; and has many small (1–4 cm broad) pilei
centrally attached and round. The fruiting body
arises from a robust, branched stipe. It is rare and
also found mostly in central and eastern North
America. Both species are most frequently found
in older hardwood stands.

Meripilus giganteus (Fr.) P. Karst.
EDIBLE

Fruiting body annual, large 40–80 cm broad with multiple pilei, overlapping from a central stipe, pileus 8–20 cm broad, brown or tinted gray with an often wavy, white margin, glabrous, dry. Flesh firm, fibrous, white 1–2 cm wide, stains slowly black when bruised. Tubes 5–8 mm deep, 3–5 pores per mm, white, black when bruised or on drying. Stipe very short, stout, centrally attached to buried wood. Odor unpleasant but not distinctive. Taste mild but somewhat acrid.

Spores 5–7 x 4.5–5.5 µm subglobose, smooth, entire, thin-walled, nonamyloid. Spore print white.

Habit and distribution: Single to several on the ground under hardwoods especially oak and beech. Found in eastern North America. Reported from Idaho but we have never seen it there. Fruiting in the late summer and fall.

Comments: Known also as *Polyporus giganteus* Fr. The pilei are larger than those of *Grifola frondosa,* which does not bruise black and has short, smooth, elliptic spores, Miller & Miller (1980) illustrate the black staining reaction. See *Bondarzewia berkeleyi* for a comparison. It is eaten, but most who have tried it rate it a poor second to *Grifola frondosa.*

Ganoderma applanatum (Pers.) Pat.
INEDIBLE

Fruiting body woody, perennial, sessile, 30–75 cm broad, a shelflike conk, gray to gray-brown, margin white, often covered with red-brown spores, dry, when wet or new appearing shellacked. Flesh soft, brown, with an easily dented, crustlike cuticle. Tubes 5–15 mm deep, pores minute, 4-6 per mm deep, bright white, but bruising brown when handled or scratched. Odor none. Taste mild.

Spores 6–12 x 5–8 µm ovoid, truncate at one end, fine internal spines, entire, thick-walled, nonamyloid. Spore print brown.

Habit and distribution: Solitary to several on logs, stumps and living hardwoods, also on conifers in northwestern North America. Widely distributed. Young buttons start in summer but continue fruiting all year.

Comments: The white pores turn brown when scratched, bruised, or handled, thus, the pore surface is widely used to etch pictures and hence the common name "Artists' Conk." The fungus produces a white rot in heartwood and sapwood as well as a butt rot of aspen (Gilbertson & Ryvarden, 1986).

Ganoderma oregonense Murrill
INEDIBLE

Fruiting body annual, very robust, sessile, up to 100 cm broad, 40 cm deep and 20 cm thick, cuticle red to reddish orange appearing shellacked. Flesh soft, white, punky when dry, cuticle easily dented. Tubes up to 3 cm deep, pores minute, 2–3 per mm, white to brown in age. Odor none. Taste unknown.

Spores 13–17 x 8–10 µm ovoid, truncate at one end, with fine internal spines, entire, thick-walled, nonamyloid. Spore print white.

Habit and distribution: Single to several on conifer snags or stumps, especially spruce, fir, and hemlock. Found in western North America. Fruiting in spring, summer, and fall.

Comments: *Ganoderma tsugae* Murrill is very similar but smaller; with smaller pores (5–6 per mm); and with somewhat smaller spores (13–15 x

7.5–8.5 µm). It is restricted to conifers, especially hemlock and fir, in eastern North America. *Ganoderma lucidum* (Curtis:Fr.) P. Karst is found on hardwood stumps and logs in eastern North America; is also sessile, but can often develop a shellacked stipe; and varies from a shellacked, dark red-brown to yellow-orange pileus. We have recorded it on beech and oak stumps and logs. It has smaller spores (9–12 x 5.5–8.0 µm). In Japan the *G. lucidum* is called Reishi or Ling Chi in Chinese. Stamets (2000) has an excellent account of its medicinal use and cultivation in Asia. We have seen it in Korea and Thailand in the wild and under cultivation. Gilbertson & Ryvarden (1986) provide more information on these species and the genus *Ganoderma* in North America.

Heterobasidion annosum (Fr.) Bref.
INEDIBLE

Fruiting body 4–15 cm broad, annual and perennial, a nearly flat pore surface with small, upturned, light brown, shelflike pilei, with a dry, wood-brown, rounded margin. Flesh tough, white. Tubes 2–3 mm deep, pores nearly round, minute 2–5 per mm, pure white to yellowish in age. Odor none. Taste unknown.

Spores 3.5–5.0 x 3–4 μm subglobose, smooth, entire, thin-walled, nonamyloid. Spore print white.

Habit and distribution: One to several, at or under the duff, around bases of live trees and on stumps or logs, on living conifers or less frequently hardwoods. Infection centers often create areas with many dead trees. Widely distributed. Fruiting in the spring and summer.

Comments: Fruiting bodies are most often annual, but old-growth trees can have large perennial conks at the ground level. This is one of the most destructive root diseases of forest and shade trees. Infection centers often develop in 20- to 40-year-old plantations of red pine and white pine in eastern North America. Southern pines are also very susceptible, and the fungus is also found on ponderosa pine and other conifers in the western United States. It may exist both as a saprophyte and parasite. The infected roots are reduced to a white spongy pulp, and the infected trees subject to wind throw.

Fometopsis pinicola (Sw.:Fr.) P. Karst.
INEDIBLE

Fruiting body a convex, perennial, robust, shelf-like conk 5–40 cm broad with a hard, zoned surface, typically black-brown followed by 2 or 3 brown or red-brown zones and a red zone near the margin, which has a very narrow white band. Flesh very tough, light wood-color. Tubes 3–5 mm deep, with 3–5 minute pores per mm, white to cream-color. Odor citrinelike when fresh and growing. Taste none.

Spores 5–9 x 3.5–4.5 μm narrowly elliptic, smooth, entire, thick-walled, nonamyloid. Spore print light yellow.

Habit and distribution: On logs, stumps, and snags of conifers and hardwoods. Widely distributed. Rarely on living trees except in Alaska and the Yukon, where it is often on wounds of living trees. Fruiting as young buttons, often with clear drops over the surface, in the spring but the perennial conks are visible all year.

Comments: Also known as *Fomes pinicola* (Sw.:Fr.) Cooke. This species is also known as the "Red Belt Fungus" and the red zone may be very broad when very vigorous and young, but in age it is mostly brown. Fresh young specimens often have liquid drops on the surface. It is very common and causes a brown, cubical rot of dead and living trees (Gilbertson & Ryvarden, 1986).

Phellinus pini (Thore:Fr.) A. Ames
INEDIBLE

Fruiting body sessile, perennial, variable from hoof-shaped to shelflike or resupinate (flat on the wood), 5–20 cm broad, surface rough, cracked, brown, reddish brown to brownish black with minute hairs which are rubbed off in age. Flesh woody, tough, yellowish brown to rusty-red. Tubes 5–6 mm deep, 2–4 pores per mm, circular or irregular in shape, ochre-orange. All parts black in 3% KOH solution. Odor none. Taste unknown.

Spores 4–6 x 3.5–5.0 µm globose to subglobose, smooth, entire, thick-walled, nonamyloid. Spore print pale brown. Cystidia 15–30 µm long, pointed, thick-walled, brown (known as setae).

Habit and distribution: On living trunks, logs, snags, and stumps of conifers. Widely distributed. Conks visible during all seasons.

Comments: Known also as *Trametes pini* Thore:Fr., this fungus causes serious loss of heartwood through decay in living conifer trees. The decay is visible as a series of small white pockets filled with white mycelium. The fruiting bodies are quite similar to a number of other species of *Phellinus* (Gilbertson & Ryvarden, 1987). *Phellinus robineae* (Murrill) Sacc. is common on locust in the eastern North America and the southwestern United States. *Phellinus everhartii* (Ellis & Galloway) A. Ames is common on oak in eastern North America. *Phellinus igniarius* (L.:Fr.) Quél. causes a white rot of heartwood of living hardwood trees in northern North America. All species of *Phellinus* have the characteristic setae and cause a white wood rot.

Fomes fomentarius (L.:Fr.) J. Kickx f.
INEDIBLE

Fruiting body, perennial, sessile, hoof-shaped, 5–15 cm wide, zonate, gray with an orange-brown zone next to the white margin, dry. Flesh woody, light brown. Tubes 8–11 mm deep, 4–5 pores per mm, light brown. Odor none. Taste unknown.

Spores 12–18 x 4–7 µm cylindric (Fig. 8), hyaline, smooth, entire, thick-walled, nonamyloid. Spore print light yellow.

Habit and distribution: Single to several on living or dead hardwood trees especially aspen, birch and alder. Widely distributed. Fruiting all season.

Comments: *Phellinus igniarius* (L.:Fr) Quél. is also hoof-shaped on living hardwoods, but the pileus is deeply cracked, gray to blackish brown; the pore surface is cinnamon to purplish brown; with small spores (5.0–6.5 x 4.5–6.0 µm). It is most common in northern North America. Both species are white rots of the heartwood of living hardwoods.

Daedalea quercina Fr.
INEDIBLE

Fruiting body perennial, sessile, tough, leathery, pileus convex 3–20 cm broad, whitish to ash-gray, fine, dry, short hairs. Flesh thick, tough, pale buff to light brown. Tubes 3–5 mm deep, pores very large, 1–3 mm wide long, irregular, with thick walls, almost lamellate, whitish to flesh-colored. Odor none. Taste unknown.

Spores 5–6 x 2–3 µm cylindric (Fig. 8), smooth, entire, thin-walled, nonamyloid. Spore print white.

Habit and distribution: Single or several on stumps and logs of hardwoods, especially oak. Found in eastern North America. Fruiting in summer and fall.

Comments: *Daedaleopsis confragosa* (Fr.) J. Schröt. has a thin, convex, zoned pileus, which is dingy, ashy-gray; the pores are mazelike and not lamellate. It has smaller pores (0.5–1.5 mm wide); large spores (7–9 x 2.0–2.5 µm). It is most common in eastern North America, and causes a brown rot of hardwoods.

Fistulina hepatica Schaeff.:Fr.
EDIBLE

Fruiting body annual, large, pileus 10–30 cm broad, nearly plane, minutely roughened, red, orange-red to liver-colored, moist. Flesh 2–6 cm thick, soft to fibrous in age, multiple zones of white to red (see inset), oozing a reddish juice when squeezed. Tubes 10–15 mm deep, 3 pores per mm, separate from each other, similar to individual pipes (see inset), white to buff, staining reddish when handled. Stipe 4–8 cm long, 1–3 cm thick, lateral, colored same as pileus. Odor mild. Taste sour.

Spores 4.0–5.5 x 3–4 µm subglobose to short elliptic, smooth, entire, thick-walled, nonamyloid. Spore print pale rusty brown to pinkish brown.

Habit and distribution: Usually single to several, on hardwood stumps or living trees at the base, usually oak. Found in eastern North America. Fruiting in the late summer and fall.

Comments: The "Beefsteak Fungus" is aptly named, since in cross-section, it has the texture of beef along with oozing red juice. It is edible but sour tasting. Older fruiting bodies should be soaked over night and the water poured off before preparing them for the table. The juice of older specimens can cause gastric upset.

Gloeophyllum sepiarium (Fr.) P. Karst.
INEDIBLE

Fruiting body sessile, annual, 1–7 cm broad, covered with dense, short hairs, zoned with colored bands, bright rusty-red to yellowish red, with a light, whitish to yellowish margin. Flesh tough, fibrous 1–3 mm thick, yellow-brown. Tubes 5–7 mm deep, pores near margin, the rest lamellate, some cross-walls, sometimes maze-like, light brown. Odor none. Taste none.

Spores 8.5–13.0 x 3.5–4.5 µm cylindric (Fig. 8), smooth, entire, thin-walled, nonamyloid. Spore print white.

Habit and distribution: Single to several on conifer logs, stumps, boards, bridge timbers, and other wood in service. Widely distributed. Fruiting in summer and fall.

Comments: Also known as *Lenzites saeparia* (Wulfen:Fr.) Fr. *Gloeophyllum trabea* (Fr.) Murrill is similar but not as hairy, even glabrous in age; pileus brown to gray-brown; with smaller spores (6.5–9.5 x 3.0–4.5 µm). It is usually on hardwoods and is an important source of decay in telephone poles and structural timber in homes and buildings throughout North America. Both species cause a brown rot. *Lenzites betulina* (Fr.) Fr. is also deeply lamellate; with a white to grayish zonation of the pileus; is a white rot of hardwoods; and widely distributed.

Cryptoporus volvatus (Peck) Shear
INEDIBLE

Fruiting body annual, sessile, pileus 1.5–5.0 cm broad, round, dull white to cream color, yellow-brown in age, glabrous, dry, surrounds the pores with a thick volva. Flesh tough, with a corky interior. Tubes 3–5 mm deep, 4–5 pores per mm, light brown, usually with discharged white spores on the surface. Odor slightly resinous. Taste slightly bitter.

Spores 10–16 x 3–5 µm cylindric (Fig. 8), smooth, entire, thin-walled, nonamyloid. Spore print white to cream color.

Habit and distribution: Several to gregarious on living, dying or recently dead conifers. Widely distributed. Fruiting spring, summer, and fall.

Comments: We have seen this fungus most often on pines in the eastern North America, but grand fir and Douglas fir along with pines are also hosts in northwestern North America. Based on our observations, we believe that bark beetles that bore into the fruiting bodies may carry the spores to uninfected trees. Once the fruiting bodies are observed on a tree, it is desirable to remove it and burn or destroy the wood to restrict its spread to healthy trees.

Laetiporus sulphureus (Bull.:Fr.) Murrill
EDIBLE

Fruiting body annual, on wood, shelflike, with an overlapping series of orange-yellow pilei, 5–25 cm broad. Flesh firm, margin soft to tough near center, white to yellowish. Tubes 3–4 mm deep, pores 2–4 per mm, bright sulphur-yellow. Stipe absent. Odor mild. Taste mild.

Spores 5–7 x 3.5–4.5 μm broadly elliptic, smooth, entire, thin-walled, nonamyloid. Spore print white.

Habit and distribution: On stumps, logs, or wounds on standing trees. Found in eastern North America. Fruiting in spring, summer, and fall.

Comments: The edible portion of this polypore is the trimmed margin of the young pilei. It is important to use only the soft, yellow edges or it becomes bitter. *Laetiporus cincinnatus* (Morgan) Burds., Banik, & Volk produces a terrestrial, large, circular cluster of the over-lapping, orange-yellow pilei and the white pores. *Laetiporus conifericola*

grows on conifer wood from California to Alaska. It has a bright orange to salmon-orange pileus and lemon-yellow pores. The Alaskans find it to have an unpleasant taste. This may reflect the substrate on which it grows. We have eaten all of the above species and enjoy them greatly. *Laetiporus persicinus* (Berk. & M. A. Curtis) Gilb. is infrequently found, has a light to dark brown pileus, pinkish to creamy tan pores, and is most often found in the Deep South and southeastern United States. It grows in rosettes on the ground or on hardwood logs or stumps. We have not eaten it. *Laetiporus gilbertsonii* Burds. has a pale salmon, orange-tan or light brown pileus and yellow to pale yellow pores. It is found on living or dead hardwoods, including oaks, *Eucalyptus,* and Carob trees on the West Coast. It is often bitter and can cause gastric upset, especially when growing on *Eucalyptus,* (Burdsall & Banik, 2001).

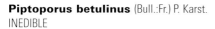

Piptoporus betulinus (Bull.:Fr.) P. Karst.
INEDIBLE

Fruiting body annual, laterally stipitate, pileus
6–25 cm broad, 5–15 cm wide, semicircular, dull
white, mouse gray to brown, margin incurved,
glabrous, dry. Flesh tough, white, 4–5 cm thick.
Tubes 8–12 mm deep, 3–5 pores per mm, white,
in age irregular almost spine-like. Stipe short,
lateral or absent, color of pileus. Odor none. Taste
unknown.

Spores 5–6 x 1.5–1.9 µm allantoid (Fig. 7),
smooth, entire, thin-walled, nonamyloid. Spore
print white.

Habit and distribution: Single to several on dead
species of birch. Found throughout the range of
birch in North America. Fruiting in spring,
summer, and fall.

Comments: Also known as *Polyporus betulinus*
Bull.:Fr., it is a brown rot usually seen on the
standing dead trees. The distinctive shape makes
it easy to identify. We have seen it on the birch in
the Appalachian Mountains, as well as commonly
further north.

Pycnoporus cinnabarinus (Jacq.:Fr.) P.
Karst.
INEDIBLE

Fruiting body annual, sessile, pileus 2–13 cm
broad, 2–6 cm wide, semicircular, sometimes
overlapping, red, coral-red to orange-red, azonate,
dry. Flesh fibrous, corky, 1.0–2.2 cm thick, orange-
red. Pores 5–15 mm deep, 3–4 per mm, round to
angular, orange to orange-red. Odor none. Taste
not distinctive.

Spores 6–8 x 2.5–3.0 µm cylindric to slightly
curved (Figs. 9 & 8), thin-walled, nonamyloid.
Spore print white.

Habit and distribution: Single or several
occasionally numerous on limbs, logs and stumps
of hardwoods, occasionally on conifers. Widely
distributed. Fruiting in summer and fall.

Comments: Also known as *Polyporus
cinnabarinus* Jacq.:Fr., it produces a white rot and
is quite common. *Pycnoporus sanguineus* (L.:Fr.)
Murrill, also on hardwoods, is very similar but has
a much thinner context (0.5 mm) and smaller
spores 5–6 x 2.0–2.5 µm. Both species are
colorless in 3% KOH. *Hapalopilus nidulans* (Fr.) P.
Karst. is cinnamon, orange to orange-brown;
somewhat similar; also a white rot of dead
hardwoods; but up to 4 cm thick. It is instantly
purple to violet with 3% KOH with short elliptic
spores, 4.0–5.5 x 2–3 µm.

Trametes versicolor (L.:Fr.) Pilát
INEDIBLE

Fruiting body sessile, annual, forming dense overlapping pilei, 2–5 cm broad, leathery, colorfully zoned white, yellow, red to green and bluish green, velvety from a dense hairy surface. Flesh tough, fibrous bends without breaking, white. Tubes 3 mm deep, pores minute, 3–5 per mm, bright white (so small they are hard to see). Odor none. Taste none.

Spores 4–7 x 1.5–2.0 µm cylindric (Fig. 8), smooth, entire, thin-walled, nonamyloid. Spore print white.

Habit and distribution: On dead limbs, stumps, and logs of hardwoods and less frequently on conifers. Widely distributed. Fruiting from late spring to fall.

Comments: Known also as *Polyporus versicolor* L.:Fr. *Trametes hirsuta* (Wulfen.:Fr.) Pilát is similar; also zoned, but with coarse hairs on the pileus, which is gray to gray-brown without the brightly colored zones of *T. versicolor*. The spores are also larger (6–9 x 2.0–2.5 µm) and *Trametes hirsuta* is also widely distributed on hardwoods in North America. Both species produce a white rot that breaks down lignin leaving the wood spongy.

Trichaptum biforme (Fr. in Klotzsch) Ryvarden
INEDIBLE

Fruiting body sessile, annual, pilei 1–6 cm broad, single to several or overlapping, hairy, light gray to whitish buff. Flesh tough, flexible, cream color. Tubes 2–5 mm deep, 3–5 pores per mm, soon splitting, irregular almost spinelike, violet to purple only fading in age to cream color or buff. Odor none. Taste unknown.

Spores 5.5–8.0 x 2.0–2.5 µm cylindric (Fig. 8), allantoid (Fig. 7), smooth, entire, thin-walled, nonamyloid. Spore print white. Cystidia clavate, thick-walled, incrusted at the apex.

Habit and distribution: On hardwood limbs, logs, stumps, and snags, often in large numbers. Widely distributed. Fruiting from late spring until fall.

Comments: Also known as *Polyporus pargamenus* Fr., it is one of the most common polypores on hardwoods in North America. It causes a white pocket rot and the decaying wood has areas of dense white mycelium that are the pockets. *Trichaptum abietinum* (Dickson:Fr.) Ryvarden is very similar with somewhat smaller fruiting bodies, but it is found on conifers. *Cerrena unicolor* (Bull.:Fr.) Murrill is imbricate with a zoned pileus that is usually covered with a growth of green algae and has mazelike pores. For additional information on this complex of species see Gilbertson and Ryvarden (1987).

FUNGI WITH A SMOOTH HYMENIUM, WITHOUT PORES, LAMELLAE, OR TEETH

APHYLLOPHORALES

This group of fungi has a smooth hymenium (spore-bearing surface) and, therefore, lacks the lamellae, ridges, teeth or spines, and pores that typify other higher fungi. Fruiting bodies like *Stereum* and *Sparassis* resemble polypores when first encountered. Examination of the fruiting body, especially with a hand lens, quickly reveals the absence of pores and directs one to this group. The species covered are mostly decomposers of wood and plant material. Only a very small number of the known species are covered in this guide. The spores are elliptic, oblong, cylindric, allantoid to tuberculate-warted with fine spines on the warts (Figs. 3, 4, 7, 8, and 8). Spore prints are white, brown, or purple-brown.

Edibility: Species of *Sparassis* are good edibles. However, the other species are either too tough or too bitter to be considered edible. Toxins are not recorded in this very large group.

KEY TO THE FUNGI WITH A SMOOTH HYMENIUM, WITHOUT PORES, LAMELLAE, OR TEETH

APHYLLOPHORALES

1. Fruiting body flat (like paint on wood), without a pileus, deep blue to indigo-blue; flesh tough, woody; on wood --- *Pulcherricium caeruleum*
1. Not as above; pileus present --- 2
    2. Fruiting body waxy, rubbery, gelatinous, undersurface with irregular ridges forming shallow, very small pores; spores 3–6 x 0.5–2.5 µm, cylindric, curved, hyaline ---- 3
    2. Fruiting body tough, flexible, but not rubbery or gelatinous; spores larger or different --- 4
3. Pileus white, densely fibrillose, pink only at margin-------------------- *Phlebia tremellosus*
3. Pileus bright pink to coral-pink --- *Phlebia incarnata*

4. Fruiting body tough, with many convex to shell-shaped pilei, 1–3 cm broad; hymenium contorted with thick and thin-walled, uneven, forked ridges, often anastomosing -- *Plicaturopsis crispa*

4. Not as above-- 5

5. Fruiting body tough and flexible, with a zoned pileus; on wood --------------------------- 6

5. Fruiting body on the ground --- 7

    6. Pileus 2.0–6.5 cm long, 0.5–7.0 cm wide, with gray, cinnamon-buff, maroon or cherry-red zones; hymenium smooth, whitish gray to pinkish buff; growing in imbricate rows, on hardwood limbs and logs ----------------- ---- *Stereum ostrea*

    6. Pileus small, 1.0–2.5 cm long, 0.8–1.5 cm wide, cinnamon-buff to cinnamon-brown zones; hymenium smooth, dull, yellowish orange, cream-buff, to dull white; in dense, wide clusters on hardwood branches, often forming pavementlike blocks on the underside of branches--- *Stereum complicatum*

7. Fruiting body flexible, rubbery, tough; in fan-shaped clusters or erect, flattened branches --- 8

7. Fruiting body a large rosette of pilei, fleshy to slightly tough ----------------------------- 9

    8. Fruiting body a cluster of erect, flattened to oval branches from a common base; odor disagreeable, foetid -- *Thelephora palmata*

    8. Fruiting body with fan-shaped or whorled clusters of pilei, 2–8 cm broad; odor none --- *Thelephora terrestris*

9. Fruiting body from a single, central point of attachment; pilei white to cream-color, fleshy --- *Sparassis crispa*

9. Fruiting body with multiple attachments to the ground; pilei somewhat zonate, slightly tough, fleshy-- *Sparassis spathulata*

      (see comments under *Sparassis crispa*)

Pulcherricium caeruleum (Lam.:Fr.) Parmasto
INEDIBLE

Fruiting body sessile, flat over the woody substrate, dry, blue to indigo-blue, in age gray-blue. Flesh 2–6 mm deep, tough, almost woody, blue. Odor none. Taste unknown.

Spores 7–9 x 4–6 µm elliptic, smooth, entire, thin-walled, nonamyloid. Spore print white.

Habit and distribution: In sheets on dead hardwoods. Found in central and especially southeastern United States. Fruiting in summer and fall.

Comments: Also known as *Corticium caeruleum* (Lam.) Fr. Ginns & Lefebvre (1993) report it on many hosts.

Phlebia tremellosa (Schrad.:Fr.) Nakasone & Burds.
INEDIBLE

Fruiting body sessile to flat in sheets. Pileus 1.0–2.0 cm wide, white, dense fibrils tinted pink at the margin. Flesh rubbery, flexible, waxy, gelatinous, dries hard and horny. Hymenium of shallow ridges, joining to form irregular pores (meruloid), reddish orange to salmon-pink, 1.5–4.0 mm thick. Odor none. Taste mild.

Spores 3–4 x 0.5–1.5 µm allantoid (Fig. 7), smooth, entire, thin-walled, nonamyloid. Spore print white. Cystidia cylindric, hyphal-like, thin-walled, hyaline.

Habit and distribution: In sheets, on decaying hardwoods and hardwood debris. Widely distributed. Fruiting in summer to late fall.

Comments: Also known as *Merulius tremellosus* Fr. The waxy gelatinous tissue and totally fertile hymenium separates this species from the polypores. *Serpula lacrimans* (Wulfen apud Jacq.:Fr.) J. Schröt. also has a meruloid, waxy, flat, brownish red fruiting body. It is found on boards in old houses, and damp cellars, usually on conifer wood in service. Breitenback & Kränzlin Vol. 2 (1986) illustrate and describe these species, which are aggressive wood decomposers.

Phlebia incarnata (Schwein.) Nakasone & Burds.
INEDIBLE

Fruiting body sessile, overlapping, 3–10 cm long. Pileus 1.5–4.0 cm wide, circular, often overlapping, minutely fibrillose, bright pink, coral-pink to light pinkish white, with often deeply scalloped margins. Flesh waxy, pliant, gelatinous, dull white. Hymenium densely ridged, often anastomosing (meruloid), forming irregular pores, dull white to light orange-white. Odor none. Taste unknown.

Spores 4–6 x 2.0–2.5 µm oblong or slightly allantoid (Figs. 4 & 7), smooth, entire, thin-walled, nonamyloid. Spore print white.

Habit and distribution: Single or several on decaying hardwoods. Found in eastern North America. Fruiting in late summer and fall, following wet weather.

Comments: Also known as *Merulius incarnatus* Schwein. We collected this species almost every year in Virginia and North Carolina.

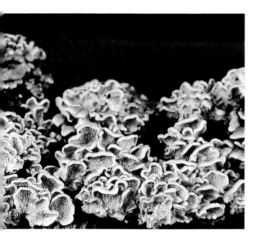

Plicaturopsis crispa (Fr.) Reid
INEDIBLE

Fruiting body sessile with multiple shelving, convex to shell-shaped, pilei 1.0–3.0 cm broad, dry, minutely fibrillose, with zones of orange-brown and a white margin. Flesh soft, white when young, soon brittle and hard. Hymenium uneven, forked ridges, often anastomosing, white to dingy gray. Odor none. Taste mild.

Spores 3–4 x 1.0–1.5 µm allantoid (Fig. 7), smooth, entire, thin-walled, weakly amyloid. Spore print white.

Habit and distribution: Gregarious on dead limbs and snags of hardwoods. Found in eastern North America. Fruiting in summer and fall.

Comments: It resembles an agaric until one examines the contorted hymenium composed of thick and thin-walled, irregular ridges. In contrast, agarics have very thin, smooth lamellae as seen with *Crepidotus mollis*.

Stereum ostrea (Blume & Nees:Fr.) Fr.
INEDIBLE

Fruiting body sessile. Pileus 1.0–6.5 cm long, 0.5–7.0 cm wide, often imbricate in rows, zonate with buff to gray or cinnamon-buff zones, toward margin darker maroon to cherry-red narrow zones, margin nearly white, dry. Flesh 0.1–0.3 cm thick, very tough, flexible, will bend in two and not break if moist and fresh. Hymenium smooth, light pinkish buff, light orange-buff to dull whitish gray. Odor none. Taste unknown.

Spores 5–7.5 x 2–3 µm cylindric (Fig. 8), smooth, entire, thin-walled, nonamyloid. Spore print white.

Habit and distribution: Broadly attached to the wood substrate, usually numerous to gregarious on hardwood logs, limbs, and stumps. Widely distributed.

Comments: There are 18 species of *Stereum* in North America. *Stereum hirsutum* (Willd.:Fr.) Gray is similar but has a dense fibrillose pileus surface.

Stereum complicatum (Fr.) Fr
INEDIBLE

Fruiting body sessile. Pileus 1.0–2.5 cm long, 0.8–1.5 cm wide, in dense clusters often circling a branch or twig, zonate with zones of bright cinnamon-buff, cinnamon-brown, with creamy buff margins, dry. Flesh 0.05–0.2 cm thick, very tough and flexible, will bend and not break. Hymenium smooth, cream-buff, cinnamon-buff to dull white. Odor none. Taste unknown.

Spores 5.0–6.5 x 2.0–2.5 µm cylindric, cylindric-curved, smooth, entire, thin-walled, nonamyloid. Spore print white.

Habit and distribution: Gregarious, often forming pavementlike blocks on the underside of branches and twigs of hardwoods. Found in eastern and central North America. Fruiting year round.

Comments: *Stereum sanguinolentum* (Alb. & Schwein.:Fr.) Fr. is found on dead conifer wood; bleeds red when cut; and has large spores 8–14 x 3–5 µm. *Stereum gausapatum* (Fr.) Fr. is found on hardwood, especially oak, logs, limbs, and stumps; also exudes a red liquid when cut or more commonly stains the hymenium red. It is larger than but otherwise similar to *S. complicatum,* which causes a white rot of hardwoods.

Thelephora palmata Scop.:Fr.
INEDIBLE

Fruiting body sessile. Pileus 3.5–6.5 cm high, of erect, oval to flattened from a common base, ends white young, soon gray to lilac or pinkish gray, almost rosettelike when mature, dry. Flesh tough, brown. Odor disagreeable, foetid. Taste unknown.

Spores 8–10 x 6–9 µm elliptic, tuberculate-warted with fine spines on the warts (Fig. 9), entire, thick-walled, nonamyloid. Spore print brown.

Habit and distribution: Single to several on the ground, under conifers. Widely distributed. Fruiting in late summer to late fall.

Comments: See comments under *Thelephora terrestris.*

Thelephora terrestris Ehrh.:Fr.
INEDIBLE

Fruiting body sessile. Pileus 2–8 cm broad, fan-shaped, in whorled clusters, often fused, dry, uneven with irregular projections, blackish brown, tinted reddish brown to deep gray-brown. Flesh 0.1–0.3 cm thick, rubbery, tough, bends but does not break, dark brown. Hymenium smooth, pale brownish drab to pale gray. Point of attachment sometimes present. Odor none. Taste mild.

Spores 8–10 x 5.0–7.5 µm elliptic, tuberculate-warted with fine spines on the warts (Fig. 9), entire, thick-walled, nonamyloid. Spore print purple-brown.

Habit and distribution: Single to several, often in clusters on the ground, mycorrhizal with conifers and hardwoods. Widespread. Fruiting in the summer and fall.

Comments: *Thelephora vialis* Schwein. is vase-shaped, somewhat yellowish with white to grayish white margins, and found under hardwoods in eastern North America. *Thelephora palmata* Scop.:Fr. is in coral-like clusters on the ground with lilac-gray branches and whitish tips. It is under conifers in North America (Ginns & Lefebere, 1993). All three species form ectomycorrhizae with forest trees. *Thelephora terrestris* also readily colonizes nursery plants in green houses.

437

Sparassis crispa Wulfen:Fr.
EDIBLE

Fruiting body in a rosette or cauliflower-like, 25–50 cm high, 15–35 cm thick, with many flattened branches, white to yellowish, with flattened tips that arise from a deeply rooted, large central stalk, 2–4 cm thick. Flesh firm, white, soft when young to somewhat tough in age. Odor not distinctive. Taste mild and pleasant.

Spores 5.0–6.5 x 3.0–3.6 µm broadly elliptic, smooth, entire, thin-walled, nonamyloid. Spore print white.

Habit and distribution: Single or occasionally several on the ground under conifers. Widely distributed. Fruiting in late summer and fall.

Comments: *Sparassis spathulata* Schwein. is an eastern species; is much more flattened and has short, flat branches; has multiple attachments to the ground; and somewhat larger spores. It is common under Virginia pine and pine/hardwoods, in sand. In addition, *S. spathulata* has light zonations (see photo below) and the flesh is tougher than *S. crispa*. Both species are edible and good, but they must be cooked slowly. Young specimens are more fleshy and are preferred. The conspicuous cauliflower-like appearance makes *Sparassis* a distinctive fungus.

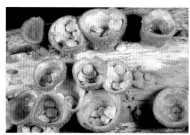

Crucibulum laeve

The orders and families in the Gasteromycetes all have one feature in common, the loss of forcible spore discharge. In place of this loss, the fruiting bodies have developed structural and physiological means of discharging their spores. The puffballs, stalked puffballs, stinkhorns, earth stars, and earth balls develop the spores within the gleba. At maturity, the gleba becomes powdery and the spores are discharged through a pore or opening in the apex of the fruiting body. Discharge is usually caused by rain drops striking the peridium, or outer skin of the fruiting body, resulting in a puff of spores that are wind disseminated. The earth balls also have a powdery gleba at maturity and the spores are then wind disseminated. Stinkhorns have a stipe or head on which the slimy green gleba develops. At maturity the green slime emits a foul odor that attracts insects. They land and eat the spores, but the slimy covering over the spores causes them to adhere to the insects feet. As the insects visit other humus piles, they leave some spores that can colonize the new location. Perhaps the most bizarre modification for spore dissemination is achieved by the bird's nest fungi. The small "eggs" that develop within the "nest" contain the basidia that produce the spores. The "eggs" are discharged by rain drops resulting in a splash cup mechanism of discharge. The sequestrate fungi are agarics and boletes in which the lamellae or pores have become contorted or modified, preventing forcible spore discharge. The fruiting body is often carried off by squirrels or other rodents. In some cases the fruiting body becomes woody and stands erect, gradually disintegrating, resulting in wind dissemination of the spores. The false truffles are hypogeous, found beneath the ground. They have oval to irregular fleshy fruiting bodies with minute locules in the gleba. The spores usually have thick-walls. At maturity the fleshy fruiting bodies omit volatile odors easily detected by rodents, which dig them up and eat them. The spores pass through the gut, unaffected, and are deposited in the feces, which effectively distributes the spores. All these structures and physiologically adapted functions create species that are able to survive and flourish in different habitats without forcibly discharging their spores.

Edibility: Puffballs in both *Calvatia* and *Lycoperdon* are widely eaten when young, white throughout and fresh. Young buttons of stinkhorns are edible, but we have never considered them all that good. Soon the odor of the mature fruiting body begins to appear and is most distasteful. Some false truffles, such as *Rhizopogon* are listed as edible, but we don't consider them to be very good. Earth balls, Sclerodermatales, are poisonous and cause severe gastric upset (Type 8 toxins). When young and fresh the gleba soon turns deep purple and has very small white locules.

EARTH STARS, PUFFBALLS, AND EARTH BALLS

The puffballs, earth stars, and earth balls all produce their spores within the fruiting body. At maturity the spores are in a powdery gleba or spore mass. The puffballs and earth stars have capillitium that are thick-walled, filamentous cells (Figs. 20-24), which proliferate throughout the gleba. Spore dispersal is achieved by means of an ostiole or pore at the apex of the fruiting body or by the splitting of the fruiting body at maturity. In either case the spores are generally wind disseminated. The spores are globose to subglobose with small warts or spines (Fig. 10) which provides them with an ability stick to surfaces, the ground, or vegetation once they make contact. The spores often have a pedicel (Fig. 15) attached or floating, when viewed with a microscope. The fruiting body is variously modified to achieve this purpose and possesses 2 or 3 outer layers called the peridium. The outer layer is the exoperidium; the second layer the mesoperidium; and the third, inner layer the endoperidium. *Lycoperdon,* for example, has only 2 layers (Fig. 37). At maturity the exoperidium sloughs off and reveals the endoperidium, where the ostiole is located. *Geastrum* has three layers and the exo- and mesoperidium split and recurve back, leaving the endoperidium, containing the exposed gleba (Fig. 38). The ostiole develops from the endoperidium The genera are distinguished as described below.

Several genera develop an ostiole or pore to accommodate dispersal of the spores. *Lycoperdon* has a gleba and often has a chambered sterile base. *Vascellum* is very similar, but has a membrane separating the gleba from the sterile base. *Disciseda* lacks a subgleba, but the exoperidium is composed of sand grains mixed with hyphae. *Bovista* has a capillitium of separate, individual capillitial units and lacks a sterile base. *Bovistella* is the same, but has a sterile base. Several genera lack the ostiole. *Calvatia* may or may not have a sterile base. *Calbovista* is similar, but has a very thick exo- and endoperidium. *Mycenastrum* is also similar, but has a thick-walled, thorny capillitium (Fig. 24) unlike the regular capillitium (Fig. 20) possessed by the other genera.

Geastrum and the earth balls are keyed out here, but fully detailed on pages 470 and 461, respectively.

Edibility: The best edible species of the puffballs are in *Calvatia* and *Lycoperdon. Calvatia gigantea, C. booniana, C. cyathiformis,* and *C. craniiformis* are the most commonly collected for the table, and all are very good edible species. Smaller species of *Lycoperdon* are also edible, but not widely eaten. There are no toxins reported and little concrete evidence for adverse reactions to species of either *Calvatia* or *Lycoperdon.*

KEY TO EARTH STARS, PUFFBALLS, & EARTH BALLS

1. Fruiting body white, firm when young, in age changing to yellow-brown, red-brown, or purple-brown, powdery -- 2

1. Fruiting body purple to dark brown and chambered when young; in age purple, purple-brown to rusty, dark brown --- 8

  2. In age, exoperidium (outer skin) sloughs off revealing an ostiole (pore) at the apex of the endoperidium (inner skin)--- 3

  2. Not as above, usually splitting open or entire peridium sloughs off leaving a naked gleba--- 7

3. Exoperidium splitting to form pointed rays, revealing a distinct ostiole -------- *Geastrum*
(see Earth Stars, page 443)

3. Not as above --- 4

  4. Fruiting body very small, 0.5–2.0 cm high; with a sand-case (acornlike) over the bottom; with a large apical ostiole------------------------------------- *Disciseda candida*

  4. Fruiting body variable in size; without a sand-case; forms an apical ostiole in age --- 5

5. Capillitium of discrete, thick-walled units with tapering branches; fruiting body white when young, metalic gray, inner peridium dingy brown to purple-brown in age --- *Bovista, Bovistella*

5. Capillitium of thick-walled, long cells, sometimes branched, less often septate; fruiting body not as above --- 6

  6. Sterile base separated from gleba by a membrane------------------ *Vascellum curtisii*

  6. Sterile base, when present, not separated by a membrane---------------- *Lycoperdon*

7. Fruiting body 4–7 cm high, 6–10 cm wide; in dry prairie or sagebrush communities, in western North America; capillitium with thornlike end cells ------ *Mycenastrum corium*

7. Not as above -- *Calvatia, Calbovista*

  8. Fruiting body, at maturity with starlike rays that are checkered on the inside; inner peridium splits at maturity; no pore develops --------------- *Astraeus hygrometricus*
(see Earth Balls, page 461)

  8. Not as above --- 9

9. Fruiting body oval to somewhat depressed, with a very hard peridium; immature gleba purple, with fine, white chambers --- *Scleroderma*
(see Earth Balls, page 461)

9. Fruiting body a rusty brown, clavate club with chambers ----------------------- *Pisolithus*
(see Earth Balls, page 461)

EARTH STARS

The earth stars are made up of a unique group of species that have developed a structure to accommodate spore discharge. They have a 3-layered peridium. The outer 2 layers, exo- and mesoperidium, split and peel back, forming pointed rays and sometimes lift the fruiting body up, exposing the third layer or endoperidium (Fig. 38). The spore sac has a peristome surrounding the single ostiole or pore, through which the spores can be discharged. The discharge occurs in nature when rain drops strike the spore sac and a puff of the powdery, dry spores is released into the air and blown away to initiate new colonies of each species. Two recent treatments of *Geastrum* are by Ponce de Leon (1968) and Sunhede (1989). Coker and Couch (1927) have an account of the southern species. *Myriostoma coliforme,* a widely distributed fungus, is unique with several pores in the spore sac. Since *Lycoperdon* has a capillitium, and the similar spores are released through an ostiole, we assumed they were related to the earth stars. Now, with new molecular techniques, we find that they are not related, and it is a prime example of convergent evolution. In fact, the species of *Lycoperdon* are decomposers, but we are not really sure of the role of *Geastrum. Geastrum* and *Myriostoma* may be mycorrhizal genera, but that possibility is still awaiting confirmation.

Edibility: None of the earth stars is edible.

KEY TO THE SPECIES OF GEASTRUM AND MYRIOSTOMA

1. Fruiting body with several pores over the spore case ------------- *Myriostoma coliforme*
1. Fruiting body with a single pore at the apex of the spore case ----------------------------- 2
    2. Spore case on a raised pedicel at maturity------- -- 3
    2. Spore case without a raised pedicel at maturity -- 4
3. Spore case with a sulcate (deeply furrowed) attachment to
    the pedicel -- *Geastrum pectinatum*
3. Spore case without a sulcate attachment ----------------------------- *Geastrum coronatum*
                        (see comments under *Geastrum pectinatum*)

 4. Spore sac arching up but remaining attached to the outer
     peridium -- *Geastrum fornicatum*

 4. Not as above -- 5

 5. Rays hygroscopic, closed tightly when fruiting body drys out ------ *Geastrum corollinum*
                   (if rays are checkered, see *Astraeus hygrometricus*)

 5. Rays not hygroscopic --- 6

     6. Rays recurving, 2–5 cm broad, leaving spore case in a shallow bowl --------------- 7

     6. Rays recurving, 5–9 cm broad, often cracking, leaving spore case in a
         deep bowl -- *Geastrum triplex*

 7. Spore case with a light brown disc, surrounding the fibrillose
     peristome -- *Geastrum saccatum*

 7. Spore case without an apical disc, only a fibrillose peristome ---- *Geastrum fimbriatum*
                   (see comments under *Geastrum saccatum*)

Myriostoma coliforme (Pers.) Corda
INEDIBLE

Fruiting body 5–10 cm broad when fully open, with 5–7 pointed rays. Spore case 4–8 cm broad, ovoid, smooth, silver-brown with several pores and supported on several, nearly fused, short stipes. Gleba white, changing to brown at maturity. Odor none. Taste unknown

Spores 4.5–7.5 µm globose, warted and partially reticulate, thick-walled, nonamyloid, yellow-brown.

Habit and distribution: Single to several, partially buried at first, in various habitats. Widely distributed throughout North America but infrequently encountered. Fruiting in summer and fall.

Comments: The placement of this fungus in this family is not certain at this time. More study needs to be carried out.

Geastrum pectinatum Pers.
INEDIBLE

Fruiting body 4–8 cm broad when fully open, with 4–8 pointed rays. Spore case 1.0–2.5 cm broad, 0.9–1.2 cm high, globose, depressed, with an apical, pointed, sulcate peristome, gray-brown to light brown. Beneath spore case is a sulcate attachment to the raised pedicel, 3–8 mm long, 1–4 mm wide (Fig. 38). A sheath forms around the pedicel at first but falls away as it matures. In age, rays recurved, raising the fruiting body from the ground. Gleba nearly white at first, soon dark brown. Odor none. Taste unknown.

Spores 4.0–5.5 µm globose, thick-walled, with warts, 1.0–1.5 µm high, nonamyloid, brown.

Habit and distribution: Single to several on the ground under hardwoods or conifers or in open grass communities, open disturbed areas, etc. Widely distributed. Fruiting in summer and fall.

Comments: *Geastrum coronatum* Pers. looks similar; has a spore case elevated on a pedicel; but it lacks the sulcate attachment to the spore case; and lacks a sheath surrounding the young pedicel, which is shown above. Both species may be found in the same habitats.

445

Geastrum fornicatum (Huds.) Fr.
INEDIBLE

Fruiting body 2–5 cm broad, 4–12 cm high when fully open. The mesoperidium splits to form 4 to 7 rays, which arch up but remain attached to the outer peridium that is sand-covered and heavy. The spore case is 0.9–4.0 cm broad, light brownish, oval, with a very short stalk or pedicel, at the apex with a fibrillose peristome surrounding the pore. Gleba mature dark brown and powdery. Odor none. Taste unknown.

Spores 5–6 μm globose, with blunt warts 0.6–1.0 μm high, thick-walled, nonamyloid, brown.

Habit and distribution: Single to several on the ground among vegetation or in dry or desert communities. It is common in southwestern United States, uncommon elsewhere. Fruiting in winter, spring, and fall, following wet weather.

Comments: The heavy sand-covered outer peridium holds the fruiting body in place and upright in heavy winds typical of the habitats in which it grows. The picture is of a specimen collected in Arizona.

Geastrum corollinum (Batsch) Hollós
INEDIBLE

Fruiting body open 2–7 cm broad when fully open, with 7–10 thin, hygroscopic rays which tightly close when dry. Spore case 0.5–2.5 cm broad, oval, depressed, glabrous, pale grayish pink, peristome not distinct, pore raised, finely fibrillose. Gleba whitish, becoming dark brown in age. Odor none. Taste unknown.

Spores 4.0–5.5 μm globose, with blunt warts 0.5 μm high, thick-walled, nonamyloid, brown.

Habit and distribution: Several to numerous, on ground among grasses, litter, and duff, often recorded near juniper. Widely distributed. Fruiting in summer and fall.

Comments: Also known as *Geastrum recolligens* (With.) Desvaux, its highly hygroscopic rays look very similar to *Astraeus hygrometricus*, but *Astraeus* has thicker, checkered rays and a fibrillose spore case. We have collected *G. corollinum* in Montana and in Oregon on Steens Mountain.

Geastrum triplex Jungh.
NONPOISONOUS

Fruiting body 5–9 cm broad when fully open, with 4–8 pointed rays, recurving toward the base, leaving the spore case sitting in a bowl, inner surface of the rays often cracked. Spore case 1.5–3.0 cm broad, 0.9–2.0 cm high, oval, depressed, gray-brown to brown, smooth with a pale, circular, apical disc and a radially fibrillose peristome surrounding the pore. Gleba white at first to dark brown and powdery at maturity. Odor none. Taste unknown..

Spores 3.5–4.5 μm globose, covered with blunt warts 1.0–1.5 μm long, thick-walled, nonamyloid, brown.

Habit and distribution: Single to several on ground under conifers and hardwoods. Widely distributed. Fruiting in summer and fall.

Comments: We have collected this species throughout the United States and in Asia, where it is also common.

Geastrum saccatum (Fr.) E. Fischer
INEDIBLE

Fruiting body 2–5 cm broad when fully open, with 4–10 pointed rays, recurving, leaving the spore case sitting in a shallow bowl. Spore case 0.6–2.0 cm broad, 0.8–1.5 cm high, oval, depressed, reddish brown with a pale light brown apical disc with conic fibrillose peristome. Gleba brown to light orange-brown. Odor none. Taste unknown.

Spores 3.5–6.0 μm globose, covered with blunt warts, 0.3–0.8 μm high, thick-walled, nonamyloid, brown.

Habit and distribution: Several to numerous on the ground under hardwoods, juniper, often around stumps. Widely distributed. Fruiting from late summer until late fall.

Comments: *Geastrum fimbriatum* (Fr.) A.H. Sm. is very similar; does not have an apical disc; has somewhat smaller spores, 3.0–3.5 μm diam, with blunt warts and partially reticulate ridges. Both species are widely distributed.

447

Disciseda candida (Schwein.) Lloyd
INEDIBLE

Fruiting body small, 0.5–2.0 cm high, 2.0–3.5 cm wide, oval and with a sand-case covering at first but usually seen with a sand-covered base (see inset) and an uncovered inner peridium with a distinct ostiole, silvery gray to slate-gray or dull light brown. The sand-case is held together by white mycelium. Gleba white, yellowish to dark brown when mature. Immature fruiting body connected to the ground by a rhizomorph, but turning over at maturity to present the ostiole on top. Odor none. Taste unknown.

Spores 3.0–5.5 µm globose, warted, with a short pedicel (Fig. 15), thick-walled, brown. Capillitium flexuous, thick-walled, occasionally branched, breaking up into short segments.

Habit and distribution: Several to gregarious on the ground in open often dry fields, dunes, desert areas or disturbed areas. Widely distributed. Fruiting spring, summer, and fall.

Comments: Often called the "Acorn Fungus" because the mature form does resemble an acorn with the basal sand-case, which remains attached (see photos). The heavy, lower sand-case enables the fruiting body to flip upright if it is upset by rain or wind. The genus is not studied in North America, but Smith & Smith (1973) and Arora (1986) provide more information on the species.

Bovista pila Berk. & M. A. Curtis
NONPOISONOUS

Fruiting body ovoid to globose, 3–4 (-8) cm wide, peridium white, fine, fuzzy, soon wearing off exposing the endoperidium, which is thin, papery, metallic to bronze-colored, soon dingy purplish brown with a well-developed round pore on top, attached to soil by a thin root-like extension. Gleba white when young to dark brown in age, powdery. Sterile base absent. Odor none. Taste unknown.

Spores 3.5–4.5 µm globose, smooth, with broken pedicels (Fig. 15), brown. Capillitium of discrete units, and a broad, main cell, with proliferating tapered branches typical of all species of *Bovista*.

Habit and distribution: Solitary, scattered, to numerous in pastures, especially where cattle have been or open woods. Widely distributed. Fruiting in summer and fall.

Comments: *Bovista plumbea* Pers. is smaller, 1–3 cm, and the outer white coat shrinks to a series of white patches, bluish gray in age. The spores are large and oval, 5–7 x 4.5–6.0 µm, and the base is attached by a pedicel, 9–14 µm long. *Bovista minor* Morgan is uncommon; small; not bluish; spores 4–5 x 3.5–4.0 µm, with long, 4–5 x 3.5–4.0 µm, tapering pedicels as in *B. pila*. The distinctive capillitium is diagnostic (Miller & Miller, 1988) and (Smith, 1951).

Bovistella radicata (Mont.) Pat.
NONPOISONOUS

Fruiting body 4–6 cm high, 5–10 cm wide, oval, white when young with a scurfy surface, granular or with connivent fibrils, light brown with a grayish tint in age, exoperidium sloughing off to reveal a papery, metallic, endoperidium with a large ostiole or pore. Gleba white young, yellowish to brown at maturity. Subgleba large, chambered, white, becoming yellowish to yellow-brown at maturity, forming a persistent base, with a stout, tapering rhizomorph extending into the ground. Odor none. Taste sweet and pleasant.

Spores 3.5–4.5 x 4.2–5.5 µm subglobose with a persistent, attached pedicel (Fig. 15), thin-walled, smooth. Capillitium of discrete units, a main cell of slightly thick-walls, and tapering branches, reddish brown in age.

Habit and distribution: Several to many on the ground in open woods, pastures or livestock holding pens. Widely distributed. Fruiting in late summer and fall.

Comments: The ample sterile base separates *Bovistella* from *Bovista*, however the unique capillitial units and spores with pedicles are the same. We have no information on its edibility. We have collected it in cow pastures.

Vascellum curtisii Berk.
NONPOISONOUS

Fruiting body 0.9–2.2 cm broad, oval, sightly depressed, not cracking in age, with white dense, short, connivent spines. Gleba white at first to olive-brown in age. Subgleba narrow, chambered, white, delineated from the gleba by a membrane, easily observed in young material. Odor mild. Taste mild.

Spores 2.8–3.5 µm globose, echinulate, thick-walled, olive-brown. Capillitium with thickened walls, branched, tapered at ends, with pores and incrusted material.

Habit and distribution: Usually several to many on bare ground, or in grass communities, and lawns. Widely distributed. Fruiting in summer and fall.

Comments: Also known as *Lycoperdon curtisii* Berk., it is too small to be considered as an edible. *Vascellum pratense* (Pers. em Quél.) Kreisel is larger, 2.5–5.0 cm high, 2–4 cm wide, with an exoperidium of spines; the subgleba is also delineated by a membrane; and has nearly smooth, globose spores, 3.5–5.5 µm. It is also found in pastures, grassy areas, and disturbed areas, and is widely distributed (Smith & Smith, 1973).

LYCOPERDON

Lycoperdon is typified by having an ostiole at maturity, and a white gleba when young, which turns from yellow-brown to dark brown, or reddish brown at maturity. The mature gleba is powdery, with thick-walled capillitium (Fig. 20), which may have pores (Fig. 21) or slits (Fig. 22), or neither. The spores are thick-walled, warted, and globose. When present, the sterile base is not separated from the gleba by a membrane, as is found in *Vascellum*. The exoperidium has warts, fibrills, or connivent fibrils, which slough off as the fruiting body matures. The species are decomposers of wood and plant parts (Miller & Miller, 1988).

Edibility: The larger species are edible when they are immature and the gleba is pure white. The taste is not outstanding and the larger species of *Calvatia* are much preferred. No toxins have been reported in the genus.

KEY TO LYCOPERDON

1. Fruiting body with a smooth to granular peridium -- 2
1. Fruiting body with cone-shaped spines or hairs on the peridium -------------------------- 3
   2. Fruiting body small, 0.8–2.0 cm wide, globose; sterile base absent --- *Lycoperdon pusillum*
   2. Fruiting body pear-shaped, larger; sterile base present-------- *Lycoperdon pyriforme*
3. Fruiting body with cone-shaped spines --------------------------------- *Lycoperdon perlatum*
3. Not as above -- 4
   4. Fruiting body brown with dark brown to black-brown, connivent fibrils -- *Lycoperdon foetidum*
   4. Not as above--- 5
5. Fruiting body small, 1–3 cm high, 1.0–4.5 cm wide, white, with low spines; exoperidium cracking and separating in patches; found on open ground ------ *Lycoperdon marginatum*
5. Not as above -- 6
   6. Fruiting body with long, dense spines, 0.3–0.6 cm long-------------------------------- 7
   6. Fruiting body with shorter, often connivent spines (0.2 cm long or less) ------------ 8
7. Spines sloughing off in age, leaving a reticulate pattern on the endoperidium --- *Lycoperdon echinatum*

7. Spines sloughing off in age, leaving a smooth, nonreticulate pattern on the
   endoperidium -- *Lycoperdon pulcherrimum*
   8. Fruiting body yellow-brown, with spines up to 0.1 cm high, often
      connivent; sterile base olive-brown to purple-brown in age; spores with
      broken pedicels --- *Lycoperdon umbrinum*
   8. Fruiting body gray-brown to light gray, with fine, soft spines, less than
      0.1 cm high and ragile connivent fibrils; sterile base white; spores with
      broken pedicels --- *Lycoperdon pedicellatum*
                          (see comments under *Lycoperdon umbrinum*)

Lycoperdon pusillum Pers.
NONPOISONOUS

Fruiting body small, 0.8–2.0 cm wide, globose, with small granules, white, ostiole (Fig. 27) or pore forming in old age. Gleba white, yellow to deep coffee-brown at maturity. Sterile base absent, but long, thin rhizomorphs proliferate from the base. Odor none. Taste mild.

Spores 3–5 µm globose, minutely spiny, thick-walled, with a very short, attached pedicel, brown. Capillitium thick-walled, branched, with small round pits.

Habit and distribution: Several to many on open hard ground, in humus and mulch beds. Widely distributed. Fruiting in spring, summer, and fall.

Comments: We have collected it most often in disturbed areas. It is probably edible, but too small to be worthwhile.

Lycoperdon pyriforme Schaeff.:Pers.
EDIBLE

Fruiting body 1.5–3.5 cm high, 1.5–4.5 cm wide, pear-shaped; exoperidium smooth to granular, but sometimes has scattered hairs at the apex, often minutely cracked, pore at apex slow to form, light tan to brown in age. Gleba white when young to olive-brown at maturity. Sterile base dull white unchanging in age, occupies lower one-third of fruiting body. Abundant rhizomorphs emanate from the base of the fruiting body and proliferate into surrounding wood. Odor unpleasant. Taste mild.

Spores 3.0–3.5 µm, globose, thick-walled, smooth, olive-brown. Capillitium thick-walled, branched, without septa.

Habit and distribution: Rarely single, most often in dense cespitose clusters on well-rotted hardwood logs and stumps, wood debris, wood mulch, and sawdust. Widely distributed. Fruiting in summer and fall.

Comments: An old, weathered spore case with an apical pore may be seen on wood at any time of the year. We have often seen large fruitings on wood mulch in gardens. The young, white fruiting bodies are edible. *Calvatia fumosa* Zeller, under conifers in western North America, is also smooth but smoky gray-brown, often cracked; with an unpleasant odor in age. It does not form a pore in age, but splits open instead.

Lycoperdon perlatum Pers.
EDIBLE

Fruiting body 3–7 cm high, 3–6 cm wide, pear-shaped, exoperidium covered with small, round, cone shaped spines, that break off, leaving noticeable round spots, dull whitish to light tan. Gleba white young to olive-brown in age, sometimes tinted purplish at maturity. Sterile base is composed of large white chambers, discoloring olive-brown in age. Odor none. Taste mild.

Spores 3.5–4.5 μm globose, thick walled with minute spines, olive-brown. Capillitium thick-walled, brown, without septa.

Habit and distribution: Single or numerous to cespitose clusters in duff and humus under hardwoods and conifers. Widely distributed. Fruiting in summer and fall.

Comments: Also known as *Lycoperdon gemmatum* Batsch, it is very common in a wide variety of habitats. The flavor is not as good as *Calvatia gigantea*. In western North America, *L. foetidum* is much more common in the conifer forests.

Lycoperdon foetidum Bonord.
EDIBLE

Fruiting body 2.5–3.5 cm high, 2.0–2.5 cm wide, oval to pyriform with a sterile base, covered densely with dark brown to black-brown, connivent fibrils over a brown ground color, when spines fall off, revealing a reticulate pattern. Gleba white to buff and dull brown at maturity. Sterile base chambered, 0.5–1.5 mm diam, dull white. Base with numerous, small, white rhizomorphs. Odor unpleasant. Taste mild.

Spores 3.5–4.8 μm globose, minute spines, thick-walled, very short pedicels, brown. Capillitium brown, thick-walled, equal, without septa, and with pores.

Habit and distribution: Several to many on the ground under or near conifers. Found in northern and western North America. Fruiting in summer and fall.

Comments: Also known as *Lycoperdon nigrescens* Pers., it appears to be closely related to *L. umbrinum*. We see it commonly in our western conifer forests, but have not eaten it.

Lycoperdon marginatum Vittad.:Moris & De Not.
EDIBLE

Fruiting body 1–3 cm high, 1–4.5 cm wide, subglobose to somewhat flattened, exoperidium white, covered with white, low, sharp spines, sometimes several fused together, cracked and flaking off in patches at maturity. Gleba firm, white to olive-brown or gray-brown, without a membrane separating it from the sterile base. Sterile base white, olive-brown, chambered. Odor none. Taste mild.

Spores 3.5–4.5 μm globose, minutely spined, thick-walled, olive-brown. Capillitium of thick-walled, slender to contorted cells, without pores.

Habit and distribution: Scattered to numerous in small clusters or even cespitose, on open ground, pastures, and golf courses. Widely distributed. Fruiting in summer and fall.

Comments: See comments under *Vascellum curtisii* which looks very similar in the field. *Lycoperdon marginatum* is too little to be considered for the table.

Lycoperdon echinatum Pers.
EDIBLE

Fruiting body 2.0–3.5 cm high, 2–4 cm wide, globose to broadly pear-shaped, over the top the exoperidium is densely covered with long spines, 3–6 mm long, some with convergent tips, white at first to dark brown (see inset), spines slough off in  age leaving a reticulate or net-like surface. Gleba white, yellowish, finally purplish. Sterile base small, not well developed, dingy white to purple-gray. Odor none. Taste mild.

Spores 4–6 μm, globose, minutely warted, thick-walled, purple-brown. Pedicels (Fig. 15) break off and are visible in slides mounted for study. Capillitium thick-walled, olive-brown, occasionally branched, with round pores.

Habit and distribution: Single or more often numerous on moss, humus, or wood debris. Found in central and eastern North America. Fruiting in late summer and fall.

Comments: *Lycoperdon pulcherrimum* Berk. & M. E. Curtis also has long spines, but they are more stout, when sloughed off peridium is not reticulate; the spores have pedicels, 10–13 μm long, usually broken off but some attached; and it is found in southern United States.

Lycoperdon umbrinum Pers.
EDIBLE

Fruiting body 1.5–8.0 cm high, 1.5–5.0 cm wide, pear-shaped, over the top the exoperidium is covered with short, slender, connivent spines, up to 1 mm high, along with some granules, honey-yellow, clay-brown to dull brown in age, ostiole at top, 3–5 mm wide, observed sooner than most. Gleba occupies rounded upper area, white but extremely variable, while maturing, olive-brown to brown, usually brown with a dull purplish hue in old age. Sterile base well developed up to one-half of total height, with large chambers, 0.5–1 mm wide, white when young to olive-brown or purplish brown in age. Odor mild to slightly unpleasant. Taste mild.

Spores 4.0–5.5 µm globose, thick-walled, with minute spines or small warts, pedicels 6–10 µm long, usually broken off, dull brown. Capillitium thick-walled, often bulbous, with many pores, dark brown.

Habit and distribution: Scattered or even in loose clusters on humus, usually but not always under conifers. Widely distributed. Fruiting in summer in north, but fall elsewhere.

Comments: *Lycoperdon pedicellatum* Peck has denser, longer spines, 1–2 mm, and pedicels 10–18 µm long, which remain attached to the spore. *Lycoperdon molle* Pers.:Pers. has a gray-brown surface, and spores with pedicels. *Lycoperdon umbrinum* var *floccosum* Lloyd is a handsome, shiny, white variety with long, wooly, soft spines. The spines are composed of a series of hairs, which are connivent and bound together.

Mycenastrum corium (Guers.:DC.) Desv.
EDIBLE

Fruiting body 4.0–7.5 cm high, 6–10 cm wide globose to slightly depressed, with flat, broad squamules and cracks forming a roughly oval to rectangular pattern, dull white, at maturity splitting into 6–9 pointed rays, which somewhat recurve exposing the ball-like gleba. Gleba white young to olive-brown and black-brown in age. Sterile base absent or very reduced and white. Odor unusual or mild. Taste pleasant, mild.

Spores 8.5–11.0 µm globose, thick-walled, with a coarse reticulum and warts, yellowish. Capillitium thick-walled, branched, with distinctive tapering, pointed, thorny end cells (Fig. 24).

Habit and distribution: Several to gregarious on the ground at low elevations in open sagebrush and saltbush dominated communities, or in grassy or shrubby wet areas in dry prairie. Found in western North America. Fruiting in spring and summer.

Comments: We have eaten this fungus and find it to have an unusual but likeable taste. We have no records of its occurrence above 3000' elevation. It is characteristically found in prairie or desert communities. A new subspecies *M. corium* var *ferrugineum* O.K. Mill., R. Brace & V. Evenson, with a rusty red gleba, has been described from Colorado (Miller et al., 2005).

CALVATIA AND CALBOVISTA

The species of *Calvatia* are the largest of the puffballs. The often orna-mented exoperidium sloughs off at maturity, exposing the thin endoperidium, which then splits open, exposing the gleba. The gleba consists of thick-walled capillitium (Fig. 20), and warted, globose spores. The basidia develop rapidly in the young, pure white gleba and are soon gone as the spores mature. The mature gleba of individual species has different colors, ranging from yellow-brown to deep purple-brown or even greenish orange to pink. Fruiting bodies range from golfball to basketball size or larger. *Calbovista* is closely related, but has a very thick peridium and tapered capillitial elements. The species of both genera are all decomposers of grass, humus, or buried wood debris.

Edibility: *Calvatia gigantea* and *C. booniana,* the largest of the species, are very fine edibles. In addition, *C. craniiformis* and *C. cyathiformis,* grapefruit size, are also delicious. They must all be harvested when the gleba is pure white. They may be kept for a day in the refrigerator, but must be used before the gleba changes color or the taste becomes unpleasant. There are no toxins reported in the genus.

KEY TO CALVATIA AND CALBOVISTA

1. Fruiting body very large, 10–35 cm high, 20–60 cm wide; sterile base absent or reduced -- 2
1. Fruiting body smaller; sterile base present--- 3
    2. Fruiting body oval to globose, smooth, white; widely distributed -- *Calvatia gigantea*
    2. Fruiting body oval, depressed to flattened, sculptured, with flat scales, white; in western North America --- *Calvatia booniana*
3. Fruiting body grapefruit size, smooth or scalloped but without raised or pyramidal warts; widely distributed --- 4
3. Fruiting body smaller or with raised or pyramidal warts; in the mountains of western North America -- 8
    4. Gleba changes from white to yellow-green, olive-brown to yellow-brown in age---- 5
    4. Gleba greenish orange, pink to purple-brown in age------------------------------------- 6

5. Fruiting body dull white, sculptured over the surface; gleba bright yellow-green to olive-brown in age; sterile base breaks down in age ---------------- *Calvatia craniiformis*
5. Fruiting body brown, cracked; gleba olive-brown to dark brown in age; sterile base persistent in age --- *Calvatia bovista*
        (see comments under *Calvatia cyathiformis*)

    6. Gleba purple to purple-brown in age; exoperidium white but soon pinkish tan to brown in age -- *Calvatia cyathiformis*
    6. Gleba greenish yellow to bright pink or purple --- 7

7. Gleba greenish-yellow; exoperidium bruising bright yellow, orange at maturity --- *Calvatia rubro-flava*
        (see comments under *Calvatia cyathiformis*)
7. Gleba bright pink to purple; exoperidium not as above, dull white ------ *Calvatia fragilis*
        (see comments under *Calvatia craniiformis*)

    8. Exoperidium with long, pointed, pyramidal warts; fruiting body pear-shaped --- *Calvatia sculpta*
    8. Exoperidium with slightly raised warts with brownish to reddish hairs at the center; fruiting body globose or slightly depressed ----------- *Calbovista subsculpta*

Calvatia gigantea (Batsch:Pers.) Lloyd
EDIBLE

Fruiting body large, 20–35 cm high, 20–55 cm wide, subglobose, exoperidium smooth, felt-like, white to light gray, yellow to olive in age, base with a thick root. Gleba white to dark olive-brown at maturity. Sterile base lacking or very reduced. Odor none young, foetid in age. Taste mild and pleasant.

Spores 3.5–5.5 x 3–5 µm subglobose to globose, minute, short spines to nearly smooth, without pedicels, olive. Capillitium thick-walled, branched with septa, small pores, brown.

Habit and distribution: Single to several together in low swales or wet areas, in woods or along the edges of meadows or in wet areas near streams. Widely distributed, but absent in the Rocky Mountains. Fruiting in late summer and fall.

Comments: *Calvatia booniana* is the "Western Giant Puffball" and rivals *C. gigantea* in size, but the sculptured surface identifies it at once. Both species are delicious edibles. *Hope's Mushroom Cookbook* (Miller, H., 1993) provides some excellent recipes.

Calvatia booniana A. H. Sm.
EDIBLE

Fruiting body large, 10–30 cm high, 20–60 cm wide, oval, depressed to flattened, surface of the exoperidium is sculptured, soon separating into large, flat scales, dull white to light tan or buff-colored, base with a small, thick, fibrous cord. Gleba white to olive-brown mature. Sterile base lacking. Odor very disagreeable in early maturity. Taste mild and pleasant.

Spores 4.0–6.5 x 3.5–5.5 µm subglobose to globose with minute spines, thick-walled, olive-brown. Capillitium thick-walled, septate, branched with very few pits, yellow-brown.

Habit and distribution: Single or several on the ground in open pastures, grassy areas, near old corrals, in especially arid habitats or micro-habitats, often near or under sagebrush. Found in western North America. Fruiting in the spring, summer, and fall.

Comments: Named for Dr. William Judson Boone, the first president of the College of Idaho, now Albertson College, who showed specimens to Dr. Smith in 1935. The "Western Giant Puffball" was described by A. H. Smith (Zeller and Smith, 1964). It is found nowhere else in the world. It has been collected and eaten since pioneer days. We find it of equal flavor to *C. gigantea.*

Calvatia craniiformis (Schwein.) Fr.
EDIBLE

Fruiting body robust 6–20 cm high, 8–20 cm wide, pear-shaped, smooth, white, exoperidium scalloped over the top, in age gray to very pale tan. Gleba white young, bright yellow-green to sordid olive-brown. Sterile base is over the lower one-third of the fruiting body, chambered, white at first, dark brown in age with white rhizomorphs from the base. Odor pleasant. Taste mild.

Spores 3.3–4.5 μm globose to subglobose, minutely spined, thick-walled, pedicel very short, yellowish. Capillitium thick-walled, infrequent branches, septate, with occasional pits.

Habit and distribution: Single to several or sometimes gregarious in grass communities, low wet areas and in hardwood forests. Found in eastern North America and southwestern United States. Fruiting in late summer and fall.

Comments: In *Calvatia cyathiformis,* the gleba mature turns purple-brown, while *C. craniiformis* has a bright yellow gleba that turns yellow-brown in age. They are both about grapefruit size and very good edibles. We like both species and have eaten them many times. *Calvatia fragilis* (Vittad.) Morgan has a gleba that changes from white to pink or purple as it matures; it is up to 8 x 5 cm in size; and is most frequently found in southern United States.

Calvatia cyathiformis (Bosc) Morgan
EDIBLE

Fruiting body 9–20 cm high, 7–16 cm wide, nearly pear-shaped but with a thick base and egg-shaped top, exoperidium is soon minutely cracked and sculptured over the top, smooth but wrinkled over the base and sides, white to light pinkish tan, brown in age. Gleba white, yellow to purple-brown in age. Sterile base is found over lower one-third of the fruiting body, chambered, white to dingy yellowish. Odor pleasant. Taste mild.

Spores 3.5–7.5 μm subglobose, with minute spines, thick-walled, purple to deep purple brown. Capillitium slightly thick-walled, occasionally branched, ends tapering, yellow-brown.

Habit and distribution: Scattered to numerous in old fields, grass, prairie or desert communities often following heavy rains. Widely distributed. Fruiting in summer and fall.

Comments: *Calvatia bovista* (Pers.) Kambly & Lee is also similar with an egg-shaped top and tapered, narrow base; the brown, exoperidium has flat areas, separated by pronounced cracks; and a dark olive-brown gleba at maturity. The sterile base is persistent and remains intact after the spores are dispersed. It is widely distributed but not common. *Calvatia rubro-flava* (Cragin) Morgan, in eastern North America, has a pinkish tan exoperidium, but all parts instantly bruise bright yellow, and are orange when dry. The gleba is greenish orange when mature. These species are all edible when the gleba is young and white (Zeller and Smith, 1964).

Calvatia sculpta (Harkn.) Lloyd
EDIBLE

Fruiting body 8–15 cm high, 8–10 cm wide, somewhat pear-shaped or egg-shaped, exoperidium is covered with distinctive, long, pointed, pyramid-shaped warts, either erect or bent over and even joined at the tip with other warts, in age peridium sloughs off leaving a naked brown spore mass. Gleba white to deep olive-brown at maturity. Sterile base is chambered, white to yellowish in age. Odor none. Taste mild.

Spores 3.5–6.5 µm globose to subglobose, minute spines, thick-walled, olive-brown. Capillitium thick-walled, infrequently branched, and with numerous pits (Fig. 21).

Habit and distribution: Single to several in duff under or near conifers at high elevations. Found in western North America. Fruiting in spring, summer, and fall during wet weather.

Comments: We have encountered this species most commonly in late June and early July. The conspicuous long pyramidal warts are the distinctive feature of this baseball-sized puffball. It is a very good edible.

Calbovista subsculpta Morse
EDIBLE

Fruiting body 6–12 cm high, 8–16 cm wide, globose or slightly depressed, covered with slightly raised, but not pointed, warts with brownish to reddish colored hairs at the center of each wart, the base often smooth to wrinkled but not warted. Gleba firm, white then red-brown or dark brown at maturity. Sterile base occupies the lower one-fourth to one-third of the fruiting body, is firm, with minute chambers, dull white, or slightly yellowish in age. Odor none. Taste pleasant.

Spores 3–5 µm globose, thin-walled, nearly smooth, hyaline to yellowish. Capillitium thin-walled, with irregular branches, and swollen thick-walled cells.

Habit and distribution: Single or several to gregarious on hard, dry road banks, stock driveways, usually near or under conifers. Found in western North America. Fruiting in late spring and summer.

Comments: This puffball is usually of softball size or sometimes larger, but never with the pointed, pyramidal warts of *Calvatia sculpta*. *Mycenastrum corium* (Guers.:DC.) Desv. is similar in size; dull white; has low blocklike cracks; but has a very reduced or absent sterile base. The capillitium has thorn-like branches (Fig. 24), and is also found at low elevations often among sagebrush or saltbush. *Calvatia subcretacea* Zeller is smaller, 1.5–4.0 cm high, 2–5 cm wide, with small, pointed, gray-tipped warts. It is found under conifers in western North America at high elevations (Miller, 1977).

EARTH BALLS

There are several features that bind the initially very different-appearing genera in the earth balls (Sclerodermatales) together. As they develop, they all have locules in which the spores mature and the young white gleba very soon turns purple or purple-brown but remains very firm. It eventually becomes powdery at maturity. The naked gleba is exposed when the peridium splits and recurves, except in *Astraeus,* which retains the endoperidium. The spores are not discharged through a well-formed ostiole or pore with an intact endoperidium. The typical capillitium of the puffballs is not present in the earth balls. *Astraeus,* unlike *Geastrum,* tears at the apex to release the spores. Lastly, *Scleroderma, Pisolithus,* and *Astraeus* are all broad host range mycorrhizal species and not decomposers as in the puffballs. *Pisolithus tinctorius* is used in conifer nurseries to form mycorrhizae with young seedlings. Guzman (1970) has a monograph of the North American species of *Scleroderma.*

Edibility: All of the species in the earth balls are poisonous, or extremely bitter and not edible, and cause severe gastric upset, Type 8 toxins.

KEY TO THE EARTH BALLS

1. Peridium splits into 7–15 pointed rays with a checkered surface; inner peridium present and covered with dense fibrils --- 2
1. Not as above -- 3
    2. Fruiting body 1–3 cm broad; widely distributed -------------- *Astraeus hygrometricus*
    2. Fruiting body 8–15 cm broad; found along West Coast of
       North America --- *Astraeus pteridus*
                    (see comments under *Astraeus hygrometricus*)
3. Fruiting body an olive to yellowish brown, clavate club, 4–25 cm tall, soon powdery, and dull brown at the apex with locules toward the base ------------ *Psolithus tinctorius*
3. Fruiting body oval to oval-depressed with a firm, purple gleba that eventually turns powdery, purple-brown at maturity with a hard peridium ----------------------------------- 4
    4. Fruiting body small, 1.5–4.5 cm broad, oval to round, smooth or with
       minute scales --- 5

    4. Not as above--- 6

5. Fruiting body dingy yellow to light reddish brown; spores 11–15 μm,
   globose, reticulate --- *Scleroderma bovista*

5. Fruiting body pale yellow-brown, sometimes with pink or reddish hues;
   spores 10–15 μm globose, spiny ------------------------------------- *Scleroderma areolatum*
                  (see comments under *Scleroderma borista*)

    6. Fruiting body brown, with a warted exoperidium, 3–6 cm broad; purple to violet-
      gray when young, with locules separated by fine, white membranes; spores with
      fine spines and particularly reticulate ridges -------- ------ *Scleroderma citrinum*

    6. Not as above, fruiting body not warted, large (4–14 cm broad), in age splitting like
      an earth star, revealing a naked gleba-- 7

7. Fruiting body with smooth, straw-colored peridium; spores 4–9 μm with warts and partial ridges -- *Scleroderma cepa*
             (see comments under *Scleroderma polyrhizon*)

7. Fruiting body with rough, often cracked, clay-colored peridium; spores 6.5–12.0 μm
   with warts and partial ridges --------------------------------------- *Scleroderma polyrhizon*

Astraeus hygrometricus (Pers.) Morgan
INEDIBLE

Fruiting body 1–3 cm broad, globose or somewhat depressed at first; outer skin splits into 7–15 pointed, checkered rays that open up and flatten out when wet, and are hygroscopic (on drying, the rays close around the spore case), opens at the top by tearing, and no regular pore is formed. The inner spore case is similar to *Geastrum* except it is covered with dense hairs. Gleba white at first, soon cocoa-brown, and divided into oval locules. Sterile base absent. Odor none. Taste unknown.

Spores 7–11 µm globose, thick-walled, with warts and spines, yellow-brown.

Habit and distribution: Scattered to numerous, in sand or sandy soil, under hardwoods and conifers. Widely distributed. Fruiting in the summer and fall.

Comments: This species has a broad host range and is mycorrhizal with many different plants. The immature gleba has locules, a characteristic of the earth balls, and not found in *Geastrum*. *Astraeus pteridus* (Shear) Zeller is much larger 8–15 cm broad when open; but otherwise appears very similar; and is only found along the West Coast.

Pisolithus tinctorius (Michx.:Pers) Coker & Couch
INEDIBLE

Fruiting body at first globose to clavate 4–12 cm broad, 4–25 cm high, and irregularly club-shaped, dull white, spotted olive-brown, yellowish brown to dingy brown in age. Peridium breaking open and disintegrates at the apex, revealing the brown powdery spores. Gleba composed of oval locules, pure white at first, becoming yellowish then dark brown and powdery when mature. Locules mature from the top down and more locules form near the base until almost the entire fruiting body is converted into a powdery mass. Odor mild young, but unpleasant in age. Taste unknown.

Spores 7–12 µm globose, with long spines, thick-walled, gleba brown.

Habit and distribution: Single to several, occasionally gregarious on ground under hardwoods and conifers. Widely distributed. Fruiting in spring, summer, and fall during wet weather.

Comments: Also known as *Pisolithus arhizus* (Scop.:Pers) Rauschert. It has a broad host range and is often an early successional mycorrhizal partner of tree seedlings. *Pisolithus tinctorius* is widely used in forestry where new pine plantations are often established with trees that have been inoculated with it.

Scleroderma bovista Fr.
Poisonous

Fruiting body ovoid, 1.5–4.0 cm tall, 2.0–4.5 cm wide, smooth or with minute scales, dingy yellowish to light reddish brown, splits or tears at the apex at maturity. Gleba when young firm, purple, with locules separated by fine white membranes, in age becoming deep purple-brown and powdery. Short stout rhizomorphs eminate from the short stipelike base. Odor none. Taste unknown.

Spores 11–15 μm globose, thick-walled, with complete reticulations, 1–2 μm high, gleba dark brown.

Habit and distribution: Single to several in sandy loam under hardwoods and conifers. Widely distributed. Fruiting in spring, summer, and fall.

Comments: The smooth exterior has led to the common name "Potato Earth Ball." It has very distinctive spores and is mycorrhizal with many different hosts. Like other earth balls, the gleba is white at first in the very young stage, soon becoming dark purple. *Scleroderma areolatum* Ehrenb. is very similar, pale yellow-brown, with minutes scales, but it has spores that are 10–15 μm globose with spines. Severe gastric upset can occur if ingested, Type 8 toxins.

Scleroderma citrinum Pers.:Pers.
POISONOUS

Fruiting body 3–6 (-12) cm broad, globose when young, depressed at maturity; brown exoperidium up to 2 mm thick, covered with cracks that set off a pattern of raised warts that may have central, somewhat darker warts, extending almost to the base, in age splitting to reveal the gleba but never star-shaped like *Astraeus*. Gleba very firm, briefly white, soon deep violet-gray to purple, with small locules separated by fine white membranes, when mature black-brown and powdery. Sterile base a slight broadening of the outer skin, white but bruising yellowish to faintly pink. Odor none. Taste bitter.

Spores 8–13 μm, globose, thick-walled, with fine spines and partial, reticulate ridges, brown.

Habit and distribution: Several or sometimes in cespitose clusters on the ground, near the base of trees, under conifers or hardwoods. Widely distributed but most common in eastern North America. Fruiting in late summer and fall.

Comments: Also known as *Scleroderma aurantium* Pers., it forms mycorrhizae with many different hosts. *Scleroderma bovista* Fr. is smaller (3–5 cm), usually smooth or sometimes cracked but without warts and with larger spores, (12–18 μm diam). Both are bitter tasting, cause severe gastric upset, and should be avoided, Type 8 toxins.

Scleroderma polyrhizum Pers.
POISONOUS

Fruiting body 4–14 cm broad, globose to depressed; exoperidium dull yellowish to clay color, very thick (almost 0.5 cm), rough, irregular cracks, in age splitting into regular lobes and recurving much like an earth star *(Geastrum),* revealing the naked, blackish brown gleba. Gleba firm, purple when young, oval locules separated by white membranes, dingy dull blackish brown and powdery in age. Numerous rhizomorphs extend from the stipelike base, which can vary in size or be almost absent. Odor none. Taste unknown.

Spores 6.5–12.0 μm globose, thick-walled, with warts and irregular ridges, spores yellow-brown.

Habit and distribution: Single or several together, on sandy banks, hard log roads, and in drainage ditches. It is mycorrhizal with hardwoods and conifers. Widely distributed but most common in eastern North America. Fruiting in summer and early fall.

Comments: Also known as *Scleroderma geaster* Fr. *Scleroderma cepa* Pers. is also large; has a smooth peridium that is roughened only in age, straw-colored; spores 4–9 μm broad with warts and partial ridges; the peridium at maturity also splits and recurves like an earth star; it is also widely distributed. Note that both of these species in the very small button stage will have a white gleba that very quickly turns purple. Both of these, if eaten, can cause severe gastric upset, Type 8 toxins.

STALKED PUFFBALLS

Most stalked puffballs initiate their growth below ground and are called hypogeous. The gleba matures within the earth, and at or near maturity the stalk or stipe elongates elevating the gleba above the ground to facilitate spore discharge. A pore or multiple pores develop over the top of the gleba and the spores discharge through the pores when raindrops hit the surface. *Battarrea* is an exception to this method of discharge. The gleba splits around the center, circumsessile dehiscence, and the entire top of the peridium "pops off" leaving the gleba exposed. The spores are then wind disseminated. The gleba in the puffballs and stalked puffballs contains a network of thick-walled, almost wirelike cells called capillitium, which separates the mature spores and allows for prolonged spore discharge caused by the impact of raindrops. The species are decomposers of roots, buried wood and other buried organic matter.

Edibility: The group is mostly woody when seen and therefore inedible, but without toxins as far as known.

KEY TO THE STALKED PUFFBALLS

1. Stalk base surrounded by a cup or volva --- 2
1. Stalk base without a cup or volva --- 4
   2. Spore case with one or several pores at the apex or over the top of the peridium -- 3
   2. Spore case splitting around the center with the top half falling away to reveal the total gleba; stalk woody and shaggy---------------------------------- *Battarrea stevenii*
3. Spore case with several pores over the peridium; stalk woody and shaggy-- *Battarraeoides digueti*
                 (see comments under *Battarrea stevenii*)
3. Spore case with a single pore at the apex; stalk smooth with longitudinal grooves -- *Chlamydopus meyenianus*
   4. Stalk dry, brittle, woody; spore case dry with an oval pore at the apex --- *Tulostoma simulans*
   4. Stalk corded, covered with a thick, sticky, gelatinous layer; spore case with red ridges at the apex --- *Calostoma cinnabarina*

Battarrea stevenii (Libosch.) Fr.
INEDIBLE

Fruiting body an ovoid spore case on a long woody stipe, which has an volva at the base. Spore case 2.5–3.5 cm high, 3–5 cm broad, oval, flattened, brown, splitting around the middle to reveal a dark brown, sticky gleba that adheres to everything it touches. Stalk 16–70 cm tall, 1–4 cm wide, equal or enlarging, dry, woody, brown, covered with shaggy, hairy scales, base is oval to nearly round with a one-layered volva 3–10 cm high, 4–12 cm wide surrounding the stipe, usually below ground. Odor and taste unknown.

Spores 5.5–8.5 x 6–8 μm subglobose, covered with thick, blunt warts, nonamyloid, brown. Capillitium of elements 27–50 x 5–6 μm called (Fig. 23) elators with thick spiral bands around each cell, unusually numerous.

Habit and distribution: Solitary or several in sagebrush prairie or deserts in the southwestern United States and western North America. Fruiting in very early spring but tough fruiting bodies may last two seasons.

Comments: A closely related species *Battarrea phalloides* (Dicks.) Pers. is reported to have a gelatinous tissue in the volva. Studies of *B. stevenii* buttons from Namibia (Jacobson et al.,1998) and Arco, Idaho show developing fruiting bodies lack any gelatinous tissues in the buttons or beyond. Even the unopened buttons below ground have a mature gleba. *Battarreoides digueti* (Pat. & Har.) Herr., a single species, is the only other species that appears even close to this strange fungus. It is very similar, also has elators (Fig. 23), but the gleba develops several pores to discharge the spores and does not split around the middle. Miller and Miller (1988) illustrate both of these genera clearly showing the differences. Both of these species are far too woody to eat. We first recorded *Battarrea stevenii* on the Yukon–Alaskan border on dry south slopes among sage. It is a decomposer and strong white rot, vital to the functioning of a desert ecosystem.

Chlamydopus meyenianus (Klotzsch) Lloyd
INEDIBLE

Fruiting body 7–40 cm high, spore case oval, light gray 2.0–3.5 cm broad with an irregular pore at the apex. Gleba rusty orange to yellow-brown and powdery at maturity. Stalk 5.0–35 cm long, 2.0–3.5 wide at apex, tapering to a narrow base, arising from a small volva 0.4–1.5 cm tall, in age longitudinally striate, woody but brittle, dry, dull gray to dull white, develops below ground emerging as the stipe expands. Odor none. Taste unknown.

Spores 5–9 μm globose, warted, thick-walled, nonamyloid, yellow-brown.

Habit and distribution: Several in the ground, in desert communities and generally low elevation arid areas. Found in southwestern and western North America. Fruiting in late fall and winter to early spring following wet weather in desert communities.

Comments: The soft, cottony, sand-covered exoperidium, see plate, is present as the fruiting body emerges from the ground but soon disappears and was only recently described by Miller (1995). It is a decomposer of dead plant roots.

Tulostoma simulans Lloyd
INEDIBLE

Fruiting body 2–4 cm high, consisting of a globose spore case, 1.0–1.5 cm wide, dark red-brown, but usually covered with dirt and debris especially on the lower case, a small globose, elevated pore at the top. Stalk 1.5–3.3 cm long, 0.3–0.4 cm wide, equal, thin, dry, dull white, tinted brown, in age the spore case disintegrates near the stalk, exposing the mature brown gleba. Odor none. Taste unknown.

Spores 4–6 µm globose with coarse, truncated warts, nonamyloid, pale yellowish. Capillitium thick-walled, branched, with swollen septa.

Habit and distribution: In troops in sand or sandy soil, often buried up to the spore case. Widely distributed. Fruiting in summer and fall or winter in the South and Southwest.

Comments: Species of *Tulostoma* are common in arid regions, in sandy soils, beaches, or sand dunes in moist temperate to subarctic regions. Coker and Couch (1928) list 10 species from eastern North America, and White (1901) has listed 15 species from the Southwest. However, a more recent monograph by Wright (1987), describes the North American as well as the world species in the genus. One must be careful to dig down under the fruiting bodies to obtain the base of the stalk. *Tulostoma* does not have a volva at the base, but other fungi do.

Calostoma cinnabarina Desv.
INEDIBLE

Fruiting body head oval 1.0–1.5 cm high, 0.8–1.5 cm broad, outer skin a thick, gelatinous, semitransparent peridium, covering the bright red, inner spore case, the gelatinous pieces fall away and appear like red seeds in the jellylike covering, leaving a bright red inner spore case; the sac has 4 to 5 raised deep red ridges at the top that break open in age to form the pore. Gleba is within a sac, powdery, buff color. Stalk 1.5–3.0 cm tall, 0.5–1.5 cm wide, equal, with longitudinal cords, pale yellow ridges, covered with a thick, semitransparent, sticky, gelatinous layer. Odor none. Taste unknown.

Spores 12–22 x 6.0–8.5 µm oblong-elliptic, pitted, appears reticulate, pale yellow.

Habit and distribution: Single to numerous or even abundant at higher elevations. Found in eastern and southern North America. Fruiting from fall to February in winter.

Comments: There are three North American species, all in eastern North America. *Calostoma lutescens* (Schw.) Burnap is a long-stalked species with a thin, gelatinous exoperidium, over a yellow spore case, capped with yellow teeth (red underneath); spores 6–8 µm globose, pitted, yellow. *Calostoma ravenelii* (Berk.) Massee has no outer gelatinous layer over the yellow to clay-colored spore case, and has cinnamon-colored teeth around the pore. It may be found at low elevations even in winter in the Southeast and its spores are 10–17 x 6.5–7.5 µm, minutely pitted, white (Castro-Mendosa et al., 1983).

469

BIRD'S NEST FUNGI (NIDULARIALES)

The curious resemblance to a bird's nest in this group makes them easy to identify. They are smaller than or about the same size as a dime and usually many fruiting bodies are found close together. The urn-shaped fruiting body or "nest" is completely enclosed at first by a cover called an epiphragm. In most species, the spores develop inside of the lens-shaped peridioles or "eggs" in the fruiting body. The spores are oval, thick-walled, and nonamyloid. At maturity the epiphragm separates exposing the peridioles. The peridioles are ejected from the "nest" when raindrops literally splash them out. *Crucibulum* and *Cyathus* both have peridioles attached to the inner wall of the fruiting body by a thin cord called the funicular cord. The cord is coiled inside a small pouch called a purse, which is found on the underside of the peridiole. When the peridioles are splashed out, the cord unfolds and often wraps around nearby twigs or grass, stems, or leaves, holding the peridiole in place until the wall disintegrates and the spores are released. *Nidularia* and *Nidula* lack the funicular cord, but instead the peridioles have a mucilaginous outer wall, which readily sticks to any surface it contacts. These species are decomposers and commonly found on sticks and woody debris. They are most often found in circles in the open, a location in which the splash cup mechanism is successful. *Sphaerobolus stellatus* differs in having a single, oval "ball" which is forcibly discharged when mature. It is similar in size and appearance but not closely related to the "Bird's nest fungi." Additional information may be found in Coker and Couch (1928), A. H. Smith (1951), and Brodie (1975).

Edibility. The very small, tough fruiting bodies are inedible. There are no reports of toxins in this group.

KEY TO THE NIDULARIALES
AND SPHAEROBOLUS

1. Fruiting body oval, minute 0.1–0.2 cm wide, splitting to form 6–8 pointed rays, like a small earth star--- *Sphaerobolus stellatus*

1. Not as above -- 2

   2. Fruiting body vase-shaped 1.0–1.5 cm tall, with a shiny, striate, interior wall; funicular cord present --- *Cyathus striatus*

   2. Fruiting body with nonstriate interior; funicular cord present or absent ------------ 3

3. Purse or funicular cord present --- 4

3. Purse or funicular cord absent -- 5

   4. Peridioles gray to black; fruiting body 0.5–1.5 cm tall, exterior brownish, densely fibrillose; spores 25–30 x 18–27 μm elliptic, thick-walled ------ *Cyathus stercoreus*

        (see comments under *Cyathus striatus*)

   4. Peridioles white; fruiting body 0.5–0.8 cm tall, exterior fine fibrillose, creamy white to cinnamon buff; spores 7–10 x 3.5–5.0 μm elliptic -------- *Crucibulum laeve*

5. Fruiting body cup-shaped, cream-color to yellowish brown, tears open revealing warm buff to dark reddish brown peridioles embedded in a sticky mucilage ---- *Nidularia farcta*

5. Fruiting body urn-shaped; white epiphragm separates, revealing brown peridioles, embedded in a sticky mucilage --------------------------------------- *Nidula niveo-tomentosa*

Sphaerobolus stellatus Tode: Pers.
INEDIBLE

Fruiting body minute 0.1–0.2 cm wide, oval depressed, convex, white to orange-buff, partially submerged in a white mat, at maturity splits to form 6–8 pointed rays, like a minute earth star, exposing the oval gleba (lower part of the plate) which is forcibly ejected, leaving an inflated sac (seen in upper part of plate). Odor none. Taste unknown.

Spores 6–10 x 4.0–6.5 µm subglobose, smooth, entire, thick-walled, nonamyloid.

Habit and distribution: Numerous on rotten wood, herbaceous debris, or dung. Widely distributed. Fruiting in spring, summer, and fall.

Comments: This curious fungus is called the "Cannon Ball" because the gleba can be forcibly discharged up to 10 or 12 feet. Bright light shining directly on the mature fruiting body triggers the ejection of the gleba. It is a decomposer of wood or lignin of all kinds. It is placed in its own family Sphaerobolaceae or more recently in the Geastraceae.

Cyathus striatus (Huds.) Wieden
INEDIBLE

Fruiting body 1.0–1.5 cm tall, 0.2–0.3 cm wide, vase-shaped, brown fibrils, with brown fibrils covering the epiphragm when immature, epiphragm parting at maturity revealing a shiny, striate interior wall with 5–12 drab, dark gray to nearly black oval peridioles at the bottom. Each peridiole contains basidia and basidiospores and possesses a purse and a coiled funicular cord. The force of rain drops discharges the peridioles and cord, which can tangle around grass blades or any object to anchor the peridiole, which disintegrates releasing the spores. Each fruiting body is attached to its woody host by a cinnamon-brown pad of mycelium. Odor none. Taste unknown.

Spores 12–22 x 8–12 µm elliptic, smooth, entire, thick-walled, nonamyloid.

Habit and distribution: Grows in groups on the ground among or on bark, sticks, mulch, and other woody debris, often in large clusters. Widely distributed. Fruiting in spring, summer, and fall after wet weather.

Comments: The purse and funicular cord occurs here and in the genus *Crucibulum. Cyathus stercoreus* (Schwein.) De Toni in Sacc. has a dense, brownish, fibrillose peridium; lacks the internal striations; has black peridioles, and larger spores 25–30 x 18–27 µm. Other genera have peridioles embedded in mucilage and lack the purse and funicular cord.

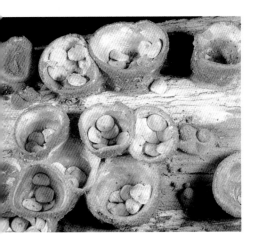

Crucibulum laeve (Huds.) Kambly
INEDIBLE

Fruiting body 0.5–0.8 cm tall, 0.6–0.8 cm wide, broad, cuplike, pale gray, buff, cinnamon to yellowish, fine fibrillose peridium, felty, minutely fibrillose epiphragm parts revealing a dull to creamy white interior with numerous small lens-shaped, white peridioles attached to the inner wall by a white funicular cord. The force of rain drops discharge the peridioles. The cord can wrap around an object anchoring the peridiole, which disintegrates releasing the spores. Odor none. Taste unknown.

Spores 7–10 x 3.5–5.0 µm elliptic, smooth, entire, slightly thick-walled, nonamyloid.

Habit and distribution: Several to numerous on wood debris, old boards, well-rotted limbs, herbaceous plant material. Widely distributed. Fruiting in spring, summer, fall, and into early winter.

Comments: Also known as *Crucibulum vulgare* Tul. & C. Tul. The very thick, single-layered, peridial wall separates this genus from *Cyathus,* which has a thinner, 3-layered, peridial wall. Both genera have the funicular cord attached to the peridiole. Along with *Cyathus striatus,* these 2 are very common circumpolar species.

Nidularia farcta (Roth.:Pers.) Fr.
INEDIBLE

Fruiting body 0.4–0.9 cm tall, 0.6–1.0 cm wide, cuplike, minutely pubescent, cream-colored to yellowish brown in age, epiphragm absent, membrane irregularly tears revealing warm buff to dark reddish brown, lens-shaped peridioles, embedded in a sticky mucilage, without a funicular cord. Odor none. Taste unknown.

Spores 5–10 x 4–6 µm oval to elliptic, smooth, entire, thick-walled, nonamyloid. Peridial hyphae thornlike, thick-walled, and branched.

Habit and distribution: Several to many on wood and wood debris of both hardwoods and conifers. Widely distributed. Fruiting in summer and fall.

Comments: Also known as *Nidularia deformis* (De Wild.:Pers.) Fr., this species has a soft fruiting body and peridioles without a purse and a funicular cord. *Nidularia pulvinata* (Schwein.) Fr. is very small, spherical, 2–10 mm wide, floccose to felty, cinnamon-brown, breaking open to reveal very small, dark brown peridioles. The exoperidium is composed of spiny branches. See photo by Sundberg and Richardson (1980). Discharge is accomplished by the splash-cup mechanism, however the mucilaginous covering allows the peridiole to adhere to objects with which it comes in contact.

Nidula niveo-tomentosa (Henn.) Lloyd
INEDIBLE

Fruiting body 0.5–0.7 cm tall, 0.3–0.6 cm wide, urn-shaped, finely fibrillose, white, epiphragm separates, revealing numerous, brown peridioles, 0.5–1.0 mm broad, embedded in a mucilage, without a purse or a funicular cord. New buttons often grow from the empty cup of old fruiting bodies. Odor none. Taste unknown.

Spores 6–9 x 4.0–5.5 µm globose to elliptic, smooth, entire, thick-walled, nonamyloid.

Habit and distribution: Several to many on twigs and herbaceous plant material. Found in western North America. Fruiting in summer and fall.

Comments: *Nidula candida* (Peck) V. S. White is larger, brown, has a flaring, tapered cup with peridioles 1.5–2.0 mm broad. It is also found in western North America. Fruiting in late summer into early winter.

STINKHORN FUNGI, PHALLALES

These strange fungi are instantly recognizable by their distinctive form as well as the green to blackish olive-green slime (gleba) over the head or arms of the fruiting body. This slimy green layer is composed of basidia and basidiospores. The very small, cylindric spores have a mucilaginous layer around them. A small amount of green slime mounted in India ink on a microscope slide will reveal this halo surrounding the spore. The disagreeable odor attracts insects, which walk over them and feed on the sticky spores, which stick to the insects' feet and become distributed as they move about from one humus pile to the next. This is certainly very different from the forcible spore discharge of preceding groups and not at all like the dry, powdery spore mass so frequently seen in the puffballs, which is wind disseminated.

Stinkhorn buttons are oval to globose, usually white at first, and firm but flaccid. The buttons are connected to the wood that is being decomposed, by cords or rhizomorphs that are often extensive into the substrate. The button is split open as the stipe expands lifting the head or fruiting head of the stinkhorn into the open. This usually coincides with the maturation of the green gleba and at this time the odor develops. The stipe is most often hollow and the chambers consist of giant cells that fill with moisture and expand producing the "growth" or extension of the stipe. At this point moisture and not nutrients are needed for the final expansion of the fruiting body. The buttons can be harvested, placed in moist soil, and they will expand in most cases, providing an opportunity to observe their growth and identify them most easily. You will probably need a well-ventilated space however!

Stinkhorns seem especially easy to introduce from other countries. *Lysurus mokusin,* described under *L. borealis* and pictured here, is an example of this. However, we also see *Clathrus ruber,* with its red latticelike fruiting body occasionally in the southern United States, and *Aseroe rubra,* with its bright red pointed arms, is also occasionally seen in mulch beds and plantings. Arora, 1986 illustrates both of these species. Stinkhorns are decomposers commonly found in flower beds mulched with wood chips in sawdust piles or in gardens. In the woods, they occur where humus has accumulated, near decayed logs or where beetle activity in trees has left wood debris on the ground.

Edibility: The rubbery to flaccid buttons are edible, but soon become smelly as they mature. Our experience is that they taste like the seasonings that are added to them. We have no great desire to eat or serve them to guests but some people enjoy them. They must be eaten before the gleba turns color.

KEY TO THE STINKHORNS, PHALLALES

1. Fruiting body with a single stipe tapering to an almost pointed apex or with a well developed head at the apex covered with green gleba ------------------------------------- 2
1. Fruiting body with several arms, which are extended or united at the apex or even latticelike with green gleba on inside surface of the arms -------------------------------- 7
  2. Fruiting body tapering to an almost pointed apex, distinct head absent, green gleba over the apex -- *Mutinus elegans*
  2. Fruiting body with a well developed head with the stipe inserted in the head; green gleba on the surface of the head --- 3
3. Fruiting body with an attached, netlike indusium hanging out from under the head -- *Dictyophora duplicata*
3. Not as above --- 4
  4. Fruiting head more or less smooth, gray-green to dark olive-green ------------------ 5
  4. Fruiting head with ridges and pits -- 6
5. Fruiting head with gray-green gleba; stipe white, volva white to light pinkish --- *Phallus ravenelii*
5. Fruiting head with blackish olive gleba; stipe very thin, pale orange to red; volva white or pinkish -- *Phallus rugulosis*
                 (see comments under *Phallus ravenelii*)
  6. Volva turns deep violet on exposure to air; fruiting head with deep ridges; gleba dark olive- green ------------------------------------- *Phallus hadriani*
  6. Volva remains white on exposure to air; fruiting head with shallow ridges; gleba light olive- green --------------------------------------- *Phallus impudicus*
                 (see comments under *Phallus hadriani*)
7. Fruiting body red, completely latticelike, or with a pink, latticelike, oval head on a red stipe -- 8

7. Not as above -- 9

    8. Fruiting body red, completely latticelike, emerging directly from the volva; green gleba on inside of the receptacle -- *Clathrus ruber*
(see illustrated visual key, page 18)

    8. Fruiting body with a latticelike, oval head with olive-green gleba in the pits; stipe pink to red, 7–9 cm tall-- *Lysurus periphragmoides*

9. Fruiting body with 5–6, erect or flattened, white to red arms ----------------------------- 10

9. Fruiting body with 3–5 arms, which arise directly from the volva and unite at the top   12

    10. Fruiting body with 6, erect, hollow arms, dull white, with olive-black gleba on the inside of the arms--- 11

    10. Fruiting body with 5–10 flattened, forked, tapering, red arms with green gleba in center; stipe chambered, red, arising from a white to pink volva ------ *Aseroe rubra*
(see comments under Stinkhorns, Phallales General, page 475)

11. Stipe white, round, chambered -- *Lysurus borealis*

11. Stipe light pink, fluted, like a 4- to 6-pointed star in cross-section ---- *Lysurus mokusin*
(see comments under Lysurus borealis)

    12. Fruiting body with 3–5 slender, pink to red, tapered arms that arise from a very short stipe and unite or touch at the top, green gleba on inside of arms--- *Pseudocolus fusiformis*

    12. Fruiting body with 4 red-chambered arms, ribbed on inside, which arise directly from the white volva; stipe absent; green gleba inside top of arms --- *Linderia columnata*

Mutinus elegans (Mont.) E. Fisch.
BUTTON IS EDIBLE

Fruiting body 6–10 cm tall, 0.8–1.1 cm wide, with a thin, often fragile stipe that tapers to a long, narrow, almost pointed apex, covered with a dark green slime, with a honey-combed, hollow, pinkish orange to bright red stipe, volva thin, membranous, white, surrounding the lower one third of the stipe. Odor slightly to strongly foetid. Taste of button is mild.

Spores 4.0–6.5 x 1.5–2.5 µm cylindric, smooth, entire, thin-walled, colorless, surrounded by a thin, transparent, sticky envelope.

Habit and distribution: Single to several on soil, humus, mulch, wood debris. Widely distributed, common in eastern North America. Fruiting in summer and fall during or after wet weather.

Comments: The slimy green spore mass covers the upper stipe without a regularly formed head, and that alone sets this genus apart from other stinkhorns. It is often confused with *Mutinus caninus* (Huds.:Pers) Fr. which has a much shorter, green, slime-covered apex and a stipe that is pinkish to red just below the green gleba but almost white, to white below. It also has a weak foetid odor. Mutinus *caninus* has very likely been introduced to North America, and is only locally encountered. The buttons are edible.

Dictyophora duplicata (Bosc) E. Fisch.
BUTTON IS EDIBLE

Fruiting body 12–17 cm tall, 2–4 cm wide, head strongly chambered and covered with a brownish olive slime; hanging out from under the lower margin of the pileus is a beautiful, pure white, skirtlike, netted veil up to 5 cm long and flaring at the bottom, but it is often collapsed and flattened against the stipe. Stipe 7–12 cm long, 3.5–4.5 cm thick, white, honey-combed, hollow, projecting from the large oval "egg" from which the fruiting body expands, leaving a membranous volva around the stipe base, attached to the ground by well-developed rhizomorphs. Odor foetid and disagreeable. Taste of buttons mild.

Spores 3.5–4.5 x 1–2 µm elliptic, smooth, entire, thin-walled, colorless, surrounded by a thin, transparent, sticky envelope.

Habit and distribution: Single or in groups in dense humus under hardwoods. Found in eastern North America. Fruiting in summer and fall during or after wet weather.

Comments: *Phallus hadriani* Vent.:Pers. looks very similar but lacks the indusium, and has the carrion-like odor; both of which attract flies and achieve insect dissemination of the spores.

Phallus ravenelii Berk. & M. A. Curtis
BUTTONS ARE EDIBLE

Fruiting body 10–16 cm tall, 1.3–1.5 cm wide; head green to gray-green, granulose, slimy to sticky with an open depression at the top. Stipe thick, equal, white, hollow, honey-combed, inserted up under the head. Button is a large oval "egg" from which the fruiting body expands, leaving a membranous, white to light pinkish volva surrounding the stipe, attached to the ground by well-developed white to pinkish rhizomorphs. Odor nauseous to foetid, sometimes detectable many yards away. Taste of buttons mild.

Spores 3–4 x 1.0–1.5 µm cylindric, smooth, entire, thin-walled, surrounded by a thin, transparent, sticky envelope.

Habit and distribution: Several or often in dense clusters in wood debris or sawdust. Found in eastern North America. Fruiting in summer and fall during or after wet weather.

Comments: The lack of a netted indusium, the smooth, green gleba, and the whitish to pinkish "eggs" separate this species from all other stinkhorns. Flies are attracted by the odor and feed as well as walk over the gray-green spore-bearing surface, thus disseminating the sticky spores. When the "egg" is cut in half, as seen in the color plate, the immature green head and the compacted stipe are revealed. There are small oval to rounded pinkish sclerotia attached to the rhizomorphs. In the button, stage both of these species are edible, but not a favorite of ours! Another species, *Phallus rugulosis* (E. Fisch.) Kuntze is tall, very thin, pale orange, tapering toward the head, which is smooth, dark blackish olive with a white, oval volva. It is occasionally seen in the eastern and southern United States. We have seen it in abundance in China.

Phallus hadriani Vent.:Pers.
BUTTON IS EDIBLE

Fruiting body 10–20 cm tall, 3.0–3.5 cm wide, head dark olive-green with irregular white ridges and deep pits, slimy and sticky, with an apical opening in age. Stipe thick, honey-combed, hollow, white to sometimes pinkish just at the base, inserted up under the head and arising from a membranous, dark pink to purple volva with rhizomorphs, which turn deep violet on exposure to air. Button a large, oval, flaccid egg, also white but becoming pinkish on exposure to air. Odor strong but not as nauseous as others. Taste of buttons mild.

Spores 3.2–4.5 x 1.5–2.5 µm cylindric, smooth, entire, thin-walled, surrounded by a thin, transparent, sticky envelope.

Habit and distribution: Single to several in mulch, leaf litter, pine duff or woody debris. Widely distributed. Fruiting in late summer or fall during or early winter on the West Coast, usually after wet weather.

Comments: *Phallus impudicus* Pers. is very similar, but the ridges are not so high; the buttons and hence the volva do not change to deep purple on exposure to the air nor do the rhizomorphs. The odor is nauseous to foetid. It is also widely distributed, but we have not found it as frequently in the southeastern United States nor in the Rocky Mountains, as on the West Coast. Very young buttons are edible for those with a strong constitution.

Lysurus periphragmoides (Kloztsch) Dring
BUTTON IS EDIBLE

Fruiting body 7–9 cm tall, head latticelike, bright pink, oval 1.0–1.6 cm thick; 1.0–1.5 cm wide, with chambered pits containing the blackish olive, slimy spores. Stipe equal, spongy, hollow, white to pinkish or reddish, arising from a firm, oval button which leaves a membranous volva. Odor strong and very disagreeable. Taste of button is mild.

Spores 3.5–4.5 x 1–2 µm cylindric, smooth, entire, yellow-brown, surrounded by a thin, transparent envelope.

Habit and distribution: Single to several, on ground in grass, apple orchards, pastures or in corn fields. Found in southeastern and southern North America. Common in the lower Central Midwest, in southern Missouri, Illinois, and Indiana. Fruiting in the spring, summer, and fall.

Comments: Also known as *Simblum sphaerocephalum* Schltdl., the oval, convex, pitted head is distinctive. This species is common in South America, but only encountered following very wet periods in southern North America. We have not eaten the buttons of this species.

Lysurus borealis (Burt.) Henn.
INEDIBLE

Fruiting body 10–12 cm tall, with 6 hollow, erect arms, dull white to pale flesh color. Gleba olive-black, slimy, located in the center of the arms. Stipe white, honey-combed, hollow, tapering toward the base, arising from a thick, membranous, white volva. Odor strong, foetid. Taste unknown.

Spores 3.0–4.5 x 1.5–2.0 µm narrowly cylindric, smooth, entire, thin-walled, olive-green, surrounded by a thin, transparent envelope.

Habit and distribution: Several on humus, mulch or wood debris. Widely distributed. Fruiting in spring, summer, and fall, during wet cool periods.

Comments: Also known as *Anthurus borealis* Burt. *Lysurus mokusin* (L.) Fr. is similar, but the stipe is fluted, 4-6 angled, and in cross-section is starlike in appearance. It is Asian and has been introduced to California, Virginia, and Maryland and, no doubt, elsewhere.

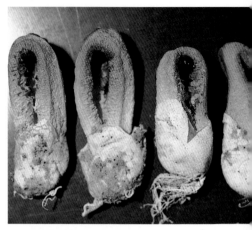

Pseudocolus fusiformis (E. Fisch.) Lloyd
NONPOISONOUS

Fruiting body 2–6 cm tall, 1.5–3.0 cm wide, with 3 to 5 long, slender, pink to red, tapering, spongy arms, arising from a short, white, tinted pink stipe, which arises from a white, membranous volva. The arms united at the apex and the slimy, green gleba forms along the inner face of the arms. Button is oval, flaccid, and white to light gray. Odor unpleasant, foetid. Taste unknown.

Spores 4.0–5.5 x 2.0–2.5 µm cylindric, smooth, entire, thin-walled, surrounded by a thin, transparent envelope.

Habit and distribution: Single to several in mulch, wood debris, or leaf litter. Found in eastern North America. Fruiting in summer and early fall.

Comments: Also known as *Pseudocolus shellenbergiae* (Sumst.) P. Micheli, it is fairly common in the southeastern United States.

Linderia columnata (Bosc) G. Cunn.
EDIBLE

Fruiting body 6–10 cm tall, 2.0–3.5 cm wide, with 4-5 hollow, bright red, spongy arms united at the top, which arise directly from the white volva, gleba dark olive-green held inside the arch at the top. Button white, flaccid, oval with white attached cords or rhizomorphs. Odor strong, of carrion. Taste in button mild.

Spores 3.5–5.0 x 2.0–2.5 µm cylindric, smooth, entire, thin-walled, surrounded by a thin, transparent envelope.

Habit and distribution: Single to several on rich soil, mulch, in gardens, lawns and open woods. Found in southeastern and southern United States. Fruiting in summer, fall, and early winter during or after wet weather.

Comments: Also known as *Clathrus columnatus* Bosc. *Clathrus ruber* P. Micheli has a red, latticelike fruiting body that emerges directly from the white volva. The green gleba is on the inside of the latticelike, hollow tubes. It is infrequently encountered in southern and western North America. The visual key illustrates this species. These are edible only in the very young buttons.

FALSE TRUFFLES

True truffles are Ascomycetes and, like the false truffles, are hypogeous or found under or just at the soil surface. False truffles are Basidiomycetes and closely related to epigeous fungi that fruit above ground. Most false truffles have minute to obvious locules in which the spores are formed. In addition to the gleba, some also have a short stipe or stipe-columella that branches and extends up into the gleba. The false truffles are mycorrhizal with trees and shrubs and many species are associated only with either hardwoods or conifers. Some are specifically found associated with specific genera, such as pines or oaks. Others are associated with one species of tree. Most species give off odors at maturity and are dug up by rodents or deer, which feed on them and, in the process of elimination, disseminate the spores. There are many species that cannot be covered in the context of a field guide. Suggested additional works include Smith and Smith, 1973; Miller and Miller, 1988; and Smith and Zeller, 1966.

Edibility: The species covered here are not edible. Unlike the true truffles, there are no reports of edible species in the false truffles. However, there are no reports of toxins.

KEY TO FALSE TRUFFLES AND TRUE TRUFFLES

1. Cross-section of the oval, irregular, or oblong fruiting body reveals locules or pores; spores are borne on basidia -- Truffles
1. Cross-section of fruiting body reveals a solid, often mottled gleba; spores develop in an ascus -- True Truffles

(see Key to True Truffles under Ascomycetes, page 529)

KEY TO FALSE TRUFFLES

1. Cross-section through point of attachment reveals a stipe-columella that branches into the gleba -- *Truncocolumella citrina*
1. Cross-section through point of attachment reveals only gleba or a very short stipe-columella -- 2
    2. Peridium very thin, dull white, soon parting to reveal large, rusty brown locules; stipe-columella very short and not branching into the gleba; odor strongly of sour milk --- *Gautieria monticola*
    2. Peridium thick; gleba with minute chambers or locules; stipe-columella absent; odor absent or not as above --------------------------------------- *Rhizopogon rubescens*

Truncocolumella citrina Zeller
INEDIBLE

Fruiting body 1.5–4.0 cm high, 2–3 cm broad, oval to egg-shaped, yellowish to dull greenish yellow, dry. Gleba olive-gray to black-brown in age, irregular chambers, separated by white branches of the columella, gelatinous to touch. Stipe-columella 0.5–1.0 cm high, 0.6–1.2 cm wide short, thick, light yellowish branches proliferates up into the gleba. Odor none. Taste unknown.

Spores 6.5–10.0 x 3.5–4.5 µm elliptic, smooth, entire, thin-walled, nonamyloid, brown in age.

Habit and distribution: Single to scattered to numerous in needle duff under conifers. Found most frequently under Douglas fir, in western North America. Fruiting in the summer and fall.

Comments: This fungus resembles a mushroom button, but when cut in half, the gleba and branching columella reveal a typical Gasteromycete. The branching stipe-columella clearly separates it from a *Rhizopogon* which has no columella. It is mycorrhizal with western conifers. Rodents and deer eat the fruiting bodies, and the spores are distributed in this manner.

Gautieria monticola Harkn.
NONPOISONOUS

Fruiting body 2–8 cm broad, oval to irregularly shaped or lobed, peridium dry, dull white to pale brownish, very thin, in age parting and revealing the glebal chambers. Gleba composed of irregular locules with thick walls and rusty brown contents, rubbery and firm when fresh. Stipe very short, 1.0–1.5 cm long, 0.4–0.7 cm wide, forming a stipe-columella. Odor very strong in age, like sour milk. Taste mild.

Spores 9–13 x 6.5–8.0 µm long elliptic to oblong, surface with deep longitudinal striations (Fig. 13) with a long apiculus, thick-walled, rusty brown.

Habit and distribution: Several in the soil or partially buried beneath the duff in conifer forests. Found in western North America. Fruiting in late summer and fall.

Comments: *Gautieria graveolens* Vittad. is similar and common in western North America under conifers, but has large oval, longitudinally striate spores 16–20 x 11–13 µm. A third common species, *Gautieria morchelliformis* Vittad., has a fruiting body 1–3 cm broad; with spores 12–18 x 8–12 µm, also longitudinally striate; and found under hardwoods throughout North America (Zeller & Dodge, 1918). We have collected all three species with the same strong odor of sour milk, but have no desire to try to eat them.

Rhizopogon rubescens Tul.
EDIBILITY UNKNOWN

Fruiting body 1–5 cm broad, globose to oval, depressed, dingy rose color with yellow cracks and depressions, stains red when bruised or on exposure to the air, base with white rhizomorphs, which penetrate into the soil. Gleba rubbery and tough, minutely chambered, white changing to honey-color or cinnamon-brown in age. Odor mild. Taste unknown.

Spores 5–8 x 2.8–3.5 μm elliptic, smooth, entire, thin-walled, nonamyloid, tinted yellowish.

Habit and distribution: Several to gregarious, buried just beneath the duff, often under five-needle pines. Widely distributed. Fruiting in summer and fall.

Comments: *Rhizopogon* is a large genus with 137 species described by Smith & Zeller (1966). There are also other genera that also occur in the duff and soil usually called "false truffles" or "gubers," in North America. They form mycorrhizae with both conifer and hardwood forest trees and shrubs. In age, most hypogeous species emit odors that attract deer, or ground squirrels and other rodents, who often feed on them and then distribute the spores in their feces. Areas should be examined where they have been digging.

SEQUESTRATE FUNGI

Sequestrate is the term for agaric fruiting bodies that are modified for successful fruiting in montane, desert or dry habitats. They often have obvious lamellate gleba, but no longer forcibly discharge spores. The spores are thick-walled and disseminated by wind as the peridium tears apart and sloughs off. As this occurs, the fruiting bodies become woody and stand erect in the desert winds. These species are widely distributed in the deserts of the world.

Edibility: The species are fleshy at first, but soon become woody and mostly inedible. However, young fruiting bodies of *Longula texensis* are edible and related to *Agaricus silvicola,* which is also edible. They, too, are soon woody and tough and become inedible. There are no toxins reported in the sequestrate fungi but most have not been tested for toxins.

KEY TO THE SEQUESTRATE FUNGI

1. Fruiting body ovate to pear-shaped, with a very short stipe (1–3 cm long)---------------- 2
1. Fruiting body convex to elongate, with a long stipe (4–30 cm long) ----------------------- 3
    2. Fruiting body pear-shaped; gleba white, but soon yellow-brown; spores subglobose, thick- walled, nonamyloid ---------------------- *Endoptychum agaricoides*
    2. Fruiting body, convex; gleba of contorted lamellae, brittle, buff in age; spores subglobose, thin-walled with amyloid warts and ridges------ *Macowanites americanus*
3. Gleba with the appearance of lamellae, white at first, soon blackening ------------------ 4
3. Gleba contorted and chambered, white at first, soon dark brown; pileus elongate, with shaggy scales; resembles unopened *Coprinus comatus* ("Shaggy Manes") -- *Podaxis pistillaris*
    4. Pileus convex; peridium white with yellow-brown tipped, raised squamules, sloughing off in age to reveal a blackish brown, hardened, lamellate gleba; fresh flesh stains yellow when bruised; without a volva surrounding the stipe base; spores without an apical pore-- *Longula texensis*
    4. Pileus convex; peridium breaks down very early; gleba black with recurved, black, lamellate plates; fresh flesh not staining yellow; a shallow volva surrounds the stipe base, often absent in age; spores with an apical pore------------ *Montagnea arenaria*

Endoptychum agaricoides Czern.
INEDIBLE

Fruiting body 1.5–10.0 cm tall, 1–7 cm wide, ovate to pear-shaped with a very short stipe. Pileus dry, white at first, light brown, pinkish brown to chocolate-brown in age, with appressed scales arranged in rows or scattered. Gleba irregular lamellae, anastomosing and intervenose, white at first to yellow-brown in age, changing from fleshy to tough and brittle in age. Stipe 1–3 cm long, 0.8–2.0 cm wide, protruding only a short way beneath the peridium, dull white, sometimes bruising yellowish, dry. Odor none. Taste mild.

Spores 7.5–9.5 x 5–7 µm subglobose to short elliptic, smooth, entire, thick-walled, 1–2 µm, nonamyloid, chocolate-brown.

Habit and distribution: Single to several on the ground in gardens, pastures, or lawns. Widely distributed. Fruiting in summer and fall usually following wet weather.

Comments: *Endoptychum depressum* Singer & A.H. Sm. is similar but with a flattened pileus and with a black-brown gleba. It is found in western North America under conifers and sometimes aspen. Both species are closely related to *Agaricus*, bruise yellow and are close to Section *Arvensis*. They could be eaten when very young buttons but soon become tough and woody. We have not tried them. Like species of *Agaricus*, they are decomposers but have contorted lamellae and do not forcibly discharge their spores. The spores are wind disseminated as the fruiting body breaks down.

Macowanites americanus Singer & A.H. Sm.
NONPOISONOUS

Fruiting body 1–4 cm tall, 1–5 cm broad. Pileus convex, flattened in center, tinted orange-pink, pink to grayish buff, or sometimes pale lilac, glabrous, surface cracking irregularly, margin enrolled, weakly viscid at first. Flesh soft, white, unchanging. Gleba of contorted lamellae, often anastamosed or even loculate, buff to orange-buff. Stipe-columella very short, 1.0–2.8 cm long, 0.4–1.2 cm wide, glabrous, white. Odor none. Taste mild.

Spores 8.5–13.5 x 7.5–11.0 µm subglobose, dark amyloid warts and short ridges, 0.5 µm high, entire, thin-walled. Cystidia long, fusiform, hyaline.

Habit and distribution: Single to several on the ground exposed or in conifer duff, under spruce, fir, Douglas fir, or pines. Found in western North America. Fruiting in early July and August as long as the wet weather continues.

Comments: Singer and Smith (1960) describe 12 species, 10 of which are found in western North America. Although they do not forcibly discharged their spores, they are collected by squirrels and cached in the crotches of tree limbs or eaten by ground squirrels. The spores are distributed in this way. *Macowanites* is a sequestrate member of the Russulales. Smith and Smith (1973) provide a key to the species.

Podaxis pistillaris (L.:Pers.) Fr.
INEDIBLE

Fruiting body 10–30 cm tall, 1.5–3.0 cm wide, elongate. Pileus dry, smooth but outer skin soon covered with large, ragged scales, appearing shaggy, pure white to tan or yellow-brown, margin appressed to the stipe, occasionally breaking and opening slightly. Gleba contorted, irregular, chambered, white to yellow, often with reddish tones and finally blackish brown, occasionally slightly deliquescent (turning to black liquid, like the "Inky Caps"). In age becoming a mass of powdery spores. Stipe 15–30 cm high, 1.0–1.5 cm thick, enlarging at the base to form a small bulb, rest equal, dry, soon scaly, same color as head, which extends through gleba to attach to the peridium in the same way as an agaric. Odor none. Taste unknown.

Spores 10–15 x 10–13 µm globose to subglobose, smooth, thick-walled, apical pore present, nonamyloid, yellow-brown.

Habit and distribution: Appears like an unopened "Shaggy Mane" *(Coprinus comatus)*. Single or in closely clustered groups; in desert regions (from 65 feet below sea level to 5,000 feet above) after seasonal rain or in irrigated fields. Found in south or southwestern North America. Fruiting during any season but most often in late winter or spring.

Comments: It is found in desert regions near the equator around the world. This is a desert adapted species related to *Coprinus comatus*. The spores are not forcibly discharged but wind disseminated when the fruiting body breaks apart.

Longula texensis (Berk. & M. A. Curt.) Zeller
EDIBLE WHEN YOUNG

Fruiting body 5–18 cm tall. Pileus 4.0–7.5 cm broad, conic, soon convex to broadly convex in age, white with yellow-brown to brown tipped raised squamules, peridium sloughing off in age revealing the lamellate gleba, dry. Flesh firm when young, white, staining light to bright yellow when bruised. Gleba irregularly lamellate, anastomosing to form cavities, white and fleshy when young, soon drab brown to blackish brown, becoming tough and brittle, free from the stipe. Stipe 4–15 cm long, 1–2 cm wide, narrowly clavate enlarging up to 4.5 cm at the base, white, staining yellow to orange-yellow when bruised, becoming woody in age, dry. Partial veil thick, white often falling away as pileus expands. Odor pleasant. Taste mild.

Spores 4.5–7.5 x 5.5–6.5 µm globose to subglobose, smooth, entire, thick-walled, apical pore absent, nonamyloid, black-brown.

Habit and distribution: Single to several or numerous, at low elevations in dry lands, sage prairie, deserts ecosystems. Found in southwestern and western North America. Fruiting in summer, late fall, winter, and spring, during or following cool, wet weather.

Comments: There is no question that this is a desert adapted *Agaricus* relative. It has a positive, bright orange, Schäffer reaction, which places it close to Section *Arvensis* in *Agaricus*. Compare this species to *Endoptychum agaricoides* Czern. which is also an *Agaricus* relative. Both species have a gleba that is not oriented for forcible spore discharge and have lost the ability to do so. Like the species of *Agaricus,* they are decomposers.

Montagnea arenaria (DC.) Zeller
INEDIBLE

Fruiting body 4–30 cm tall. Pileus 1–5 cm broad, convex to plane or depressed in age with a fragile peridium that breaks down very early. Gleba gray but very soon black, in wet weather with a black, sticky, partial deliquescence, soon with recurved, lamellate, gussets (black plates), which harden but are brittle and slowly eroded by the wind. Stipe 2.5–20.0 cm long, 0.2–1.5 cm wide, equal or tapering downward, hollow, tough to woody with scattered loose fibrils, dingy white, longitudinally grooved. Volva dull white, saclike, thick and double layered, usually embedded in soil or sand. Odor none. Taste unknown

Spores 7–22 x 4.5–14.0 μm ovoid, oblong to broadly elliptic, smooth, thick-walled with a hyaline apical pore, black.

Habit and distribution: Solitary, scattered to gregarious in dry areas or deserts, dry river beds, sand dunes and other disturbed areas. Widely distributed. Fruiting during or after periods of wet weather, often in the late fall or winter in the desert Southwest.

Comments: A highly variable fruiting body with a wide range of spore sizes. The amount of variable substrate, moisture conditions, temperature, and wind most likely contribute to the variability. The spores are very thick-walled and pigmented and will germinate in very short order after years in a herbarium collection. It is related to the Coprinaceae and close to *Coprinus comatus*. A desert decomposer as a root rot, it often fruits under or near sage (*Artemisia tridentata* Nutt.) and other desert plants.

HETEROBASIDIOMYCETES

Tremella mesenterica

The jelly fungi are the one group within this division of Basidiomycetes that is treated here. They have very different basidia, which are often septate or like tuning forks, and are more closely related to the rust fungi. However, their jellylike fruiting bodies and very characteristic shapes and coloration, usually bright orange, yellow, pink to white makes them distinctive and very visible. The spores are often septate and have several cells. The hymenium is usually smooth, except in *Pseudohydnum gelatinousum* (page 494) which has spines and the spores are forcibly discharged. They usually fruit during or just after wet weather. They are decomposers of wood and found on stumps, logs, and limbs as well as humus on the ground. The bright yellow species have long been called "Witches' Butter," see photo above.

JELLY FUNGI

The name refers to the gelatinous fruiting bodies that are usually found on logs, stumps, and twigs, but some are also on the ground. The ones covered here belong to three different orders in the Heterobasidiomycetes, including the Tremellales, Dacrymycetales, and Auriculariales. The spores are borne over the surface of the fruiting bodies on basidia that are structurally different from those found in the other Basidiomycetes covered in this field guide. The bright yellow to yellow-orange species look like butter and are commonly referred to as "Witches' Butter." The majority of the species fruit on decayed wood in cool, moist weather and soon disappear in dry weather. In the southern United States and the West Coast, they are frequently encountered in the winter months when it is cool and moist. Most of them are recognized by their distinctive fruiting bodies.

Edibility: *Auricularia auricula* (Hook.) Underw. is the only species in North America that is commonly eaten. In the Western Mountains it is often so abundant near melting snowbanks that large quantities can be collected. In China and the Far East, a closely related species, *Auricularia polytricha* (Mont.) Sacc., is widely eaten and grown commercially, dried, and used as a flavoring for soup. It is commonly called "Cloud Ears" *(Yung Ngo)* or "Wood Ears" *(Muk Ngo)* in China or *Kikurage* in Japan. Stamets (2000) explained the growth and cultivation of this jelly fungus. Most other jelly fungi are either too small or tasteless to be worth eating, but there are no reports of toxins.

KEY TO THE JELLY FUNGI

1. Fruiting body 4–15 cm broad with erect, often fused branches, tough, waxy, cream-color; on the ground, in woods ----------------------------------- *Tremellodendron pallidum*

1. Not as above, if on ground and branched, soft and not waxy, tough --------------------- 2

   2. Fruiting body 1–5 cm broad, translucent with white spines beneath the pileus-- *Pseudohydnum gelatinosum*

   2. Not as above--- 3

3. Fruiting body with erect fingers, fan-shaped, or in leaflike clusters; on wood or on the ground --- 4

3. Fruiting body with lobes, gelatinous clusters or earlike lobes; on wood ----------------- 7

   4. Fruiting body 8–20 cm broad of erect fingerlike branches or leaflike clusters ------ 5

   4. Fruiting body 3–10 cm tall, erect, single fruiting bodies, gelatinous, golden yellow, pink or rose-colored --- 6

5. Fruiting body with erect, fingerlike branches, sometimes interconnected below, white to cinnamon -- *Tremella reticulata*

5. Fruiting body with leaflike, thin, lobed branches, reddish brown to pale brown --- *Tremella foliacea*

   6. Fruiting body with coral-like, golden yellow, gelatinous branches -- *Calocera cornea*

   6. Fruiting body pink to rose, fan-shaped to somewhat lobed -- *Phlogiotis helvelloides*

7. Fruiting body orange-brown to reddish brown, thick, gelatinous earlike lobes; flesh firm and gelatinous --- *Auricularia auricula*

7. Not as above --- 8

   8. Fruiting body blackish olive-brown, in sheets, often folded with numerous, black-brown small warts--- *Excidia glandulosa*

   8. Fruiting body gelatinous, yellow, yellow-orange or very small and orange, tinted green --- 9

9. Fruiting bodies arise on a bed of white mycelium --- 10

9. Fruiting bodies without any white mycelium; lobed and convoluted orange to golden yellow -- *Tremella mesenterica*

   10. Fruiting body 1–6 cm broad, multiple lobes, yellow-orange to orange-red--- *Dacrymyces palmatus*

   10. Fruiting body 0.5–3.0 mm broad, round, flattened, orange, tinted green; usually numerous-- *Dacrymyces minor*

       (see comments under *Dacrymyces palmatus*)

Tremellodendron pallidum (Schwein.) Burt
NONPOISONOUS

Fruiting body 4–15 cm broad, 5–10 cm high, with a series of fused, erect branches, flattened at tips or a rosette, white, light cream-color below, sometimes in age greenish from algae, waxy appearing. Flesh white, very tough, will bend and not break. Odor none. Taste none.

Spores 7.5–11.0 x 4.0–6.5 µm narrowly elliptic, smooth, entire, thin-walled, nonamyloid.

Habit and distribution: Single or in scattered clusters on the ground, under hardwoods or mixed hardwood/conifer stands. Found in eastern and central North America; rare under oak in southwestern United States. Fruiting in summer and fall.

Comments: Also known as *Tremellodendron schweinitzii* (Peck) G. F. Atk. Recent studies suggest that this species may be ectomycorrhizal with hardwoods. This role is unusual for a member of the jelly fungi. Like grass, it is edible but who cares!

Pseudohydnum gelatinosum (Fr.) P. Karst.
NONPOISONOUS

Fruiting body 1–5 cm broad, pileus convex, gelatinous with a whitish, translucent appearance. Hymenium beneath covered with short teethlike, white spines. Stipe short lateral and most common in some specimens but in others the stipe is upright, longer, and supports the laterally attached head. Odor none. Taste bland.

Spores 5–7 µm subglobose, smooth, entire, thin-walled, nonamyloid.

Habit and distribution: Several to numerous on well-rotted wood. Widely distributed. Fruiting in spring, summer, fall, and early winter in the south, after wet weather.

Comments: This is the only jelly fungus with teeth. None of the hydnums have small translucent fruiting bodies. It is tasteless.

Tremella reticulata (Berk.) Farl.
INEDIBLE

Fruiting body 8–14 cm broad, consisting of erect fingerlike branches, appear inflated, ends single or forked, light yellowish, cream color or whitish, firm, elastic. Flesh gelatinous, rubbery. Odor none. Taste unknown.

Spores 9–11 x 5–6 µm elliptic, smooth, entire, thin-walled, nonamyloid.

Habit and distribution: Single, rarely more, on the ground in humus or decaying wood in many habitats. Found in eastern North America. Fruiting in late summer and fall.

Tremella foliacea Pers.:Fr.
INEDIBLE

Fruiting body 8–20 cm broad, consisting of a leaf-like, cluster, thin-lobed, gelatinous, pale brown. Flesh gelatinous, rubbery. Odor none. Taste mild.

Spores 8–10 x 6–9 µm subglobose to short elliptic, smooth, entire, thin-walled, nonamyloid.

Habit and distribution: On decaying logs, limbs and stumps, usually hardwoods, but occasionally on conifer wood. Widely distributed. Fruiting in late summer and fall, following wet weather.

Comments: It is not poisonous, but does not have any taste.

Calocera cornea (Batsch:Fr.) Fr.
INEDIBLE

Fruiting body 3–10 cm tall, 0.1–0.3 cm wide, narrow, slender, cylindric, sometimes forked, pliant, orange-yellow to golden-yellow, viscid. Odor none. Taste unknown

Spores 7–10 x 2.5–4.5 µm slightly allantoid (Fig.7), smooth, entire, thin-walled, one cross-wall only at maturity, nonamyloid.

Habit and distribution: Several to numerous on hardwood logs and stumps. Widely distributed. Fruiting in late summer and fall, following wet weather.

Comments: It can be easily confused with a coral fungus. The pliant, viscid fruiting body is different from most coral fungi, which are brittle and moist to dry. *Calocera viscosa* (Pers.:Fr.) Fr. is somewhat larger, forked, similar in color, but found on conifer logs and stumps, and both have spores with one cross-wall.

Phlogiotis helvelloides (Fr.) G. W. Martin
EDIBLE

Fruiting body 3–8 cm tall, 2–6 cm wide, fan-shaped to somewhat lobed, pink to rose, smooth, gelatinous. Flesh gelatinous, flexible. Stipe narrows below, pink to rose with white mycelium surrounding the base. Odor none. Taste pleasant.

Spores 9.5–12.0 x 4–6 µm narrowly elliptic, smooth, entire, thin-walled, nonamyloid.

Habit and distribution: Several to numerous under conifers on hard-packed ground or in well-decayed conifer debris. Widely distributed. Fruiting in spring, summer, and fall following wet weather.

Comments: We have seen large fruitings of this beautiful fungus under western conifer stands, but elsewhere it seems to be only occasionally encountered.

Auricularia auricula (Hook.) Underw.
EDIBLE

Fruiting body large, 3–15 cm broad, thick, gelatinous, ear-like lobes, often several from one point of attachment, orange-brown to dark red-brown, smooth on top but often ribbed beneath, dries very tough and hard. Flesh very firm, gelatinous. Odor none. Taste mild.

Spores 12–16 x 4–6 µm allantoid (Fig. 7), smooth, entire, thin-walled, nonamyloid.

Habit and distribution: Several to abundant on logs and wood of conifers, less common on hardwoods. Widely distributed. Fruiting during cool wet periods from early spring until late fall.

Comments: This fungus is common just after the snow melts in western North America. It is raised on inoculated logs, dried, and sold in the market in Asia. In China where it is commonly called Yung Ng or Muk Ng, it is used in soups and stir-fry dishes. It is one of the few jelly fungi that tastes good and is large enough to be of practical interest as an edible.

Exidia glandulosa Bull.:Fr.
NONPOISONOUS

Fruiting body 5–15 cm long usually in narrow rows, folded or leaflike to contorted, blackish olive-brown with numerous, soft and thin, small, black-brown warts, gelatinous. Flesh firm, gelatinous. Odor none. Taste none.

Spores 8–16 x 3–5 µm allntoid (Fig. 7), smooth, entire, thin-walled, nonamyloid.

Habit and distribution: Several to clusters or in sheets, on the limbs, logs and stumps of hardwoods, during periods of cool wet weather. Widely distributed. Fruiting in the spring and again in the fall.

Comments: It is too thin to be confused with *Auricularia auricula,* but does superficially resemble it. It is tasteless and not edible.

Tremella mesenterica (Gray) Pers.
INEDIBLE

Fruiting body 2–10 cm broad, 3–4 cm thick, lobed and convoluted, even brainlike, orange to golden-yellow, tough, gelatinous. Spores borne over the upright lobes. Odor none. Taste mild.

Spores 10–14 x 7.5–9.0 μm elliptic, smooth, entire, thin-walled, nonamyloid.

Habit and distribution: It is usually single to several on hardwood limbs, logs and stumps. Widely distributed. Fruiting in late summer and fall following wet weather.

Comments: This fungus is often called "Witches' Butter." Unlike *Dacrymyces palmatus,* the fruiting bodies are not surrounded by white mycelium, but otherwise they sometimes resemble each other.

Dacrymyces palmatus (Schwein.) Bres.
NONPOISONOUS

Fruiting body 1–6 cm broad, a lobed mass of gelatinous, tough tissue, yellow-orange to orange-red with whitish mycelium surrounding the point of attachment. Flesh soft, gelatinous. Odor none. Taste unpleasant.

Spores 17–25 x 6–8 μm oblong to sausage-shaped, up to seven cross-walls, smooth, entire, thin-walled, nonamyloid.

Habit and distribution: Often abundant on well rotted conifer limbs, logs, and stumps. Widely distributed. Fruiting in early spring to summer.

Comments: The fruiting bodies arise from a bed of white mycelium unlike *Tremella. Dacrymyces minor* Peck has very small, 0.5–3 mm, flattened, orange, tinted green, fruiting bodies and fruits in eastern North America in late winter to early spring. It is often gregarious on rotten wood.

ASCOMYCETES

Morchella elata

The Ascomycetes are composed of fungi that produce spores in a sac or ascus (Fig. 18). The spores of the vast majority are produced in a cylindrical ascus and are forcibly discharged from the ascus when they are mature. True morels (see photo to left), false morels, and cup fungi have this type of spore discharge. Truffles, which develop and mature in the soil, have oval, pear-shaped, or irregularly shaped asci. They rely on volatile odors to attract rodents and deer to dig them up and disseminate the thick-walled, often ornamented spores. See comments under Truffles, page 529.

For convenience, the Ascomycetes are divided into visually recognizable groups, which can then be keyed out more easily. It is also helpful, but not necessary, to use a microscope to aid in the identifications. Of the many species of Ascomycetes, we have selected some of the most common ones to describe and illustrate.

Edibility: One of the most popular and distinctive groups of edible mushrooms collected by a wide variety of people are the morels. Nationwide, it is a springtime ritual to go hunting for "merkles," "mountain fish," or just morels. False morels have also been hunted for many years, but the recognized presence of gyromitrin (monomethylhydrazine) (Type 5 toxins) in some species raises a caution flag. We now recommend that species of *Gyromitra* be avoided.

KEY TO THE ASCOMYCETES

1. Stipe tough, fleshy, or brittle, well-developed-- 2
1. Stipe very small (0.1–0.3 cm wide) or absent --- 4
   2. Fruiting head with well-developed ridges and pits ------------------------ True Morels
   2. Fruiting head not as above -- 3
3. Fruiting head wrinkled to infolded, lower margin free or nearly so,
   3–10 cm broad-- False Morels
3. Fruiting head clavate, irregularly shaped or a small, rounded, wrinkled head (0.8–2.0
   cm wide) --- Earth Tongues and Look Alikes
   4. Fruiting body a small cup or shallow saucerlike disc
     (0.2–4.0 cm wide) --- Small Cup Fungi
   4. Not as above--- 5
5. Fruiting body a bright white, yellow-green to green or orange or orange-red,
   pustulate growth over the lamellae or pores or entire fruiting body of agarics,
   boletes, and polypores-- *Hypomyces*
5. Not as above --- 6
   6. Fruiting body spherical, oval, irregular, potato-like, growing in the soil ------ Truffles
   6. Not as above -- 7
7. Fruiting body ear-shaped or lacking development on one side; single or in a dense,
   cespitose cluster -- Ear Fungi
7. Fruiting body not as above --- Large Cup Fungi

TRUE MORELS

All true morels have a head with distinctive ridges and pits and a stipe. In most species the head is attached all the way around at the bottom to the stipe. However, two species have the lower part of the head free from the stipe. The true morels are hollow inside in contrast to the false morels, which have a soft, cottony, white internal tissue that may collapse in age. True morels fruit in the early spring, depending on the weather, from March in the South. At high elevations, in Canada for example, spring comes as late as late July. Morels are found in a wide variety of habitats with *Morchella elata,* the "Black Morel," most often associated with conifers. The other species are found under or near hardwoods or in mulch beds and a variety in non-forest habitats. An in-depth reference work by Weber (1988) provides additional information.

Edibility: Truly one of the best edible groups of mushrooms, morels are widely hunted throughout North America and the rest of the world. They can be dried and kept in sealed plastic bags or glass jars for several years and will quickly revive in warm water. We find the taste is the same or better than the fresh specimens, but is enhanced by drying and so one can use fewer dried specimens in cooking. There are no toxins present, but we recommend cooking all true morels before eating. Some people experience gastric upsets after eating *Ptychoverpa bohemica.* Recipes can be found in *Hope's Mushroom Cookbook,* Miller (1993).

KEY TO THE TRUE MORELS

1. Fruiting head attached at the apex or part way and hanging skirtlike ---------------------- 2
1. Fruiting head not free, attached firmly to the stipe ------------------------------------- 3
   2. Fruiting head attached at the apex only and hanging skirtlike; spores very large (60–85 x 17–22 µm) --- *Ptychoverpa bohemica*
   2. Fruiting head attached part way and only the lower half hanging skirtlike; spores smaller (21–26 x 11.5–15.0 µm) ----------------------------------- *Morchella semilibera*
3. Fruiting head with black to black-brown ridges, conic to rounded with elongated, longitudinally arranged ridges and pits --- *Morchella elata*
3. Not as above --- 4
   4. Fruiting head with white ridges and brown pits ------------------ *Morchella deliciosa*
   4. Fruiting head with yellow to caramel-brown ridges and pits -- *Morchella esculenta*

Ptychoverpa bohemica (Krombh.) Boud.
EDIBLE FOR SOME

Fruiting body 5–21 cm tall, head 2–5 cm high, 2.0–3.5 cm wide, conic, flaring to campanulate in age, attached at the apex of the stipe, long ridges extend from the apex to the margin with inner irregular ridges, light brown to dark brown in age. Flesh brittle, soft cottony white tissue in the stipe, partially collapses in age. Stipe 5–15 cm long, 1.0–2.5 cm wide, enlarging toward the base, white, minutely tomentose, becoming fragile in age. Odor mild. Taste mild.

Spores 60–85 x 17–22 μm oblong, thin-walled, hyaline, smooth, nonamyloid, cream colored. Asci nonamyloid.

Habit and distribution: Single to numerous on the ground most often under hardwoods or mixed woods. Widely distributed. Fruiting very early in the spring usually before the morels.

Comments: Also known as *Verpa bohemica* (Kromb.) Schröter, the asci are 2-spored and the longest of any stipitate, larger Ascomycetes. Some people become ill after eating this species, experiencing a lack of coordination and suffering gastric upset. Lincoff and Mitchel (1977) note that symptoms are especially likely if eaten in quantity or for several days in a row. Weber (1988) recommends avoiding this species altogether. We have not eaten this species and don't recommend it.

Morchella semilibera (DC.:Fr.) Lév.
EDIBLE

Fruiting body 2.5–20.0 cm tall, head 2–4 cm high, 2.0–3.5 cm wide, conic to rounded, with elongated, longitudinally arranged brown ridges and pits, hanging skirtlike, flaring out in age, partially attached halfway to the top of the stipe. Flesh brittle, interior hollow. Stipe 2–10 cm long, 1–3 cm wide, equal, white to yellowish with fine granular material on the surface. Odor pleasant. Taste mild.

Spores 21–26 x 11.5–15.0 μm elliptic, smooth, thin-walled, hyaline, nonamyloid, yellow. Asci nonamyloid.

Habit and distribution: Single to several on the ground in sandy soil under oak and beech, or along streams under cottonwood and willows. Widely distributed. Fruiting a bit earlier than the other morels.

Comments: The "Half Free Morel" is the smallest of the morels usually 4–10 cm tall and is often fruiting before the other species. *Ptychoverpa bohemica* (Krombh.) Boud. is usually larger; has much larger spores; white cottony tissue in stipe; and has the head attached at the apex of the stipe.

Morchella elata Fr.
EDIBLE

Fruiting body 5–25 cm tall, head 3–11 cm high, 3–8 cm wide, conical to rounded with elongated, longitudinally arranged ridges and pits, brown at first, but soon with black to black-brown ridges and dark brown pits. Flesh brittle, interior hollow. Stipe 4–13 cm high, 2.5–7.0 cm wide, smooth to irregularly fluted and gnarled, roughened, white surface. Odor pleasant. Taste mild.

Spores 23–30 x 11.5–18.0 μm elliptic, smooth, thin-walled, hyaline, nonamyloid, cream to light buff. Asci nonamyloid.

Habit and distribution: Single, several or gregarious on the ground under or near conifers. Widely distributed. Fruiting in early spring.

Comments: Also known as *Morchella angusticeps* Peck and *M. conica* Pers., the "Black Morel" is most often conical with radially aligned elongate pits, but in western North America, it is often ovoid to rounded and robust, but still has the typical black-brown ridges. There is also a wide range of spring fruiting depending on the latitude north and the elevation of the habitat. It is a delicious edible, and when found in quantity, one we dry for later use.

Morchella deliciosa Fr.
EDIBLE

Fruiting body 2–11 cm tall, head 2.0–4.5 cm high, 1.5–3.5 cm wide, broadly conic, rounded, with irregular white ridges and brown pits. Flesh brittle, interior hollow. Stipe 2.5–6.0 cm long, 0.9–3.0 cm wide, smooth, fluted, or folded, dull white to cream colored. Odor pleasant. Taste mild and pleasant.

Spores 18–22 x 10–13 μm elliptic, smooth, thin-walled, nonamyloid, cream color. Asci nonamyloid.

Habit and distribution: Single or several on the ground under dying elm trees, mulch beds, and humus, in a wide variety of habitats. Widely distributed. Fruiting in the early spring or along the California coast even in winter.

Comments: The "White Morel" is generally smaller than the "Yellow" or "Black Morel." It is not found in conifer habitats but shows up irregularly in a variety of habitats. One should remember that further north or up higher in elevation, spring comes later in the year. We have found morels at Moraine Lake in Banff Provincial Park, Canada, on July 26. Arora (1986) reports it fruiting in mid-winter in California as well as in the spring. It is a fine edible species.

Morchella esculenta Pers.:St.-Amans
EDIBLE

Fruiting body 8–22 cm tall, head 4–11 cm high, 3–12 cm wide, oval to conical or pine cone-shaped, with ridges and pits, irregularly arranged, yellow-brown to caramel-brown. Flesh brittle, interior hollow. Stipe 3–11 cm high, 1.5–5.5 cm wide, nearly equal, minutely pubescent, dull white to pinkish buff. Odor none. Taste mild.

Spores 18–24 x 10–14 µm elliptic, thin-walled, hyaline, nonamyloid, buff or orange-buff. Asci nonamyloid.

Habit and distribution: Single, several, or gregarious on the ground in a wide variety of habitats. Widely distributed. Fruiting in early spring.

Comments: The "Yellow Morel" most often fruits between April 20th and May 10th in Virginia and the southeastern United States, but at 5,000 feet elevation in Idaho in late May and early June. This is a delicious edible, but we caution people to cook them before eating them. Dried morels can be placed in a sealed bag and kept for several years. When soaked in warm water they revive and have lost none of their flavor. A very large form of this species, up to 22 cm high with a head 10–12 cm wide and a very large stipe, is called *Morchella crassipes* Fr. We have found it near rivers in rich, bottom land soil.

FALSE MORELS AND ALLIES

False morels and allies have a wrinkled, smooth, conic, oval or cup-shaped fruiting head, but never with ridges and pits. A stipe is always present, but very reduced in *Discina,* to a short, fluted base. All species have brittle flesh and are some shade of brown to dull, whitish brown. The species of *Helvella* have either cups or saddle-shaped heads and a smooth to fluted stipe. *Gyromitra* has a typically oval to rounded, wrinkled, very fragile head that is attached only at the apex and is suspended skirtlike around the stipe. Many of the species have spores that are ornamented, and/or have a sterile area at each end of the spore, which is called an apiculus (Fig. 19b). True morels do not have this feature. Tylutki (1979) and Weber (1972 & 1988) have more information.

Edibility: Some members of the genus *Gyromitra* are eaten, but poisoning also occurs in this group. Gyromitrin (monomethylhydrazine (MMH), Type 5 toxins) occurs in an unknown number of species of *Gyromitra* (Spoerke & Rumak, 1994). The toxin is volatile and driven off when cooked or in the water when soaked. However, inhaled steam from cooking or using the water in which soaking took place can cause strong toxic results. *Gyromitra ambigua,* which occurs in northern North America, is a very toxic member of the genus. We recommend that all species of *Gyromitra, Discina,* and *Helvella* be avoided.

KEY TO THE FALSE MORELS AND ALLIES

1. Fruiting body without a true stipe; hymenium a smooth, brown disc; ascus nonamyloid --- *Discina perlata*
1. Fruiting body with a stipe; head wrinkled to saddle-shaped -------------------------------- 2
   2. Fruiting body with a wrinkled head and free or mostly free margin ------ *Gyromitra*
   2. Fruiting body with a cuplike, saddle-shaped or conic or campanulate head and a free margin --- 3
3. Fruiting body a stipe with a cuplike or saddle-shaped head ---------------------- *Helvella*
3. Fruiting body with a conic to campanulate head ------------------------------ *Verpa conica*

Discina perlata Fr.
EDIBLE

Fruiting body 4–9 cm broad, a shallow cup, more or less plane or with the margin turned up or down, exterior often veined, brown to dark-brown. Flesh brittle, white. Stipe very short, up to 3 cm long, white, usually fluted or ribbed. Odor mild. Taste mild.

Spores 27–45 x 12–16 µm elliptic, apiculate, pointed ends (Fig. 19b), minutely warted to reticulate, thin-walled, nonamyloid, white. Asci nonamyloid.

Habit and distribution: Single to numerous, in conifer woods on ground or rotten wood. Widely distributed. Fruiting in spring and early summer.

Comments: Also know as *Gyromitra perlata* (Fr.) Harmaja, it is usually referred to as "Pig's Ears." There are several species that can only be properly identified using a microscope to study the ascospores, illustrated by Abbott & Currah (1997). We do not recommend eating any *Discina*, since one is not able to easily identify the species and the presence of toxins in many species is not known.

KEY TO GYROMITRA

1. Fruiting body robust, 15–20 cm tall; head 5–11 cm high, deeply folded, almost pitlike; spores reticulate-warted; found in southeastern, south-central, and southern United States --- *Gyromitra caroliniana*
1. Not as above --- 2
    2. Fruiting body very fragile; stipe deeply ribbed, tinted pink to rose; found in western North America; fruiting from spring to fall ----------------------- *Gyromitra californica*
    2. Not as above--- 3
3. Found in western North America; head convoluted and lobed but not saddle-shaped; either (a) fruiting under or near melting snowbanks or (b) not in the early spring; spores apiculate or not --- 4
3. Widely distributed or in the southeastern, central and southern United States -------- 6
    4. Fruiting near or from under snowbanks; stipe broad, 3–6 cm wide; spores with a flattened apiculus-- *Gyromitra montana*
    4. Fruiting later in the spring or in late summer and fall; spores not apiculate -------- 5
5. Fruiting later in the spring; stipe narrow, 1–3 cm wide -------------- *Gyromitra esculenta*
5. Fruiting in late summer and fall--- *Gyromitra infula*
    6. Fruiting in the spring; southeastern, central and southern United States -- *Gyromitra fastigiata*
    6. Fruiting in the late summer and fall; widely distributed-------------- *Gyromitra infula*

Gyromitra caroliniana (Bosc:Fr.) Fr.
NONPOISONOUS

Fruiting body 15–20 cm tall, robust, head 5–11 cm high, 6–13 cm wide, deeply folded almost pitlike, almost loculate in cross-section, reddish brown to deep blackish brown, margin closely appressed to the stipe. Flesh brittle, stipe stuffed solidly with soft white tissue. Stipe 15–20 cm high, 5–11 cm wide, massive, white feltlike surface, fluted and irregularly rounded, discolored somewhat when rubbed or handled. Odor mild. Taste mild.

Spores 27–33 x 12–14 µm elliptic, reticulated warted surface with an apiculus (Fig. 19b) at each end, thin-walled, hyaline, nonamyloid, cream-color. Asci nonamyloid.

Habit and distribution: One to several on the ground under hardwoods. Found in southeastern, south central, and southern United States. Fruiting in very early spring, March and April.

Comments: This is the largest of the *Gyromitra* species with convoluted folds that form locules and the interior is densely packed with tissue. It is commonly eaten in Missouri, Iowa, and Kansas where it is often referred to as "The Big Red." However, it does contain hydrazines volitilized when cooked. We recommend that it should not be eaten. (Tiffany, Litt., et al. 1998)

Gyromitra californica (W. Phillips) Raitviir
POISONOUS

Fruiting body 2.5–8.5 cm tall, head 1.5–8.0 cm high, 2.5–14.0 cm wide, convex, lobed, surface wrinkled, yellow-brown when young, dark brown to black-brown in age, margin hanging free, not clinging to the stipe. Flesh very brittle, stipe interior stuffed with cottony white tissue but soon hollow. Stipe 2.5–8.0 cm high, 1–6 cm wide, deeply ribbed with sharp edges, minutely tomentose, white, tinted pink to rose especially over the lower stipe. Odor mild. Taste mild.

Spores 14–20 x 7.5–10.0 µm elliptic, minutely roughened, thin-walled, hyaline, nonapiculate, nonamyloid, white. Asci nonamyloid.

Habit and distribution: Solitary to numerous on ground or well decayed wood debris, under or near conifers. Found in western North America. Fruiting in spring, summer and fall.

Comments: Also known as *Pseudorhizina californica* (W. Phillips) Harmaja, it is closely related to *Gyromitra sphaerospora* (Peck) Sacc (*Pseudorhizina sphaerospora* (Peck) Pouzar), which has globose spores, 8.5–10.5 µm. It is occasionally found in northern North America throughout the boreal forest. Both species are suspected of containing monomethyhydrazine (MMH) (Type 5 toxins) and should be avoided.

Gyromitra montana Harmaja
NONPOISONOUS

Fruiting body 9–20 cm tall, head 4–7 cm high, 3–7 cm wide, with deep lobes and convolutions, yellow-brown to caramel-brown remaining so until very old, then dark brown, attached at the apex, but margin closely clasps the stipe. Flesh firm but brittle, stipe stuffed with cottony white mycelium which collapses in age. Stipe 6–15 cm high, 3.0–6.5 cm wide, longitudinally fluted or ribbed, minutely felted, white remaining so or with slight brown stains where handled. Odor mild. Taste mild.

Spores 26–35 (-39) x 11–15 μm elliptic, with a flattened apiculus at each end (Fig. 17), surface minutely warted, thin-walled, nonamyloid, cream color. Asci nonamyloid.

Habit and distribution: Single, but most often several, fruiting just under or at the edge or very near melting snowbanks, very occasionally some distance away. Found in western North America. Fruiting in the spring during the snow melt in May to early July.

Comments: *Gyromitra gigas* (Krombh.) Quél. has traditionally been the name given to this species. Breitenback & Kränzlin (1981) in Europe describe *G. gigas* with much smaller spores, which have a more prominent apiculus. We have eaten this species with no problems. However, with monomethylhydrazines (Type 5 toxins) present in *G. esculenta,* which occurs in the same habitats, we do not recommend eating any *Gyromitra.*

Gyromitra esculenta (Pers.:Fr.) Fr.
POISONOUS

Fruiting body 5–18 cm tall, head 5–6 cm high, 6–9 cm wide, convoluted and lobed, yellow-brown young, becoming brown to blackish brown at maturity, attached at apex. Flesh brittle, stipe at first stuffed with white cottony mycelium that collapses in age, becoming hollow. Stipe 5–14 cm high, 1–3 cm wide, minutely tomentose, fluted to irregular in shape, cream-color with shades of brown to red-brown. Odor mild. Taste mild.

Spores 19–26 x 10.0–13.5 μm broadly elliptic, nonapiculate, thin-walled, hyaline, nonamyloid, cream-color. Asci nonamyloid.

Habit and distribution: Single, several to gregarious, sometimes in clusters, on the ground, under conifers. Found in western North America. Fruiting in spring, usually late April to late June depending on elevation.

Comments: This species contains Monomethylhydrazine (Type 5 toxins). Cooking drives off the toxins, but the steam can be inhaled, and the cook can be toxified. The toxins can kill red blood cells and cause liver damage. We strongly recommend against eating this species. *Gyromitra ambigua* (P. Karst.) Harmaja is very similar but has smaller spores (22–30 x 7.5–12 μm) and is also poisonous. We have found it in Idaho, and it is distributed north into western Canada (Abbott & Currah, 1997). See also comments under *Gyromitra gigas* (Krombh.) Quél.

Gyromitra infula (Schaeff.:Fr.) Quél.
POISONOUS

Fruiting body 8–13 cm tall, head 2.5–8.0 cm high, 2–8 cm wide, saddle-shaped to lobed, surface wrinkled, margin fused with the pileus, orange-brown to dark red-brown in age. Flesh brittle, stipe with cottony contents to hollow in age. Stipe 8–10 cm high, 1–3 cm wide, pale pinkish cream to grayish brown, minutely tomentose sometime fluted just at the base. Odor mild. Taste mild.

Spores 17–22 x 6.5–9.5 µm elliptic, minutely rugose, nonapiculate, nonamyloid, cream-color. Asci nonamyloid.

Habit and distribution: Several to numerous on the ground under conifers and hardwoods. Widely distributed. Fruiting in late summer and fall.

Comments: Spoerke and Rumack (1994) report the presence of monomethylhydrazine (Type 5 toxins) in this species, and so it should be avoided. It is a fall fruiting false morel, a fruiting pattern shared only by *Gyromitra californica* (W. Phillips) Raitv., which fruits from spring to fall.

Gyromitra fastigiata (Krombh.) Rehm
POISONOUS

Fruiting body 5–10 cm tall, head 4–7 cm high, 3–9 cm wide, saddle-shaped, often with two adjacent lobes appressed to each other, surface wrinkled, red-brown, chestnut-brown margin closely appressed to the stipe. Flesh brittle, stipe interior with soft white cottony tissue. Stipe 5–10 cm tall, 1.8–4.0 cm wide, pinkish to pure white in age, minutely felty, somewhat fluted, slightly larger at the base. Odor mild. Taste mild.

Spores 26–34 x 10–15 µm fusiform, with a prominent apiculus at each end (Fig. 19b), surface low reticulate warted, thin-walled, hyaline, nonamyloid, white. Asci nonamyloid.

Habit and distribution: Single to several on the ground under hardwood forests. Found in southeastern, central, and southern United States. Fruiting in April and May.

Comments: Usually not found in quantity so at this time analysis for monomethylhydrazine (MMH) has not been carried out. However, closely related species have MMH, and we recommend against eating this species. The distinctive spore morphology and size ease the problem of identification. *Gyromitra brunnea* Underw. is a synonym of *G. fastigiata* (Weber, 1988).

KEY TO HELVELLA

1. Fruiting body a deep or shallow cup -- 2
1. Fruiting body head saddle-shaped, smooth or wrinkled; stipe smooth or ribbed -------- 3
    2. Fruiting body a deep cup; stipe contiguous with cup and
       deeply ribbed -- *Helvella acetabula*
    2. Fruiting body a shallow cup; stipe slender, mouse gray, densely
       pubescent -- *Helvella macropus*
3. Stipe smooth, white; head light brown -------------------------------------- *Helvella elastica*
3. Stipe ribbed to deeply ribbed; head gray to gray-black or white to pale cream ---------- 4
    4. Stipe deeply ribbed; head gray to gray-black------------------------ *Helvella lacunosa*
    4. Stipe ribbed; head white to pale cream --------------------------------- *Helvella crispa*

Helvella acetabula (L.:Fr.) Quél.
INEDIBLE

Fruiting body 2–8 cm broad, deeply cupulate, 0.5–2.0 cm deep, light to dark brown, light brown exterior. Flesh brittle, white. Stipe 1–2 cm long, 0.8–4.5 cm wide, white, contiguous with cup, prominently ribbed. Odor mild. Taste mild.

Spores 18–22 x 12–14 µm elliptic, smooth, thin-walled, hyaline. Asci nonamyloid.

Habit and distribution: Single to several on ground in many habitats. Widely distributed. Fruiting in spring and early summer.

Comments: Also known as *Paxina acetabulum* (L.) Kuntze, it is set apart from other larger Ascomycetes because of its large cup with the prominent external ribs. We recommend avoiding it because closely related species contain gyromitrin, Type 5 toxins.

Helvella macropus (Pers.:Fr.) P. Karst.
INEDIBLE

Fruiting body 2–6 cm tall, head 0.3–1.2 cm high, 2.0–3.5 cm wide a shallow cup or nearly flat in age, interior gray-brown to yellow-brown, exterior mouse gray to mouse gray-brown, densely pubescent (minutely fibrillose). Flesh brittle, light gray, solid in stipe. Stipe 2–6 cm high, 0.1–0.6 cm wide, mouse gray, round, densely pubescent. Odor mild. Taste unknown.

Spores 18–25 x 11–12 µm subfusiform, thin-walled, hyaline, smooth to minutely warted, nonamyloid, with one large central oil drop. Asci nonamyloid.

Habit and distribution: Solitary to numerous in humus or soil under hardwoods or sometimes conifers. Widely distributed. Fruiting in summer and fall.

Comments: Also known as *Paxina hispida* (Schaeff.) Seaver and *Macropodia macropus* (Fr.) Fuckel. We have collected this distinctive species in Idaho and Virginia. The spores are borne inside the cup.

Helvella elastica Bull.:Fr.
INEDIBLE

Fruiting body 5–10 cm tall, head 2–3 cm broad, saddle-shaped, glabrous, light brown. Flesh brittle, white. Stipe 2–10 cm high, 0.2–0.8 cm wide, equal, smooth, white. Odor mild. Taste unknown.

Spores 18–22 x 11–13 µm elliptic, smooth, hyaline, with one oil drop. Asci nonamyloid.

Habit and distribution: Single to several on the ground in woods under both hardwoods and conifers. Widely distributed. Fruiting in summer and fall.

Comments: It is found in a wide variety of habitats fruiting up to frost in the fall (Weber, 1972).

Helvella lacunosa Fr.
NONPOISONOUS

Fruiting body 6–11 cm tall, head 1–5 cm high, 2–6 cm wide, saddle-shaped, somewhat wrinkled to convoluted, gray to gray-black. Flesh brittle, gray. Stipe 6–11 cm long, 1.5–2.0 cm wide, equal, deeply ribbed, anastomosing with cavities, nearly white, to gray tinted olive or yellowish to bright yellow. Odor none. Taste unknown.

Spores 15–20 x 11–13 µm elliptic, smooth, thin-walled, nonamyloid, with one large central oil drop, white. Asci nonamyloid.

Habit and distribution: Single or several on wet soil, often in burned areas. Widely distributed. Fruiting in the fall.

Comments: We would not recommend eating it because of the closely related, toxic, nonedible or poisonous species with which it could be confused.

Helvella crispa Scop.:Fr.
INEDIBLE

Fruiting body 6–12 cm tall, head 1–5 cm high, 1–5 cm wide, saddle-shaped to irregularly lobed, white to pale cream or buff, minutely tomentose, margin inrolled at first. Flesh brittle, internally chambered, white. Stipe 6–12 cm high, 1.5–3.0 cm wide, enlarged somewhat toward the base, rounded, ribbed to chambered, white to cream to gray-brown. Odor mild. Taste unknown.

Spores 17–24 x 10–13 µm broadly elliptic, thin-walled, hyaline, nonamyloid with one large oil drop, white, Asci nonamyloid.

Habit and distribution: Single to several on the ground in litter or grass under conifers and hardwoods. Widely distributed. Fruiting in late summer to fall.

Comments: We do not recommend eating this species since there are closely related species which are poisonous.

Verpa conica (O. F. Müll.) Swartz:Pers.
EDIBLE

Fruiting body 3–6 cm tall, head 1–3 cm high, 1.5–3.0 cm wide, conic to campanulate, nearly smooth, orange-brown to brown, white beneath, attached at the apex, hanging skirt-like. Flesh brittle, in the stipe a soft, cottony, white tissue which collapses in age. Stipe 3–6 cm long, 0.8–1.5 cm wide, nearly equal, smooth white. Odor pleasant. Taste mild.

Spores 22–26 x 12–16 µm, elliptic, smooth, thin-walled, hyaline, nonamyloid, cream colored. Asci nonamyloid.

Habit and distribution: Single to several on the ground, in a wide variety of habitats. Widely distributed. Fruiting in the early spring.

Comments: It is edible but rather small and the true morels are better tasting. Although usually considered with the true morels, it is treated here for convenience.

EARTH TONGUES AND LOOK ALIKES

A group of unrelated Ascomycetes that have stipitate, club-shaped to spathulate fruiting bodies are described in this section. Several have a distinctive head. They are smaller than the false morels and are often found in different habitats. *Cordyceps,* which are parasitic on insects and a truffle, are separated from the earth tongues, which grow on the ground or on well-decayed wood. The species of *Cordyceps* have on the upper surface small pustules that are called perithecia. These are flasks that contain the spores. The earth tongues have an exposed spore-bearing surface over the top or apex of the fruiting body.

Edibility: These are small, tasteless mushrooms that are not eaten. There are no reports of toxins in this group. Many, however, have not been tested for toxins.

KEY TO EARTH TONGUES AND LOOK ALIKES

1. Fruiting body club-shaped or with a round and ball-like; surface with small pustules, and with a sandpaper-like flesh; orange-red, yellow or with a round, olive-brown head; parasitic on insects or truffles ------- 2
1. Fruiting body surface without pustules, not parasitic on insects or truffles ------- 4
   2. Fruiting body with an olive-brown, round and ball-like head; emerging from below the soil surface and growing under ground on the truffle *Elaphomyces* ------- *Cordyceps capitata*
      (see comments under *Cordyceps militaris*)
   2. Fruiting body club-shaped with pustules but without a round head, orange-red to yellow; parasitic on insect larvae or pupae------- 3
3. Fruiting body club-shaped, orange to orange-red ------- *Cordyceps militaris*
3. Fruiting body bright yellow ------- *Cordyceps melolanthae*
      (see comments under *Cordyceps militaris*)
   4. Fruiting body with a small, wrinkled head ------- 5
   4. Fruiting body club-shaped or spatulate ------- 7
5. Fruiting head oval to irregular, creamy pink to light brownish pink ---- *Cudonia circinans*
5. Fruiting head oval, wrinkled, viscid to gelatinous, yellow-orange to dark olive-green ------- 6

  6. Fruiting head bright orange-yellow to yellowish olive, and viscid to

    moist and rubbery -- *Leotia lubrica*

  6. Fruiting head dark olive-green --- *Leotia viscosa*

              (see comments under *Leotia lubrica*)

7. Fruiting body black to brown, flattened to clavate; flesh firm and brittle to tough and

 like charcoal -- 8

7. Not as above -- 9

  8. Fruiting body firm but brittle, clavate, flattened, black to

    black-brown-- *Geoglossum simile*

  8. Fruiting body tough, carbonaceous, club-shaped, cylindric to irregular

    in shape -- *Xylaria polymorpha*

9. Fruiting body with a bright yellow, elliptic, ovoid head, clearly separate

 from the stipe -- 10

9. Fruiting body flattened, spoon-shaped or irregular in form, not clearly

 separate from the stipe --- 11

  10. Stipe slim, pure white; found on floating leaves or on moss

    in wet areas --- *Mitrula paludosa*

  10. Stipe thicker, bright yellow and tufted; on humus and well-

    decayed wood -- *Microglossum rufum*

         (see comments under *Mitrula paludosa*)

11. Fruiting body flattened, club-shaped to irregular in form, light yellow to straw colored;

 on soil in conifer woods --- *Neolecta irregularis*

11. Fruiting body flattened, spoon-shaped or spathulate, light yellow-brown; on soil and

 conifer litter -- *Spathularia velutipes*

Cordyceps militaris (Fr.) Link
INEDIBLE

Fruiting body 2–5 cm tall, narrowly club-shaped with minute orange to orange-red pustules (perithecia) over the upper one-half, tapering below to a white stipe that arises from the larvae and /or pupae of insects. Odor none. Taste unknown.

Spores 250–350 x 1.0–1.5 μm hyphal-like, soon segmenting to form spores 3.5–6.0 x 1.0–1.5 μm, hyaline, thin-walled, nonamyloid. Asci long cylindric, nonamyloid.

Habit and distribution: Single to several on the ground or in humus or well-decayed wood. Widely distributed. Fruiting in late summer and fall.

Comments: *Cordyceps melolanthae* (Tul.) Sacc. is similar, usually larger, but bright yellow to pale yellowish white and not as common. *Cordyceps capitata* (Fr.) Link, with a round, olive-brown head, grows from several species of the truffle *Elaphomyces,* which it parasitizes. Mains (1957a, 1958) describes 41 species of *Cordyceps* on insects and seven species parasitizing *Elaphomyces.*

Cudonia circinans Pers.:Fr.
INEDIBLE

Fruiting body 2–6 cm tall, head 0.5–2.0 cm wide, recurved, oval, wrinkled, thin, creamy pink to light brownish pink. Flesh brittle, whitish pink. Stipe 1.5–5.0 cm high, 0.1–0.6 cm wide, enlarging toward base, sometimes longitudinally striate especially near the apex, pinkish brown to light brown. Odor mild. Taste unknown.

Spores 30–45 x 1.8–2.2 μm needlelike, somewhat curved, thin-walled, multi-septate, nonamyloid. Asci nonamyloid.

Habit and distribution: Several to gregarious on humus, well-decayed wood, under or near conifers. Widely distributed. Fruiting in late summer and fall.

Comments: It looks like a small *Gyromitra,* but the needlelike spores separate it from the false morels. *Cudonia monticola* Mains is much larger, up to 10 cm tall; the brown head is 2.0–3.5 cm broad. It fruits from the early spring to early summer in the western mountains (Tylutki, 1979).

Geoglossum simile Peck
INEDIBLE

Fruiting body 2–7 cm tall, head flattened, clavate, 0.2–1.2 cm wide, black to black-brown. Flesh firm but brittle. Stipe 1.0–4.5 cm long, 0.1–0.5 cm wide, round, to fluted, minutely pubescent, black. Odor mild. Taste unknown.

Spores 75–105 x 6–9 μm narrowly clavate, somewhat curved, with 7 septa or more, black, nonamyloid. Asci nonamyloid. Paraphyses present, setae absent.

Habit and distribution: Single, or several to numerous on humus, rotten wood, often in moss. Found in eastern North America. Fruiting in late spring, summer, and early fall.

Comments: Mains (1954) recognizes 12 species of *Geoglossum* in North America and 9 species of *Trichoglossum*. *Trichoglossum* has abundant, black, pointed setae in the hymenium and stipe. Both genera are found widely distributed in North America, but microscopic observation is necessary to distinguish between them. They are uniformly dark brown to black.

Leotia lubrica (Scop.) Pers.
INEDIBLE

Fruiting body 3–7 cm tall, head 1.0–1.5 cm wide, oval, incurved, wrinkled, viscid, gelatinous, yellow-orange, often with an olive tint. Flesh brittle, cream color. Stipe 2–6 cm high, 0.5–1.0 cm wide, round, viscid, white tinted buff. Odor mild. Taste unknown.

Spores 16–24 x 4–6 µm cylindric-oblong, 3-5 septa, smooth, thin-walled, nonamyloid. Asci nonamyloid.

Habit and distribution: Several to abundant on soil or litter in hardwood and conifer forests. Widely distributed. Fruiting in summer and fall.

Comments: *Leotia viscosa* Fr. on the right in the plate is very similar but the head is dark olive-green. It is also widely distributed and viscid when fresh. Neither species is edible.

Mitrula paludosa Fr.
INEDIBLE

Fruiting body 2–6 cm tall, head 0.8–1.0 cm wide, elliptic-ovoid, bright orange-yellow, clearly separate from the stipe. Stipe 1–4.5 cm high, 0.2–0.3 cm wide, pure white, moist, sometimes slightly larger at the base. Odor mild. Taste unknown.

Spores 10–18 x 2.5–3.0 µm elliptic, hyaline, smooth, sometimes one septate, nonamyloid. Asci with weakly amyloid tips.

Habit and distribution: Several to gregarious on very wet to floating leaves or in sphagnum on needles. Widely distributed. Fruiting after wet weather in spring, summer, and fall.

Comments: Also known as *Mitrula phalloides* (Bull.) Chevall. We have collected it on floating matts of oak leaves in the fall. *Microglossum rufum* (Schwein.) Underw. also has a bright yellow head along with a bright yellow stipe with yellow tufts over the surface. It is found in humus and well-decayed wood and illustrated by Roody (2003). *Mitrula abietis* Fr. is a small species with a light brown cylindric head, very common on needles of conifers in northern and western North America.

Neolecta irregularis (Peck) Korf & J. D. Rogers
INEDIBLE

Fruiting body 1.8–3.0 cm tall, apex 1–2 cm broad, flattened to contorted, club-shaped, to irregular in form, bright yellow. Stipe 1–2 cm high, 0.2–0.5 cm wide, yellowish white. Odor none. Taste unknown.

Spores 6–10 x 4–5 µm elliptic, smooth, thin-walled, nonamyloid. Asci nonamyloid.

Habit and distribution: Solitary to cespitose clusters on soil in conifer woods. Widely distributed. Fruiting in summer and fall.

Comments: Also known as *Mitrula irregularis* (Peck) E. J. Durand, it is frequently mistaken for a *Clavaria*. A microscope will quickly demonstrate the present of asci and ascospores.

Spathularia velutipes M. C. Cooke & Farlow
INEDIBLE

Fruiting body 2–5 cm tall, head fan-shaped to spoon-shaped, 1–3 cm wide, yellow brown. Stipe 2–4 cm high, 0.3–0.5 cm wide, longitudinally ribbed and fluted, reddish-brown. Odor none. Taste unknown.

Spores 35–45 x 2.0–2.5 µm cylindric, thin-walled, multi-septate, hyaline, nonamyloid. Asci nonamyloid.

Habit and distribution: Several to gregarious, on the ground, in humus, or rotten wood, under conifers. Widely distributed. Fruiting in late summer and fall.

Comments: *Spathularia flavida* Pers.:Fr. is similar with a yellowish, flattened or fan-shaped head, but it has a yellow stipe. It is also found in litter under pine and is widely distributed.

Xylaria polymorpha (Pers.:Mérat) Grev.
INEDIBLE

Fruiting body club-shaped, cylindrical, fingerlike or irregular in shape, dull black, 4–8 cm long, 1.0–2.5 cm thick. Flesh tough, white. If white, see comments below.

Spores 18–32 x 5–9 µm narrow, fusiform, slightly curved, flattened on one side, dark brown, nonamyloid. Asci with amyloid tips.

Habit and distribution: Single, several, or in cespitose clusters or even branched, on logs and stumps of hardwoods. Widely distributed. Fruiting in summer and fall.

Comments: "Dead Man's Fingers" is common on dead hardwood logs, limbs, and stumps, found in eastern North America. Young fruiting bodies in early summer are initially covered with a white powder, which is the asexual spores. Later, it becomes black and has embedded, flasklike fruiting bodies (perithecia) that contain the ascospores. *Xylaria hypoxylon* (L.:Fr.) Grev. is much thinner and highly branched; also black at maturity; and occurs in the same habitats.

SMALL CUP FUNGI

This section contains very small cup fungi (0.5–4.0 cm wide), without stipes or with stipes up to 10 cm long. They are often brightly colored and often fruit in large numbers. They are found on logs, stumps, rotten wood, and wood debris. The assemblage treated here are a selection of the more common and distinctive of the several hundred known species present in North America. Seaver (1961) has the most complete treatment of this group of Inoperculate Ascomycetes.

Edibility: They are too small or too tough to be considered edible.

KEY TO THE SMALL CUP FUNGI

1. Fruiting body with a short to long (0.1–10.0 cm), narrow (0.1–0.3 cm) stipe ----------- 2
1. Fruiting body without a stipe -- 4
 2. Fruiting body and associated wood bright green to bluish green; stipe very short (0.1–0.2 cm long) --- *Chlorosplenium aeruginascens*
 2. Fruiting body bright red to light brown; stipe long, with or without hyaline hairs ---- 3
3. Fruiting body hymenium bright red; exterior and stipe clothed in long, rigid, white hairs; not attached to a black sclerotium -------------------------------------- *Microstoma floccosa*
3. Fruiting body hymenium light brown; stipe smooth; attached to a black sclerotium -- *Sclerotinia tuberosa*
 4. Flesh tough, gelatinous, rubbery; often cespitose; on hardwood limbs and logs and stumps-- 5
 4. Flesh brittle and fragile; on ground, mulch, buried wood, plant debris ------------- 6
5. Fruiting body black, 1–4 cm wide; with a shiny, black, shallow cup -- *Bulgaria inquinans*
5. Fruiting body black-brown, 1.5–3.5 cm wide; with a reddish brown, shallow cup -- *Galiella rufa*
 6. Fruiting body a creamy white to yellowish cup with a white, toothed margin --- *Tarzetta catinus*
 6. Fruiting body orange-red to reddish orange -- 7
7. Fruiting body a shallow, reddish orange, saucerlike disc; margin with brown, pointed hairs; on wood debris and plant material ----------------------------- *Scutellinia scutellata*
7. Fruiting body an orange-red cup; margin white toothed; on charcoal and burned wood --- *Geopyxis carbonaria*

Chlorosplenium aeruginascens (Nyl.)
P. Karst.
INEDIBLE

Fruiting body a small cup 0.2–0.6 cm wide, with a short stipe 0.1–0.2 cm long, bright green to blue-green over both cup and stipe. Flesh firm, light green. Odor none. Taste unknown.

Spores 5–10 x 1.2–2.5 μm cylindric, smooth, thin-walled, hyaline, nonamyloid. Asci narrowly clavate, with amyloid tips.

Habit and distribution: Numerous, on decayed hardwood limbs and logs. Widely distributed. Fruiting in spring summer and fall, after wet weather.

Comments: Also known as *Chlorociboria aeruginosa* (Oeder) Seaver. The mycelium is unique in that it turns the wood green, so it is obvious when the fungus is present.

Microstoma floccosa (Schwein.) Raitv.
INEDIBLE

Fruiting body a cup and stipe 4–6 cm tall. Cup 0.5–0.8 cm wide, red, clothed in long, hyaline to white, rigid hairs, hymenium bright red. Stipe 3–5 cm high, 0.1–0.3 cm wide, white, also clothed in long, rigid, white, hyaline hairs. Odor none. Taste unknown.

Spores 20–35 x 15–17 μm elliptic, thin-walled, smooth, hyaline, nonamyloid. Asci nonamyloid.

Habit and distribution: Several to numerous and often cespitose on sometimes buried, hardwood sticks. Found in eastern North America. Fruiting in late spring and summer.

Comments: Also known as *Plectania floccosa* (Schwein.) Seaver. This beautiful cup fungus is common in the southeastern United States, but found as far north as Quebec according to Pomerleau (1980).

Sclerotinia tuberosa (Hedw.:Fr.) Fuckel
INEDIBLE

Fruiting bodies small cups 1.0–1.5 cm broad, brown. Flesh brittle. Stipe 3–10 cm long, 0.1–0.2 cm wide, light brown, borne on a small, oval, black knot of fungus tissue (sclerotium). Odor none. Taste none.

Spores 12–17 x 6–9 μm elliptic, smooth, thin-walled, containing two oil drops, nonamyloid. Asci amyloid with a pore at apex.

Habit and distribution: Several together on the ground in wood debris. Widely distributed. Fruiting in the early spring about the same time as the morels.

Comments: There are a number of small cup fungi on stipes in the Ascomycetes described and illustrated by Seaver (1951). This species is usually found associated with and growing on the roots of species of *Anemone,* which is a small, spring wildflower.

Bulgaria inquinans Fr.
INEDIBLE

Fruiting body 1–4 cm, wide short, cylindric to rounded, expanding to form a short, thick, black base with the shiny, black hymenium lining a concave to shallow cup. Flesh tough, gelatinous rubbery, black. Odor mild. Taste unknown.

Spores 10–17 x 6–7 μm elliptic, lemon-shaped, smooth, dark brown, nonamyloid. Asci amyloid at apex.

Habit and distribution: Several to numerous, often in cespitose clusters, on the bark of recently fallen hardwood trees especially oak, beech, and birch. Widely distributed. Fruiting in the fall.

Comments: Also known as *Phaeobulgaria inquinans* (Pers.) Nannf., it is especially common on oaks, both in the East and on the West Coast.

Galiella rufa (Schwein.) Nannf. & Korf
INEDIBLE

Fruiting body 1.5 3.5 cm wide, forming a shallow cup with a toothlike margin, smooth, hymenium, reddish brown to orange-brown, exterior black-brown with black fibrils. Flesh tough, translucent, gelatinous and rubbery. Odor mild. Taste unknown.

Spores 10–22 x 8–10 µm elliptic, thin-walled, finely warted, nonamyloid. Asci nonamyloid.

Habit and distribution: Solitary, but more often several or in cespitose clusters on hardwood branches and logs. Found in eastern North America. Fruiting in late summer and fall.

Comments: Know also as *Bulgaria rufa* Schwein. It is similar to *Bulgaria inquinans* which has a shiny black hymenium.

Tarzetta catinus (Holmsk.:Fr.) Korf & J. K. Rogers
INEDIBLE

Fruiting body 1.0–2.5 cm high, 1–4 cm wide, cup-shaped, hymenium creamy white to yellowish orange, or yellowish tan, margin white, minutely toothed (crenate), exterior dull white, minutely granular. Flesh brittle, white. Odor mild. Taste unknown.

Spores 20–24 x 11–13 µm elliptical, thin-walled, hyaline, smooth, nonamyloid, with two oil drops per spore. Asci nonamyloid.

Habit and distribution: Several to gregarious on the ground in gardens, mulch beds under hardwoods and conifers. Widely distributed. Fruiting in spring, summer, and fall during wet weather.

Comments: Also known as *Pustularia catinus* (Holmsk.:Fr.) Fuckel. *Geopyxis vulcanalis* resembles it but has no oil drops in the spores, which are not as broad (15–21 x 8–11 µm).

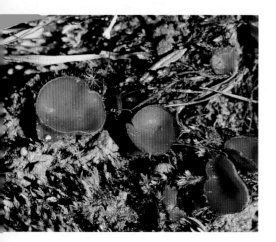

Scutellinia scutellata (L.:Fr.) Lamb.
INEDIBLE

Fruiting body a shallow, sessile, saucer-like disc, 0.5–2.2 cm wide, hymenium reddish orange to orange, smooth, margin with thick-walled, pointed, brown, pigmented, hairs 1.0–1.5 mm long, exterior hairy, light orange. Flesh thin, fragile. Stipe very short extend to the wood. Odor none. Taste unknown.

Spores 19–22 x 11.5–14.5 µm broadly elliptic, minutely warted, with small oil drops, nonamyloid. Asci nonamyloid.

Habit and distribution: Single to most often several or gregarious on hardwood and conifer wood and wood debris. Widely distributed. Fruiting in the spring and fall during cool wet weather.

Comments: There are a number of North American species. *Scutellinia umbrarum* (Fr.) Lamb. is found in the western mountains, usually on the ground. *Humaria hemispherica* (Wiggers:Fr.) Fuckel is larger, 1–3 cm broad; has a whitish gray hymenium; a fuzzy, brown exterior; and the cup margin is clothed in thick-walled, pointed hairs. It is found on humus and rotten wood.

Geopyxis carbonaria (Alb.& Schwein.) Sacc.
INEDIBLE

Fruiting body cup-shaped, 0.5–1.0 cm high, 0.5–1.5 cm wide, hymenium orange-red, margin minutely white toothed (crenate), exterior dull yellowish. Flesh fragile, yellowish. Stipe 0.2–0.3 cm high, 0.1 cm wide. Odor mild. Taste unknown.

Spores 12–18 x 6–9 µm elliptic, thin-walled, smooth, nonamyloid. Asci nonamyloid.

Habit and distribution: Several to gregarious on burned ground, charcoal, wood or organic debris. Widely distributed. Fruiting following wet weather spring, summer, or fall.

Comments: *Geopyxis vulcanalis* (Peck) Sacc. is similar; found on unburned, conifer litter; has a light yellow hymenium; and elliptic spores 15–21 x 8–11 µm.

HYPOMYCES

The species of *Hypomyces* are parasites of higher fungi, both Basidiomycetes and Ascomycetes. The spore-bearing surface is most often attached, aborting the normal growth of the lamellae of agarics or hymenium of boletes, polypores, and cup fungi. In many cases the entire fruiting body is covered by the parasite. The spores of the *Hypomyces* develop in small flask-shaped fruiting bodies, each called a perithecium, which appear as pustules on the surface of the invaded host and gives the surface a fine, sandpaper-like feeling. The asci are nonamyloid.

Edibility: Most of the 15 to 20 species are inedible. However, *Hypomyces lactifluorum* is a popular exception. We know of no negative reports following the ingestion of this species and conclude that it must invade only edible species of *Russula* and *Lactarius*.

KEY TO HYPOMYCES

1. Fruiting body an orange to orange-red parasite over the lamellae, stipe and pileus of agarics (*Russula* and *Lactarius*) ------------------------------------- *Hypomyces lactifluorum*
1. Fruiting body, when parasitized become white or green ----------------------------------- 2
    2. Fruiting body is bright green and invades the lamellae of Russula --- *Hypomyces luteovirens*
               (see comments under *Hypomyces lactifluorum*)
    2. Fruiting body of *Amanita* invaded and becomes a white, amorphous club -- *Hypomyces hyalinus*
               (see comments under *Hypomyces lactifluorum*)

Hypomyces lactifluorum (Schwein.) C. Tul.
EDIBLE

Fruiting body a bright orange parasite which grows over the stipe, lamellae, and eventually the pileus of species of *Russula* and *Lactarius*. The parasite grows quickly in very wet weather making it difficult to identify the host mushroom. *Lactarius deceptivus* and *Russula brevipes* are two which we have found as hosts, but there are certainly others. The parasite covers the lamellae leaving only blunt radial ridges. Pustule-like, small, orange swellings called perithecia on the parasite contain the spores.

Spores 30–40 x 6–8 µm spindle-shaped, with an apiculus (Fig. 19b) at each end, minutely warted, 1–2 celled. Asci cylindric, nonamyloid.

Habit and distribution: Single, several, or numerous, on mushrooms. Widely distributed. Fruiting following wet weather in summer and fall.

Comments: It is a highly prized edible mushroom. Since we have no knowledge of any one

becoming sick after eating "The Lobster," we assume that it only parasitizes edible mushrooms. *Hypomyces luteovirens* (Fr.) C. Tul., is bright green; commonly invades only the lamellae of Russula species; and is widely distributed (see photo below). *Hypomyces hyalinus* (Schwein.:Fr.) C. Tul. parasitizes species of *Amanita* turning them into white clubs, unrecognizable as agarics. It is found in eastern North America, and since the host is unknown should not be eaten.

TRUFFLES

The truffles are well known by almost everyone but few ever see them in nature. They develop in the soil and are not visible to the casual observer and are mycorrhizal with trees. In fact they are often associated specifically with a given tree species such as eastern white pine and Douglas fir. Fruiting often occurs in winter and early spring when other fleshy fungi are not fruiting. At maturity they produce a specific odor that attracts rodents, deer, and insects. The rodents and deer dig them up and eat them. The spores are unaffected, move through the alimentary canal, and survive to germinate and establish more colonies of the species.

Edibility: Some species of truffles are edible and sought after by gourmet cooks to enhance the flavor of their dishes. We have eaten some wonderful meals in Europe and North America which have included truffles in the recipes.

There are more than 55 species of truffles in North America and many are described and illustrated by Gilkey (1939) and Castellano et al. (1980). Truffles are being commercially grown here in the United States. Information can be found at http://natruffling.org on the North American Truffling Society web site.

KEY TO THE TRUFFLES

1. Fruiting in eastern North America -- 2
1. Fruiting in western North America -- 3
    2. Fruiting body red-brown to orange-brown, large, 2–7 cm wide --*Tuber canaliculatum*
    2. Fruiting body creamy white, small, 0.6–1.8 cm wide---------------------- *Tuber shearii*
              (see comments under *Tuber canaliculatum*)
3. Fruiting body dark violet, brown, to black; spores smooth, thick-walled, lemon-shaped, 74–80 x 24–32 μm--- *Leucangium carthusiana*
3. Not as above --- 4
    4. Fruiting body light buff to tinted light brown; fruiting from late January to June, under Douglas fir --- *Tuber gibbosum*
    4. Fruiting body develops orange-brown to red-brown areas; fruiting from October to January, under Douglas fir-- *Tuber oregonense* ined.
              (see comments under *Tuber gibbosum*)

Tuber canaliculatum Gilkey
NONPOISONOUS

Fruiting body 2–7 cm broad, 2–4 cm high, ovoid, oval depressed, irregularly furrowed, red-brown to orange-brown in the furrows, surface dry with low warts. Gleba very firm, marbled brownish gray to deep gray in age with puzzlelike white veins creating pockets of spores. Odor when mature sweet not pleasant. Taste mild.

Spores 45–60 x 40–50 µm globose to subglobose, reticulate (up to 5 µm high), dark brown, nonamyloid. Asci globose to pear-shaped with a short stalk, thin-walled, nonamyloid.

Habit and distribution: Several to gregarious, just beneath soil surface, under eastern white pine. Found in eastern North America or wherever it has been planted. Fruiting from October to December.

Comments: We did not find this species edible, but a reliable fruiting occurs in the late fall in Virginia under eastern white pine, 20 years and more old. In tests we gave it to some laboratory mice who enjoyed it very much. We also synthesized mycorrhizae with it and eastern white pine in our growth chambers. *Tuber shearii* Harkn. is a small, oval, creamy white, 0.6–1.8 cm wide species; also found with eastern white pine but as young as 15 years old. Its spores are subglobose, 35–56 x 28–42 µm, with large reticulations.

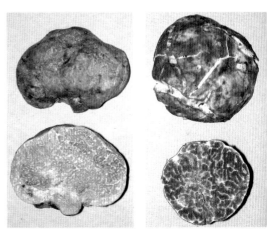

Leucangium carthusiana (Tul. & C. Tul.) Paol.
EDIBLE

Fruiting body oval to rounded, 1–7 cm broad, surface uneven, granular, dark violet, brown to black-brown. Gleba buff, olive-buff to pinkish buff, marbled with white veins and oval locules where the spores are concentrated, maturing to gray or olive-brown. Odor fungoid, pungent, or slightly garliclike. Taste pleasant mild.

Spores 74–80 x 24–32 µm lemon-shaped, one end pointed, thick-walled, smooth, nonamyloid. Asci broadly elliptic, stipitate, nonamyloid.

Habit and distribution: Several to many in the soil under conifers or oaks. Found in western North America. Fruiting in early spring and summer.

Comments: Also known as *Picoa carthusiana* Tul. and the "Oregon Black Truffle." We have collected it in March in California under oak but also later on in the spring. It is one of the very good truffles that we have eaten. Gilkey (1939) describes the species and illustrates the spores. The genus *Tuber* has spores that are oval to globose and ornamented.

Tuber gibbosum Harkn.
EDIBLE

Fruiting body oval, rounded to lobed 1–6 cm broad, light buff to tinted light brown, becoming somewhat darker brown when mature, minutely pubescent. Gleba firm, brown to purple-brown, marbled with white veins. Odor pleasant. Taste mild but like garlic when mature.

Spores 35–52 x 17–39 µm elliptic, reticulate, thick-walled, yellow-brown, nonamyloid. Asci oval thin-walled, nonamyloid.

Habit and distribution: Several to numerous, in the soil, under Douglas fir. Found at 2,000 feet elevation or lower, in northern California, Oregon, Washington to Vancouver British Columbia, Canada, west of the Cascade and Sierra Mountains. Fruiting from late January to June.

Comments: The "Oregon White Truffle" is a highly desirable edible. A second very good edible truffle, tentatively named *Tuber oregonense* by Dr. James Trappe, is very similar and fruits from October to January (see photo on right). However, it develops orange-brown to red-brown areas not found with *Tuber gibbosum*. It occurs in the same habitats and is also associated with Douglas fir. We have eaten both *T. gibbosum* and *T. magnatum* Paol., the "European White Truffle," and enjoyed them very much.

EAR FUNGI

There are two common genera, *Otidia* and *Wynnea* that develop an ear-shaped fruiting body. Two species of *Wynnea* are found only in eastern North America. However, *Otidia* species are widely distributed and in a wide variety of habitats.

Edibility: Both genera should be avoided. Severe gastric upset (Type 8 toxins) can result.

Otidia leporina (Fr.) Fuckel
POISONOUS

Fruiting body sessile 1–4 cm tall, 1–3 cm wide, ear-shaped, curled, open on one side, smooth orange to orange-buff, exterior bright orange to orange. Flesh brittle, light orange. Odor none. Taste unknown.

Spores 10–14 x 6–8 µm elliptic, smooth, two oil drops, thin-walled, nonamyloid. Asci nonamyloid.

Habit and distribution: Several to numerous in conifer duff under conifer forests. Widely distributed. Fruiting in late summer and fall.

Comments: *Otidia alutacea* (Fr.) Massee has a gray-brown hymenium; pale brown exterior; elliptic spores, 14–17 x 6–9 µm; and is found under hardwoods and conifer stands. Ingestion of the species can cause severe gastric upset (Type 8 toxins), therefore we avoid all species of *Otidia*.

Wynnea americana Thaxt.
POISONOUS?

Fruiting body 6–13 cm tall, 1.0–4.5 cm wide, ear-shaped, narrowing at the apex, joined together in a tight cluster of several to many, on 4–5 short branches from a common central base 2.5–3.5 cm long, 1.0–1.5 cm wide, hymenium dark red to purplish red, exterior granular, blackish brown to black-brown. Odor none. Taste unknown.

Spores 35–40 x 12–14 µm fusiform, with distinct longitudinal ridges, pale brown, thick-walled, non-amyloid. Asci nonamyloid.

Habit and distribution: Single, sometimes more than one cluster, under hardwoods and hardwood/conifer forests. Found in the Appalachian Mountains and generally in eastern North America. Fruiting from late summer to late fall.

Comments: *Wynnea sparassoides* Pfister is an unusual species with a very complex loculate more or less oval head 6–8 cm wide on a very stout stipe up to 30 cm long by 2–2.5 cm wide. Both species are uncommon and were collected by us in Virginia and North Carolina. They are tough and are not edible. Their role in nature is unknown.

LARGE CUP FUNGI

The cup fungi treated here are mostly 3–12 cm broad and, with only two exceptions, are fragile or brittle and all lack a stipe and are sessile. They form a more or less cup-shaped fruiting body called an apothecium, which has a smooth hymenium and ranges in color from bright yellow, orange, and red to brown and even black-brown. For users of a microscope, the species in the genus *Peziza* have an amyloid (dark blue) ascus tip. The rest covered here have nonamyloid asci. The species grow on the ground, in humus or plant debris and on rotten wood.

Edibility: Spoerke & Rumack (1994) list *Sarcosphaera crassa* as poisonous. There are no other toxic species in this group. However, some people eat *Aleuria aurantia,* but it has no taste and is very thin and fragile.

KEY TO THE LARGE CUP FUNGI

1. Fruiting body a large cup fungus; hymenium bright orange, yellow, scarlet, pink or violet; asci nonamyloid -- 2
1. Fruiting body not colored as above-- 5
   2. Hymenium bright orange with or without blue-green stains -------------------------- 3
   2. Hymenium scarlet, pink or violet -- 4
3. Hymenium bright orange without blue-green stains ----------------------- *Aleuria aurantia*
3. Hymenium bright orange with blue-green stains ----------------------- *Caloscypha fulgens*
   4. Hymenium scarlet-- *Sarcoscypha austriaca*
   4. Hymenium pink to violet-- *Sarcosphaera crassa*
5. Fruiting body yellow-brown to dark brown, brittle; tips of the asci amyloid-------- *Peziza*
5. Fruiting body tough to rubbery, pliant, a robust cup or deep urn-shaped, asci nonamyloid -- 6
   6. Fruiting body tough, fibrous, deep urn-shaped; found in eastern North America --- *Urnula craterium*
   6. Fruiting body a robust, rubbery, shiny black, shallow disc; flesh filled with transparent gel; found in conifer forests ------------------------- *Sarcosoma mexicana*

Aleuria aurantia (Fr.) Fuckel
EDIBLE

Fruiting body sessile, 3–8 cm wide, cup-shaped to irregularly cupulate, bright orange, exterior pale orange, slightly roughened, margin splitting in age. Flesh brittle, light orange. Odor mild. Taste mild.

Spores 18–22 x 9–10 µm elliptic, reticulate ridged, nonamyloid. Asci nonamyloid. Paraphyses with orange contents.

Habit and distribution: Several to abundant on sandy, hard soil, during moist weather. Widely distributed. Fruiting in spring, summer, and fall, during wet weather.

Comments: A striking species referred to as the "Orange Peel," it is a decomposer. *Aleuria rhenana* Fuckel is small 1–3 cm wide, cuplike; with a white stipe; and found occasionally under conifers. Both are edible but bland, with very little flesh, and are not very interesting. In conifer habitats, if one encounters a similar orange species with areas tinted blue-green, see *Caloscypha fulgens*.

Caloscypha fulgens (Pers.) Boud.
NONPOISONOUS

Fruiting body sessile, 1–5 cm broad, margin wavy, pale to bright orange with blue-green stains mostly on the exterior. Flesh brittle. Odor none. Taste mild.

Spores 6–8 µm globose, thin-walled, smooth, nonamyloid. Asci nonamyloid.

Habit and distribution: In clusters on soil under spruce and fir. Widely distributed but common in the western mountains. Fruiting in spring or early summer during cool weather.

Comments: This colorful species is a spruce seed pathogen. It invades squirrel caches, killing 90% of the seeds. Beneath large clusters of fruiting bodies one can often find many decayed spruce cones (Paden, et al., 1978).

Sarcoscypha austriaca (Beck.:Sacc.)
Boud.
INEDIBLE

Fruiting body sessile, 2–6 cm broad, hymenium scarlet, exterior whitish buff tinted pink. Flesh brittle cream. Odor mild. Taste mild.

Spores 25–36 x 9–13 µm narrowly elliptic, truncate, thin-walled, hyaline, nonamyloid. Asci nonamyloid.

Habit and distribution: Single or several on sticks. Found in eastern North America. Fruiting in the early spring.

Comments: *Sarcoscypha coccinea* (Jacq.:Fr.) Lamb., also known as the "Scarlet Cup," is a conspicuous component of the early spring or occasionally late fall fungus flora during cold weather. Found along coastal western North America, it does not have the truncate spores but is identical macroscopically. *Sarcoscypha occidentalis* (Schwein.) Sacc has a small, bright red to purple-red, deep cup (0.5–2.0 cm wide) on a white stipe,1–3 cm long. It is found on hardwood twigs in central, eastern and southern North America according to Harrington (1990).

Sarcosphaeria crassa (Santi) Pouzar
EDIBLE

Fruiting body sessile, a deep round cup 4–15 cm wide, buried in soil, white but soon pink to violet, splitting crownlike into 7-10 rays, exterior dull white to cream color. Flesh soft, brittle. Odor none. Taste mild.

Spores 15–18 x 8–9 µm elliptic, truncated ends, thin-walled, smooth, nonamyloid. Asci nonamyloid.

Habit and distribution: Several to numerous over large areas, just at the surface of the ground in conifer and hardwood forests. Widely distributed.. Fruiting in spring and early summer.

Comments: Also known as *Sarcosphaera coronaria* (Jacq.:M. C. Cooke) Boud. and *Sarcosphaera eximia* (Durieu & Lév.) Maire. It is numerous in the spring in the western mountains. We have eaten this, but it requires much cleaning, and there is little flavor. There are some reports of gastric problems with the ingestion of this fungus, so caution should be taken.

KEY TO PEZIZA

1. Fruiting body 1.0–3.5 cm broad, hymenium pale violet to reddish violet; associated with burned soil -- *Peziza violacea*
1. Fruiting body larger and hymenium not violet -- 2
    2. Fruiting body 5–12 cm broad; hymenium pale to dark brown, exterior white or pale whitish brown; spores smooth --- *Peziza repanda*
    2. Fruiting body not as above --- 3
3. Growing in homes, damp cellars, bathrooms, greenhouses, on wood, sheet rock, and plaster; spores with a partial reticulum ---------------------------------- *Peziza domiciliana*
                                        (see comments under *Peziza badia*)
3. Growing on ground or well-decayed wood, under hardwoods and conifers ------------- 4
    4. Fruiting body 3–10 cm broad; hymenium and exterior dark brown; spores with a partial reticulum -- *Peziza badia*
    4. Fruiting body 3–10 cm broad; hymenium and exterior yellow-brown; spores minutely warted -- *Peziza badioconfusa*
                             (see comments under *Peziza badia*)

Peziza violacea Pers.
INEDIBLE

Fruiting body sessile 1.0–3.5 cm broad, deeply cupulate at first, soon open and saucerlike, smooth, pale violet young to dark violet or reddish violet in age, margin even, exterior whitish young to pinkish gray to grayish violet. Flesh brittle, pale pinkish to pale purple. Odor mild. Taste unknown.

Spores 13–16 x 7–9 µm elliptic, thin-walled, hyaline, nonamyloid, smooth, with two oil drops. Ascus with amyloid apex.

Habit and distribution: Scattered to gregarious on burned soil and debris. Widely distributed. Fruiting in spring, summer, and fall.

Comments: The pigmentation varies considerable depending on the age and climate where fruiting bodies are growing.

Peziza repanda Pers.:Fr.
NONPOISONOUS

Fruiting body sessile 5–12 cm broad, cupulate to smooth pale brown to dark brown, margin sometimes recurved or somewhat enfolded, exterior minutely pubescent, white or very pale whitish brown. Flesh brittle, brown. Point of attachment very short and white. Odor mild. Taste mild.

Spores 14–16 x 8–10 µm elliptic thin-walled, smooth, nonamyloid, without oil bodies. Ascus with an amyloid apex.

Habit and distribution: Single or more often gregarious, on rotten conifer and hardwood logs, limbs, and debris. Widely distributed. Fruiting spring, summer and fall, following wet weather.

Comments: *Peziza varia* Hedw.:Fr. is very similar but has spores with a minutely warted surface. Most species of *Peziza* have too little flesh and taste to be considered edible!

Peziza badia Pers.:Mérot
NONPOISONOUS

Fruiting body 3–10 cm wide, sessile, cupulate, smooth, dark brown, margin often wavy, exterior dark brown, smooth. Flesh soft, brittle, light brown. White mycelium at point of attachment. Odor mild. Taste mild.

Spores 15–19 x 7–10 μm elliptic, thin-walled, with two oil drops, one larger than the other, surface with a partial reticulum, nonamyloid. Upper half of the ascus amyloid.

Habit and distribution: Several to numerous on the ground or on well-decayed wood, under conifers or hardwoods. Widely distributed. Fruiting in summer and fall.

Comments: *Peziza badioconfusa* Korf, also widely distributed, is very similar but has warted spores. *Peziza domiciliana* M. C. Cooke is very similar; yellow-brown; found on rotten wood, sheet rock, and plaster in homes, damp cellars, bathrooms, and occasionally in greenhouses; and the spores are elliptic, 13–16 x 8–10 μm, smooth, hyaline.

Urnula craterium (Schwein.) Fr.
INEDIBLE

Fruiting body deep urn-shaped, 7–10 cm tall, urn brown to blackish brown in age. 4–6 cm high, 3–4.5 cm wide, brownish black. Flesh tough and fibrous. Stipe 3–4 cm long, 0.6–0.9 cm wide, black, smooth. Odor none. Taste unknown.

Spores 25–35 x 12–14 μm elliptic, smooth, thin-walled, hyaline, nonamyloid. Asci nonamyloid.

Habit and distribution: Several to cespitose clusters on decayed hardwood sticks, limbs, stumps, and logs. Found in eastern North America. Fruiting in early spring and summer.

Comments: Often called the "Gray Urn," the young cespitose clusters are club-shaped and closed at first. They gradually split open at the apex to reveal the deep, urn-shaped, black hymenium. *Urnula craterium* is a parasite, causing a canker of oaks, hickories, basswood, beech, and other hardwoods. It fruits from the infected branches or logs after they have fallen to the ground, Sinclair, et al., 1987.

Sarcosoma mexicana (Ellis & Holoway) Paden & Tylutki
INEDIBLE

Fruiting body a robust shallow cup or disc 6–11 cm tall, 6–14 cm wide, shiny, black, exterior wrinkled, black, minutely fibrous. Flesh rubbery, pliant, filled with dense, transparent gel shown in the lower photo. Odor none. Taste unknown.

Spores 23–34 x 10–14 µm elliptic, smooth, hyaline, thin-walled. nonamyloid. Asci nonamyloid.

Habit and distribution: Several to numerous, often in cespitose clusters of 4-7, on rotten conifer wood in conifer forests. Widely distributed. Fruiting following wet weather in spring, summer, and fall.

Comments: In some years, we have found large fruitings in June in Idaho. The fruiting bodies are very heavy and, in one case, we broke a pack basket transporting a large collection. Tylutki (1979) gives more details on the species of *Sarcosoma*.

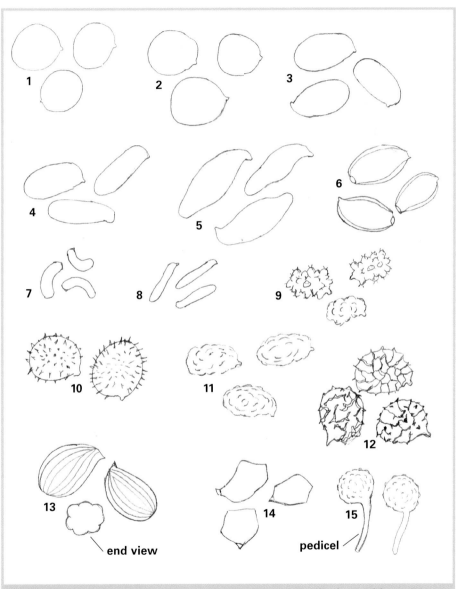

Basidiospores Figs. 1–15. 1. globose. **2.** subglobose. **3.** elliptic. **4.** oblong. **5.** subfusiform. **6.** apical germ pore, thick-walled. **7.** allantoid. **8.** cylindric. **9.** warted with spines or tuberculate-warted. **10.** spiny. **11.** rugose or wrinkled. **12.** reticulate, reticulate-warted. **13.** longitudinally striate (note end view). **14.** angular (4- to 6-sided). **15.** spore with pedicel.

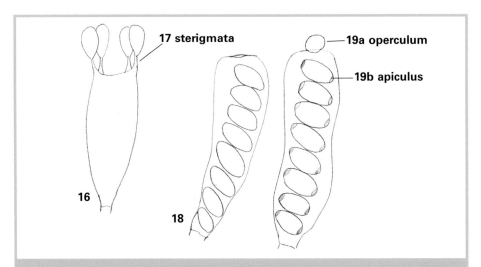

16. basidium. 17. sterigmata (sterigma). 18 ascus with 8 ascospores. 19. ascus with 8 ascospores. 19a. lid or operculum. 19b. apiculus on ends of ascospore.

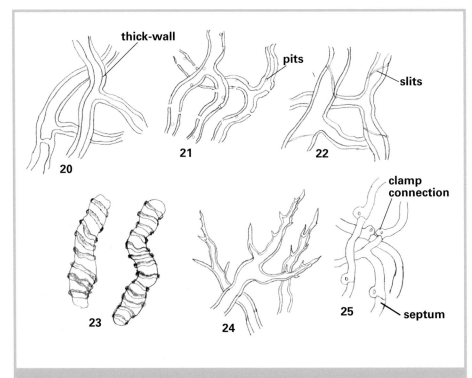

20. thick-walled capillitium. 21. thick-walled capillitium with pits. 22. thick-walled capillitium with slits. 23. elators in gleba. 24. thick-walled thorny capillitium. 25. thin-walled hyphae with clamp connections.

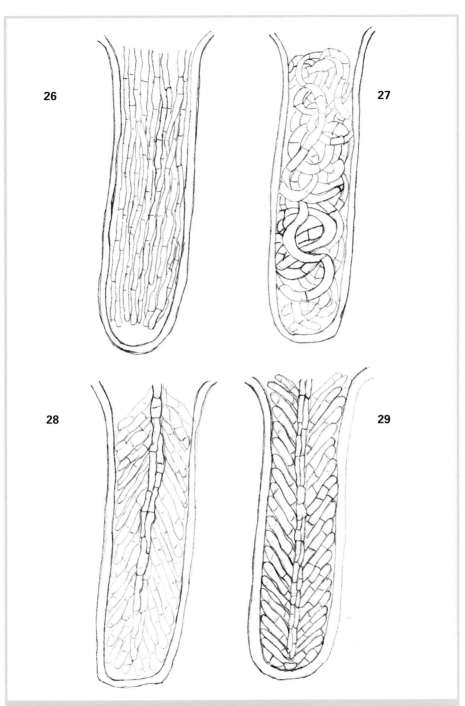

Longitudinal sections of: 26. parallel lamellar hyphae. 27. interwoven lamellar hyphae. 28. divergent lamellar hyphae. 29. convergent lamellar hyphae.

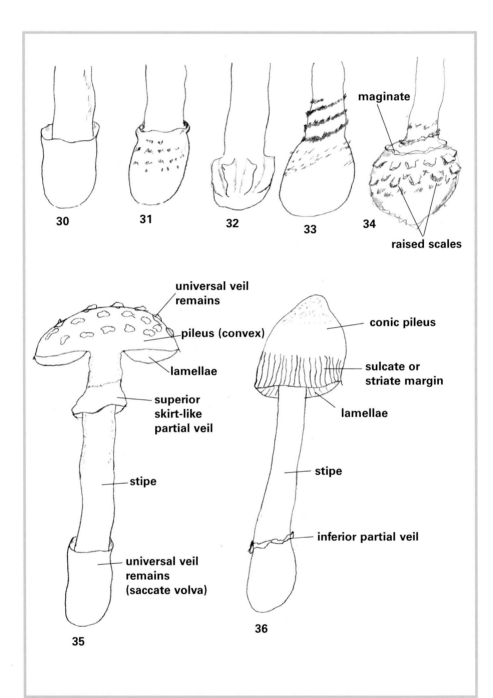

30. saccate stipe base. 31. marginate bulb at stipe base. 32. cleft base of stipe. 33. rings of volval tissue at stipe base. 34. abrupt bulb with scale. 35. fruiting body of an agaric with a superior partial veil and a universal veil. 36. conic fruiting body with a striate margin and an inferior partial veil.

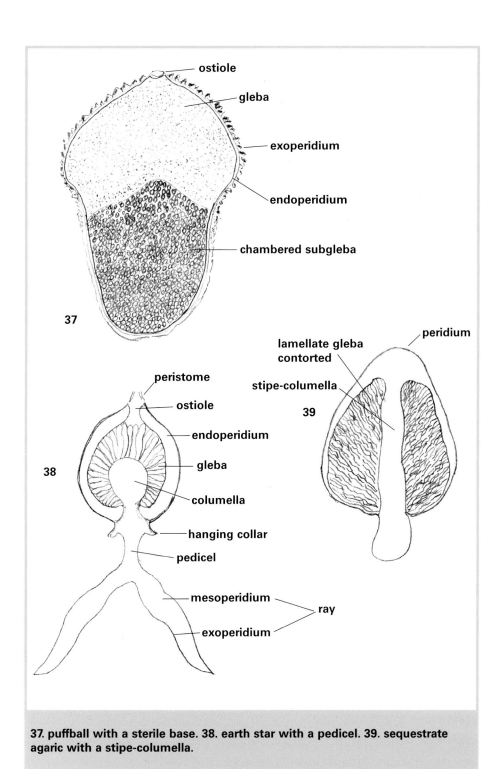

37. puffball with a sterile base. 38. earth star with a pedicel. 39. sequestrate agaric with a stipe-columella.

GLOSSARY

acrid: burning or peppery tasting

adnate: lamellae broadly attached to the stipe

aerolate: finely cracked

allantoid: curved and sausage-shaped (Fig. 7)

amyloid: staining blue, blue-gray to blackish violet in Melzer's solution

anastomosing: connecting crosswise to form a veinlike network

angular: 4- to 6-sided spores of *Entoloma* (Fig. 14)

annular ring: a distinct ring on the stipe (Figs. 35, 36)

annular zone: an indistinct ring or zone of fibrils on the stipe

annulus: a ring of tissue left on the stipe by the torn partial veil (Fig. 6)

apex: uppermost portion of the stipe or the very top part

apical pore: a small opening located at the spore apex (Fig. 6)

apiculus: a short projection on the spore of Basidiomycetes, which attaches the spore to the sterigmata (Figs. 3, 19), or the sterile ends of ascospores in species of *Gyromitra*

apothecium: an open Ascomycete hymenium, typical of a cup fungus or the pits on a morel, where the spores are formed

Ascomycetes: a group of fungi which have spores formed in an ascus (Fig. 18)

ascus, asci: a sac or sacs in which spores of Ascomycetes are produced (Fig. 18)

attenuate: gradually narrowed

basal mycelium: an entangled mass of hyphae located at the base of the stipe

basidiolichen: a fungus consisting of algae and fungal hyphae, see *Lichenomphalia*

basidium (a): sexual cell or cells of basidiomycetes that give rise to the spores (Fig. 16)

boletinoid: radially arranged and elongated pores, as in *Suillus*

brown cubical rot: brown-stained lignin in a small, cubical pattern left when mycelium decomposes the cellulose in wood

bulb: a swollen base of the stipe (Fig. 34)

buttons: immature mushrooms

campanulate: bell-shaped

canescence: a pale hoary down

capillitium: sterile, threadlike, often branched, thick-walled hyphae in the gleba of puffballs, earth stars, etc. (Figs. 20–24)

capitate: having a small knob at the apex of a cystidium

caulocystidia: sterile cells or hairs located on the surface of the stipe

cespitose: marked by several stipes arising close together, but not joined

cheilocystidia: sterile cells located on the edge of the lamellae

cristate: having dainty, fine branches with fine tips, as in *Clavulina*

chrysocystidia: cystidia that contain yellow, oval, oil bodies, as seen in 3% KOH

clamp connections: small semicircular branches at the septum on hyphae of many, but not all, basidiomycetes (Fig. 25)

clavate: club-shaped

close: the spacing of lamellae halfway between crowded and subdistant

columella: sterile center within an earth star (Fig. 38)

conks: perennial, woody fruiting bodies, see *Fomes*

conifer: a cone-bearing tree, such as pine or spruce

connivent: having pointed fibrils, usually in fours, which nod together, as on the exoperidium of puffballs

convergent evolution: two unrelated fungi, such as *Geastrum* and *Astraeus,* that have evolved the same functional structures

convergent hyphae: hyphae like a V on either side from the center of the lamellae (Fig. 29)

corrugate: coarsely wrinkled or ridged

cortinous: having a silky, weblike, partial veil (found in *Cortinarius*)

crenulate: very finely scalloped

cystidia: sterile cells that may project from the pileus, lamellae or stipe

decurrent: when lamellae descend down the stipe

dehiscence: opening by a slit or pore or by tearing, as found in the puffballs

deliquescent: when lamellae liquefy into an inky mass, see *Coprinaceae*

depressed: having the disc lower than the margin of the pileus, or tubes sunken around the stipe

dextrinoid: dark red to red-brown color in Melzer's solution

dichotomous: repeatedly dividing in twos, see *Clavicovona*

disc: the central portion of the surface of the pileus

divergent hyphae: hyphae diverging like an inverted V on either side from the center of the lamellae (Fig. 28) as in the Amanitaceae

duff: cast off needles and plant parts on the forest floor

eccentric: attached off center

ectomycorrhizae: a symbiotic relationship between fungus and plant (see introduction)

eggs: common name of the peridioles, which contain the spores, in the Bird's nest fungi

elators: thick-walled cells in the gleba in *Battarrea* (Fig. 23)

elliptic: having spores rounded on both ends with curved sides (Fig. 3)

endoperidium: innermost layer of a puffball or earth ball (Figs. 37, 38)

entire: of spores that do not have an apical pore (Figs. 1–3)

epiphragm: covering over the young fruiting body of the Bird's nest fungi

epigeous: having a fruiting body that develops above the ground

exoperidium: outer layer of a puffball or earth ball (Figs. 37, 38)

fairy ring: a circle in which fungi grow, usually in lawns or meadows

farinaceous: having an odor of fresh meal

fascicles: small bundles of hairs

fenugreek: odor of sweet clover

ferric sulphate (FeSO₄): a 3% solution of $FeSO_4$ yields a green reaction on the fresh flesh of some fungi as in *Ramaria*

fibrillose-scaly: having scales composed of fibrils that are more or less flattened

fibrils: minute threadlike hairs

fimbriate: finely torn or fringed

floccose: having tufts of soft, cottony material

fluted: having sharp-cornered ridges extending down the stipe as in *Helvella lacunosa*

fruiting body: the entire portion of a fungus developed for production of spores

funicular cord: a cord attached to the peridioles of bird's nest fungi

gastromycetes: Basidiomycetes that have spores developing within the fruiting body and do not forcibly discharge their spores

genus: a group of similar species, closely related, i.e. *Amanita*

glabrous: smooth, bald, lacking scales, fibrils, etc.

glandular dots: sticky drops or glands composed of caulocystidia, i.e. on the stipe of *Suillus*

gleba: a spore mass contained within a peridium in the Basidiomycetes, such as *Lycoperdon, Tulostoma,* or Ascomycetes, such as *Tuber* (Fig. 37)

globose: having round or spherical spores (Fig. 1)

glutinous: of a sticky, gluelike, pectinous material

gussets: individual, upraised, black plates, see *Montagnea arenaria*

hardwoods: trees with broad leaves, i.e. birch, beech, oak, aspen, maple, etc.

heart wood: the inner, usually dead wood, of a tree trunk

hirsute: covered with a dense layer of long, stiff hairs

homogeneous: having uniform composition

humus: partially decomposed plant material

hyaline: transparent, colorless

hygrophanous: watery, typically of a pileus changing color on drying

hygroscopic: repeatedly absorbing water, opening up, contracting, and closing on drying

hymenium: the spore-bearing surface such as lamellae of an agaric or pits of a morel

hyphae: microscopic, threadlike filaments (Fig. 25)

hypogeous: of fruiting bodies arising beneath the surface of the ground

imbricate: overlapping like shingles

indusium: a netlike "skirt" in *Dictyophora duplicata,* that is attached beneath the head

infundibuliform: deeply depressed in center of the pileus

inoperculate: having an ascus that has a pore and not a lid through which the spores are discharged

intervenose: having conspicuous, ridgelike veins between the lamellae or ridges of chanterelles and some agarics

interwoven: in cross-section, the lamellar trama have hyphae that are intertwined (Fig. 27)

KOH: potassium hydroxide, usually made-up in a 3% or 10% concentration in water

lacerated: appearing torn or shredded

lamellae (a): the hymenium of flat plates on which the spores are borne in the agarics (Figs. 35, 36)

lamellar hyphae: the supporting sterile, internal tissue of the lamellae (Figs. 26–29)

lamellulae: short lamellae that do not reach the stipe

latex: a juice that may be milky or watery, white or colored, see *Lactarius* and *Mycena*

locules: an area of gleba partitioned by a membrane, see *Scleroderma* and *Pisolithus*

longitudinally striate: having minute furrows or lines down the stipe or on spores (Fig. 13)

margin: edge of the pileus or lamellae

marginate bulb: ring of tissue at the top of the basal bulb, see *Amanita* (Fig. 31)

mealy: smelling of fresh grain or having a granular appearance

Melzer's solution: contains 20 cc H_2O, 1.5 g potassium iodide, 0.5 g iodine and 20 g chloral hydrate, used to test for the amyloid (blue) reaction of spores and cell walls

merulioid: having a pliant, waxy, gelatinous flesh, see *Phlebia tremullosa*

mesoperidium: the middle peridial layer of puffballs or earth stars (Fig. 38)

metuloids: modified thick-walled cystidia, often encrusted with lime, see *Pluteus*

mucronate: tipped with an abrupt, short, sharp point

mycelium: collective name for the filamentous hyphae of the vegetative fungus plant

mycorrhizal: a mutualistic relationship between the mycelium of a fungus and the tiny, short roots of green plants

ochraceous: having shades of orange-yellow

ochre: warm buff to ochraceous-orange color

operculate: having a small lid, typical of the ascus in many Ascomycetes (Fig. 19a)

ostiole: a pore in the top of the peridium of puffballs through which the spores escape (Fig. 37)

paraphyses: sterile supporting filaments located between asci in the Ascomycetes

parallel hyphae: in cross-section, the cells of the lamellar trama which lie side by side (Fig. 26)

parasitized: of living tissue of a plant or animal attacked and killed by a fungus

partial veil: a covering that extends from the unopened margin of the mushroom pileus to the stipe (Fig. 35)

pedicel: a long tubelike extension on the spores of many puffballs (Fig. 15) or short stalk on an earth star (Fig. 38)

peridiole: small chambers in the gleba delineated by thin, white to yellow membranes, see *Scleroderma*, or the "eggs" in the bird's nest fungi

peridium: the outer skin of fruiting bodies such as puffballs

peristome: the circular area surrounding the ostiole on some Gasteromycetes (Fig. 38)

perithecium (a): small flask or flasks where the spores are borne, embedded in fungus tissue, see *Xylaria* and *Hypomyces*

pileipellis: the outer layer of the pileus

pileocystidia: cystidia located on the surface of the pileus

pileotrama: the supporting tissue of the pileus located between the pileipellis and the spore-bearing surface

pileus (ei): the mushroom cap or caps (Fig. 35)

pip-shaped: teardrop-shaped

pits (of capillitium): small, round holes in the puffball capillitium (Fig. 21)

plage: a smooth area near the point of attachment on a spore, see *Galerina*

plane: having a flat surface

pleurocystidia: cystidia located on the face of the lamellae or within tubes of a bolete

plicate: folded and resembling a fan

pore: a small opening that may be round, angular or elongated

pore surface: the layer formed by the outermost end of the tubes, as in the polypores

pruinose: covered with a white, powdery substance

pubescent: covered with a layer of short, soft, downy hair

purse: pouch in which the funicular cord develops and is stored, see Bird's nest fungi

putative ectomycorrhizae: assumed to be mycorrhizal, but not proven

pyriform: pear-shaped

radially striate: having minute furrows or lines spreading from a common center

rays: the starlike, pointed peridium of the mature earth star (Fig. 12)

reticulum: a netlike arrangement or network over stipe, pileus or spore surface (Fig. 12)

rhizomorph: a cord or strand composed of mycelium, which penetrates the substrate

rimose: having tiny cracks or crevices

rugose: coarsely wrinkled spore (Fig. 11) or pileus surface

saccate: having a loose baglike volva that surrounds the base of the stipe, see *Amanita* and *Volvariella* (Fig. 30)

sand-case: an exoperidium composed of hyphae and sand particles, i.e. *Disciseda*

sapwood: the living, outer layer of a tree trunk

scabers: tufts of dark hairs on the stipe of *Leccinum*

scales: projections or tearing of the pileus or stipe surface, forming small, flattened or erect fanlike decorations

sclerotium: a hard, usually black, knot of fungus tissue

secotioid: appearing like an unopened agaric or bolete, usually with a stipe-columella

sequestrate: having a fruiting body that has evolved from ancestors with an exposed hymenium and forcible spore discharge but no longer forcibly discharges its spores, see *Longula* and *Gastroboletus*

septum (a): hyphal cell or cells divided by crosswalls (Fig. 25)

serrate: toothed, like the edge of a saw blade

sessile: lacking a stipe

setae: sharp pointed steril cells, a type of cystidium

Shäffer's reaction: the bright orange reaction at the point where the flesh is streaked with aniline and crossed with a streak of nitric acid, see *Longula* and *Agaricus*

siderophilous granulations: dark purple to purplish black particles observed in the basidia of some fungi stained with acetocarmine, see *Lyophyllum*

skeletal hyphae: a type of thick-walled hyphae found in the polypores, hydnums, etc.

sphaerocysts: a cluster of more or less globose cells in the pileipellis or trama, see *Russula*

spiny: having minute projections on the spore surface (Fig. 10), or on capillitium of *Mycenastrum* (Fig. 24)

spore print: a deposit of spores left on paper when the hymenium is placed on it. Needed to obtain the spore color.

squamulose: covered with minute, often ill-defined scales

sterigmata: attachment of spores to the basidia (Fig. 17)

sterile base: the sterile tissue beneath the gleba (Fig. 37)

stipe: technical term for the stem or stalk of a fungus (Fig. 35)

stipe-columella: a sterile, stalklike structure that extends from outside to inside the fruiting body of some Gasteromycetes (Fig. 39)

striate: having minute, radiating furrows or lines, often on the pileus margin (Fig. 36)

strigose: having thick, stiff, usually erect hairs

subdistant: spacing of the lamellae halfway between close and distant

subfusiform: more or less spindle-shaped (Fig. 5)

substrate: food source on which a fungus is growing, i.e. decaying wood, pine cones, or leaves

sulcate: grooved (Fig. 36)

superior annulus: located on the upper portion of the stipe (Fig. 35)

taiga: northern region of boreal conifers

thick-walled: of cell walls, which are secondarily thickened (Fig. 20)

thin-walled: of cell walls, which are not secondarily thickened (Fig. 25)

tomentose: densely matted and wooly

translucent-striate: the appearance of striations caused by edges of the lamellae, visible through the unusually thin pileus tissue, see *Mycena*

truncate: appearing to have an end cut off

tuberculate: with small projecting warts or knobs (Fig. 9)

tubes: tiny hollow cylinders in which the spores of boletes or polypores are produced

µm: micrometer (micron) = 1000 µm per mm

umbilicate: shaped like a navel (often in center of the pileus)

umbo: a knob or abruptly raised area in the center of the pileus

universal veil: a tissue surrounding the mushroom button (Fig. 35)

ventricose: of cells in the middle of the trama that are swollen in the middle and tapering in either direction

viscid: sticky to the touch

volva: the remains of the universal veil located at or surrounding the base of the stipe or as patches on the pileus (Fig. 30, 35)

BIBLIOGRAPHY

Abbot, S.P.& R.S. Currah. 1997. The Helvellaceae: Systematic Revision and Occurrence in Northern and Northwestern North America. *Mycotaxon* 62:1–125.

Aime, M.C., R. Vilgalys, & O.K. Miller Jr. 2005. The Crepidotaceae (Basidiomycota, Agaricales): Phylogeny and taxonomy of the genera and revision of the family based on molecular evidence. *Am. Jour. of Botany* 92:74–82.

Ammirati, J.F. 1989. *Dermocybe, Subgenus Dermocybe,* Section Sanquineae in Northern California. *Mycotaxon* 34:21–36.

Ammirati, J.F. & A.H. Smith. 1977. Studies in the genus *Cortinarius* III: section *Dermocybe,* New North American Species. *Mycotaxon* 5:381–97.

Ammirati, J.F., J.A. Traquair, & P.A. Horgen. 1985. *Poisonous Mushrooms of Canada.* Fitzhenry & Whiteside, Ltd. Markham, Ontario, Canada, 396p.

Antonin, V., R.E. Halling, &.E. Noordeloos.1997. Generic concepts within the groups of *Marasmius* and *Collybia* sensu lato. *Mycotaxon* 63:359–68.

Arora, D. 1986. *Mushrooms Demystified* (2nd ed.), Ten Speed Press, Berkeley, Calif., 959p.

Baird, R.E. 1986. *Type studies of North American and other related taxa of stipitate hydnums: Genera Bankera, Hydnellum, Phellodon, Sarcodon.* J. Cramer, Stuttgart, Germany, 89p.

Baroni, T.J. 1981. *A Revision of the Genus Rhodocybe Maire* (Agaricales). J. Cramer, Vaduz, 194p.

Bedry, R., G. Deffieux, E.E. Creppy, J.P. Pomies, J.M. Ragnaud, M. Dupon, D. Neau, C. Gabinski, S. De Witte, J. C. Chapalain & P. Godeau. 2001. Wild-Mushroom intoxication as a cause of Rhabdomyolysis. *N. Engl. J. Med.* 345(11): 798–802

Bessette, A.E. & W.J. Sundberg. 1987. *A Quick Reference Guide to Mushrooms of North America.* Macmillan Publishing Co. Inc., New York, N.Y., 173p.

Bessette, A.E., A.R. Bessette & D.W. Fischer. 1997. *Mushrooms of Northeastern North America.* Syracuse University Press, Syracuse, N.Y., 582p.

Bessette, A.E., O.K. Miller, A. Bessette & H. Miller. 1995. *Mushrooms of North America in Color, A Field Guide Companion to Seldom Illustrated Fungi.* Syracuse University Press, Syracuse, N.Y. 172p.

Bessette, A.E., W.C. Roody, & A.R. Bessette. 2000. *North American Boletes.* Syracuse University Press, Syracuse, N.Y., 396p.

Bigelow, H.E. 1973. The Genus *Clitocybula. Mycologia* 65:1101–16.

Bigelow, H.E. 1978. The Cantharelloid Fungi of New England and Adjacent Areas. *Mycologia* 70:707–56.

Bigelow, H.E. 1982. *North American Species of Clitocybe Part I*. J. Cramer, Vaduz, 280p.

Bigelow, H.E. 1985. *North American Species of Clitocybe Part II*. J. Cramer, Vaduz, 471p.

Boertmann, D. 2000. *The genus Hygrocybe. Svampetryk,* Tilst, Denmark, 184p.

Both, E.E. 1993. *The Boletes of North America A Compendium*. Buffalo Science Museum, Buffalo, N.Y., 436p.

Breitenback, J. & F. Kränzlin *1981.Pilz der Schweiz. Band 1. Ascomyceten. Mykologia,* Lucerne, Schweiz, 313p.

Breitenback, J. & F. Kränzlin. 1986. *Fungi of Switzerland Vol. 2. Non Gilled Fungi. Mykologia,* Lucerne, Switzerland, 412p.

Breitenback, J. & F. Kränzlin. 1991. *Fungi of Switzerland Vol. 3. Boletes and Agarics, 1st part.* Mykologia, Lucerne, Switzerland, 361p.

Breitenback, J. & F. Kränzlin 1995. *Fungi of Switzerland Vol. 4. Agarics 2nd part. Mykologia* Lucerne, Switzerland, 368p.

Breitenback, J. & F. Kränzlin 2000. *Fungi of Switzerland Vol. 5. Agarics 3rd part.* Cortinari- aceae. *Mykologia* Lucerne, Switzerland, 338p.

Brodie, H.J. 1975. *The Bird's Nest Fungi.* University of Toronto Press, Toronto, Canada.

Bruns, T.D., T.M. Szaro, M. Gardis, K.W. Cullings, J.J. Pan, D.L. Taylor, T.R. Horton, A. Kret- zer, M. Garbelotto, & Y. Li 1998. A sequence database for the identification of ectomyc- orrhizal basidiomycetes by phylogenetic analysis. *Molecular Ecology* 7:257–72.

Burdsall, H.H. & T.J. Volk. 1993. *The state of taxonomy of the genus Armillaria. McIlvainea* 11:4–12.

Burdsall, H.H. & M.T. Banik. 2001. The Genus *Laetiporus* in North America IN: Lindsey & Nakasone. A Celebration of Over 50 Years in Mycology. *Harvard Papers in Botany* 6:43–55.

Castellano, M.A., J.M. Trappe, Z. Maser, & C. Maser. 1989. *Key to Spores of Hypogeous Fungi of North Temerate Forests with special reference to animal mycophagy.* Mad River Press, Eureka, Calif., 186p.

Castro-Mendoza, E., O.K. Miller, Jr., & D.A. Stetler. 1983. Basidiospore wall ultrastructure and tissue system morphology in the genus *Calostoma* in North America. *Mycologia* 75:36–45.

Coker, W.C. 1917. The Amanitas of the Eastern United States. *Elisha Mitchell Scientific Soc.* 33:1–88.

Coker, W.C. 1923. *The Club and Coral Mushrooms (Clavarias) of the United States and Canada.* Dover Inc. New York, N.Y., 208p.

Coker, W.C. & J.N. Couch. 1928. *The Gasteromycetes of the Eastern United States and Canada.* The University of North Carolina Press, Chapel Hill, 201p.

Corner, E.J.H. 1967. *Clavaria and Allied Genera.* Biddles Ltd., Guilford, Great Britain, 740p.

Cotter, H. Van T. & O.K. Miller, Jr. 1985. Sclerotia of *Boletinellus merulioides* in Nature. *Mycologia* 77:927–31.

Cripps, C. I. 1997. The genus *Inocybe* in Montana aspen stands. *Mycologia* 89:670–88.

Dähncke, R.M. & S.M. Dähncke. 1979. *700 Pilze in Farbfotos.* AT Verlag, Stuttgart, Germany, 686p.

Desjardin, D.E. 1987. *The Agaricales (Gilled Fungi) of California 7. Tricholomataceae I.* Mad River Press, Eureka, Calif., 99p.

Evenson, V.S. 1997. *Mushrooms of Colorado and the Southern Rocky Mountains.* Westcliff Pub. 207p.

Farr, E.R., O.K. Miller, Jr. & D.F. Farr. 1977. Biosystematic studies in the *Pholiota aurivella* species complex. *Can. J. Bot.* 55:1167 1180.

Geesteranus, R.A.M. 1975. *Die Terrestrischen Stachelpilze Europas (The Terrestrial Hydnums of Europe).* North-Holland Publishing Co., Amsterdam, 127p.

Gilbertson, R.L. & L. Ryvarden 1986. *North Americal Polypores Vol. 1.* Fungiflora Oslo, Norway. 1–433.

Gilbertson, R.L &, L. Ryvarden 1987. *North American Polypores Vol. 2.* Fungiflora Oslo, Norway. 437–885

Gilkey, H.M. 1939. *Tuberales of North America.* Oregon State College, Corvalllis, Ore., 63p.

Gilliam, T.S. 1976. The genus *Marasmius* in the Northeastern United States and adjacent Canada. *Mycotaxon* 4:1–144.

Gillman, L.S. & O.K. Miller, Jr. 1977. A study of the boreal, alpine, and arctic species of *Melanoleuca. Mycologia* 69:927–51.

Ginns, J. 1985. *Hericium* in North America: cultural characteristics and mating behavior. *Can. J. Bot.* 63:1551–63.

Ginns, J.& M.N. Lefebvre. 1993. Lignicolous Corticioid Fungi (Basidiomycota) of North America. *Mycological Memoir* 19, APS Press, 247p.

Guzman, G. 1970. Monografia del Genera *Scleroderma* Pers. Emend Fr. *Darwiniana* 16:233–407.

Guzman, G. 1983. *The Genus Psilocybe.* J. Cramer, Vaduz, 439p.

Hall, I.R., S.L. Stephenson, P.K. Buchanan, W. Yun, A.L.J. Cole. 2003. *Edible and Poisonous Mushrooms of the World.* Timber Press Inc., Christchurch, NZ, 371p.

Harrington, F.A. 1990. *Sacroscypha* in North America (Pezizales, Sarcoscyphaceae) *Mycotaxon* 38:417–58.

Harrison, K. 1961. *The Stipitate Hydnums of Nova Scotia Publ. 1099.* Canada Department of Agriculture, Ottawa, Canada, 60p.

Hesler, L.R. 1967. *Entoloma in Southeastern North America.* J. Cramer, Stuttgart, Germany, 196p.

Hesler, L.R. 1969. *North American Species of Gymnopilus.* Hafner Publishing Co., New York, N.Y., 117p.

Hesler, L.R. & A.H. Smith 1963. *North American Species of Hygrophorus.* University of Tennessee Press, Knoxville, 416p.

Hesler, L.R. & A.H. Smith 1965. *North American Species of Crepidotus.* Hafner Publishing Co., New York, N.Y., 168p.

Hesler, L.R. & A.H. Smith 1979. *North American Species of Lactarius.* University of Michigan Press, Ann Arbor, 841p.

Horak, E. & O.K. Miller. 1992. *Phaeogalera and Galerina* in Arctic-Subarctic Alaska (USA) and the Yukon Territory (Canada). *Can. J. Bot.* 70:414–33.

Huffman, D.M., L.H. Tiffany & G. Knaphus. 1989. *Mushrooms of the Midcontinental United States.* Iowa State University Press, Ames, Iowa, 326p.

Jacobson, K.M., P.J. Jacobson, & O.K. Miller 1998. The autecology of *Battarrea stevenii* in ephemeral rivers of southwestern Africa. *Mycol. Res. 103:* 9–17.

Jenkins, D.T. 1986. *Amanita of North America.* Mad River Press, Eureka, Calif., 197p.

Kauffman, C.H. 1918. *The Agaricaceae of Michigan.* Johnson Reprint Corp., 924p.

Kerrigan, R.W. 1986. *The Agaricales of California 6. Agaricaceae.* Mad River Press, Eureka, Calif., 62p.

Kibby, G. 1992. *Mushrooms and Other Fungi.* American Nature Guides. Smithmark Publishing, New York, N.Y., 192p.

Kibby, G. & R. Fatto 1990. *Keys to the Species of Russula in Northeastern North America.* Kibby-Fatto Enterprises, 61p.

Kimbrough, J. 2000. *Common Florida Mushrooms.* University of Florida Extension, Gainesville, 342p.

Kirchmair, M., R. Pöder, C.G. Huber, & O.K. Miller, Jr. 2002. Chemotaxonomical and morphological observations in the genus *Omphalotus* (Omphalotaceae). *Persoonia* 17:583–600.

Largent, D., D. Johnson, & R. Watling. 1980. *How to Identify Mushrooms to Genus III: Microscopic Features.* Mad River Press, Eureka, Calif., 148p.

Largent, D. 1985. The Agaricales (Gilled Fungi) of California. 5. Hygrophoraceae, 208p. In: H.D. Thiers, ed., *Agaricales of California.* Mad River Press, Eureka, Calif.

Largent, D. 1994. *Entolomatoid Fungi of the Western United States and Alaska.* Mad River Press Eureka, Calif., 495p.

Lentz, P.L. 1955. *Stereum* and Allied Genera of Fungi in the Upper Mississippi Valley. Agriculture Monograph No.24, USDA, 74p.

Lincoff, G. & D.H. Mitchel. 1977. *Toxic and Hallucinogenic Mushroom Poisoning.* Van Nostrand Reinhold Co., New York, N.Y., 267p.

Mains, E.B. 1954. North American Species of *Geoglossum* and *Trichoglossum. Mycologia* 46:586–631.

Mains, E.B. 1957. Species of *Cordyceps* Parasitic on *Elaphomyces. Bull. Torrey Bot. Club* 84:243–51.

Mains, E.B. 1958. North American Entomogenous Species of *Cordyceps. Mycologia* 50:169–222.

Marr, C.D. & D.E. Stuntz 1973. *Ramaria of Western Washington.* J. Cramer, Leutershausen, Germany, 232p.

McKenny, M., D.E. Stuntz & J.E. Ammirati. 1991. *The New Savory Wild Mushroom.* University of Washington Press, Seattle, 249p.

McIlvaine, C. & R.K. Macadam. 1973. *One Thousand American Fungi, rev. ed.* Something Else Press, West Glover, Vt., 729p.

Methven, A.S. 1990. *The genus Clavariadelphus in North America.* J. Cramer, Stuttgart, Germany, 192p.

Methven, A.S. 1997. The Agaricales (Gilled Fungi) of California. 10. Russulaceae II *Lactarius* 78p. In: H.D. Thiers, ed., *Agaricales of California.* Mad River Press, Eureka, Calif.

Metzler, S., V.T. Metzler, & O.K. Miller Jr. 1992. *Mushrooms of Texas.* University of Texas Press, Austin, 350p.

Miller, H.H. 1993. *Hope's Mushroom Cookbook.* Mad River Press, Eureka, Calif., 220p.

Miller, O.K. Jr. 1968. A revision of the genus *Xeromphalina. Mycologia* 50:156–88.

Miller, O.K. Jr. 1966. A new western species of *Chroogomphus. Mycologia* 58:855–61.

Miller, O.K. Jr. 1970. The genus *Panellus* in North America. *Michigan Botanist* 9:17–30.

Miller, O.K. Jr. 1971. The genus *Gomphidius* with a revised description of the Gomphidiaceae and a key to the genera. *Mycologia* 63:1129–63.

Miller, O.K. Jr. 1971. The genus *Lentinellus Mycologia* 63:333–69.

Miller, O.K., Jr. 1977. *Mushrooms of North America*. E. P. Dutton, Inc. New York, N.Y., 350p.

Miller, O.K., Jr. 1984. A New Species of *Hygrophorus* from North America. *Mycologia* 76:816–19.

Miller, O.K. Jr. 1993. Observations on the genus *Cystoderma* in Alaska. Arctic and Alpine Mycology 3. *Bibl. Mycol.* 150:161–69.

Miller, O.K., Jr. 1995. Observations on unusual Gasteromycetes from North America. *Documents Mycologique* 25:259–67.

Miller, O.K. Jr. 2003. The Gomphidiaceae revisited: a worldwide perspective. *Mycologia* 95:176–83.

Miller, O.K., Jr. and M.C. Aime. 2001. Systematic, ecology and world distribution in the genus *Chroogomphus* (Gomphidiaceae). In: Misra, J.K., Horn, B.W., eds. *Trichomycetes and other fungal groups*. Science Publishers, Inc. Enfield, N.H., p. 314–33.

Miller O.K. Jr. & V. Evenson. 2001. Observations on the alpine tundra species of *Hebeloma* in Colorado. *Gilbertson Honorary Volume, Harvard Papers* 6:155–62.

Miller, O.K., Jr. & D.E. Farr. 1975. *Index of the Common Fungi of North America. (Synonymy and Common Names)*. Bibliotheca Mycologica. 44:206p.

Miller, O.K., Jr. & H.H. Miller. 1980. *Mushrooms in Color: How to Know Them, Where to Find Them, What to Avoid*. E. P. Dutton Inc., New York, N.Y., 286p.

Miller, O.K., Jr. & H.H. Miller. 1988. *Gasteromycetes: Morphological and Developmental Features with Keys to the Orders, Families and Genera*. Mad River Press, Eureka, Calif. 157p.

Miller, O.K., Jr., M.C. Aime, F.J. Camacho, U. Peintner. 2002. Two new species of *Gomphidius* from the Western United States and Eastern Siberia. *Mycologia* 94:1044–50.

Miller, O.K. Jr., R.L. Brace, & V. Evenson. 2005. A new subspecies of *Mycenastrum corium* from Colorado. *Mycologia* 97:530–33.

Miller, O.K., T.J. Volk, & A.E. Bessette. 1996. A new genus, *Leucopholiota*, in the Tricholomataceae (Agaricales) to Accomodate an unusual taxon. *Mycologia* 88:137–39.

Moncalvo, J.M., R. Vilgalys, S.A. Redhead, J.E. Johnson, T.Y. James, M.C. Aime, V. Hofstetter, S. Veredui, E. Larsen, T.J. Baroni, G. Thorn, S. Jacobson, H. Clémençon, O.K. Miller. 2002. One hundred and seventeen clades of Eugarics. *Molecular, Phylogenetics, and Evolution* 23:357–400.

Moser, M. 1983. *Keys to Agarics and Boleti*. Whitefriars Press, Tonbridge, Great Britain, 535p.

Mueller, G.M. 1992. Systematics of *Laccaria* (Agaricales) in the Conteniental United States and Canada, with Discussions on Extralimital Taxa and Descriptions of Extant Types. *Fieldiana, Botany New Series* 30:1–158.

Noordeloos, M.E. 1987. *Entoloma* (Agaricales) in Europe. *Nova Hedwigia* 91:1–419.

Nooderloos, M.E., Th.W. Kuyper, & E.C. Vellinga. 2001. *Flora Agaricina Neerlandica Vol 5*. A.A. Balkema, 169p.

Norvell, L. L. & S. A. Redhead 2000. *Phaeocollybia* in western North America 2: the vernal *P. pleurocystidiata* sp. nov. and *P. carmanahensis* reconsidered. Mycologia 92(5):984–91.

Orton, P.D. & R. Watling 1979. *British Fungus Flora, Agarics and Boleti 2. Coprinaceae: Coprinus*. Royal Botanic Garden, Edinburgh, 149p.

Overholts, L.O. 1953. *The Polyporaceae of the United States, Alaska, and Canada*. Univ. of Mich. Press, Ann Arbor, MI, 444p.

Paden, J.W., J.R. Sutherland, & T.A.D. Woods. 1978. *Calocypha fulgens* (Ascomycetidae, Pezizales): the perfect state of the conifer seed pathogen *eniculodendron pyriforme* (Deuteromycotina) Hyphomycetes. *Can J. Bot.* 56:2375–79.

Petersen, R.H. 1968. *The genus Clavulinopsis in North America*. Hafner Publishing Co., New York, N.Y., 39p.

Petersen, R.H. 1988. Vernally fruiting taxa of *Ramaria* from the Pacific Northwest. *Mycotaxon* 33:101–44.

Pilát, A. 1951. The Bohemian species of the genus *Agaricus*. *Acta Museum Nationalis Pragae* 7:3–142.

Pomerleau, R. 1980. *Flore Des Champignons au Québec*. Les Éditions la Presse, Ottawa, 623p.

Pomerleau, R. 1966. Les Amanitas du Québec. *Le Nat. Can.* 93:861–87.

Ponce de Leon, Patricio. 1968. A Revision of the Family Geastraceae. *Fieldiana* 31:303–49.

Redhead, S. 1980. The genus *Strobilurus* (Agaricales) in Canada with notes on extralimital species. *Can. J. Bot.* 58:68–83.

Redhead, S. 1986. Mycological Observations 15–16: On *Omphalia* and *Pleurotus*. *Mycologia* 78:522–28.

Redhead, S. 1986. The genus *Crinipellis* Pat. in Canada. *Atti del Centro Studi per la Flora Mediterranea* 6:175–99.

Redhead, S.A. & J. Ginns. 1980. *Cyptotrama asprata* (Agaricales) from North America and notes on five other species of *Cyptotrama* sect. *Xerulina*. *Can. J. Bot.* 58:731–40.

Redhead, S.A., J. Ginns, & R.A. Shoemaker. 1987. The *Xerula (Collybia, Oudemansiella) radicata* complex in Canada. *Mycotaxon* 30:357–405.

Redhead, S.A., R. Vilgalys, J-M. Moncalvo, J. Johnson & J.S. Hopple, Jr. 2001. *Coprinus* Pers. and the disposition of *Coprinus* species *sensu lato*. *Taxon* 50:203–41.

Roody, W.C. 2003. *Mushrooms of West Virginia and the Central Appalachians*. University Press of Kentucky, Lexington, 520p.

Schalkwijk-Barendsen, H.M.E. 1991. *Mushrooms of Western Canada*. Lone Pine Press, Edmonton, Alberta, Canada, 414p.

Seaver, F.J. 1951a. *North American Cup Fungi, Inoperculates*. Hafner Publishing Co., New York, N.Y., 428p.

Seaver, F. J. 1961. *North American Cup Fungi, Operculates*. Hafner Publishing Co., New York, N.Y., 377p.

Shaffer, R.L. 1957. *Volvariella* in North America. *Mycologia* 69:545–79.

Shaffer, R.L. 1964. Subsection *Lactarioideae* of *Russula*. *Mycologia* 56:202–31.

Shaffer, R. L.1972. North American Russulas of the Subsection Foetentinae. *Mycologia* 64:1008–53.

Shanks, K. M.1997. *Tricholoma. The Agaricales (Gilled Fungi) of California II. Tricholomataceae*. Mad River Press Inc., Eureka, Calif., 54p.

Shaw, C.G. III & G.A. Kile. 1991. *Armillaria Root Disease*. Agriculture Handbook No. 691, U.S.D.A. Washington, D.C., 233p.

Sinclair, W. A., H.H. Lym & W.T. Johnson. 1987. *Diseases of Trees and Shrubs*. Comstock Publ. Assoc., Cornell University Press, Ithaca, N.Y., 574p.

Singer, R. & A.H. Smith. 1943. A monograph of the genus *Leucopaxillus* Boursier. *Mich. Acad Sci.* 28:85–132.

Singer, R. & A.H. Smith. 1960. Studies on Secotiaceous Fungi IX The Astrogastraceous Series. *Bull. Torrey Bot. Club* 21:1–112.

Smith, A.H. 1941. Studies of North American Agarics I. *Cont. Univ. of Mich. Herbarium* 4:3–73.

Smith, A.H. 1947. *North American Species of Mycena*. University of Michigan Press, Ann Arbor, 521p.

Smith, A.H. 1949. *Mushrooms in their Natural Habitats*. Sawyer's Inc., Portland, Ore., 626p.

Smith, A.H. 1951. The North American Species of *Naematoloma*. *Mycologia* 43:467–521.

Smith, A.H. 1951. *Puffballs and their Allies in Michigan*. University of Michigan Press, Ann Arbor, 131p.

Smith, A.H. 1960. *Tricholomopsis* (Agaricales) in the Western Hemisphere. *Brittonia* 12:41–70.

Smith, A.H. 1972. The North American Species of *Psathyrella. Memoirs New York Botanical Garden* 24:1–632.

Smith, A.H. & R. Singer. 1945. A Monograph of the Genus *Cystoderma. Mich. Acad. Sci.* 30:71–124.

Smith, A.H., H. V. Smith, & N. S. Weber. 1979. *How to Know the Gilled Mushrooms.* W.C. Brown Inc., Dubuque, Iowa, 334p.

Smith, A.H. & H.D. Thiers 1964. *A contribution toward a monograph of North American species of Suillus.* University of Michigan Press, Ann Arbor, 116p.

Smith, A.H. & H.D. Thiers 1969. Hypogeous *Cortinarii. Mycologia* 61:526–36.

Smith, A.H. & H.D. Thiers 1971. *The Boletes of Michigan.* University of Michigan Press, Ann Arbor, 428p.

Smith, A.H., H.D. Thiers, & O.K. Miller. 1965. The species of *Suillus* and *Fuscoboletinus* of the Priest River Experimental Forest and Vicinity, Priest River, Idaho. *Lloydia* 28:120–38.

Smith, A.H. & S.M. Zeller 1966. A preliminary account of the North American species of *Rhizopogon. Memoirs, New York Botanical Garden* 14:1–178.

Smith, H.V. 1954. The Genus *Limacella* in North America. *Lloydia* 17:307–28.

Smith, H.V. & A.H. Smith 1973. *How to Know the Non Gilled Fleshy Fungi.* Wm. C. Brown Inc., Dubuque, Iowa, 402p.

Snell, W.H. & E.A. Dick. 1970. *The Boleti of Northeastern North America.* Verlag Von J. Cramer, Lehre, 115p.

Spoerke, D.G. & R.H. Rumack 1994. *Handbook of Mushroom Poisoning, Diagnosis and Treatment.* CRC Press, West Palm Beach, Fla., 456p.

Stamets, P. 1996. *Psilocybin Mushrooms of the World.* Ten Speed Press, Berkeley, Calif., 245p.

Stamets, P. 2000. *Growing Gourmet & Medicinal Mushrooms,* 3rd ed. Mycomedia Production. Berkeley, Calif., 574p.

Sundberg, W.J, & J.A. Richardson. 1980. *Mushrooms and Other Fungi of Land Between the Lakes.* Department of Botany, Southern Illinois University, Carbondale, 60p.

Sunhede, S. 1989. Geastraceae (Basidiomycotina) Morphology, Ecology, and Systematics with Special Emphasis on the North European Species. Synopsis Fungorum I. *Fungiflora,* Oslo, Norway.

Thiers, H.D. 1975. *California Mushrooms, A Field Guide to the Boletes.* Hafner Press, New York, N.Y., 261p.

Thiers, H.D. 1982. *The Agaricales (Gilled Fungi) of California 1. Amanitaceae.* Mad River Press, Eureka, Calif., 51p.

Thiers, H.D. 1997. *The Agaricales (Gilled Fungi) of California. 9. Russulaceae I.* Mad River Press, Eureka, Calif., 192p.

Thorn, R.G. & D.W. Malloch. 1993. Species of *Cortinarius* subgenus *Leprocybe,* sections *Orellani* and *Linonei* in North America. *Can. J. Bot* 72:520–32.

Tiffany, L.H., Knaphus, G. & D.M. Huffman 1998. Distribution and Ecology of the Morels and False Morels of Iowa. *Jour. Iowa Acad. Sci.* 105:1–15.

Tuloss, R.E. 1988. *Amanita sinicoflava:* A new species from Eastern North America. *Mycotaxon* 32:421–31.

Tylutki, E.E. 1979. *Mushrooms of Idaho and the Pacific Northwest: Discomycetes.* University of Idaho Press, Moscow, Idaho, 133p.

Vellinga, E.C. 1990. Pluteaceae Kotl. & P. In: *Flora Agaricina Neerlandica Vol. 2.* Balkema, Rotterdam, 137p.

Vellinga, E.C., R.P.J. de Kok & T.D. Bruns, 2003. Phylogeny and taxonomy of *Macrolepiota* (Agaricaceae). *Mycologia* 95: 442–56.

Vilgalys, R. & O.K. Miller Jr. 1983. Biological species in the *Collybia dryophila* Group in North America. *Mycologia* 75:707–22.

Vilgalys, R., A. Smith, B.L. Sun & O.K. Miller. 1992. Intersterility groups in *Pleurotus ostreatus* from the continental United States and adjacent Canada. *Can. J. Bot.* 71:113–28.

Watling, R. 1982. *British Fungus Flora 3 Bolbitiaceae: Agrocybe, Bolbitius & Conocybe* Royal Botanic Garden, Edinburgh, 139p.

Watling, R. & O.K. Miller. 1987. Observations on the Bolbitiaceae–30 *Agaricus callistus* Peck. *Mycologia* 79:310–13.

Weber, N.S. 1972. The Genus *Helvella* in Michigan. *Michigan Botanist* 11:147–201.

Weber, N.S. 1988. *A Morel Hunter's Companion, A Guide to the True Morels and False Morels of Michigan.* Two Peninsula Press, Lansing, Mich., 209p.

Wells, V.L. & P.E. Kempton. 1968. A preliminary study of *Clavariadelphus* in North America. *Michigan Botanist* 7:35–57.

White, V.S. 1901. The Tulostomataceae of North America. *Bull. Torrey Bot. Club* 28:421–43.

Wright, J.E. 1987. *The Genus Tulostoma (Gasteromycetes), A World Monograph.* J. Cramer, Stuttgart, Germany, 338p.

Zeller, S.M. & C.W. Dodge. 1918. *Gautieria* in North America. *Ann. Missouri Bot. Gard.* 5:133–42.

Zeller, S.M. & A.H. Smith. 1964. The genus *Calvatia* in North America. *Lloydia* 27:148–86.

INDEX

Note: Numbers in bold indicate the page where the main descriptions of the species and genera are found; other references lead to secondary mentions.

ABOUT THE AUTHORS

The Millers, Dr. Orson Miller, and his wife, Hope, have worked extensively in North America, including Alaska and Canada, as well as Europe, Australia, New Zealand, and parts of Asia More recently they have carried out field work in Biodiversity studies in the Greater Antilles and Belize. Currently, they are engaged in a National Science Foundation Study of the Biodiversity of the Great Smoky Mountain National Park.

Dr. Orson K. Miller Jr. and Hope H. Miller

Orson is a Professor Emeritus of Botany and Curator of Fungi from Virginia Tech where he spent 32 years. His students are professors and researchers in academia and industry at home and abroad. He has previously authored six books on fungi, three of which he collaborated on with Hope. Orson has written more than 150 scientific papers in which he authored 105 new species, genera, and combinations new to science. He continues his research in his retirement. He is past president of the Mycological Society of America (MSA) and a Fellow of the American Association for the Advancement of Science. He received the William Weston Award for Teaching Excellence in 1989 and Distinguished Mycologist Award from MSA in 1997, the Thomas Jefferson Medal for Outstanding Contributions to Natural Science in 1999, and the North American Mycological Association Award for Contributions to Amateur Mycology in 1981.

Hope has authored a mushroom cookbook containing more than 320 recipes using both wild and commercial mushrooms. She has been Orson's constant companion in the field doing all manner of support work, such as collecting, recording, culturing, drying, and storing the fungi. She has been on television, radio, the Denver Botanical Gardens, and many forays and mycology classes doing cooking demonstrations, she taught classes at the Open University at Virginia Tech on "How to Know Your Mushrooms," lectured at a workshop in Thailand explaining collecting, recording, and preservation of fungi, and has been the recorder at more than 100 fungus forays. She has also had a cooking column in the local Blacksburg newspaper and has received the Life Time Achievement Award for Contributions to Amateur Mycology from the Texas Mycological Society.